THE
Hero in Eclipse
IN
VICTORIAN FICTION

THE
Hero in Eclipse
IN VICTORIAN FICTION

BY

MARIO PRAZ

TRANSLATED FROM THE ITALIAN

BY

ANGUS DAVIDSON

GEOFFREY CUMBERLEGE

OXFORD UNIVERSITY PRESS

LONDON   NEW YORK   TORONTO

1956

Oxford University Press, Amen House, London E.C.4
GLASGOW NEW YORK TORONTO MELBOURNE WELLINGTON
BOMBAY CALCUTTA MADRAS KARACHI CAPE TOWN IBADAN
Geoffrey Cumberlege, Publisher to the University

———

PRINTED IN GREAT BRITAIN

Contents

List of Illustrations

LIST OF ILLUSTRATIONS

INTRODUCTION

Genre Painting and the Novel

Those innumerable *genre* pieces—conversation, music, play—were in truth
the equivalent of novel-reading for that day. . . .

WALTER PATER, Sebastian van Storck

I

ONE of the tritest maxims of writers on the history of
culture is that the spread of any new form of taste
manifests itself in literature before it makes its appearance in the visual arts. The vogue of the ἐκφράσεις in
the Hellenistic period, and of the Picturesque during the
eighteenth century (when Claude, Salvator Rosa, and the
Dutch painters opened the eyes of writers to a new appreciation of landscape) do not provide the only exceptions. There
are aspects of the narrative literature of the nineteenth century that are less satisfactorily accounted for by a scrutiny
of literary tradition than by reference to the *genre* painting
—the Dutch, especially—which flourished from the seventeenth century onwards.[1]

The thriving state of trade in the Dutch United Provinces in the seventeenth century was a repetition, on a
somewhat larger scale perhaps, of the phenomenon that
had occurred in the republics of Italy three centuries before :
now it was Dutch ships that penetrated into every sea (their
merchant fleet was twice as large as that of all other nations
together), Dutch banks carried on the cosmopolitan tradition of the banks of Florence and Siena, Amsterdam
became the market of the world. As previously in Italy,
commercial prosperity brought with it prosperity in the arts ;
but, while in Italy, where the influence of the Church was
still prevalent, the citizen had not desired any reproduction
of himself except as the figure of a donor at the foot of a
sacred group, and scenes of everyday life, in order to be
thought worthy of the immortality of art, had to be dressed

up as scenes from the Bible, in Holland, on the other hand, the decay of sacred art as a result of Protestantism was a circumstance favourable to the development of the art of portraiture and the interior scene, and of *genre* painting in general. What before had been marginal (the figure of the donor), or mere background (landscape, small groups of figures), now, owing to the very fact that the divine element had evaporated, occupied the foreground.[2] Houses, rather than churches, were now decorated, houses with rooms which became more and more elaborately adorned, though they still retained their small proportions—the proportions of what in an Italian palace would have been a study or closet; hence the prevalence of small-scale painting. More deliberately than elsewhere, art in Holland aimed at giving satisfaction and delight, and at the edification of the severe, prosperous caste whose highest spiritual life evolved in an arid, rarefied atmosphere like that of the white, unadorned churches, those bare shells that were designed to reverberate with the voice of the preacher or the sound of the organ accompanying the hymns. Satisfaction was given by the reproduction of the features of the family in its own surroundings, amongst its own possessions and its pets. Delight was produced by landscape painting (elegy), rustic scenes such as the *bambocciate*,[3] *kermesses* (comedy or uproarious farce). Edification was provided by the pleasing illustration of fables and proverbs, by series of pictures exemplifying vice, and so on. With the exclusion of all transcendental aims, the painter's attention could be devoted to the rendering of material objects with complete and sincere abandonment, to the enjoyment of their richness, their quality, their charm. Hence, in the greatest of these painters (especially in Vermeer), the firm intensity of contemplation that charges the object represented with a fullness of energy undiverted by any metaphysical intention. The portrait-painters did not aim at investing their models with ideal qualities; the models remained in the picture just as they were in life, and their features did not have to conform to any pious or warlike pattern. They remained just what they were, essentially bourgeois.[4] And so, in this school of painting, realism triumphs.

Anecdote also triumphs: it is a *genre* painting which reflects the practical spirit characteristic of the Dutch—and indeed of the bourgeois everywhere—for whom painting, besides being painting, must tell a story, amusing or edifying, better still both witty and edifying at the same time (*miscere utile dulci*). Literature becomes subordinated to the visual image; it is the epoch of Jacob Cats, the poet of proverbs and allegories illustrated with charming vignettes; moral instruction goes hand in hand with the painting of customs and manners. Deeper qualities then emerge in this type of painting. Realism is spiritualized through intensity of vision, attaining, in the highest examples, the quality of inwardness and becoming 'intimism'; and, since it reproduces the joys of prosperity and peace, it suffuses these paintings with an air of great earthly security: moments of everyday life thus become intimations of eternity. This is true of Terborch, Pieter de Hooch, and particularly Vermeer.

It has been rightly said that Vermeer seems to hold up a mirror to the world; but it is an enchanted mirror. Everyday things take upon themselves a mute magnificence; they are steeped in an atmosphere purer than that of this earth. Invoking no divine presence in his pictures, Vermeer yet portrays a peace more divine than that of the paradises depicted in the canvases of others. No one could yearn to find himself in the restless turmoil of writhing bodies that is the Paradise of Michelangelo or Tintoretto; but what peace desired of man has ever held greater enchantment than that which breathes from Vermeer's interiors? Quite rightly have that great solemnity, that firm, undisturbed serenity brought to mind similar aspects in Piero della Francesca: colour, in these painters, tends naturally towards a pearl-like light, a sense of peace translated into purely visual terms. The feeling of satisfaction produced by the setting, by rare stuffs, polished glass, cunningly arranged objects, becomes ecstatic; the soul of the beholder comes forth from itself and plunges, unreservedly, into the thing seen. A map hanging on a wall, a majolica vase, a pearl in a woman's ear, have, as it were, a Platonic value as archetypes: they are, *par excellence*, the objects they represent. The transfiguration of everyday things could go no farther. Thus Vermeer, from the very beginning of this bourgeois art, was the forerunner, in painting, of those who, centuries later, were to be the supreme products of that same art in literature (it was not for nothing that Proust alluded, in various passages, to Vermeer as to an exquisite thing unknown to the vulgar and profane such as Odette and Albertine: 'Do you know the Vermeers?' Albertine answered 'no': she thought she was being asked about living people). Generations and generations of realistic novelists were to pass by before a similar transfiguration of everyday matters was reached in literature. Vermeer's visions and those of Proust unfold in an atmosphere of perfect silence: a solemn, utterly quiet accumulation of magic particles.[5]

This sphere of elegiac calm is one of the farthest points arrived at by bourgeois art, which, in its purest essence, is an art of tranquillity, of immobility transmuted into dream. We see this also in Terborch, who—without however attaining to Vermeer's intensity of contemplation—embraces his interior scenes with a cold, detached, precise eye, sensible only of the qualities, of the varying exquisiteness of the material world, so that flesh, glass, tapestries, silks are fused, with the gentlest possible transition, into a soft, barely indicated harmony in which each thing has an accent peculiar to itself though it speaks only in the faintest whisper. His is an atmosphere of suspense—of a suspense that is most easily noticeable in a picture with a musical subject such as the *Concert* in the Kaiser-Friedrich Museum. The lack of communication between the faces of the performers—one keeps her eyes bent on the spinet, the other turns her back upon us as she plays her viola da gamba—removes all anecdotic, sentimental interest: the eye feasts itself upon a careful still life, upon the silk of garments, the softness of a fur tippet, the smooth back of a neck, the almost hieratic, intangible remoteness of the woman's bust, like a silver reliquary, as she sits behind the spinet. And the harmony generated by the contemplation of this exquisite still life is, precisely—translated into bars of modulated silence—the sound that we should hear if the voices of the instruments could reach us. Pieter de Hooch has an extremely clever expedient for making us aware of the solemn silence of interiors and courtyards: through a perspective of rooms or a lateral passage more luminous than the rest of the picture, a figure retires or approaches: we imagine the sound of a footstep echoing in a magical void. The sound, like that of a stone falling into a quiet pool, is a comment upon the immense surrounding silence.

The interior painting which descends in a direct line from the portrait of the merchant Arnolfini and his wife,[6] painted by Jan Van Eyck in 1434, achieves its supreme formula in Vermeer, Terborch, and de Hooch. Before Van Eyck, if interiors were painted, they were either of St. Jerome's study with the shelf of books and the lion lying curled up like a faithful dog, or of St. Anne's bedroom, with the women intent on bathing the divine infant girl.[7] With the Arnolfini portrait, the sacred episode disappeared: the relation between the interior and its occupants became that of everyday life. Motionless as a waxen statue, the man in his wine-brown robe keeps his eyes fixed on the floor while he stretches out his palm with puppet-like stiffness to the big-bellied woman in her long green gown edged with white fur; round about them are familiar objects, the bed and the great chair covered in red, the brass chandelier, the clogs, the elegant pair of red shoes, the oranges on the chest beneath the window, and, in the foreground, pretty as a fluffy toy, the little *griffon* dog. In a round mirror on the wall the group and the whole room are reflected as though in a miniature—the reflection of a reflection, for the immobility of the figures is already beyond reality; and yet with the greatest, the most faultless care to reproduce reality in all its most minute details, even to the transparent shadow of the amber rosary on the wall, even to the shapes of the people who stand outside the door reflected in the round mirror, facing the married pair, even to the miniatures that radiate from the circular frame of the mirror itself. There is no breath of sentiment in the scene; it is a group in a rarefied atmosphere, a first realistic study, with no attempt made to embellish or animate the figures; a long, patient pose, forerunner of the daguerreotype: husband and wife fixed for ever in a gesture that makes plain the bond between them, as in the groups that recline upon the lids of Etruscan sarcophagi.[8]

The history of this bourgeois art interests us here because of the progressive infiltration into it of sentimental, humorous, and pathetic elements, and because of its addiction to narrative. In Gabriel Metsu the spell of that crystalline air is already broken, of that world fixed for ever in a posture of loveliness, that is to be found in Terborch and in Vermeer. No story could be invented about Terborch's *Music Lesson*, and it would be very difficult to put together a tale on the subject of the same artist's *Curiosity* (Bache Collection, New York), in which a lady sits writing a letter in a richly decorated Dutch room, while a friend, standing behind her, bends over her shoulder, in a pose which— more than the expression of her face—betrays curiosity; and in front of the writing-table stands a third lady, who casts her eyes vaguely in the direction of a little dog. But Gabriel Metsu, combining the two subjects of music and curiosity in his *Lovers of Music*, presents us with a real pantomime, in the woman whose eyes are pursuing some thought or fantasy of her own and who interrupts the writing of her letter to hear the notes the other woman is drawing from her lute, and the chubby-faced gallant who is leaning on the back of the chair upon which she sits, as though he had come up very quietly behind her and were finding affectionate expressions directed to himself in the letter at which he is peeping. *The Intruder* is the title of another picture (in the National Gallery, Washington): in this the serving-maid is holding back the impetuous young cavalier who early in the morning bursts into the chamber of his beloved just as she is getting out of bed and putting her bare feet to the floor; she reproves the young dandy with a look of irritation, while the elderly woman sitting in the corner seems to be regarding the unexpected irruption with benevolence. It was from these gallant and amorous little pictures (a favourite composition was that of a beautiful young woman and her admirer at a table, he sitting smiling beside her with one arm round her waist and, in the other hand, a glass sparkling with golden wine, while the table before them is spread for a feast) and from the gallant,

lascivious paintings of Jan Steen (some of them, not published in monographs on the subject, are carried rather far)
that the French eighteenth century was later to draw its
inspiration. It is rarely that Vermeer indulges in anecdote:
one of his 'Women Reading' (Amsterdam) stops her lute-
playing to look at the note which the smiling servant-maid
has brought her, and questions her with her eyes; but the
most famous of them, the one in Dresden, does nothing
more than provide an excuse for a play of lights and reflections. In a pair of small pictures by Metsu (formerly in the
Beit Collection, London) we see, in one, a young man in the
act of writing a love-letter, his lips slightly parted as though
to whisper the sweet words that he is writing down, in the
other, a lady turning to the window in order to read the
letter, while the maid who has brought it to her loiters to
gaze at a picture on the wall, which is left partly uncovered
by the curtain. A comparison between this and the severe
'Woman Reading' of Vermeer gives the full measure of
difference between the loftiest and the most ordinary utter-
ances of this bourgeois painting. It might be said that the
curtain, which in Vermeer's picture has a purely pictorial
value, has become, in Metsu's, an element in an anecdotic
ensemble. In two pictures of sick persons Metsu's subject-
matter appears to be a decided foreshadowing of a certain
department of nineteenth-century taste. In the *Sick Child*
(Steengracht Collection, The Hague) the mother has lifted
the little invalid from his bed, and the child, languidly, his
eyes fixed on nothing, abandons himself to her; the mother's
gesture is caressing but discreet, and her face as she bends
down betrays no emotion. The note of pathos is barely
hinted at here, whereas in the *Sick Woman* in the Kaiser-
Friedrich Museum it is heavily stressed: drowsy with a
sleep that brings no refreshment, she sits with her head
sunk into a pillow that rests against the back of her chair,
her pale face, exhausted by pain, against the pale background of the cushion, and seems to be groaning in a subdued fashion; the servant-maid comes towards her, her
handkerchief held to her eyes; the sentimentality of the
picture culminates in the maid's sobbing. Compare this with
the treatment of the same subject—the sick woman in an

armchair, her head resting on a pillow—by a contemporary of Vermeer and de Hooch, Jacob Vrel. His *Convalescent*, who sits dozing near the hearth with her head against a pillow balanced on the back of the chair, has a face less stricken than that of Metsu's invalid: the picture, with the pets crouching at their mistress's feet, suggests only absorption and profound silence; it touches no lacerating note, it does not aim at forcing tears from the compassionate spectator. Not that Vrel, elsewhere, is lacking in a decidedly tendentious tone. But the melancholy, the agoraphobia, one might well call it, of this painter (so much does he delight to enclose himself in narrow spaces, in nameless by-streets, in hidden rooms at the ends of narrow lanes) are apparent in the painting itself; they emanate from the *ensemble*, they do not announce themselves descriptively. Vrel breathes absorption and melancholy, as Fra Angelico breathes serenity. Sometimes his asceticism (he has been called the painter of *béguinages*) expresses itself in very bold inventions. In *Woman combing a little Girl's hair* (Detroit Museum) the *genre* (treated, for instance, by Terborch in *Boy picking fleas from a Dog*, at Munich, and in *Mother combing her Daughter's hair*, Mauritshuis) becomes subsidiary: there is indeed, on the right of the picture, the group of the mother delousing her little girl's head, and on the left, intent on looking out of the door, the little brother, while the hoop and stick on the floor tell of play abandoned; but the true feeling of the picture is given by the bare wall dominating the centre, its surface only slightly broken, at one side, by the cloak hanging on it: this wall gives the impression that the people in the picture are immured alive. Or, again, Vrel excludes light altogether, and paints darkness; an interior window behind whose glass lies a murky room; a child's face pressed against the pane in the thick gloom. It is a pity that Huysmans, the nineteenth-century bourgeois in whom realism and sensuality, having passed the point of ripeness, decay in an atmosphere of *putridero*, did not know Vrel's pictures, which would have supported his own aspirations towards mystic nihilism; for Vrel's art —a phrase from John Donne's *Nocturnall upon S. Lucie's Day* is appropriate—

did expresse
A quintessence even from nothingnesse,
From dull privations, and leane emptinesse. . . .

In Vrel, too, Huysmans would have discovered the first
artist to be inspired by the fascination of mean streets in
out-of-the-way quarters, precursor of Dickens, the painter
of the London slums—except that the effects of intense
melancholy obtained by Dickens through an accumulation
of dazzling details were achieved by Vrel with a very different economy of means. But the important thing to be
observed here is that this aspect of bourgeois nineteenth-
century narrative literature—the love of poor and humble
quarters of towns—is sometimes also to be found in seventeenth-century Dutch painting. Usually the *genre* painters
in Holland who specialized in urban painting concentrated
upon illustrious monuments or the larger arteries of towns:
this is so in Berckheyde, van der Heyde, Nicolas Hals.
Few painters troubled to reproduce humble streets—except Vermeer in his view of a quiet corner of Delft, with a
woman sitting in a doorway at her embroidery and another
one busy in the passage to the little courtyard; and, more
than anyone, Vrel, with his narrow streets in which the
picturesque façades and odd roofs of the buildings, the
curious shop-signs, the irregular pavements, seem to be
speaking a human language: Vrel plunges into these little
lanes with a voluptuous pleasure in hiding, in escaping
from the great world.

The painting of interiors (even without human figures,
as in an anonymous picture in the Louvre, which, through
an open door with a bunch of keys hanging from the key-
hole, shows a portion of a room with a table, a chair, and
two pictures, one of them a Terborch: the only sign of
human presence being a pair of slippers on the threshold)
and also of humble corners of towns, are two aspects of
bourgeois art that are clearly shown as early as the seventeenth century, with a characteristic sentimental notation.
Dutch painting is also the first to take on a colouring of
humour or satire. Even in the countenances of the *Money
Changers* (of which so many replicas exist) of Quentin
Matsys and of Marinus van Roymerswaale—busy

counting and weighing money, with their sinister criminals' faces, at a table laden with groschen and florins and bills— we can already discern characteristics that Dickens was later to impress upon his figures of misers and money-lenders: familiar figures of the commercial and bourgeois world portrayed with the sharpest realism. In the Dutch painters the unbridled and superficial world of Flemish *bambocciate*, as seen in the work of Breughel, Brouwer, and Teniers, is tempered with good-natured ease. The bacchanal atmosphere of Jordaens is softened into that of a little family party in Metsu (*The Feast of the Kings*, Munich). The theme of Jordaens and Metsu is also treated by Jan Steen (Cassel): in this too the plebeian revelry of the Flemish painter gives place to a crackling bourgeois humour. The agreeable settings that we have already encountered in Terborch and Metsu become, in Steen, shrill with gibes and laughter. Steen knows how to seize upon the comic aspect of every situation; even his sick women are only sick for a joke. There is one, for instance, whose head, as usual, is supported by a pillow, as in the pictures of Vrel and Metsu; but this one seems prepared to make a fuss as the doctor feels her pulse; and in any case attention is not concentrated upon her any more than upon the utensils of ordinary life: the lute hanging on the wall, the footwarmer on the floor and, on it, the bottle containing the sample of urine and the linen thread used by the doctor. In another small picture (Print Room, The Hague) the subject is a lady who is sick from love; in others, they suffer from perfectly ordinary headaches, or from indigestion, and the accessories, in Rabelaisian fashion, are brought into prominent notice— the chamber-pot, the phial containing the urine, if not actually the enema syringe. The beautiful invalid in the Pannwitz Collection, Heemstede, lies on the bed with her bosom uncovered, while the sprightly old doctor, with a paunch like Mr. Punch himself, takes away the syringe from the elderly female relation and places his hand on his chest, as much as to say: '*I'll* see to it'; the whole atmosphere throbs with comic expectation. Steen touches notes that were to be rediscovered in the nineteenth century by artists such as Spitzweg and Dickens. A pompous silken

curtain, exactly similar to the one which, in a picture by
Pieter de Hooch, opens upon the Burgomasters' Hall in
the Town Hall of Amsterdam, rises in a decorative manner,
in Steen, upon a coarse tavern scene; a solemn doorway
frames a view of a bed on whose edge sits a woman putting
on her stockings. These are witticisms translated into
painting, and in Steen, truly, the art of the painter is often
subordinated to the subject, so that he becomes a mere
illustrator. In a picture such as *The Gallant Offering* (Brussels)—it has been said—the satirical point underlying the
anecdote already foreshadows Hogarth, except that, whereas in Steen a popular, sensual art is on the point of declining
into epigrammatic rationalism, in Hogarth the painting is
going the opposite way: starting as moralistic illustration,
it ends by exalting itself into art.

But clear pointers towards Hogarth are by no means
lacking in Steen—in the series of 'dissolute families', for
instance, who give themselves up to riotous junketing while
round them children and animals vie with each other to
reduce the house to ruin: in contrast to them there are
pious families gathered round a sober table, saying grace
before the meal. One of the 'dissolute families' (in the
Schloss Collection, Paris) especially claims our attention.
Beside the table, which is laid for a meal and covered with
glasses and decanters and a formidable peacock pie, sit the
dissolute husband and wife, plunged in sleep; on the floor
there is a confused mass of overturned and scattered objects,
amongst which the children are playing. The positions of
the husband and wife, particularly the abandoned attitude
of the husband, recall irresistibly the famous breakfast
scene in Hogarth's *Marriage à la Mode*. Even the Hogarthian manner of stressing the moral of a picture by means
of some symbolic object or animal has its antecedents in
Steen. The fantastic clock in the room where Hogarth's
breakfast scene is set is a hybrid hotchpotch—a china cat
on an ormolu clock, surrounded by foliage amongst which
fish are swimming; and underneath, a figure like a Buddha,
from the navel of which issue snakelike arms carrying
candles. It is, as it were, a symbol of ill-assorted matrimony.
In this 'dissolute family' by Steen the monkey disarranging

the papers on the floor and the flaunting peacock's tail on the table are emblems taken bodily from popular engravings of the vices. The brothel scene in the *Rake's Progress* recalls typical scenes in Steen—the one in the Louvre, for instance, in which the man has collapsed, blind drunk, into the lap of the half-stunned courtesan who is raising her wine-glass; another girl is removing the watch from the wretch's pocket and passing it over to a long-nosed procuress, who has already seized upon his cloak and sword. In the revellings of the *Rake's Progress* the courtesan holds one hand inside the drunken young man's shirt, while, with the other, she hands his stolen watch to her accomplice; in the opposite corner another courtesan is in the act of slipping on her shoe, in an attitude that very frequently recurs in pictures by Steen.

In scenes of tipsy women Steen does not really attain to the macabre satire of the Hogarth of *Gin Lane*; there is always, in him, a background of rich laughter, even when he is pointing a moral, as in the picture of a party of drunken women—one of them staggering, another roaring with laughter—returning home with a gay male companion and stared at by the whole village; by way of comment he puts in a pig raising its snout from its sty. It is not at all surprising that Steen should have a tendency towards the moral emblem, considering how very widely diffused emblems of this kind were in Holland; Breughel, with his illustrated proverbs, had been one of the Holy Fathers of *genre* painting. The collections of Jacob Cats, and especially that of Johan de Brune (*Emblemata of Zinnewerck*, 1624) abound in little scenes of bourgeois interiors with a moral point.

And so, when, shortly after 1730, William Hogarth started his first series of 'pictur'd morals' with the *Harlot's Progress*, he certainly had no right to boast, as he did, that he had put his hand to 'a field not broken up in any country or any age'. 'I thought both writers and painters had, in the historical style, totally overlooked that intermediate species of subject, which may be placed between the sublime and the grotesque.' Hogarth was not discovering a new province any more than, ten years later, was Chardin, when he devoted himself to the delineation of humble bourgeois interiors. Bourgeois art had already, in Holland, touched all its principal chords.⁹

*   *   *   *   *

II

Hogarth carried to an extreme a moralizing tendency that was already to be observed in Steen, and jeopardized the balance between pictorial expression and edifying content to such a point that he caused Charles Lamb to say: 'His graphic representations are indeed books: they have the teeming, fruitful, suggestive meaning of *words*. Other pictures we look at,—his prints we read.' And again, *à propos* of *Gin Lane*: 'Every thing in the print, to use a vulgar expression, *tells*.' These are words which, in the mouth of Lamb, were meant to be words of praise, but we have learnt from much of the painting of the nineteenth century, burdened, as it was, with highly intellectualized intentions, that they can, on the other hand, be turned to imply disapproval. But, just because it is so easily translatable into words, Hogarth's painting, if, in a sense, it is closely connected with the literature, particularly the satirical literature, of his age—owing to its presentment of every facet of the everyday world Lamb compares his painting to the best novels of Fielding and Smollett—does, also, anticipate the nineteenth-century novel, especially that of Dickens, with his satirical portraits and his impressions of the London slums. No one had undertaken to describe the latter before Dickens, but there are very clear precedents in the work of Hogarth. Look, for instance, at *Morning*, in the *Four Times of the Day* series (1738).

Henry Fielding, when (in *Tom Jones*, 1749) he is describing the appearance of Miss Bridget Allworthy, compares her to the lady on her way to Covent Garden church in that particular print of Hogarth's. It can be said that, in this case, painting had preceded literature in the delineation of a type; but there is more than that in Hogarth's *Morning*, there is the feeling of poor life and low life in London, and especially of the background of that life: tall, desolate

houses beneath an inclement winter sky, a description of
which would be vainly sought in the novelists of the
eighteenth century; for that, we have to wait until Dickens.
With regard to *Gin Lane* again, Lamb relates the impression of a friend—that not merely are the human figures
laden with significance, but 'every thing else in the print
contributes to bewilder and stupefy,—the very houses . . .
tumbling all about in various directions, seem drunk—
seem absolutely reeling from the effect of that diabolical
spirit of phrenzy which goes forth over the whole composition'. And in Dickens, indeed, we see the very landscape
charged with ethical content, animated as though with
a sinister character and a sinister intention of its own (the
corner of the Thames, for example, where Quilp lives and
dies). There is no story-teller of Hogarth's time in whom
we find so minutely picturesque an interior as that of *The
Strolling Players*, which Horace Walpole, who was well
versed in the picturesque, declared to be Hogarth's masterpiece. It is not until the novelists of the nineteenth century
that we find the minute descriptions, producing an effect
almost of hallucination by the preciseness of their observed
detail, which can claim equality with this painting, and
also similar contrasts of misery and grandiloquence (the
misery, in this case, of the strolling players contrasting with
their fabulous disguises). Further, with regard to the expressions of Hogarth's faces, to that richness so highly
praised by Lamb, certainly in comparison with them the
characterizations of Fielding and Smollett appear summary; it is only in Dickens—who was indeed nourished by
these eighteenth-century novelists, but who made a great
advance on his own account—that we can review so imposing a portrait-gallery. Lamb, seeking a literary counterpart
to the *Rake's Progress*, had to go back to Shakespeare's
Timon of Athens; but it does not seem to us that this parallel
can be sustained when we think how much nearer Dickens
came to Hogarth's mixture of grotesque and tragic. A spirit
of observation so acute that 'tables, and chairs and joint-
stools in Hogarth, are living and significant things'; subjects drawn from everyday life rather than from history or
fable; finally, edification and an ability to move the feelings:

there is no doubt that, in all these qualities, Hogarth is the precursor of the nineteenth-century novel.

Satire and humour there were, in the eighteenth century, but, as Lamb says: 'Hogarth has been often imitated in his satirical vein, sometimes in his humorous; but very few have attempted to rival him in his moral walk.' There is indeed a moral, edifying purpose, illustrated with a subject taken boldly from the most prosaic kind of life, to be found in *The History of George Barnwell* (1731) by George Lillo— the tragedy of a merchant apprentice seduced and led to perdition by a courtesan, a drama which, in its simple-minded ethical pattern (like a popular print), is certainly a near relation to the parallel careers of the industrious and the lazy apprentices in Hogarth's *Industry and Idleness*; but, both in Lillo and in his follower Edward Moore (*The Gamester*, 1753) there is a conspicuous lack of those qualities of observation, of that study of contrast between grotesque and painful, that we find in Hogarth.

Lillo and Moore nevertheless, with their tearful comedies, have without doubt a close relationship to the moralistic painting of Greuze, through their influence on their ad-mirer and imitator Diderot, who maintained: 'As for me, I consider that if a dramatic work is well made and well played, the stage should offer the spectator as many real pictures as there are moments favourable to the painter in the course of the action.' A similarly theatrical point of view is, moreover, dominant in Hogarth, and perhaps that is why Charles Lamb, himself a passionate theatregoer, exalted him to the stars; perhaps that is why the comparison with Shakespeare's plays came spontaneously to his mind. 'I . . . wished to compose pictures on canvas similar to representations on the stage, and further hope that they will be . . . criticized by the same criterion', declared Hogarth. '. . . I have endeavoured to treat my subjects as a dramatic writer: my picture is my stage, and men and women my players, who by means of certain actions and gestures are to exhibit a dumb show.' Hogarth was speak-ing of himself as *author* rather than as *artist*; it was as if he considered himself a comic writer as, in a sublime manner, Shakespeare had been, and as Dickens was to be later.

Hazlitt reaffirmed this connexion with literature when he included Hogarth in his *Lectures on the English Comic Writers*. Nor is this the first case of painting inspired by stage action. And yet, in this whole game of exchanges between literature and art, we can see how very small is the literary premiss (the plays of a writer like Lillo), and how, in effect, it was the development of situations and subjects employed in painting (even if through stage interpretation) which influenced subsequent literary evolution.

For there is a truly convincing relationship between the founder of the English pictorial tradition, William Hogarth, and the patriarch of the English novel, Henry Fielding. It is convincing because Fielding was guided by the same principles as Hogarth; in fact, he actually regarded the work of the painter as his model.

From the literary point of view, it is clear, Fielding can be traced back to Cervantes, and if one wishes to seek a national model, in literature, for his satire of manners, one may think of Ben Jonson; but parallels with *Don Quixote*, however close (to take one case amongst a great many, the scene in Lady Booby's house at the end of *Joseph Andrews*, during which various persons exchange beds in the dark, recalls the celebrated tavern scene in which Don Quixote believes the monstrous Maritornes to be a lovely *châtelaine*: and the rough, bearded Mrs. Slipslop is indeed an English Maritornes), are hardly enough to provide the key to Fielding's art; and on the other hand, the satire of Ben Jonson, who made an effort to be a realist and to scourge the social abuses of the century ('to imitate justice and instruct to life' was the task assigned by Jonson to comic wit),[10] was too deferential to classical models (too easily did he transfer himself in imagination to the Rome of the Caesars) for his barbs aimed at the traditional vices— avarice, lechery, drunkenness—to hit their targets well and truly; while his attacks of more immediate purpose, such as those on the Puritans, do little more than graze the skin.

Fielding also (and this is yet another characteristic he has in common with Cervantes) came from the theatre; from 1727 to 1737 he wrote for the stage; only later did

1. SIR EDWIN LANDSEER. Queen Victoria, the Prince Consort and the Princess Royal, at Windsor (*Windsor Castle. Reproduced by gracious permission of Her Majesty The Queen*)

2. VAN EYCK. Arnolfini and his Wife (*London, National Gallery.
Reproduced by courtesy of the Trustees*)

he venture upon narrative prose, introducing into it the
vivacity of his dialogue in order to break the monotony of
a continuous story, and thus becoming the founder—
rather than Defoe (as V. S. Pritchett has well observed in
The Living Novel)[11]—of the tradition of the English novel.
Only an author with experience of stage plots could have
kept control of so closely woven a web as that of *Tom Jones*,
and in fact Coleridge quotes it as one of the three most perfect plots he knew, in company with those of two plays, the
Oedipus Rex of Sophocles and Ben Jonson's *Alchemist*. Certain episodes in *Tom Jones* seem lifted bodily from the
theatre, such as that in which both Lady Bellaston and later
her maid are concealed behind the curtain in Tom's room.
In Hogarth the theatrical tendency proclaims itself when,
for instance, he shows two successive moments of a single
episode, as in *The Game of Draughts*.[12] If, as regards moral
instruction, he clung to a popular form of the type exempli-
fied in the well-known pair of compositions, *Death of the
Righteous Man* and *Death of the Sinner*, as regards dramatic
representation he almost showed the way to the strip cartoons of today. The pictures in the series of the *Industrious
Apprentice* and the *Idle Apprentice* are like scenes in a play;
the attitudes, the expressions of the characters suggest
dialogue. Fielding had the idea of putting words into the
mouths of Hogarth's characters, sometimes by directly
referring to them: we have already heard the novelist assur-
ing us that his Bridget Allworthy, in *Tom Jones*, is like the
lady on her way to Covent Garden church in Hogarth's
Morning; Partridge's wife looks exactly like the woman
pouring out tea in the third engraving of the *Harlot's Progress*; and Thwackum, the conscientious, brutal chaplain
who takes charge of Tom's upbringing, resembles, as one
drop of water resembles another, the guardian and chastiser
of the courtesans in Bridewell, in the fifth of the same series.
Often, when Fielding is imagining the facial expressions of
his characters, he quotes Hogarth: it is thus in *Joseph
Andrews*, thus in *Amelia* when he wishes to describe the
effervescent Mrs. Matthews, and so on.[13] And not only are
the characters Hogarthian whose resemblance Fielding
himself proclaims, but others, too, seem to be drawn from

those famous engravings—Jonathan Wild, for instance, or the unnamed lord who is the seducer in *Amelia*, and all the figures of the malefactors in the introductory chapter on Newgate in that same novel. At a certain point in *Tom Jones* Fielding amuses himself by inverting the distinguishing qualities in the careers of the industrious and the idle apprentices, for he tells us that everyone thought that Tom would end up on the gallows because he committed small thefts (like the idle apprentice in one of Hogarth's pictures) and was disrespectful to his masters, and we see his behaviour in an even worse light when we compare it with the virtues of Blifil: but in the novel it is Tom who is the hero and the hypocritical Blifil his antagonist.[14]

Fielding had as sharp an eye as Hogarth for rough, ill-formed physical types. Yet, with all that, the art of both always stops short of caricature. There is, in their figures, too strong, too pungent a human flavour for it to be possible to laugh at them as though they were queer arabesques. As Lamb said: 'Of the severer class of Hogarth's performances, enough, I trust, has been said to shew that they do not merely shock and repulse; that there is in them the "scorn of vice" and the "pity" too; something to touch the heart, and keep alive the sense of moral beauty; the "lacrymae rerum", and the sorrowing by which the heart is made better.' Both these artists plunge their roots into the most vital of human experience. Take, for example, the celebrated passage in *Tom Jones* (Book V, chap. 10) in which Tom is absorbed in enthusiastic meditations upon the charms of Sophia and is saying to himself that no other woman could ever have so much attraction for him, when Molly Seagrim comes along with a pitchfork in her hand, straight from haymaking, 'without a gown, in a shift that was somewhat of the coarsest, and none of the cleanest, bedewed likewise with some odoriferous effluvia, the produce of the day's labour', goes up to Tom, and a few moments later he disappears with her into the bushes. Hogarth's derelicts and *goujats* are often sinister, but never caricatures: we feel ourselves shudder in their presence, because we discover the same human material in them as in ourselves. And that is the reason why Hogarth's prints are

so effective, even today—that they do not confine themselves to telling a commonplace story of vice punished
and virtue rewarded, but lay bare the social sores of the
eighteenth century and reveal the dark and terrible sides
of a period which only a superficial conception can present
in a wholly Arcadian, refined light. It was against the
cruelty and hypocrisy of his time that Hogarth launched
his bill of indictment; for the central figures of his pictures
—the dissolute couple, the prostitute, the scapegrace, the
idle and the industrious apprentices—are the principal
characters only in name: it is the whole surroundings in
which they live that are denounced, as Michael Ayrton
well observes. When Hogarth shows us his scapegrace who
ends up in a lunatic asylum, he is not upholding the satisfaction of right-thinking people at so well-deserved a fate,
but is anxious, above all, that we should become aware of
the horrifying treatment of the insane in hospitals, and of
the terrible destiny of a young man led astray by the parasites who, in the other pictures of the series, crowd round
their newly-rich victim in order to do him homage. And
when he shows us the prostitute who finishes in Bridewell,
it is not so much that he wishes to edify us by the just
retribution of vice as to offer us the spectacle of a victim
crushed by a savage penal code. Hogarth reserves his vitriol
for the go-betweens and pettifoggers and charlatans who
throng his paintings. Fielding satirizes legal advisers,
magistrates, police spies, officers of the law, and night
watchmen. It was an age of bestial licence and violent,
inhuman repression—excesses which leapt to the eye.
Hogarth and Fielding fought against these abuses, the
former declaring that, if his *Four Stages of Cruelty* succeeded
in checking cruelty towards animals in London, he would
be 'more proud of having been the author' than if he had
painted Raphael's cartoons; the latter inculcating reforming tendencies into the English novel, from the very beginning. Dickens, in the following century, was to follow his
example, combating social evils which were less clear but
more insidious than those denounced by Fielding: the
crowd of hellish parasites in eighteenth-century society was
succeeded by the Pecksniffs and the Gradgrinds.

III

1755, the year in which Greuze's *Father Explaining the Bible to his Children* was exhibited at the Salon, marks an important date in the establishment of bourgeois art. In this type of sentimental work painting and literature again follow each other closely; if the Greuze of the melodramatic pictures bears traces of the theatre of Lillo and La Chaussée, *sensiblerie* on the other hand also finds in him its most pronounced expression before it appears in *La Nouvelle Héloïse* (1761), in *Émile*, in *The Vicar of Wakefield* (1766). The *Father Explaining the Bible* is a complete realization of Greuze's ingenuous moralistic intention to produce serious domestic painting, in dim tones—Protestant painting, as it were. The young man came from the provinces, and he expressed, in this picture, the depths of his own spirit; he made no concessions to fashion, in fact he had so little belief that the picture could be destined for success that he did not exhibit it for quite a long time, until M. de la Live de Jully discovered it. Its enthusiastic welcome by the public, and his marriage to Gabrielle Babuti, were, both of them, circumstances that transformed Greuze the sincere moralist into Greuze the painter of ambiguous innocences as described by the Goncourts. He thought he had touched the heart of his contemporaries, but they—to make use of the Goncourts' appropriate comparison—belonged to the race of Valmont in the *Liaisons dangereuses*, who slipped in a work of charity between two evil deeds. He thought he was marrying a middle-class woman who would turn into a model mother, *une mère bien-aimée*, and found himself, instead, tied to a libertine. The painter's underlying sensuality was thus fostered, and if this was perhaps a good thing for his painting in itself, for it became clothed with a kind of reflection of the exuberance of Rubens, another result of it was an artificial, equivocal character in his representations of virtue. Sensuality is transparently visible even in his most innocent-looking pictures—in the abandoned poses of the figures, in the disorder of garments; it declares itself in such curious adulterations as *La Cruche cassée*, *Le Miroir brisé*, *La Cage vide*, arch little symbols of lost vir-

ginity in which Greuze seems to be making the same speech
to the public as was made by so many seventeenth-century
allegorists: if you want to enjoy the picture, you can do so;
and if you like to be instructed by its moral, so much the
better. The spirit in which these languid, innocent creatures
are painted can be seen from reading the description of
Sophie in Rousseau's *Émile* (1761):

> A peine est-elle jolie ... mais on ne sauroit avoir ... une physio-
> nomie plus touchante. ... Sa parure est très modeste en apparence
> et très coquette en effet; elle n'étale point ses charmes, elle les
> couvre, mais en les couvrant elle sait les faire imaginer. En la voyant
> on dit, Voilà une fille modeste et sage; mais tant qu'on reste auprès
> d'elle, les yeux et le cœur errent sur toute sa personne sans qu'on
> puisse les en détacher, et l'on diroit que tout cet ajustement si simple
> n'est mis à sa place que pour en être ôté pièce à pièce par l'imagination.

Or think of La Volanges in the *Liaisons*—that innocent
young girl who was a living invitation to venery. And so
Greuze became the most perfect expression of the artificial
fashion for moralizing which was prevalent in decadent
eighteenth-century society—he, the painter who had been
encouraged by Diderot to think of himself as a healthy
plebeian predestined to react against the licentious manner
of Boucher, he, the painter who would have liked to be a
French Hogarth, representing *Bazile et Thibaud, ou les deux
éducations* in a series of edifying pictures, the conclusion
of which was that Thibaud, the murderer, was condemned
to death by none other than his old friend Bazile, now
a deputy judge of assize; such being the consequences of
a good or bad upbringing, just as, similarly, in *Industry and
Idleness*, the industrious apprentice, having become Sheriff
of London, sends the idle apprentice to be hanged at
Tyburn. For Hogarth had become no less popular in
France than in England, and there was no paterfamilias
who did not acquire his engravings to keep before his
children's eyes as incentives to perseverance in the paths of
virtue.[15] The fundamental ambiguity in Greuze's painting
did not prevent its being taken for true coin by observers
who lacked the perception of a Gautier or a Goncourt;
faced with *La Mort du paralytique*, *La Dame de charité*,
La Veuve inconsolable, *La Malédiction paternelle*, or *Le Fils*

puni, they felt themselves seized by emotions sometimes sweet, sometimes passionate. Of all eighteenth-century painters, Greuze was the only one who found favour in the eyes of the virtuous bourgeois of the middle of the following century. In the photographic minuteness of his settings, the humbleness of his domestic subjects, the declamatory ostentation of pictures such as *La Malédiction paternelle*, Dickens's contemporaries discerned a spirit in harmony with their own taste, without realizing that Greuze's exaltation of Duty and Virtue was to a great extent a solemn game—even if involuntary.

The ethical trend to be observed in Greuze was indeed merely one aspect of a much larger phenomenon: the precise, realistic examination of a whole world which until then had been little exploited by painters, in France, at any rate—the humble, intimate world of the bourgeoisie. It was the final result of an artistic revolution which had begun, in Italy, with Caravaggio, who, for ideal, heroic types, had substituted his own plebeian figures taken from life, without the slightest attempt at idealization.[16] The descendants of Caravaggio and the Dutch painters were, in France, the three brothers Le Nain, and they created for themselves their own province amongst solid, sober peasants and middle-class lovers of good living and family virtues. Families—consisting generally of one older person and a troop of peasant children—cluster together in communal, earthy life and stare at you as though your entrance into the place had made them jump (Antoine Le Nain); peasants amongst their humble huts or on their cottage doorsteps, or in moments of respite from toil in the open country (the rustic, smiling girl carrying a basket in the *Halte du cavalier*, in the Victoria and Albert Museum, assumes the dignity of an eternal type like Wordsworth's monumental Solitary Reaper), or, again, taken by surprise in workshop or at table, distracted for a moment by your presence and yet without relinquishing their quietness which is that of the eternal things of the earth (Louis Le Nain); or, with a little more movement—farm-labourers in procession, leading a heifer and raising glasses of wine, like an ancient sacrificial *cortège*, or bourgeois busy at the

card table, or girls dancing a slow measure to the music of
a violin (Mathieu Le Nain): all these scenes have nothing
anecdotal about them (unless we wish to see an anecdote
in a grace before meat, or a return from the fields, or a game
of cards), nor any moralistic intention, either; they are
solid realism well satisfied with itself, a realism whose
unique, monotonous originality is in no way disturbed by
a Neapolitan note here, a Spanish note there, a Dutch one
somewhere else. These were the *bambocciate* of the French,
produced in order to satisfy a taste which perhaps wel-
comed the intimate note of the brothers Le Nain and the
superficial picturesqueness of a Sébastien Bourdon with
the same eagerness. In the *bambocciate* of the brothers Le
Nain—more than in the lively Dutch, and more than in
the Neapolitans and the Spaniards, with whom the image
always fixes some pronounced gesture—one feels the
affinity of such *genre* painting with still life: or rather,
both types were 'nature in repose', according to the word
used in Holland, Germany, and England (*Still-leven*,
Stilleben, still life). This confirms the absence of the anecdotal and the edifying which has already been mentioned.

The affinity between the two branches—'nature in repose' and *genre* painting—is also very clearly seen in
Greuze's great contemporary, Chardin, whose name is
especially coupled with his for having given artistic expression to the 'third estate'. In Greuze and in Chardin there
exist, indeed, the opposite poles between which bourgeois
inspiration was to oscillate during the whole of the nineteenth century: on the one hand melodramatic sentiment,
on the other, concentration of thought, intimacy, realistic
observation sublimated into poetry. Like the brothers Le
Nain, like Greuze too, in his own way (his *Gâteau des rois*,
for instance, merely modernizes the subject of the Feast of
the Epiphany, as treated by Jordaens, Metsu, Steen, &c.)
Chardin links up with the Dutch painters, the first to
have given artistic expression to the life of the bourgeoisie.
The cultural background is the same; the subjects are the
same: women attending to their duties in humble rooms,
the industrious mother, the grace before meat, the morning
toilet, the governess questioning the child, the housewife

preparing convalescent food, children intent on their houses
of cards. The warm dusk, the visible silence of the surroundings, the look on the faces, generally drawn in profile,
half turned away—all these invite to meditation; as does
also the alignment of persons and things on the same plane
of importance, which is, in fact, simply their pictorial value.
A typical example is *Menu de maigre*, in which the ready-
laid table has at least the same degree of relief as the
woman's figure. And this aesthetic levelling is quite a
different thing from the social levelling which people sought
to regard as the 'novelty' in Chardin, as though he had
invented bourgeois painting, or introduced it into France,
for some kind of political reason. It would appear to have
been, rather, a practical matter; for it was in order to find
new subjects—hitherto he had limited himself to still life
—that Chardin chose that very field of activity which,
though it had previously been explored in France (Abraham Bosse, Bourdon, the Le Nain brothers), had since
become a special province of the Dutch (Chardin's pictures
were vaguely described as being 'in the taste of Teniers'):
a field which comprised interiors of middle-class houses
and the lives of industrious, virtuous, humble people—
subjects that were not of so much interest to the middle
classes themselves as they were to the great, who were
moved by the same curiosity as they had previously shown
in the matter of rustic life, regarded, sometimes, as racily
realistic, sometimes as idyllic. It has been observed, in fact,
that those who acquired Chardin's small *genre* pictures
were the royal collectors of Russia and Sweden, were counts
and princes and cavaliers; nor, furthermore, does the idea
of a good, modest, middle-class Chardin (the *bonhomme*
Chardin), exactly reproducing his own surroundings, seem
altogether sound, for his inventory declares him to have
been the owner of furniture that was positively sumptuous,
and he was far cleverer about his own affairs than he chose
to show himself to apologists, who in his case became
almost hagiographers. But, whatever there may have been
behind the scenes, psychologically, in Chardin's painting,
never has the poetry of ordinary life, of everyday objects
and foods, been exalted to so high a place as it was by him.[17]

In place of the opulence of the Dutch settings—rare crystal, sumptuous carpets, silks and velvets: a type of setting that Chardin used only in the most Dutch, and the earliest (1732), of his *genre* pictures, the *Lady sealing a Letter*, at Potsdam—we have simple glasses and crockery—sometimes a bare stone floor—cotton prints and woollen stuffs. What was said of Crabbe, that he was 'a Pope in woollen stockings', might be also said of Chardin: 'a Vermeer in woollen stockings'. Once upon a time a certain nobility of subject-matter seemed necessary to artists; but from the seventeenth century onwards people began to realize that poetry does not have to be sought after in the rare, the heroic, the unusual: it can be found in the most trivial objects around us. Like Charles Lamb, later on, Chardin had no need to move out of his own quarter of the town— even, in fact, out of his own parlour—in order to have his imagination stimulated. His figures—usually house- wives—are sparing of gesture; reserved, modest, they give scarcely a hint of movement; on their faces is no play of expression; certainly this art, in contrast to that of a Hogarth or a Greuze, owes nothing to the theatre. Thus, in painting, Chardin achieves an ideal which, according to modern terminology, might be termed that of everyday lyricism, the same ideal that was to be the aim of so much eighteenth- and early nineteenth-century literature, follow- ing the most diverse roads (Flaubert, the Goncourts, the Patmore of *The Angel in the House*, Trollope in his happier moments, and later the George Moore of *Esther Waters*, Proust, Virginia Woolf). And the secret of his supreme success has to be sought in his technique, a *legato* technique if ever there was one, in which each colour acts as a mirror to its neighbour, all contrast being thus muted, and the whole being fused by imperceptible gradations into a com- pact harmony, extremely rich beneath its appearance of monotony; a technique that, if one wishes to find a com- parison in literature, reminds one of the verbal orchestra- tions of Proust and Virginia Woolf.

Having thus passed in review the Holy Fathers of *genre* painting, it is not our intention to pause over the minor masters, such as for instance, in France, Étienne Aubry, a list of whose subjects sufficiently reveals the bourgeois limits of his inspiration (maternal correction, domestic employments, the farewell to the nurse, the first lesson in brotherly friendship, or—in the melodramatic manner of Greuze—the broken marriage, the repentant son returning to his father's house); or Louis Boilly, who gives a neo-classic smoothness and elegance to a style derived from the Dutch, and who also painted scenes of bourgeois life—the café, the billiard-room, the departure of the coach, little dramatic scenes with a flavour of gallantry, grotesque faces like those of Leonardo and Hogarth. But, from the second half of the eighteenth century onwards *genre* painters are legion; the little Dutch pictures come to be sought after for private galleries, and are reproduced in ladies' almanacs.[18] Sir Walter Scott, in his pictures of interiors, has much in common with *genre* painting, and, in the famous description of the family gathered round the corpse of the drowned sailor in *The Antiquary*, observes: 'In the inside of the cottage, was a scene which our Wilkie alone could have painted, with that exquisite feeling of nature that characterizes his enchanting productions.' Scott claims kinship with David Wilkie, disciple of the Dutch, while the humour of Dickens finds parallels in Thomas Rowlandson and George Cruikshank.

The vein of sniggering coarseness that we have already noted in Jan Steen is predominant, without any moralistic restraint, in Rowlandson. The latter, though he derives straight from Hogarth, has no desire, like Hogarth, to depict virtue and vice, or to evolve schemes for edifying the public; on the contrary, he abandons himself, in a frenzy of ardour, to his passion for representing the exuberant life of the masses, a life in which the feminine element plays a large part—rubicund women with bosoms bursting forth from their clothes and legs ignorant of the restraining influence of petticoats. Hogarth's actors move according to the dramatic laws of the stage, but there is no aura of the theatre left in Rowlandson's figures, whose bacchic saraband has all the freedom of expansion of life itself. He is a Rubens who has descended to the level of the popular print, but who has remained a supreme master of drawing, without the awkwardnesses shown in Épinal prints. In Rowlandson we can observe in full flower the primitive Anglo-Saxon exuberance which was gradually to be suffocated by bourgeois morality, the same exuberance that lends so fresh a flavour to many of Dickens's pages, weighed down though it is by a superstructure of middle-class conventions.[19] Cruikshank, formed in the school of the famous political caricaturist Gillray, began with satires on fashion (*Fashionable Monstrosities*) and refined his humorous inspiration by contact with the German writers of fairy-tales (A. von Chamisso, whose *Peter Schlemihl*, the man without a shadow, he illustrated; and the brothers Grimm, to whose fairy-stories he provided a pictorial commentary), thus arriving at the combination of romantic and grotesque that was to make him the ideal illustrator of Dickens. In fact, it might be said that—at the beginning, anyhow—the work of the writer Dickens ranks below that of the illustrator Cruikshank, so satisfactory a formula has the latter already found for what Dickens is still struggling to say. Cruikshank's *London in the early Morning* needs nothing more than a background of deserted streets with a solitary policeman, a stall with hot drinks in the foreground, a chilly-looking man drinking, and a little boy who seems wholly engaged in rubbing his hands together and stretching himself, to suggest completely the raw atmosphere of early morning. Dickens, on the other hand, launches out into a long essay that has all the appearance of a composition by a diligent schoolboy trying to remember all the things he saw one day when he happened to leave the house early. It was to his contact with the German Romantics that Cruikshank owed that mixture of fearsome and grotesque which distinguishes some of his most successful *Oliver Twist* illustrations; but however fearsome the scene may be there is always a streak of humour in him, as so often happens with Dickens. With the years, the moralistic side of Cruikshank became accentuated; he became the apostle of temperance, and when he was seventy painted a colossal picture in oils, *The Worship of Bacchus*, a terrifying work which, in attempting to give a general survey illustrating all the episodes to which drinking can give rise, achieves the crowded complication of a Hieronymus Bosch. In a bourgeois, positivist century, this had a significance equivalent to that of the *Universal Judgement* in the Sistine Chapel in the time of Michelangelo —except that in Cruikshank the scenes of felicity over which Bacchus presides are revealed as a mere make-believe against the frightful background of ruins and disasters caused by alcohol.[20]

The affinity between Cruikshank and Dickens is obvious at the first glance, and no further example of it is necessary than Cruikshank's picture *The Runaway Knock* (W. T. Spencer Collection, London), in which the solemn, pompous butler is coming out of a house at a corner—the front of the house adorned, in the Victorian manner, with creepers and a clump of hollyhocks—and staring, with bulging eyes, in the opposite direction to that in which the street arabs who have knocked at the door for a joke are making their escape; in front of the butler, a troop of lazy, spoilt lap-dogs, no less grotesque than he, rushes barking down the steps, scattering in all directions, while inside the bow-window can be seen the faces of the owners of the house, disturbed by the sudden uproar, and even the parrot on its perch still beating its wings in alarm. The picture is a satire upon those same comfortable bourgeois, the Podsnaps and their friends, against whom Dickens's barbs were aimed. Certain aspects of Dickens and Cruikshank correspond so perfectly that their ways of expressing themselves are like translations of the same range of humour into two different media—drawing and the written word. In any case, between 1830 and 1860 English painting, with its emphasis on subject, on the moral to be inculcated, the story to be told, was a branch almost of literature, rather than of painting. The public demanded that a picture should contain a moral, an anecdote: even in the previous century the Frenchman, Laugier, had made the pronouncement: 'L'invention est l'endroit où brille le génie du peintre. ... Son tableau parfaitement bien inventé, quand même il serait médiocrement peint, réussira beaucoup mieux que s'il était du pinceau le plus excellent avec une invention médiocre. ... Il faut que le peintre soit poète dans l'invention' (*Manière de bien juger les ouvrages de peinture*, 1771). Sentimental interest during the Victorian period reached such a point that Frith's famous painting, *Ramsgate Sands*, was severely criticized because the crowd on the beach contains no figure of a tender mother fussing over a convalescent child. Painters took great pains to load their pictures with meaning and suggestion,[21] story-tellers to convey the living image of things by means of a minute, 'picturesque' descriptiveness. *Ut pictura poesis* had become the golden rule—more than it ever had been, more than it ever was to be again—of nineteenth-century narrative literature.

NOTES TO THE INTRODUCTION

[1] This relationship between Dutch painting and nineteenth-century narrative has been noticed from time to time. For example, by Hegel in the *Vorlesungen über die Aesthetik* (1832), and by G. A. Sala (*Dutch Pictures, with some Sketches in the Flemish Manner*, London, 1861, Preface, p. viii): 'There are the Teniers, the Gerard Douws, the Ostades, and the Metzus—the great makers of minutiae, but surpassingly gifted likewise in skilful draughtsmanship, in harmonious composition, in brilliant colour, in exquisite finish. Such admirable exemplars answer, perhaps, to our Goldsmiths, our Lambs, our Leigh Hunts, and our Washington Irvings. I will name no living writer for fear of being howled at.' And, even more clearly, Walter Pater, in the passage from *Sebastian van Storck* (*Imaginary Portraits*) quoted at the beginning of this chapter.

[2] A similar phenomenon is to be found in literature, in the decadence and disappearance of the epic poem, and in the birth of the bourgeois form which corresponds to the epic poem and the drama, the novel. Henry Fuseli, who was, in theory, an upholder of the heroic and historical in painting, said at the beginning of the nineteenth century that modern art in Holland had been reduced to 'chronicle small beer' (cf. Shakespeare, *Othello*, ii. i. 161, and *2 Henry IV*, ii. ii. 8 et seq.), that is, to occupying itself with everyday things, (*The Mind of Henry Fuseli*, Selections from his Writings with an Introductory Study by Eudo C. Mason, London, Routledge & Kegan Paul, 1951, p. 278): the phrase is echoed in that manifesto of bourgeois art, Thackeray's *Small-Beer Chronicle*, see below, p. 248.

[3] A type of painting of rustic scenes, so called after the nickname—'Il Bamboccio' (Fr. *bamboche*)—of the seventeenth-century Dutch painter Peter van Laer, chief of the band of Dutch painters in Rome between 1625 and 1638.

[4] See the just observations of Max J. Friedländer in *Landscape, Portrait, Still Life* (Oxford, Bruno Cassirer, 1949, p. 105) on the anti-emphatic,

anti-baroque spirit of the Dutch: 'The Dutch view of the world, taken by and large, is objective, modest and patient. . . . They knew what they were depicting, and guarded against depicting anything they did not know.' To this subject of their specialization could be applied what Thackeray says in the *Small-Beer Chronicle*, see below, p. 250.

5 See, on Proust and Vermeer, R. Huyghe in *L'Amour de l'art*, 1936, i, and G. Macchia in *L'Immagine* (Rome), No. 16 (1950), and in *Il Tempo* (Rome), Jan. 14th, 1954 (*Con Marcel Proust alla ricerca di un pittore*).

6 It has recently been maintained that the subject of the portrait is the painter himself and his wife. See M. W. Brockwell, 'The Pseudo-Arnolfini Portrait in the National Gallery', in *The Connoisseur*, May 1953.

7 With regard to the bourgeois influence on this type of iconography, see F. Antal, *Florentine Painting and its Social Background*, London, 1947, p. 145, and especially pp. 355–6: the tendency to secularize birth-chamber scenes of the Nativity of Christ, of John the Baptist, or of the Virgin, on the birthday plates (*deschi da parto*) given away as presents on the occasion of the birth of a child. The intimate quality of *genre* painting seems already to be present in the scene of the birth of the Madonna in the Asciano altarpiece, attributed by Bernard Berenson to Sassetta. See B. Berenson, *The Sienese Painters of the Franciscan Legend*, Dent, 1910, pp. 56–57:

> It is a domestic scene carried out with that sense of every little action and every little circumstance having an almost sacramental value, the indispensable precision of ritual, which sense it is the sole business of justifiable *genre* painting to communicate. Ennobled comfort, cheerfulness, daintiness are the soul's perfumes exhaled from such a treatment of the subject. You hear the pleasant crackle of the fire on the hearth, and yet you breathe the sun-enlivened air of the out-of-doors; you get a charming glimpse of a little garden with its wall, its flower-beds and its solitary tree. At the time when this masterpiece of *genre* was painted it could have had but few rivals in European art.

8 The interpretation of this picture round about 1850 is symptomatic of the taste, and, in fact, of the need for anecdote, of the nineteenth century. Viardot, in *Les Musées d'Angleterre* (Paris, 1852), saw in the picture a scene of chiromancy: the man is trying to read in the palm of the woman's hand the future of the child whose birth she appears to be expecting. Laborde, in *La Renaissance des arts à la cour de France* (Paris, 1855, ii), gives the picture a title characteristic of nineteenth-century *genre* painting, *La Légalisation*: the man solemnly raises his right hand in order to testify, in the presence of a crowd of witnesses gathered at the door, that the baby whose birth the lady is obviously expecting is his own; to accentuate this fact Van Eyck has surrounded the mirror with ten other smaller mirrors, each one reflecting the scene from its own exact perspective, with a minuteness and a faithfulness which are truly noteworthy (less noteworthy are the minuteness and the faithfulness of Laborde, who did not take the trouble to observe that the scenes in the little round pictures round the mirror represent the Passion of Christ!). As for the facial expressions, which seem to be quite impassive, C. Phillips, in *The Fortnightly Review* of Oct. 1902, considers that the husband's expression is filled with emotion at his wife's pregnant condition: 'A moment of the holiest emotion, though it is made

manifest neither by word nor gesture, transfigures to a solemn beauty a
countenance of an almost grotesque ugliness.'

⁹ The influence of Hogarth made itself felt even in Russia, in the *genre*
pictures of Fedotov; see I. D. Leschinsky, *Pavel Andreevich Fedotov*,
Leningrad and Moscow, 1946, especially pp. 78–80.

¹⁰ As has been shown by L. C. Knights in *Drama and Society in the Age
of Jonson*, 1937, and, more recently, by Helena Watts Baum in *The Satiric
and the Didactic in Ben Jonson's Comedy*, Chapel Hill, The University of
North Carolina Press, 1947.

¹¹ London, Chatto & Windus, 1946.

¹² See nos. 4 and 5 in *Hogarth's Drawings*, collected by Michael Ayrton
and Bernard Denvir, London, Avalon Press, 1948.

¹³ A detailed list of these direct references is to be found in Robert
Etheridge Moore, *Hogarth's Literary Relationships*, University of Minne-
sota Press, 1949, pp. 122 et seq.

¹⁴ Fielding shows affinities with Hogarth even in his dramatic works.
The Lottery (1731) and *The Covent Garden Tragedy* (1732) may be compared with *A Harlot's Progress*, and *Pasquin* (1736) recalls the theatrical
satires of Hogarth's first prints. See, for these and other parallels, R.
Etheridge Moore, op. cit., who summarizes thus (p. 121):

He had drawn occasionally from Hogarth during his play-writing career.
When he came to compose a novel, to create a continuous story enacted by
individual characters, he could find the recipe waiting for him in Hogarth. ...
Joseph Andrews did not appear until 1742, ample time for Fielding to have
formulated the new philosophy of composition set forth in the famous preface,
a philosophy which he partially explains by direct reference to Hogarth's art.
In fine, all his comedies of manners were written without the influence of Hogarth,
and are wholly barren; *Joseph Andrews*, however, burst upon the world in full
flower of Hogarthian influence, and is one of the eternal marvels of English
humor.

Certainly there was also, in it, the confessed influence of Cervantes and
the unconfessed influence of Marivaux's *Paysan parvenu*. 'Yet consider the
Hogarthian element in the preface, consider that the two artists' outlook on
life is much alike, that they portray the same people doing the same things,
that they openly admire each other's work, and that they are close friends
to boot; then it seems certain that the younger and still unsettled learned
from the older and eminently successful.'

¹⁵ For the relationship between painting and literature in eighteenth-
century France see the essay by Louis Hautecœur, 'Le Sentimentalisme
dans la peinture française de Greuze à David', in the *Gazette des Beaux-
Arts*, 1909, i, pp. 159–76 and 269–86. Hautecœur strongly emphasizes
the literary factors, but then recognizes that, of the two, it was perhaps
Greuze who first inspired Diderot: 'D'ailleurs, Greuze ne remporte d'abord
que peu de succès auprès des critiques: on trouvait son genre "trop bas":
ce n'est que dix ans après, à l'époque de la *Nouvelle Héloïse*, que Greuze
réunit tous les suffrages avec son *Accordée du Village*.' And if it is true that
he adds, immediately afterwards, that 'entre 1753 et 1761, à l'époque où
se répandit la littérature sentimentale ... la peinture se prit à l'imiter et ...

se [fixa] les thèmes', it is no less true that the fashion had been fore-shadowed by a painter, Greuze.

[16] On Caravaggio see below, note to p. 392.

[17] Proust, in a letter to the editor of the *Revue hebdomadaire* (quoted by Charles Briand, *Le Secret de Marcel Proust*, Paris, Lefebvre, 1950, pp. 241–2), wrote:

Je viens d'écrire une petite étude de philosophie de l'art si le terme n'est pas trop prétentieux où j'essaye de montrer comment les grands peintres nous initient à la connaissance et à l'amour du monde extérieur, comment ils sont ceux 'par qui nos yeux sont déclos' et ouverts en effet sur le monde. C'est l'œuvre de Chardin que je prends dans cette étude comme exemple et j'essaye de montrer son influence sur notre vie, quel charme et quelle sagesse elle répand sur nos plus humbles journées en nous initiant à la vie de la nature morte. Croyez-vous que cet essai pourrait intéresser les lecteurs de la Revue Hebdomadaire?

On Dutch painting Proust wrote ('Tableaux de genre du souvenir', re-printed in *Les Plaisirs et les jours*, edition *Œuvres complètes*, Paris, *Nouvelle Revue française*, ix, 1935, p. 209):

Nous avons certains souvenirs qui sont comme la peinture hollandaise de notre mémoire, tableaux de genre où les personnages sont souvent de condition médiocre, pris à un moment bien simple de leur existence, sans événements solen-nels, parfois sans événements du tout, dans un cadre nullement extraordi-naire et sans grandeur. Le naturel des caractères et l'innocence de la scène en font l'agrément, l'éloignement met entre elle et nous une lumière douce qui la baigne de beauté.

[18] A review, albeit incomplete, of the enormous field of *genre* painting can be seen in Lothar Brieger, *Das Genrebild*, Die Entwicklung der bürger-lichen Malerei, Munich, Delphin-Verlag, 1922. See also Odette Aubrat, *La Peinture de genre en Angleterre de la mort de Hogarth au Préraphaélisme*, Paris, Maison du livre français (1935).

[19] If no one except Wilkie could have worthily depicted the scene described by Scott in the passage given above, who but Rowlandson could have done justice to this description of Sleary's company of mountebanks, in *Hard Times* (chap. vi)?

There were two or three handsome young women among them, with their two or three husbands, and their two or three mothers, and their eight or nine little children, who did the fairy business when required. The father of one of the families was in the habit of balancing the father of another of the families on the top of a great pole; the father of a third family often made a pyramid of both those fathers, with Master Kidderminster for the apex, and himself for the base; all the fathers could dance upon rolling casks, stand upon bottles, catch knives and balls, twirl hand-basins, ride upon anything, jump over everything, and stick at nothing. All the mothers could (and did) dance upon the slack wire and the tight-rope, and perform rapid acts on bare-backed steeds; none of them were at all particular in respect of showing their legs; and one of them, alone in a Greek chariot, drove six in hand into every town they came to. They all assumed to be mighty rakish and knowing, they were not very tidy in their private dresses, they were not at all orderly in their domestic arrangements, and the combined literature of the whole company would have produced but a poor

3. VERMEËR. Woman Reading (*Dresden Art Gallery*)

4. TERBORCH. The Concert (*Berlin, Kaiser-Friedrich Museum*)

letter on any subject. Yet there was a remarkable gentleness and childishness about these people, a special inaptitude for any kind of sharp practice, and an untiring readiness to help and pity one another, deserving often of as much respect, and always of as much generous construction, as the every-day virtues of any class of people in the world.

[20] *The Worship of Bacchus* might well seem to be a translation on to canvas of a fantasy such as is to be found in chapter xlvii of *Dombey and Son*: 'Oh for a good spirit who would take the house-tops off, with a more potent and benignant hand than the lame demon in the tale, and show a Christian people what dark shapes issue from amidst their homes, to swell the retinue of the Destroying Angel as he moves forth among them!'

[21] One need only think of the pictures of Augustus Egg, or of a Pre-Raphaelite such as Holman Hunt, whose *Awakening Conscience* was quoted by Ruskin in *Modern Painters* as an example of 'painting taking its proper place beside literature': the tragedy of the girl's lost virtue is suggested in the symbols that surround her—the luxurious, vulgar furnishings, the cat playing with a dead bird on the carpet, the gilded tapestry, with the fowls of the air feeding upon the ripened corn, the picture above the fireplace, with its single drooping figure, the *Woman taken in Adultery*; indeed, according to Ruskin (article in *The Times* of May 25th, 1854), even 'the very hem of the poor girl's dress, at which the painter has laboured so closely, thread by thread, has story in it, if we think how soon its pure whiteness may be soiled with dust and rain, her outcast feet failing in the street . . .' (see my essay on the Pre-Raphaelites in *La Casa della Fama*, Milan–Naples, Ricciardi, 1952, pp. 256 et seq.). This tendency, as I have already observed, goes back to Steen and Hogarth. Thackeray, discussing the latter painter in *The English Humourists*, pauses to enumerate the significant details, and to remark upon the persistent recurrence of the coronet, in old Lord Squanderfield's room in Hogarth's print:

Pride and pomposity appear in every accessory surrounding the Earl. . . . His coronet is everywhere. . . . The pictures round the room are sly hints indicating the situation of the parties about to marry. A martyr is led to the fire; Andromeda is offered to sacrifice; Judith is going to slay Holofernes. There is the ancestor of the house (in the picture it is the Earl himself as a young man), with a comet over his head, indicating that the career of the family is to be brilliant and brief.

PART ONE

Romanticism turns Bourgeois

Coleridge and Wordsworth

I SHALL not waste many words in defence of the use of the term 'Victorian' which will recur frequently in the course of this volume, since the discussion I have published elsewhere,[1] on the subject of a similar approximate term, 'romantic', holds equally good here. Like 'gothic', 'baroque', and 'Biedermeier' (of which it is, in a way, the English parallel), 'Victorian' is a term born out of a reaction—a summary definition and a summary act of justice on the part of later generations who, reacting to a certain taste, or, to employ a word in fashion at present, a certain 'climate', tried to fix its characteristics as the negative of the positive which they intended to bring into use. And, like those other terms, 'Victorian', having in the end lost its uncomplimentary tone, has survived as a useful approximation to indicate a phase of the habits and sensibilities that developed in England during a great part of the nineteenth century. It is more useful, in this case, than the term 'bourgeois'—with which after all it might be considered to correspond—since, in the matter of literature, Jean de Meung, even as far back as the end of the thirteenth century, presented all the characters that are typical of the bourgeoisie, while the bourgeois note was predominant in seventeenth-century art in Holland (as we have already had occasion to observe in the preceding pages) and played also so important a part in the eighteenth century in England (Addison has been called 'the first of the Victorians') and in the countries where English influence was paramount, that the term 'bourgeois' becomes clearly too generic, whereas 'Victorian' has a much more closely circumscribed local colour.

From the point of view of aesthetics it is easy to maintain—as I have already remarked in connexion with the word 'romantic'—the inadequacy, the positive inconsistency, even, of these 'ambiguous historical concepts' that we have called approximations. The argument against them appears, however, to resolve itself in the main into a dilemma of this kind: baroque, romantic, &c. either denote art, in which case they denote 'the beautiful' in the universal, and only admissible, sense of that word, or they denote a fashion, a vogue, in which case they stand for a negative concept, something that does not exist.[2] And this is a dilemma which would invite us to take no account of certain aspects, even in the work of the great artists, which are far from negligible, as I have tried to show with regard to Shakespeare.[3] In any case such a strict attitude is not always reflected in the practical conduct of those who make an intransigent theoretical profession of it: opponents of categories of taste have been known to have recourse, not to 'ambiguous historical concepts', but to rhetorical concepts (sub-categories of the beautiful, such as the pleasing, &c.), which, besides being even more ambiguous, are worn threadbare from the excessive use made of them in former times.

These approximations are intended merely to indicate where the accent falls, and acquire their meaning only within the compass of specified historical periods. It is thus that certain characteristics, sporadically visible earlier, appear so plentifully during the nineteenth century as to colour the whole epoch. Foretastes of Victorianism and of Biedermeier are to be found, for example, in seventeenth-century Holland; and yet, on the other hand, not all the writers, uniformly, of the epoch of Queen Victoria are 'Victorian' in the qualifying sense in which we use the word. But that is the dominant tone. What Gabetti wrote[4] on the subject of Biedermeier (a concept which he criticizes, in any case): 'It was the slow and unobtrusive, yet widespread, process of assimilation by which the German spirit of the period adapted the entire riches of the spiritual conquests of Romanticism to be an adornment for the quiet, bourgeois *Gemütlichkeit* of its own life. . . . And everything was lowered in tone, reduced in colour, diminished in intensity of vibrations'—might well be repeated of Victorianism. A conspicuous example of the alteration in tone in the second decade of the nineteenth century can be seen in the work, and in the success throughout Europe, of the Danish sculptor Thorwaldsen.[5]

Parallel with that of Biedermeier, though with differences caused by the different historical circumstances of the two countries, was the process by which Romanticism in England gradually turned bourgeois, the process that culminated in the Victorian epoch. For there can be observed, even in the great Romantics, a falling-back from extreme positions, a slowing-down into a quiet conformism, a dissemination of Romantic ideas in such a way as to make them accessible to the middle classes.

* * * * *

Coleridge, who at first had preached fervently in favour of liberty and against violence and the sceptred and bloody tyrants, fell back later upon a defensive, Christian ideal, with *Fears in Solitude* (1798). The beginning and ending of this poem, inspired by a love of his own land in the gentler and humbler aspects of its landscape, have a pastoral tone, a tone of elegiac quietism that might well be termed Biedermeier:

> A green and silent spot; amid the hills,
> A small and silent dell! O'er stiller place
> No singing sky-lark ever poised himself.
> The hills are heathy, save that swelling slope,
> Which hath a gay and gorgeous covering on,
> All golden with the never-bloomless furze,
> Which now blooms most profusely: but the dell,
> Bathed by the mist, is fresh and delicate
> As vernal corn-field, or the unripe flax,
> When, through its half-transparent stalks, at eve,
> The level sunshine glimmers with green light.
> Oh! 'tis a quiet spirit-healing nook!
> Which all, methinks, would love; but chiefly he,
> The humble man, who, in his youthful years,
> Knew just so much of folly, as had made
> His early manhood more securely wise!
> Here he might lie on fern or withered heath,
> While from the singing lark (that sings unseen
> The minstrelsy that solitude loves best),
> And from the sun, and from the breezy air,

Sweet influences trembled o'er his frame;
And he, with many feelings, many thoughts,
Made up a meditative joy, and found
Religious meanings in the forms of Nature!

Then, after exhorting his fellow countrymen to—

repel an impious foe,
Impious and false, a light yet cruel race,
Who laugh away all virtue, mingling mirth
With deeds of murder—

a race that promises freedom, but then—

cheat(s) the heart
Of faith and quiet hope, and all that soothes,
And all that lifts the spirit—

the poet lingers again to contemplate the land in its most
affectionately human aspect:

Now farewell,
Farewell, awhile, O soft and silent spot!

The poet leaves this 'quiet and surrounded nook' (note
how often, in this poem, the idea of the quiet refuge recurs),
and, standing on the brow of the hill, sweeps the whole
landscape with his eye:

And now, beloved Stowey! I behold
The church-tower, and, methinks, the four huge elms
Clustering, which mark the mansion of my friend;
And close behind them, hidden from my view,
Is my own lowly cottage, where my babe
And my babe's mother dwell in peace! With light
And quickened footsteps thitherward I tend,
Remembering thee, O green and silent dell!
And grateful, that by nature's quietness
And solitary musings, all my heart
Is softened, and made worthy to indulge
Love, and the thoughts that yearn for human kind.

All enthusiasm for the French Revolution having been
extinguished in Coleridge thanks to the influence of the
anti-Jacobin Burke, there developed in him those conservative tendencies that were later to be formulated in his

work *On the Constitution of the Church and State* (1830). Coleridge's conception of the State is a way of meeting a difficulty, one of those compromises that became so typical of the Victorian age. With a mixture of idealism and realism, he wants all manifestations of life to be permeated by the Christian spirit (Coleridge's religious position remained all his life 'a kind of religious twilight' between evangelicalism and philosophic deism); on the other hand he makes a clear separation between the sphere of Christianity and the sphere of politics: the necessity of the State to aim at power must be recognized, but at the same time moral rules are enunciated to which politics must conform. He rejects revolution and is for a gradual, natural evolution of the life of the State: and it was exactly in this direction that English politics in the Victorian era were to develop. In fact Coleridge, according to Basil Willey,[6] was the direct precursor of the modern developments of the English Socialist State, with its vast network of social services of every kind. As to Coleridge's insistence upon the Christian spirit, it may be observed that Biedermeier also is so permeated by it that somebody, considering this to be its principal aspect, even went so far as to suggest that the period should be called the 'second Christian Renaissance'; while it is evident that the widespread diffusion of this spirit is one of the aspects of the reaction against Romantic 'titanism', and of bourgeois expansiveness and good nature.

*   *   *   *   *

Even more typical than Coleridge's evolution was that of Wordsworth. Wordsworth had been a sympathetic spectator of the first episodes of the French Revolution:

> But Europe at that time was thrilled with joy,
> France standing on the top of golden hours,
> And human nature seeming born again—
> *(The Prelude*, vi. 339–41).

which seems almost to echo Virgil's: 'Magnus ab integro saeclorum nascitur ordo.' However it is not very difficult to see that his enthusiasm was not that of a real revolutionary,[7] but of a bourgeois rejoicing at the feeling of expansiveness in a free civil life, of an Englishman who, brought up in

> . . . a Republic, where all stood thus far
> Upon equal ground; that we were brothers all
> In honour, as in one community,
> Scholars and gentlemen . . .
>
> (ix. 226–9).

is delighted to see the same principles triumphing elsewhere. He is present at a festive banquet of delegates returning from the Convention (vi. 384 et seq.), and the scene makes one think of one of those pictures of Dutch marksmen's clubs (*Doelen*) painted by Frans Hals. Later, when far more formidable events supervened, Wordsworth, though still retaining his faith in his own idyllic concept of Revolution—the joyous company of dancers round the tree of Freedom—began to be gravely troubled. The vision of the September massacres made him sleepless, and, meditating in the silence of the night in Paris, he felt as though in 'a wood where tigers roam' (x. 63–93). Wordsworth's support of the French Revolution, however, had been, in the first place, by no means remote and theoretical; he did not go to the extremes of Blake's *Marriage of Heaven and Hell*, but he too, up to a point, thought:

> —they
> The wisest whose opinions stooped the least
> To known restraints.

The emancipation of man must extend not merely to politics, but also to sexual relations, to the family; love must be a law unto itself; for a moment Wordsworth considered himself authorized by the principles of revolution to indulge the ardour of his own youthful blood. Then came the adventure with Annette Vallon, the episode that was to weigh heavily, later, upon the moral life of the mature Wordsworth—to such an extent that, as an old man, standing in front of Canova's *Cupid and Psyche* enlaced in voluptuous embrace, he exclaimed: 'Demons!' Herbert Read[8] has rightly stressed the interdependence of

his emotional and his intellectual development. Wordsworth's remorse for his desertion of Annette was transmuted unconsciously into hatred for the object of his dead
passion, and, on the plane of consciousness, transferred
itself into hatred for all the things associated with that
passion. So Wordsworth 'gradually renounced the cause
of France and then the cause of the Revolution, and finally
the cause of humanity'. Through this process of emotional
compensation, the puritan in Wordsworth got the better
of the disciple of Rousseau, and from love as passion he
took refuge in love as affection, in the domestic idyll, as is
well illustrated by the group of poems dedicated to Lucy.
And Lucy, the 'violet by a mossy stone half-hidden from
the eye', appeared as the genius of the land to which the
poet returned after wandering on foreign soil:

> I travelled among unknown men,
>   In lands beyond the sea;
> Nor, England! did I know till then
>   What love I bore to thee.
>
> 'Tis past, that melancholy dream!
>   Nor will I quit thy shore
> A second time; for still I seem
>   To love thee more and more.
>
> Among thy mountains did I feel
>   The joy of my desire;
> And she I cherished turned her wheel
>   Beside an English fire.

That is the true soul of Wordsworth, a Biedermeier soul.
The Revolution had been a youthful lapse; as Professor
Grierson remarks:[9] 'France of the Revolution his mistress
was; England and her morals, customs, prejudices, became
his wife.' His revolutionary experiment had the effect of
turning Wordsworth from politics to introspection, from
society to Nature: to the world of the Lakes, the little
world of his own childhood, to the recalling of the profound
emotions impressed upon his senses by the lake at Esthwaite
and amongst the Cumberland and Westmorland hills. Now
this 'conversion', this retreat from the wider world of social

and political struggle to the small, intimate world of family
affections (his sister Dorothy), of 'little, nameless unremembered acts Of kindness and of love',[10] of simple
creatures of the fields, of contact with the Infinite through
'a grain of sand'[11]—all this has a parallel with what happened in Germany and there received the name of Biedermeier. The poet absorbs a contemplative joy from the
landscape like the pleasure of the bee amongst flowers.[12]
Sensations of peace, of serenity, are continually commemorated in the magnificent descriptions of the poet's
youthful years in the first books of *The Prelude*:

> oh, then, the calm
> And dead still water lay upon my mind
> Even with a weight of pleasure, and the sky,
> Never before so beautiful, sank down
> Into my heart, and held me like a dream.[13]

And again:

> and I stood and watched
> Till all was tranquil as a dreamless sleep.
>
> .   .   .   .   .
>
> Even then
> I held unconscious intercourse with beauty
> Old as creation, drinking in a pure
> Organic pleasure from the silver wreaths
> Of curling mists, or from the level plain
> Of waters coloured by impending clouds.[14]

Immensely solemn, spacious landscapes, these, like the
landscapes of Kaspar David Friedrich. The feeling that
the poet draws from Nature is one of 'organic pleasure': the
peace of Nature becomes, as it were, an emblem of the peace
to which moral man should aspire. And happiness is no
longer to be sought in some Utopia, in dreams of the
Revolution or of Godwin's social regeneration:

> Not in Utopia—subterranean fields,—
> Or some secreted island, Heaven knows where!
> But in the very world, which is the world
> Of all of us,—the place where, in the end,
> We find our happiness, or not at all![15]

Happiness must be sought upon this humble earth on

which we live: a concept which was to become fundamental in George Eliot's conception of life. A Biedermeier concept, as are also the poems written at the beginning of the century, which are animated as though by a sense of rebirth, like that of a convalescent. And the poet turns to the birds, to the linnet, the blackbird, the lark, which know the ways of wisdom better than man with all his books.[16] A Romantic like Shelley was to enlarge a similar concept to cosmic proportions; he appealed to the lark to teach him even half the gladness that it felt, so that he might enchant the world with the harmonious madness that would flow from his lips. To Wordsworth the blackbird, the lark, seem to be examples of a perfect life:

> With Nature never do they wage
> A foolish strife; they see
> A happy youth, and their old age
> Is beautiful and free.[17]

The stars in their unchangeable courses, the patient hills that endure without complaint the sun's ardours and the shock of the storm, the days and the seasons in their comings and goings, the birds, the flowers, the clouds—these things, to Wordsworth, seem never to be rebellious or weary: their life appears to him not only beautiful, but full of a profound sense of joy, a joy in which men could have a share if they would discover the law of their own being, and obey it without murmuring.[18] That is the form in which reaction to the revolutionary gospel of freedom manifests itself in Wordsworth: for the Romantics Nature was the symbol of freedom, for him it becomes the symbol of law. This Wordsworth who wished to draw from Nature a continual lesson of life, of joy, of love, was to become the ideal poet of the Victorians. They recognized themselves in him, who was their forerunner in so many respects. What, for instance, could be more Victorian than this sentimental little picture from *The Prelude* (viii. 843–58), written in 1805?

> 'Twas a Man
> Whom I saw sitting in an open square
> Close to an iron paling that fenced in

The spacious grass-plot; on the corner stone
Of the low wall in which the pales were fixed
Sat this one man, and with a sickly babe
Upon his knee, whom he had thither brought
For sunshine, and to breathe the fresher air.
Of those who passed, and me who looked at him,
He took no note; but in his brawny arms
(The artificer was to the elbow bare
And from his work this moment had been stolen)
He held the child, and, bending over it,
As if he were afraid both of the sun
And of the air which he had come to seek,
He eyed it with unutterable love.[19]

Does this not give a foretaste of Dickens's little pictures, such as the one in chapter xlvi of *The Old Curiosity Shop*, with the group formed by Nell's ingenuous schoolmaster and the old grandfather? It was not only his interest and pleasure in the humble aspects of life and society that placed Wordsworth, even then, within the ambit of Victorian sensibility, but his finding in these things a rival theme to challenge comparison with the heroic, which had hitherto held the stage in poetry, his discovery of a note more truly moving, more genuinely heroic, in humble people than in the great and celebrated: a note first touched by Gray in his famous *Elegy in a Country Churchyard*. Wordsworth does not seek lessons of wisdom from books, but from the living experience of contact with the men whom he meets in the streets:

When I began to inquire,
To watch and question those I met, and held
Familiar talk with them, the lonely roads
Were schools to me in which I daily read
With most delight the passions of mankind,
There saw into the depth of human souls,
Souls that appear to have no depth at all
To vulgar eyes . . .
                                . . . There I heard,
From mouths of lowly men and of obscure
A tale of honour; sounds in unison
With loftiest promises of good and fair.

.   .   .   .   .

Of these, said I, shall be my Song; of these,
If future years mature me for the task,
Will I record the praises, asking Verse
Deal boldly with substantial things, in truth
And sanctity of passion, speak of these
That justice may be done, obeisance paid
Where it is due: thus haply shall I teach,
Inspire, through unadulterated ears
Pour rapture, tenderness, and hope, my theme
No other than the very heart of man. . . .[20]

We know how Wordsworth wrote *Peter Bell*, the tale of
the travelling potter made sensible to the voices of Nature
and of moral life by the strong impression he received at
the sight of a drowned man shown him by the ass staring
intently into the water (an incident that lent itself to several
parodies), with the object of proving that 'the imagination
not only does not require for its exercise the intervention
of supernatural agency, but that, though such agency be
excluded, the faculty may be called forth as imperiously,
and for kindred results of pleasure, by incidents, within
the compass of poetic probability, in the humblest depart-
ments of daily life'.[21] And in the Prologue:

Long have I loved what I behold,
The night that calms, the day that cheers;
The common growth of mother-earth
Suffices me—her tears, her mirth,
Her humblest mirth and tears.

The dragon's wing, the magic ring,
I shall not covet for my dower,
If I along that lowly way
With sympathetic heart may stray,
And with a soul of power.

What interests Wordsworth is not the dignity of the
protagonist, but the interior conflict aroused in him by the
strong impression he has received; he invokes the spirits
of moral consciousness—'the Spirits of the Mind'—asking
them to leave for a moment men of more elevated percep-
tions, in order to rouse souls like that of Peter Bell:

> But might I give advice to you,
> Whom in my fear I love so well;
> From men of pensive virtue go,
> Dread Beings! and your empire show
> On hearts like that of Peter Bell.

And so, remorse for his own ferocity towards animals, and compassion for the dead man, penetrate into Peter Bell's wild, rough soul; he thinks again of his wife, or rather, of one of his wives (he had had six), a girl from the mountains who had died of a broken heart owing to Peter's disorderly life:

> And now the Spirits of the Mind
> Are busy with poor Peter Bell.

The very title of the poem *The Idiot Boy* seems to go against all traditional preconceptions of decorum. And yet it is to the Muses that the poet turns, to those same sacred Muses invoked for very different themes by his predecessors, praying them to teach him how to tell the tale of the idiot's adventure:

> I to the Muses have been bound
> These fourteen years, by strong indentures:
> O gentle Muses! let me tell
> But half of what to him befell;
> He surely met with strange adventures.

The invocation is not without irony, for it does not serve to introduce any exceptional adventure, merely the discovery that the idiot had stopped to indulge in reverie beside the moonlit waterfall, while his horse quietly cropped the grass:

> O gentle Muses! is this kind?
> Why will ye thus my suit repel?
> Why of your further aid bereave me?
> And can ye thus unfriended leave me;
> Ye Muses! whom I love so well?

He seems here to catch one of those inflexions—how deliberately humorous it is impossible to say—that are the true property of England's first bourgeois poet, Chaucer.

5. TERBORCH. The Music Lesson (*London, National Gallery.
Reproduced by courtesy of the Trustees*)

6. TERBORCH. Curiosity (*Bache Collection, New York*)

Elsewhere, in the old and solitary leech-gatherer in *Resolu-tion and Independence*, whom he compares to a rock trans-ported by an ancient glacier and left 'couched on the bald top of an eminence', and in the *Solitary Reaper*, the poet achieved a monumental quality of truly heroic proportions, the sublimation of the humble, democratic prompting given him by some nameless, earthy being, who became thus transfigured into a creature of myth and legend. But the old leech-gatherer, the reaper, no less than Peter Bell, the idiot, the blind Highland boy, and finally the old wandering Scottish pedlar whom Wordsworth makes his spokesman in *The Excursion* (thereby exposing himself to the sarcasms of the critic Jeffrey)—all these are the result of a deliberate programme to discover the nucleus of a lofty spiritual message in some humble human vicissi-tude, and in simple, childlike people, to whom Wordsworth attributed primitive virtues (and in this myth lay his differ-ence from the Victorians, in whom all mythology of this kind had been obliterated); a humble vicissitude, which could be told to children into the bargain ('. . . and now, my little Bess, We've reached at last the promised Tale. . .'). These figures are so many aspects of the type of objective correlative that Wordsworth sought for his inspiration. There can be no doubt that the French Revolution, if it did not give the first impulse, must certainly have stimulated the poet towards this democratization of the heroic, which is brought about at the cost of the poet's being content to portray his figures in the vaguest and most indeterminate manner—like the solitary reaper, a figure but faintly seen beneath the uncertain light of a nordic sky. As soon as the poet descends to details, the contrast between appearances and the meanings with which he wishes to charge them cannot be reconciled (as happened in the synthesis of the seventeenth-century metaphysical poets, who were animated by 'heroical wit') but comes out in involuntary parody. Thus in the famous lines of *Peter Bell* (later cut out), in which the potter asks himself what can be the object floating in the river: after naming various objects of Romantic terror (the distorted face of the moon, the spectral image of a cloud, a gallows, a coffin, a grisly idol, a ring of fairies, a demon condemned to eternal punishment), he wonders:

> Is it a party in a parlour?
> Cramm'd just as they on earth were cramm'd—
> Some sipping punch, some sipping tea,
> But, as you by their faces see,
> All silent and all damn'd?[22]

Here the terrifying sight of a company of corpses sitting in rigid attitudes round a table, some of them drinking tea and some punch, resolves itself into a bourgeois curiosity, a corner in a museum of waxworks.

Read side by side with Coleridge's *Ancient Mariner*, *Peter Bell* offers the clearest possible example of the democratization of the heroic that had been accomplished in Wordsworth. Compare the image of the sea-tossed ship in Coleridge's poem:

> Then like a pawing horse let go
> She made a sudden bound—

with Wordsworth's reversed image, which reads almost like a parody:

> Now—like a tempest-shattered bark,
> That overwhelmed and prostrate lies,
> And in a moment to the verge
> Is lifted of a foaming surge—
> Full suddenly the Ass doth rise!

What damages Wordsworth's poetry is not the introduction of common, humble objects (these could be introduced without peril into the poetry of Donne and Herbert), but their introduction into an atmosphere which still, both by metre and diction, holds a suggestion of the heroic tradition. The little blind Highland boy ventures out to sea in a wash-tub, and this is how the poet writes:

> But say, what was it? Thought of fear!
> Well may ye tremble when ye hear!
> —A Household Tub, like one of those
> Which women use to wash their clothes,
> This carried the blind Boy.

And what is the spiritual message with which the poet

wishes to invest the blind child's adventure? A warning to reconcile oneself with this humble life, when aspirations and dreams fail! The blind boy had ventured out to sea in his tub upon the quiet waters of a Scottish inlet, and, after a moment of intense joy as he was carried away by the tide, was brought home again by sailors in a rowing-boat; from that moment he became resigned:

> Thus, after he had fondly braved
> The perilous deep, the Boy was saved;
> And, though his fancies had been wild,
> Yet he was pleased and reconciled
> To live in peace on shore.[23]

The adventure resolves itself into a moral exercise like that of *Struwwelpeter*, or *Shock-headed Peter* (the well-known educative, terrifico-humorous manual of the Biedermeier period): the symbol is brought into service for a humble book of children's allegorical tales. The same can be said of very many poems in which the feeling for Nature, the original nucleus of Wordsworth's inspiration, is translated, not into immediate expression, but into a considered and discursive exposition. Take for example the lines on *The Redbreast chasing the Butterfly*. Their author might well have been the schoolmaster Gottlieb Biedermeier, or—which is the same thing—Luigi Sailer who, in the very middle of the nineteenth century, wrote that well-known Italian nursery poem, *La Vispa Teresa*:

> Art thou the bird whom Man loves best,
> The pious bird with scarlet breast,
>   Our little English robin;
> The bird that comes about our doors
> When Autumn winds are sobbing?
>
> .   .   .   .   .
>
> The bird that by some name or other
> All men who know thee call their brother,
> The darling of children and men?
> Could Father Adam open his eyes
> And see this sight beneath the skies,
> He'd wish to close them again.
>
> .   .   .   .   .

What ailed thee, Robin, that thou couldst pursue
   A beautiful creature,
   That is gentle by nature?
   Beneath the summer sky
   From flower to flower let him fly;
'Tis all that he wishes to do.

       .   .   .   .   .

His beautiful wings in crimson are drest,
A crimson as bright as thine own:
Wouldst thou be happy in thy nest,
O pious Bird! whom man loves best,
Love him, or leave him alone![24]

It was the Wordsworth who stuck meticulously to the
circumstances and the minutest accessory details of the
country scene whom the Victorians, deservedly, were to
have as their Poet Laureate: the Wordsworth who besprinkled the humblest events with ideal and ethical notions,
the poet of the *Ode to Duty*. This ode marks a characteristic
reaction against Romantic aspirations after unlimited freedom. The poet seeks refuge in Duty as if in a quiet harbour, a sure defence against temptations:

   From vain temptations dost set free;
   And calm'st the weary strife of frail humanity!

Duty is a support and a joyfully accepted rule:

   But thee I now would serve more strictly, if I may.

   Through no disturbance of my soul,
   Or strong compunction in me wrought,
   I supplicate for thy control;
   But in the quietness of thought:
   Me this unchartered freedom tires;
   I feel the weight of chance-desires:
   My hopes no more must change their name,
   I long for a repose that ever is the same. . . .

       .   .   .   .   .

   To humble functions, awful Power!
   I call thee: I myself commend
   Unto thy guidance from this hour;
   Oh, let my weakness have an end!

Give unto me, made lowly wise,
The spirit of self-sacrifice;
The confidence of reason give;
And in the light of truth thy Bondman let me live!

This was the conservative Wordsworth, the pillar of Church and State, who wrote the sonnet *Long-favoured England!*, in which, 'monstrous theories of alien growth' having been banished, he invoked rules of government derived from eternal truth, which should 'work to cheer—Not scourge, to save the People—not destroy'. In 1832, frightened by what were likely to be the inevitable consequences of the first Reform Bill, which transferred political power from the landowning to the industrial class, thus implying the decay of privilege, of property, and of religion, he who had formerly been a democratic 'patriot' on the French pattern thought, now, of taking refuge in Austria: he wrote that he would seek the quietest corner he could find in the middle of Austria (an aspiration which could hardly have been more Biedermeier);[25] and in fact, the ideal that he had had in prospect in his *Addresses to the Freeholders of Westmoreland* (1818) had been a system of temperate feudalism, a social pyramid held together by the moral cement of personal loyalty, lacking only the figure of the Emperor to make it identical with the Austrian régime. As regards the Church, Wordsworth emphasized the traces of the Catholic past which survive in English Protestantism, and in the *Ecclesiastical Sketches* of 1822 he anticipated the tendency which later, with his disciple John Keble, was to blossom forth into the Oxford Movement. Here again one might speak of a Christian Renaissance, as in Germany; but it is obvious that the phenomenon really derived from the deliberate restriction of horizon, the concentration upon the close-at-hand, the concrete, the intimate, that were the natural reaction from Romantic revolts and disintegrations. The Wordsworth of the *Ode to Duty* and the *Ecclesiastical Sonnets* marks the opposite pole to the Romantic creed of Blake expressed in *The Marriage of Heaven and Hell* and *The Everlasting Gospel*.

Sir Walter Scott

THE novels of Sir Walter Scott made a notable contribution to the process by which Romanticism turned bourgeois. Their enormous success is explained by the fact that, in Scott, romantic subjects were brought within the reach of all, and were seasoned with so many pinches of common sense, of humour, of picturesqueness of the most obvious kind, that they became acceptable, without the slightest effort, in bourgeois circles. This was recognized by Keats, in a letter of January 1818: 'The Grand parts of Scott are within the reach of more Minds that [*sic*] the finest humours in Humphrey Clincker[26]—I forget whether that fine thing of the Sargeant is Fielding's or Smollet's but it gives me more pleasure that [*sic*] the whole Novel of the Antiquary.'

Scott, far too sensible, wisely avoided the intoxicating delights of the mysterious and the terrible, so dear to the authors of the 'tales of terror', 'Monk' Lewis and Mrs. Radcliffe; one of his novels, *Guy Mannering*, is made to hinge upon astrology, but even in the preface he warns the reader not to take this dead science too seriously:

It appeared, on mature consideration, that Astrology, though its influence was once received and admitted by Bacon himself, does not now retain influence over the general mind sufficient even to constitute the mainspring of a romance. Besides, it occurred, that to do justice to such a subject would have required not only more talent than the author could be conscious of possessing, but also involved doctrines and discussions of a nature too serious for his purpose, and for the character of the narrative.

And so Scott makes use of the horoscope incident in the story in a way that is half humorous; he does not draw any sensational advantage from it; on the other hand, in order to retain some of its effect, he falls back upon a compromise: 'So strangely can imagination deceive even those by whose volition it has been excited, that Mannering, while gazing upon these brilliant bodies, was half inclined to believe in the influence ascribed to them by superstition over human events.' And farther on, after explaining the curious co-incidences that seemed, in this specific case, to corroborate the influence of the stars: 'It will be readily believed, that, in mentioning this circumstance, we lay no weight what-ever upon the pretended information thus conveyed. But it often happens, such is our natural love for the marvellous, that we willingly contribute our own efforts to beguile our better judgments.' A similar necessity to justify, to explain, is visible in Manzoni: it is a disillusioned, cautious, honest attitude, characteristically bourgeois. Nor does Scott intro-duce a ghostly manifestation in a bedroom at night without giving the reader due instructions which explain, in the light of reason, that there is nothing supernatural about it. Sometimes, in fact, the appearance of ghosts provides an opportunity for a comic episode. This occurs in *Ivanhoe*: towards the end of the novel, Cedric says to Wilfred-Ivanhoe that, as regards the Lady Rowena, two years of mourning will have to be observed for the defunct Athel-stane: 'It seemed as if Cedric's words had raised a spectre; for scarce had he uttered them ere the door flew open, and Athelstane, arrayed in the garments of the grave, stood before them, pale, haggard, and like something arisen from the dead!' At this point, in case possibly the reader might have been seized by a romantic shudder, there is a note ready to pour cold water upon him. The note reads: 'The resuscitation of Athelstane has been much criticized, as too violent a breach of probability, even for a work of such fantastic character. It was a *tour de force*, to which the author was compelled to have recourse, by the vehement entreaties of his friend and printer, who was inconsolable on the Saxon being conveyed to the tomb.' But the scene changes into farce. Athelstane tells how the monks, who had been designated as his heirs at his death, had tried to persuade him that he was indeed defunct, and in purgatory; and finally he throws himself upon the food and makes a hearty meal. The deliberate humorous and bourgeois exploitation of incidents of a romantic nature on the part of Scott calls to mind the similar manner in which the bourgeois Chaucer took some useful hints from the *Divina*

Commedia, in his *Hous of Fame*—Chaucer who turned the
terrible episode of Count Ugolino into a thing of pathos
and sentiment, Chaucer who does not venture upon the
high seas but coasts along the shore. And the best of Scott
is not to be sought in his conventional pictures of Gothic
manor-houses and effects of storm-ridden Nature or unbridled passions—pictures in which he inclines towards
the oleographic; but, as is well known, in his descriptions
of Scottish habits and customs, such as those that occupy
the whole of the first part of *The Pirate*; or in small scenes
of intimate interiors, like the famous scene of the relations
gathered round the corpse of the drowned sailor, in *The
Antiquary*:

> At a little distance stood the father, whose rugged weather-beaten
> countenance, shaded by his grizzled hair, had faced many a stormy
> night and night-like day. . . . His glance was directed sidelong to-
> wards the coffin. . . . In another corner of the cottage, her face
> covered by her apron, which was flung over it, sat the mother—the
> nature of her grief sufficiently indicated by the wringing of her
> hands, and the convulsive agitation of the bosom. . . . Two of her
> gossips, officiously whispering into her ear the commonplace topic
> of resignation under irremediable misfortune, seemed as if they were
> endeavouring to stun the grief which they could not console. The
> sorrow of the children was mingled with wonder at the preparations
> they beheld around them. . . . But the figure of the old grandmother
> was the most remarkable of the sorrowing group. . . . She seemed
> every now and then mechanically to resume the motion of twirling
> her spindle. . . . She would then cast her eyes about, as if surprised
> at missing the usual implements of her industry, and appear struck
> by the black colour of the gown in which they had dressed her,
> and embarrassed by the number of persons by whom she was sur-
> rounded. . . .

And so on. Now, at the beginning of this scene, Scott had
written the words we have already had occasion to quote:[27]
'In the inside of the cottage, was a scene which our Wilkie
alone could have painted, with that exquisite feeling of
nature that characterizes his enchanting productions.' Indeed, the Scottish painter Sir David Wilkie provides the
exact parallel to Scott's descriptive passages, not merely
because, as Ruskin observed, his art 'touches passions

which all feel, and expresses truths which all can recognize',
but because it invites the observer to study the play of
feelings on the faces of his characters, and tends to enlarge
the circle of extra-pictorial associations to which a picture
can give rise, to such an extent that its purely pictorial
qualities become subordinated. One of his first works,
Peasants (1806), already foreshadows the characteristics
and the limits of Wilkie's art. The group looks as if it had
been taken bodily from one of Adriaen van Ostade's tavern
scenes; particular importance is given to the 'contrast of
character' that sent his contemporaries into ecstasies. *The
Blind Fiddler* (1807), *The Village Festival, Blind Man's Buff*
(1811), &c., recall Teniers and Jan Steen; *The Sick Lady*
(1809) and *The Letter of Introduction* (1814) bring to Scotland subjects widely circulated in Holland by such painters
as Metsu and Steen; and comparison might also be made—
as has indeed been done—with certain pages of Goldsmith,
if he, too, had not been preceded, in the study of interiors
and of shades of expression on the protagonists' faces in
everyday, commonplace episodes, by the great bourgeois
Dutch painters, whom we discussed in the Introduction.
The true 'intimism' of the Dutch was never attained either
by Wilkie or by Scott; they stop short at its antecedents,
the *bambocciate*, the scenes in the tavern or at the fair, the
interiors of peasants' houses: they continue the tradition
which, starting with painters such as Brouwer, Teniers,
and Ostade, was to melt away in the nineteenth century
with the Hungarian Munkacsy and his humble followers
(in Italy, for example, Gaetano Clerici of Reggio). They
delight to add a colouring of pathos or melodrama to the
contrast of character—a development that the Dutch barely
hinted at, as we have seen—as Scott did in the funeral
episode described above, and Wilkie in *Distraining for Rent*,
in *Reading the Will*, in *The Parish Beadle*, and in *The
Chelsea Pensioners listening to the News of Waterloo*. The
subject of this last picture (painted between 1816 and
1822) is very characteristic of the Biedermeier point of
view that was making headway throughout Europe. And
it is curious that it should have been the Duke of Wellington himself who gave Wilkie the idea for it. Battle pictures

commissioned by Napoleon from his official artists were always scenes of the battlefield itself; nor, before that time, had anyone thought of doing otherwise. But the Iron Duke, true leader of the Allies as he was, had clearly, in his temperament, an alloy of some metal more tractable than iron. Towards the end of his life he was to be immortalized by painters in the role of the kind old grandfather—by Winterhalter, in the act of offering, with a bow, a casket to the infant Prince Arthur in the arms of Queen Victoria, while the Prince Consort stands by, the perfect image of Saint Joseph in this new version of the Visit of the Magi; by Robert Thorburn, in the midst of his grandchildren who are playing on the Brussels carpet in his library, a kind and gentle patriarch with his arm round the shoulders of his favourite, Victoria, who looks tenderly at him as she offers him a rose. This was the Duke of Wellington about the year 1850; on the morrow of Waterloo he had suggested to Wilkie that he should commemorate the battle by painting a picture of a group of old soldiers—Chelsea Pensioners—sitting at the door of an inn, perhaps playing at skittles, telling each other of their ancient feats of valour: a suggestion that Wilkie developed by making one of the veterans read out aloud the news bulletin of the Battle of Waterloo. The various emotions aroused by the reading are depicted on the faces and in the acts of the audience; particularly admired was the expression of the old woman intently following the reading behind the back of the soldier who holds the newspaper, an expression that appeared admirably contrasted with those of the rest of the bystanders. But the picture breaks up into a variety of episodes—groups of young women and children, dogs playing, a mounted cavalryman who stops and leans back attentively in his saddle; every aspect of popular life is represented in this quiet suburban scene dominated by the trees and the wide sky, a scene as calm as, years later, was the view of Milan in a similar picture by Domenico Induno, *Arrival of the News of the Peace of Villafranca* (1860). De Quincey described groups of people celebrating at the passing of the coach which brought the news of victory, in his *English Mail-Coach*; for the bourgeois century took pleasure in immortalizing great historical events in this indirect but moving fashion; and even Stendhal was to give marginal, episodic reflections of the Battle of Waterloo in the famous chapters of *La Chartreuse de Parme*. Not that Wilkie did not also attempt a frontal attack upon the celebrated scenes of history; but his pictures then became mere melodramatic spectacles, groups of masked, attitudinizing figures like those in an opera (it suffices to mention *The Preaching of John Knox*), scenographic *tours de force* (and this applies to all nineteenth-century historical painting) such as could only be redeemed by the music of a Verdi. And only music could give any sense to the mechanically contrived historical novels that Scott was publishing from 1819 onwards, he also, like Wilkie, having been led astray into drowning the notes of the authentic bagpipe, his own natural instrument, beneath the ear-splitting blasts of the epic trumpet. To give some indication of the taste which found its ideal in Wilkie's anecdotal painting, it will be remembered that a critic found fault with the universally admired *Blind Man's Buff* on the ground that Wilkie seemed to him to be degenerating, to be running the risk of lowering himself to the level of a Watteau (Jan Steen's would have been the more proper name to mention, since Wilkie's painting derives from Steen's *Twelfth Night Feast* at Buckingham Palace). This anecdotal quality in Wilkie and Scott gave new life and vigour to the bourgeois inspiration which had been visible even in the Elizabethan theatre, in plays such as *The Shoemaker's Holiday*, made for the gratification of the burgesses of the City. The richness of anecdote is in sharp contrast to the conventional characterization of the figures, serious or tragic: look, for instance, at Wilkie's *Maid of Saragossa* (1828), pale sister of the Madonnas of Murillo, or, in Scott, at the gallery of fascinating bandits—reduced and sweetened versions of the Byronic *homme fatal*—of honest young men who attain, after various vicissitudes, to the summit of their dreams, of angelic maidens, of gipsy-women and picturesque beggars, and so on. Look at the portrait of Minna Troil in *The Pirate*, a portrait as sweet and pleasing as the type of woman who was shortly afterwards to become so widely known from lithographs, a portrait which ends like this:

In short, notwithstanding our wish to have avoided that hackneyed simile of an angel, we cannot avoid saying there was something in the serious beauty of her aspect, in the measured, yet graceful ease of her motions, in the music of her voice, and the serene purity of her eye, that seemed as if Minna Troil belonged naturally to some higher and better sphere, and was only the chance visitant of a world that was not worthy of her.

It is the translation into bourgeois terms of the angelic woman of the *stil nuovo*:

E par che sia una cosa venuta
Da cielo in terra a miracol mostrare.

In the same way the Madonnas of Overbeck and the 'Nazarenes'—Biedermeier 'mystics'—were to provide a bourgeois equivalent of the Virgins of the Primitives. And in the same Biedermeier taste was the contrast of two opposite types of beauty—the sisters Minna and Brenda in *The Pirate*, Rebecca and Rowena in *Ivanhoe*, &c.—a theme already treated by Greuze in *The Two Friends* and *The Two Sisters* (or *The Comparison*); by Madame Vigée-Lebrun in *The Two Sisters*; by William Owen in *The Sisters*; and frequently repeated later by painters about 1840 (for example, *Blonde and Brunette* by Dubufe, *Italy and Germany* by Overbeck, &c.).

A discussion of Scott's humour would bring us to considerations of the same nature. It is a humour that exercises itself upon a sense of the comic generated by mechanical repetition; but it is this mechanical quality that is the very backbone of human habits and prejudices and traditions: Dandie Dinmont's dogs, all 'Peppers' and 'Mustards', or a retort like that of Bertram to the vain and fatuous Sir Robert Hazlewood: 'I really do not see, sir, as there is an old Hazlewood and a young Hazlewood, why there should not be an old and a young Vanbeest Brown'—a reply that left the other man indignant and disconcerted as though it had been a mortal offence to the noble line of his forefathers. It is an episode of a bourgeois type of humour which considers the upper classes' sense of superiority ridiculous;

this same sense of superiority was laughed at by Manzoni in *I Promessi Sposi*.

Collecting-mania and scientific pretension, which Flaubert later held up to ridicule in *Bouvard et Pécuchet*, his satire on the bourgeoisie, are salient characteristics in Scott. Thus, after he had made one of the characters in *The Pirate* find some gold and silver coins in one of the ancient rooms at Stourburgh, on that remote Nordic shore which forms the background of the novel, he was delighted to hear of the actual discovery of such coins in that same region, a discovery that gave a colour of truth to what had previously seemed one of the most improbable fictions in the book. He even pauses, in the course of the book, to guarantee the authenticity of the scene in the witch's cavern, referring to the superstitions of Zetland; in fact, the novelist inserted the incident with the express purpose of preserving the memory of a curious old custom 'in a narrative connected with Scottish antiquities'. This collector's precision urges Scott to give minute descriptions, as if he were drawing up an inventory, of the furniture and costumes in his historical novels, thus starting a tradition in literature (here too, precedents can be found in Dutch painting) which became universal amongst nineteenth-century novelists (one has only to think of Balzac, of Hugo, of Zola). For instance, in *Ivanhoe*, he describes point by point the dress of a Saxon swineherd, and those of the jester Wamba and of the epicurean friar: and Chaucer, the Chaucer of the portraits of the Canterbury pilgrims in the famous Prologue, is the model here. Such descriptions are not to be found in Dante, nor in the heroic romances of La Calprenède, of Gomberville, of Madeleine and George de Scudéry, romances that mirrored an aristocratic culture, as indeed was the culture of Dante. Here, for example, is Scott's description of Cedric's dress:

His dress was a tunic of forest green, furred at the throat and cuffs with what was called minever; a kind of fur inferior in quality to ermine, and formed, it is believed, of the skin of the grey squirrel. . . . Behind his seat was hung a scarlet cloth cloak lined with fur, and a cap of the same materials richly embroidered, which completed the dress of the opulent landholder when he chose to go forth.

It reads like a fashion-book. There was even 'a small white truncheon which lay by Cedric's trencher, for the purpose of repelling the advances of his four-legged dependents' (an elegant circumlocution for 'dogs'). In this way the historical romance becomes like Madame Tussaud's, a museum of waxworks which are supposed to give a sense of life and its settings. And when the Prior and the Templar present themselves to Cedric, there is another description of clothes; and when the Jew appears, there is at once an inventory of his garments, and when Rebecca arrives at the tournament, it is her dress which first strikes Scott's imagination; and when De Bracy is preparing to seduce Rowena, Scott makes a digression on his way of dressing, with historical references of this kind:

We have already noticed the extravagant fashion of the shoes at this period, and the points of Maurice de Bracy's might have challenged the prize of extravagance with the gayest, being turned up and twisted like the horns of a ram. Such was the dress of a gallant of the period; and, in the present instance, that effect was aided by the handsome person and good demeanour of the wearer, whose manners partook alike of the grace of a courtier, and the frankness of a soldier.

The same care was used in describing apartments; thus, after describing that of the Lady Rowena:

Yet let not modern beauty envy the magnificence of a Saxon princess. The walls of the apartment were so ill finished, and so full of crevices, that the rich hangings shook to the night blast, and, in despite of a sort of screen intended to protect them from the wind, the flame of the torches streamed sideways into the air, like the unfurled pennon of a chieftain. Magnificence there was, with some rude attempt at taste; but of comfort there was little, and, being unknown, it was unmissed.

It is well known how Scott translated into real life this passion for the minute trappings of habit and custom, creating at Abbotsford a sumptuously furnished abode in the Gothic style. He loved antique objects not so much for their intrinsic beauty as for the persons and deeds they commemorated; Tippoo Sahib's scimitar, a Scottish broadsword from the battlefield of Flodden, a pair of spurs which were a relic of Bannockburn, a gun that Rob Roy had handled, the pulpit from which Ralph Erskine had preached at Dunfermline, the iron stocks with which Wishart had been fastened to the block at St. Andrews, a chair carved out of the beams of the house in which Wallace had been betrayed. Stained-glass windows contained the likenesses of the Scottish kings as they appeared on a ceiling in Stirling Castle; coats of arms all round the walls of the entrance hall recorded all the families with which Sir Walter boasted kinship; the fireplace in the same room was one of the ogives from the cloister at Melrose; the courtyard was adorned with medallions of the ancient Cross of Edinburgh, and with Roman bas-reliefs from the ancient colony of Petreia which had afterwards become Old Penrith. From his bedroom he could come down into his study by way of a secret staircase, like Louis XI in *Quentin Durward*, and his Armoury transported him back to the days of Richard Cœur de Lion.

As in the old times, Sir Walter, lord of his own castle, also administered justice in the guise of Sheriff of Selkirk; justly and humanely he applied the laws of his ancestors with none of those inclinations towards reformation that were beginning to agitate England, for the French Revolution had seemed to him merely a subversion of law and a threat to sound local tradition, his patriotism being entirely local, rooted in the cult of the smallest social unit, the village, the parish. His servants and dependants were like members of one single family, and Sir Walter occupied himself with their affairs as though they were his own; he distributed presents among them, and after a rustic celebration picked up in his carriage anyone who, having had too much to drink, had fallen by the wayside.

We see him in Wilkie's well-known picture, now in the National Portrait Gallery of Scotland, surrounded by his family, who have put on peasant clothes for the occasion, as if for an eighteenth-century pastoral: he sits with his stick and his old, battered white hat; on one side of him stand the women, the handsome milkmaids with their pails (Sophia Charlotte and Anne Scott) and the peasant-woman with a basket on her arm, and, on the other, the village wag with his hands in his waistcoat pockets and his sprightly expression (Sir Adam Ferguson), the young gamekeeper (Scott's elder son) with his gun and the hare he has killed, and an old man with a tartan plaid over his shoulder, while in the background can be seen gentle, monotonous ranges of hills, of a dull green: these are his own people, this is his own country. The picture breathes a sense of peace and patriarchal satisfaction, of that good-natured solidity which is one of the dominant notes of the nineteenth century. It is this Scott, this Scottish laird with the very provincial accent and the kindly sense of humour, this creator of *bambocciate* in the Dutch manner, who, bereft of the fictitious background of second-hand medieval stage-scenery with which he loved to surround himself, lives on as one of the forerunners of Victorian bourgeois literature: and it was this aspect of him—which escaped, or appeared of secondary importance to, so many of his contemporaries, especially on the Continent—that was to make so strong an impression upon his great Italian follower, Manzoni.

7. METSU. Lovers of Music (*The Hague, Mauritshuis*)

8. JAN STEEN. Morning Toilet (*London, Buckingham Palace. Reproduced by gracious permission of Her Majesty The Queen*)

Charles Lamb

IF anticipations of Victorianism are to be found in the later work of Coleridge and Wordsworth and in that of Scott, it is more especially in the group of so-called 'eccentrics' that one can discern the first signs of the atmosphere of attenuated Romanticism tempered with bourgeois kindliness and humour that was to be a dominant characteristic of the Victorian age. What Charles Lamb says about his dreams in his essay on *Witches, and other Night Fears* might be taken as an image both of his own work and of that of the other two transitional writers associated with him in histories of literature, De Quincey and Peacock. Taking as his point of departure a little poem by Barry Cornwall, *A Dream* (1819), Lamb imagines that he too is dreaming of the triumph of Neptune and Amphitrite—

with the customary train [of tritons] sounding their conches before me (I myself, you may be sure, the leading god), and jollily we went careering over the main, till just where Ino Leucothea should have greeted me (I think it was Ino) with a white embrace, the billows gradually subsiding, fell from a sea roughness to a sea calm, and thence to a river motion, and that river (as happens in the familiarisation of dreams) was no other than the gentle Thames, which landed me in the wafture of a placid wave or two, alone, safe and inglorious, somewhere at the foot of Lambeth Palace.

The pretended sea-god ends by putting on his slippers; the adventure has the flavour of one of Heine's jokes.

We know how narrow was Lamb's universe. F. V. Morley[28] has shown us his life as a passage from physical enclosures to moral enclosures. From Christ's Hospital to the Temple, from cloister to cloister, with brief country interludes; then, in 1793, when his father, owing to the death of his employer, had to leave the Inner Temple, the tide of London swept against the family, now no longer under the protection of any quiet cloister walls. The disaster that decided Lamb's future, his sister Mary's attack of violent insanity (September 1796), and, consequent upon it, the heavy responsibilities that came to weigh upon Charles (he undertook the guardianship of his sister, who, apart from periodical attacks, was a creature of exquisite sensibility and intelligence), then drove him to build moral walls around his wounded soul. On one side, with Mr. Morley, we see a Romantic writer's personality, hinted at in a few youthful compositions, but gradually drying up as all hope of a normal life recedes; on the other, a new character, assumed for purposes of defence, and developing until it comes to full flower in the essayist Elia. Humour became a defence, as did self-projection into an idyllic past, the cultivation of childlikeness, the cult of antiquity; a similar interpretation can be given to Lamb's passion for the fantastic world of the theatre, and to his other, less innocent, refuges, wine and tobacco. And so the story of Lamb's life might well be read in a passage of the essay *Blakesmoor in H - - - shire*:

> So far from a wish to roam, I would have drawn, methought, still closer the fences of my chosen prison; and have been hemmed in by a yet securer cincture of those excluding garden walls. I could have exclaimed with that garden-loving poet [Andrew Marvell]—
>
>> Bind me, ye woodbines, in your 'twines,
>> Curl me about, ye gadding vines;
>> And oh so close your circles lace,
>> That I may never leave this place;
>> But, lest your fetters prove too weak,
>> Ere I your silken bondage break,
>> Do you, O brambles, chain me too,
>> And, courteous briars, nail me through!

Nevertheless it still remains doubtful whether 'this green hedge, that hides so large a part Of the remote horizon from my view'[29] was really an artificial hedge constructed by Lamb round his most secret self, as a defence, or whether it was not, rather, that the circle of his interests had been a restricted one from the very beginning, and that the personality of the potential Romantic claimed by Mr. Morley is, to a great extent, a myth.

Now there is undoubtedly a Romantic accent in Lamb's

early works; but it is a mere Romanticism of manner, pointing quite decidedly towards Biedermeier. There are a few sonnets of melancholy recollection of the past, which caused contemporary criticism to classify him amongst the 'plaintive' poets; there was a little gloomy story (*The Tale of Rosamund Gray and Old Blind Margaret*); and a play in blank verse which testifies to the loving study its author had made of his Elizabethan models. The best things of this period were some lines written in 1798, fraught with an atmosphere of sentimentalism that is a direct forerunner of certain Victorian attitudes of mind, especially in Tennyson (*The Old Familiar Faces*). Here are accents of a languid, intimate, bourgeois Romanticism: family affections contemplated with nostalgia and with a gentle pain that is not devoid of a certain pleasure. And if we consider Lamb's life after the critical year of his domestic tragedy, in the few episodes that interrupted its monotony and also in his letters, we cannot fail to be convinced that we are face to face with a typical Biedermeier. Lamb's first letters are addressed to Coleridge, a short time after the tragedy, and show a soul still hesitating in its aims and expressions. Lamb wants to be guided and instructed by Coleridge; the accent is on the Christian note, and here too some people may see Christian renaissance rather than bourgeois sentiment; but in any case this is not the manner in which true Romantics react; they are titanic rebels, or tumultuous Christians, but not resigned, not murmuring timid prayers. In the pathetic accents of a soul tried by savage calamity, we can find nothing to justify Mr. Morley's conjecture of a Lamb who sought to control, to deflect, to appease an ambitious and tormented self. Certainly he had ambitions: he liked children, he would have liked to have a family. Moreover, nothing is more characteristic than the way in which love manifested itself in Lamb's life. Apart from one shy, youthful idyll (whose object was Anne Simmons, the 'Alice W - - - n' of the *Essays of Elia*), love made one more appearance in his life, and that was when the 'divine plain face' of the actress Fanny Kelly (who is hinted at in the essay *Barbara S - - -*) kept his thoughts occupied. Lamb proposed marriage, in a letter full of simplicity and feeling and deliberately devoid of emphasis—far from romantic, in fact; then, when she besought him not to persist, bore his disappointment like a man of spirit; and the friendship between the two protagonists in this brief drama (the exchange of letters was accomplished in one day) then continued as cordially as before. *Dream-Children*, the most deeply felt of the *Essays of Elia*, gives immortal expression to the most human of desires; it is the quintessence of the spirit of bourgeois intimacy. So that Elia, far from concealing a potentially Romantic Lamb, as it were behind a mask, appears to bring a brief, miraculous flowering to a mind which, in ordinary life, was limited in its interests, was typical, in fact, of the middle class. In this ability to express the quintessence of bourgeois feeling lies the reason for Lamb's immense popularity during the Victorian epoch, and for his canonization which was proclaimed by the high priest of the most bourgeois type of Victorianism, Thackeray; the reason, also, for his popularity today amongst people whom otherwise one would not expect to be attracted by a different aspect of Lamb, his delight in learned quotation.

How limited were Lamb's interests is illustrated with singular clearness in his letters. We do not ask Elia to tell us what he thought of a period full of great historical events—as was that in which he flourished—but we are surprised to find so few references to it in the letters of Charles Lamb. Elia's essay on *Newspapers* mentions 'our first boyish heats kindled by the French Revolution', but Lamb writes to Thomas Manning (March 1st, 1800):[30]

Public affairs—except as they touch upon me, and so turn into private, I cannot whip up my mind to feel any interest in. I grieve, indeed, that War and Nature and Mr. Pitt . . . should have conspired to call up three necessaries, simple commoners as our fathers knew them, into the upper house of Luxuries; Bread, and Beer, and Coals. . . . But as to France and Frenchmen, and the Abbé Sieyès and his constitutions, I cannot make these present times present to me. I read histories of the past, and I live in them; although, to abstract senses, they are far less momentous than the noises which keep Europe awake. I am reading Burnet's *Own Times*. . . . Burnet's good old prattle I can bring present to my mind—I can make the revolution present to me; the French Revolution, by a converse perversity in my nature, I fling as far *from* me. . . .

The year 1814, which marked the end of the Napoleonic era, meant little more to Lamb than the profanation of Hyde Park on the occasion of the celebrations for the peace between England and France:[31]

The very colour of green is vanished, the whole surface of Hyde Park is dry crumbling sand (Arabia Arenosa), not a vestige or hint of grass ever having grown there, booths and drinking places go all round it for a mile and half I am confident—I might say two miles in circuit—the stench of liquors, *bad* tobacco, dirty people and provisions, conquers the air and we are stifled and suffocated in Hyde Park. . . . Meantime I confess to have smoked one delicious Pipe in one of the cleanliest and goodliest of the booths . . . in company with some of the guards that had been in France and a fine French girl (habited like a Princess of Banditti) which one of the dogs had transported from the Garonne to the Serpentine. The unusual scene, in H. Park, by Candlelight in open air, good tobacco, bottled stout, made it look like an interval in a campaign, a repose after battle, I almost fancied scars smarting and was ready to club a story with my comrades of some of my lying deeds. . . .

Half a century later, W. P. Frith was to paint his pictures of crowds in the same spirit. We find no more allusions to political events in Lamb's letters until 1830. For many Englishmen the French Revolution was no more than a distant hurricane; but the social discontent round about 1830 affected their pockets more closely: the acts of incendiarism, result of the agricultural depression and in opposition to the advent of machines, could not but terrify the English leisured classes, who spent a great part of their lives in their country houses. Lamb was living then at Enfield, and although in the long run he found life dull there, incendiarism was more than he bargained for in the way of distraction. He might regret that the Gunpowder Plot of two centuries before had not been effective—'There would have been so glorious an explosion!'[32]—but while he took delight in calling to memory the picturesque figure of Guy Fawkes, the incendiary of the time of James I (Lamb himself, as a young man, had, on account of his pinched

appearance, been hailed by some cheerful revellers at Lud-
gate Hill, one Fifth of November, as the 'real Guy', and
had been carried by them in a kind of grotesque triumphal
procession), he could not help finding the actual presence
of nineteenth-century incendiaries of some personal incon-
venience. As a result, for the first time in his letters we find
him discussing the welfare of England with George Dyer:
'It was never good times in England since the poor began
to speculate upon their condition. . . .'33 Formerly, the
peasants had reflected no more than their own horses; now,
with a 'box of phosphorus' in his pocket, the rustic could
'write his distaste in flames' and feel himself transformed
into an 'exterminating angel'; no doubt this is 'a march of
Science; but who shall beat the drums for its retreat?' The
previous night, seven haystacks and a number of barns had
been reduced to ashes; at this rate 'the food for the inhabitants of earth will quickly disappear. Hot rolls may
say: *Fuimus panes, fuit quartern-loaf, et ingens gloria
Apple-pasty-orum*. That the good old munching system
may last thy time and mine, good un-incendiary George,
is the devout prayer of thine, To the last crust, CH. LAMB.'34

   The limited nature of Lamb's interests is made clear by
that extraordinary event in his life, his journey to Paris in
1822, apparently undertaken with the object of learning
a little French to teach to his adopted daughter, Emma
Isola; and we can imagine the reluctance with which Lamb
must have decided upon it, attached as he was to his own
native land, in fact to his own parish ('I do not willingly
admit of strange beliefs or out-of-the-way creeds or places.
. . . I am a Christian, Englishman, Londoner, Templar').35
His letters to his friends from Paris seem written according
to a fixed recipe; they contain, indeed, very little more than
a recipe—of the way in which to cook frogs (a French dish
which has never ceased to fill the English with astonishment).36 Frogs, and a counterfeit portrait of Shakespeare
in the possession of Talma, were the two most vivid impressions that Lamb brought back from Paris; and also the old
books on the *quais*, and the picturesque crowds. He wrote
to his sister, who, owing to an indisposition, had had to
remain at Amiens: 'You must walk all along the Borough

side of the Seine facing the Tuileries. There is a mile and
a half of print shops and book stalls. If the latter were but
English! Then there is a place where the Paris people put
all their dead people and bring 'em flowers and dolls and
ginger bread nuts and sonnets and such trifles. And that is
all I think worth seeing as sights, except that the streets
and shops of Paris are themselves the best sight.'[37] The
principal themes of what may be called—applying to Lamb
Coleridge's remark about Cowper—the 'divine chit-chat'
of Elia, are touched upon in these brief notes from Paris:
his epicurean interest in tit-bits, which suggested some of
the happiest passages in his letters and his famous *Dissertation upon Roast Pig*, his epicurean love of old books, his
enthusiasm for the animated streets of a great capital, the
thrill of life at second hand communicated to the innocent
'Carlagnolus' (doubly tethered to a humdrum existence,
owing to his employment and also to his sister) by contact
with the crowd:

A garden was the primitive prison till man with promethean
felicity and boldness luckily sinned himself out of it. Thence followed Babylon, Nineveh, Venice, London, haberdashers, goldsmiths, taverns, playhouses, satires, epigrams, puns—these all came
in on the town part, and the thither side of innocence.[38]

Throughout the whole of Lamb's letters we find him
praising the gay life of London, even to those aspects of it
which a Victorian would have determinedly ignored, the
whores, the drunken scenes. 'The wonder of these sights
impels me into night-walks about her crowded streets, and
I often shed tears in the motley Strand from fulness of joy
at so much Life.'[39] Life as a thing seen or as a thing read:
Lamb's enthusiasm for London is paralleled by the attrac-
tiveness, to him, of the atmosphere of violence in Elizabethan drama, of the adventures of thieves and prostitutes
related by Defoe; and he seems indeed a true forerunner of
the Goncourts and Walter Pater in his supposition of the
balefulness of the beauty of Leonardo's women: the
'Leonardos of Oxford made my mouth water', he wrote
to Hazlitt on November 10th, 1805;[40] '. . . I had not
settled my notions of Beauty. I have now for ever!—the

small head, the long Eye,—that sort of peering curve, the wicked Italian mischief! the stick-at-nothing, Herodias'-daughter kind of grace. You understand me.' (Farther on in the same letter: 'Vittoria Corombona, a spunky Italian Lady, a Leonardo one, nick-named the White Devil, being on her trial for murder . . .'). Thus, by such roundabout ways, Lamb's instinctive desire for life was compelled to satisfy itself, a desire which a contemporary (Walter Wilson) noted in him: 'He had an instinctive desire for life, and I have heard him say, in his own strong language, when a young man, that he would rather live on board the gallies than not live at all.'

In the style of Sir Thomas Browne's *Religio Medici* ('Holy-water and Crucifix (dangerous to the common people)'—wrote Browne—'deceive not my judgment, nor abuse my devotion at all: I am, I confess, naturally inclined to that which misguided Zeal terms Superstition,' &c.) Charles Lamb made, in *The Londoner*, his own profession of faith, wrote his own *Religio Laici*:

> The very deformities of London, which give distaste to others, from habit do not displease me. The endless succession of shops where *Fancy miscalled Folly* is supplied with perpetual gauds and toys, excite in me no puritanical aversion. I gladly behold every appetite supplied with its proper food. . . .

The sub-title of Lamb's letters might well be *Religio Laici*, or in fact, *Religio Burgensis*, so thoroughly does the figure that emerges from them display characteristics of a particular class, characteristics which Lamb has in common with an author in other respects so very different, Flaubert. To counteract the impression of narrowness which emanates from the greater part of Lamb's letters, one must turn to the *Essays of Elia*, in which, from narrowness, is distilled poetry.

In the essays, Elia talks to us about himself, about his life with his 'cousin' (that is, his sister), about his college friends, the places of his childhood, his holiday walks, the different aspects of his beloved London: in this typically bourgeois love of town life Lamb is much closer to Dr. Johnson, Boswell, and the eighteenth century in general than to the Romantics; Johnson preferred Fleet Street, with its busy hum, to the quiet of Greenwich Park, and the smell of the flares in a theatre to the fragrance of a May evening, and Boswell declared: 'Fleet Street is in my mind more delightful than Tempe.' Lamb talks to us also about his favourite authors, about the theatre which he loved so passionately, he confides to us his tastes, his antipathies, and the fancies that pass through his head, with the apparent capriciousness of a live conversation; we come upon him talking to his 'cousin' about the time when they were poor, when it was a pleasure to spend a few shillings sometimes on a book or a print, a pleasure mingled with regret for the small amount saved that had been dissipated, whereas now that they were comfortably off they could spend money whenever they liked on prints or books, and yet they no longer felt the pleasure of spending; on another occasion he talks to us about the great emptiness he felt after giving up his employment, and how he missed the Sunday holidays of the old days, which were, really and truly, rather melancholy, and how the week's summer holiday was more like an anxious chase after pleasure than pleasure itself, but expectation was everything; every day of the week and every month of the year was then coloured in relation to the holiday, according to whether it was far off or near at hand, whereas now that it was always holidays it was never holidays, and there were no longer the walks and the visits to the country which at the moment did not appear to be anything much, but which afterwards continued always to haunt the memory. All this Elia tells us in a style that follows the gentle, uninterrupted flow of his memories, in long sentences that seem anxious to tell everything: what appeared, in Mary, to be a chaos of extravagant recollections, was, in Charles, a quiet mirror of the past. See, in fact, what Lamb said in a letter about his sick sister:[41]

When she is not violent her rambling chat is better to me than the sense and sanity of this world. . . . Her memory is unnaturally strong; and from ages past, if we may so call the earliest records of our poor life, she fetches thousands of names and things that never would have dawned upon me again, and thousands from the ten years she lived before me. What took place from early girlhood to her coming of age principally lives again (every important thing and every trifle) in her brain with the vividness of real presence. For twelve hours incessantly she will pour out without intermission all her past life, forgetting nothing, pouring out name after name . . . as a dream; sense and nonsense; truths and errors huddled together; a medley between inspiration and possession.

Characteristic of the *Essays of Elia*, side by side with their exquisiteness of form, with their jewel-like decoration of learned allusion—like inlay-work, as though their author took a collector's or a decorator's pleasure in arranging erudite reminiscences in admirably appropriate positions—is the deliberate absence of emphasis, the anti-rhetorical quality, the refusal to go over to the full orchestra in the manner of the Romantics; the desire to preserve a muted tone, making use of humour to extinguish any over-adventurous flare-up. For instance, in his *Chapter on Ears* he confesses himself, in a joking and quite unpretentious way, to be insensible to classical music; and he is not at all ashamed of appearing pedestrian, as we have seen at the beginning of this chapter, on the subject of dreams (*Witches, and other Night-Fears*): 'For the credit of my imagination, I am almost ashamed to say how tame and prosaic my dreams are grown. They are never romantic, seldom even rural.' And he likes to linger over the humbler aspects of important people, for example over the modest beginnings of a great actress, in the delicious essay *Barbara S - - -*, in which he goes into ecstasies over the little blotted and scrawled notebooks containing the small parts she had acted as a beginner. *Old China* discusses the subjects—so very Biedermeier—of pieces of china displayed in neat order in a glass-fronted cabinet, and of things remembered, the latter also being contemplated facet by facet, like painted, shining little cups. Lamb's masterpiece, *Dream-Children*, with its mixture of wit and heart-ache, anticipates the first part of *David Copperfield*; except that Dickens rarely succeeded in being so soberly pathetic.[42]

Thomas De Quincey

ONE would hardly expect, at the first glance, to find bourgeois tendencies in the life of the opium-eater Thomas De Quincey, who aroused the admiration of the anti-bourgeois Baudelaire. He would seem, in fact, in many respects to be a forerunner of the Decadents, typical artist as he was, with his wandering life, his disorganized method of work, his incapability of adapting himself to family life. He would cut a much better figure, it might be thought, in the discussion of a different current in nineteenth-century literature, the current I dealt with in *The Romantic Agony*—to such an extent is algolagnia the dominant factor in his life: to such a point, indeed, that one wonders whether his being reduced to playing hide-and-seek with his creditors (who were certainly very threatening) was not also due to an appetite for persecution. This suspicion finds support in a letter from his daughter, Mrs. Baird-Smith: 'It was an accepted fact among us that he was able when saturated with opium to persuade himself and delighted to persuade himself (the excitement of terror was a real delight to him) that he was dogged by dark and mysterious foes.' Even his bitter conviction, during the last years of his life, that he was nothing more than a journalist, appears to have given him the satisfaction of humiliation. Furthermore, all his life De Quincey had a morbid interest in criminal trials. This and other things would indeed seem to give substance to the report, current on the Continent, that De Quincey was a forerunner of the Decadents. But *The Confessions of an Opium Eater* and *Murder considered as One of the Fine Arts* represent a very small section of De Quincey's work, and besides, the *Confessions* contain only a few pages of Decadent interest, and *Murder* is a humorous evasion of an obsession; moreover De Quincey's life, if it is not the life of a bourgeois, if it provides—as one of his modern biographers has written[43]—'one of the saddest careers in literary history', with its perpetual struggle to reduce the doses of opium and its burden of debt, has not really many resemblances to the lives of the *poètes maudits*. Edward Sackville-West, author of the best biographical study of De Quincey,[44] declares the continental point of view to be preposterous, which sets the author of the *Confessions* beside such figures as Huysmans and Beardsley, and treats his work as a kind of pendant to the *Fleurs du Mal*: 'Nothing could be more at variance with the facts. To regard him as a decadent, *fin-de-siècle* figure is fundamentally to misconceive the nature of his being.'

We find ourselves faced, in fact, with an ambiguous figure, characteristic of a period of transition. The violent physical disturbances artificially produced by opium brought to the surface the raw elements of a nature which was essentially poetic, but which at the same time tended to avoid developing that particular one amongst the mental faculties. So that we find in De Quincey's work, consciously dominated as it was by intellect and logic (he made plans for works on philosophy and economics, and accumulated an immense mass of information which he later put to use in the numberless newspaper articles in which, all too often, he dissipated his talent), the reappearance, at intervals, of the fantastic vein brought to light by opium. The dreams produced by opium caused a flaw in the structure of a personality that had been deliberately orientated to harmonize with a bourgeois atmosphere. De Quincey's conscious attempts to create Romantic art have all the characteristics of a tradition in decay: he seems like the last, imitative survivor of a moribund school, that of the 'tales of terror'. The sensationalism of *Klosterheim* (1832), for instance, derives from Mrs. Radcliffe, combined with historical scenes in the manner of Scott. Like Mrs. Radcliffe, De Quincey makes an effort to create an atmosphere of terror, only to dissipate the 'terrific' elements in incidents that are very far from supernatural.

In works of this kind De Quincey is doing no more than echo a defunct manner; with his attack on Goethe's *Wilhelm Meister*, however, he foreshadows the moralistic criticism of the Victorians. The eighteenth-century, Casa-

novan character of Goethe's novel offends his moral sense,
already set towards the sorry standards that were to prevail
under Queen Victoria. He did not feel its fullness of life
either as an eighteenth-century critic or as a Romantic
would have felt it; as a Victorian, he judged it to be merely
indecent. The first part of this attack, published in the
London Magazine of August 1824, was later omitted by
De Quincey from the complete collection of his works: it
poured contempt upon the figure of Goethe in terms of
vulgar jocularity. But what interests us here is his criticism
of the novel. The female characters in it are passed in
review, and found to be depraved, worthless, corrupt. In
certain passages De Quincey's analysis resembles that of
Macaulay: the tone of moral indignation is veiled with
irony. For example:

> Even from personal uncleanliness Mr. Goethe thinks it possible
> to derive a grace. 'The white négligé' of Philina, because it was
> 'not superstitiously clean,' is said to have given her 'a frank and
> domestic air'. But the highest scene of this nature is the bedroom
> of Mariana: it passes all belief; 'Combs, soap, towels, *with the traces
> of their use*, were not concealed. Music, portions of plays, and pairs
> of shoes, washes and Italian flowers, pincushions, hair skewers,
> rouge-pots and ribbons, books and straw-hats—all were united by
> a common element, powder and dust.' This is the room into which
> she introduces her lover; and this is by no means the worst part of
> the description: the last sentence is too bad for quotation, and ap-
> pears to have been the joint product of Dean Swift and a German
> Sentimentalist.

And what is this last sentence, which modesty forbids
De Quincey to quote? It is hard to believe one's eyes: it is
neither more nor less than this perfectly innocent passage:

> It seemed to Wilhelm, as he put aside her corset in order to place
> himself at the pianoforte, or, again, laid her skirt on the bed so that
> he could sit down, or as she herself, with unaffected coolness, made
> no attempt to conceal from him certain natural things [*manches
> Natürliche*] that for decorum's sake are usually kept hidden from
> others—it seemed to Wilhelm, I say, that he felt closer to her every
> moment, as if their intimacy were being strengthened by invisible
> bonds.

De Quincey's modesty is in complete accordance with

the canons of the Victorian age, when the subject of intimate
female garments 'became a social taboo which must never
be referred to lest it recalled anatomical facts, and those (as
a Victorian lady so admirably expressed it) "are not things,
my dear, that we speak of; indeed, we try not even to think
of them" '.[45] De Quincey also says:

> How Laertes came by his hatred of women, and the abominable
> history of his 'double wounds', the reader must look for in Mr.
> Goethe: in German novels such things may be tolerated, as also in
> English brothels; and it may be sought for in either place; but for
> us, *nous autres Anglois*,
>
> > 'Non licet esse tam disertis
> > Qui musas colimus severiores.'[46]

Nous autres Anglois: such a thing would never have been
said, in a similar case, by the contemporaries of Fielding,
of Smollett, of Sterne; but De Quincey talks like a Victorian, like an Englishman of the period during which
there was formed, abroad, the conception—still current—
of British narrow-mindedness and hypocrisy.[47] According
to De Quincey, the English vocabulary has no name for
the role the Baroness plays when she interferes in the
Countess's love-affairs (but it had—with a vengeance!—
in Shakespeare's time); English patience cannot tolerate
that a young unmarried woman, designed for a model
of propriety and good sense, should, in her first conversation with a young man, recount the adulterous
intrigues of her supposed mother, even though she pro-
tects herself by adding: 'Alas! that I should have to say so
of my mother.' 'Adultery, by way of displaying her virgin
modesty!' exclaims De Quincey, in the feeling tones of
a preacher, 'her mother's adultery in testimony of her filial
piety!' And what is the point of this 'volunteer exposure of
her mother's depravity . . . by a young "German maiden"
dressed in men's clothes to a strolling player whom she had
never seen or heard of before'? It has no point at all: the
episode is related for nothing but 'its own inherent attractions'! De Quincey's irony on the subject of Serlo's love-
affairs becomes unbridled. 'Our English brains', he says,
among other things, 'whirl at the thought of the cycles and

epicycles, the vortices, the osculating curves' which the
chain of couples recorded in a speech by Philina 'would
describe' ('Aurelia pursues her faithless swain, thou her, I
thee, her brother me'—a situation that Goethe himself may
well have taken from an English work, none other than the
Midsummer Night's Dream). Finally De Quincey goes on
to examine the character of Mignon, and finds in it 'the
most unequivocal evidence of depraved taste and defective
sensibility':

First of all, Mignon is the offspring of an incestuous connexion
between a brother and sister. Here let us pause one moment to point
the reader's attention to Mr. Goethe, who is now at his old tricks,
—never relying on the grand high-road sensibilities of human
nature, but always travelling into bypaths of unnatural or un-
hallowed interest. Suicide, adultery, incest, monstrous situations, or
manifestations of supernatural power, are the stimulants to which
he constantly resorts in order to rouse his own feelings, originally
feeble, and, long before the date of this work, grown torpid from
artificial excitement.

Let us, in our turn, 'pause one moment'. De Quincey's
words somehow sound familiar; they call to mind, in fact,
certain other words, the words used by the moralizing,
hypocritical Jules Janin to condemn the works of the Marquis de Sade![48]

The preference of the bourgeois De Quincey, then, is not
for the aristocratic Goethe; his favourite German author is
the one who was the idol of Biedermeier, Jean Paul Richter.
In his mixture of pathos and humour, perfect 'as Corinthian
brass', he considers Richter 'by far the most eminent artist
in that way since the time of Shakespeare'—far superior to
Sterne. Jean Paul's coruscating wit sends him into ecstasies;
furthermore, 'everywhere a spirit of kindness prevails: his
satire is everywhere playful, delicate, and clad in smiles,—
never bitter, scornful, or malignant'. This eulogy corresponds exactly to the spirit and contents of *Punch*, the
humorous journal which was to be born in the Victorian
era. Jean Paul, in fact, maintains in everything the golden
mean; he never indulges in excesses, he tempers the pathetic
with the grotesque, he veils satire with benignity. And
finally, to complete the picture of the perfect bourgeois,

there is in him no lack of the tendency towards moral judgment and social reform. Typical, amongst all the extracts from Richter that De Quincey gives at the end of his essay,[49] is the first, which tells of the happy life of a Swedish parish priest—a picture of the 'intimist' type which breathes peace and quiet affections, and is suffused with a grey magic of its own, as can be judged from these passages:

Thus if it be the afternoon of Christmas-day; but, if it be any other afternoon, visitors, perhaps, come and bring their well-bred, grown-up daughters. Like the fashionable world in London, he dines at sunset; that is to say, like the *un*-fashionable world of London, he dines at two o'clock; and he drinks coffee by moonlight; and the parsonage-house becomes an enchanted palace of pleasure, gleaming with twilight, starlight, and moonlight. Or, perhaps he goes over to the schoolmaster, who is teaching his afternoon school: there, by the candle-light, he gathers round his knees all the scholars, as if —being the children of his spiritual children—they must therefore be his own grandchildren; and with delightful words he wins their attention, and pours knowledge into their docile hearts.

In contrast to this little winter picture, which breathes the good-humoured grace of a *genre* painting by Waldmüller, here is a summer picture, of one of those interminable Northern summer days, followed by its brief, luminous night:

The priest will not allow his company to depart: he detains them in the parsonage garden, where, says he, every one that chooses may slumber away in beautiful bowers the brief, warm hours until the reappearance of the sun. This proposal is generally adopted, and the garden is occupied: many a lovely pair are making believe to sleep, but, in fact, are holding each other by the hand. The happy priest walks up and down through the parterres. Coolness comes, and a few stars. His night-violets and gilly-flowers open and breathe out their powerful odours. To the north, from the eternal morning of the pole, exhales as it were a golden dawn. The priest thinks of the village of his childhood far away in Germany; he thinks of the life of man, his hopes, and his aspirations; and he is calm and at peace with himself. Then all at once starts up the morning sun in his freshness. Some there are in the garden who would fain confound it with the evening sun, and close their eyes again; but the larks betray all, and awaken every sleeper from bower to bower.

Then again begin pleasure and morning in their pomp of radiance; and almost I could persuade myself to delineate the course of this day also, though it differs from its predecessor hardly by so much as the leaf of a rose-bud.

De Quincey, in his best works, aimed at a mixture of the intimate, the pathetic, the fantastic, and the humorous; and nowhere did he succeed in this so well as in the work which is considered his masterpiece, *The English Mail-Coach*, published in *Blackwood's Magazine* in the full Victorian period, in 1849. The work, in its final form, consists of three sections entitled respectively: *The Glory of Motion*; *The Vision of Sudden Death*; *Dream-Fugue, founded on the preceding Theme of Sudden Death*. The first part, the least notable, is a combination of newspaper article and autobiographical essay; it sets forth the advantages of travelling by mail-coach, with divagations and anecdotes, and tells of De Quincey's first experiments in this method of locomotion; the various personal themes are then summarized in a kind of full-orchestra finale, in which they are woven together according to a musical design—a technique De Quincey had learnt from Hoffmann, though his own fantastic opium dreams also contributed to it. With his mail-coach journeys was associated the image of a girl, Fanny, who was generally to be seen as the coach passed through the forest near Marlborough, during the summer months; she was the granddaughter of the coachman, who, although like Fanny he had roses in his cheeks (*his* roses came from drinking), had the stiffness of a crocodile when it was a question of turning round. The picture of this coachman in his braided livery is brought into the finale, which has the character not so much of opium dreams as of the fantastic choreographies of nineteenth-century ballets, or of the oddities of Christmas decorations; the logical thread is as obvious as the wires which regulated the wings of those stage sylphs:

If, therefore, the crocodile does *not* change, all things else undeniably *do*: even the shadow of the pyramids grows less. And often the restoration in vision of Fanny and the Bath road makes me too pathetically sensible of that truth. Out of the darkness, if I happen to call back the image of Fanny, up rises suddenly from a gulf of forty years a rose in June: or, if I think for an instant of the rose in

June, up rises the heavenly face of Fanny. One after the other, like the antiphonies in the choral service, rise Fanny and the rose in June, then back again the rose in June and Fanny. Then come both together, as in a chorus—roses and Fannies, Fannies and roses, without end, thick as blossoms in paradise. [*This calls to mind certain choreographic effects in a ballet, with rows of ballerinas all dressed the same, and all making the same movements.*] Then comes a venerable crocodile, in a royal livery of scarlet and gold, with sixteen capes; and the crocodile is driving four-in-hand from the box of the Bath mail. And suddenly we upon the mail are pulled up by a mighty dial, sculptured with the hours, that mingle with the heavens and the heavenly host. Then all at once we are arrived at Marlborough forest, amongst the lovely households of the roe-deer; the deer and their fawns retire into the dewy thickets; the thickets are rich with roses; once again the roses call up the sweet countenance of Fanny; and she, being the grand-daughter of a crocodile, awakens a dreadful host of semi-legendary animals—griffins, dragons, basilisks, sphinxes —till at length the whole vision of fighting images crowds into one towering armorial shield, a vast emblazonry of human charities and human loveliness that have perished, but quartered heraldically with unutterable and demoniac natures, whilst over all rises, as a sur- mounting crest, one fair female hand, with the forefinger pointing, in sweet, sorrowful admonition, upwards to heaven, where is sculp- tured the eternal writing which proclaims the frailty of earth and her children.

A close comparison between this passage in its final form and the original as it appeared in *Blackwood* (five times as long) will reveal how De Quincey sacrificed not only re- dundancies, but, with them, certain passages of a more intimate and heartfelt significance, which remind one of Proust in the complication of their analysis: their theme is the horror we feel in dreams, and their origin lies in what De Quincey calls a double personality (that 'double' which provided sustenance for so much Romantic literature),[50] but which we should call the subconscious.

The last part of the first section of *The English Mail- Coach* shows the coach in its function of spreading the news of the English victories over Napoleon, and is full of lively *genre* pictures in the purest bourgeois taste. Here is the beflagged mail-coach coming out at sunset through the London suburbs: old and young come to the windows to acclaim it as it passes; the beggar forgets his infirmities and rises up in exultation at the victory; women and children, from garrets and cellars 'look with loving eyes upon our gay ribbons and our martial laurels' and throw kisses and wave handkerchiefs or aprons or anything that 'will express an aerial jubilation'. The coach meets a private carriage:

The weather being so warm, the glasses are all down; and one may read, as on the stage of a theatre, everything that goes on within. It contains three ladies—one likely to be 'mamma', and two of seventeen or eighteen, who are probably her daughters. What lovely animation, what beautiful unpremeditated pantomime, explaining to us every syllable that passes, in these ingenuous girls! By the sudden start and raising of the hands on first discovering our laurelled equipage, by the sudden movement and appeal to the elder lady from both of them, and by the heightened colour on their animated countenances, we can almost hear them saying, 'See, see! Look at their laurels! Oh, mamma! there has been a great battle in Spain; and it has been a great victory.' In a moment we are on the point of passing them. We passengers—I on the box, and the two on the roof behind me—raise our hats to the ladies; the coachman makes his professional salute with the whip; the guard even, though punctilious on the matter of his dignity as an officer under the crown, touches his hat. The ladies move to us, in return, with a winning graciousness of gesture; all smile on each side in a way that nobody could misunderstand, and that nothing short of a grand national sympathy could so instantaneously prompt.

This little scene, and another a little farther on, at night, by the light of torches (De Quincey describes it as 'a picture at once scenical and affecting, theatrical and holy'), seek to produce, with words, effects which properly belong to the field of *genre* painting, which triumphed throughout Europe during the nineteenth century (Boilly in France, Frith in England, J. P. Krafft, L. Russ in Austria, F. Krüger and W. Brücke the Younger in Germany, Induno in Italy, and so on; for these painters of great public scenes are legion). The play of expression on the innumerable faces of a crowd during an experience shared in common —the departure of a coach or a train, a fair, a horse race, a regatta or a military review, the arrival of political news— these are the things that the painters and story-tellers of the flourishing bourgeoisie seek to grasp in their works of

art: in these scenes the crowd is no longer a background
of walkers-on, grouped about one or more central figures,
as in the court painting of the centuries of aristocratic rule;
no longer are they anonymous spectators of the meeting of
a pope or an emperor, or of similar historical happenings—
a mere ornamental border for the great ones of the earth;
what now counts is the separate repercussion of facts, the
small individual drama which is clearly traced in the foreground and which, multiplying itself, confers upon the
picture the analytical, anecdotal character that belongs to
the bourgeois century: history seen as a domestic chronicle.
We have already had occasion to mention this point of view
when speaking, àpropos of Sir Walter Scott, of Wilkie's
Chelsea Pensioners listening to the News of Waterloo. We are
already in the atmosphere of Thackeray's 'novel without
a hero'.

The second part of *The English Mail-Coach* opens with
a dissertation of journalistic-encyclopaedic character on the
subject of sudden death, and goes on to relate an adventure
which happened to the author in 1817 or 1818. One clear
August night De Quincey, under the influence of a dose
of opium, was seated on the box of a mail-coach, when he
saw that the coachman was asleep, and was witness of a
threatened collision between the heavy, fast-moving vehicle
and a 'frail reedy gig' containing two lovers whose thoughts
were far distant:

Before us lay an avenue straight as an arrow, six hundred yards,
perhaps, in length; and the umbrageous trees, which rose in a regular
line from either side, meeting high overhead, gave to it the character
of a cathedral aisle. These trees lent a deeper solemnity to the early
light; but there was still light enough to perceive, at the further end
of this Gothic aisle, a frail reedy gig, in which were seated a young
man, and by his side a young lady. Ah, young sir! what are you
about? If it is requisite that you should whisper your communications to this young lady—though really I see nobody, at an hour
and on a road so solitary, likely to overhear you—is it therefore
requisite that you should carry your lips forward to hers? The little
carriage is creeping on at one mile an hour; and the parties within
it, being thus tenderly engaged, are naturally bending down their
heads. Between them and eternity, to all human calculation, there
is but a minute and a half.

And on the box of the swiftly-charging vehicle, beside the slumbering coachman, sits the narrator, with staring eyes and mind half-paralysed with opium. The idyllic bourgeois picture changes to a nightmare; the two planes upon which the spirit of De Quincey moves, the Biedermeier plane, as we may call it, and the metaphysical, opium-conditioned plane—the two planes cross. And the last vision we have, after the disaster has been miraculously avoided, is that of the young woman, who, crazy with terror, rises and sinks up and down upon her seat, waving her arms: 'from the silence and deep peace of this saintly summer night. . . .' Death had leaped upon her, 'Death . . . with all the equipage of his terrors, and the tiger roar of his voice.' This image, which no one but that painter of nightmares who achieved fame in England at the end of the eighteenth and the beginning of the nineteenth centuries —Fuseli—could have represented in a picture, remained for ever before De Quincey's eyes; upon it was founded the brilliant fantasy, conceived in the manner of a musical fugue, which is contained in the third part. Reality and dream are mingled in the author's hallucinated mind; he sees himself in the guise of the lover, and seems to be transported in a vessel over tropic seas, while on another ship is the girl, and the two vessels almost collide; then the girl goes farther away and appears and disappears amongst furious waves; later on, she is swallowed up by quicksands, while De Quincey is powerless to save her. The funeral march is succeeded by a hymn of victory, and the coach, taking up again the final motif of the first part, becomes a triumphal chariot and bears all over the world the news of the victory of Waterloo; it sweeps, by night, into a mighty cathedral, which soon turns into a solemn, turreted necropolis where repose all those who have died for England in a thousand battles, from Crécy to Trafalgar; and then the theme of the nightmare comes back again: the coach meets 'a carriage as frail as flowers' in which is the girl, and threatens to overturn it. De Quincey rises in horror, and there also rises, from one of the tombs, a 'Dying Trumpeter sculptured on a bas-relief', who sounds his trumpet, and lo! the horses drawing the coach come to a stop, they too 'frozen to a bas-relief'. 'Afar off, in a vast recess, rose three mighty windows to the clouds; and . . . at height insuperable to man, rose an altar of purest alabaster', in a halo of unearthly light, in which the woman appears again, 'sinking, rising, raving, despairing', and by her side kneels her guardian angel, his face hidden by his wings, weeping and pleading for her. And so, with this paradisal Victorian-lithograph vision, the strange work comes to an end, a work in which can be detected reminiscences of Piranesi's *Prisons*—greatly admired by De Quincey—, of the fantastic tales of Hoffmann,[51] and perhaps of the stage effects in the romantic ballets so popular during the nineteenth century.

From humble, commonplace starting-points, De Quincey escapes at once into a magic universe. This can be seen in the pencil portrait of him and his family by J. Archer. Dressed in white, the two daughters play with the granddaughter, and appear to ignore the black figure of the man who sits, bending forward, beside them—and yet so far away—with his eyes staring into the void. He is in their world, he is sitting in the same armchair against whose back leans Emily, the younger daughter: in the Victorian drawing-room that echoes with the baby's gay chatter, De Quincey contemplates the solemn, piteous processions which arise from the fumes of opium.

Thomas Love Peacock

FUNDAMENTALLY bourgeois, also, are the life and works of the third of the 'eccentrics' who form as it were a bridge of transition between Romanticism and the Victorian age—Thomas Love Peacock (1785–1866). Son of a London glass merchant, and finding his father's business little to his taste, he lived for some years, after he left his school at Englefield Green, on his own income, writing verses in a classical and moralistic style. He soon developed an affection for the British Museum, but knew nothing of the Romantic Muse except that tender little elegiac spirit, all eighteenth-century in feeling, the 'gentle nymph Melancholy', which accompanied him on his solitary rambles through rural England. He meditated upon the flight of time, upon the decline of men and empires, and his *Visions of Love* (a short poem of 1806) harmonizes an honest if tepid love with domestic pleasures and the delights of learning. This is what woman meant in his life:

> To strew its short but weary way with Flow'rs,
> New hopes to raise, new feelings to impart,
> For this to man was lovely woman given.

The woman in the house ends by being a vehicle of comfort no less than the library:

> The classic bookcase deck'd with learning's store,
> Rich in historic truth and bardic lore.

In winter, at the fireside, they will recall the time when he was courting her, her 'angelic blushes', her timid smiles, the mute language of her eyes; together they will read the poets, in chronological order—Homer, Virgil, Shakespeare, Milton, Gray, Ossian. She will play the harp, they will have friends to see them, she will perform good works, visiting the widow and orphan: the vision of conjugal life develops panoramically, as in an illustrated almanac for ladies. Time will cool the ardour of passion, but mutual esteem will remain; and when time is ripe, husband and

wife will meet again in the abodes of the just.[52] A perfect
Biedermeier picture.

Peacock's sentimental resources, like those of a small,
prudent republic, are of modest proportions, but his ex-
penditure is so limited that the amounts paid in cannot but
suffice to counterbalance it. No wonder a nature of this
sort could find all the nourishment it needed in the arcadies
of Guarini and Metastasio. In 1807, at the age of twenty-
two, he became engaged, but the girl's family thought it
better to marry her off to a more advantageous party; the
new bride died in the following year. These circumstances,
which would have overwhelmed a Romantic, darkened the
soul of Peacock with only a faint shadow of delicate sadness,
and even before the faithless young woman died, he had
already written her epitaph in the perfectly commonplace
lines *Beneath a Cypress Shade*—a poem which of course
found its way into the Parnassus of the Victorian Palgrave,
The Golden Treasury:

> I dug, beneath the cypress shade,
>   What well might seem an elfin's grave;
> And every pledge in earth I laid,
>   That erst thy false affection gave.
>
> I pressed them down the sod beneath;
>   I placed one mossy stone above;
> And twined the rose's fading wreath
>   Around the sepulchre of love.
>
> Frail as thy love, the flowers were dead,
>   Ere yet the evening sun was set:
> But years shall see the cypress spread,
>   Immutable as my regret.

Some biographers of Peacock have given too much importance to this idyll, attributing to it a decisive influence
upon his character; but the most authoritative of them,
J.-J. Mayoux, reduces it, quite rightly, to very modest
proportions: '. . . après les toutes premières années, qui
nous échappent, la vie de Peacock est l'expression de son
caractère, auquel les événements s'intègrent et s'harmoni-
sent avec une facilité merveilleuse'. The figure of Peacock
was clearly drawn, from the beginning, as it was to remain

always. He was an intellectual, a solitary of average sensibility: his tastes in the sphere of feeling were simple; all he wanted was a type of woman without surprises or profundities, provided she had sweetness, gaiety, and good health. It is true that he went wandering up hill and down dale with his big Newfoundland dog, but not in the manner of a Romantic in search of an unattainable land of dreams, an 'anywhere out of the world'; merely as an idle man who knew how necessary it was to wander in order to appreciate the pleasure of staying still, and to renew the landscape around himself in order to be able to keep himself fresh for the stimulus of beauty. The great occupation of his life was reading. The philosophers of the latter part of the eighteenth and the beginning of the nineteenth century gave, in the end, a precise orientation to his imagination. Rather than become intoxicated with German metaphysics and attach himself to the greatest, Peacock found delight in taking sips at the secondary philosophers, those who maintained out-of-date positions and were easy and pleasant to read; in William Drummond's *Academical Questions* and Horne Tooke's *Diversions of Purley* he found models of dialectics which confuted with brilliant superficiality and covered with identical ridicule both the then new Kant and a certain comic old-fashioned philosopher, Lord Monboddo, a strange sort of Don Quixote with a head stuffed full of ancient metaphysics. The culminating moment of the *Diversions of Purley* supplies, for Peacock, a firm starting-point:[53]

> *True* is a past participle of the verb *treothan, confidere*, to Think, to Believe firmly, to be thoroughly persuaded of, to Trow. . . . *True* . . . means simply and merely—*that which is Trowed*. . . . Truth supposes mankind. . . . If no man, no Truth. There is therefore no such thing as eternal, immutable, everlasting Truth; unless mankind, *such as they are at present*, be also eternal, immutable, and everlasting. Two persons may contradict each other, and yet both speak Truth: for the Truth of one person may be opposite to the Truth of another. . . .

This is a debasement of truth to the level of opinion, a raising of opinion and conferring upon it the rank of sole truth; it is giving the same value to all variations of the spirit. Peacock was to adopt this point of view both by natural affinity and almost by instinct. As a result of these readings he developed a habit of learned scepticism of an elegant eighteenth-century type.

In 1812 this tepid-souled dabbler in philosophy came into contact with a soul of very different temper, that of Shelley. The Hookhams, publishers of both poets, paved the way for the meeting by sending Shelley Peacock's *Genius of the Thames* and *Palmyra* to read. The two formed a close friendship, owing, perhaps, to the very diversity of their temperaments: one, an aristocratic, revolutionary idealist, the other a bourgeois, conservative positivist. While, during those years, Peacock was leading the hermit-like life of a sage, with an almost complete lack of external history except for the dates of his visits to Wales, Shelley was being driven on by an urgent longing for clamorous action, for Prometheus-like gesture, and was leading a nomadic life, the nomadic life of a Romantic, attracting eccentric types of women into his orbit. At Lynmouth, for instance, a whole harem collected round this perfectly chaste sultan: it was composed of Harriet ('my Harriet'), her sister Eliza, and the governess Elizabeth Hitchener ('my Portia'), a feminist and a republican, who had been his correspondent for a long time and was, so to speak, invested with the office of receiving the dictates of the Shelleyan doctrine and replying to them. Shelley also invited Fanny Imlay, Godwin's step-daughter, but without success. The Shelley of that period had a certain affinity with another strange Rousseau-esque apostle of our own day, D. H. Lawrence, especially as he appears in the books of Mabel Dodge Luhan and Dorothy Brett. One taste in common—if nothing else—Peacock and Shelley had, that of amusing themselves with launching paper boats on the quiet waters of canals: a taste which, so far as Shelley is concerned, is illumined with a curious symbolic gleam when one thinks of his tragic end. But no less significant is the sequel that this innocent amusement had in the life of the bourgeois Peacock. In 1836, as an Examiner to the East India Company, he induced the Company to build iron steamboats for the Indian lines of communication, both internal and ex-

ternal; he provided plans, suggested movable keels that
drew no more than five feet of water for the navigation of
the shallower rivers, and superintended the construction
of the ships which could also carry, if required, guns of
large calibre. On October 16th, 1846, he received personal
congratulations from Lord Auckland, First Lord of the
Admiralty.

Shelley and Peacock, moreover, in the formation of this
close friendship, gave proof of a largeness of comprehen-
sion that is not easily imaginable from the rather generalized
outlines of their characters which are usually given us:
Peacock must have been more generous and considerate
than the comic spirit with which the critics have summarily
identified him might lead one to expect, and Shelley must
have tempered the enthusiasm of his vision with a wider
and more tolerant sense of humanity's accepted standards.
It is also interesting to note—as Professor Mayoux has
done—certain analogies between Shelley's *The Revolt of
Islam* and *Prince Athanase* on the one hand, and Peacock's
Ahrimanes and *Rhododaphne* on the other. But Shelley was
destined to impregnate Peacock with a very different kind
of inspiration: the Shelley who devoured the 'tales of
terror', who was the author of *Zastrozzi* and *St. Irvyne*
with their bandits and caverns, their tragic loves, their
sinister or superhuman spirits—the Shelley whom an
Italian-American student of the subject, Michele Ren-
zulli, has tried (with, to tell the truth, inadequate ability) to
throw light upon[54]—supplied Peacock with the prototype
of Scythrop, the young hero of *Nightmare Abbey* (1818),
a gracefully-treated caricature which amused Shelley himself, who by then was considerably past that stage of
development. *Nightmare Abbey* is not therefore, as some
critics have tried to show, an abuse of intimacy and an
evidence of unpardonable indelicacy, still less an involuntary confession on the part of Peacock that he did not
understand the real, essential Shelley. Scythrop's dilemma
between his two loves, Marionetta and Celinda-Stella, is
more or less a repetition of Shelley's dilemma between
Harriet and Mary; but before accusing Peacock of indelicacy we must remember that Shelley was merely

translating into real life a situation adumbrated by himself in *St. Irvyne,* when the noble brigand Wolfstein hesitates between Megalena and Olympia, who—like Harriet, later —kills herself for love: Shelley's situation in 1814 was, in fact, a typical Romantic situation, and Peacock, in *Nightmare Abbey,* was merely isolating a typical side of his friend, a side which had more to do with the history of manners than with the history of a particular man. Scythrop's adventure is the prettiest of anti-Romantic moralities, whereas the real adventure of Shelley, between Harriet and Mary, has about it something sordid and sinister. The sentimental intrigue in *Nightmare Abbey* is more a caricature of Shelleyan Romantic behaviour than of Shelley's own love-affairs. Other aspects of Romanticism were satirized by Peacock in *Nightmare Abbey*: Coleridge's metaphysics in the character of Mr. Flosky, and Byronism in Mr. Cypress.

Shelley himself, in any case, had given the initial idea for the novel, when he wrote, in the Preface to *The Revolt of Islam* (end of 1817): 'Gloom and misanthropy [in consequence of the failure of the French Revolution] have become the characteristics of the age in which we live, the solace of a disappointment that unconsciously finds relief only in the wilful exaggeration of its own despair. This influence has tainted the literature of the age with the hopelessness of the minds from which it flows. . . . Our works of fiction and poetry have been over-shadowed by the same infectious gloom. . . .' The correspondence of Shelley and Peacock reveals how well they agreed on the subject of *Nightmare Abbey*. On May 30th, 1818, Peacock wrote: 'I have almost finished *Nightmare Abbey*. I think it necessary to "make a stand" against the "encroachments" of black bile. The fourth canto of *Childe Harold* is really too bad. I cannot consent to be *auditor tantum* of this systematical "poisoning" of the "mind" of the "reading public".' To which Shelley replied: 'You tell me that you have finished *Nightmare Abbey*. I hope that you have given the enemy no quarter. Remember, it is a sacred war. We have found an excellent quotation in Ben Jonson's *Every Man in his Humour*. . . .' To which Peacock answers: 'Your quotation from Jonson is singularly applicable, and I shall

certainly turn it to account.' He made use of it, in fact, in
Nightmare Abbey, and it is worth recording here, since it is
typical of the bourgeois attitude towards Romantic melancholy:

MATTHEW. Oh! it's your only fine humour, sir. Your true melancholy breeds your perfect fine wit, sir. I am melancholy myself,
divers times, sir, and then do I no more but take pen and paper
presently, and overflow you half a score or a dozen of sonnets
at a sitting.

STEPHEN. Truly, sir, and I love such things out of measure.

MATTHEW. Why, I pray you, sir, make use of my study: it's at your
service.

STEPHEN. I thank you, sir, I shall be bold, I warrant you. Have you
a stool there, to be melancholy upon?[55]

And, in the same correspondence with Shelley, Peacock
clinches the point that the object of *Nightmare Abbey* was
to unmask some of the morbid aspects of contemporary
literature. Peacock himself, as we have seen, had started
as a worshipper of the melancholy Muse, even if his melancholy had been of a very mild type: and now, here he is,
criticizing an aspect whose symptoms he had observed in
himself. He is, then, a typically transitional figure.

There is a second motto at the beginning of *Nightmare
Abbey* which also casts light upon the author's nature. It is
taken from Rabelais:[56]

Ay esleu gasouiller et siffler oye, comme dit le proverbe, entre
les cygnes, plustost que d'estre entre tant de gentils poëtes et faconds
orateurs mut du tout estimé.

The comparison between a goose and our bourgeois
author, in the midst of a chorus of romantic swans, could
hardly be more appropriate.

The period of studious and rustic leisure had of necessity to come to an end for Peacock with his entry into the
service of the East India Company in 1816; in 1819 he
thought to approach still nearer to the ordinary life of
mankind by getting married, and with this end in view
wrote to a young Welsh lady whom he had not seen for
eight years, Jane Gryffydh, declaring that 'the greatest

blessing this world could bestow on me would be to make you my wife'. It makes one think of the marriage of Traddles in *David Copperfield*. Professor Mayoux wittily remarks: 'Jane était évidemment du bois dont sont faites les femmes des philosophes': she accepted the proposal. The final passage of Peacock's letter is worth recording, for it is an illustration of the opposite pole to the Romantic epistolary style:

> The same circumstances which have given me prosperity confine me to London, and to the duties of the department with which the East India Company has entrusted me: yet I can absent myself for a few days once in every year: if you sanction my wishes, with what delight should I employ them in bringing you to my home! If this be but a baseless dream—if I am even no more in your estimation than the sands on the sea-shore—yet I am sure, as I have already said, that you will answer me with the same candor with which I have written. Whatever may be your sentiments, the feelings with which I now write to you, and which more than eight years of absence and silence have neither obliterated nor diminished, will convince you that I never can be otherwise than most sincerely and most affectionately your friend.

A curious marriage, crowned, moreover, with a numerous offspring. One consequence of Peacock's new circumstances was that he was parted both from poetry and from Shelley; but, amongst the correspondence of the two men of letters during this period, there is one request from Shelley, in 1821, to his friend who was now an influential official at India House, which strikes the imagination: Shelley was seeking employment as political counsellor to an Indian prince! When Shelley died in 1822, Peacock and Byron were the executors of his will, but, Byron being unable to discharge his function, the task fell to Peacock, who had considerable difficulty in reconciling the demands of Shelley's father with those of his widow, who, in any case, did not much care for Peacock.

Peacock's intellectual evolution had, in the meantime, turned in the direction of utilitarianism, of a system of practical morality firmly anchored in the rude reality of the quest for personal advantage. To utilitarian criticism he brought a well-sharpened wedge for the felling of certain selected trees in the forest of false values. The intellectual anarchism of *Maid Marian* (written chiefly towards the end of 1819, and published in 1822), a typical work of the period of the Holy Alliance, far surpasses, in boldness, even the position of utilitarian criticism. The main point of the story lies in the close approximation made by Peacock of the hero Richard Cœur de Lion to the brigand Robin Hood:

Their Richard is a hero, and our Robin is a thief: marry, your hero guts an exchequer, while your thief disembowels a portmanteau; your hero sacks a city, while your thief sacks a cellar: your hero marauds on a larger scale, and that is all the difference. . . . But two of a trade cannot agree: therefore your hero makes laws to get rid of your thief . . . for might is right, and the strong make laws for the weak, and they that make laws to serve their own turn do also make morals to give colour to their laws.

It is an anti-heroic conclusion, of a bourgeois scepticism, and belonging to the tradition that goes far back to Jean de Meung. I have said that the work is typical of the period of the Holy Alliance, of the reaffirmation of legitimism by force against the desire of the peoples. The outlaw's code presents, in satirical form, that same might disguised as right which was the basis of the Holy Alliance: this is satire from the point of view of the bitter common sense of a liberal bourgeois:

The principles of our society are six: Legitimacy, Equity, Hospitality, Chivalry, Chastity, and Courtesy.
The articles of legitimacy are four:

I. Our government is legitimate, and our society is founded on the one golden rule of right, consecrated by the universal consent of mankind, and by the practice of all ages, individuals, and nations: namely, To keep what we have, and to catch what we can.

II. Our government being legitimate, all our proceedings shall be legitimate: wherefore we declare war against the whole world, and every forester is by this legitimate declaration legitimately invested with a roving commission, to make lawful prize of everything that comes in his way.

III. All forest laws but our own we declare to be null and void.

IV. All such of the old laws of England as do not in any way interfere with, or militate against, the views of this honourable assembly, we will loyally adhere to and maintain. The rest we declare null and void as far as relates to ourselves, in all cases wherein a vigour beyond the law may be conducive to our own interest and preservation.

At India House Peacock had, first as colleague, then as superior, James Mill, a sceptic in matters of psychology, he too under the influence of Horne Tooke's analyses, and, in that respect, prepared to be on terms of easy understanding with Peacock; whereas another side of Mill, that of the zealous partisan of political economy and commercialism, was calculated rather to excite Peacock's vein of parody; not so provocatively, however, as his son, John Stuart, the sentimental, ascetic economist—a sort of Shelley without beauty or imagination, without music and without grace. Peacock reacted to the inhuman aridity of Jeremy Bentham's utilitarianism by seeking a humanistic way out, John Stuart Mill a humanitarian. Peacock was not a radical with philosophic tendencies like Bentham, but a radical philosopher, and he soon realized that the sophism of 'progress' was a mental sedative more dangerous, because more seductive, than the sophism of those who were attacked by Bentham, those who exalted the wisdom of the ancients—a struggle in which the antagonism between ancients and moderns, which had raged furiously ever since the Renaissance, still continued.

In *The Misfortunes of Elphin* (which appeared at the beginning of 1829), after exposing the absurdity of the anti-reformist arguments through the mouth of the corrupt official, Seithenyn, a confirmed drunkard, Peacock finally concludes that, in the story of humanity, *plus ça change, plus c'est la même chose*. Not that Peacock takes no interest in the idea of reform; but he concentrates upon his task as an intellectual, as the champion of clarity, the champion of mental effort against common, trite ideas, against the platitudes by which the world allows itself to be guided. And so, with gay cynicism and a healthy exaggeration, he demolishes the whole work of humanity, tearing off the mask.[57] Peacock is here carrying on the stream of bour-

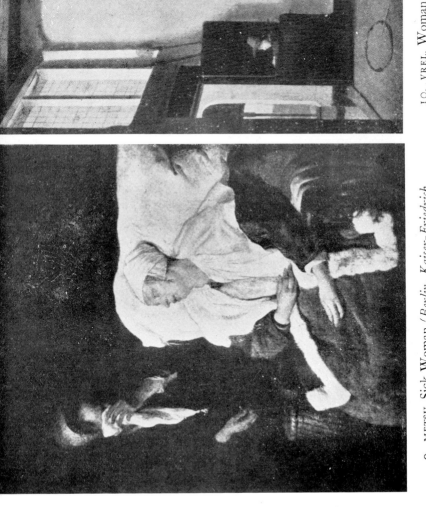

9. METSU. Sick Woman (*Berlin, Kaiser-Friedrich Museum*)

10. VREL. Woman combing a little Girl's hair (*Detroit Museum*)

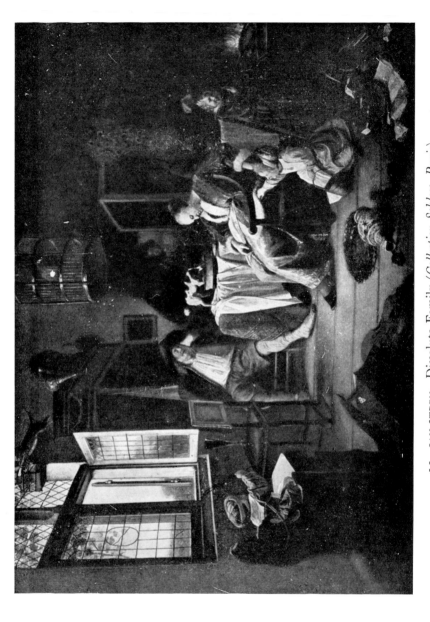

11. JAN STEEN Dissolute Family (*Collection Schloss, Paris*)

geois satire which had produced Voltaire's *Contes philoso-phiques*, and which was later to produce Anatole France. It is also possible to discern, on the other hand, the con-nexion with Rousseau's idea that sees happiness in primi-tive simplicity, when Peacock shows that force transformed into pseudo-right is infinitely more oppressive than brute force, that ignorance which has become pseudo-science is worse than sheer ignorance, that abuses refined and com-plicated by being transformed into institutions are more deadly than visible abuses. Here we shall not, of course, compare Peacock with the typical Victorian bourgeois, who satisfied himself with pretences; it was rather the bourgeois of the eighteenth century that survived in him.

But perhaps the ultimate depth of Peacock's philosophy is to be found in a passage in *Crotchet Castle*, another dia-lectical novel in the spirit of Aristophanes that appeared at the beginning of 1831, where one of the characters says, of the controversy between the economist and the medievalist: 'Gentlemen, you will never settle this controversy, till you have first settled what is good for man in this world; the great question, *de finibus*, which has puzzled all philo-sophers.' The Peacock of *Crotchet Castle* insists upon the fundamental individualism of man. But whereas the utili-tarians who, in the economic field, clung to individualistic and liberal doctrines—free competition, free negotiation between capital and labour—believed at the same time in the coercive force of good political institutions to secure the happiness of man, Peacock displayed an opposite con-tradiction. An individualist both by temperament and by profound conviction, Peacock never tired of hurling sar-casms at political, legal, and all kinds of institutions, whether ancient or modern, and felt the need of legislation precisely in that economic sphere in which individuals, thanks to capitalist policy, no longer encountered each other as such, and in which some people, in face of the weakness of the subordinate masses, found themselves in-vested with a power monstrous in itself and yet, often, unrelated to their personal worth.

The bourgeois quality of Peacock is well illustrated by his attitude towards the masses, as revealed in *Crotchet*

Castle. Incendiarism, of which we have already spoken in
relation to Lamb, provoked, in Peacock, a reaction similar
to that of the conservative Lamb; he makes use, ironically,
of the same expression—the 'march of mind'—which the
Conservatives used to stigmatize the revolutionary spirit.
One of the characters in *Crotchet Castle* says: 'The march
of mind . . . has marched into my rick-yard, and set my
stacks on fire, with chemical materials, most scientifically
compounded.' Also: 'The policeman, who was sent down
to examine, says my house has been broken open on the
most scientific principles. All this comes of education.'
And, whereas Peacock had already reproved Burke for
using the expression 'swinish multitude', he now himself
starts talking about the 'rabble-rout'.

But *Crotchet Castle* already presents us with a Peacock
who has become at the same time both dense and dried-up:
he had, in the meantime, come under the influence of the
French 'romans gais'—Pigault-Lebrun, Paul de Kock (no
less than 144 volumes by this novelist were found in Peacock's library at his death!), and even *Le Compère Mathieu*
by that sinister character, the rebel priest Henri Joseph
Du Laurens, a nihilistic and scabrous novel which, in
accordance with the custom in vogue during those years
in France to find an excuse for the most suspect works,
concluded by pretending that its intention had been to
make fun of the nihilistic principles paraded throughout
the book, and by holding up, as its true philosophy, the
ideal of a quiet life in accordance with the dictates of
self-respect, justice, and moderation. Peacock's article *On
French Comic Romances*, which appeared in the *London
Review* of 1835–6, throws light on the conception he had
formed of the function of the 'roman gai': an intense love
and a clear apprehension of the truth, he says, are both of
them essential in comic compositions of the first rank. So
that Peacock's own work, outwardly comic, is evidently
serious in intention: the eternal *ridendo dicere verum*. His
mission is the search for truth, without fear, without reserve,
almost without concern for anybody.[58] Nevertheless, while
Peacock gives free play to his satirical and destructive vein
in order to pull down everything that appears to be super-

structure, he still fails to find the ultimate truth which alone could justify such devastation; and, as Professor Mayoux observes, the psycho-analysis of social communities has its dangers, for the most useful and solid constructions can rest on rotten foundations, provided nobody knows it.

In a nerveless work such as *Crotchet Castle* we witness the breaking of the precarious balance between heart and brain which had still persisted in *The Misfortunes of Elphin*. This balance was replaced by a double figure: on one side a positive Peacock for whom reality is without veils, or even worse than it really is, on the other, a Peacock becoming more and more sentimental with age, and contenting himself with a facile idealism well protected from all hazardous tests. The two bourgeois figures—the eighteenth-century one who produced the philosophic novels *à la* Voltaire, and the nineteenth-century one who is already coloured with sentimentalism and easy Victorian optimism—meet together in that singular transitional figure which is Peacock.

In 1836 James Mill died, and Peacock succeeded him in the important position of Examiner at India House; he busied himself, with recognized competence, in public works, especially in the application of steam navigation to the communications of India, as we have already said. One of Peacock's daughters, Mary Ellen, having been left a widow in 1844 by the death of her husband Edward Nicolls, a naval lieutenant, in 1849 met and agreed to marry Meredith—a union which was destined to come to a dramatic end. In 1862 Peacock finished his last, very slight work, a translation of a famous Italian Cinquecento comedy, *Gl'Ingannati*. Tended, till his very last years, by an adopted daughter, he died at the height of the Victorian period; as Professor Mayoux says, 'il cultive son jardin, il grogne, il sentimentalise, il hellénise, il relit Dickens et s'attendrit, il préside à des fêtes d'enfants le premier jour de mai . . . .'.

With regard to Peacock's poetry, its formula, as Professor Mayoux has well observed, was the opposite of Wordsworth's: it was not 'emotion recollected in tranquillity', but 'tranquillity recollected with emotion'. And in this reversal lies the whole meaning of the literary revolution that was in process of being accomplished: on the far side, Romanticism, on this side Biedermeier. Poe praised Peacock's poem *Rhododaphne* as being 'brimful of music'. Peacock, however, as a poet, lacks truly intimate experience of the beauty that is his constant aim, and the sensuous appeal of this musical poetry is indirect, reflected, as it were, not gushing naturally from an image-generating sensation; it is, in fact, the poetical exercise of an intellectual.

The most notable part of Peacock's work is the tales, which form a link in the development of English literature between Ben Jonson's comedy of humour, Restoration comedy, and Voltaire's novels on the one hand (with, in the background, Rabelais), and, on the other, the modern intellectual novels of Meredith, and, in an even more obvious way, of Norman Douglas and Aldous Huxley. The style of Peacock's novels is descriptive rather than suggestive, with a tendency towards the exploiting of pedantry for comic effect, and towards Rabelaisian redundancy (for an example of pedantry: 'Mr. Cranium being utterly destitute of natatorial skill was in immediate danger of final submersion'). It is a style which, even when it achieves beauty, at the same time reveals a flaw—the omnipresent feeling of an illusory charm. The rhythm of this style is not spontaneous, but is, rather, of an architectonic order, as carefully controlled as a dance-figure, very different from Voltaire's rhythm, which is elastic and boundlessly free. Amongst the expedients for achieving comic effect, the least convincing is perhaps the very ancient one of giving the characters names which crystallize the characteristics that the author intends to parody. Peacock, in this field, attains subtleties which might well have made him the subject of a comic portrait by Proust (of the type of the philologist in *Sodome et Gomorrhe*). For instance, the name of Lord Anophel Achthar in *Melincourt* means: 'terrae pondus inutile', ἀνωφελ(ὲς) ἄχθ(ος) ἀρ(ούρης). The most successful comic effects are obtained by means of encounters between the manifold typical characters: theories and theorists, manias and maniacs, cranks of every kind butt into each other on almost every page of Peacock with automatic regularity—that automatic quality in which, according to

Bergson, the essence of laughter consists. This may become monotonous, but it may sometimes produce an irresistibly comic result, as in the description of Lord Littlebrain's garden in *Headlong Hall*, and in the suggestion of an atmosphere of complete idiocy which is given forth by the refrain: 'And there is Lord Littlebrain, rowing in an elegant boat... and there is Lord Littlebrain walking under it . . . and there you see Lord Littlebrain, on the top of the pavilion, enjoying the prospect with a telescope... and there you see Lord Littlebrain looking out of the window...' (chap. vi). But Peacock's taste for suddenly upsetting the balance, for turning somersaults, for the reduction of the human body to its material and geometrical elements, belongs to a far coarser type of humour: this is a taste which Professor Mayoux sets alongside that other taste for Rabelaisian enumerations, for avalanches of words, helter-skelter.

The architectonic tendency dominates not only the style but also the choice of characters; especially in *Headlong Hall*, which displays all Peacock's salient characteristics. There, the central group is of a perfect symmetry: Foster on one side, Escot opposite him, Jenkinson in the middle: thesis, antithesis, synthesis personified, as in a popular print. Creator of the 'novel of talk', Peacock, with his elegant distorting mirror, gives an oblique reflection of modes and manners and opinions, reducing the vast Romantic heaven, torn by a hundred blasts, to a storm in a teacup: there rises again in him, beneath a superficial Romantic patina which soon flakes away, a kind of eighteenth-century spirit, which, however, has coarsened and grown bourgeois.

In this band of eccentrics, who form the bridge of transition between Romanticism and the Victorian age, no more than a bare mention need be made of Hazlitt, who, notwithstanding his cult of violent action and energy which bring to mind a writer such as Stendhal, still turns back towards the eighteenth century in his desire for purism unadorned, and treats all subjects with a good sense that keeps to generalities and grows rigid in its fixedness of design.[59] With another essayist, Macaulay, we find ourselves, on the other hand, in the atmosphere of full Victorianism.

Macaulay

THE case of Macaulay as a writer presents some affinities with that of Hazlitt. He too seems to have been born 'all of a piece'; he shows scarcely any development, but has, from the very beginning, his own superficial perfection—in this case a showy perfection which makes him the idol of the average reader. Son of a philanthropist and abolitionist, Zachary Macaulay, he gave signs from the earliest age (he was born in 1800) of precocious genius and exceptional memory: he read voraciously and spoke like a printed book; at seven he began a compendium of universal history, at eight he wrote a treatise to convert the natives of Malabar to Christianity (a very different kind of homage from that which Baudelaire was to pay, many years later, to that same people, in his lines *A une Malabaraise*); after learning by heart Scott's *Lay of the Last Minstrel* and *Marmion*, he felt inspired to compose poems and hymns; he echoed Scott in a poem upon Olaus Magnus, a supposed ancestor of the Macaulays. Sent to school in 1812, he learnt with astonishing rapidity; in October 1818 he entered Trinity College, Cambridge, where he occupied himself with politics, becoming a convinced Liberal; in 1822 he won the annual college prize with an essay on William III, conceived in a style which already had the characteristics that were to develop in his maturity. In 1826 he passed his bar examination, but gave up this profession after a short time, finding Parliament more attractive than the Law Courts: he gave a first example of his eloquence, publicly praised in the *Edinburgh Review*, with a speech at a meeting of the Anti-Slavery Society, on June 24th, 1824. In the meantime he had started contributing to reviews, and in the August 1825 number of the *Edinburgh Review* his first essay appeared, on Milton. This essay had an immense success, for which the way was paved, undoubtedly, by the reputation this young man of great promise already had amongst his friends. His articles were

now published one after the other in the *Edinburgh Review*,
eclipsing all others.

Having been elected for the borough of Calne, Macaulay
made his maiden speech in Parliament on April 5th, 1830,
in favour of Robert Grant's Bill to revoke the restrictions
suffered by the Jews; another speech, on the second reading
of the Reform Bill, drew praises even from his opponent,
Sir Robert Peel, and finally established, for good and all,
Macaulay's reputation as a Parliamentary speaker. He was
received at Holland House, the centre of political, literary,
and artistic life in London, presented to the most celebrated
figures of the day, and flattered on all sides.

Macaulay's economic situation was, nevertheless, embarrassed, because his father's affairs had gone from bad
to worse, to the point when Macaulay had been forced to
sell the gold medals he had won at the University. But
with the passing of the Reform Act in June 1832 and the
triumph of the Grey Ministry, Macaulay was in favour
with the party in power, and was appointed one of the six
Commissioners of the Board of Control (a body of inspec-
tors instituted by Pitt to supervise the East India Company
to which the government of India was then entrusted).
His manifold public occupations did not allow him much
free time for literary activity, but by rising each morning
at five he managed to continue his contributions to the
Edinburgh Review. Elected member of Parliament for the
new constituency of Leeds, in 1833, he played a predominant part in the Bill for the abolition of slavery. In
1834 he was appointed to the Supreme Council of India
with a salary of £10,000 a year, which allowed him to put
aside very large sums for the alleviation of his father's
disastrous financial state and for paying off his creditors.
One of Macaulay's sisters, Hannah, was married in 1834
to Charles Trevelyan, who was then in the employ of
the East India Company, and the new home provided
Macaulay with the domestic surroundings which were all
that his emotional life needed; for he never married, and
it does not appear that he ever had any amorous relationship.

Macaulay lived in Calcutta until the end of 1837. He

applied his liberal mind to the study of the complex problems presented by the handing over of the administration of India from the East India Company to the Government: he defended the freedom of the press, he championed the equality of natives and Europeans in the eyes of the law, and, as chairman of the committee of Public Instruction, upheld the precedence of English over Indian studies; and, above all, he supervised the compilation of the Penal Code and the Code of Criminal Procedure for India, which were published at the end of 1837 and showed evidence of admirable preparation, surprising in one who, like him, had had only very slight practical experience of the Law.

Having returned to Europe in the autumn of 1838, he travelled in Italy, collecting material for his *Lays of Ancient Rome* (published in 1842). In March 1839 he started work on his *History of England*, which, according to his intention, was to embrace the period from the Revolution of 1688 to the death of George III. In 1839 he was elected member for Edinburgh, and shortly afterwards entered the Cabinet as Secretary of State for War, in which office he defended the Government's action over the war in China. When Lord Melbourne's Cabinet fell in 1841, Macaulay was able to devote himself once more to the composition of his *History*; in 1843 he collected his *Essays* in one volume, which enjoyed immense popularity. In November 1848 appeared the first two volumes of the *History of England*, which met with a success comparable only with that of Scott, Dickens, and the *Tales in Verse* of Byron: 13,000 copies were sold in four months. On July 19th, 1853, suffering from a serious affection of the heart, he delivered his last speech in Parliament. In December 1855 appeared the third and fourth volumes of the *History*, the sale of which surpassed all precedents in the United States, except for the Bible. In ten weeks 26,500 copies were sold, and the publishing firm of Longmans paid to Macaulay, in March 1856, a sum of £20,000 for author's rights—which is still regarded by the firm as a phenomenon in the annals of publishing.

In May 1856 Macaulay took up residence in a pleasant villa on Campden Hill—Holly Lodge—with a large garden which he took to cultivating with loving care. His last years were spent between his books, the pleasures of society, the affection of his relations, and his usual little autumn travels. In August 1857 he became Baron Macaulay of Rothley. His life came to a quiet end as he was sitting in his library; he was buried in Westminster Abbey.

This brief biographical sketch is all we need to be able to discern in Macaulay the figure of the perfect bourgeois. Excellent pupil, winner of medals at school, a good worker who from the first made full use of his gifts, including his prodigious memory, one who utilized every odd moment of time (the list of books he read on board ship on his voyages to and from India is famous); an admirable employee, thrifty, content to enjoy the cordial, comfortable routine of family life without entangling himself in any of those relationships, passionate or intensely emotional, which are generally implicit in such a routine. A kind of good-natured uncle, of domestic cat that finds its own comforts without risking any inconveniences. And it is, indeed, to the fireside and the warm slippers that Macaulay's *Essays* summon their eulogist, Taine:

> La solide reliure, la table symétrique, la préface, les chapitres substantiels alignés comme des soldats en bataille, tout vous ordonne de prendre un fauteuil, d'endosser une robe de chambre, de mettre vos pieds au feu, et d'étudier; vous ne devez pas moins à l'homme grave qui se présente à vous armé de six cents pages de texte et de trois ans de réflexion.

Serene, energetic, healthy, with a mind free of passion and emotion: as I have said, there was no trace either of sexual passion or of religious feeling. God, for him, is an important personage with whom Great Britain is upon terms of cordial understanding. It was John Mitchel who observed that in Macaulay's *History* there is 'a tone of polite, though distant recognition of Almighty God, as one of the Great Powers. . . . British civilization gives Him assurances of friendly relations.' He is on the side of religious tolerance, but if the churches are to be free, that is not to say that they are to interfere in affairs of State: his conception is inflexibly Erastian,[60] that is, for the supremacy of the State in ecclesiastical affairs. It is the attitude of the enlightened bourgeois of the nineteenth century. He despised theology. In chapter xvii of his *History* he says: 'In theology, the interval is small indeed between Aristotle and a child, between Archimedes and a naked savage.' And, in a passage which probably alludes to Newman's conversion to Catholicism: 'Inquisitive and restless spirits take refuge from their own scepticism in the bosom of a church which pretends to infallibility, and, after questioning the existence of a Deity, bring themselves to worship a wafer.' And elsewhere he mocks at the 'absurd metaphysics' of Dante. In a letter of November 1840 he says he has no inclination to split a hair in four over the Eucharist, but prefers to write about Wycherley and the other 'good-for-nothing fellows'. The mysteries of the Faith gave him no sort of thrill, either of emotion, or even of interest. His was a nature exactly opposite to that of Chateaubriand. Macaulay's views on the relation between Church and State are formulated, particularly, in one of the most lucid of his essays, *Gladstone on Church and State*. His idea of the State is the bourgeois, liberal idea, which goes back to Beccaria, who denied any concept of the interest and value of the State as distinct from, and superior to, the interest and value of the individuals who compose the aggregate of society. For Macaulay, the State exists for the comfort of the individual: 'it is designed to protect our persons and our property, . . . to compel us to satisfy our wants, not by rapine, but by industry, . . . to compel us to decide our differences, not by the strong hand, but by arbitration, . . . to direct our whole force, as that of one man, against any other society which may offer us injury.' These, he says, are the only actions for which the State machine is expressly adapted, the only actions that wise governments set before themselves as their principal object.

Taine has already recognized this: love of justice, one of Macaulay's salient characteristics, becomes, in him, a passion when it is a question of political freedom. He adds: 'Macaulay l'aime par intérêt, parce qu'elle est la seule garantie des biens, du bonheur et de la vie des particuliers.' It is the traditional English conception of political freedom as the guarantee of the enjoyment of private property, which, in the Victorian bourgeois, Macaulay, assumes an almost lyrical intensity: it is the mainspring of his *History*. Whoever attacks this freedom becomes his enemy, and the figure of James II, the tyrant and bigot, is so hardly treated by him that another book was needed— by Hilaire Belloc—before it became possible to see him in a tolerable light. Fawning and flattery of a sovereign are stigmatized by him in pungent epigrams. For instance, Pitt, when he was at college, wrote some Latin verses on the death of George I; in this composition 'the Muses are earnestly entreated to weep over the urn of Caesar; for Caesar, says the Poet, loved the Muses; Caesar, who could not read a line of Pope, and who loved nothing but punch and fat women'. Macaulay's political attitude, serviceable for epigrams, was less so for writing history: for to see the world in black and white, in crude contrasts, does not make for reliability. For the proper temper of the historian, narrative ability is not enough. Macaulay possessed this, as will be seen, in the highest degree; but subtlety is needed too, a feeling for the finer shades. Macaulay's mentality was that of a politician, of one who over-simplifies, and its lucid but limited method of classification is no doubt good for swaying an assembly, but not for satisfying the kind of fireside reader imagined by Taine—unless the fireside is to be reserved entirely for fairy-tales. Lytton Strachey, in *Portraits in Miniature*, aptly compares the portraits of party politicians which fill Macaulay's pages, to steel engravings, crude, obvious, lacking in half-lights and subtle gradations. But the politician in Macaulay was not merely devoid of subtlety; he had a 'preposterous optimism', he saw the epoch in which he was living as the culminating point and justification of the whole preceding course of history; and the Revolution of 1688 appeared to him to have been accomplished on purpose to prepare the advent of Queen Victoria. The England of his day was for him an inexhaustible source of pride. Thus, as Strachey observed, he could not refrain, when writing of the landing of William of Orange at Torbay, from drawing the contrast between Torbay at that time and the modern Torquay. At that time, in 1688, 'the huts of ploughmen and fishermen were thinly scattered over what is now the site of crowded marts and of luxurious pavilions'. And he could not refrain from flattering his bourgeois reader with a vision of Torquay at the present day. 'The inhabitants are about ten thousand in number. The newly-built churches and chapels, the baths and libraries, the hotels and public gardens, the infirmary and the museum, the white streets, rising terrace above terrace, the gay villas peeping from the midst of shrubberies and flower beds, present a spectacle widely different from any that in the seventeenth century England could show.' There is another passage, which is famous, on the improvement in road communications: 'before treatment' and 'after treatment'. It is, in fact, the mentality that was to find popular expression in that famous Italian ballet, *Excelsior* (1881): a more trumpery type of enlightenment than that of the eighteenth century, the Victorian, positivist type. References to his own period, inserted to excite the reader's interest, are always present in Macaulay. This also was noted by Taine:

Macaulay a toujours devant les yeux des imaginations anglaises, remplies par des images anglaises, je veux dire par le souvenir détaillé et présent d'une rue de Londres, d'un cellier à spiritueux, d'une allée de pauvres, d'une après-midi à Hyde Park, d'un paysage humide et vert, d'une maison blanche et garnie de lierre à la campagne, d'un clergyman en cravate blanche, d'un matelot en casquette de cuir.

To such an extent was the England of his day the greatest thing to which the human race can aspire, that he cannot imagine any different goal for the progress of India towards happiness. His tone of voice, on this subject, becomes warm and prophetic:

The destinies of our Indian empire are covered with thick darkness. It is difficult to form any conjecture as to the fate reserved for a state which resembles no other in history, and which forms by itself a separate class of political phenomena. The laws which regulate its growth and its decay are still unknown to us. It may be that the public mind of India may expand under our system till it has outgrown that system; that by good government we may educate our subjects into a capacity for better government; that, having become instructed in European knowledge, they may, in some future age, demand European institutions. Whether such a day will ever come I know not. But never will I attempt to avert or to retard it. Whenever it comes, it will be the proudest day in English history. To have found a great people sunk in the lowest depths of slavery and superstition, to have so ruled them as to have made them desirous and capable of all the privileges of citizens, would indeed be a title to glory all our own. The sceptre may pass away from us. Unforeseen accidents may derange our most profound schemes of policy. Victory may be inconstant to our arms. But there are triumphs which are followed by no reverse. There is an empire exempt from all natural causes of decay. Those triumphs are the pacific triumphs of reason over barbarism; that empire is the imperishable empire of our arts and our morals, our literature and our laws.

This is the highest point touched by Macaulay's liberalism: an almost religious mission to enlighten inferior peoples; later, with Kipling, it was to become the 'white man's burden'. Imperialism sublimated to an apostolate.

As a thinker Macaulay was the incarnate ideal of the positivist epoch, the ideal of a triumphant simplification. Here too, he was at the last extremity of a tradition, the tradition of English experimentalism gloriously initiated by Bacon and established through bitter controversies between the up-to-date men of learning and the followers of Aristotle during the seventeenth century: the tradition of which the keystone was the foundation of the Royal Society. But in Macaulay the complexity of science was simplified into an elegant gesture, the kind of gesture that was to arrive later, with Enrico Ferri, in Italy.

In one of his essays Macaulay imagines a disciple of Epictetus and a disciple of Bacon travelling together:

They come to a village where the small-pox has just begun to rage, and find houses shut up, intercourse suspended, the sick abandoned, mothers weeping in terror over their children. The Stoic assures the dismayed population that there is nothing bad in the small-pox, and that to a wise man disease, deformity, death, the loss of friends are not evils. The Baconian takes out a lancet and begins to vaccinate. They find a body of miners in great dismay. An explosion of noisome vapours has just killed many of those who were at work; and the survivors are afraid to venture into the cavern. The Stoic assures them that such an accident is nothing but a mere ἀποπροηγμένον [that is, a thing of secondary importance, from ἀπο-προάγω]. The Baconian, who has no such fine word at his command, contents himself with devising a safety-lamp. They find a ship-wrecked merchant wringing his hands on the shore. His vessel with an inestimable cargo has just gone down, and he is reduced in a moment from opulence to beggary. The Stoic exhorts him not to seek happiness in things which lie without himself, and repeats the whole chapter of Epictetus Πρὸς τοὺς τὴν ἀπορίαν δεδοικότας [For those who fear poverty]. The Baconian constructs a diving-bell, goes down in it, and returns with the most precious effects from the wreck. It would be easy to multiply illustrations of the difference between the philosophy of thorns and the philosophy of fruit, the philosophy of words and the philosophy of works.

A brilliant anecdote, which might be reminiscent of situations in the *Contes philosophiques*, if it did not lack Vol-taire's flexible elegance, and if thesis and antithesis, black and white, did not balance each other with a mechanical monotony which acquires an unintentionally grotesque quality. For such as Macaulay, clearly, the Great Exhibi-tion of 1851, with all its new inventions, must have been a fane more worthy of reverence than Westminster Abbey. And we can imagine him greeting the advent of photo-graphy as an invention that would allow mankind to dis-pense with the services of men like Raphael and Titian: for a picture is a difficult and laborious affair, which may not always succeed, whereas a photograph, provided a few prescribed rules are followed, is infallible.

As I have said, Macaulay restates the same position as the first experimentalists who followed in Bacon's footsteps. In Thomas Sprat's *History of the Royal Society* (1667) we find the remark that the sceptical, scrupulous, diligent observer of nature is nearer to the modest, meek, severe Christian than is the proud and speculative intellect. Science and Christianity have the same humanitarian ob-ject, for Christ himself, by feeding the hungry, healing the lame, and opening the eyes of the blind, showed that 'it is the most honourable labour to study the benefit of Mankind; to help their infirmities; to supply their wants; to ease their burdens. . . . All which may be called *Philosophical Works* perform'd by an *Almighty Hand*. . . .' Miracles are God's

'divine experiments'. Science, religion, and humanitarianism are here in close interrelationship. Sprat contrasted
the utilitarian value of science with the inutility of the
ancient philosophy. These ideas of the Baconians were
already being opposed by sensible criticisms on the part
of contemporaries, which are valid also in the case of
Macaulay. Thus Meric Casaubon, son of the great human-
ist, in a letter to Peter Du Moulin (Cambridge 1669),
criticized the idea just put forward by Sprat, saying that,
at that rate, brewers and bakers, smiths and horse-doctors
would have to be considered superior to those who hitherto
had appeared as the great lights of learning; but that the
soul of man, on the contrary, was of more importance than
his body, since upon it true happiness depends. Casaubon
held up to ridicule the belief that experimental science
could 'moralize' man, and mocked at the claim of Gas-
sendi, who said he had learned to control his passions by
observing how the blood of a louse, when it was angered,
all rushed to its tail.[61] How far Macaulay's ideas coincided
with those of the supporters of the Royal Society in the
seventeenth century can be seen from the exact similarity
of his language to that of George Thomson, a doctor, who,
in Μισοχυμίας "Ελεγχος in Vindication of My Lord Bacon
(London, 1671), maintained that an unlearned, laborious
empiricist produced, in his opinion, more real, useful knowledge than the 'most learned Academick in Europe, who
studies Words more than Works, a Library more than a
Laboratory' (Works contrasted with Words, as in the passage
from Macaulay quoted above), and goes on to exclaim:
' 'Tis Works, not Words; Things, not Thinking; Pyro-
technie, not Philologie; Operation, not meerly Specula-
tion, must justifie us Physicians.'

Macaulay's supreme object is the useful: the improvement of the comfort of the individual, and that which
serves to create it. The purpose of the various branches of
science is to tame nature and bring it into the service of
man. And man's aim is to rejoice as he contemplates his
own progress—a little god taking his rest on the seventh
day. Philosophy serves no purpose unless it serves to invent
'labour-saving devices': the test of it, for instance, is to be

seen in the kitchen. Progress means to have one's whole
dinner ready prepared in tins; progress is predigested
food, the prefabricated house. Macaulay, in front of anything, asks himself: what use does it serve? Does it serve
'for the relief of man's estate'? Seen from this point of
view, the horizon of human activity becomes not a little
restricted, and it is impossible to see, for example, what
place poetry has in it. As Mark Pattison concluded: 'He is
in accord with the average sentiment of orthodox and
stereotyped humanity on the relative value of the objects
and motives of human endeavour. And this commonplace
materialism is one of the secrets of his popularity, and one
of the qualities which guarantee that that popularity will
be enduring.'

The practical end is, therefore, naturally, always present
in the mind of Macaulay as a writer. This has been recognized even by his eulogists. Taine, for instance:

Il n'est pas véritablement philosophe: la médiocrité de ses premiers
chapitres sur l'ancienne histoire d'Angleterre le prouve assez; mais
sa force de raisonnement, ses habitudes de classification et d'ordre
mettent l'unité dans son histoire. Il n'est pas véritablement artiste:
quand il fait une peinture, il songe toujours à prouver quelque chose;
il insère des dissertations aux endroits les plus touchants; il n'a ni
grâce, ni légèreté, ni vivacité, ni finesse, mais une mémoire éton-
nante . . . un grand talent d'avocat . . . une connaissance précise des
faits précis et petits qui attachent l'attention, font illusion, diversi-
fient, animent et échauffent un récit.

The curious thing is that Taine, who in these few sentences says almost all that unfavourable critics could say
of Macaulay, yet recognizes his genius: 'Le génie con-
centre. Il se mesure au nombre des souvenirs et des idées
qu'il ramasse en un seul point. Ce que Macaulay en ras-
semble est énorme.' Genius is memory, Macaulay has a
prodigious memory, *ergo* he is a genius. In point of fact
the definition of genius can be suitably applied to Macaulay
provided it is qualified in this way: he is an advocate of
genius. He has studied rhetoric from the classics, and from
the classics he has learnt rhythm and flow of language. He
knows, to a nicety, the art of the peroration and the art of

12. HOGARTH. Breakfast (Marriage à la Mode) (*London, National Gallery. Reproduced by courtesy of the Trustees*)

13. JAN STEEN. Brothel Scene (*Paris, Louvre*)

invective. He has immense clarity, due, partly, to his
faculty for simplification, and partly to his desire to convince an average audience. No one knows how to explain
better than he, and no one explains as much. As Taine
remarks, it is as though Macaulay were making a wager
with his reader, and saying to him:

> Be as absent in mind, as stupid, as ignorant as you please; in vain
> you will be absent in mind, you shall listen to me; in vain you will
> be stupid, you shall understand; in vain you will be ignorant, you
> shall learn. I will repeat the same idea in so many different forms, I
> will make it sensible by such familiar and precise examples, I will
> announce it so clearly at the beginning, I will resume it so carefully
> at the end, I will mark the divisions so well, follow the order of
> ideas so exactly, I will display so great a desire to enlighten and con-
> vince you, that you cannot help being enlightened and convinced.

He leaves nothing to be guessed by the reader; his is
a 'history without tears'; everywhere he smooths the pathway in front of us; we climb gradually without noticing
the hill, and in the end we find ourselves right at the top
of the peak. Macaulay is the most comfortable of historians.

He is judge, he is advocate, he declaims, he preaches,
he scatters flowers amongst his own compact arguments.
Here, for example, from his essay on Milton, is his retort
to the defenders of Charles I, who said the king was a good
father and a good husband:

> We charge him with having broken his coronation oath; and we
> are told that he kept his marriage vow! We accuse him of having
> given up his people to the merciless inflictions of the most hot-
> headed and hard-hearted of prelates; and the defence is, that he
> took his little son on his knee and kissed him! We censure him for
> having violated the articles of the Petition of Right, after having,
> for good and valuable consideration, promised to observe them; and
> we are informed that he was accustomed to hear prayers at six
> o'clock in the morning! It is to such considerations as these, together
> with his Vandyke dress, his handsome face, and his peaked beard,
> that he owes, we verily believe, most of his popularity with the
> present generation.

Sometimes he can handle his ironic barbs with a good
nature that relates him to Scott and Manzoni; as with

them, his irony is of a characteristically bourgeois kind. Here is an example from his essay on the *War of the Succession in Spain*:

They therefore gave the command to Lord Galway, an experienced veteran, a man who was in war what Molière's doctors were in medicine, who thought it much more honourable to fail according to rule, than to succeed by innovation, and who would have been very much ashamed of himself if he had taken Monjuich by means so strange as those which Peterborough employed. This great commander conducted the campaign of 1707 in the most scientific manner. On the plain of Almanza he encountered the army of the Bourbons. He drew up his troops according to the methods prescribed by the best writers, and in a few hours lost eighteen thousand men, a hundred and twenty standards, all his baggage and all his artillery.

One thinks of Manzoni's Don Ferrante, or of the German generals in Tolstoy's *War and Peace*. And one understands why Macaulay felt a liking for Jane Austen, why he had, in fact, a veritable cult for that novelist with her sharp, bourgeois, eighteenth-century wit.

But all Macaulay's qualities are connected with oratory. His essays are by nature spoken attacks, arising from the kind of polemical reviewing typical of the contributors to the *Edinburgh Review*, in which both censure and praise were equally marked by insolence. And so deeply imbued with oratory was Macaulay's cast of mind that his style is the same, whether in an essay or a speech. This quality, it is obvious, makes the essays superlatively convincing for the average reader who dislikes erudite treatises and footnotes: Macaulay is responsible for many distortions of historical figures which have become current—for example Bacon, Warren Hastings.

Macaulay knows the art of persuasion to a nicety. In writing history his first preoccupation is with the reading public; he wants to 'produce something which shall for a few days supersede the last fashionable novel on the tables of young ladies'. In an essay on *History* (1828) he maintains that 'a truly great historian would reclaim those materials which the novelist has appropriated'. Scott, following in the footsteps of the historians, had 'constructed out of their

gleanings, works which, even considered as histories, are
scarcely less valuable than theirs'. The ideal was to com-
bine the picturesqueness of Scott with the intellectual interest of Hume or Clarendon. And it cannot be denied that
Macaulay often succeeds in his intention: once the limitations of his horizon are recognized, and the emptiness that
lies behind so many of his highly-coloured, sonorous pages,
it has to be admitted that he possesses a great constructive
ability and a great splendour—oratorical though it may be
—of exposition. It is a splendour that one soon gets to the
bottom of, for his style can be analysed and dissected as
easily as that of D'Annunzio. The habitual mechanism of
Macaulay's period consists of a series of simple parallel
phrases; or, if it is more complex, the subordinate clauses
are subdivided into new pairs and parallels, marked by
antitheses of language coupled with repetitions of rhythm.
For example:

> The *war between wit and Puritanism* soon became a *war between
> wit and morality*. The hostility excited by a grotesque caricature of
> *virtue* did not spare *virtue* herself. *Whatever* the canting Round-
> head had regarded with reverence was insulted. *Whatever* he had
> proscribed was favoured. Because he had been *scrupulous* about trifles,
> all *scruples* were treated with derision. . . . To that sanctimonious
> *jargon* which was his Shibboleth, was opposed another *jargon* not
> less absurd and much more odious.

The essay on Machiavelli can serve as an illustration:
elegant simplifications of facts (the resurgence of literature
after the age of barbarism, the nomad races, the mercenary
forces, the portraits of Renaissance Italians, the type of
sixteenth-century ambassador, the decadence of Venice,
&c.), definitions that impress without defining ('The *Man-
dragola*, in particular, is superior to the best of Goldoni,
and inferior only to the best of Molière'), some epigrammatic thrusts ('He would think it madness to declare open
hostilities against rivals whom he might stab in a friendly
embrace, or poison in a consecrated wafer'), digressions
(on Shakespeare, &c.), comparisons (Montesquieu and
Machiavelli), and finally a criticism of Machiavelli for not
having recognized in his works 'with sufficient clearness

... the great principle, that societies and laws exist only for the purpose of increasing the sum of private happiness'.

A middling nature, 'commonplace', as Carlyle found ('unhappily without divine idea'), he debased great things to the level of materialism, and elevated, to almost mystical pinnacles, the mediocre things to which his bourgeois spirit felt itself drawn. For instance, he composed a eulogy of Addison which would never lead one to suspect the latter's mediocre side, the side for which he has been described as 'the first of the Victorians'.

But, even with all the reservations that can be made upon his value as a historian, upon his lack of philosophic profundity, upon the mechanical quality of his style—which Taine called 'un peu uniforme, sans flexibilité ni douceur', and which Lytton Strachey judged thus: 'His sentences have no warmth and no curves; the embracing fluidity of love is lacking' (pointing out this quality in relation to the absence of sexual passion in the life of the man himself)[62] —all the critics come, more or less, to the same conclusion as Taine. Oliver Elton, for instance: 'There is his fabric, with its great shining surface, its solid skilful grandiose architecture, its bold bright colouring, which must be judged, in fairness, from a little distance off; it has a pillar broken, a façade tarnished here and there; but the thing stands.' Strachey ends his essay with a eulogy of Macaulay's purely narrative passages, of his accounts, for instance, of the trial of the Bishops, of the siege of Derry, of the Battle of Killiecrankie:

To write so is to write magnificently, and if one has to be a Philistine to bring off those particular effects one can only say, so much the better for the Philistine. But it is not only in certain passages that Macaulay triumphs. His whole History is conditioned by a supreme sense of the narrative form. It presses on, with masterly precipitation, from start to finish. Everything falls into place. Unsatisfying characters, superficial descriptions, jejune reflections, are seen to be no longer of importance in themselves—they are merely stages in the development of the narrative. They are part of the pattern—the enthralling, ever-shifting pattern of the perfect kaleidoscope. A work of art? Yes, there is no denying it: the Philistine was

also an artist. And there he is—squat, square and perpetually talking
—on Parnassus.

And, at the beginning of the essay, where he gives its
whole content as though in a nutshell:

A coarse texture of mind—a metallic style—an itch for the
obvious and the emphatic—a middle-class, Victorian complacency
—it is all too true; Philistine is, in fact, the only word to fit the
case; and yet, by dint of sheer power of writing, the Philistine has
reached Parnassus.

NOTES TO PART I

[1] In the Introduction to *The Romantic Agony*, Oxford University Press,
1951 (2nd ed.).

[2] The line followed in this case by writers on aesthetics has a curious
resemblance to the arguments of the neo-classical theorists, who admitted
only ideal and universal forms. See, for example, Henry Fuseli (*History of
Art*, 1808, p. 218, cit. in *The Mind of Henry Fuseli*, Selections from his
Writings with an Introductory Study by Eudo C. Mason, London, Routledge & Kegan Paul, 1951, p. 245): 'Michelangelo appeared and soon felt
that the candidate of legitimate fame is to build his works, not on the
imbecile forms of a degenerate race, disorganised by clime, country, education, laws and society; not on the transient refinements of fashion or local
sentiment, unintelligible beyond their circle and century to the rest of
mankind; but to graft them on Nature's everlasting forms and those general
feelings of humanity, which no time can efface, no mode of society
obliterate.' Fortunately Fuseli did not always, in practice, follow this precept, the observance of which contributed to the insipid, monotonous
character of so much of the artistic production of the time. Far more fertile
is the principle formulated by Baudelaire in *L'Art romantique*: 'Le beau est
fait d'un élément éternel, invariable, dont la quantité est excessivement
difficile à déterminer, et d'un élément relatif, circonstanciel, qui sera, si l'on
veut, tour à tour ou tout ensemble, l'époque, la mode, la morale, la passion.
Sans ce second élément, qui est comme l'enveloppe amusante, titillante,
apéritive, du gâteau, le premier élément serait indigestible, inappréciable,
non adapté et non approprié à la nature humaine.'

[3] In *Rivista italiana del dramma*, July 15th, 1938 and July 15th, 1940;
these studies were later reprinted in *Ricerche anglo-italiane*, Rome, Edizioni
di Storia e Letteratura, 1946.

[4] In *Studi germanici*, i, 1935, p. 699. The name Biedermaier was an
invention of the poet Ludwig Eichrodt (1827–92), who, in *Fliegende*

Blätter in 1855 and the following years, published parodies of the poems of a humble Swabian schoolmaster, Samuel Friedrich Sauter, whom he renamed Biedermaier. (These were republished in book form as *Biedermaiers Liederlust* in 1869, and a new edition, *Das Buch Biedermaier*, appeared in 1911.) 'Simple good-heartedness', according to Eichrodt, was the keynote of Sauter's poems, and 'a naïve observance of the simplest relationships of life'. He sings the small joys of a restricted life with an eye to their utilitarian aspects. 'With a scanty wage this worthy man finds in the depths of his simple, upright and serene Swabian soul the precious source which helps him to banish the cares of family life and to bear the burdens of his profession. . . .' Biederm*a*ier became Biederm*e*ier, and the term was adopted in Germany in the first place as a term of mockery (just as Gothic and Baroque had been used as derisive terms) to describe typical aspects of the bourgeois culture of the nineteenth century. The term is chiefly current nowadays to describe the style of furniture which came after the Empire style; but it has also been extended to the whole bourgeois *Weltanschauung*. Thus 'Biedermeier' is both a style and a conception of the world, of a small world of good sense and good manners, domestic pleasures and the cult of a gentle, well-groomed Nature, subservience to sane principles, minute love of the concrete, with, from time to time, a few flights on the wings of a mild and perhaps slightly melancholy dream. It is a world of bourgeois morality and bourgeois art, avoiding extremes, conciliating, eclectic, half classical, half romantic, which maintained its balance roughly from 1815 to 1870 (the initial date might be put back, just as the final date could certainly be brought forward). Not all the art and literature of the nineteenth century comes under the definition, but it is the dominant note, the background, the unfailing ingredient even in the great artists and writers. This, at any rate, is maintained by the German professors who have proclaimed the formula in the *Deutsche Vierteljahrsschrift für Literaturwissenschaft und Geistesgeschichte* (1935), and, as far as Germany is concerned, there is no doubt that the formula fits very well. (The 1931 issue of the *Deutsche Vierteljahrsschrift* also contains three essays on Biedermeier. And see Rudolf Majut, 'Das literarische Biedermeier: Aufriß und Probleme', in *Germanisch-Romanische Monatsschrift*, Band XX, 1932, pp. 401 et seq.

⁵ See the chapter *Il cavaliere Alberto* in my volume *Il Gusto neo-classico*, Florence, Sansoni, 1940.

⁶ Basil Willey, *Nineteenth Century Studies*, Coleridge to Matthew Arnold, London, Chatto & Windus, 1949, pp. 46–47.

⁷ Malcolm Elwin, *The First Romantics*, London, Macdonald, 1947, p. 54, remarks: 'Wordsworth at his best was a rebel *malgré lui*; fate for a time cast him among the persecuted and free-thinking minority, but he always wanted to be on the side of self-righteous convention.' See also pp. 58–59: his brother Richard, in 1794, recommended him to 'be cautious in writing or expressing your political opinions. By the suspension of the Habeas Corpus Act the Ministers have great powers'—a recommendation with which Wordsworth fell into line: 'At twenty-four the revolutionary, the rebel, the reformer, was "very cautious"; increasing

with years, caution was to grow a blight on his character, till a morbid, old-maidish fear of life fastened like a fungus to strangle his genius.'

8 *Wordsworth*, London, Faber & Faber, 1930 (reprint 1949), p. 117.

9 H. J. C. Grierson, *Milton and Wordsworth*, Poets and Prophets, A Study of their Reactions to Political Events, Cambridge University Press, 1937.

10 *Lines composed a few miles above Tintern Abbey*, l. 33.

11 Cf. W. Blake, *Auguries of Innocence*: 'To see a World in a Grain of Sand, And a Heaven in a Wild Flower, Hold Infinity in the palm of your hand, And Eternity in an hour.'

12 '. . . gathering as it seemed Through every hair-breadth in that field of light New pleasure like a bee among the flowers', *The Prelude*, i. 579–80.

13 *The Prelude*, ii. 170–4.

14 *The Prelude*, i. 462–3, 561–6.

15 *The Prelude*, xi. 141–4.

16 *The Tables Turned*: 'Books! 'tis a dull and endless strife: Come, hear the woodland linnet, How sweet his music! on my life, There's more of wisdom in it. . . . One impulse from a vernal wood May teach you more of man, Of moral evil and of good, Than all the sages can.'

17 *The Fountain*, ll. 41–44.

18 See *Ode to Duty*; the sonnet *Nuns fret not . . .*, in which occurs the phrase 'the weight of too much liberty'; *To a Skylark*, where the lark is called 'type of the wise who soar, but never roam'. See also Grierson, *Milton and Wordsworth*, op. cit., p. 173.

19 The final version (*Prelude*, vii. 604–18) was remodelled by the poet himself.

20 *The Prelude*, xii. 161–8, 181–4, 231–40 (1805–6).

21 Constable, whose affinity with Wordsworth has been repeatedly stressed (see Kenneth Clark, *English Romantic Poets and Landscape Painting*, 1945, and *Landscape into Art*, London, Murray, 1949, pp. 74–79; E. Cecchi, 'Il giovane Wordsworth e la poesia di paesaggio', in *English Miscellany* vol. i (1950), wrote:

What were the habits of Claude and the Poussins? Though surrounded with palaces filled with pictures, they made the fields their chief place of study. . . . We derive the pleasure of surprise from the works of the best Dutch painters in finding how much interest their art, when in perfection, can give to the most ordinary subjects. Those are cold critics who turn from their works and wish the same skill had been rendered a vehicle for more elevated stories . . . and it may always be doubted whether those who do not relish the works of the Dutch and Flemish schools, whatever raptures they may affect in speaking of the schools of Italy, are capable of fully appreciating the latter; for a true taste is never a half taste.

22 Charles Lamb quotes this passage jestingly in one of the *Essays of Elia* (*Chapter on Ears*). It appears that it was suggested by an anecdote told by Mrs. Basil Montagu.

23 Cf. Humphry House in *The New Statesman and Nation*, Mar. 29th, 1947. The moral of Dorothea Brooke's adventure in George Eliot's *Middlemarch* is not very different.

²⁴ *The Redbreast chasing the Butterfly.* The redbreast is called 'pious' because of the popular belief (which spread from Germany and Lorraine to Brittany and across to England) that it furnishes a covering of leaves and moss for corpses abandoned in the woods. In the famous sixteenth-century popular ballad, *The Children in the Wood*, the redbreast thus covers the two children's bodies.

²⁵ It was, on the other hand, Metternich who took refuge in England, during the revolution of 1848.

²⁶ The novel by Smollett.   ²⁷ See above, p. 26.

²⁸ *Lamb before Elia*, London, Cape, 1932.

²⁹ Leopardi's *Infinito* (trans. Iris Origo): '. . . questa siepe, che da tanta parte Dell'ultimo orizzonte il guardo esclude'.

³⁰ *The Letters of Charles and Mary Lamb*, ed. E. V. Lucas, London, Dent and Methuen, 1935, 3 vols.; vol. i, pp. 176–7. De Quincey (*Recollections of Charles Lamb*, in the 3rd vol. of his *Works*, ed. Masson) says of Lamb: 'Politics—what cared he for politics?'

³¹ *Letters*, vol. ii, pp. 127–8.

³² Opinion recorded by Carlyle.   ³³ *Letters*, vol. iii, p. 299.

³⁴ Parody of a passage in the *Aeneid*, ii. 325: *Fuimus Troes, fuit Ilium, et ingens gloria Teucrorum.*

³⁵ *Letters*, vol. ii, p. 164.

³⁶ See my essay 'Su Charles Lamb cento anni dopo la morte', in *Studi e svaghi inglesi*, Florence, Sansoni, 1937.

³⁷ *Letters*, vol. ii, p. 329.   ³⁸ *Letters*, vol. iii, p. 242.

³⁹ *Letters*, vol. i, p. 241.   ⁴⁰ *Letters*, vol. i, p. 410.

⁴¹ *Letters*, vol. iii, p. 401.

⁴² How close Dickens could come to the style of Lamb in *Dream-Children* is shown by a passage in *The Old Curiosity Shop* (chap. xvii):

> Then growing garrulous upon a theme which was new to one listener though it were but a child, she told her how she had wept and moaned and prayed to die herself, when this [her husband's death] happened; and how when she first came to that place, a young creature strong in love and grief, she had hoped that her heart was breaking as it seemed to be. But that time passed by, and although she continued to be sad when she came there, still she could bear to come, and so went on until it was pain no longer, but a solemn pleasure, and a duty she had learned to like. And now that five-and-fifty years were gone, she spoke of the dead man as if he had been her son or grandson, with a kind of pity for his youth, growing out of her own old age, and an exalting of his strength and manly beauty as compared with her own weakness and decay; and yet she spoke about him as her husband too, and thinking of herself in connexion with him, as she used to be and not as she was now, talked of their meeting in another world as if he were dead but yesterday, and she, separated from her former self, were thinking of the happiness of that comely girl who seemed to have died with him.

And later on in the same novel (chap. xxv):

> Then he would stop and tell them what the sick child had said last night, and how he had longed to be among them once again; and such was the poor schoolmaster's gentle and affectionate manner, that the boys seemed quite remorseful

that they had worried him so much, and were absolutely quiet; eating no apples, cutting no names, inflicting no pinches, and making no grimaces, for full two minutes afterwards.

Side by side with these passages of Dickens, Lamb's whole essay should be read: the type of inspiration, the tone, the style, indeed closely resemble each other. For instance:

Then I went on to say, how religious and how good their great-grandmother Field was, how beloved and respected by every body, though she was not indeed the mistress of this great house. . . . And then I told how, when she came to die . . . . Then I told what a tall, upright, graceful person their great-grandmother Field once was; and how in her youth she was esteemed the best dancer—here Alice's little right foot played an involuntary movement . . .—the best dancer, I was saying, in the county, till a cruel disease called a cancer came and bowed her down with pain; but could never bend her good spirits, or make them stoop, but they were still upright because she was so good and religious. Then I told how she was used. . . . Then I told how good she was to all her grandchildren, having us to the great-house in the holydays . . . how I never could be tired with roaming about that huge mansion . . . sometimes in the spacious old-fashioned gardens . . . and how the nectarines and peaches hung upon the walls, without my ever offering to pluck them. . . . Here John slyly deposited back upon the plate a bunch of grapes. . . . Then, in somewhat a more heightened tone, I told how, though their great-grandmother Field loved all her grandchildren, yet in an especial manner she might be said to love their uncle . . . and how I bore his death as I thought pretty well at first, but afterwards it haunted and haunted me. . . . Here the children fell a-crying, etc.

Yet another comparison: in the same novel of Dickens, Mrs. Jarley, with her high opinion of waxworks, reminds us of Mrs. Battle and her love of the 'rigour of the game' of whist, in Lamb's *Mrs. Battle's Opinions on Whist*; one thinks again of *Dream-Children* when the Marchioness interrupts her story and is left in perplexity as Swiveller, in bed, forms a great cone by gathering up his knees under the bed-clothes and assuming an expression of the utmost concern. 'The small servant pausing, and holding up her finger, the cone gently disappeared, though the look of concern did not.' This mixture of tenderness and humour which pervades essays like *Dream-Children* and *Barbara S——*, is to be found again in the childish memories of *David Copperfield*.

43 H. A. Eaton, *Thomas De Quincey*, A Biography, Oxford University Press, 1936.
44 E. Sackville-West, *A Flame in Sunlight*, The Life and Work of Thomas De Quincey, London, Cassell, 1936.
45 C. Willett Cunnington, *Feminine Attitudes in the Nineteenth Century*, London, Heinemann, 1935; see also C. Willett and Phillis Cunnington, *The History of Underclothes*, London, Michael Joseph, 1951, pp. 153–4.
46 Martial, ix. 11.
47 On this subject, see the book by the Dutch author G. J. Renier, *The English: Are they Human?* Williams & Norgate, new ed. 1931.
48 Cf. M. Praz, *The Romantic Agony*, Oxford University Press, 1951 (2nd ed.), pp. 125–6. It is curious to note that, in our own time, the

conception of love in *Wilhelm Meister* has been denounced as scandalous by the author of *Lady Chatterley's Lover* (D. H. Lawrence was of opinion that, in Goethe's novel, love was perversely conceived as an education, a means to culture, and women were treated as mere instruments).

[49] See vol. xi of *The Collected Writings of Thomas De Quincey*, ed. D. Masson, Edinburgh, Adam & Charles Black, 1890; the essay appeared originally in the *London Magazine* of Dec. 1821, followed by the extracts, 'Analects from Richter'. In the same volume is to be found the essay 'Goethe as reflected in his novel of Wilhelm Meister'.

[50] See Ralph Tymms, *Doubles in Literary Psychology*, Cambridge, Bowes & Bowes, 1949.

[51] There are many passages which invite comparison with Hoffmann's *Princess Brambilla* and *The Golden Pot*. In this latter tale (*Seventh Wake* [*Siebente Vigilie*]), for instance, the girl with the angelic face wringing her uplifted hands as though invoking the protection of the angels during the magic rite that terrifies her—seen by a traveller in a passing coach who feels an impulse to rush to her protection; but the postilion furiously sounds his horn and the vision vanishes in a thick mist. And, in *Princess Brambilla* (chap. ii):

And so the whole company, shouting loudly for help, is carried off through the air by a monstrous vulture.... And now the prison changes into a great hall with rows of columns adorned with wreaths of flowers, in the middle of which stands a lofty and sumptuous throne. Delicious music is heard, from drums and pipes and timbrels. A splendid procession approaches; Harlequin is borne along in a palanquin by four Moors. . . .

And later (chap. viii):

When he had finished reading, the Magician closed the book again and at the same moment burning vapours issued from the silver funnel that he bore on his head, and entirely filled the hall. Beneath a harmonious pealing of bells and a sound of harps and trumpets, everything began to move and to melt together. The dome rose upward and became a joyous rainbow, the columns were transformed into tall palm-trees, the golden cloth fell to earth and became a many-coloured, shining, flowery carpet, and the great crystal mirror dissolved into a clear and splendid lake. . . . Suddenly the music, the rejoicing, the singing, all ceased. . . .

[52] See J.-J. Mayoux, *Un Épicurien anglais, Thomas Love Peacock*, Paris, Nizet et Bastard, 1933, pp. 24 et seq.

[53] Mayoux, op. cit., p. 65.

[54] *La Poesia di Shelley*, Foligno–Rome, Campitelli, 1932.

[55] Act III, scene 1.

[56] Prologue to Book V.

[57] Mayoux, op. cit., p. 387.

[58] Mayoux, op. cit., pp. 446–7.

[59] I wrote on Hazlitt in *English Studies*, xiii (1931) and in *La Stampa*, Dec. 30th, 1930.

[60] Erastus (i.e. Liebler) was a doctor in Heidelberg in the sixteenth century: he rebelled particularly against the tyrannical use of excommunication by the Calvinist Church.

[61] See R. F. Jones, *Ancients and Moderns*, Washington University Studies, 1936, p. 242.

[62] Cf. Matthew Arnold's description: 'The external characteristic being a hard metallic movement with nothing of the soft play of life, and the internal characteristic being a perpetual semblance of hitting the right nail on the head without the reality.'

PART TWO

The Decline of the Hero

Charles Dickens

In Dickens, that born writer, there is to be found—as though in a convex mirror—a lively and fascinating picture of the Victorian age both in its overt tastes and its latent impulses. The Swiss professor, Friedrich Brie, in applying the term Biedermeier to England, found the essential requisites of this bourgeois type in Dickens. 'His bourgeois-humanitarian instincts protect him from all tendency towards the supernatural, the marvellous, the revolutionary, from all exaltation of passion.' Goodness and quiet happiness are his ideals, as is made clear from the story of David Copperfield, the virtuous bourgeois youth who, through privations and harsh experiences, finds at last his own quiet harbour of refuge. The contrasting character, James Steerforth, the fascinating, untrammelled aristocrat, capricious, arrogant, seducer of women, is as it were the symbol of the Romantic poet in the guise in which he appeared in England, in Byron particularly, and with a few allusions to Shelley as well (his death in a shipwreck during a storm). This pair of opposites is equivalent, in the language of Dickens, to Carlyle's 'Close your Byron, open your Goethe'.

In sexual relationships, the novelist Dickens is the champion of the strictest orthodoxy; adultery has no charms for him. It might be said of him that he truly keeps in mind the precept of the puritan American professor Charles Eliot Norton, that 'no great work of the imagination had ever been based on illicit passion'. Take, for instance, the episode in *David Copperfield* of the youthful wife of the pedantic old Dr. Strong, a kind of Victorian reincarnation of Dr. Johnson. The reader may, for some time, suspect that Mrs. Strong has an understanding with Jack Maldon, her brilliant, teasing cousin. Imagine what a French novelist, a George Sand (to say nothing of a Flaubert) would have made of the episode! However, when the mystery of this relationship is unveiled, one finds that Mrs.

Strong has kept herself pure, in spite of the fact that her mother, a pimping busybody, has tried to throw her into the arms of temptation:

It was at that time that mama was most solicitous about my cousin Maldon. I had liked him ... very much. We had been little lovers once. If circumstances had not happened otherwise, I might have come to persuade myself that I really loved him, and might have married him, and been most wretched. There can be no disparity in marriage like unsuitability of mind and purpose. .... There is nothing that we have in common. I have long found that there is nothing. If I were thankful to my husband for no more, instead of for so much, I should be thankful to him for having saved me from the first mistaken impulse of my undisciplined heart.

The departure of Maldon to India, which had appeared at the time, in the novel, as an expedient to cut short his adulterous relations with Annie Strong, turns out to have been merely for the sake of advancement in his career. It was only on the night of his departure that Maldon disclosed his feelings to Annie:

That night I knew he had a false and thankless heart. I saw a double meaning, then, in Mr. Wickfield's scrutiny of me. I perceived, for the first time, the dark suspicion that shadowed my life.

This imaginary guilt was enough to oppress her heart beneath 'a load of shame and grief', 'the unhappiness and burden of my secret'; but now she can lift her eyes to the dear face of Dr. Strong, 'revered as a father's, loved as a husband's, sacred to me in my childhood as a friend's, and solemnly declare that in my lightest thought I had never wronged you; never wavered in the love and the fidelity I owe you!'

Oh, hold me to your heart, my husband! Never cast me out! Do not think or speak of disparity between us, for there is none, except in all my many imperfections. Every succeeding year I have known this better, as I have esteemed you more and more. Oh, take me to your heart, my husband, for my love was founded on a rock, and it endures!

A passionate confession, if you like; but one which makes passion coincident with regularity, not with the

illicit, as with the Romantics. A confession, in fact, which
fits perfectly into the Victorian conception of life.

In the relations between Edith Granger and Carker, in
Dombey and Son, we also reach the point of an appearance
—but no more than an appearance—of illicit love; this,
it seems, was thanks to the intervention of Jeffrey the
critic, who, in collecting his own essays, boasted that his
chief title to the memory of mankind was his effort to
maintain moral standards. Edith flees to France from her
husband's insolent cruelties, with Carker, Granger's dis-
loyal dependant; and they stay in a hired apartment whose
specious splendours reveal, by daylight, traces of shabbiness and neglect. Dickens intended that Edith should
become Carker's mistress, but as a result of Jeffrey's objec-
tions he changed his mind. Here is what happens instead.
Waiters from a nearby restaurant enter, bringing an exquisite supper into the luxurious apartment—the classic
nest of adultery in the French novel. Upon Carker's arrival
Edith, embraced by him, shows signs of fainting. Is she
overcome with joy? No, she 'had only shrunk and shivered',
but she draws herself up to her full height and, placing her
hand on the back of an armchair, waits with face immovable
and staring eyes. Supper is served and the waiters are
dismissed, in spite of their protests. While Carker is fastening the door, Edith, who had already assured herself of a
means of escape by putting the key of another smaller door
on its outer side, 'brings a knife within her reach upon the
table'. 'How strange to come here by yourself, my love!'
says Carker:

'What!' she returned. Her tone was so harsh; the quick turn of
her head so fierce. . . .

Carker goes on to speak, on his side, of the journey he
has planned to Sicily, which is to be their place of retreat:

'In the idlest and easiest part of the world, my soul, we'll both
seek compensation for old slavery.' He was coming gaily towards her,
when, in an instant, she caught the knife up from the table, and
started one pace back. 'Stand still!' she said, 'or I shall murder you!'

A melodramatic scene[1] follows, in which Edith cures
Carker for ever of his dreams of Sicilian ease ('You have

fallen on Sicilian days and sensual rest, too soon') by revealing that she has fled with him, the parasite and tool of her
tyrannical husband, only in order that her husband may
be the more deeply wounded:

> I single out in you the meanest man I know, the parasite and
> tool of the proud tyrant, that his wound may go the deeper and may
> rankle more. . . . I have thrown my fame and good name to the
> winds! I have resolved to bear the shame that will attach to me—
> resolved to know that it attaches falsely—that you know it too—
> and that he does not, never can, and never shall. I'll die and make
> no sign. For this I am here alone with you, at the dead of night.
> For this, I have met you here, in a false name, as your wife. . . .

Edith's revenge is on a line with that of the Duchess of
Sierra-Leone in Barbey d'Aurevilly's famous story *La Vengeance d'une femme* (in *Les Diaboliques*, 1874), who, as wife
of a Spanish grandee, avenges herself on her husband by
dragging his name in the dirt.

Finally, with a diabolical smile, Edith tells Carker that,
like all betrayers, he has been betrayed, and that her husband has been informed of his presence there; and—no
sooner said than done—there is a furious sound of the bell
ringing. Edith, taking advantage of Carker's momentary
distraction, escapes by the door of which she had hidden
the key, while Carker, in a panic at being discovered by
his patron, whose voice he can now hear, also escapes. At
the very moment of catching a train at a country station,
he sees the man from whom he has fled, rushes on to the
lines, is run over by the train and his 'mutilated fragments'
cast into the air. *Dombey and Son* belongs to 1847–8, and
perhaps this was the first character in a novel to finish under
the wheels of a train: it is that, rather than the spectacular
punishment of an adulterer, which is all that can interest
us today in this grotesque episode. A similar occurrence,
with a very different force of meaning, was to be made use
of by Tolstoy in *Anna Karenina*.[2]

No halo of beauty surrounds the guilt of Martha, the
lost girl, nor of Emily, who, in her youthful aberration,
allows herself to be seduced by Steerforth. Their stories
find their perfect allegory in Greuze's *Innocence enchaînée*

par l'amour et suivie du repentir. Their guilt seems to them immense, inexpiable. Martha, feeling herself lost, 'a solitary curse to myself, a living disgrace to everyone I come near', wishes to kill herself, then redeems herself by the good deed of helping Emily's uncle to find his niece, thus putting her back upon the straight path; and finally, having emigrated to Australia, gets married and goes to live in the bush, cut off, with her companion, from all human society. Emily expiates her youthful folly by devoting herself to works of charity and nursing the sick, disgusted, for ever, with sex; she travels great distances in order to give lessons to children, to look after invalids, or to perform some kind action with the object of getting girls married (but never attends their weddings); she is beloved by old and young, and sought out by people in trouble. On the other hand, if these fallen women are not, by their very guilt, rendered poetical, as with the Romantics, no more are they painted in realistic colours, in such a way as to present a picture that would be really adapted to impress the moral sense. Nancy, in *Oliver Twist*, is little more than a cipher: of the surroundings in which she moves, of the language that must have been spoken there, Dickens gives no exact idea; he never hints, even obscurely—as Humphry House has pointed out—at the fact that the atmosphere of iniquity in which Oliver lived in London must have been 'drenched in sex', since the women like Nancy who had the task of entrapping young men into the haunts of evil life certainly made use with them of every form of low seduction.

This dislike of too realistic detail is not in any case limited, in Dickens, to sexual life; Mr. House has also pointed out how, even with the great pile of adjectives at his command, Dickens, in describing the London under-world, never defines precisely the more repugnant objects, but speaks of 'polluted air, foul with every impurity that is poisonous to health and life' (*Dombey and Son*, chap. xlvii), says that 'the air was impregnated with filthy odours', and that 'drunken men and women were positively wallowing in filth' (*Oliver Twist*, chap. viii). 'Dirt' is a word that recurs frequently in Dickens's descriptions of London, which do not go beyond generic terms of this kind.[3] Mr.

House has tried to penetrate into the origin of this Victorian prudery. The middle class became sensible of the horrors of poverty and filth, and sharpened sensibility was accompanied, on the one hand, by a wish to turn away from them, on the other by a wish to cure them; but the cure could only come about if the evils were exposed in their full foulness, and this, 'dainty delicacy' did not like to hear: hence a vicious circle from which Dickens never quite escaped.[4] For frankness, which never abandons him when he is denouncing injustices, cruelties, and humbug, fades away when he seeks to denounce the more revolting consequences, in sex, drink, and dirt, of bad social conditions. Mr. House observes that this aspect of Dickens is characteristic of the morality of a middle, ambiguous class. Whereas writers of popular origin, or those who belonged to the upper classes, described vice, even in the Victorian age, with human realism, Dickens was, on the one hand, too far removed, both by habits and social class and feeling, from such things to assimilate them fully (he was ashamed when he thought of having once been a manual worker), and yet was not remote enough to be able to treat them with detachment. It was not merely convention that prevented Dickens from speaking freely: there was the conflict within himself. And so it is that, at the time of his separation from his wife, he himself provided a typical case of Victorian hypocrisy.

It is only recently[5] that full light has been thrown upon Dickens's passion for the actress Ellen Ternan, who first attracted the novelist's attention by her exquisite modesty, bursting into tears because she had to show her legs on the stage in the part of Atalanta; and then ended by making him lose his head completely when she acted the part of the pupil, and Dickens himself that of the elderly, love-sick drawing-master, in the farce *Uncle John*. Dickens, rejuvenated by passion, felt more and more disgusted by the apathetic forgivingness and incomprehension of his wife; he was unwilling to share a bedroom with her any longer, and ordered a partition to be put up between his room and hers —a structure which makes one think of some solemn, sinister episode in a bourgeois drama. Finally it came to a legal separation, to which he attracted the attention of the public[6] by an incautious insertion in *Household Words* (June 12th, 1858) in which he declared that the rumours on the subject of his domestic affairs were 'abominably false, and that whosoever repeats one of them after this denial, will lie as wilfully and as foully as it is possible for any false witness to lie before Heaven and earth'. In a successive public communication he then laid the responsibility for the separation upon incompatibility of character; and he finished by declaring that the initiative for the separation came from his entirely passive wife, whom he accused directly of a mental disorder—a separation which was due, simply and solely, to his violent love for an eighteen-year-old girl, and to the youthful infatuation which made him look upon his own children as so many brothers and sisters, and upon his wife as a disgusting old hag (he himself dyed his hair and looked like an old man at forty-six). In the words of his daughter, Dickens seemed 'like a madman' about the young actress,[7] for whom he took a house in the then rural district of Peckham, Windsor Lodge, paying the rent under the false name of Charles Tringham. 'Like the piano legs and mantelpieces of the Victorian era', observes Una Pope-Hennessy, 'the tenancy of this house was well covered up.' Many years later the tenants of the house used to point out two trees in the garden (a quince and a sumach) in the shade of which 'Mr. Tringham' was accustomed to sit, busy writing a mysterious tale (*The Mystery of Edwin Drood*). What makes a painful impression in the whole of this affair is not really the fact of his adultery but, alongside and in contrast with his curious exhibitionism, the series of subterfuges, the shabby expedients, to which Dickens had recourse in order to avoid calling things by their real names—in life, as in art—as far as sex was concerned. In life Dickens obeyed, unrestrainedly, the impulses of his own heart; but in his works he put his readers on their guard against these same undisciplined impulses. We have seen the case of Mrs. Strong. Let us draw a parallel between it and Fielding's *Tom Jones*.

If one compares the protagonist of *David Copperfield*

with the protagonist of *Tom Jones* (and Dickens, as is well
known, took Fielding as his source of inspiration), it is
possible to get a very clear notion of the difference of
position of the two novelists with regard to their heroes.
Fielding's moral attitude hinges upon 'natural goodness of
heart', which in his eyes redeems every fault; and Tom's
instinctive goodness displays itself continually in effusions
of sentimental rhetoric. This is a process of veneering; and
it is in conformity with the spirit that animated, essentially,
Greuze's family scenes. But behind this veneer Tom Jones
is very far from being a saint: bourgeois morality in Fielding's time, as in that of Defoe, was still, to a great extent,
a make-believe; and a Victorian of the calibre of Thackeray
could say, quite rightly, of Tom Jones: 'Too much of the
plum cake and rewards of life fall to that boisterous, swaggering young scapegrace.' In *Tom Jones* too we have a
hypocritical rascal, Blifil, contrasted, like Uriah Heep in
David Copperfield, with the hero of the novel. Blifil hates
Tom, who has won the affection of the lovely Sophia, Squire
Western's daughter; Heep hates David who has won the
affection (although he himself does not know to what
extent) of the lovely and virtuous Agnes Wickfield, after
whom Heep aspires. But then, what kind of a hero is Tom
Jones? He has an intrigue with Molly Seagrim, the woodman's daughter—though in this case he is more the
seduced than the seducer; he nearly lets himself be caught
by Sophia in the arms of the adventuress Mrs. Waters;
he has an intrigue with Lady Bellaston—the woman who
sets a perfidious trap for Sophia in order to make her marry
the dissolute and questionable Lord Fellamar—and here
too Sophia runs right into him one night when he is going
to keep an appointment with Lady Bellaston: and he has
many other complicated and far from edifying adventures
typical of the century in which he lived. What, on the other
hand, comes between David and Agnes, the Victorian re-
incarnations of Tom and Sophia? Merely Dora, a thought-
less little creature with whom David at first falls in love
'from the first mistaken impulse of my undisciplined heart'
—according to Mrs. Strong's phrase which David ponders
in his innermost consciousness. The heart therefore must

be disciplined, must mistrust its first spontaneous movements, which may be misleading: a complete reversal of
the principle in *Tom Jones*, and in accordance with Victorian morality. Goodness, therefore, and quiet happiness
are the ideals, and the guide towards those ideals—a new
Beatrice—is Agnes Wickfield, the angel descended upon
earth, idealized figure of the perfect woman, drawn according to the dictates of the bland classicism which inspired
the painters of 'beauties' round about 1840 (e.g. Hayez,
in Italy). Agnes appears to us like a quiet angel keeping
watch upon a tomb, 'one solemn hand pointing towards
heaven'. It is thus when Dora dies in her arms, and it is
thus right to the end of the novel. One should read the
whole scene of David's courtship of Agnes after his return
from abroad (chap. lx), in that atmosphere of peace in
which the feminine figure is surrounded with a sisterly,
motherly aura as she sits playing one of her old tunes on
the piano:

> You remember, when you came down to me in our little room
> —pointing upward, Agnes? . . . As you were then, my sister, I
> have often thought since, you have ever been to me. Ever pointing
> upward, Agnes; ever leading me to something better; ever direct-
> ing me to higher things! . . . I want you to know, yet don't know
> how to tell you, that all my life long I shall look up to you, and be
> guided by you, as I have been through the darkness that is past. . . .
> Until I die, my dearest sister, I shall see you always before me,
> pointing upward!

The end of the scene is like one of those mawkish lithographs of the period:

> . . . Thinking of her, pointing upward, [I] thought of her as
> pointing to that sky above me, where, in the mystery to come, I
> might yet love her with a love unknown on earth, and tell her what
> the strife had been within me when I loved her here.

From the very beginning Agnes had appeared bathed
in a kind of religious light: 'the soft light of the coloured
window in the church, seen long ago, falls on her always,
and on me when I am near her, and on everything around.'
The Victorian sentiment that idealized woman as a weak,

angelic creature, is well illustrated by the beginning of chapter xxiii in *David Copperfield*:

When I awoke in the morning I thought very much of little Em'ly, and her emotion last night, after Martha had left. I felt as if I had come into the knowledge of those domestic weaknesses and tendernesses in a sacred confidence, and that to disclose them, even to Steerforth, would be wrong. I had no gentler feeling towards anyone than towards the pretty creature who had been my playmate, and whom I have always been persuaded, and shall always be persuaded, to my dying day, I then devotedly loved. The repetition to any ears—even to Steerforth's—of what she had been unable to repress when her heart lay open to me by an accident, I felt would be a rough deed, unworthy of myself, unworthy of the light of our poor childhood, which I always saw encircling her head. I made a resolution, therefore, to keep it in my own breast; and there it gave her image a new grace.

It is with the angelic image of Agnes that the novel ends:

O Agnes, O my soul, so may thy face be by me when I close my life indeed; so may I, when realities are melting from me like the shadows which I now dismiss, still find thee near me, pointing upward![8]

It is certainly not in figures like that of Agnes that we must look for Dickens's true originality, nor, in general, in the figures of the protagonists of his novels. Fielding made his heroes move according to the inspiration of his own personal taste, except that he tied a label on to them in order to make them acceptable to the virtuous public; but with Dickens current moral standards penetrated right into the heart of the novelist: his heroes are figures conceived in accordance with the neo-classicism which, in the bourgeois nineteenth century, inspired sepulchral monuments: they are angels with mild, stupid faces. Look at Oliver Twist, for instance, whom Dickens wished to set up as a counterblast to the idealization of the common criminal by the Romantics (he was aiming, particularly, at Ainsworth and Bulwer Lytton), thereby showing, also, that giving oneself over to a life of crime is not the idle and amusing experience that the Romantic story-tellers imagined it to be. In *Oliver Twist* also, be it noted, there is the stock figure of the woman of evil life (like Martha in *David Copperfield*) who tries to redeem herself by performing a good action (Nancy). Oliver is little more than a puppet; and the illustrator, Cruikshank, has interpreted his character well in giving him the fair, long, sad face of a neo-classic angel, in the midst of the saraband of demons from the London underworld.[9]

All, however, was not going well behind the comfortable façade of Dickens's novels—the exaltation of the domestic hearth (even if only that of the Micawbers), the goodness, the humanitarianism, the humour, the repugnance for all realistic representation of sex, of cruelty, of dirt. Nothing that could not be read *virginibus puerisque*.[10] The incident in Dickens's conjugal life seems to disfigure that comfortable façade with an alarming crack—if not an absolutely fatal one, like that of the House of Usher. And it was not the only crack.

When, before the last War, a French professor, Lafourcade by name, who had made a study of Swinburne's sadism, stressed the recurrence of sadistic elements in Dickens's work and hinted[11] that Dickens took pleasure in lingering over ghastly details[12] and had a keen appetite for the sights of the Morgue,[13] people may have thought that he had hopelessly impaired his vision by poring over the works of the Divine Marquis.[14] And in truth it is certainly not the darkest scenes of *Oliver Twist* that we recall when we think of Dickens, but rather Pickwick, and the old coaching days, and the most human and idyllic parts of *David Copperfield*. The melodramatic Dickens, contemporary of Sue and of so many other sensational novelists, we willingly forget. And so one may well be surprised when one reads, in Una Pope-Hennessy's biography, of certain episodes in the last period of Dickens's life. After the separation from his wife in 1858, in order to meet his ever-increasing expenses, Dickens devoted himself to lucrative lecture tours; for if, in his novels, he sincerely despised riches, in practical life he confessed that 'at the age of fifty-five or fifty-six, the idea of making a very great addition to one's capital in half a year is immense'. He read famous episodes from his own novels, impersonating the characters, counterfeiting their voices, like a very clever actor such as Fregoli. The effect on his audience was immense. In those days, perhaps to make up for the repressions of real life, people were very easily moved at public spectacles. Imagine: in 1862 Dickens was present, in Paris, at a performance of *Orphée* with Madame Viardot, and afterwards was taken round to the actress's dressing-room 'disfigured as he was by crying'; but not many days passed before he had his revenge, on the occasion of one of his readings of *The Cricket on the Hearth*, at the house of the painter, Ary Scheffer. When Madame Viardot, who was present, was asked to sing, she was unable to do so, because she was still choking with the tears produced by his reading.

Amongst the repertory of Dickens's readings there began to figure, in 1868, a ferocious episode from *Oliver Twist*: the murder of Nancy by Bill Sikes. Before performing it in public Dickens tried it out before a select circle of literary men and critics, and so effectively did he impersonate the Jew Fagin, the demoniac Sikes, and Nancy, the victim (now exquisitely pathetic, now hysterical in her last desperate appeal) that his hearers were left as though under the influence of a hypnotic spell. 'You may rely upon it', a doctor warned him before the public reading, 'that if only one woman cries out when you murder the girl, there will be a contagion of hysteria all over the place.' For this reading Dickens had the platform arranged like a proper stage, with a maroon-coloured backcloth and wings; and when, after the reading was over, the gas reflectors, which had been concentrated upon the performer, were turned, as he had ordered, on to the auditorium, he saw that, although the ladies, in their many-coloured dresses, looked like a 'great bed of flowers and diamonds', their faces were pale and horror-stricken. At Clifton the same reading produced 'a contagion of fainting'; and there were similar effects at Bath and Torquay. To Dickens, this 'atrocious novelty' became more and more of a star turn in his cycles of readings; he repeated it with a frequency that alarmed his agent, since it recoiled upon the reader himself. After one of these readings, in January 1870, Dickens's pulse-rate rose from 72 to 112, and a quarter of an hour's rest on a sofa was required before his breathing returned to normal. Such emotions must certainly have contributed to the apoplectic stroke from which the novelist died in that same year.

At that time he was also considering the writing of *The Mystery of Edwin Drood*, the unfinished novel which hinges upon a murder mystery that English critics have struggled hard to solve. If, as seems certain,[15] Edwin Drood was the victim of a ritual sacrifice by an initiate of the fierce cult of Kali, what more convincing prefigurement of the *collages* of Max Ernst[16] could be imagined than this invention of Dickens? An exotic cult, a dark plot, a type of murderer— Jasper—like a character in a certain kind of sensational film; and, as a façade to all this, a silent, sleepy, mouldering, Victorian provincial town, in whose shadows there seems to be a ferment of human corruption, a town pervaded by the earthy smell that emanates from the crypt of the ancient cathedral;[17] an opium den, a Gothic cathedral whose architecture hints at the sinister splendour of a Hindu temple, as in a Gustave Moreau picture: what more terrifying *collage à la* Max Ernst can be imagined than this? And if, with Edmund Wilson, we go so far as to see, in Jasper's double soul, an adumbration of the author himself and of his moral conflicts, and a way of escape from a criminal obsession that had been with him ever since his tragic youthful experiences in the boot-blacking factory, we shall have difficulty indeed in reconciling all this with the traditional figure of Dickens—the good Dickens who created Pickwick and Mr. Micawber, David Copperfield and Little Dorrit—and with the heavy hangings and cross-stitch embroidery of a Victorian drawing-room. Dickens's personal case may assume, in our eyes, a symbolic value, for the century's subconscious stratum was a turbid one; and when, in 1866, Swinburne flustered the Victorians with the sadistic cruelty of *Anactoria* and the *Dolores* litanies, instead of being astonished by the contrast between such daring expressions and the atmosphere out of which they arose, we should, on the contrary, see in them a clear verification of the intimate and profound relation between the two.

*   *   *   *   *

To the Victorians, of course, these intimate contradictions in Dickens's character, this contrast between his repressed instincts and his ethical conformism, were not apparent. He made a complete conquest of the English public because he expressed, better than any other writer, its tastes and tendencies. Even the reforming tendency, the sense of responsibility for the lives of humble people, the benevolence, the 'Christmas spirit', may seem to us today, detached from their surroundings, far more original and typical aspects of Dickens than they were within the compass of their own period. He was not really the only one to denounce abuses and call attention to a whole series of social facts; poverty, and the problems of poverty, were widely-diffused preoccupations at the time. Nor did his originality consist in making use of the novel for propaganda, for here too he was not the only one; it lay, undoubtedly, in his giving, in his works, so much more than mere propaganda that their survival is in no way qualified by it.

As a propagandist, Dickens can be considered, according to Mr. House's definition, a journalist of genius, and Mr. House's book is a necessary corrective to the thesis of another recent critic, inspired by the Russian Marxist critique, T. A. Jackson,[18] who sees in Dickens a downright radical.

Mr. Jackson admits that Dickens, by origin and on the surface, was a petit bourgeois, a Biedermeier; but a Biedermeier who was unable to forget having seen his father in the debtors' prison, and having himself suffered hell, as a child, in the boot-blacking factory. It is true, he says, that Dickens, like any God-fearing citizen, poured contempt and ridicule, in *Barnaby Rudge*, upon the popular movements that were the forerunners of socialist agitation— but on this occasion he was misled by the tendentious conservative press; it is true that in *American Notes* he showed a fastidiousness towards certain habits of American democracy such as only a bourgeois who pretends to some knowledge of good manners could feel—but in this case the writer was under the influence of Mrs. Dickens; it is true that the Dickens of the *Christmas Books*, who is, for so many, the most characteristic, could in no circumstances find favour with a Marxist critic[19]—but here he was only adopting a convention for commercial purposes. The real Dickens was not an acquiescent petit bourgeois, i.e. a Biedermeier, Mr. Jackson maintains, but a petit bourgeois in full revolt, who ended, without in the least realizing it, by writing the fiercest possible accusation against the bourgeois society that had given him birth: a figure very different from the conventional one of a Dickens transformed by success and comfort into a snob and a reactionary. Nor, it seems, did Dickens belong to the school of bourgeois socialists whom Marx and Engels stigmatized in the Communist Manifesto, for he was not taken in by the moralizings and the philanthropy of the Victorian age, which served as a mere mask for capitalist rapacity. The note of optimism is only to be found in the first novels, when the writer believed in the inevitable triumph of virtue, and in an enlightened humanitarianism that was capable of smoothing out the difference between rich and poor: an expression of this state of mind is Mr. Pickwick, the prosperous business man from whom radiates a benevolence so great that his bald and shining skull seems almost to be surrounded with a halo of sanctity. But Pickwick is soon contrasted with Pecksniff, whose universal benevolence is merely the mask of a cold and rapacious egoism. Dickens's experience of America, which revealed to him the corrupting influence of power and wealth, changed his conception of life: the author of *Martin Chuzzlewit*, according to Mr. Jackson, was now no longer a Biedermeier.[20] And the author of *David Copperfield* finds good people only among the lower middle class and the proletariat—Micawber, Tommy Traddles, the Peggotty family (cf. in *Great Expectations*, Joe Gargery)—whereas the seducers, the rascals, the liars —Steerforth, Murdstone, Spenlow—are recruited from the upper classes and the wealthy bourgeoisie. In *Hard Times* Dickens attacks the ethics of capitalism as portrayed by the Manchester school of economists; in *Little Dorrit* he shows vice going hand in hand with riches, virtue with poverty, and displays so much sympathy for the masses as to achieve a tone that is positively revolutionary; and

A Tale of Two Cities, for Mr. Jackson, is a hymn to revolution. *Great Expectations*—which had a happy ending only because of Bulwer Lytton's intervention—represents, as though in a parable, the final failure of optimism and of the Victorian compromise. As Dickens gradually lost faith in reforms, says Mr. Jackson, he felt himself urged on towards a revolutionary solution, and started the revolution in his own home, by separating from his wife: thus he shook both the pillars of bourgeois society, the Law and the Family. Contempt for the bourgeoisie is the dominant note in *Our Mutual Friend*: long past are the days when Biedermeier acquired a halo of sanctity with Pickwick; the typical bourgeois is now called Podsnap, who does not admit the existence of anything that is contrary to his own personal satisfaction, who knows the ways of Providence to a nicety; and 'it was very remarkable (and must have been very comfortable) that what Providence meant, was invariably what Mr. Podsnap meant'. If Pickwick was a saint in bourgeois clothes, Podsnap is undoubtedly the Evil One dressed up as a typical Victorian of 1860.[21] But, the bourgeois Heaven having collapsed, Dickens was unable to find another one, and that was his tragedy.[22]

Was Dickens really as adventurous and original a radical as Mr. Jackson makes him out? Let us even admit it to be true that he does not find his good people anywhere except in the lower middle class and the proletariat, and his seducers, rascals, and liars amongst the upper classes and the wealthy bourgeoisie. But are his youthful heroes really proletarians? Nicholas Nickleby, Martin Chuzzlewit, Edward Chester, David Copperfield, John Harmon—they are all 'walking gentlemen' of noble appearance, as George Orwell remarks,[23] people with soft hands rather than calloused palms, who speak the King's English, not popular slang. Little Pip in *Great Expectations*, for instance, was brought up by people who spoke the Essex dialect, but he himself, from his tenderest childhood, speaks the English of the upper classes. And what of the novelist's ideal of life? His heroes, once they have made money and settled down, not merely no longer work, but do not even occupy their leisure with the energetic pastimes to which Fielding's

heroes devoted themselves.[24] They live and multiply themselves in happy families, suitable for portrayal in 'conversation pieces', those typical pictures of the Victorian era.

The ideal to be striven after, then, appears to be something like this: a hundred thousand pounds, a quaint old
house with plenty of ivy on it, a sweetly womanly wife,
a horde of children, and no work. Everything is safe, soft,
peaceful and, above all, domestic. In the moss-grown
churchyard down the road are the graves of the loved ones
who passed away before the happy ending happened. The
servants are comic and feudal, the children prattle round
your feet, the old friends sit at your fireside, talking of
past days, there is the endless succession of enormous
meals, the cold punch and sherry negus, the feather beds
and warming-pans, the Christmas parties with charades
and blind man's buff; but nothing ever happens, except
the yearly childbirth. This is the ideal happy ending of
Dickens's novels, in Orwell's words. An ideal which could
not possibly be more Biedermeier.

Mr. House, on the other hand, observes that Dickens
was not connected, in any decided manner, with any of the
radical currents of his time, neither did he start one of his
own; but, at least in his first novels, strove to depict a type
of individual who might become a centre for the diffusion
of reformist sentiment and might point out the way to a
better social order. He did not, however, conceive this type
of individual on a heroic plane in the manner of Carlyle;
heroic, superhuman virtues were beyond his Biedermeier
range: it was the simplest and most ordinary kinds of
human goodness that he contented himself with displaying
in intensified form, in characters created to meet the taste
of those who were not professed thinkers and philan-
thropists. His champions of goodness were figures of
popular art like Épinal prints. There is stressed in these
characters, in a form which comes very near caricature, a
certain generic benevolence quite devoid of any reference
to the controversies and ambitions of the time. And this
mixture of generic quality and exaggeration has the result
of making these characters appear to us today almost like
monstrous grotesques. Mr. House observes (p. 51):

We cannot now read about Pickwick in his more consciously benevolent moods, Brownlow, the Cheerybles, and Garland without some impatience: when they are not unpleasant they are tedious, and the parts they play in their plots are too mechanical. In particular, Dickens's trick of stressing peculiarities of look or manner or dress, which is so brilliantly successful in comic or grotesque figures like Pecksniff or Quilp, tends to make these benevolent old boys revert to the butt-type, from which Mr. Pickwick set out. . . . For us the caricaturist's themes detract too much from the dignity of what is meant to be admirable.

Dickens's attitude of general benevolence shows itself in little Biedermeier pictures of the type of Spitzweg's,[25] in which a gossipy and a humorous manner are allied, in piquant contrast, with a poetic atmosphere, with a bounteousness of clear skies or a freshness of orchards and gabled roofs which look like a translation into paint of the 'God 's in his heaven, all 's right with the world' of Browning's *Pippa passes*. These benevolent characters of Dickens are as it were messengers—slightly grotesque angels like those of Chagall—of the Christmas spirit, the spirit of *Bescherung*, of universal largesse, which, from the *Christmas Books*, has diffused its halo over the whole work of Dickens, becoming, in our memories, its salient characteristic. It is an atmosphere of generosity, of reconciliation, of compensation for everyone, a limited bourgeois paradise, lit by the candles of the holy eve and adorned with holly and mistletoe. In this fairy-tale atmosphere, subtle psychology is not to be expected in the characters: Scrooge's conversion is brought about as if by the wave of a magic wand; there is no more psychology in such transformations than there is in the transition from one dance figure to another in a ballet. And the panacea—in a bourgeois world dominated by money—is nothing else than a bag of jingling coins distributed by a typical Biedermeier philanthropist, a 'good rich man'—whether he calls himself Pickwick, Cheeryble, old Chuzzlewit, Scrooge, or Boffin.[26] A naïve reaction on Dickens's part to the savage social background laid bare by the Malthusian theories which were then frightening everybody! Malthus saw no salvation for civilization except in continence, in the closing of taverns, in birth-control, in

14. HOGARTH. Orgies (The Rake's Progress) (*London, Sir John Soane's Museum. By courtesy of the Trustees*)

15. HOGARTH. Gin Lane

the abolition of all recreation, and in rigid economy for the poorer classes: therefore one clung tightly to the puritan exclusion of amusements (which may offer incentives to vice and error) from the celebration of Sunday, which, in nineteenth-century England, became the most tedious day of the week.[27]

Discipline and restriction were therefore preached to the poor. And then comes Dickens, setting up against all this prudence the *Bescherung* of the Christmas spirit, the fabulous generosity of the Cheerybles and of the repentant Scrooge, the groaning dish carried to the table, the steaming punch-bowl, the 'eating with joy', almost according to the teaching of St. Philip Neri!

In Micawber, the improvident, the prolific, Dickens created a flagrant contradiction to the theory of Malthus, and by showing him in the end as an excellent Colonial magistrate, sought to overthrow the Malthusian conclusion with regard to individuals of this stamp. Fundamental, 'natural' goodness of man, virtue crowned with success even upon earth, like invested capital paying substantial dividends; and paradise turns out to be like a quiet village Sunday, a vision evoked by Dickens to confute the puritan condemnation of Sunday pastimes. The picture might have been painted by Waldmüller, the painter of idyllic Austrian village scenes:[28]

I was travelling in the west of England a summer or two back, and was induced by the beauty of the scenery, and the seclusion of the spot, to remain for the night in a small village, distant about seventy miles from London. The next morning was Sunday; and I walked out, towards the church. Groups of people—the whole population of the little hamlet apparently—were hastening in the same direction. Cheerful and good-humoured congratulations were heard on all sides, as neighbours overtook each other, and walked on in company. Occasionally I passed an aged couple, whose married daughter and her husband were loitering by the side of the old people, accommodating their rate of walking to their feeble pace, while a little knot of children hurried on before; stout young labourers in clean round frocks; and buxom girls with healthy, laughing faces, were plentifully sprinkled about in couples, and the whole scene was one of quiet and tranquil contentment, irresistibly captivating. The morning was bright and pleasant, the hedges were green and blooming, and a thousand delicious scents were wafted on the air, from the wild flowers which blossomed on either side of the footpath. The little church was one of those venerable simple buildings which abound in the English counties; half overgrown with moss and ivy, and standing in the centre of a little plot of ground, which, but for the green mounds with which it was studded, might have passed for a lovely meadow. I fancied that the old clanking bell which was now summoning the congregation together, would seem less terrible when it rung out the knell of a departed soul, than I had ever deemed possible before—that the sound would tell only of a welcome to calmness and rest, amidst the most peaceful and tranquil scene in nature.

I followed into the church. . . . The impressive service of the Church of England was spoken—not merely *read*—by a grey-headed minister, and the responses delivered by his auditors, with an air of sincere devotion as far removed from affectation or display, as from coldness or indifference. . . .

On coming out of church, the villagers wait in the churchyard for the clergyman, to salute him and ask his advice, and there are tasty little *genre* scenes like this:

That [the clergyman] was fond of his joke, I discovered from overhearing him ask a stout, fresh-coloured young fellow, with a very pretty bashful-looking girl on his arm, 'when those banns were to be put up?'—an inquiry which made the young fellow more fresh-coloured, and the girl more bashful, and which, strange to say, caused a great many other girls who were standing round, to colour up also, and look anywhere but in the faces of their male companions.

As I approached this spot in the evening about half an hour before sunset, I was surprised to hear the hum of voices, and occasionally a shout of merriment from the meadow beyond the churchyard; which I found, when I reached the stile, to be occasioned by a very animated game of cricket, in which the boys and young men of the place were engaged, while the females and old people were scattered about: some seated on the grass watching the progress of the game, and others sauntering about in groups of two or three, gathering little nosegays of wild roses and hedge flowers.

Another little *genre* scene: an old man giving a cricket lesson to a young man, while the latter throws an occasional glance at the old man's granddaughter, who is standing by. And when the young man is at the wicket and still throws a glance at the pair from time to time, the old man thinks it is 'an appeal to his judgment of a particular hit', but the blush on the girl's face and the downcast look of her bright eye shows for whom these glances were really intended. It was the clergyman himself who had established the cricket-field, and had provided the stumps and bats and balls and everything. Dickens concludes: 'It is such scenes as this, I would see near London, on a Sunday evening.' The scene has a family resemblance to the description of a day in the life of a parish priest by Jean Paul which made such an impression on De Quincey.

No more quietist, bourgeois—in fact Biedermeier— ideal could be imagined than this vague and sentimental form of Christian socialism. Taine was perfectly right in thinking that Dickens's work could be summed up in the following formula:[29]

> Au fond, les romans de Dickens se réduisent tous à une phrase, et la voici: Soyez bons et aimez; il n'y a de vraie joie que dans les émotions du cœur: la sensibilité est tout l'homme.

And as for his exaltation of the goodness of humble people, upon which hinges so much of Mr. Jackson's thesis on Dickens's radicalism, it is not inapt to record a criticism from *Blackwood's Magazine*, June 1855, which is quoted by Mr. Humphry House:

> We cannot but express our conviction that it is to the fact that he represents a class that he owes his speedy elevation to the top of the wave of popular favour. He is a man of very liberal sentiments—an assailer of constituted wrongs and authorities—one of the advocates in the plea of Poor *versus* Rich, to the progress of which he has lent no small aid in his day. But he is, notwithstanding, perhaps more distinctly than any other author of the time, a *class* writer, the historian and representative of one circle in the many ranks of our social scale. Despite their descents into the lowest class, and their occasional flights into the less familiar ground of fashion, it is the air and breath of middle-class respectability which fills the books of Mr. Dickens.[30]

Arguing from the point of view of Mr. Jackson, one sees no reason why one should not discover a radical in Tennyson too, considering that he declaimed violently against the inequality of the social classes and the injustice of the rich in his poem *Maud*; and one wonders whether, in view of this aspect of Tennyson, one can agree with Mr. Edmund Wilson when he says that, of the great Victorian writers, Dickens was the one who took up the most antagonistic attitude towards the Victorian period itself. But, as Mr. House well observes, such declamations, far from infrequent throughout Victorian literature, were intended rather to deny class differences between the bourgeoisie and the aristocracy—recruited for so many centuries, in England, from the very ranks of the bourgeoisie —than to advocate any real equality between *all* social classes. In the Victorian age anyone might, in fact, be called a radical—according to the vague acceptation of the term—if he felt sympathy for the humiliated and oppressed, for the 'underdog', for the petit bourgeois, the humble employee who needs so little to make him happy. Dickens saw clearly the negative side of the legislation in force, but contributed nothing constructive towards a future society; and if his ideals appear to coincide partly with those of the Chartist Movement, he recoiled in horror always from the thought of armed revolution and violence; for him, the correction of social injustices must come from above, from the rich and powerful who had been converted like Scrooge, not from the subversive hatred of the masses. His fear of revolutionary unrest was the same as that which we found in Lamb,[31] and when he depicted, in gloomy nightmare colours, the Gordon Riots and, even more, the hysterical scenes of the Terror, he was thinking not so much of those episodes of half a century before, as of what might happen in 1840. Horror of the bestiality latent in man made of him a pacifist, a bourgeois; his attacks were directed against abuses of administration, never aimed at political forms (although Mr. Wilson wishes to see in him a rebel, in opposition to institutions of every kind, in consequence of the spiritual trauma already mentioned);[32] and the affinities of his ideals with those of the Chartists became apparent chiefly when that movement, having lost its hold over the mob and the mob's innate violence, became merged with the general aspirations towards reform. Reform, certainly, and the elimination of abuses; but with no disturbance of established order, no angry crowds in the streets. An enlightened bourgeois, in fact, not a hot-headed radical. The forms of disorder that attracted him all came under the heading of the picturesque; the disorder that, socially, repelled him was decanted into artistic representation—slums, and extravagant types such as Micawber and Dick and positively morbid ones like Miss Havisham; and it was the picturesque of *genre* painting, as introduced by the Dutch, with whom Dickens had in common, not only his vein of caprice, but his meticulous care for detail, for the minute instruments of arts and crafts, for 'still life'. Even his satire on the administration of the law resolves itself, to a great extent, into still-life pictures of emblems—the Exchequer tally-sticks, the waxen seals on legal documents, the red tape round files of papers, and such-like ancient and picturesque stationery.

What, in him, may seem to be realism is merely delight in the picturesque: consider the minuteness with which he describes the appearance and the workings of inanimate objects. He is debarred from true realism partly by his tendency towards theatricalism (he is a scene-painter rather than a scrupulous, notary-like annotator *à la* Balzac; and like his minor characters, his stage-scenes also are evolved with a distorting, caricaturist's eye,[33] the eye, too, of a collector of *bric-à-brac*), partly by his Victorian repugnance for everything that is crude and offensive to delicacy.

We have already considered an episode from *Dombey and Son* which was conceived in terms of the theatre.[34] Behind his landscapes we are often aware of the wings and the backcloth and the stage machinery,[35] just as his typical lesser characters consist often of nothing more than a few curiosities of speech and rattled-off picturesque expressions hung up on an empty wire frame, or a wickerwork lay figure. But the skill, the *verve*, of the artist are such that one does not notice the emptiness.[36]

But before true realism, the realism that does not shrink from wretched human details, even of things to which a transcendent significance is attached, Dickens revolted. A typical case, quoted by Mr. House, is Dickens's reaction

to Millais's *The Carpenter's Shop*, in which the family of
Christ is depicted as a real family of humble artisans:[37]

You come—in this Royal Academy Exhibition, which is familiar
with the works of Wilkie, Collins, Etty, Eastlake, Mulready, Leslie,
Maclise, Turner, Stanfield, Landseer, Roberts, Danby, Creswick,
Lee, Webster, Herbert, Dyce, Cope,[38] and others who would have
been renowned as great masters in any age or country—you come,
in this place, to the contemplation of a Holy Family. You will have
the goodness to discharge from your minds all Post-Raphael ideas,
all religious aspirations, all elevating thoughts; all tender, awful,
sorrowing, ennobling, sacred, graceful, or beautiful associations; and
to prepare yourself as befits such a subject—pre-Raphaelly considered—for the lowest depths of what is mean, odious, repulsive,
and revolting.

You behold the interior of a carpenter's shop. In the foreground
of that carpenter's shop is a hideous, wry-necked, blubbering, red-
headed boy, in a bed-gown, who appears to have received a poke in
the hand from the stick of another boy with whom he has been
playing in an adjacent gutter, and to be holding it up for the contemplation of a kneeling woman, so horrible in her ugliness, that
(supposing it were possible for any human creature to exist for
a moment with that dislocated throat) she would stand out from the
rest of the company as a Monster, in the vilest cabaret in France,
or the lowest gin-shop in England. Two almost naked carpenters,
master and journeyman, worthy companions of this agreeable female,
are working at their trade; a boy, with some small flavour of
humanity in him, is entering with a vessel of water; and nobody is
paying any attention to a snuffy old woman who seems to have
mistaken that shop for the tobacconist's next door, and to be hopelessly waiting at the counter to be served with half an ounce of her
favourite mixture. Wherever it is possible to express ugliness of
feature, limb, or attitude, you have it expressed. Such men as the
carpenters might be undressed in any hospital where dirty drunkards,
in a high state of varicose veins, are received. Their very toes have
walked out of Saint Giles's.

How much more realistic than Dickens were the Dutch
painters who sought to add touches of humanity—even if
of vulgar humanity—to their sacred figures, and who
placed the latter in scenes that reproduced faithfully their
own everyday surroundings! Look for instance at Jan
Lievens's (1607–74) *Annunciation* (Barber Collection, Bir-
mingham): the angel, looking like a fat priest in his long

blue tunic, appears to a woman of the most ordinary type sitting on a straw-bottomed chair, with arms outstretched in a gesture which it would be hard to reconcile with the solemn words *Ecce ancilla Domini*: a translation of the supernatural into terms of everyday life, anticipating Millais's picture which gave offence to Dickens.

*   *   *   *   *

Dickens's aspirations towards reform, his criticisms of the administration in force, found a favourable medium in the development of the novel in the nineteenth century.[39] And by 'development of the novel' I mean, first of all, the conditions of publishing, which in a certain sense determined the character of the nineteenth-century novel. At the beginning of the century, in accordance with a tradition started and enforced by Sir Walter Scott, a novel had to be a work in three volumes (about 300,000 words), to be sold at the very high price of $1\frac{1}{2}$ guineas: such a work could be acquired only by the wealthy, and circulated chiefly by means of the circulating libraries. But, a little after 1820, serial novels began to appear, at the price of a shilling for each part: *The Adventures of Tom and Jerry* by the feeble, prolix Pierce Egan (a book about London life in the Regency period, in which you would search in vain for the somehow rather bland flavour of contemporary gossipiness that is to be found in the series of little French volumes by De Jouy devoted to the investigations of the 'Hermite de la Chaussée-d'Antin'; a book which nevertheless was the delight of Thackeray at school) was the first experiment in a method which was later to produce the *Pickwick Club*. The form of publication had a certain influence upon the character of the work: thus, while the three-volume novel had to be padded out with adventitious disquisitions and descriptions and tedious discourses and the so-called 'pauses for reflection'—thus provoking that picturesque image (of Saintsbury's) of 'a sandwich with a sawdust filling'—the serial novel induced in its authors a need to maintain the lively interest of the reader by various methods such as, in the better cases, suspense designed to sharpen curiosity at the end of a part, or, in the worst (especially in Charles

Reade), some sensational incident which, at the end of a part, had the same function as the epigrammatic close of a sonnet. Collins's formula was famous: 'Make 'em laugh, make 'em cry; make 'em wait.' In this way were created the conditions favourable to the 'sensation novel', the origins of which, on the other hand, must be sought in the quarry of the 'tales of terror' of the end of the eighteenth century (Mrs. Radcliffe, 'Monk' Lewis). The tendency towards sensationalism, the cheaply-priced serial novel, and the utilization of narrative literature for social ends were simultaneous phenomena: for none of these was Dickens responsible, but he was able to give them all full play in his work, thus conferring upon it a physiognomy which, at first glance, carries us far away from our 'Biedermeier' definition—in fact, appears to contradict it. One common element marks all these aspects of his work: democratization, vulgarization.

The sensational is no longer the mysterious, the semi-supernatural, of Mrs. Radcliffe and Lewis; from the tale of terror was born the Byron hero, the *homme fatal* who was later to end his career of democratization with Eugène Sue (while in England, as we have already pointed out with regard to Steerforth in *David Copperfield*, he was destined to be put in the pillory and then to disappear); and there was also born the conditioned, implicitly self-cancelling supernatural of Scott. The place of the supernatural was now taken by a different kind of sensationalism—the kind that provides sustenance for the crime columns in the newspapers—and the novelist was to find, within the compass of society, horrors and mysteries better suited to the bourgeoisie than the hocus-pocus of the tales of terror. Instead of demons there would be criminals, instead of the mystery of a medieval castle, the mystery of a crime; and so it was that the man who was cleverest of all, during the Victorian epoch, at raising an intellectual thrill, Wilkie Collins, initiated the detective story, that positive, bourgeois type of fairy-tale.

Moreover, with the advent of the serial novel and the enormous increase in circulation, the novelist, who had previously been the pariah of literature, came to be the

writer who made the most conspicuous profits, and felt
himself invested with a power that had some affinities with
political power, since the novel lent itself admirably as a
vehicle of ideas. The profession of novelist could be just as
remunerative as that of lawyer: on this point we have explicit declarations from those very men of letters who took
this path, for example, Trollope. And so, while the Biedermeier spirit of the Victorian bourgeoisie was made incarnate pre-eminently by domestic novels of the type of *Vanity
Fair* which appeared in the old three-volume form and in
the more expensive magazines, the agitation of the lower
middle class, the emotion-hunger of the people, the whole
ferment that was active beneath the crust of the Victorian
compromise, found their outlet in the serial novels which
were, as a matter of course, sensational. Dickens was the
creator of the 'popular magazines' whose price did not
exceed one shilling (*Household Words, All the Year Round*);
with the sensational tendency that was the inevitable fruit
of this type of publication he combined, in himself, a natural
propensity for the dramatic, and a conception of the novel
as drama, together with the ability to gather up a number
of threads and then untie them again in a series of melodramatic episodes towards the end (it might be said that, in
a sense, just as Scott's novels occupied the place of dramatic
literature for the Romantics, so did those of Dickens for the
Victorians).

Through the press, thanks to the revolution in publishing just mentioned, the novelist was able to make an appeal
to a vast public, as the Elizabethan dramatists had done
through the stage and as film writers do today: and indeed
the Victorian sensational novel represents the same phenomenon of drama for the masses. On one side, therefore,
there is the distortion, for melodramatic ends, of the world
as observed, an arbitrary dramatization of the plot that
verges on the grotesque. In *David Copperfield*, for instance,
the scene between Peggotty and Mrs. Steerforth is of the
type calculated to make a hit in the popular theatre of
the nineteenth century—scenes with conflicts between the
parents of the two lovers, between the deserted woman and
the mother of her seducer, between the neglected wife and

the fortunate mistress, &c., all of them conflicts and con-
frontations typical of bourgeois moral and social feeling.
Observe also the schematic method of presentation and the
perspective pattern of such situations. In *Great Expectations*,
for example, Estella is the creature of Miss Havisham's
hatred, Pip the creature of the convict Magwitch's love:
parallelism and contrast. Magwitch, the felon, wants to
make of Pip a gentleman to put all other gentlemen to
shame ('I'll show a better gentleman than the whole kit of
you put together'); Miss Havisham, who had been deserted
by her betrothed, wants to make of Estella a *femme fatale*
who shall inspire unrequited love in all men. Estella has an
unhappy marriage; Magwitch's wealth, destined for Pip,
is confiscated by the State. On one side, melodramatic distortions of this kind; on the other, the novelist's desire to
call attention to truths which bourgeois conventions set
out to ignore. Hence a complex of the arbitrary and the
audacious, of the stereotyped, the artificial and the liberal,
which constitutes the character *sui generis* of Dickens the
professional novelist (distinct, as will be seen, from the
artist). And, within the compass of dramatic expression—
a genuine gift with Dickens, and one profoundly rooted,
as Mr. Wilson has remarked,[40] in the lack of balance in his
own nature—we must make a distinction between the
dramatization of the plot, which is always mechanical,
artificial, melodramatic, absurd, and the dramatization of
the characters, by which the latter express themselves in
dialogues that are usually animated with the very colours
of life; and into these dialogues, as has been universally
and accurately observed, Dickens puts the greater part of
his force—more than he puts into his plots, or into his
episodes, or even into his descriptions.[41] The characters
move, they speak, they do not analyse, nor do they analyse
themselves: this external dramatic quality produces its
greatest effects with comic characters.

But before we proceed to a study of 'what is alive' in
Dickens, something should be said of his formula for the
novel. This formula, as extracted from the whole series of
his novels, from *Oliver Twist* to *The Mystery of Edwin
Drood*, is: melodrama, combined with grotesque and

humorous elaboration of the characters. Two contrasting tones, from whose combined effect was to be born that diverse and picturesque world which had been the ideal of the Romantics. Victor Hugo's formula was not very different: the same mixture of elements, in fact, that he saw in Gothic architecture—figures of angels and gargoyles of grinning demons, laughter side by side with pathos. Dickens's formula for the novel up till 1859 is: a single or double melodrama flanked by scenes of exuberant garrulity in which an *ad libitum* quantity of minor characters are brought into prominence: tragedy and farce juxtaposed. After 1859 (*A Tale of Two Cities*) these scenes of eccentric figures come to be more and more subordinated to a more rigorous narrative unity. The melodramatic part is characterized by externality: tragic quality is not manifested by means of analysis—a method which was later to become the special property of Henry James and Joseph Conrad—but is a mere surface consisting of gestures, acts, words: the characters are launched one against the other like mechanical playthings, toy trains, or they go into reverse, like Scrooge who turns, point-blank, from bad to good, or Dombey who, having reformed, becomes a model father and thus, as Taine remarks, spoils a good novel. Even when Dickens wishes to analyse the mixture of good and bad in the same individual, he has to represent the two coexistent elements to himself in a material, artificial way, constructing the figure of John Jasper, in *The Mystery of Edwin Drood*, as a double personality,[42] on the one hand the respectable choir-master of a Victorian cathedral, on the other the Thug, follower of the ferocious cult of Kali— thus, in fact, calling in the help of the exotic and the strange. At the end of a novel a review of the characters and their successive fortunes is like the final tableau in a theatre of automatons, whose mechanism runs down after their final bow; see, for example, *David Copperfield*. This kind of formula was common at the time: we find it again, for instance, in Soulié's *Mémoires du diable*.

A novel of this sort culminates in commonplace effects, with violent lights and shades; the figures lose all contact with reality and assume the sinister fixed, exasperated

expressions of wax dolls; it is a foretaste of the Grand Guignol. Surprise effects (especially the classic expedient of the
rediscovery of relations), coincidences, chance retributions,
these are the tricks that have discredited the type of novel
cultivated by Dickens, which does not differ very much, in
this respect, from the method of such writers as Soulié and
Sue.[43] Gissing, though he was an admirer of Dickens,
remarked, on the subject of his coincidences: 'It seems
never to have occurred to him, thus far in his career [at the
time of *Bleak House*] that novels and fairy tales . . . should
obey different laws in the matter of incident.'[44] Look, for
instance, at the construction of *Oliver Twist*. Oliver, a
foundling brought up at the expense of the parish, is in
fact the illegitimate son of a very rich gentleman and of
a woman who, as a result of her fall, had been reduced to the
workhouse, where Oliver is born. He spends some years
there, and the unhappiness of his life is increased by the
meanness and brutality of the workhouse administrators.
Oliver is the victim, particularly, of the parish beadle,
Bumble, who takes a sadistic pleasure in whipping him.
Sensationalism goes hand in hand with the denunciation
of the so-called educational system suffered by unfortunates
born in Oliver's circumstances. Bound apprentice to an
undertaker, Oliver finds his destiny has not improved and
decides that any sort of change could not make it worse.
So he runs away to London, and on the way falls in with
a boy (who later turns out to be The Artful Dodger) who
offers him a lodging with the gang directed by Fagin, an
old Jewish receiver who lives in a mouldering house in
a dark corner of the slums. Thus Oliver becomes a new
recruit in the gang of thieves. At one moment he is helped
by Mr. Brownlow (whom in fact one discovers later to be
his grandfather), but he is snatched away again by the
gang. His next expedition is made with Bill Sikes, a house-
breaker; Oliver is lowered through a little window into the
interior of an outhouse, somewhere in the country, so that
he may open the door to his accomplices, but receives a
gunshot wound in the process. He is saved a second time
by Mrs. Maylie and her *protégée* Rose, who treat him with
kindness and bring him up. In his first thieving expedition,

as already mentioned, Oliver had encountered his grand-father; in this second one, he stumbles into the house of an aunt. In the meantime a sinister character, Monks, has made his appearance; he has an interest in the total ruin of Oliver, and makes the gang of thieves acquainted with his wish, so that an unexpected source of gain is opened up to them. And this sinister personage is none other than Oliver's half-brother. Oliver, in fact, was the illegitimate son of Edwin Leefold and of the poor girl Agnes Fleming, Rose's sister. Leefold's wife had revealed to Agnes's father that his daughter's seducer was her own husband; the old man died of a broken heart, and the girl fled from the village. Monks had sworn to his own mother on her death-bed that he would persecute the illegitimate scion of the family, and therefore was seeking to compromise him irremediably with the criminals. Nancy, Bill Sikes's wretched companion, takes pity on Oliver and communi-cates Monks' plot to ruin Oliver to Mr. Brownlow, whom she knows to take an interest in the boy. But she falls under suspicion, is tracked down by the chief of the gang, is con-demned to disappear; it is Sikes who is deputed to dispose of her, and he does so. And now the moment has arrived when things have to take a different turn and the guilty have to be punished. The murderer Sikes is pursued and, as he attempts to flee, accidentally hangs himself while trying to lower himself from a roof by means of a rope; the rest of the gang are delivered over to justice and Fagin is condemned to death; he goes mad in his cell. Monks is forced to confess; he emigrates and dies in prison. Bumble ends his career as an inmate of the workhouse he had formerly governed. Oliver is adopted by Mr. Brownlow.

The plot contains all the classic elements of the sensa-tional novel: recognition scenes, coincidences that have something of the miraculous about them (the houses of his relations seem to attract Oliver like magnets), stage effects. There are figures from the Chamber of Horrors: Bill Sikes acts and speaks like an ogre. When Fagin is preparing him for the announcement of Nancy's perfidy, he begins by asking him what he would do if The Artful Dodger had betrayed him: 'I'd grind his skull under the iron heel of my boot into as many grains as there are hairs upon his head', replies the criminal. 'What if *I* did it?' asks Fagin. 'If I was tried along with you', retorted the other, 'I'd fall upon you with them [the irons] in the open court, and beat your brains out afore the people.' And so, seeing that Sikes, for the sake of avenging himself, would have respect for no one, Fagin discloses the name of the guilty one, brandishing one hand aloft, as the foam flows from his lips. 'Hell's fire!' roars Sikes, and rushes off to his wretched mistress, whose face he bashes in with the butt of his pistol; and, as if that were not enough, he finishes her off with a heavy club. It is not long before the murderer is pursued: his dog betrays the place where he is lodging, and a crowd surrounds the house where the criminal had hoped to conceal himself. Sikes, finding himself trapped inside the house, goes to the window and defies his persecutors: 'Do your worst! I'll cheat you yet!' At which, 'of all the terrific yells that ever fell on mortal ears, none could exceed the cry of the infuriated throng'. Sikes thinks to escape by letting himself down from the roof into a ditch behind the house; but when he reaches the roof-top, he discovers that the tide has gone out, and the ditch is a mere 'bed of mud'. Realizing his intention and that it is impossible for him to put it into effect, the crowd 'raised a cry of triumphant execration to which all their previous shouting had been whispers'. Still Sikes does not despair of escaping by way of the ditch; he fastens the rope round the chimney-stack, and is on the point of securing the running loop at its other end beneath his armpits, when, just at that moment, as he is looking back on to the roof, he throws his arms above his head and utters a yell of terror:

'The eyes again!' he cried in an unearthly shriek. Staggering as if struck by lightning, he lost his balance and tumbled over the parapet. The noose was at his neck. It ran up with his weight, tight as a bow-string, and swift as the arrow it speeds. He fell for five-and-thirty feet. There was a sudden jerk, a terrific convulsion of the limbs; and there he hung, with the open knife clenched in his stiffening hand. . . . A dog which had lain concealed till now, ran backwards and forwards on the parapet with a dismal howl, and, collecting himself for a spring, jumped for the dead man's shoulders.

Missing his aim, he fell into the ditch, turning completely over as he went; and striking his head against a stone, dashed out his brains.

A list of similar horrors could be made for other novels of Dickens. Quilp, in *The Old Curiosity Shop*, a kind of evil Quasimodo—in the organization of the novel this deformed figure has, actually, an opposite function to that of the monster in *Notre-Dame de Paris*, the function of persecutor instead of that of saviour—tries to persuade us how terrible he is by eating eggs with their shells on and drinking boiling rum. And if Sikes, in *Oliver Twist*, did no more than threaten to bash out Fagin's brains with his hand-cuffs, Magwitch, in *Great Expectations*, does indeed attempt, with his handcuffs, to kill his enemy Compeyson. In *Bleak House* we have nine varieties of grotesque and violent deaths. Mr. Brook dies by 'spontaneous combustion', Lady Ded-lock's first lover poisons himself, Miss Flite, who wanders perpetually through the corridors of the law-courts, dies from madness and inanition, Jo the crossing-sweeper, pursued by the police, dies from exposure, Lady Dedlock dies of cold and a broken heart on her lover's grave— a mournful episode of the kind that Max Ernst uses with such relish for his *collages*—Tulkinghorn is killed by a shot from a gun, and the French maid who has killed him will end up, it is to be understood, on the gallows. In *Great Expectations*, which however belongs to a period when Dickens had refined his technique, we have escaped con-victs (the novel, in fact, opens in a sensational manner), a woman who has been deserted on her wedding day, who becomes a monomaniac and lives in the sinister atmosphere of a house with perpetually darkened windows, while her wedding-cake moulders on the fully-laid table and her wedding-dress falls to rags upon her back; until—cul-minating horror—the unfortunate creature catches fire at the hearth and is consumed like a torch. In the same novel a criminal apprentice, Orlick, bashes in Mrs. Gargery's skull with a chain, and very nearly bashes in Pip's, too, with a hammer. Finally the fight between the two convicts, Magwitch and Compeyson, ends with one being drowned and the other dying from the wounds he has received. The

adventures of this pair of criminals, which are merely hinted
at in the novel, include a seduction, an infanticide, and a
fight between two women in which one is strangled.

Because of this sensational side to his novels Dickens
was classified by Thackeray amongst the authors of so-
called 'Newgate Fiction'. The name of 'Newgate Novels'
was applied to certain novels written between 1830 and
1840 with, as protagonist, a noble criminal, that is, a
criminal endowed with generous and sympathetic qualities.
Bulwer Lytton, in particular, with *Paul Clifford* and *Eugene
Aram*, provided examples of this type of character, which
descends in direct line from the Byronic hero and therefore
constitutes the final development in the transformation of
the Montoni-Schedoni type in the works of Mrs. Radcliffe
(*The Mysteries of Udolpho; The Italian*). Byron had presented
the Corsair as a heroic ruffian with a thousand vices and
one single virtue; it was Bulwer Lytton's task to multiply
the virtues of the type, and to show his crimes in a light
which did not preclude, but in fact invited, the compassion
and regret of the reader. Thus the Byronic hero came to
be adapted to the bourgeois age; thus, also, he was made
to serve as a pretext for attacking the way in which justice
was administered in England. *Paul Clifford* was intended
to be a denunciation of the penal code, to 'draw attention
to two crimes in our penal institutions, viz. a vicious prison
discipline and a sanguinary criminal code—the habit of
corrupting the boy by the very punishment that ought to
redeem him, and then hanging the man, at the first occasion,
as the easiest way of getting rid of our blunders. Between
the example of crime which the tyro learns in the prison
yard, and the terrible levity with which the mob gather
about the drop at Newgate, there is a connection which
a writer may be pardoned for quitting loftier regions of
imagination to trace and detect.' Nevertheless there is
a great difference between Bulwer Lytton's noble aims and
their translation into practice: in reality he is more concerned with constructing a convincing tale in a vein then
popular, than with denouncing the influence of the penal
code upon the increase of crime. Bulwer Lytton was merely
exploiting the popularity of a certain type of character—

16. CHARDIN. Grace before Meat (*Paris, Louvre*)

17. GREUZE. L'Accordée du village (*Paris, Louvre*)

18. GREUZE. La Malédiction paternelle (*Paris, Louvre*)

the Byronic hero—just as Dickens, ten or fifteen years later, with *Oliver Twist* and *Barnaby Rudge*, exploited the methods of the Newgate School. And in truth Dickens's programme in the preface to *Oliver Twist* sounds very like Bulwer Lytton's programme quoted above. Dickens declares that, having found in the books about criminals known to him that the criminal was surrounded by a certain glamour, he himself intended to describe 'a knot of such associates in crime as really do exist; to paint them in all their deformity, in all their wretchedness, in all the squalid poverty of their lives; to show them as they really are, for ever skulking uneasily through the dirtiest paths of life, with the great, black, ghastly gallows closing up their prospect'. We have already seen with what limitations this so-called 'reality' of Dickens must be interpreted. Thackeray, nevertheless, associates *Oliver Twist* with the novels of Bulwer Lytton, Ainsworth, and Whitehead, and mentions it together with them in the preface to his *Catherine*, which appeared in *Fraser's Magazine* in 1839 and 1840. Thackeray's book was intended to tell the story of a real female delinquent, derived from the Newgate registers, its object being to put an end to the ambiguity between virtue and vice caused by novels like those of Bulwer Lytton; his moralistic satire continued later with *Barry Lyndon* (1844) and *George de Barnwell* (in *Punch*, 1847), in which latter—with its title like that of Lillo's famous play and its style that resembles the pompous manner of Bulwer Lytton—he sought to stigmatize the attempts of novelists to portray noble, delicate criminals (thus George, the future murderer, when he is a chemist's boy reads Homer in Greek behind the counter, impresses the Foreign Secretary with his profound knowledge of the French language and French politics, &c.). Thackeray, in short, is an incarnation of the bourgeois reaction against the portrayal of the honourable bandit, of the murderer so gentle that he steps aside to avoid crushing a worm. But the Newgate School, which lasted barely ten years and vanished owing to the violent reaction of the Victorian bourgeoisie against this kind of embellishment of vice, served as a bridge between the tale of terror of the end of

the eighteenth and the beginning of the nineteenth century, and the 'sensation novel' of the middle of the nineteenth century: it accentuated the melodramatic method
of terrifying effects elaborated simply for their own sake—
a thing which did not occur, for instance, in Scott, in whose
work stage effects are not lacking, but where there is no
insistence on effects which are repellent and teratological.
The sensationalism of Dickens is well illustrated by his
excessive use of chance retribution. In *The Old Curiosity
Shop*, before describing the horrible body of Quilp in the
mud of the Thames, Dickens remarks:

> Retribution, which often travels slowly—especially when heaviest,
> had tracked his footsteps with a sure and certain scent and was gain-
> ing on him fast. Unmindful of her stealthy tread, her victim holds
> his course in fancied triumph. Still at his heels she comes, and once
> afoot, is never turned aside.

Retribution in the novels of Dickens has all the violence
of a natural phenomenon, against which human energies
avail nothing. Quilp and Steerforth are drowned, Bill Sikes
kills himself involuntarily, Rigaud Blandois in *Little Dorrit*
is crushed by the collapse of a building, Carker is cut to
pieces by a train, Madame Defarge in *A Tale of Two Cities*
is dispatched by an accidentally-fired pistol, the perfidy of
Sir John Chester in *Barnaby Rudge* is punished by the death
of his son, in the same way as is Ralph Nickleby's ignoble
vengeance on Nicholas. These extraordinary happenings
were intended, by Dickens and the other sensational
novelists, to exemplify the intervention of Providence.
With this object, Steerforth's body is thrown up on the
beach at Yarmouth in view of the house he had dishonoured.
Sensationalism placed itself at the service of theology and
morality. But the extent to which this sensationalism was
a mere external recipe, unconnected with the more genuine
tendencies of these writers, can be seen from the case of
Trollope—a Biedermeier novelist *par excellence*—who was
also of the opinion that narrative should make use of sensational incidents, and made use of them himself in his
novels, yet subordinated sensationalism to the study of
character. Both he and Thackeray dislike the melodramatic

and the heroic; in them, even violent scenes are tempered
with humour. And this, of course, is the typical Biedermeier attitude towards sensationalism; the anti-heroic attitude that we shall find in Thackeray, in George Eliot, in
those novelists who exerted themselves to look beyond the
external aspect of deeds into the souls of their characters.
But Dickens does not know this concentration of thought;
about him there is nothing introspective; he conceives his
world dramatically, and any kind of dramatization serves
his purpose. Action, gesture, dialogue—these are what
matter to him. And so the result is that the most interesting
characters turn out to be those who contribute little or
nothing to the development of the plot—characters such
as Mr. Micawber, Mrs. Gamp, Flora Finching, Mr.
Crummles. What is the significance of this? It means
probably that Dickens was born to be a writer of 'sketches',
of character-essays, such as are to be found in *Sketches by
Boz* and in the best essays in *The Uncommercial Traveller*;
and that he adapted himself without repugnance to the
mechanics of the novel because there was in his nature,
besides the artist, the practical man, the lawyer who takes
pleasure in a showy piece of reasoning, in a complicated
argument, a theatrical prosecution or defence. It has been
said[45] that the *Sketches by Boz* contain, in a raw state, the
material of the future novels; it might more properly be
said that the material of the essays has, in the novels, been
squeezed out to the last possible drop, so that its fresh,
vigorous spirit may enliven a huge cask of ordinary wine.
His novels are often like towns whose centres are dull and
conventional and tedious—like the centres of so many of
the industrial towns that arose in England during the Victorian period—but which have picturesque suburbs, and
a few little streets and blind alleys and out-of-the-way lanes
that have survived from the original, ancient nucleus of the
town. We shall have occasion to return to this point later on.

Dickens, although of the moral fibre of the reformer of
manners, was, fundamentally, a slave to the mechanical
conventions of the novel, and was incapable of adapting his
means of expression to his nature; or rather, of the two
types of novel prevalent in the Victorian era—the 'low-

pressure' type of domestic novel in three volumes, with its
painstaking, analytical character-painting, and the 'high-
pressure' type of sensational novel, concerned entirely with
externals—he preferred the latter as being the one which
best satisfied his dramatic instinct, his need of a huge public
to move and to stimulate, and—last but not least—his need
of immediate revenue so as to achieve a comfortable position in life.

And so it is that Dickens is unable to write a Christmas
tale without creating a fictitious, artificial scaffolding, with
disguises, mistaken identities, lost heirs, and all the other
expedients hallowed by an ancient narrative tradition that
goes back to the Hellenistic period. After pages of delicious
humorous conversation, he remembers that he must get
on with his plot, must give a pull to the big cardboard
machine that he drags along behind him; and at once he
plunges, with the utmost indifference, into this lifeless
matter, not realizing that here he is dealing with shadows,
failing to distinguish between the light of reflectors and
footlights, and the light of the sun. For, to put it briefly,
all critical discussion of Dickens comes down to this: his
obvious lack of taste and culture. He treats gold and tinsel
with the same fervour, the same feverishness; for he never
has time to stop and calculate. There is in him a feverish
activity, and to nourish it anything serves; just as Cellini,
lacking the bronze for the casting of the Perseus, threw
into the mould pewter platters and any metal he could lay
hands on. There are some lines in one of his letters to
Forster which throw a light on his character:

... however strange it is never to be at rest, and never satisfied, and
ever trying after something that is never reached, and to be always
laden with plot and plan and care and worry, how clear it is that it
must be, and that one is driven by an irresistible might until the
journey is worked out. It is much better to go on and fret, than to
stop and fret. As for repose—for some men there's no such thing in
life.

This restlessness could not but have an influence upon
his vision of the external world—which is that of a reporter,
as indeed he was, with a pencil always ready for jotting
down notes in shorthand. And as a shorthand-writer, it is

well known, Dickens began; the most efficient shorthand-writer in the kingdom. In his world he makes puppets converse with living figures, Mr. Carker with Toots; Nancy in the underworld is side by side with Charles Bates. Restlessness prevents Dickens's pages from ever becoming languid: a feverish agitation permeates plot, dialogue, landscape, communicates an ephemeral liveliness to commonplaces and lifeless passages: so that the most usual effect of his pages is dazzling.

Just as he lacks taste in the choice of his means of expression, accepting the sensational novel for its innate propensity to the dramatic, so he lacks taste also in his choice of emotions, as Lord David Cecil has observed.[46] Charles Reade was a sensationalist, but a virile one: he knew the limits to the portrayal of the pathetic; but Dickens has no restraint; just as anything serves to make up the plot, so is it in the case of pathos; the subtlest and the coarsest means avail him equally. In *Dream-Children* Lamb was able to achieve the highest note of pathos without ever losing his own particular air of chastity, always keeping control over his feelings; so that it is not vulgar tears he calls forth, but a sad and at the same time exalted *Stimmung*, a sublimation which is art. To this, Dickens does indeed attain in the first part of *David Copperfield*. The end of the first chapter of that novel, for example, is very close to Lamb: 'No. I lay in my basket, and my mother lay in her bed; but Betsey Trotwood Copperfield was for ever in the land of dreams and shadows....' This recalls the closing passage of Lamb's *Dream-Children*: 'While I stood gazing, both the children gradually grew fainter to my view, receding and still receding . . . "We are nothing; less than nothing, and dreams. . . ." ' &c. But, side by side with his successes, how many cases there are in which Dickens, dragged on by his fret and fever, exaggerates, over-labours a passage, and produces inferior work! It is as though one of Greuze's pathetic scenes—I am reminded again of the pictorial antecedents of this particular tendency—were taken up again by Boilly, the portrayer of grotesque faces. Yet even this comparison is not really just; for Dickens's caricature is not always so shameless; it is sometimes an insidious thing; his creative energy is such that it deceives the reader, who, for a moment, is drawn along in spite of himself, until, reconsidering the scene after a first impression, he comes to despise the artificial method by which the feeling has been provoked, and includes the whole of Dickens's work in one undiscriminating condemnation, as happened in England at the end of the last century. Dickens is lacking, above all, in moderation: he is not content with stirring the emotions, but has to squeeze out the very last drop. The account of the death and funeral of Little Nell in *The Old Curiosity Shop* is a foretaste of the worst swoonings of that classic of nineteenth-century mawkishness, Edmondo De Amicis's *Cuore*, and vulgarizes a feeling that Lamb would have touched with a few airy lines. One well-known passage of this episode (chap. lxxii) is enough to show how mannered, how oleographic is this pathos of Dickens:

And now the bell—the bell she had so often heard by night and day, and listened to with solemn pleasure almost as a living voice—rang its remorseless toll for her, so young, so beautiful, so good. Decrepit age, and vigorous life, and blooming youth, and helpless infancy, poured forth—on crutches, in the pride of strength and health, in the full blush of promise, in the mere dawn of life—to gather round her tomb. Old men were there, whose eyes were dim and senses failing—grandmothers, who might have died ten years ago, and still been old—the deaf, the blind, the lame, the palsied, the living dead in many shapes and forms, to see the closing of that early grave. What was the death it would shut in, to that which still could crawl and creep above it!

Along the crowded path they bore her now; pure as the newly-fallen snow that covered it; whose day on earth has been as fleeting. Under that porch, where she had sat when Heaven in its mercy brought her to that peaceful spot, she passed again, and the old church received her in its quiet shade.

They carried her to one old nook, where she had many and many a time sat musing, and laid their burden softly on the pavement. The light streamed on it through the coloured window—a window, where the boughs of trees were ever rustling in the summer, and where the birds sang sweetly all day long. With every breath of air that stirred among those branches in the sunshine, some trembling, changing light would fall upon her grave.

Earth to earth, ashes to ashes, dust to dust. Many a young hand dropped in its little wreath, many a stifled sob was heard. Some—and they were not a few—knelt down. All were sincere and truthful in their sorrow.

The service done, the mourners stood apart, and the villagers closed round to look into the grave before the pavement-stone should be replaced. One called to mind how he had seen her sitting on that very spot, and how her book had fallen on her lap, and she was gazing with a pensive face upon the sky. Another told how he had wondered much that one so delicate as she, should be so bold; how she had never feared to enter the church alone at night, but had loved to linger there when all was quiet, and even to climb the tower stair, with no more light than that of the moon rays stealing through the loopholes in the thick old wall. A whisper went about among the oldest there, that she had seen and talked with angels; and when they called to mind how she had looked, and spoken, and her early death, some thought it might be so, indeed. Thus, coming to the grave in little knots, and glancing down, and giving place to others, and falling off in whispering groups of three or four, the church was cleared in time of all but the sexton and the mourning friends.

They saw the vault covered and the stone fixed down. Then, when the dusk of evening had come on, and not a sound disturbed the sacred stillness of the place—when the bright moon poured in her light on tomb and monument, on pillar, wall, and arch, and most of all (it seemed to them) upon her quiet grave—in that calm time, when all outward things and inward thoughts teem with assurances of immortality, and worldly hopes and fears are humbled in the dust before them—then, with tranquil and submissive hearts they turned away, and left the child with God.

Oh! it is hard to take to heart the lesson that such deaths will teach, but let no man reject it, for it is one that all must learn, and is a mighty, universal Truth. When Death strikes down the innocent and young, for every fragile form from which he lets the panting spirit free, a hundred virtues rise, in shapes of mercy, charity, and love, to walk the world, and bless it. Of every tear that sorrowing mortals shed on such green graves, some good is born, some gentler nature comes. In the Destroyer's steps there spring up bright creations that defy his power, and his dark path becomes a way of light to Heaven.[47]

In its way the death of Little Nell is treated with as much exaggeration as that with which Donne, in *First Anniversary*, treated the death of Elizabeth Drury, by whose disappearance the whole universe ceased to exist: two kinds of rhetoric, the seventeenth-century kind, full of conceits, the nineteenth-century, lachrymose. The death of Nell and other pathetic scenes of the same sort have become proverbial as illustrations of Dickens's bad taste; one more quotation will suffice to exemplify that same taste, which was commonly current in the Victorian age—a passage from *Oliver Twist* (chap. xxxv), the dialogue between Harry Maylie and the convalescent Rose:

'I was brought here, by the most dreadful and agonising of all apprehensions,' said the young man; 'the fear of losing the one dear being on whom my every wish and hope are fixed. You had been dying: trembling between earth and heaven. We know that when the young, the beautiful, and good, are visited with sickness, their pure spirits insensibly turn towards their bright home of lasting rest; we know, Heaven help us! that the best and fairest of our kind, too often fade in blooming.'

There were tears in the eyes of the gentle girl, as these words were spoken: and when one fell upon the flower over which she bent, and glistened brightly in its cup, making it more beautiful, it seemed as though the outpouring of her fresh young heart, claimed kindred naturally, with the loveliest things in nature.

And mark the commonplaces of pathos that grace this speech of Harry's:

'. . . Rose, Rose, to know that you were passing away like some soft shadow, which a light from above casts upon the earth . . . to feel that you belonged to that bright sphere whither so many of the fairest and the best have winged their early flight. . . .'

*   *   *   *   *

We have observed Dickens the sensational and Dickens the pathetic, and have mentioned his social crusade: these are the capital letters in his alphabet; and if we are to judge him by these showy characters on his title-page we should certainly find no fault with the taste of the end of the century and the Edwardian era, which, taking Dickens literally, condemned him wholesale. *His* sensationalism—to say the least—is not *our* sensationalism, and even if his skill as a story-teller succeeds in keeping our attention fixed, we have no difficulty in seeing the strings being pulled and smiling at the performance. His campaigns in favour of this or that reform may interest the modern historian, and may even go so far as to lend themselves, as we have seen, to Marxist interpretations; but obviously it is not there that Dickens's art lies. And finally, his pathos no longer moves us, it has an old-fashioned smell about it; and even if the extremes to which Dickens carries all these tendencies, even if his own ardour, seem always to constitute an imposing and genial phenomenon, it is not possible to pass sentence upon his work in its entirety, as a single whole, without wronging the novelist's memory.

The Dickens who appeals to the moderns, on the other hand—the Dickens I have hinted at, more than once; and this is the moment to treat of him at greater length—is the original, the more genuine Dickens, the one who would always have been a writer of the first rank—not a Dickens of minor importance—if the fashion for the serial novel and the course of English social evolution had not directed his activity into paths other than the essay and the *genre* picture. It is not an arbitrary conception of Dickens that we are seeking to carve out from the complete figure of the artist. It is, rather, the Dickens that appears in the foreground of all his novels, the Dickens we remember when the mechanically contrived plots, the melodramatic catastrophes, the outbursts of tears have been cast into oblivion.

There comes into my mind, in this connexion, Breughel's picture of *St. John the Baptist preaching* (Museum of Fine Arts, Budapest). What do we see in this picture? A crowd of people of every social class assembled in a forest, within sight of a pleasant river in which is mirrored a distant town: there are townsmen, artisans, peasants, gypsies, monks of various orders, and our eye runs over the picturesque throng until, in the midst of it, in the background, it picks out the figure of the man who should be the protagonist of the picture, St. John, preaching.[48] Thackeray, in *Vanity Fair*, wrote deliberately a 'novel without a hero' and fixed his whole attention on the study of character—of characters far from heroic. Dickens appears to set great store by the figure of the hero, but his heroes, his protagonists, with the exception of David Copperfield and Pickwick, are puppets; so that his novels, too, in

a different way, end up by being 'novels without a hero'.
Like a Flemish or Dutch painter, the thing that Dickens[49]
concentrates chiefly upon, in itself, is the setting, the
studies of lesser figures. The 'extra' characters stimulate
his imagination in quite a different way from the *dramatis
personae*. Like Jan Steen, who, when he painted *The Marriage of Cana*, was interested not so much in the miracle
as in the picturesque figures crowding the staircase at the
top of which the table is spread. Or Metsu, who, when
engaged in painting *Lazarus and the Rich Man* (about
1654; the picture is at Strasbourg), imagines, certainly, a
sumptuous setting, as iconographic tradition demands; but
the figure that first strikes our fancy is that of the serving-
maid who is solemnly carrying in some succulent dish. And
just as we should not demand religious depth from Steen
and Metsu when they depict a Biblical story, so we must
not demand characters of tragedy from Dickens—even
though he wants to make us believe that terrible tragedies
are his principal business. Dante's Ugolino episode became, in Chaucer, a *genre* picture—a family dying of
hunger; and just as Chaucer excelled in depicting the
characters of his narrators rather than in the tales themselves—the figure of the Wife of Bath is certainly his most
genuine creation—and as Ben Jonson was successful in
his 'humours' and composed, in *Bartholomew Fair*, a play
made up of lively little figures and disjointed episodes—so
we must visualize Dickens in this same English, bourgeois
tradition.

Light is thrown upon Dickens's sources of inspiration
by what J. B. Priestley wrote in an essay on Walter de la
Mare:[50]

There is a lesser order of geniuses who create worlds for themselves that have a distinct life of their own, but are obviously different, running obliquely, from the actual world we know, and it
appears to me that such writers (Dickens is the type) build up their
little universes from their childish impressions and carry forward
with them into manhood their early imaginings and memories.
What they do not understand and cannot enter into imaginatively
during their youth they never do understand, not, at least, for the
purposes of their art. The world of the imaginative child is made up

of impressions that are largely at the mercy of his reading. Dickens
spent his childhood among the odd figures that loafed about Ports-
mouth, Chatham, and Camden Town, and his earliest reading gave
him a pair of spectacles through which these odd figures looked even
more grotesque than they actually were, so that for the remainder
of his life he moved in a world of queer shapes and violent ever-
recurring gestures. Afterwards he met many new types of men and
women, counting some of them among his intimates, that he tried
very earnestly to portray, but he never succeeded in dowering them
with that superhuman vitality which animates his other characters,
for the simple reason that such persons, belonging as they did to
a world he only knew later in life, never entered into his childish
memories and imagination, which represented the animating principle, the pulsating heart, of all his work. A Shakespeare could have
swept them all in, a Dickens could not. One mark of all the writers
who belong to this class is their weakness in portraying normal,
somewhat commonplace and sensible persons, who hardly exist in
a child's world. Figures of terror and figures of fun, fearful or
adorable monsters like Fagin and Micawber or Quilp and Mrs.
Gamp, the vast shadows thrown by a few odd personages in the
flickering taper-light of a child's terror or glee, these alone are the
characters to which they can give an intense life of their own.

If we seek for a moment—by what is certainly an anti-
historical hypothesis—to imagine how Dickens might have
developed in a period of different tastes from that in which
he flourished, we realize, perhaps with some surprise, that
the road which presented itself most naturally to him was
that of the essay on things observed: he was a sublime
reporter, and it is to be regretted that essays like some of
those in his *Uncommercial Traveller* do not form a larger
proportion of his work.[51] Let us see, for instance, how he
talks of the City churches (*City of London Churches*); here
are one or two passages that give the very essence of the
thing described:

The opening of the service recalls my wandering thoughts. I then
find, to my astonishment, that I have been, and still am, taking
a strong kind of invisible snuff, up my nose, into my eyes, and down
my throat. I wink, sneeze, and cough. The clerk sneezes; the
clergyman winks; the unseen organist sneezes and coughs (and
probably winks); all our little party wink, sneeze, and cough. The
snuff seems to be made of the decay of matting, wood, cloth, stone,

iron, earth, and something else. Is the something else, the decay of dead citizens in the vaults below? As sure as Death it is! Not only in the cold, damp February day, do we cough and sneeze dead citizens, all through the service, but dead citizens have got into the very bellows of the organ, and half choked the same. We stamp our feet to warm them, and dead citizens arise in heavy clouds. Dead citizens stick upon the walls, and lie pulverised on the sounding-board over the clergyman's head, and, when a gust of air comes, tumble down upon him. . . .

. . . In other cases, rot and mildew and dead citizens formed the uppermost scent, while, infused into it in a dreamy way not at all displeasing, was the staple character of the neighbourhood. In the churches about Mark Lane, for example, there was a dry whiff of wheat; and I accidentally struck an airy sample of barley out of an aged hassock in one of them. From Rood Lane to Tower Street, and thereabouts, there was often a subtle flavour of wine: sometimes of tea. One church near Mincing Lane smelt like a druggist's drawer. Behind the Monument the service had a flavour of damaged oranges, which, a little further down towards the river, tempered into herrings, and gradually toned into a cosmopolitan blast of fish. In one church, the exact counterpart of the church in the Rake's Progress where the hero is being married to the horrible old lady, there was no speciality of atmosphere, until the organ shook a perfume of hides all over us from some adjacent warehouse.

I said 'things observed': but things observed through a peculiar distorting lens, fantastically distorted. Every artist's imagination distorts, but though within certain limits it is possible to speak of interpretation rather than distortion, Dickens's world is akin to that of Doré, of Hugo, of Breughel, and of the gargoyles on Gothic cathedrals. It has about it some quality of hallucination. That same tendency to the hallucinatory which, when applied to a plot, leads to those monstrous developments already alluded to, creates, when applied to a setting or a character, something more alive than life, sketches outlines with a swift, sure imprint which only a malicious judgement can call caricature.[52]

Dickens has the caricaturist's lightning stroke, his power to make a synthetic recapitulation of a character's picturesque essence. Take, for example, Littimer, Steerforth's manservant: 'every peculiarity that he had he made respectable. If his nose had been upside-down, he would

have made that respectable.' Having laid his finger on the
key of the character, Dickens invents racy variations upon
it: 'When I undrew the curtains and looked out of bed, I
saw him, in an equable temperature of respectability, unaffected by the east wind of January, and not even breathing
frostily, standing my boots right and left in the first dancing
position, and blowing specks of dust off my coat as he laid
it down like a baby.' When he consults his watch, he opens
the lid with as much gravity as if it had been 'an oracular
oyster'. 'Another of his characteristics—no use of superla-
tives. A cool calm medium always. . . . He went out,
shutting the door as delicately as if I had just fallen into
a sweet sleep on which my life depended.' The greatest possible effect is to be obtained by displaying this model servant against the Bohemian background of the Micawber
family, as happens in chapter xxviii. Or consider this convincing description of Mrs. Micawber's voice: '. . . a small,
thin, flat voice, which I remembered to have considered,
when I first knew her, the very table-beer of acoustics'.
Dora's bird-like aunts (*David Copperfield*, chap. xl) are a
caricature such as might be found in Edward Lear's *Book
of Nonsense*. Caricature invests, also, inanimate objects: in
Great Expectations, for instance, a bed is 'a despotic monster
of a four-post bedstead, straddling over the whole place',
the rush-light 'an object like the ghost of a walking-cane'.
In *Edwin Drood* the low travellers' inn, 'The Travellers'
Twopenny', is 'a house all warped and distorted, like the
morals of the travellers'.

    At other times the caricature is of an obvious, farcical
kind, irresistible but cheap—for example, David's aunt's
holy horror of donkeys, and fear that they will trample her
garden:

'I am convinced' said my aunt, laying her hand with melancholy
firmness on the table, 'that Dick's character is not a character to
keep the donkeys off. I am confident he wants strength of purpose.
I ought to have left Janet at home, instead, and then my mind
might perhaps have been at ease. If ever there was a donkey
trespassing on my green,' said my aunt, with emphasis 'there was
one this afternoon at four o'clock. A cold feeling came over me
from head to foot, and I *know* it was a donkey!'

Another recurrent trait in her character is the fear of fires, which provides an easy starting-point for comic passages: each time she hears a vehicle in the distance she thinks it is the fire-engine rushing to put out a fire. The constant harping on such traits causes some of Dickens's characters to look like automata that make the same gesture over and over again. Another comic invention, unfailing in its effect, is the famous one of Spenlow and Jorkins, this also being of the type of mechanical drollery which Bergson once discussed in his well-known essay on laughter. Dickens, in his caricaturist vein, is always ready to invent a comic figure or situation. To quote *David Copperfield* again: 'Mrs. Waterbrook, who was a large lady—or who wore a large dress: I don't exactly know which, for I don't know which was dress and which was lady—came sailing in.' He pullulates with comic inventions which would make the fortune of a film director of today; for instance when David makes his declaration to Dora while the dog barks: 'The more I raved, the more Jip barked. Each of us, in his own way, got more mad every moment.'

And yet it is—let it be said at once—an art of the moment. Dickens presents people with extreme liveliness; he sees them gesticulating and acting, from outside; but he is not in possession of the organic principle that underlies their personalities. Or he thinks to get possession of it by reducing it to the mechanical level of a 'humour' *à la* Ben Jonson.[53] In the case of Uriah Heep, who repeats always the same gestures, the same words—that eternal 'Master-Mister' when he turns to David—he never gets away from these external signs, as though he were afraid of losing his way. It is the same with Quilp, who at every moment feels himself to be dominated by his own private longing to do something fantastic or apelike, and when he speaks to Nell does so in the sugared tones of the Wolf in Little Red Riding-Hood. Even of the period of his youth, the period which, as has been said, left the deepest marks upon him— the period when he lived in contact with the poor—Dickens does not give a realistic picture. Thus his descriptions of London are, *par excellence*, the thing that they set out to be; they extract all the picturesque data from reality and magnify them. Dickens, having stopped at the stage of childish fantasy, was fascinated by dwarfs and giants,[54] by houses made of boats,[55] by wedding-cakes full of spiders,[56] by the trite contrast between spring and death, by puppet-theatres in cemeteries,[57] by impossible analogies and illogical resemblances (of which there are so many in the discourses of Sam Weller), by names like Pumblechook and Gradgrind and Chuzzlewit. One sees here again his kinship with Hugo, the describer of the *cour des miracles*, the lover of names such as Goulatromba, Wapentake, Quasimodo. Except that, whereas Hugo himself speaks, in the first person, the figurative language suggested to him by his observation of the world, Dickens often puts it into the mouths of his characters—Micawber, for instance, or Flora Finching. Both these writers are in favour of violent chiaroscuro. When faced with aspects of life that could not be thus distorted by the imagination, Dickens's art fails. When for example he has to describe a good and virtuous girl like Agnes Wickfield, he gives us, as we have seen, an insipid angel, a wax doll.

Where he is unrivalled is in his descriptions of the chaotic, picturesque, sinister London of 1820–30: this is his background, and such a background would suffice to throw a halo of fable round any story.[58] And the London of Dickens has, in the end, imposed itself upon the imagination of posterity. When Pío Baroja gives a novel the title of *La ciudad de la niebla*, he is thinking, not so much of the real London, as of the phantom city described in the first chapter of *Bleak House*:

London. Michaelmas Term lately over, and the Lord Chancellor sitting in Lincoln's Inn Hall. Implacable November weather. As much mud in the streets as if the waters had but newly retired from the face of the earth, and it would not be wonderful to meet a Megalosaurus, forty feet long or so, waddling like an elephantine lizard up Holborn Hill. Smoke lowering down from chimney-pots, making a soft black drizzle, with flakes of soot in it as big as full-grown snowflakes—gone into mourning, one might imagine, for the death of the sun. Dogs, undistinguishable in mire. Horses, scarcely better; splashed to their very blinkers. Foot passengers, jostling one another's umbrellas, in a general infection of ill-temper, and losing their foot-hold at street-corners, where tens of thousands of other foot passengers have been slipping and sliding since the day broke (if this day ever broke), adding new deposits to the crust upon crust of mud, sticking at those points tenaciously to the pavement, and accumulating at compound interest.

Fog everywhere. Fog up the river, where it flows among green aits and meadows; fog down the river, where it rolls defiled among the tiers of shipping, and the waterside pollutions of a great (and dirty) city. Fog on the Essex marshes, fog on the Kentish heights. Fog creeping into the cabooses of collier-brigs; fog lying out on the yards, and hovering in the rigging of great ships; fog drooping on the gunwales of barges and small boats. Fog in the eyes and throats of ancient Greenwich pensioners, wheezing by the firesides of their wards; fog in the stem and bowl of the afternoon pipe of the wrathful skipper, down in his close cabin; fog cruelly pinching the toes and fingers of his shivering little 'prentice boy on deck. Chance people on the bridges peeping over the parapets into a nether sky of fog, with fog all round them, as if they were up in a balloon, and hanging in the misty clouds.

Gas looming through the fog in divers places in the streets, much as the sun may, from the spongy fields, be seen to loom by husbandman and ploughboy. Most of the shops lighted two hours before their time—as the gas seems to know, for it has a haggard and unwilling look.

The raw afternoon is rawest, and the dense fog is densest, and the muddy streets are muddiest, near that leaden-headed old obstruction, appropriate ornament for the threshold of a leaden-headed old corporation—Temple Bar. And hard by Temple Bar, in Lincoln's Inn Hall, at the very heart of the fog, sits the Lord High Chancellor in his High Court of Chancery.

It was of this city—the modern, bourgeois parallel of the infernal cities described by the epic poets of preceding centuries—that Huysmans was thinking when his hero Des Esseintes, in *A Rebours*, was preparing to undertake a journey to London simply for the sake of seeing something so perversely melancholy and sinister that it would give him a feeling of exaltation:

La lecture de Dickens commença lentement à agir dans un sens inattendu, déterminant des visions de l'existence anglaise qu'il ruminait pendant des heures. . . . Cet abominable temps de brouillard et de pluie aidait encore à ses pensées, en appuyant les souvenirs de ses lectures, en lui mettant la constante image sous les yeux d'un pays de brume et de boue. . . . Un Londres pluvieux, colossal, immense, puant la fonte échauffée et la suie . . . puis des enfilades de docks s'étendaient à perte de vue, pleins de grues, de cabestans, de ballots. . . . Tout cela s'agitait sur des rives, dans des entrepôts gigantesques, baignés par l'eau teigneuse et sourde d'une imaginaire Tamise.

See, for example, again in *Bleak House*, the description of a gloomy quarter of London, Tom-all-alone: the very name seems symbolic of the place itself (chap. xxii); or, in *David Copperfield* (chap. xlvii) the corner of the Thames whither Martha goes to kill herself:

The neighbourhood was a dreary one at that time; as oppressive, sad, and solitary by night, as any about London. There were neither wharves nor houses on the melancholy waste of road near the great blank prison. A sluggish ditch deposited its mud at the prison walls. Coarse grass and rank weeds straggled over all the marshy land in the vicinity. In one part, carcases of houses, inauspiciously begun and never finished, rotted away. In another, the ground was cumbered with rusty iron monsters of steam-boilers, wheels, cranks, pipes, furnaces, paddles, anchors, diving-bells, windmill-sails, and I know not what strange objects, accumulated by some speculator, and grovelling in the dust, underneath which—having sunk into the soil of their own weight in wet weather—they had the appearance of vainly trying to hide themselves. The clash and glare of sundry fiery Works upon the river-side, arose by night to disturb everything except the heavy and unbroken smoke that poured out of their chimneys. Slimy gaps and causeways, winding among old wooden piles, with a sickly substance clinging to the latter, like green hair, and the rags of last year's handbills offering rewards for drowned men fluttering above high-water mark, led down through the ooze and slush to the ebb-tide. There was a story that one of the pits dug for the dead in the time of the Great Plague was hereabout; and a blighting influence seemed to have proceeded from it over the whole place. Or else it looked as if it had gradually decomposed into that nightmare condition, out of the overflowings of the polluted stream.

Or again, this description of poor, unhealthy slum quarters of the town, in *Oliver Twist* (chap. l):

Near to that part of the Thames on which the church at Rother-hithe abuts, where the buildings on the banks are dirtiest and the vessels on the river blackest with the dust of colliers and the smoke of close-built low-roofed houses, there exists, at the present day, the filthiest, the strangest, the most extraordinary of the many localities that are hidden in London, wholly unknown, even by name, to the great mass of its inhabitants.

To reach this place, the visitor has to penetrate through a maze of close, narrow, and muddy streets, thronged by the roughest and poorest of waterside people, and devoted to the traffic they may be supposed to occasion. The cheapest and least delicate provisions are heaped in the shops; the coarsest and commonest articles of wearing apparel dangle at the salesman's door, and stream from the house-parapet and windows. Jostling with unemployed labourers of the lowest class, ballast-heavers, coal-whippers, brazen women, ragged children, and the very raff and refuse of the river, he makes his way with difficulty along, assailed by offensive sights and smells from the narrow alleys which branch off on the right and left, and deafened by the clash of ponderous waggons that bear great piles of merchandise from the stacks of warehouses that rise from every corner. Arriving, at length, in streets remoter and less-frequented than those through which he has passed, he walks beneath tottering house-fronts projecting over the pavement, dismantled walls that seem to totter as he passes, chimneys half crushed half hesitating to fall, windows guarded by rusty iron bars that time and dirt have almost eaten away, and every imaginable sign of desolation and neglect.

In such a neighbourhood, beyond Dockhead in the borough of Southwark, stands Jacob's Island, surrounded by a muddy ditch, six or eight feet deep, and fifteen or twenty wide when the tide is in, once called Mill Pond, but known in these days as Folly Ditch. It is a creek or inlet from the Thames, and can always be filled at high water by opening the sluices at the Lead Mills from which it took its old name. At such times, a stranger, looking from one of the wooden bridges thrown across it at Mill-lane, will see the inhabitants of the houses on either side lowering from their back doors and windows, buckets, pails, domestic utensils of all kinds, in which to haul the water up; and when his eye is turned from these operations to the houses themselves, his utmost astonishment will be excited by the scene before him. Crazy wooden galleries common to the backs of half-a-dozen houses, with holes from which to look upon the slime beneath; windows, broken and patched: with poles thrust out, on which to dry the linen that is never there; rooms so small, so filthy, so confined, that the air would seem too tainted even for the dirt and squalor which they shelter; wooden chambers thrusting themselves out above the mud, and threatening to fall into it—as some have done; dirt-besmeared walls and decaying founda-

tions; every repulsive lineament of poverty, every loathsome indication of filth, rot, and garbage; all these ornament the banks of Folly
Ditch.

Similar pictures of prodigious desolation are to be found
in every one of Dickens's novels, for example in *The Old
Curiosity Shop*, chap. xv, where it is easy to observe how
Dickens achieves his effects by a bewildering accumulation
of significant details, presenting a tightly packed, swarming, vibrant whole. In this novel, especially, Dickens was
the first to depict the new landscape that had been created
in the suburbs of large towns and in mining districts by the
industrial civilization then coming to birth. In chapter xliv
we have the description of a foundry, a composition which,
like so many others by Dickens of the same type, later
found its pictorial equivalent in Doré's *London* illustrations; and in chapter xlv there is this description of the
suburb of an industrial town:

A long suburb of red brick houses,—some with patches of garden-
ground, where coal-dust and factory smoke darkened the shrinking
leaves, and coarse rank flowers; and where the struggling vegetation
sickened and sank under the hot breath of kiln and furnace, making
them by its presence seem yet more blighting and unwholesome
than in the town itself,—a long, flat, straggling suburb passed, they
came by slow degrees upon a cheerless region, where not a blade of
grass was seen to grow; where not a bud put forth its promise in the
spring; where nothing green could live but on the surface of the
stagnant pools, which here and there lay idly sweltering by the
black roadside.

Advancing more and more into the shadow of this mournful
place, its dark depressing influence stole upon their spirits, and filled
them with a dismal gloom. On every side, and far as the eye could
see into the heavy distance, tall chimneys, crowding on each other,
and presenting that endless repetition of the same dull, ugly form,
which is the horror of oppressive dreams, poured out their plague
of smoke, obscured the light, and made foul the melancholy air.
On mounds of ashes by the wayside, sheltered only by a few rough
boards, or rotten pent-house roofs, strange engines spun and writhed
like tortured creatures; clanking their iron chains, shrieking in their
rapid whirl from time to time as though in torment unendurable,
and making the ground tremble with their agonies. Dismantled
houses here and there appeared, tottering to the earth, propped up

by fragments of others that had fallen down, unroofed, windowless, blackened, desolate, but yet inhabited. Men, women, children, wan in their looks and ragged in attire, tended the engines, fed their tributary fires, begged upon the road, or scowled half-naked from the doorless houses. Then came more of the wrathful monsters, whose like they almost seemed to be in their wildness and their untamed air, screeching and turning round and round again; and still, before, behind, and to the right and left, was the same interminable perspective of brick towers, never ceasing in their black vomit, blasting all things living or inanimate, shutting out the face of day, and closing in on all these horrors with a dense dark cloud.

But night-time in this dreadful spot!—night, when the smoke was changed to fire; when every chimney spirted up its flame; and places, that had been dark vaults all day, now shone red-hot, with figures moving to and fro within their blazing jaws, and calling to one another with hoarse cries—night, when the noise of every strange machine was aggravated by the darkness; when the people near them looked wilder and more savage; when bands of unemployed labourers paraded in the roads, or clustered by torchlight round their leaders, who told them in stern language of their wrongs, and urged them on to frightful cries and threats; when maddened men, armed with sword and firebrand, spurning the tears and prayers of women who would restrain them, rushed forth on errands of terror and destruction, to work no ruin half so surely as their own —night, when carts came rumbling by, filled with rude coffins (for contagious disease and death had been busy with the living crops); when orphans cried, and distracted women shrieked and followed in their wake—night, when some called for bread, and some for drink to drown their cares; and some with tears, and some with staggering feet, and some with bloodshot eyes, went brooding home —night, which, unlike the night that Heaven sends on earth, brought with it no peace, nor quiet, nor signs of blessed sleep—who shall tell the terrors of the night to that young wandering child?[59]

In this last passage the arrangement of the sentences becomes precipitate, eloquent, almost lyrical, to evoke an apocalyptic vision, a vision already seen, even at the beginning of the century (in 1811) by Robert Southey in the Black Country: 'There is something very striking in that sort of hell above ground—hills of scoria, an atmosphere of smoke, and huge black piles, consisting chiefly of chimneys and furnaces, grouped together in the finest style of the damnable picturesque.' It was exactly this 'damnable

picturesque' that Dickens made into his own special province: he excels particularly in his descriptions of desolate
places; for instance our memories of *Great Expectations* are
all coloured by the powerful initial picture of the dreary
marshland, and by that other picture of Miss Havisham's
sinister house and of the empty, abandoned brewery. There
is nothing arbitrary in seeing a connexion between this
taste for the gloomy and Dickens's infatuation for reading
terrifying scenes from his own novels, of which we have
already spoken.

Elsewhere, it is quiet corners of London that Dickens
describes—no less melancholy in their peacefulness than
was the infernal scene quoted above, in its turmoil of agitation. Here is a little stunted garden at the back of one of
those typical London houses (*Nicholas Nickleby*, chap. ii):

Some London houses have a melancholy little plot of ground
behind them, usually fenced in by four high whitewashed walls, and
frowned upon by stacks of chimneys: in which there withers on,
from year to year, a crippled tree, that makes a show of putting
forth a few leaves late in autumn when other trees shed theirs, and,
drooping in the effort, lingers on, all crackled and smoke-dried, till
the following season, when it repeats the same process, and perhaps
if the weather be particularly genial, even tempts some rheumatic
sparrow to chirrup in its branches. People sometimes call these dark
yards 'gardens'; it is not supposed that they were ever planted, but
rather that they are pieces of unreclaimed land, with the withered
vegetation of the original brick-field. No man thinks of walking in
this desolate place, or of turning it to any account. A few hampers,
half-a-dozen broken bottles, and such-like rubbish, may be thrown
there, when the tenant first moves in, but nothing more; and there
they remain until he goes away again: the damp straw taking just as
long to moulder as it thinks proper: and mingling with the scanty
box, and stunted everbrowns, and broken flower-pots, that are
scattered mournfully about—a prey to 'blacks' and dirt.

Fountain Court (in *Martin Chuzzlewit*, chap. xlv) offers
a similar picture; or, in *Nicholas Nickleby* again, see the
description of City Square (chap. xxxvii) or that of 'The
Rules' near the debtors' prison (chap. xlvi), or, finally, the
description of Snow Hill (chap. iv), another sinister corner
of London near Newgate, the character of which, in

comparison with its immaculate name, and linked, in piquant contrast, with the name of the Saracen's Head Inn, could not fail to appeal to Dickens's acute sense of the picturesque.

Dickens invests places and aspects of landscape almost with personalities, so that they become coloured by good or evil intentions—a kind of anthropomorphism which Proust was later to derive from him.[60] We have already seen examples of this anthropomorphism when we spoke of caricature extended to inanimate objects; representative of all is the half-page containing the description of Podsnap's silver, which seems to reflect the character of its owners (in *Our Mutual Friend*, chap. xi):

> Hideous solidity was the characteristic of the Podsnap plate. Everything was made to look as heavy as it could, and to take up as much room as possible. Everything said boastfully, 'Here you have as much of me in my ugliness as if I were only lead; but I am so many ounces of precious metal worth so much an ounce;— wouldn't you like to melt me down?' A corpulent straggling epergne, blotched all over as if it had broken out in an eruption rather than been ornamented, delivered this address from an unsightly silver platform in the centre of the table. Four silver wine-coolers, each furnished with four staring heads, each head obtrusively carrying a big silver ring in each of its ears, conveyed the sentiment up and down the table, and handed it on to the pot-bellied silver salt-cellars. All the big silver spoons and forks widened the mouths of the company expressly for the purpose of thrusting the sentiment down their throats with every morsel they ate.
>
> The majority of the guests were like the plate, and included several heavy articles weighing ever so much. . . .

Just as Dickens knows how to find the picturesque detail in inanimate things, so he also finds, as we have already noted, the picturesque feature, the lively, memorable phrase, in conversations: his pages are a series of *genre* pictures. It has been justly observed that it is principally the minor and the least important artists who hand on to posterity the flavour peculiar to a period, its manners, its feeling towards its surroundings, whereas the great artists seem to be outside any specific place or time, to be universal. Dickens, in this respect, must be classed with the small rather than the great masters. Where but in a Victorian keepsake should we find a scene that 'dates' as this one does (*Old Curiosity Shop*, chap. xxv)? 'She took some needle-work from her basket, and sat herself down upon a stool beside the lattice, where the honeysuckle and woodbine entwined their tender stems, and stealing into the room filled it with their delicious breath.' And the description of David Copperfield, as a child, in church during the sermon, is a perfect parallel to a picture by George Cruik-shank, *The Disturber Detected*.[61] In *David Copperfield*, again, this little picture of David and Emily sitting on the step of the house made out of a boat, which might well have been painted by William Mulready:

> The best times were when she sat quietly at work in the doorway, and I sat on the wooden step at her feet, reading to her. It seems to me, at this hour, that I have never seen such sunlight as on those bright April afternoons; that I have never seen such a sunny little figure as I used to see, sitting in the doorway of the old boat; that I have never beheld such sky, such water, such glorified ships sailing away into golden air.

Here is another little picture from *David Copperfield* which might be entitled 'The Orphan':

> The room was as neat as Janet or my aunt. As I laid down my pen, a moment since, to think of it, the air from the sea came blowing in again, mixed with the perfume of the flowers; and I saw the old-fashioned furniture brightly rubbed and polished, my aunt's inviolable chair and table by the round green fan in the bow-window, the drugget-covered carpet, the cat, the kettle-holder, the two canaries, the old china, the punch-bowl full of dried rose-leaves, the tall press guarding all sorts of bottles and pots, and, wonderfully out of keeping with the rest, my dusty self upon the sofa, taking note of everything.

The next picture, again from the same novel, might be entitled 'The Unfaithful Wife', and might have found its painter in Augustus Egg. Dr. Strong was reading a 'state-ment of a theory out of [his] interminable Dictionary', while his wife, who has just taken leave of Jack Maldon,[62] sits on a stool at his feet:

> . . . She was looking up at him. But, with such a face as I never saw. It was so beautiful in its form, it was so ashy pale, it was so

fixed in its abstraction, it was so full of a wild, sleep-walking, dreamy horror of I don't know what. The eyes were wide open, and her brown hair fell in two rich clusters on her shoulders, and on her white dress, disordered by the want of the lost ribbon. Distinctly as I recollect her look, I cannot say of what it was expressive. I cannot even say of what it is expressive to me now, rising again before my older judgment. Penitence, humiliation, shame, pride, love, and trustfulness—I see them all; and in them all, I see that horror of I don't know what.

This one is an interior in the Dutch taste:

It was not in the coffee-room that I found Steerforth expecting me, but in a snug private apartment, red-curtained and Turkey-carpeted, where the fire burnt bright, and a fine hot breakfast was set forth on a table covered with a clean cloth; and a cheerful miniature of the room, the fire, the breakfast, Steerforth, and all, was shining in the little round mirror over the sideboard.

Another Victorian keepsake picture, this one of Dora Spenlow against the background of a greenhouse:

We loitered along in front of [the geraniums], and Dora often stopped to admire this one or that one, and I stopped to admire the same one, and Dora, laughing, held the dog up childishly, to smell the flowers; and if we were not all three in Fairyland, certainly *I* was. The scent of a geranium leaf, at this day, strikes me with a half comical, half serious wonder as to what change has come over me in a moment; and then I see a straw hat and blue ribbons, and a quantity of curls, and a little black dog being held up, in two slender arms, against a bank of blossoms and bright leaves.

Dora always carries with her an exquisitely Victorian atmosphere. To make a signal to David, for instance, she hangs up a cage of little birds at the drawing-room window; and when David asks her if she can love a beggar, the girl begs him not to be 'dreadful':

'Don't talk about being poor, and working hard!' said Dora, nestling closer to me. 'Oh, don't, don't!'

'My dearest love,' said I, 'the crust well-earned—'

'Oh, yes; but I don't want to hear any more about crusts!' said Dora. 'And Jip must have a mutton-chop every day at twelve, or he'll die!'

This passage recalls Frith's picture *The Crossing-Sweeper*

—the ragged, bare-footed urchin sweeping the street for
the lovely lady to cross it; she raises her elegant skirts as
she does so, and her face is framed in lace and bows of
ribbon—a picture that is to such an extent the quintessence
of the Victorian scene that it was appropriately chosen for
the jacket of Professor G. M. Young's book, *Victorian
England, the Portrait of an Age.*

And the house of the newly married couple, David and
Dora, with everything new and shining, the flowers on the
carpets looking as if freshly gathered, the green leaves on
the wallpaper as if they had just come out, and the spotless
muslin of the curtains, and the 'blushing rose-coloured
furniture', and Dora's garden hat with blue ribbons hanging on the peg, and the guitar-case: what more typical
interior could be imagined?

Another little picture, still from *David Copperfield*,
which might have, as title, 'The Wanderer' (Peggotty in
search of his niece):

'When I come to any town,' he pursued, 'I found the inn, and
waited about the yard till someone turned up (some one mostly did)
as know'd English. Then I told how that I was on my way to seek
my niece, and they told me what manner of gentlefolks was in the
house, and I waited to see any as seemed like her, going in or out.
When it warn't Em'ly, I went on agen. By little and little, when
I come to a new village or that, among the poor people, I found they
know'd about me. They would set me down at their cottage doors,
and give me what-not fur to eat and drink, and show me where to
sleep; and many a woman, Mas'r Davy, as has had a daughter of
about Em'ly's age, I've found a waiting for me, at Our Saviour's
Cross outside the village, fur to do me sim'lar kindnesses. Some has
had daughters as was dead. And God only knows how good them
mothers was to me! . . . They would often put their children—
partic'lar their little girls,' said Mr. Peggotty, 'upon my knee; and
many a time you might have seen me sitting at their doors, when
night was coming on, a'most as if they'd been my darling's children.
Oh, my darling!'

A touching picture, the desolate man with the children
on his knee, at the door of these humble cottages; a Biedermeier picture, recalling the little scenes of Waldmüller,
Danhauser, and Peter Fendi.

There are many *genre* pictures from Dickens's novels
that linger in the memory—David Copperfield dining at
the inn and allowing the cunning waiter to carry off his
portions of food, Pickwick stumbling into a lady's bedroom, and a great many others whose flavour is all in the
words which the novelist puts into his characters' mouths:
triumphs not of psychology but of style, for Dickens has
the gift of the genial stroke of humour, as when, in *Martin
Chuzzlewit*, Mrs. Gamp, speaking of the wickedness of
Mrs. Prig, says in an unwitting parody of the Biblical style:
'But the words she spoke of Mrs. Harris lambs could not
forgive . . . nor worms forget', or when she makes the
pronouncement: 'Rich folks may ride on camels but it
ain't so easy for 'em to see out of a needle's eye.' Remarks
in which the blunder has about it an almost metaphysical
lustre. It is thus when Bumble, in *Oliver Twist*, gets angry
with the poor who never stop asking for food and coal:
'Give 'em an apron full of coals to-day, and they'll come
back for another the day after to-morrow, as brazen as
alabaster', in which the absurd juxtaposition of brass
and alabaster mingles with the colour contrast between
alabaster and coal, so that at first one thinks for a moment
that it is a faulty recollection of phrase (such as, e.g. 'a skin
as fair as alabaster') that has caused the amusing verbal
catastrophe. Sometimes a simple juxtaposition of words
produces an astonishment of the kind that was so dear to
the hearts of the Baroque school of writers. On the subject
of Peggotty's snoring, David says (chap. iii): 'I could not
have believed unless I had heard her do it, that one defence-
less woman could have snored so much.' And when Peggotty
the sailor washes himself in hot water, he comes out 'so
rubicund, that I couldn't help thinking his face had this in
common with the lobsters, crabs, and crawfish—that it
went into the hot water very black and came out very red'.
Dickens shares the taste for the paradoxical comparison
with the metaphysical writers, and in this baroque tendency
he again resembles Victor Hugo. When, for example,
David and Little Emily are sitting side by side on their
little locker, with Mr. Peggotty and Ham smiling at
them: 'They had something of the sort of pleasure in us,

I suppose, that they might have had in a pretty toy, or a pocket model of the Colosseum.'

Great art, but wholly external: picturesque stage settings of squalid town life; picturesque little *genre* scenes, pathetic, comic, or sentimental; picturesque passages of dialogue.[63] The picturesque is a bizarre design or pattern that the eye of a certain type of artist discovers in things: at farthest, such an artist will reach the point of seeing, in some object or arrangement of objects, some kind of allusion to a spiritual and moral world which he is incapable of representing by any other means except conventionally. The minuteness of Dickens's symbolism recalls Hogarth, the Hogarth of the breakfast scene in *Marriage à-la-mode*; so in *David Copperfield* (chap. viii), the rooks' nests torn down by the wind are the desolate symbol of Copperfield's own destroyed nest; the sheet of paper covered with drawings of skeletons that Traddles gives David to comfort him after his mother is dead, is a mannerism on the part of Traddles which all at once becomes significant; and a whole list of other analogous symbols might be made from the same novel—the appearance of Emily accompanied by the hammering on the coffins at the end of the courtyard; the blind beggar whom David finds under Agnes's windows, who murmurs: 'Blind! blind! blind!', the word describing David's blindness in not seeing that Agnes is the woman he ought to love; Uriah Heep's old mother watching David and Agnes while she plies her knitting-needles at something that looks like a net ('she showed in the firelight like an ill-looking enchantress, baulked as yet by the radiant goodness opposite, but getting ready for a cast of her net by-and-by'); and in *Great Expectations*, Miss Havisham's house with its walled-up windows and gratings and its front door barred with chains, symbols of its owner's spiritual confinement. The eloquence of external things is exploited by Dickens just as it is in our own day by film directors, who isolate an object, a significant detail, to make it say something that words could not express. And the measure of Dickens's art can be given by a comparison between a passage from *King Lear* (Act v, scene iii) and a passage from *The Old Curiosity Shop*.

And my poor fool is hang'd! [says the old King] No, no, no life!
Why should a dog, a horse, a rat, have life,
And thou no breath at all? Thou'lt come no more,
Never, never, never, never, never!

The cry is human, direct, utterly natural, universal: it was
written in the seventeenth century; it might have been
written today. And now we are in Little Nell's room, and
she is dead: 'Her little bird—a poor slight thing the pressure of a finger would have crushed—was stirring nimbly in
its cage; and the strong heart of its child-mistress was mute
and motionless for ever.' This little allegorical picture,
with its suggestion of an interior and its somewhat laboured
antithesis, could have been conceived only by a Biedermeier artist, with his eye open to every possible picturesque
contrast.

William Makepeace Thackeray

WE are so accustomed to the Dickens–Thackeray contrast that, if we seek to find, in the one, the characteristics of the Victorian bourgeois outlook, we might well think that the other must necessarily be outside its range. It is not, in fact, possible to see history thus in black and white, after the manner of Macaulay: Victorian characteristics are to be found in both of them, and if both—as was bound to happen with original writers —dissociate themselves, in some respects, from their surroundings, the stress of reaction is more decided in Dickens, who, as we have seen, felt more sympathy for the working class, than in Thackeray, whose reaction against snob conventionalism was made, in reality, in the name of another kind of conventionalism, that of disillusioned common sense. Thackeray, to put it briefly, was an ironist through repressed romanticism. His character can be grasped at one glance in a photograph taken during his second lecture tour in America:[64] the curve of the tight lips is an unmistakable evidence of repression; the eyes, with their hard, penetrating look enlivened by an amused attentiveness, express an ironic, humorous view of the world; the indeterminate arch of the eyebrows, with its hint of emotionalism and excitability and its clouded, almost lachrymose air, contrasts with the half-pitiless, half-amused expression of the eyes; above all, the right-hand half of the face wears a twisted, detached smile, while the left half is solemn and severe. Thackeray was solidly anchored to the predominant bourgeois ethics of his time, and derived material for caricature from his moralistic abhorrence of all excess.

Let us first take a brief glance at his life. Born at Alipur, a suburb of Calcutta, on July 18th, 1811, Thackeray lost, at the age of four, his father (who, following the family tradition,[65] had set out to make his fortune in the service of the East India Company); he was sent to be educated in England. During the voyage the ship touched at St. Helena, and the child was taken by the native servant for a long walk over rocks and hills, to see a garden in which a man was walking. The servant said to him: 'That is he! That is Bonaparte! He eats three sheep every day, and all the little children he can lay hands on!' This was the first view Thackeray had of a 'hero': and it was to colour his conception of heroism and superman-ism for the whole of his life.[66] Entrusted to the care of relations, Thackeray spent his childhood almost exclusively in the company of women, amongst whom was a great-grandmother who was a curious relic of the eighteenth century (can this perhaps have contributed to Thackeray's predilection for that century of harmonious elegance?). The neighbourhood (Fareham) appears to have been inhabited chiefly by the widows and spinster daughters of naval officers; upon the walls of every respectable house hung large portraits of officers in uniform, amongst pictures of shipwrecks and naval battles; Thackeray's grandmother, an imposing old lady with a lofty halo of white hair and a face still beautiful, carried a long tortoiseshell cane, and handled her snuff-box and gold toothpick with exquisite grace. This limitation to female society made Thackeray incapable of mixing with his contemporaries at Charterhouse, where he was from 1822 to 1828: the sense of loneliness and of actual despair which he felt during those years at school was not to be without effect upon his future attitude towards the world; his gentle ways, his lack of skill at games and his short sight made him an obvious victim for coarser, more robust boys. The brutality of certain aspects of English public school life left indelible traces upon him, for he had his nose broken in a tussle with one of his companions (George Stovin Venables, who remained his friend all his life), and suffered permanent disfigurement. This disfigurement increased his abnormal sensitiveness which, later on, made him shy of revealing himself openly and caused him to adopt pseudonyms—although he claimed that he took refuge in this expedient so as not to lose the esteem of the public, which would not tolerate that the same author should produce, at the same time, works of quite different character and in periodicals of varying prestige. The disfigurement extended its effect, with the years, to the expression of his whole face. Being inclined to imagine that his appearance aroused a feeling of ridicule, Thackeray erected a defence of sardonic wit, affecting to mock at himself in order to forestall others, and mocking at the weak points of others so that no one should feel himself to be without defects or superior. Hence his sarcasm, to which his face lent itself only too well, hence his agony if obliged to make a public speech, and hence also those outbursts of rage whenever he was unkindly criticized, and, on the other hand, his pathetic gratitude if someone showed no sign of considering him different to other people, especially if that someone was a pretty woman.[67]

Thackeray's mother had married in 1818 a major of the Bengal Engineers, Henry Carmichael-Smyth, whose earlier wooing of her had been thwarted by her family.[68] The dependence of the orphan on his mother had been aggravated by his separation from her when, at the age of six, he was sent home to England: in fact, that separation made such a deep impression on him that throughout his life Thackeray betrayed an almost pathological aversion to saying good-bye, and whenever the relation between mother and child became his theme in one of his novels, he indulged in an uncontrolled mawkishness which went beyond the average Victorian sensibility in such cases. Mr. J. Y. T. Greig[69] has convincingly argued that by 'possessing' him, Thackeray's mother arrested his emotional growth, so that at forty he was still almost as firmly tied to her as he was at fourteen: his own marriage, which might have freed him from such dependence, came to an end tragically, as we shall see.[70] Much of Thackeray's conformism with Victorian points of view (as, for instance, his attitude to women and sex) was due, consciously or unconsciously, to the continuing influence of his mother.[71]

In 1821 Mrs. Carmichael-Smyth had come back to England and had settled with her husband first at Addiscombe, then at Ottery St. Mary, where Thackeray joined her: he was later to describe this period in *Pendennis*. But he did not stay long with the Carmichael-Smyths; in February 1829 he entered Trinity College, Cambridge.

He remained at the University only until the Easter vacation of 1830, profiting little from studies towards which he did not feel attracted; there he came to know a few contemporaries who were destined to become famous, especially Tennyson and Edward FitzGerald; he took pleasure in literary conversations and debates, and contributed humorous verse (which he had started composing very early in life), together with lively caricatures, to a university paper, the *Snob*.[72] It was chiefly at this period that he read and assimilated the works of Swift, Sterne, Addison, Steele, Pope, and Goldsmith. He had spent the summer vacation of 1829 in Paris, studying French and German; in 1830 he was at Cologne and, more especially, at Weimar, where he stayed several months, enjoying the simplicity and affability of that little court, and coming into contact with Goethe, but admiring Schiller more highly, 'whose religion and morals were unexceptionable'.[73] He had ideas of a diplomatic career, but decided on the law.

In 1831 he started upon his legal career in the Middle Temple, but preferred the society of men of letters and artists, so that when, in 1832, he came into possession of his patrimony, he acquired and directed a literary journal (the *National Standard and Journal of Literature*), to which he contributed letters from Paris. There he was now studying painting; but after a year he felt discouraged—so much so that he wrote on one occasion in the year 1835 to his friend Frank Stone, the painter: 'I have become latterly so disgusted with myself and art and everything belonging to it, that for a month past I have been lying on sofas reading novels, and never touching a pencil.' Partly through the unfortunate enterprise of the journal (which ceased publication in February 1834, after only one year of life), and, even more, through gambling,[74] he lost almost the whole of the estate he had inherited from his father, and was reduced to living upon his talent as a journalist and caricaturist. He suggested to Dickens, after the death of Robert Seymour in April 1836, that he should illustrate the *Pickwick Papers*, but without result; in the same year he published his first little volume (London and Paris): *Flore et Zéphyr*, eight lithographs of satirical drawings; he also

19. CRUIKSHANK. The Runaway Knock

20. MARGARET GILLIES. William and Mary Wordsworth (*Grasmere,
Wordsworth's House. By courtesy of the Trustees of Dove Cottage*)

became Paris correspondent of the *Constitutional*, an ultra-liberal paper to the foundation of which his stepfather had contributed. Relying upon his salary from this paper, Thackeray in that same year married Isabella Getkin Creagh Shawe, daughter of an Irish colonel who had seen service in India. But the paper failed after six months, almost ruining its backer (Smyth, prototype of Colonel Newcome in *The Newcomes*, resembled the hero of that novel in his weakness for absurd speculations). Thackeray decided to take upon himself the heavy burden of paying the debts incurred by his stepfather in this disastrous undertaking, but only succeeded in doing so completely with the success of *Vanity Fair*, since his first works, such as *The Yellowplush Papers*, written for *Fraser's Magazine* in 1838 (in which high society is viewed through the mentality of a servant, Mr. Yellowplush), and *The Paris Sketch Book* (1840, under the pseudonym of Michael Angelo Titmarsh) did not have a large audience. To make Thackeray's situation even more painful, a domestic tragedy befell him in 1840: his wife, after giving birth to a third daughter (the second had died in 1839) became mentally afflicted, and, notwithstanding repeated attempts at treatment—Thackeray took her to Paris, and later to Germany—she never recovered her reason for the whole of the rest of her life (she lived till 1894). No wonder therefore, observes Professor Lionel Stevenson,[75] that Thackeray came to look upon life with bitterness, after such blows had fallen upon him. As a child, having lost his father, he had been taken from the beloved family circle to be brought up amongst strangers; when his mother returned to England, with another husband, Thackeray merely spent brief holidays with his family. At school, as already described, a misfortune altered his physical appearance and rendered it grotesque; then, as he was entering upon the enjoyment of a life of leisure and dilettante interests, he had lost his patrimony mainly through the ill-advised confidence that he himself and his relations had placed in their fellow men; and, being thus cut adrift from the normal security of his social class, had found himself obliged to earn his living by his pen because he had no qualifications for any other profession. Having married and settled down, he had seen—after a very few years of happiness and a struggle to provide for the needs of his new family on an extremely modest income—the ruin of his family life through his wife's losing her reason, an affliction worse than her death would have been. Certainly there had been enough to give him a feeling of disillusioned detachment from life, the attitude of a puppet-showman who looks upon his own world as a half-serious melodrama.

Having parted from his wife and entrusted his daughters to the care of their grandparents, Thackeray sought to maintain himself on his journalistic earnings, publishing, in various newspapers and reviews (among them *Punch*, to which he was invited to contribute in 1842, the year after its foundation), under various pseudonyms (he had caught the habit of using pseudonyms from the example of William Maginn, editor of *Fraser's Magazine*), critical articles, fantasies, sketches, and novels; amongst the sketches the most famous are those which appeared in *Punch* in 1846–7 (*The Snobs of England by One of Themselves*) and were reprinted in 1848 as *The Book of Snobs*, in which, under the common denominator of 'snobism',[76] the author satirizes, harshly and in detail, all the failings of the English, or indeed of humanity (he concluded that it was perhaps impossible for a Briton not to be a snob, to some extent): thus *The Book of Snobs* carries on the tradition of Erasmus's *In Praise of Folly*. Although Thackeray takes up the attitude of a humorist, there is very little humour, and even less good-humour, in these sketches by an arid, exasperated pen. He deserved the name better for the facile parodies of novelists which appeared in *Punch* in 1847 (the *Prize Novelists*, slight, tasty trifles in their day, which any unusual journalist might have written); for the short burlesques *A Legend of the Rhine* (1845), *Rebecca and Rowena: a Romance upon Romance* (1850: a re-elaboration of *Proposal for a Continuation of 'Ivanhoe'*, published in *Fraser's Magazine* in 1846); for the grotesque tale *The Rose and the Ring, or The History of Prince Giglio and Prince Bulbo: a Fireside Pantomime for great and small Children* (1855); and for his comic verses, although the best of these, the

Ballad of Bouillabaisse (which appeared in *Punch* in 1849)—
on the memories recalled by a certain corner in a restaurant
in Paris where the writer, in company with his young
wife and his friends, had been in the habit of eating
bouillabaisse—was, as we shall see, more bitter than gay.
Indeed, as has been observed,[77] as a novelist Thackeray
matured slowly; he arrived at literature through disappointment in his own attempts at painting: he developed
a talent, not as a painter, but as a caricaturist (though, with
regard to drawing, he remained always an amateur), and
his first literary productions are also those of a caricaturist
—productions which show not the slightest sign of the
future inventor of characters and plots. Even with *Vanity
Fair*, his first idea was to write a humorous work: the sub-
title of the first instalment was: *Pen and Pencil Sketches of
English Society.*

Originally intended as caricature was his first novel,
The Luck of Barry Lyndon (it appeared under this title in
Fraser's Magazine in 1844; it was later entitled *The Memoirs
of Barry Lyndon, Esq., By Himself*); written in reaction
against the romantic portrayal of criminals which, deriving
from Byron, continued in Bulwer Lytton and others, it had
no success. Like Fielding's Jonathan Wild, the protagonist
of Thackeray's novel, an impudent Irishman, recounts the
deeds in his career as adventurer and rascal as though they
were the most natural things in the world. Thus caricature of a particular *genre*, the Newgate School, started
Thackeray on the form of the novel. An adventuress is
also the leading figure in the novel that made Thackeray
famous, *Vanity Fair*, which was published in monthly instalments from January 1847 to July 1848, according to the
method made fashionable by Dickens.

The success of *Vanity Fair* was gradual; Thackeray's contemporaries weighed his merits against those of Dickens,
and, while the latter remained by far the more popular
novelist, Thackeray appealed to the more cultivated public
and the critics. In May 1848 he was called to the Bar,
probably with the intention of obtaining a post in the
magistrature with the help of his friend Monckton Milnes
(later Lord Houghton): he would thus have been following

in the footsteps of Fielding. But since, in order to be nominated, it was necessary to have practised at the Bar for seven years, the project came to nothing. Thackeray, having reduced his contributions to *Punch* (they ceased altogether in 1854; in 1851 he had declared his disagreement with the paper on account of its attacks on Napoleon III), now dedicated himself to the composition of novels. For many years his amorous devotion to the wife of a clergyman, Mrs. Jane Octavia Brookfield, a chronic invalid, was the only support he had in his loneliness and depression. His platonic relations with this lady, whom he took pleasure in calling his sister, drew remonstrances from her uncle, Henry Hallam the historian, who tore asunder the modest veil that covered the relationship and declared its true nature, which Thackeray, making the husband's approval the excuse of his platonic courtship, had been repressing. Later, however, his relations with the husband deteriorated, and Mrs. Brookfield resigned herself to acting the part of the loyal wife and breaking off her amorous friendship with Thackeray. Kept in check by the Victorian code of manners, they suffered and in the end consoled themselves with the smug pride of having remained virtuous.

Vanity Fair was followed by *Pendennis* (published in instalments, 1848–50), a kind of pendant to its contemporary *David Copperfield*, and itself by no means devoid of melodramatic elements which, though not at all in harmony with the peaceful, bourgeois style of the book, were demanded by the taste of the period—such as the violent scene between Major Pendennis and his servant Morgan, leading to the unmasking of the latter; the discovery, on the part of Foker, that Altamont-Amory is Blanche's father; the further identification of Altamont with an escaped convict, thanks to a tell-tale tattooed arm—the kind of recognition-scene that formed the mainstay of Dickens's novels. The place of Agnes in the novel by Dickens is taken, in Thackeray's, by Laura, in whom Pendennis finally recognizes the ideal mate—the modest girl who would be satisfied to act as servant to Pen and his future wife, simply in order to stay near him. 'For years I

had an angel under my tent, and let her go.' 'And you are
the dearest and best of women—the dearest, the dearest
and the best. Teach me my duty. Pray for me that I may
do it—pure heart. God bless you—God bless you, my
sister': these are words that immediately make one think
of David's words to Agnes.[78] In *Pendennis* Thackeray
reproduced, fantastically, the experiences of his own youthful years (for instance, Ottery St. Mary becomes Clavering
St. Mary), not however to the point of allowing complete
identification of the characters; another novel of contemporary life is *The Newcomes* (1853–5), in which occurs one
of the few genuinely pathetic episodes of Thackeray's
work, the death of Colonel Newcome, a generous, noble
soul, innocent as a child; the novel, as usual, is more the
narrative of a family history than an adventure-story with
a definite plot.

Henry Esmond, on the other hand (1851–2; the autobiography of a man who grows up during the reign of
Queen Anne, a work to be admired for the correctness of
its historical perspective and for its bright-coloured, lively
portrait of a beautiful woman, a lover of ostentation, the
imperious, treacherous Beatrix, whose ambitions were to
be disappointed like those of Becky Sharp—a portrait
which seems an incarnation of the ideal of the painters of
the period he is dealing with),[79] and its sequel, *The Virginians* (1857–9)—these are historical novels, but of a
different type from the choreographies of Scott, and with
a closer affinity to Dutch interior painting. With the success of these novels came prosperity, and Thackeray was
received with enthusiasm by the very world against which
his satire was aimed. In order to provide for his daughters,
he followed Dickens's example and gave lucrative courses
of lectures, both in England (*The English Humourists of the
Eighteenth Century*, 1851, published in book form in 1853)
and in America (1852–3 and 1855–6: in this second tour
he read his essays on *The Four Georges*, published in 1860).
In 1853 he went to Rome, where an attack of tertian ague
further undermined his health, which had not been robust
ever since an illness he had had in 1849 (probably typhoid
fever): anxieties and convivial excesses (in which he

indulged in order to combat his painful feeling of loneliness after his wife lost her reason) shortened his life. This decline can be felt in *The Virginians*, and even more in his last novels which appeared in the *Cornhill Magazine*, in which, nevertheless, some of his best essays, *The Roundabout Papers*, were also published. He died of an apoplectic stroke on the night of December 23rd–24th, 1864.

*   *   *   *   *

To his own generation Thackeray appeared a misanthrope, an egoist; and even nowadays it is not uncommon to find him described as a cynic. Here, it was said, was a writer who found fault with everything, who ruthlessly removed every veil from every human act, who, as Charlotte Brontë wrote in a letter, 'likes to dissect an ulcer or an aneurism, has pleasure in putting his cruel knife or probe into quivering living flesh'. Or—to use another image—the reading of *Vanity Fair* acted like a cold douche, was even like diving into icy water, 'that first cold plunge into *Vanity Fair*'. Here was an author who penetrated into men's hearts and brains, displaying them in all their nakedness, beneath a crude light: 'la clairvoyance des deux cents premières pages de *Vanity Fair* est admirable et mortelle', wrote Cazamian. In this novel (with the sub-title *A Novel without a Hero*) virtue seems destined to founder and perish, while Falsity, Injustice and Villainy triumph everywhere. In it the contrast is drawn between the career of Becky Sharp, the intelligent, treacherous upstart, and that of the virtuous, pretty, silly Amelia Sedley. Becky's father had been a drunken, penniless artist, her mother a French dancer (Thackeray is careful to give his adventurers some non-English blood; note that Barry Lyndon was an Irishman); even as a child Becky had learned to deceive and flatter in order to obtain favours; moreover her early experience of artistic circles makes her despise the shabby decorum of Miss Pinkerton's school where she goes as an apprentice teacher of French, and also, later, the conventionality and moral standards of the bourgeoisie, and the ineptitude of the upper classes, with which she comes, successively, into contact. So Becky applies herself, without any scruples, to making her fortune by taking advantage of people who are socially superior to her. First she tries to catch the brother of Amelia, the girl of good family whom she has known at school, then, having become governess in the house of the old cynic, Sir Pitt Crawley, she insinuates herself into his good graces and those of his rich sister Miss Crawley; the baronet, on his wife's death, offers to marry her, and it then comes to light that Becky is already secretly married to Rawdon, Sir Pitt's second son and Miss Crawley's favourite —cavalry officer, gambler, and duellist: this false step on Becky's part rouses the old man's anger, and loses Rawdon the inheritance he had expected from his aunt. Later on Becky comes to an understanding with George Osborne, another officer, who has married Amelia on the insistence of his fellow soldier Captain Dobbin and in spite of his own wish to have nothing more to do with her because his father, having come to know of the financial catastrophe of the Sedleys, had forbidden the marriage. Becky's intrigue with George, whom his wife loves blindly, takes place on the eve of Waterloo, where George meets his death. In spite of her poverty and low origin, Becky manages to make her way in the high society of Paris and London; she allows herself to be kept by Lord Steyne without the knowledge of her husband, who, having caught them together, makes a scene and breaks off relations with her. After a vagabond life in places of doubtful repute on the Continent, the adventuress rediscovers Amelia's brother, the fat Jos Sedley, her old flame, and constitutes herself his nurse, until finally he, in abject terror of her, leaves her part of his fortune as he is dying. Becky, assuming a mask or respectability, piety, and philanthropy, is well received in the society of Bath and Cheltenham, where she is thought to be a victim of ill-treatment. Amelia lives a life of poverty and humiliation, comforted by the faithful Dobbin, whom she at last consents to marry when Becky reveals to her how she had been betrayed by the dead George, whose memory she had revered.

The novelist's intention was to teach a 'dark moral', by showing 'a set of people living without God in the world . . . greedy, pompous men, perfectly self-satisfied for the most part, and at ease about their superior virtue'; and amongst these people, considered by the novelist himself to be 'odious' (with the exception of Dobbin and of Miss Briggs, Miss Crawley's lady companion), Amelia alone, after long delay, redeems herself, because, although foolish, she is endowed with a 'quality above most people'—love.

A plot of this kind, hinging upon a couple of young women, one of whom is vicious and leads a life of pleasure, while the other, virtuous, suffers a long series of afflictions, fits into a well-defined scheme of novel-writing which enjoyed great success in France round about 1830.[80] The prototype of this genus of novel was hidden away in the darkness of that section of the library known as the *enfer*; it was the diptych, *Justine, ou les malheurs de la vertu*, and *Juliette, ou les prospérités du vice*, by de Sade; and a modernized form, *Les Mémoires du diable*, by Frédéric Soulié, had appeared in 1837. In a diary of Thackeray relating to 1844, at the date February 22nd, we find: 'Read in that astonishingly corrupt book *Les Mémoires du diable*.' Soulié too—as Thackeray did later—satirized contemporary society, which honoured vice when powerful and hypocritical, and oppressed virtue. Soulié, of course, derives from the tradition of the 'tales of terror', Thackeray from that of the polished eighteenth-century novel, and there is no similarity whatever between the two novelists in the way in which they treat the subject. In Soulié's pages duels, poisonings, murders, parricides, adulteries, incests and the condemnation of innocent victims follow close upon one another, and the grim phantasmagoria is dominated by the figure of a dandified Beelzebub with a 'hideux sourire' and a 'fauve regard de cannibale, contemplant la victime qu'il va dévorer'. The virtuous ladies languish in prisons or asylums, or kill themselves from despair, while the prostitutes and the murderesses pass for paragons of virtue in the eyes of the world. Caroline, the virtuous sister of the protagonist Luizzi and the victim of every sort of outrage, arrives dressed as a beggar, to save her brother, at the place which Juliette, the wicked sister, had left to pursue a career of vice, where, also, Luizzi meets her in all the pomp of luxury.

There is a curious familiarity in the choice of theme between Soulié's cheap trash and the great novel that Thackeray published ten years later—misfortunes of virtue and prosperity of vice; and the author, in each case, traces back all human actions to impure motives, and abandons himself to an orgy of moral sadism. Las Vergnas observes:[81]

Quand il [*Thackeray*] porte sur le monde son regard aigu, il va droit aux retraites ténébreuses, aux repaires souterrains du Mal. Ces êtres que nous côtoyons, que nous aimons peut-être, ô stupeur! ce sont des gredins, des faussaires, des malfaiteurs au plein sens du mot. Rebecca Sharp, Beatrix Castlewood [*to extend this analysis to all Thackeray's novels*], Lady Kew, Blanche Amory, Mrs. Mackenzie, pour ne citer que les plus illustres, sont des intrigantes, des rouées, des égoïstes, qui sèment autour d'elles le malheur et la ruine.

In the original conclusion of *Barry Lyndon* Thackeray had remarked that poetic justice is an illusion on the part of the novelist:

Justice, forsooth! Does human life exhibit justice after this fashion? Is it the good always who ride in gold coaches, and the wicked who go to the workhouse? Is a humbug never preferred before a capable man? Does the world always reward merit, never worship cant, never raise mediocrity to distinction? never crowd to hear a donkey braying from a pulpit, nor ever buy the tenth edition of a fool's book? Sometimes the contrary occurs, so that fools and wise, bad men and good, are more or less lucky in their turn, and honesty is 'the best policy', or not, as the case may be.

At moments it might really seem as if Thackeray possessed the magic lamp of Soulié's devil, as when, in one of *The Roundabout Papers*, *On a Medal of George IV*, he wonders how many murderers there are amongst people that we meet in the ordinary way, how many criminals are to be found at an ordinary tea-party; how many things the people we meet have to conceal, far more serious than 'a yellow cheek behind a raddle of rouge'. Like those medieval artists who sometimes portrayed a putrid corpse at the back with a splendid, sumptuous, youthful figure in front, Thackeray never ceases to evoke the repulsive moral skeleton side by side with the rosy outward appearance.

The appellation of 'cynic' which many people in his own time bestowed upon Thackeray is not, in truth, very convincing to us moderns; and in any case, how could a real, thorough-going cynic, one who painted vice in all its deformity, have found success in the Victorian age, prudish as it was? Let us not be deceived by the strong expressions of Charlotte Brontë and others: Thackeray found favour with the public, he was admired and honoured. Charlotte Brontë herself, who was shocked at Thackeray's admiration for Fielding (the blemishes upon whose private life Thackeray had, in any case, exaggerated), saying that the hour she had spent in listening to Thackeray's lecture on Fielding had been a painful one—'I felt Thackeray was dangerously wrong. Had I a brother yet living I should tremble to let him read Thackeray's lecture on Fielding'— on the other hand found this also to say, on the subject of a comparison between the two novelists: 'They say he is like Fielding. . . . He resembles Fielding as an eagle does a vulture: Fielding could stoop on carrion, but Thackeray never does.' And this remark is to be found in the long dedication of *Jane Eyre* to Thackeray, whom she sees as a man with a prophetic mission, as a warning voice: 'I have alluded to him, Reader, because I think I see in him an intellect profounder and more unique than his contemporaries have yet recognized; because I regard him as the first social regenerator of the day—as the very master of that working corps who would restore to rectitude the warped system of things. . .'[82] Mrs. Gaskell also wrote: 'Whatever vinegar and gall, whatever idle froth a book of Thackeray's may contain, it has no dregs, you never go and wash your hands when you put it down nor rinse your mouth to take away the flavour of a degraded soul. Perverse he may be and he is, but, to do him justice, not degraded—no, never!' This remark by the spruce, well-bred Victorian authoress tells us more about Thackeray's 'cynicism' than many disquisitions. Bitter indeed he was, but bitter as quinine is bitter, with a bitterness that, if the Victorians tolerated it, must also have had its healing virtues.

In that Victorian society whose prudishness we find it

hard, nowadays, to imagine, Thackeray passed for a realist, and a realist reaction is indeed proclaimed by his words of preface to *Pendennis*:

Since the author of *Tom Jones* was buried, no writer of fiction among us has been permitted to depict to his utmost power a MAN. We must drape him, and give him a certain conventional simper. Society will not tolerate the Natural in our Art. Many ladies have remonstrated and subscribers left me, because in the course of the story, I described a young man resisting and affected by temptation. My object was to say, that he had the passions to feel, and the manliness and generosity to overcome them. You will not hear—it is best to know it—what moves in the real world, what passes in society, in the clubs, colleges, mess-rooms—what is the life and talk of your sons. A little more frankness than is customary has been attempted in this story; with no bad desire on the writer's part, it is hoped, and with no ill consequence to any reader. If truth is not always pleasant, at any rate truth is best, from whatever chair—from those whence graver writers or thinkers argue, as from that at which the story-teller sits as he concludes his labour, and bids his kind reader farewell.

Thackeray believed, then, that he was being a terrible realist and unmasking the frauds of society when, for instance, in *Vanity Fair*, he turned to his readers and said, apropos of Becky, Jos, and Lord Steyne: 'Such people there are, dear reader—let us have at them with might and main.' But, in respect of *Pendennis*, can one really speak of realism in connexion with a scene like the one between Mr. Bows and Pendennis about Fanny Bolton, which concludes in so oleographically edifying a manner?

And had not Thackeray, in *Vanity Fair* (chap. lxiv), made this symptomatic declaration?

We must pass over a part of Mrs. Rebecca Crawley's biography with that lightness and delicacy which the world demands—the moral world, that has, perhaps, no particular objection to vice, but an insuperable repugnance to hearing vice called by its proper name. There are things we do and know perfectly well in Vanity Fair, though we never speak of them. . . . I defy anyone to say that our Becky, who has certainly some vices, has not been presented to the public in a perfectly genteel and inoffensive manner. In describing this siren, singing and smiling, coaxing and cajoling, the author, with modest pride, asks his readers all round, has he once forgotten the laws of politeness, and showed the monster's hideous tail above water? No! Those who like may peep down under waves that are pretty transparent, and see it writhing and twirling, diabolically hideous and slimy, flapping amongst bones, or curling round corpses; but above the water-line, I ask, has not everything been proper, agreeable, and decorous, and has any the most squeamish immoralist in Vanity Fair a right to cry fie? When, however, the siren disappears and dives below, down among the dead men, the water of course grows turbid over her, and it is labour lost to look into it ever so curiously. . . . We had best not examine the fiendish marine cannibals, revelling and feasting on their wretched pickled victims.

If we compare Thackeray with a true realist—beside whom he has sometimes been arbitrarily placed—Flaubert (and realist is perhaps not the correct term for Flaubert either; or only as an approximation—one might perhaps call him an integralist), the difference leaps to the eye. Thackeray himself said of *Madame Bovary*: 'It is the heartless cold-blooded story of the downfall and degradation of a woman.'[83] It follows, therefore, that *Vanity Fair* cannot be described in the same terms. So little, indeed, is *Vanity Fair* a realistic novel, sticking close to life in all its complexity, that Thackeray's pen stops, paralysed, when confronted with great emotions, either of the sublime kind, or of the lowest, those of the senses. The realism of *Vanity Fair*—if one wishes to make use of the word—is in fact a paralysed realism, impaired by reticences and *sous-entendus*. Consider how the whole plot hinges, at one moment, upon the fact that Becky Sharp is Lord Steyne's mistress. But is she really? Thackeray never says so except indirectly— and there is no chance of finding descriptions of private meetings between the two lovers, such as we should certainly find with a French novelist. The most suspicious attitude in which we are ever allowed to catch Lord Steyne in Becky's company, is when he leans against the sofa upon which she is sitting and performs the gesture of kissing her hand. To Thackeray, the situation must have seemed highly compromising. In *Pendennis* Blanche's frivolity is demonstrated in the same way. 'Our little Siren was at her piano.' Blanche is singing at the piano, like a siren, with the fascinated Foker beside her, when Pendennis unexpectedly drops in and discovers, in this way, that he has been betrayed. In connexion with 'proofs' of this kind, it is not irrelevant to quote a letter from Flaubert to Louise Colet, dated 1852, on the subject of Lamartine's Graziella:

> Et d'abord, pour parler clair, la baise-t-il ou ne la baise-t-il pas? Ce ne sont pas des êtres humains, mais des mannequins. Que c'est beau ces histoires d'amour où la chose principale est tellement entourée dé mystère que l'on ne sait à quoi s'en tenir, l'union sexuelle étant reléguée systématiquement dans l'ombre comme boire, manger, pisser, etc. Le parti pris m'agace. . . . Mais non, il faut faire du convenu, du faux. Il faut que les dames vous lisent. O mensonge! mensonge! que tu es bête!

And it is interesting, in order to realize the conditions in the two societies, the English and the French, to hear Thackeray cry Lies! to Victorian society, and Flaubert cry Lies! to Thackeray himself. So true is it that everything is relative.

When the question arose of his giving his lectures on *The Four Georges* in England, Thackeray tried them out in front of an audience of friends and acquaintances: another listener whom the lecturer eyed with trepidation was his own sixteen-year-old Minny, since there had been some complaints that parts of the lecture were unsuited to innocent young ears. He could have no peace until he could be certain that it contained no cause for scandal; but she, too, was satisfied. In America Thackeray's manservant had remarked that 'the (first) lecture was too smutty for the fair sex', and Thackeray had recognized this in a letter to Frank Fladgate, one of his greatest friends at the Garrick Club: 'The people did not know what to make of George I and his strumpets. Morality was staggered.' At Richmond, Virginia, just as he was embarking on the questionable narrative of the royal favourites, he had been 'horrified to notice a score of little schoolgirls occupying the front rows'.

When Elizabeth Barrett Browning sent her poem *Lord Walter's Wife* to the *Cornhill Magazine*, Thackeray, who edited the review, found himself much embarrassed because this poem contained 'an account of unlawful passion felt by a man for a woman'. Thackeray kept the poem in a drawer for many months, feeling, in respect of it, like a man who has to have a tooth out and is afraid to face the dentist; finally he sent it back to the poetess with a long letter of excuses, praising the composition for its qualities of 'pure doctrine and real modesty and pure ethics', and its authoress for being one of 'the best wives, mothers, women in the world', but explaining that there were squeamish people amongst the readers of the review who would certainly make trouble if the poem were published. Mrs. Browning then sent him a blameless poem entitled *The North and the South*, inspired by a visit of Hans Andersen. A story by Trollope was rejected for the same reason, and the latter remarked: '*Virginibus puerisque*! That was the gist of his objection. There was a project in a gentleman's mind—as told in my story—to run away with a married woman! Thackeray's letter was very kind, very regretful —full of apology for such treatment to such a contributor. But—*virginibus puerisque*!'

To follow up the comparison with the French, one should read those pages of the *Paris Sketch Book* in which Thackeray is shocked by the 'horrors' of Balzac and of the plays of Dumas; one should also remember that when Thackeray, on his way back from his second tour in America, stopped in Paris and went twice to the theatre, on both occasions he left the house at the end of the second act, because the plays were too 'wicked'; one was *Le Juif errant*, the other *La Dame aux camélias*. However, he recommended people to read the novels of Monsieur de Bernard (whose name one would seek in vain in a history of literature), 'who has painted actual manners without those monstrous and terrible exaggerations in which late French writers have indulged; and who, if he occasionally wounds the English sense of propriety (as what French man or woman alive will not?), does so more by slighting than by outraging it, as, with their laborious descriptions of all sorts of imaginable wickedness, some of his brethren of the press have done'. Thackeray finds this Bernard 'more remarkable than any other French author, to our notion, for writing like a gentleman: there is ease, grace and *ton* in his style which, if we judge aright, cannot be discovered

in Balzac, or Soulié, or Dumas'. Certainly the plays of
Dumas and Hugo, which Thackeray treats as a joke
(though he adored Dumas's historical novels) had something frenzied and ridiculous about them—but who is
their rival and competitor? Monsieur de Bernard, the
gentleman-author![84]

We come, then, to this conclusion: Thackeray is indeed
bitter and harsh, but he remains always a gentleman, he
remains, that is, within the framework of Victorian society;
he is a cynic in yellow gloves, respectful, when all is said
and done, of the conventions. He does not truly see life
as it is, but with a caricature-like distortion which is
conditioned by the exigencies of morality, and it is thanks
to this moralizing tendency that his criticism is acceptable
to an extremely moral society; he does not depict vice either
under alluring forms, as the French did, or under forms so
totally repugnant that they shock the moral sense, but
rather as it is depicted by a preacher,[85] so that it remains
always in the world of logic and argument and never
descends to the point of direct, emotional contact. The
thrill of intuitive, electrical contact is lacking in Thackeray:
his appeal is to the mind of his reader rather than to his
emotional experience.

This is the bourgeois, the Biedermeier aspect of this
so-called cynic: he is a moralist, he carries on, in a less
agreeble, less artistic form, the work of correcting manners
that had been begun by Addison—Addison whom he finds
to be synonymous with perfection. Thackeray is, as we
shall see, essentially anti-heroic; yet he presents the figure
of Addison (in *The English Humourists*) as that of a being
without faults, natural, good, noble, smiling, courteous,
calm: a humorist who never loses the urbanity of a gentleman, a gentleman not only in manner, but—which is more
important—in character, for he has perfect self-control and
serenity of spirit. Addison, for Thackeray, is almost the
only proof of the possibility of perfection in man, he is—
as far as Thackeray's conception could reach—a superman,
almost as Goethe is nowadays represented by some modern
writers: 'It is in the nature of such lords of intellect to be
solitary—they are in the world, but not of it; and our minor

struggles, brawls, successes, pass under them. . . . He must have stooped to put himself on a level with most men.' And it is noteworthy that Macaulay, too, bowed down before Addison as before a model: which confirms, on the one hand, the description of 'Victorian *ante litteram*' given to Addison by Professor Bonamy Dobrée, and, on the other, signifies a community of ideals in Thackeray and Macaulay —both of them Victorians, though of different types.

Thackeray's method, too, of taking the reader aside and commenting in a familiar fashion upon the spectacle of the world, recalls Addison's and Fielding's benevolent, confidential tone; except that in Thackeray this kind of urbane conversation acquires an even more bourgeois tinge: the writer, in his slippers, delivers his comments from the fireside. It is a method that accentuates the rhythm of passing time, the sense of slow corrosion brought about by the years and by human passions and weaknesses, but it prevents the story from taking a dramatic course: plot is forgotten in the moral analysis of character.

Instead of *The Spectator* club, it is, with Thackeray, the snobs' club: but life is always analysed according to plan, never directly: Addison's sketches carry on the tradition of Ben Jonson's 'humours', and Thackeray's *Snobs of England*, too, are 'characters', samples, generalizations. Descended from a family which (as already mentioned) could count among its numbers at least nineteen clergymen, Thackeray was born with the vocation of a lay preacher; and Taine observed that it would be possible to dig out of his novels a volume or two of essays in the manner of La Bruyère or Addison. In any case Thackeray himself does not hesitate to reveal that his mission is that of lay preacher; he said this in conversations with friends, he wrote it in various pages of his novels. In one chapter (the thirty-eighth) of *The Newcomes*, for example, we read:

This book is all about the world and a respectable family dwelling in it. It is not a sermon, except where it cannot help itself, and the speaker pursuing the destiny of his narrative finds such a homily before him. O friend, in your life and mine, don't we light upon such sermons daily? don't we see at home as well as amongst our neighbours that battle betwixt Evil and Good? Here on one side is

21. DAVID WILKIE. Chelsea Pensioners (*London, Victoria and Albert Museum. Crown Copyright*)

22. R. THORBURN. The Duke of Wellington and his grandchildren (*Stratfield Saye House, Reading.*)

Self and Ambition and Advancement, and Right and Love on the other. Which shall we let to triumph for ourselves, which for our children?

His preaching vocation is evident even in the most vivid episodes of his best novels. See, for instance, chapter vi of Book III of *Esmond*, where Esmond gives Beatrix the news of Hamilton's death—Hamilton who had represented the crowning of all her worldly ambitions. Beatrix wants to make Esmond admire the great gold salver with the Hamilton arms upon it ('a pretty piece of vanity', says Esmond); at the first hint of the fatal news, she drops the salver on the floor (its fall, it is hardly necessary to point out, is a symbol of the ruin of Beatrix's splendid ambitions), and believes that Hamilton has left her from unfaithfulness. The speech in which Esmond tells her how matters stand has all the tone of a sermon: 'Vain and cruel woman! kneel and thank the awful Heaven which awards life and death, and chastises pride', &c. And, when he alludes to the tradesmen who have brought their sumptuous wares to the house in connexion with Beatrix's approaching marriage: 'The army of Vanity Fair, waiting without, gathered up all their fripperies and fled aghast.' For Thackeray's 'homily' manner see also the passage in *Pendennis* on the subject of Fanny Bolton's condemnation by all honest women, and the novelist's warning to the latter, or his other warning to 'the Clarissas of this life'. 'O you poor little ignorant vain foolish maidens!' &c. And his observations on the chain of universal love intended by the Creator, in the *Journey from Cornhill to Grand Cairo*. This preaching vocation becomes more and more accentuated in Thackeray's career, so that the last works, such as *The Adventures of Philip*, are practically sermons pure and simple. There is no mistaking the pulpit tone in phrases such as: 'Oh blessed they on whose pillow no remorse sits! Happy those who have escaped temptation!' or again: 'Honour your father and mother. Amen. May his days be long who fulfils the command.' In *The Roundabout Papers* the account of a recent infamous crime (*On two Roundabout Papers which I intended to write*), or of the singularity of certain gifts which place people above the common run of humanity (*A Mississippi Bubble*), or of the ignominious end of a dishonest public figure (*On a Pear-tree*) suggest the perorations of real sermons; and in the essay *On a Medal of George IV* the argument is transported on to the moral plane in this way: 'Ah, friend, may our coin, battered, and clipped, and defaced though it be, be proved to be Sterling Silver on the day of the Great Assay!'

*   *   *   *   *

But it is, in point of fact, from the depths of disillusioned meditations upon mortality and the impermanence of all human things (ancient themes of the preacher) that a breath of poetry most often arises, in Thackeray's pages. As early as 1839 (in *Catherine*), in front of a copy of the *Daily Post* of a hundred and ten years before, in which there was an account of the murder of Hayes and the execution of the culprits, he had exclaimed:

> Think of it! it has been read by Belinda at her toilet, scanned at 'Button's' and 'Will's', sneered at by wits, talked of in palaces and cottages, by a busy race in wigs, red heels, hoops, patches, and rags of all variety—a busy race that hath long since plunged and vanished in the unfathomable gulf towards which we march so briskly. Where are they? 'Afflavit Deus'—and they are gone! Hark! is not the same wind roaring still that shall sweep us down? and yonder stands the compositor at his types who shall put up a pretty paragraph some day to say how, '*Yesterday*, at his house in Grosvenor Square,' or 'At Botany Bay, universally regretted,' died So-and-So.

And in the sixth chapter of the third book of *Esmond*, Esmond, returning from Kensington, where he has announced Hamilton's death to Beatrix, meets the street-criers shouting the news and sees the town coming to life in the sunny, early, November morning:

> The world was going to its business again, although dukes lay dead and ladies mourned for them. . . . So night and day pass away, and to-morrow comes, and our place knows us not.[86] Esmond thought of the courier now galloping on the North road, to inform him who was Earl of Arran yesterday that he was Duke of Hamilton to-day; and of a thousand great schemes, hopes, ambitions, that were alive in the gallant heart, beating a few hours since, and now in a little dust quiescent.

So also in *Pendennis* (chap. xxxvi):

At this time of his life Mr. Pen beheld all sorts of places and men; and very likely did not know how much he enjoyed himself until long after, when balls gave him no pleasure, neither did farces make him laugh; nor did the tavern joke produce the least excitement in him; nor did the loveliest dancer that ever showed her ancles cause him to stir from his chair after dinner. At his present mature age all these pleasures are over: and the times have passed away too. It is but a very very few years since—but the time is gone, and most of the men. Bludyer will no more bully authors or cheat landlords of their score. Shandon, the learned and thriftless, the witty and unwise, sleeps his last sleep. They buried honest Doolan the other day: never will he cringe or flatter, never pull long-bow or empty whiskey-noggin any more.

A little farther on Thackeray reflects upon intimate details of the private life of certain old dandies or bucks who study to appear youthful, and imagines how, 'if any parson in Pimlico or St. James's were to order the beadles to bring [such a one] into the middle aisle, and there set him in an armchair, and make a text of him, and preach about him to the congregation, [he] could be turned to a wholesome use for once in his life, and might be surprised to find that some good thoughts came out of him'. Such a sermon, one supposes, might have sounded like some of Donne's: 'Thou hast a desire to please some *eyes*, when thou hast much to doe, not to displease every *Nose*; and thou wilt solicit an adulterous entrance into their beds who, if they should but see thee goe into thine own bed, would need no other mortification, nor answer to thy solicitation' (Sermon XX).

And again in *Pendennis* (chap. xli):

The bloom disappears off the face of poetry after you begin to shave. You can't get up that naturalness and artless rosy tint in after days. Your cheeks are pale, and have got faded by exposure to evening parties, and you are obliged to take curling-irons, and macassar, and the deuce-knows-what to your whiskers; they curl ambrosially, and you are very grand and genteel, and so forth; but, ah! Pen, the spring time was the best.

Of the passage on Congreve in *The English Humourists*:

I have read two or three of Congreve's plays over before speaking of him; and my feelings were rather like those, which I daresay most of us here have had, at Pompeii, looking at the Poet's house and the relics of an orgy: a dried wine jar or two, a charred supper-table, the breast of a dancing-girl pressed against the ashes, the laughing skull of a joker, a perfect stillness round about, as the cicerone twangs the moral, and the blue sky shines calmly over the ruin. The Congreve muse is dead, and her song choked in Time's ashes. We gaze at the skeleton, and wonder at the life which once revelled in its mad veins. We take the skull up, and muse over the frolic and daring, the wit, scorn, passion, hope, desire, with which that empty bowl once fermented. We think of the glances that allured, the tears that melted, of the bright eyes that shone in those vacant sockets; and of lips whispering love, and cheeks dimpling with smiles, that once covered yon ghastly yellow framework. They used to call those teeth pearls once. See! there's the cup she drank from, the gold chain she wore on her neck, the vase which held the rouge for her cheeks, her looking-glass, and the harp she used to dance to. Instead of a feast we find a gravestone, and in place of a mistress, a few bones.

Thackeray's repressed romanticism—we shall have occasion to return to this point later—'took vent', as one critic (Emerson Grant Sutcliffe) has remarked, 'in the sentiment and didacticism which so oddly colour his satire'. Hence his continually taking his reader aside, his turning to him with a perpetually implied 'de te fabula', his alteration of the 'dear brethren' of the pulpit into the layman's 'my friend'. M. Las Vergnas, taking up a remark by Charles Whibley ('He acts like the sheep-dog to his characters'), goes so far as to write:

Il est indéniable que Thackeray a considéré ses personnages comme autant de brebis égarées, et si, de la métaphore du troupeau, il fallait retenir quelque trait, ce serait, non pas l'image brutale du chien, mais celle, au double sens heureux des termes, du pasteur grave et doux.

And M. Las Vergnas asks himself, what else is *Pendennis* but a series of reflections upon man, a kind of animated psychological treatise, a philosophy in action? And is not *Vanity Fair* a sermon on a text from Ecclesiastes? Thackeray might be consulted for moral advice by the chance opening of the page—*sortes thackerayanae*. Yet is this accessory quality in the novel, which M. Las Vergnas considers much more noteworthy than the plot itself, really so rich in shades and subtleties of meaning as the French critic supposes? Thackeray's reflections stand out prominently against the narrative plot, they are pointers placed continually in the margin of the page, and—which is worse—they are usually trite and pedestrian in character. For Thackeray had no original, revolutionary view of the world; his morality is 'correct', like his gentlemanly suit of clothes. A gentleman is a man who has nothing showy either in his clothes or in his manners. The quality of a gentleman is a golden mean, an avoidance of all excess, an admirable mediocrity.

This, then, was why Thackeray, in spite of his bitterness, found favour with the Victorians: because he was a preacher, and because he was a non-revolutionary preacher. He was like the boatswain who beat time for the oarsmen in a galley; he whipped the lazy ones, but did not seek to impose upon them a different 'time' from the one they already had. The Victorian age had several writers who took upon themselves this boatswain's function: but a Carlyle, an Arnold, wished to alter the rhythm of the rowers, to quicken it up. Thackeray alone was the boatswain elect, the one who did not claim to work miracles, who kept to the old rhythm.

And so, in contrast to Carlyle who exalts the hero, whom he puts forward as a combined reproof and pattern to an anti-heroic, bourgeois age, Thackeray sets himself up as deliberately anti-heroic, even to the title of his most famous novel—*Vanity Fair, a Novel without a Hero*. The virtuous, in his novels, are intellectually inferior to the wicked, and all claim to superhuman or heroic qualities is excluded, even from virtue, to a point when the reader begins to wonder whether virtue and imbecility are not the same thing. Christian humility? This quality, certainly, has been observed in Thackeray, and corresponds perfectly to one of the aspects of Biedermeier, that of the revival of Christian meekness and resignation.

It is indeed possible, remembering certain episodes in Thackeray's life, to imagine, in him, a secret life dominated by a profound sense of religion. Listening to a choir of boys in St. Paul's, he hid his tear-streaming face in his hands. And in Edinburgh, walking one Sunday evening with some friends and seeing on Corstorphine Hill, outlined against the sky, a wooden crane taking on the form of a cross, he 'gave utterance in a tremulous, gentle and rapid voice, to what all were feeling, in the word "Calvary".'[87] The return of the group of friends, with a sense of solemnity hanging over them and Thackeray talking humbly of his simple faith in God and his Saviour, is truly Biedermeier. He believed, fundamentally, in virtue and simplicity. When William B. Reed asked him what had most struck him in America, he answered: 'You know what a virtue-proud people we English are. We think we have got it all to ourselves. Now, what most impresses me here is that I find homes as pure as ours, firesides like ours, domestic virtues as gentle; the English language, though the accent be a little different, with its home-like melody; and the Common Prayer book in your families.' And when he moved into the house in Queen Anne style which he had built for himself in Kensington towards the end of his life, he wrote in his diary a solemn prayer: 'I pray Almighty God that the words I write in this house may be pure and honest; that they be dictated by no personal spite, unworthy motive, or unjust greed for gain; that they may tell the truth as far as I know it; and tend to promote love and peace among men, for the sake of Christ our Lord.' Speaking of Addison, after praising some verses of his on the stars, verses which leave us moderns cold, he went on:

It seems to me those verses shine like the stars. They shine out of a great deep calm. When he turns to Heaven, a Sabbath comes over that man's mind: and his face lights up from it with a glory of thanks and prayer. His sense of religion stirs through his whole being. In the fields, in the town: looking at the birds in the trees: at the children in the streets: in the morning or in the moonlight: over his books in his own room: in a happy party at a country merry-making or a town assembly, good-will and peace to God's creatures, and love and awe of Him who made them, fill his pure heart and shine from his kind face.... A life prosperous and beautiful—a calm death—an immense fame and affection afterwards for his happy and spotless name.

Like the hermit crab, Thackeray was imperfectly covered by his shell of sarcasm: the cynic was also a man of piety and sensibility. Carlyle described Thackeray to Lord Houghton as a man of enormous size, fierce, with eyes overflowing with tears, but not a *strong* man. And in a letter to Emerson he said almost the same thing: 'A *big*, fierce, weeping, hungry man; not a strong one.' Mrs. Story, who saw him in Rome, after she had lost a child through gastric fever, found Thackeray deeply moved by her grief: 'Once he surprised me when I had in my hand a little worn shoe which had for me an intense association; he shed tears over it with me and understood what it meant to me as few could have done. Under what people called his cynical exterior and manner, his was the kindest and truest heart that ever beat.' And Martin, the 'Bon Gaultier' of the famous comic ballads which were very like those of Thackeray, declared outright: 'In fact, of all men I have known he was the most tender-hearted; in this respect, indeed, almost womanly.' Once, in America, at the Baxters' house, Thackeray took up a copy of *Pendennis* in the drawing-room, skimmed through a few pages of it with an odd smile on his face, and finally exlaimed: 'Yes, it is very like—it is certainly very like.' 'Like whom, Mr. Thackeray?' 'Oh, like me, to be sure; Pendennis is very like me.' 'Surely not,' protested Mrs. Baxter; 'Pendennis was so weak!' 'Ah, well, Mrs. Baxter,' he replied, with a shrug of his broad shoulders, 'your humble servant is not very strong.' The character of Philip, also, in *The Adventures of Philip*, is a transparent self-portrait of Thackeray: 'He had a childish sensibility for what was tender, helpless, pretty, or pathetic; and a mighty scorn of imposture, wherever he found it.'

Certain of his characters, who reproduce aspects of his own soul such as are revealed to us from his letters, are melancholy, charitable, resigned, like Biedermeier Christians: Dobbin, for instance, or Warrington, and above all Colonel Newcome, whose death scene Thackeray himself could never read with a dry eye. A friend bears witness to this: 'When he came to the final "Adsum" the tears which had been swelling his lids for some time trickled down his face and the last word was almost an inarticulate sob.'

There are some lines by Thackeray, *To a very old Woman*, which breathe a simple faith; and it was not for nothing that they were translated from a Biedermeier German poet (M. Las Vergnas fails to notice this)—La Motte Fouqué ('Und du gingst einst, die Myrt' im Haare'):

> And thou wert once a maiden fair,
>   A blushing virgin warm and young:
> With myrtles wreathed in golden hair,
> And glossy brow that knew no care—
>   Upon a bridegroom's arm you hung.
>
> The golden locks are silvered now,
>   The blushing cheek is pale and wan;
> The spring may bloom, the autumn glow,
> All's one—in chimney corner thou
>   Sitt'st shivering on.—
>
> A moment—and thou sink'st to rest!
> To wake perhaps an angel blest
>   In the bright presence of thy Lord.
> Oh, weary is life's path to all!
> Hard is the strife, and light the fall,
>   But wondrous the reward!

On the subject of which lines—especially knowing them to be a translation—we shall not go so far as to say, with M. Las Vergnas: 'Il est consolant de savoir qu'il a écrit ces vers, où il a dit son attente assurée de la consolation suprême.' But in any case it is noteworthy that Thackeray should have chosen them.

This aspect of Thackeray, with thoughts turned towards religion, becomes accentuated in his later life, but we also find traces of it in his youthful essays, for example in the *Pictorial Rhapsody* which appeared in *Fraser's Magazine* in June 1840, in which he considers that the greatest painting is a hymn of gratitude to God:

The view of a picture of the highest order does always, like the view of the stars in a calm night, or a fair quiet landscape in sunshine, fill the mind with an inexpressible content and gratitude towards the Maker who has created such beautiful things for our use. And as the poet has told us how, not out of a wide landscape merely, or a sublime expanse of glittering stars, but of any very humble thing, we may gather the same delightful reflections (as out of a small flower, that brings us 'thoughts that do often lie too deep for tears')—in like manner we do not want grand pictures and elaborate yards of canvas so to affect us.

The criterion for judging the value of a picture is: to what extent does it touch the heart?

The best paintings address themselves to the best feelings of it [your heart]. . . . Skill and handling are great parts of a painter's trade, but heart is the first; this is God's direct gift to him, and cannot be got in any academy, or under any master. Look about, therefore, for pictures, be they large or small, finished well or ill, landscapes, portraits, figure-pieces, pen-and-ink sketches, or what not, that contain sentiment and great ideas. He who possesses these will be sure to express them more or less well. Never mind about the manner. He who possesses them not may draw and colour to perfection, and yet be no artist.

Thackeray finds that Eastlake possesses this sentiment: his painting is as pure as a Sabbath-hymn sung by the voices of children, as can be seen in the picture *The Salutation of the Aged Friars*: this 'brings the spectator to a delightful peaceful state of mind, and gives him matter to ponder upon long after'. And what is the edifying subject of this picture? A group of innocent, happy-looking Italian peasants approaches a couple of monks; a little boy comes forward with a flower, which he offers to the elder of the two monks, and the old man blesses him. It is true, observes Thackeray, that there are several faults in this picture: the shadows are too red, the whites are excessive, the faces are repetitions of those in other works by the same artist, the drawing is lacking in vigour, the flesh tints lack variety,

—but the merits of the performance incomparably exceed them [the faults], and these are of the purely sentimental and intellectual kind. What a tender grace and purity in the female heads! If Mr. Eastlake repeats his model often, at least he has been very lucky in finding or making her: indeed, I don't know in any painter, ancient or modern, such a charming character of female beauty. The countenances of the monks are full of unction: the children, with their mild-beaming eyes, are fresh with recollections of heaven. There is no affectation of middle-age mannerism, such as silly Germans and silly Frenchmen are wont to call Catholic art, and the picture is truly Catholic in consequence, having about it what the Sternhold and Hopkins hymn[88] calls 'solemn mirth', and giving the spectator the utmost possible pleasure in viewing it.

He suggests that coloured lithographs should be taken of the Sternhold and Hopkins hymn... the picture to decorate the rooms of the poor: they would be 'such placid, pious companions for a man's study, that the continual presence of them could not fail to purify his taste and his heart'. Further on he also praises two 'delightful' little pictures by Cope, whose subjects are sufficiently indicated by the 'mottoes' that inspired them: 'Help thy father in his age, and despise him not when thou art in thy full strength'; and 'Reject not the affliction of the afflicted, neither turn away thy face from a poor man.' He finds extremely pathetic and edifying a picture by Biard which depicts a slave-girl in the act of being branded: 'God bless you, Monsieur Biard, for painting it. It stirs the heart more than a hundred thousand tracts, reports, or sermons. . . . Let it hang along with the Hogarths in the National Gallery: it is as good as the best of them.' What a wonderful weapon the painter possesses for spreading the idea of goodness!—concludes the Biedermeier Thackeray. He is less moved by large sacred pictures than by small compositions such as *La prière* by Trimolet (*On Men and Pictures*, in *Fraser's Magazine*, July 1841: *A propos of a Walk in the Louvre*):

A man and his wife are kneeling at an old-fashioned praying desk and the woman clasps a little sickly-looking child in her arms, and all three are praying as earnestly as their simple hearts will let them. The man is a limner or painter of missals, by trade, as we fancy. One of his works lies upon the praying desk, and it is evident that he can paint no more that day, for the sun is just set behind the old-fashioned roofs of the houses in the narrow street of the old city where he lives.

This quiet little picture gave great pleasure to Thackeray, who, in half a dozen visits to the Exhibition, had become 'perfectly acquainted with all the circumstances of the life of the honest missal illuminator and his wife, here praying at the end of their day's work in the calm summer evening'. Thackeray's ideal in painting is Biedermeier: 'quiet scenes of humour and pathos', little domestic pictures (*Picture Gossip*, in *Fraser's Magazine*, June 1845). In his article *On Men and Pictures* we find him admiring a youthful picture by Raphael (possibly a copy, observes Thackeray, but what does that matter?) which represents 'two young people walking hand in hand in a garden', with an expression of 'solemn mirth': behind them is a meadow, at the far end of the meadow a cottage, and close by, a river 'environed by certain prim-looking trees':

> It is impossible for any person who has a sentiment for the art to look at this picture without feeling indescribably moved and pleased by it. It acts upon you—how? How does a beautiful, pious, tender air of Mozart act upon you? What is there in it that should make you happy and gentle, and fill you with all sorts of good thoughts and kindly feelings? . . . the sensual effort in this case carries one quite away from the earth, and up to something that is very like heaven.

Perhaps, he writes, he is wrong in saying that Raphael at thirty had lost the delightful innocence and purity that made his works at twenty so divine; perhaps the 'quaintnesses and imperfections of manner' that can be observed in his early work are the reason why they appear, to Thackeray, so singularly attractive:

> At least among painters of the present day, I feel myself more disposed to recognize spiritual beauties in those whose powers of execution are manifestly incomplete, than in artists whose hands are skilful and manner formed.

He prefers 'honest, hearty representations, which work upon good, simple feeling in a good downright way', and which, if they are not works of art, are certainly works that can do a great deal of good and make honest people happy. On the other hand he turns his face away from Delacroix's *Naufrage de Don Juan*; how can the painter 'dash down such savage histories . . . and fill people's minds with thoughts so dreadful?' What is the use of being made uncomfortable? In an article in the *Pictorial Times* of May 13th, 1843, on the Royal Academy, he recognizes a certain progress in the English school of painting:

> They paint from the heart more than of old, and less from the old heroic, absurd, incomprehensible unattainable rules.

They no longer attempt grandiose subjects. Milton has yielded place to *Gil Blas* and *The Vicar of Wakefield*. The heroic has been deposed; our artists cultivate, instead, the pathetic and the familiar:

A gentle sentiment, an agreeable, quiet incident, a tea-table tragedy, suffices for the most part their gentle powers. Nor surely ought we to quarrel at all with this prevalent mode. . . . We have wisely given up pretending that we were interested in such [the ancient, heroic, allegorical subject], and confess a partiality for more simple and homely themes.

And he passes in review a series of small pictures of this type. Among others is a picture by Charles Landseer, *The Monks of Rubrosi*, a *genre* painting of a kind destined to become a stock type during the nineteenth century (the German Eduard von Grützner later made a speciality of similar monkish episodes):

The scene is extremely cheerful, fresh and brilliant; the land-scape almost as good as the figures, and these are all good. Two grave-looking, aristocratic fathers of the abbey have been fly-fishing; the couple of humbler brethren in brown are busy at a hamper of good things; a gallant young sportsman in green velvet lies on the grass and toasts a pretty lass that is somehow waiting upon their reverences. The picture is not only good, but has the further good quality of being *pleasant*; and some clever artist will do no harm in condescending so far to suit the general taste.

He compares this picture with one by Poole inspired by an episode of the Great Plague in London, a picture too gloomy to decorate any sort of surroundings. So also in the article *May Gambols* he finds fault, for the same reasons, with another of Poole's pictures, *The Moors beleaguered in Valencia* (a spectacle of people in the extremities of hunger), and a picture by Leahy, *Lady Jane Grey praying before Execution*:

The coarse fury of Zurbaran and Morales is as far below the sweet and beneficent calm of Murillo as a butcher is beneath a hero. Don't let us have any more of these hideous exhibitions—these Ghoul festivals. It may be remembered that Amina in *The Arabian Nights*, who liked churchyard suppers, could only eat a grain of rice when she came to natural food. There is a good deal of sly satire in the apologue which might be applied to many (especially French) literary and pictorial artists of the convulsionary school.

He considers nevertheless that Charles Landseer goes too far in making solemn themes domestic, as in the picture of *Noah's Ark*. 'No painter', he remarks (*May Gambols*, in *Fraser's Magazine*, June 1844), 'has a right to treat great historical subjects in such a fashion.' In this essay Thackeray reacts to some extent against artists condescending to sentimental, pretty subjects. He finds fault with Redgrave's picture inspired by *The Song of the Shirt* and with the same artist's *Marriage Morning*, and condemns Frank Stone, and Delaroche's *Holy Family*, for sentimentality. And in *Picture Gossip* (*Fraser's Magazine*, June 1845) he disapproves of the bourgeois treatment of the subject in *Moses' Mother parting with him before leaving him in the bulrushes*, by Eddis. He also reacts, in the same article, against the 'decidedly spoony' quality of Redgrave's *The Governess* (she is sitting in the deserted schoolroom, with the piano open and a copy of 'Home, sweet Home' on the music-stand, and a tray with tea and bread-and-butter which she, in her homesickness, has not touched) and also against another sentimental picture, *Arrival of the Overland Mail*, which shows a lady receiving the communication of the death of her husband, whose portrait, in major's uniform, hangs upon the wall. 'Sentiment [as Walker said in *The Original*][89] is like garlic in made dishes: it should be felt everywhere and seen nowhere.' He praises Frith (*The Good Pastor*) for having observed proper proportions. Let asses set about painting big historical pictures; Frith prefers the humble path where flowers grow in abundance and children prattle in the byways. This is the kind of painting that should be cultivated today, he says: 'kindly, beautiful, inspiring delicate sympathies, and awakening tender good-humour'. *The Good Pastor* illustrates 'the right sort of sentiment':

The dear old parson with his congregation of old and young clustered round him; the little ones plucking him by the gown, with wondering eyes, half-roguery, half-terror; the smoke is curling up from the cottage chimneys in a peaceful, Sabbath sort of way; the three village quidnuncs are chattering together at the churchyard stile; there's a poor girl seated there on a stone, who has been crossed

in love evidently, and looks anxiously to the parson for a little doubtful consolation. That's the real sort of sentiment—there's no need
of a great, clumsy, black-edged letter to placard her misery, as
it were, after Mr. Redgrave's fashion; the sentiment is only the
more sincere for being unobtrusive, and the spectator gives his compassion the more readily, because the unfortunate object makes no
coarse demand upon his pity.

Certain figures in the picture make Thackeray think of
Greuze and Teniers.

There was nothing he abhorred so much as French
classical painting: David, Girodet and the rest of them (the
'Imperio-Davido-classical school', as he called them) were
impostors. He disliked the subjects of their pictures—
'Orestes pursued by every variety of Furies; numbers of
little wolf-sucking Romuluses; Hectors and Andromaches
in a complication of parting embraces', and so on; and in
each one of these large paintings the usual accessories of
the sublime—white cloaks, white urns, white columns,
white statues, with every other colour participating in the
same pale or livid marmoreal hue. The most conspicuous
examples of the sublime were to be sought in murders or
deaths of illustrious figures, the death of Lucretia, of Zeno-
bia, of Hector, of Caesar, of Eudamidas—a fifth-act-of-a-
tragedy classicism, ideas of beauty and sublimity that seem
to be taken from the bloody melodramas of the *boulevard*:[90]

Fancy living in a room with David's *sans-culotte* Leonidas staring
perpetually in your face! . . . I think in my heart I am fonder of
pretty third-rate pictures than of your great thundering first-rates.
. . . Let us thank Heaven, my dear sir, for according to us the power
to taste and appreciate the pleasures of mediocrity.

He spared no praises, however, to Mulready, Wilkie,
and Eastlake: he considered Mulready's colouring as brilliant as that of Van Eyck, and judged that the day would
come when a picture by him would be as much sought after
'as a Hemlinck [i.e. Memling] or a Gerard Dow . . .
nowadays'. He found Etty's pictures immodest, but his
colour sublime as Titian's, and his painting worthy to rank
with that of Rubens. He admired Turner's *Fighting Témé-
raire*, but deplored his pea-green skies, crimson-lake trees,

and orange and purple grass', &c.—his impressionism, in fact. He praised Danby for his picture *The Deluge*, which was superior to Poussin and to Turner. He extolled the minute realism of Maclise's still life painting: 'This young man has the greatest power of hand that was ever had, perhaps, by any painter in any time or country.' He extolled Landseer for similar virtues: 'Fido [in *Fido's Bath*] is wonderful, and so are the sponges, and hair-brushes, and looking-glass, prepared for the dog's bath.' Elsewhere he praised Landseer's *The Stag*: the enormous stag in a snowy landscape, beside a great blue Northern lake, 'stalks over the snow down to the shore. . . . In a word, your teeth begin to clatter as you look at the picture, and it can't properly be seen without a greatcoat.' For classical sculpture he had no liking: it appeared to him cold (*A Pictorial Rhapsody*, in *Fraser's Magazine*, June 1840):

> Look at Apollo the divine: there is no blood in his marble veins, no warmth in his bosom, no fire or speculation in his dull, awful eyes. Laocoon writhes and twists in his anguish that never can, in the breast of any spectator, create the smallest degree of pity. . . . Such monsters of beauty are quite out of the reach of human sympathy.

And, coming from such considerations to a little picture by Eastlake, he finds that 'out of a homely subject, and a few simple figures not at all wonderful for excessive beauty and grandeur, the artist can make something infinitely more beautiful than Medicean Venuses, and sublimer than Pythian Apollos'. Eastlake has in truth something ot Raphael's fire, 'a tender, yearning sympathy and love for God's beautiful world and creatures.' And after praising, as we have already seen, the grace and tender sentiment of Eastlake's pictures, he regrets that the portrait of Miss Bury which Eastlake is now exhibiting is too realistic in comparison with the ideal image of the same woman that he showed six years before, which had been engraved for one of the *Annals*. Here the lovely lady looks as though she were not wearing a corset: 'O beautiful lily-bearer of six years since! you should not have appeared like a mortal after having once shone upon us as an angel.' From which it can be seen that Thackeray was inimical to the heroic manner of 1810, but not to the sugary and sentimental manner of 1840. A picture by Mulready which he invites his reader to admire, a little further on, with the title *First Love*, represents a 'young fellow, so solemn, so tender, whispering into the ear of that dear girl . . . who is folding a pair of slim arms round a little baby, and making believe to nurse it,' in the shade of some trees by a stile. A more Victorian picture could not be imagined—just as nothing could be more Victorian than the version he gives, a little later, of a strophe of Horace (*Odes*, iii. 2), in which he renders: 'Vetabo, qui Cereris sacrum vulgarit arcanae' by 'And fly the wretch who dares to strip Love of its sacred mystery', and: 'sub iisdem sit trabibus' by 'My loyal legs I would not stretch Beneath the same mahogany'. The drawings of Chalon, with their 'satins and lace . . . and charming little lap-dogs', surpass, in his eyes, the magic of Watteau and Lancret.

* * * * *

The 'humble Christian' aspect of Thackeray emphasized by M. Las Vergnas is, nevertheless, far less conspicuous than another aspect of him which we encounter at every step—his anti-heroic feeling. We have just given a sample of his tastes in the matter of painting. In his novels, not merely does he describe mediocre persons, but, as has already been mentioned, he does not portray such persons at moments when they rise above themselves through some overwhelming emotion:

> What passed between that lady and the boy is not of import. A veil should be thrown over those sacred emotions of love and grief. The maternal passion is a sacred mystery to me (*Pendennis*, chap. ii).

> I do not care to pursue this last scene. Let us close the door as the children kneel by the sufferer's bedside, and to the old man's petition for forgiveness, and to the young girl's sobbing vows of love and fondness, say a reverent Amen (*Adventures of Philip*, chap. xxix).

The very conception that Thackeray formed of the superior man is an anti-heroic conception. The hero, for Thackeray, is not an exceptional man; he is, rather, a man just like other men who only 'in the presence of the great occasion' is capable of showing his superiority over other men; when the critical moment is over, he falls back into normality, into mediocrity. Thackeray's conception of the hero, therefore, is relative, not absolute.[91] His ideal is not so much an individual, as a rule of conduct—the gentleman, as we have seen above:

> What is it to be a gentleman? Is it to have lofty aims, to lead a pure life, to keep your honour virgin; to have the esteem of your fellow-citizens, and the love of your fireside; to bear good fortune meekly; to suffer evil with constancy; and through evil or good to maintain truth always? Show me the happy man whose life exhibits these qualities, and him we will salute as gentleman, whatever his rank may be (*The Four Georges: George IV*).

A critic, Walter Frewen Lord, has given an essay on Thackeray the title of *The Apostle of Mediocrity*.[92] For the great figures of history, according to Thackeray, are different from other men only at moments of crisis; yet the thing upon which he insists is not the moment of crisis, the apotheosis of the character concerned, but rather his ordinary condition. Read, for instance, his essay on Louis XIV, in the *Meditations at Versailles* chapter of the *Paris Sketch Book*. It is an anti-heroic outburst: the French had exalted 'le Roi Soleil', and Thackeray tries with all his might to deprive him of all lustre:

> The city [of Versailles] was peopled with parasites, who daily came to do worship before the creator of these wonders—the Great King. 'Dieu seul est grand', said courtly Massillon; but next to him, as the prelate thought, was certainly Louis, his viceregent here upon earth—God's lieutenant-governor of the world,—before whom courtiers used to fall on their knees, and shade their eyes, as if the light of his countenance, like the sun, which shone supreme in heaven, the type of him, was too dazzling to bear.
>
> Did ever the sun shine upon such a king before, in such a palace? —or, rather, did such a king ever shine upon the sun? When Majesty came out of his chamber, in the midst of his superhuman splendours, viz. in his cinnamon-coloured coat, embroidered with diamonds; his pyramid of a wig [*Thackeray observes in a footnote*: It is fine to think that, in the days of his youth, his Majesty Louis XIV used to *powder his wig with gold-dust*]; his red-heeled shoes, that lifted him four inches from the ground, 'that he scarcely

Q

seemed to touch'; when he came out, blazing upon the dukes and duchesses that waited his rising,—what could the latter do, but cover their eyes, and wink, and tremble? And did he not himself believe, as he stood there, on his high heels, under his ambrosial periwig, that there was something in him more than man—something above Fate?

Thackeray examines the panegyric of Louis XIV written by a Jesuit, and makes a mock of the terms 'l'invincible', 'le sage', &c., bestowed upon him by his flatterer (he refers to a 'book of medals [dedicated] to the august Infants of France': this is evidently the *Histoire du roy Louis-le-Grand par les médailles, emblêmes, devises*, &c., by Father Claude-François Menestrier, 1689).

'Look at this Galerie des Glaces,' cries Monsieur Vatout, staggering with surprise at the appearance of the room, two hundred and forty-two feet long, and forty high; 'here it was that Louis displayed all the grandeur of royalty; and such was the splendour of his court, and the luxury of the times, that this immense room could hardly contain the crowd of courtiers that pressed around the monarch.' Wonderful! wonderful! Eight thousand four hundred and sixty square feet of courtiers! Give a square yard to each, and you have a matter of three thousand of them. Think of three thousand courtiers per day, and all the chopping and changing of them for near forty years; some of them dying, some getting their wishes, and retiring to their provinces to enjoy their plunder: some disgraced, and going home to pine away out of the light of the sun; new ones perpetually arriving,—pushing, squeezing, for their place, in the crowded Galerie des Glaces. A quarter of a million of noble countenances, at the very least, must those glasses have reflected. Rouge, diamonds, ribands, patches, upon the faces of smiling ladies: towering periwigs, sleek-shaven crowns, tufted moustaches, scars, and grizzled whiskers, worn by ministers, priests, dandies, and grim old commanders.—So many faces, O ye gods! and every one of them lies! So many tongues, vowing devotion and respectful love to the great king in his six-inch wig; and only poor La Vallière's, amongst them all, which had a word of truth for the dull ears of Louis of Bourbon. . . .

She goes, and the finished hero never sheds a tear. What a noble pitch of stoicism to have reached! Our Louis was so great, that the little woes of mean people were beyond him: his friends died, his mistresses left him; his children, one by one, were cut off before his eyes, and great Louis is not moved, in the slightest degree! As how, indeed, should a god be moved?

I have often liked to think about this strange character in the world, who moved in it, bearing about a full belief of his own infallibility; teaching his generals the art of war, his ministers the science of government, his wits taste, his courtiers dress; ordering deserts to become gardens, turning villages into palaces, at a breath; and, indeed, the august figure of the man, as he towers upon his throne, cannot fail to inspire one with respect and awe:—how grand those flowing locks appear; how awful that sceptre; how magnificent those flowing robes! In Louis, surely, if in any one, the majesty of kinghood is represented.

But let us make a closer analysis of this 'hero as king', as Carlyle would have said:

But a king is not every inch a king, for all the poet may say; and it is curious to see how much precise majesty there is in that majestic figure of Ludovicus Rex. In the plate opposite, we have endeavoured to make the exact calculation.

The plate shows three figures: the clothes in a heroic pose upon a faceless dummy with stick-like arms and legs; on the far side the King in these same clothes, in the same solemn pose in which a certain famous portrait (by Hyacinthe Rigaud; in the Louvre) shows him; while in the centre is a horrible little old man, bald and paunchy, in shoes without any high heels, one hand in his waistcoat pocket and the other leaning on a stick.[93]

The idea of kingly dignity is equally strong in the two outer figures; and you see, at once, that majesty is made out of the wig, the high-heeled shoes, and cloak, all fleurs-de-lis bespangled. As for the little, lean, shrivelled, paunchy old man, of five feet two, in a jacket and breeches, there is no majesty in *him*, at any rate; and yet he has just stept out of that very suit of clothes. Put the wig and shoes on him, and he is six feet high [like the giants in *Rheingold*]; —the other fripperies, and he stands before you majestic, imperial, and heroic! Thus do barbers and cobblers make the gods that we worship: for do we not all worship him? Yes; though we all know him to be stupid, heartless, short, of doubtful personal courage, worship and admire him we must; and have set up, in our hearts, a grand image of him, endowed with wit, magnanimity, valour, and enormous heroical stature.

And what magnanimous acts are attributed to him! or, rather, how differently do we view the actions of heroes and common men, and find that the same thing shall be a wonderful virtue in the former, which, in the latter, is only an ordinary act of duty. . . .

Do not let us abuse poor old Louis, on account of this monstrous pride; but only lay it to the charge of the fools who believed and worshipped it. If, honest man, he believed himself to be almost a god, it was only because thousands of people had told him so—people, only half liars, too, who did, in the depths of their slavish respect, admire the man almost as much as they said they did.

In the same chapter Thackeray shakes his head over the question of military glory:

We will not examine all the glories of France, as here they are portrayed in pictures and marble: catalogues are written about these miles of canvas, representing all the revolutionary battles, from Valmy to Waterloo,—all the triumphs of Louis XIV—all the mistresses of his successor—and all the great men who have flourished since the French empire began. Military heroes are most of these—fierce constables in shining steel, marshals in voluminous wigs, and brave grenadiers in bearskin caps; some dozens of whom gained crowns, principalities, dukedoms; some hundreds, plunder and epaulets; some millions, death in African sands, or in icy Russian plains, under the guidance, and for the good, of that arch-hero, Napoleon. By far the greater part of 'all the glories' of France (as of most other countries) is made up of these military men; and a fine satire it is, on the cowardice of mankind, that they pay such an extraordinary homage to the virtue called courage, filling their history books with tales about it, and nothing but it.[94]

As for the reverse side of the medal in this unmasking of hypocrisy preached by Thackeray, it is nothing more nor less than the negation of the epic spirit. Thackeray carries on and accentuates the bourgeois attitude towards the military which had been taking shape ever since the Renaissance Humanists; but his negation of glory is far more all-embracing; he preaches not merely the vanity of earthly things, but actually denies the possibility of man being 'great' in any way or on any occasion. In *The Four Georges*, he says:

We are not the Historic Muse, but her ladyship's attendant, talebearer—*valet de chambre*—for whom no man is a hero.[95]

In *Vanity Fair*, instead of a description of the Battle of Waterloo, we have little detached scenes of episodes in

Brussels, like so many Dutch *genre* pictures: life in the elegant meeting-places of the English society that has arrived with the army; the ball; George Osborne who, before leaving for the battle, meditates beside the bed where his wife is sleeping, until finally the whole city awakes to the sound of the trumpets and drums of the infantry and the bagpipes of the Scots. It is the moment of the battle, and Thackeray writes:

> We do not claim to rank among the military novelists. Our place is with the non-combatants. When the decks are cleared for action we go below and wait meekly. . . . We shall go no farther with the —th than to the city gate: and leaving Major O'Dowd to his duty, come back to the Major's wife, and the ladies, and the baggage.

The past lives for him more truly in its humble than in its grandiose documentations: *Tom Jones* is more instructive than the official history-books; a volume of Smollett or *The Spectator* carries a greater amount of truth than a volume of history which purports to be all true; from a work of fiction can be gathered 'the expression of the life of the time; of the manners, of the movement, the dress, the pleasures, the laughter, the ridicules of society—the old times live again'.[96] The same can be said of the caricatures and lithographs of life in Paris. And his intention, in his lectures on the Hanoverian kings (*The Four Georges*), was not to speak of battles, of politics, of statesmen and measures of state, but 'to sketch the manners and life of the old world', to amuse his audience 'for a few hours with talk about the old society'; he delights in such trifling chronicles, he takes pleasure in attributing the downfall of the Stuarts and the changing of the course of history to the Pretender's followers' stopping to powder their hair instead of starting an assault upon the Rock at Edinburgh: all this for a *pulveris exigui jactu*, a 'little toss of powder for the hair'. He dwells less upon battles than upon the episode of the soldiers who were flogged for wearing the oak-bough, the Stuart emblem, in their hats; he prefers the *genre* picture to the great historical piece. When speaking of George II he begins like this:

> On the afternoon of the 14th of June, 1727, two horsemen

might have been perceived galloping along the road from Chelsea to Richmond. The foremost, cased in the jackboots of the period, was a broad-faced, jolly-looking, and very corpulent cavalier, *etc.*[97]

He appreciates Sir Robert Walpole, who 'gave Englishmen no conquests, but . . . peace, and ease, and freedom; the three per cents nearly at par, and wheat at five and six-and-twenty shillings a quarter'. Speaking of the reign of George III:

It is to the middle class we must look for the safety of England: the working educated men, . . . the good clergy not corrupted into parasites by hopes of preferment; the tradesmen rising into manly opulence; the painters pursuing their gentle calling; the men of letters in their quiet studies: these are the men whom we love and like to read of in the last age. How small the grandees and the men of pleasure look beside them!

And when he reflects upon the legends of the Crusades as exalted by Scott, he declares that Saladin was a pearl of refinement in comparison with the brutal Richard Cœur-de-Lion, the beef-eater, and thanks heaven that grocers rule the world nowadays instead of barons.[98] To adopt the terminology of the Stock Exchange, whereas Carlyle tries to raise prices, and is a 'bull', Thackeray tries to bring prices down, and is a 'bear'. And since he does not allow 'great' men, even less does he allow that worship of the great which is snobbery, that affectation of living in contact with the finest flower of society. Yet this attitude of wishing to reduce values is due not merely to a spirit of mediocrity; it is due also to another bourgeois quality: honesty, modesty. Thackeray detests pose; his pet aversion, the snob, is nothing more than a *poseur*. Hence his disapproval of the truculent romanticism of Byron, and his contrasting of the poet's heroines, his Leilas and Gulnaras, with a simple Somersetshire peasant-girl:

Give me a fresh, dewy, healthy rose out of Somersetshire; not one of those superb, tawdry, unwholesome exotics, which are only good to make poems about. Lord Byron wrote more cant of this sort than any poet I know of. . . . That man *never* wrote from his heart. He got up rapture and enthusiasm with an eye to the public. . . .

He used also to relate sarcastically how excited Tennyson would become when declaiming *Ulysses*, especially at the line: 'And see the great Achilles, whom we knew.' 'He went through the streets', said Thackeray, 'screaming about his great Achilles, whom we knew, as if we had all made the acquaintance of that gentleman, and were very proud of it.'

Great was the surprise of the Americans, fresh from the experience of Dickens's histrionics, when they had the opportunity to observe the demeanour of Thackeray. Here is the account of an eye-witness (from the *New York Evening Post*):

Few expected to see so large a man; he is gigantic, six feet four at least. . . . Then there was a notion in the minds of many that there must be something dashing and 'fast' in his appearance, whereas his costume was perfectly plain; the expression of his face grave and earnest; his address perfectly unaffected. . . . The most striking feature in his whole manner was the utter absence of affectation of any kind. He did not permit himself to appear conscious that he was an object of peculiar interest to the audience, neither was he guilty of the greater error of not appearing to care whether they were interested in him or not. In other words, he inspired his audience with a respect for him, as a man proportioned to the admiration which his books have inspired for him as an author.

And Theodore Roosevelt wrote to his children: 'Of course the fundamental difference is that Thackeray was a gentleman, and Dickens was not.' He had indeed the quality of sincerity, a critical habit of mistrusting, of not trusting, himself, an uneasiness. There is a southern Italian expression for 'being afraid'—'*Non mi fido*—I don't trust myself'. And of such stuff it is obvious that heroes are not made. The origin of this attitude is to be sought in the rude shock suffered by his sense of security, his self-confidence, when, as a child of six, he was torn abruptly from his family circle to be brought up among strangers in England. Just as, furthermore, the sudden curtailment of maternal caresses left in him a deposit of repressed nostalgia, of pent-up sentimentality, kept in shamefaced subjection.

This also was one of the reasons for the many grotesque pseudonyms used by Thackeray in his early work—his hesitation in putting his name to any act or any written word; this was the reason for the modest sub-title of *Vanity Fair—Pen and Pencil Sketches of English Society*, implying short descriptive articles rather than a novel in the full sense of the word, a series of little scenes, almost, as in Ben Jonson's *Bartholomew Fair*. And this was the reason, too, for the grotesque, caricaturish, ironical tone which is habitual to Thackeray: the ironist stands aside from life, he does not involve himself in it; he is commentator, not poet. Hence the repression of emotional impulses, the perpetual damper on all 'feeling'. He had a habit of tearing up letters in which he had let himself go in some sentimental effusion. A typical case of this occurred when, on leaving New York, he had to part from the Baxters, whose elder daughter, the eighteen-year-old Sally, he admired, considering her to be a living portrait of Beatrix in *Esmond*. At first he feared he had been too bold in kissing the girls good-bye; as soon as he reached Boston he started writing them a long letter, only to put it in the fire as being too fond and sentimental; a second letter suffered the same fate; and only the next day was he able to express his gratitude in his usual whimsical, bantering vein.[99]

Professor Lionel Stevenson remarks:[100]

The cruelty of some of his sneers at namby-pamby sentimentalism was almost masochistic; he was lacerating a shrinking victim within himself, which had been driven into hiding on his earliest school-day at Southampton and terrified beyond recovery by the crassness of Charterhouse. The only outlet for this suppressed and distorted softness was in sudden flashes of austere moralistic disapproval.

Let us consider the *Ballad of Bouillabaisse*. Its theme is the same as that of Lamb's *The Old Familiar Faces*, but whereas Lamb, in this poem, abandoned himself completely to the nostalgia of regret, with his disconsolate refrain: 'All, all are gone, the old familiar faces':

> Ghost-like I paced round the haunts of my childhood;
> Earth seem'd a desert I was bound to traverse,
>   Seeking to find the old familiar faces . . .
> How some they have died, and some they have left me,
> And some are taken from me; all are departed;
>   All, all are gone, the old familiar faces—

Thackeray, in the *Ballad of Bouillabaisse*, is determined to
be a 'bear' even from his very title, which in itself is 'price-
lowering': his tone has almost the playfulness of the Italian
cinquecentists' lines in praise of the gudgeon, of eels, &c.
And what could be more non-committal than the note of
deliberate parody at the beginning? The ballad tells of
a tavern where the cooking is good:

> A street there is in Paris famous,
>   For which no rhyme our language yields,
> Rue Neuve des Petits Champs its name is—
>   The New Street of the Little Fields.
> And here's an inn, not rich and splendid,
>   But still in comfortable case;
> The which in youth I oft attended,
>   To eat a bowl of Bouillabaisse.

A pedestrian beginning, on the bourgeois-Ariosto-like note
of the *parva sed apta mihi*. In the second stanza is a description in verse of the famous fish soup:

> This Bouillabaisse a noble dish is—
>   A sort of soup or broth or brew,
> Or hotchpotch of all sorts of fishes,
>   That Greenwich never could outdo;
> Green herbs, red peppers, mussels, saffron,
>   Soles, onions, garlic, roach, and dace:
> All these you eat at TERRÉ's tavern,
>   In that one dish of Bouillabaisse.

What follows could not be more bourgeois, with its trite
theme of the jovial monk, reminiscent of the *genre* pictures
in vogue during the nineteenth century, which we have
already mentioned:

> Indeed, a rich and savoury stew 'tis;
>   And true philosophers, methinks,
> Who love all sorts of natural beauties,
>   Should love good victuals and good drinks.
> And Cordelier or Benedictine
>   Might gladly, sure, his lot embrace,
> Nor find a fast-day too afflicting,
>   Which served him up a Bouillabaisse.

The poet returns to the tavern after several years, and

nothing seems changed; the red-cheeked oyster-woman is
still at the door. But when he asks the waiter: 'How 's
Monsieur TERRÉ, waiter, pray?' a sad note creeps in, but
is quickly smothered:

> 'Monsieur is dead this many a day'.
> 'It is the lot of saint and sinner,
>   So honest TERRÉ's run his race'.
> 'What will Monsieur require for dinner?'
>   'Say, do you still cook Bouillabaisse?'
>
> 'Oh, oui, Monsieur', 's the waiter's answer;
>   'Quel vin Monsieur désire-t-il?'
> 'Tell me a good one'.—'That I can, Sir:
>   The Chambertin with yellow seal'.
> 'So TERRÉ's gone', I say, and sink in
>   My old accustom'd corner-place;
> 'He's done with feasting and with drinking,
>   With Burgundy and Bouillabaisse'.

The accent becomes more nostalgic, but the rhymes continue to be jocular:

> My old accustom'd corner here is,
>   The table still is in the nook;
> Ah! vanish'd many a busy year is
>   This well-known chair since last I took.
> When first I saw ye, *cari luoghi*,
>   I'd scarce a beard upon my face,
> And now a grizzled, grim old fogy,
>   I sit and wait for Bouillabaisse.
>
> Where are you, old companions trusty
>   Of early days here met to dine?
> Come, waiter! quick, a flagon crusty—
>   I'll pledge them in the good old wine.
> The kind old voices and old faces
>   My memory can quick retrace;
> Around the board they take their places
>   And share the wine and Bouillabaisse.
>
> There's JACK has made a wondrous marriage;
>   There's laughing TOM is laughing yet;
> There's brave AUGUSTUS drives his carriage;
>   There's poor old FRED in the *Gazette*;

On JAMES's head the grass is growing:
  Good Lord! the world has wagged apace
Since here we set the claret flowing,
  And drank, and ate the Bouillabaisse.

Ah me! how quick the days are flitting!
  I mind me of a time that's gone,
When here I'd sit, as now I'm sitting,
  In this same place—but not alone.
A fair young form was nestled near me,
  A dear, dear face looked fondly up.
And sweetly spoke and smiled to cheer me
  —There's no one now to share my cup.

So ends the stanza, without the refrain, and we plunge into
the full tide of pathos; but the poet recovers himself, and,
after dots representing an interruption, brings his verses to
an end, once more in a jovial manner though his face is
lined with tears:

I drink it as the Fates ordain it.
  Come, fill it, and have done with rhymes:
Fill up the lonely glass, and drain it
  In memory of dear old times.
Welcome the wine, whate'er the seal is;
  And sit you down and say your grace
With thankful heart, whate'er the meal is.
  —Here comes the smoking Bouillabaisse.[101]

In *Charity and Humour* Thackeray exclaims:

Humour! If tears are the alms of gentle spirits, and may be
counted, as sure they may, among the sweetest of life's charities,—
of that kindly sensibility, and sweet sudden emotion, which exhibits
itself at the eyes, I know no such provocative as humour. It is an
irresistible sympathiser; it surprises you into compassion; you are
laughing and disarmed, and suddenly forced into tears. . . . Humour!
humour is the mistress of tears; she knows the way to the *fons
lachrymarum*, strikes in dry and rugged places with her enchanting
wand, and bids the fountain gush and sparkle. She has refreshed
myriads more from her natural springs, than ever tragedy has
watered from her pompous old urn.

*   *   *   *   *

Convivial humour acts, in the *Ballad of Bouillabaisse*, as
a conductor to sentimental emotionalism, and that this

must have vibrated strongly in Thackeray is indicated by, for instance, a passage in *Lovel the Widower* (chap. iv):

> Oh! the whole world throbs with vain heartpangs, and tosses and heaves with longing, unfulfilled desires! All night, and all over the world, bitter tears are dropping as regular as the dew, and cruel memories are haunting the pillow. Close my hot eyes, kind Sleep! Do not visit it, dear delusive images out of the Past!

The feeling of desolation, of disconsolate loneliness, which is perhaps the strongest feeling in Thackeray, lies at the root of his melancholy—a feeling that dates back to his school years, when the small boy felt himself a stranger amongst the other boys, isolated amongst his hostile contemporaries at Charterhouse. His was a case of heartbroken solipsism, of loss of contact with the world, characteristic of an extreme stage of bourgeois individualism. Forced back upon himself, the individual becomes reserved, unsociable, mistrustful of contacts, shy even of sympathy——'the horrible pain of sympathy'—seeking every possible pretext to react against sympathy by becoming aggressive. Thackeray was capable of feeling an emotion more strongly in memory, when it was already too late and manifested itself only in a void; in *Esmond* (Book I, chap. ix) we read of acts of kindness accepted as a matter of course, almost without thanks, until later, when they are remembered many years afterwards, and tears of gratitude are shed:[102]

> Then forgotten tones of love recur to us, and kind glances shine out of the past—oh so bright and clear!—oh so longed after!—because they are out of reach: as holiday music from within-side a prison wall—or sunshine seen through the bars; more prized because unattainable—more bright because of the contrast of present darkness and solitude, whence there is no escape.

One might think he took a kind of painful, voluptuous pleasure in this frustration of affection.

And, as if to illustrate the moulding of destiny upon character—each man has the life his character merits—Thackeray's destiny was that of a solitary. Events took it upon themselves to confirm him in his situation. The domestic fireside that formed his innermost ideal soon failed him; and he became a frequenter of clubs, and sought a family amongst strangers—he who 'was made for the nursery folly and had no home . . . the very anguish of the heart drove his soul to the waste of clubland' (Quiller-Couch). One can see, from Thackeray's correspondence, how his heart bled; his external sarcasm is but the reaction of a character that is tender, reserved, cautious, and therefore unable to find an outlet for feeling, and furious at being thus bottled up. His shyness about his own emotions is revealed, for instance, in the recurrence of the adjective 'blushing' in this passage from *Esmond* (Book III, chap. vii):

> And tender and blushing faintly with a benediction in her eyes, the gentle creature [Lady Castlewood] kissed him. They walked out hand in hand, through the old court, and to the terrace-walk, where the grass was glistening with dew, and the birds in the green woods above were singing their delicious choruses under the blushing morning sky.

And the two lovers recall a thousand memories of their youth, beautiful and sad.

Thackeray's daughter, Anne Thackeray Ritchie, compared her father with Goldsmith for tenderness of heart; to Trollope he was tender as charity itself; to M. Las Vergnas he comes near to Steele, because his breast swells equally with kindness towards all mankind—'one whose own breast exuberated with human kindness' (these were the words used by Thackeray of Steele in the *English Humourists*). Characteristic is this passage from *Esmond* (Book II, chap. vi), in which the writer asks himself what is the ambition to become famous, compared with love:

> To be rich, to be famous? What do these profit a year hence, when other names sound louder than yours, when you lie hidden away under ground, along with the idle titles engraven on your coffin? But only true love lives after you—follows your memory with secret blessing—or precedes you, and intercedes for you. *Non omnis moriar*—if dying, I yet live in a tender heart or two; nor am lost and hopeless living, if a sainted departed soul still loves and prays for me.

This passage finds a parallel in his letters—in one, for example, to his beloved Mrs. Brookfield:

> I swear the best thought I have is to remember that I shall have

your love surviving me and with a constant tenderness blessing my memory. I can't all perish living in your heart.

That Thackeray's sentimentality, if it had been completely unfolded, might have been of a sickly kind, irritating to us moderns, albeit typically Victorian, can be seen from certain phrases that escape him in moments of inattention—the phrase in the *Ballad of Bouillabaisse*, for instance: 'A fair young form was nestled near me', alluding to his wife who is spiritually dead; or, in *Pendennis*, this apostrophe to a bunch of flowers: 'Poor little silent flowers! You'll be dead to-morrow. What business had you to show your red cheeks in this dingy place?'; or this expression of pity for Fanny: '*Little* Fanny was very much changed by the fever and agitation, and passion and despair, which the past three weeks had poured upon the head of that *little* victim'; or, in *The Virginians*, when he wishes to describe virginal love, impatient and shy: 'Hop back to thy perch, and cover thy head with thy wing, thou tremulous little fluttering creature!'—a picture of a little bird that seems to be taken straight from a Victorian keepsake. In the same novel can be seen these further expressions of tearful and emblematic sentimentality:[103]

> You remember. It may be all dead and buried; but in a moment, up it springs out of its grave, and looks, and smiles, and whispers as of yore when it clung to your arm, and dropped fresh tears on your heart. It is here, and alive, did I say? O far far away! O lonely hearth and cold ashes! Here is the vase, but the roses are gone; here is the shore, and yonder the ship was moored; but the anchors are up, and it has sailed away for ever.

Thackeray's loftiest notes are concerned with the 'sacred and secret' family affections—notes which give the essence of the Biedermeier world. Thus, in *Esmond* (Book III, chap. xiii):

> That happiness, which hath subsequently crowned [my life], cannot be written in words; 'tis of its nature sacred and secret, and not to be spoken of,[104] though the heart be ever so full of thankfulness, save to Heaven and the One Ear alone—to one fond being, the truest, and tenderest, and purest wife ever man was blest with.

There follows a paean of praise to conjugal love:

In the name of my wife, I write the completion of hope and the summit of happiness. To have such a love is the one blessing, in comparison of which all earthly joy is of no value; and to think of her is to praise God. . . . The tender matron, as beautiful in her autumn, and as pure as virgins in their spring, with blushes of love and 'eyes of meek surrender', yielded to my respectful importunity, and consented to share my home. Let the last words I write thank her, and bless her who hath blessed it.

Esmond ends with an idyllic picture of the new family transplanted to the shores of the Potomac, in a halcyon St. Martin's-summer climate, amongst negro slaves 'the happiest and merriest, I think, in all this country', a picture which calls to mind the rosiest ideals of the eighteenth-century bourgeoisie. Lady Castlewood is an incarnation of the angel-woman (whom we have already met in Dickens, in Agnes Wickfield)—the angel-woman who is described in *Pendennis* (chap. ii) as follows:

I think it is not national prejudice which makes me believe that a high-bred English lady is the most complete of all Heaven's subjects in this world. In whom else do you see so much grace, and so much virtue; so much faith, and so much tenderness; with such a perfect refinement and chastity? And by high-bred ladies I don't mean duchesses and countesses. Be they ever so high in station, they can be but ladies, and no more. But almost every man who lives in the world has the happiness, let us hope, of counting a few such persons amongst his circle of acquaintance—women in whose angelical natures there is something awful, as well as beautiful, to contemplate; at whose feet the wildest and fiercest of us must fall down and humble ourselves, in admiration of that adorable purity which never seems to do or to think wrong.[105]

And again, still apropos of Pendennis's mother (chap. lvii): 'an angel, transfigured and glorified with love—for which love, as for the greatest of the bounties and wonders of God's provision for us, let us kneel and thank Our Father.' The death of Pendennis's mother, and that of Colonel Newcome, give Thackeray the opportunity for scenes of pathos in which it can be said that he in no way lags behind Dickens's tearful episodes of young people's deaths. Such was the taste of the period.

The tone of Thackeray's sentimentalism is naturally, when it displays itself, elegiac. Elegiac, too, and not cruel (as they would be, were the novelist perfectly logical) are the endings of Thackeray's novels. It has been rightly said:[106] 'Thackeray is a romanticist since he avoids many a logical outcome of circumstances by killing off somebody and blinding the reader with a tear-drenched handkerchief.'

Elegiac and melancholy, also, is Thackeray's attitude towards modern progress. In this he is a bourgeois of the Lamb type, not of the Macaulay type which hails the latest scientific discoveries with delight. The eyes of Thackeray are turned towards the past. Look, for example, at the essay *De Juventute* in the *Roundabout Papers*:

We who have lived before railways were made, belong to another world. In how many hours could the Prince of Wales drive from Brighton to London, with a light carriage built expressly, and relays of horses longing to gallop the next stage? Do you remember Sir Somebody, the coachman of the Age, who took our half-crown so affably? It was only yesterday; but what a gulf between now and then! *Then* was the old world. Stage-coaches, more or less swift, riding-horses, pack-horses, highwaymen, knights in armour, Norman invaders, Roman legends, Druids, Ancient Britons painted blue, and so forth—all these belong to the old period. I will concede a halt in the midst of it, and allow that gunpowder and printing tended to modernize the world. But your railroad starts the new era, and we of a certain age belong to the new time and the old one. . . . We have stepped out of the old world on to 'Brunel's'[107] vast deck, and across the waters *ingens patet tellus*. . . . [The old world] lies on the other side of yonder embankments. You young folks have never seen it; and Waterloo is to you no more than Agincourt, and George IV than Sardanapalus. We elderly people have lived in that prae-railroad world, which has passed into limbo and vanished from under us. I tell you it was firm under our feet once, and not long ago. They have raised those railroad embankments up, and shut off the old world that was behind them. Climb up that bank on which the irons are laid, and look to the other side —it is gone. There *is* no other side. Try and catch yesterday. Where is it? . . . We who lived before railways, and survive out of the ancient world, are like Father Noah and his family out of the Ark. The children will gather round and say to us patriarchs, 'Tell us, grandpapa, about the old world.' And we shall mumble our old

23. DAVID WILKIE. Sir Walter Scott and his Family at Abbotsford (*Edinburgh, Scottish National Portrait Gallery. By permission of the National Galleries of Scotland*)

24. F. S. CARY. Charles Lamb and his sister Mary (*London, National Portrait Gallery*)

stories; and we shall drop off one by one; and there will be fewer and fewer of us, and these very old and feeble. . . . We who lived before railways are antediluvians—we must pass away. We are growing scarcer every day; and old—old—very old relics of the times when George was still fighting the Dragon.

In *Meditations at Versailles* the regret for the pre-railway era has the true accent of Elia, recalling the time when people travelled from Paris to Versailles in a slow omnibus:

The old *coucous* are all gone, and their place knows them no longer. Smooth asphaltum terraces, tawdry lamps, and great hideous Egyptian obelisks, have frightened them away from the pleasant station they used to occupy under the trees of the Champs Elysées; and though the old *coucous* were just the most uncomfortable vehicles that human ingenuity ever constructed, one can't help looking back to the days of their existence with a tender regret, for there was pleasure, then, in the little trip of three leagues; and who ever had pleasure in a railroad journey? Does any reader of this venture to say that, on such a voyage, he ever dared to be pleasant? Do the most hardened stokers joke with one another? I don't believe it. Look into every single car of the train, and you will see that every single face is solemn. They take their seats gravely, and are silent, for the most part, during the journey; they dare not look out of window, for fear of being blinded by the smoke that comes whizzing by, or of losing their heads in one of the windows of the down train; they ride for miles in utter damp and darkness; through awful pipes of brick, that have been run pitilessly through the bowels of gentle mother earth, the cast-iron Frankenstein of an engine gallops on, puffing and screaming. Does any man pretend to say that he *enjoys* the journey?—he might as well say that he enjoyed having his hair cut; he bears it, but that is all: he will not allow the world to laugh at him, for any exhibition of slavish fear; and pretends, therefore, to be at his ease; but he *is* afraid, nay, ought to be, under the circumstances. I am sure Hannibal or Napoleon would, were they locked suddenly into a car; there kept close prisoners for a certain number of hours, and whirled along at this dizzy pace. You can't stop, if you would;—you may die, but you can't stop; the engine may explode upon the road, and up you go along with it; or, may be a bolter, and take a fancy to go down a hill, or into a river: all this you must bear, for the privilege of travelling twenty miles an hour.

In the essay *De Juventute* he laments the dancers of his

own day, ecstatically reeling off the celebrated names of the
artists of the past: 'Ah, Ronzi de Begnis, thou lovely one!
Ah, Caradori, thou smiling angel! Ah, Malibran! . . . and
the exquisite young Taglioni . . .'—and he deplores the
deterioration of beauty on the stage since the days of
George IV: 'Think of Sontag! I remember her in *Otello*
and the *Donna del Lago* in '28. I remember being behind
the scenes at the opera (where numbers of us young fellows
of fashion used to go), and seeing Sontag let her hair fall
down over her shoulders previous to her murder by Don-
zelli. Young fellows have never seen beauty like *that*, heard
such a voice, seen such hair, such eyes.' And even though
he refuses to be called a *laudator temporis acti* (there were
even some artists who did not please him, and he was
'thankful to live in times when men no longer have the
temptation to write so as to call blushes on women's cheeks,
and would shame to whisper wicked allusions to honest
boys', as for example did Sterne), he yet regrets the pastry-
tartlets of once upon a time, and the period when he delighted in the novels of Walter Scott, 'the kindly, the
generous, the pure':

How well I remember the type and the brownish paper of the
old duodecimo *Tales of My Landlord*! I have never dared to read
The Pirate, and *The Bride of Lammermoor*, or *Kenilworth*, from
that day to this, because the finale is unhappy, and people die, and
are murdered at the end. But *Ivanhoe*, and *Quentin Durward*! Oh!
for a half-holiday, and a quiet corner, and one of those books again!

And whereas now 'every London man is weary and
blasé' there was 'an enjoyment of life in these young bucks
of 1823 which contrasts strangely with our feelings of
1860': when the young bucks took 'a *turn* or two in Bond
Street, a *stroll* through Piccadilly, a *look in* at Tattersall's,
a *ramble* through Pall Mall, and a *strut* on the Corinthian
path,' until dinner-time came, 'when a few glasses of Tom's
rich wines soon put them on the *qui vive*'. And the day
came to an end amid the amusements of Vauxhall. 'Vauxhall is gone, but the wines which could occasion such a
delightful perversion of the intellect as to enable it to enjoy
ample pleasures there, what were they?'

That is the reason why Thackeray's novels are by preference set in the past, and that is why the most successful
parts of them are always the descriptions of the protagonists' youth—Pendennis, Clive, Warrington, Philip.
It is romantic, this idolizing of the past; but romantic in
a calm, middle-class, Biedermeier manner. He recalls the
Temple in the days of Pendennis's youth: 'The festivity
of that period revives in our memory; but how dingy the
pleasure-garden has grown, how tattered the garlands look,
how scant and old the company. . . . Grey hairs have come
on. . . . Well, friend, let us walk through the day, sober and
sad, but friendly.' So drawn does he feel to the eighteenth
century that he almost ceases to be conscious of the period
in which he is living: like Lamb, he might exclaim: 'I cannot
make these present times present to me'; he imagines himself to be as much at home in the eighteenth as in the nineteenth century; Oxford and Bolingbroke are of as much
interest to him as Russell and Palmerston. Sometimes he
wonders which of these two centuries he really belongs to,
since, as he says, he spends his days in one and his evenings
in the other. The 'disenchanted' Thackeray, then, reserved
his sense of wonder and enchantment for the past. He too
projected himself into a form of exoticism. And he wrote
Esmond in the language of the past. Of the past, it was
chiefly the private life, the family atmosphere, that he saw;
not the great political events, the social and economic currents. Angellier said, of Thackeray's historical novels: 'Au
lieu des peintures à fresques et à tendances épiques des
romans historiques de W. Scott, c'est de l'art hollandais.
C'est le roman historique d'un peintre de l'école hollandaise,
intime, familier, et non héroïque.' To which it must be
observed that the best things in Scott also are Dutch pictures, as we have already remarked. Thackeray, then, sees
the past in the light of a dream; and he sees the past as an
environment, as an atmosphere, not in the form of great
historical figures. It is a curious contradiction in him that,
on the one hand, he demolishes the epic point of view, on
the other, he yearns nostalgically towards the past; this is
his fundamental ambiguity—to be anti-romantic but not
satisfied with the present.

One of the most conspicuous Biedermeier characteristics appears to be lacking in Thackeray: the love of nature, the loving, minute description of landscape. In the *Notes on a Journey from Cornhill to Grand Cairo* we read:

There are a set of emotions about which a man had best be shy of talking lightly,—and the feelings excited by contemplating this vast, magnificent, harmonious Nature are among these. The view of it inspires a delight and ecstasy which is not only hard to describe, but which has something secret in it that a man should not utter loudly. Hope, memory, humility, tender yearnings towards dear friends, and inexpressible love and reverence towards the Power which created the infinite universe blazing above eternally, and the vast ocean shining and rolling around—fill the heart with a solemn, humble happiness, that a person dwelling in a city has rarely occasion to enjoy.

This vague, ineffable emotion leaves no room for paintings in miniature. But *genre* paintings are not lacking in Thackeray, and they are usually pictures of interiors, often humorous, in the Dutch manner. Look, for instance, in *Pendennis*, at the little tea-table scenes that Thackeray portrays, at the picture of Pendennis's tête-à-tête with the actress Miss Fotheringay, in which the lady does not understand even a tenth part of what her admirer is saying to her, and, though pretending to listen, is thinking of commonplace, practical matters; or, a little farther on, Miss Fotheringay being given a lesson in acting by the cripple, 'little Mr. Bows'; or the same lady falling asleep at the end of her day's work and snoring 'as resolutely and as regularly as a porter'; and, again, the young men's awkward attempts to throw roses to the actress on the stage; and Pendennis and his tutor, the curate Smirke, lingering over their glasses after dinner, and Smirke recalling the true and tender women he had known, and 'casting up his eyes towards the ceiling, and heaving a sigh as if evoking some being dear and unmentionable, took up his glass and drained it, and the rosy liquor began to suffuse his face' (which makes one think of that scene of sprightly ecclesiastics in the act of raising their wine-glasses, which so frequently inspired the *genre* painters of the nineteenth century); or again, the lively double scene, worthy the brush of a Frith, in which Thackeray shows us the drawing-rooms and parks of Kensington on a summer evening, or the scene in which Pen is convalescent at Lamb Court in the Temple, and his friends go off to bed at the sound of the chimes from St. Clement's church. More rarely landscape creeps into the *genre* scene, as when Dr. Portman rises from the table to go and meet the dean's wife as she walks on the lawn with her pink parasol 'over her lovely head' and her children playing around her: the doctor offers her his arm, 'and they sauntered over the ancient velvet lawn, which had been mowed and rolled for immemorial Deans, in that easy, quiet, comfortable manner, in which people of middle age and good temper walk after a good dinner, in a calm golden summer evening, when the sun has but just sunk behind the enormous cathedral towers, and the sickle-shaped moon is going every instant higher in the heavens'. It is a picture *à la* Spitzweg, and, like Spitzweg, Thackeray likes to derive his inspiration from the quiet air of a golden summer evening. Or again let us cull this pretty picture (in *The Four Georges*) of the young actresses curtseying to Dr. Johnson: '. . . youth, folly, gaiety, tenderly surveyed by wisdom's merciful, pure eyes.'

When he travels, Thackeray has no curiosity except about human beings and their customs, and he judges them —unless he is deliberately intending to teach the English a lesson, as in certain chapters of the *Paris Sketch Book*— from a purely insular point of view. Characteristic are some of his judgements on the French, on their Revolution which is nothing but 'a caricature of freedom', on their Empire which has been 'a caricature of glory'. Thackeray's anti-heroic feeling grows sharper when he is abroad; if he detests romantic flights in his own country, those that he observes on the other side of the Channel seem to him merely grotesque caricature; and he points his barbs against the neo-mysticism of George Sand (in the chapter *Madame Sand and the New Apocalypse*):

While in David's time art and religion were only a caricature of Heathenism; now, on the contrary, these two commodities are imported from Germany; and distorted caricatures originally, are still farther distorted on passing the frontier. I trust in Heaven that

German art and religion will take no hold in our country (where there is a fund of roast beef, that will expel any such humbug in the end); but these sprightly Frenchmen have relished the mystical doctrines mightily; and having watched the Germans, with their sanctified looks, and quaint imitations of the old times, and mysterious transcendental talk, are aping many of their fashions, as well and solemnly as they can: not very solemnly, God wot; for I think one should always prepare to grin when a Frenchman looks particularly grave, being sure that there is something false and ridiculous lurking under the owl-like solemnity.

After this preamble, Thackeray makes a violent attack upon George Sand and the 'immorality' of her novels. He says, for example, of *Lélia*:

A wonderful book indeed, gorgeous in eloquence, and rich in magnificent poetry; a regular topsyturvyfication of morality, a thieves' and prostitutes' apotheosis. This book has received some late enlargements and emendations by the writer; it contains her notions on morals, which, as we have said, are so peculiar, that, alas! they can only be mentioned here, not particularized: but, of *Spiridion*, we may write a few pages, as it is her religious manifesto

And he concludes his analysis of *Spiridion* like this: 'There is always, I think, such a dash of the ridiculous in the French sublime.'

He congratulates himself, when writing of the manner in which a certain trial, *l'affaire* Peytel, had been conducted in France: 'Thank God that, in England, things are not managed so.' And, on the subject of French novels: 'French novels are a picture of French life, a pretty society!' Many more illustrations could be given of the limited nature of Thackeray's horizon.

*   *   *   *   *

Such being the limitations of Thackeray the man, we shall not be surprised to find analogous limitations in Thackeray the artist. Speaking of the deceased Laman Blanchard in *Fraser's Magazine* (March 1846), he adopts Dr. Johnson's point of view that profit is the true incentive of the literary profession ('No man but a blockhead ever wrote, except for money'):

Bread, in the main, is the incentive. . . . If only men of genius were to write, Lord help us! how many books would there be?

How many people are there even capable of appreciating genius?...
To do your work honestly, to amuse and instruct your reader of
to-day, to die when your time comes, and go hence with as clean
a breast as may be; may these be all yours and ours, by God's will.
Let us be content with our *status* as literary craftsmen, telling the
truth as far as may be, hitting no foul blow, condescending to no
servile puffery, filling not a very lofty, but a manly and honourable
part.

It is a bourgeois conception of the man of letters. To a
friend he confessed: 'I have a six-penny talent and so have
you. Ours is small beer, but, you see, it is the right tap.'
Once when Tennyson had recited two passages from
Catullus to him in order to illustrate their tender feeling,
Thackeray, after remarking that he himself would be
capable of doing even better, thought it over during the
night and, in the morning, filled with contrition, wrote:
'When I have dined, sometimes I believe myself to be
equal to the greatest painters and poets. The delusion goes
off; and then I know what a small fiddle mine is and what
small tunes I play upon it.' One of the essays in the *Roundabout Papers* is called *Small-Beer Chronicle* and develops
the theme: do not seek to appear more than you really are.
Let us observe, to begin with, that, although Thackeray
professed to have derived his inspiration for the *Roundabout
Papers* from Montaigne and the *Letters* of Howell,[108] these
essays of his are very far from possessing the charm of
the Frenchman's. The subjects of his 'humble essays' are
characteristic of the artist's Biedermeier soul: he lingers
over a description of the peaceful little Swiss town of Chur
(*On a Lazy Idle Boy*); he interests himself in the touching
and mysterious circumstance of two children whom he
first sees, well dressed and accompanied by a lady, in the
train between Frankfurt and Heidelberg, and then comes
upon again, neglected-looking and in company with a
rough man (the father?), in other places (*On Two Children
in Black*); he makes humorous reflections upon the vanity
of titles and badges of honour (*On Ribbons*); and of dearly
paid honours (*Autour de mon chapeau*); he regrets the days
of his youth (*De Juventute*); he is moved by the pathetic
life of Thomas Hood (*On a Joke I once heard from the late*

Thomas Hood); he evokes the image of a Christmas tree
(*Round about the Christmas Tree*); he speaks of kind thoughts
and the sweet feeling of ineffable gratitude at the sight of
a fair scene of nature, or of a bunch of lively children at
play, or of a group of flowers by the hedge-side from which
comes the song of a bird (*On two Roundabout Papers which
I intended to write*); he exhorts people to be kind to the
aged occupants of workhouses (*On some Carp at Sans-
souci*); he speaks of the quiet amusements of old age (*Autour
de mon chapeau*); and he abandons himself to a gentle
recollection of the *carillon* at Antwerp (*A Roundabout
Journey*). The essay entitled *Small-Beer Chronicle* (July
1861) is the most characteristic of all, and is worth quoting
at length:

Not long since, at a certain banquet, I had the good fortune to
sit by Doctor Polymathesis, who knows everything, and who, about
the time when the claret made its appearance, mentioned that old
dictum of the grumbling Oxford Don, that 'ALL CLARET *would be
port if it could!*'[109] Imbibing a bumper of one or the other not
ungratefully, I thought to myself, 'Here, surely, Mr. Roundabout,
is a good text for one of your reverence's sermons.' Let us apply to
the human race, dear brethren, what is here said of the vintages of
Portugal and Gascony, and we shall have no difficulty in perceiving
how many clarets aspire to be ports in their way; how most men
and women of our acquaintance, how we ourselves, are Aquitainians
giving ourselves Lusitanian airs; how we wish to have credit for
being stronger, braver, more beautiful, more worthy than we really
are.

Nay, the beginning of this hypocrisy—a desire to excel, a desire
to be hearty, fruity, generous, strength-imparting—is a virtuous and
noble ambition; and it is most difficult for a man in his own case, or
his neighbour's, to say at what point this ambition transgresses the
boundary of virtue, and becomes vanity, pretence, and self-seeking.
You are a poor man, let us say, showing a bold face to adverse
fortune, and wearing a confident aspect. Your purse is very narrow,
but you owe no man a penny; your means are scanty, but your
wifes' gown is decent; your old coat well brushed; your children at
a good school; you grumble to no one; ask favours of no one;
truckle to no neighbours on account of their superior rank, or (a
worse, and a meaner, and a more common crime still) envy none
for their better fortune. To all outward appearances you are as well
to do as your neighbours, who have thrice your income. There may

be in this case some little mixture of pretension in your life and behaviour. You certainly *do* put on a smiling face whilst fortune is pinching you. Your wife and girls, so smart and neat at evening-parties, are cutting, patching and cobbling all day to make both ends of life's haberdashery meet. You give a friend a bottle of wine on occasion, but are content yourself with a glass of whisky-and-water. You avoid a cab, saying that of all things you like to walk home after dinner (which you know, my good friend, is a fib). I grant you that in this scheme of life there does enter ever so little hypocrisy; that this claret is loaded, as it were; but your desire to *portify* yourself is amiable, is pardonable, is perhaps honourable: and were there no other hypocrisies than yours in the world we should be a set of worthy fellows; and sermonizers, moralizers, satirizers, would have to hold their tongues, and go to some other trade to get a living.

But you know you *will* step over that boundary line of virtue and modesty, into the district where humbug and vanity begin, and there the moralizer catches you and makes an example of you. For instance, in a certain novel in another place my friend Mr. Talbot Twysden[110] is mentioned—a man whom you and I know to be a wretched ordinaire, but who persists in treating himself as if he was the finest '20 port. In our Britain there are hundreds of men like him; for ever striving to swell beyond their natural size, to strain beyond their natural strength, to step beyond their natural stride. Search, search within your own waistcoats, dear brethren—*you* know in your hearts, which of your ordinaire qualities you would pass off, and fain consider as first-rate port. And why not you yourself, Mr. Preacher? says the congregation. Dearly beloved, neither in nor out of this pulpit do I profess to be bigger, or cleverer, or wiser, or better than any of you. A short while since, a certain Reviewer announced that I gave myself great pretensions as a philosopher. I a philosopher! I advance pretensions! My dear Saturday friend, And you? . . .

No, I do not, as far as I know, try to be port at all; but offer in these presents, a sound, genuine ordinaire, at 18s. per doz. let us say, grown on my own hill-side, and offered *de bonne cœur* to those who will sit down under my *tonnelle*, and have a half-hour's drink and gossip. It is none of your hot porto, my friend. I know there is much better and stronger liquor elsewhere. Some pronounce it sour: some say it is thin; some that it has wofully lost its flavour. This may or may not be true. There are good and bad years; years that surprise everybody; years of which the produce is small and bad, or rich and plentiful. But if my tap is not genuine it is naught, and no man should give himself the trouble to drink it. I do not even say that I would be port if I could; knowing that port (by which I would imply much stronger, deeper, richer, and more durable liquor than my vineyard can furnish) is not relished by all palates, or suitable to all heads. We will assume, then, dear brother, that you and I are tolerably modest people; and, ourselves being thus out of the question, proceed to show how pretentious our neighbours are, and how very many of them would be port if they could. . . .

'I was walking with Mr. Fox'—and sure this anecdote comes very pat after the grapes—'I was walking with Mr. Fox in the Louvre,' says Benjamin West (*apud* some paper I have just been reading), 'and I remarked how many people turned round to look at *me*. This shows the respect of the French for the fine arts.' This is a curious instance of a very small claret indeed, which imagined itself to be port of the strongest body. There are not many instances of a faith so deep, so simple, so satisfactory as this. I have met many who would like to be port; but with few of the Gascon sort, who absolutely believed they *were* port. George III believed in West's port, and thought Reynolds' overrated stuff. When I saw West's pictures at Philadelphia, I looked at them with astonishment and awe. Hide, blushing glory, hide your head under your old nightcap. O immortality! is this the end of you? Did any of you, my dear brethren, ever try and read 'Blackmore's Poems', or the 'Epics of Baour-Lormian,' or the 'Henriade', or—what shall we say?—Pollok's 'Course of Time'? They were thought to be more lasting than brass by some people, and where are they now? And *our* masterpieces of literature—*our* ports—that, if not immortal, at any rate are to last their fifty, their hundred years—oh, sirs, don't you think a very small cellar will hold them?

Those poor people in brass, on pedestals, hectoring about Trafalgar Square and that neighbourhood, don't you think many of them —apart even from the ridiculous execution—cut rather a ridiculous figure, and that we are too eager to set up our ordinaire heroism and talent for port? A Duke of Wellington or two I will grant, though even of these idols a moderate supply will be sufficient. Some years ago a famous and witty French critic was in London, with whom I walked the streets. I am ashamed to say that I informed him (being in hopes that he was about to write some papers regarding the manners and customs of this country) that all the statues he saw represented the Duke of Wellington. That on the arch opposite Apsley House? the Duke in a cloak, and cocked-hat, on horseback. That behind Apsley House in an airy fig-leaf costume? the Duke again. That in Cockspur Street? the Duke with a pig-tail—and so on. I showed him an army of Dukes. There are many bronze heroes who after a few years look already as foolish, awkward, and out of place as a man, say at Shoolbred's or Swan and

Edgar's. For example, those three Grenadiers in Pall Mall, who have been up only a few months, don't you pity those unhappy household troops, who have to stand frowning and looking fierce there; and think they would like to step down and go to barracks? That they fought very bravely there is no doubt; but so did the Russians fight very bravely; and the French fight very bravely; and so did Colonel Jones and the 99th, and Colonel Brown and the 100th; and I say again that ordinaire should not give itself port airs, and that an honest ordinaire would blush to be found swaggering so. I am sure if you could consult the Duke of York, who is impaled on his column between the two clubs, and ask his late Royal Highness whether he thought he ought to remain there, he would say no. A brave, worthy man, not a braggart or boaster, to be put upon that heroic perch must be painful to him. . . . They have got a statue of Thomas Moore at Dublin, I hear. Is he on horseback? Some men should have, say, a fifty years' lease of glory. After a while some gentlemen now in brass should go to the melting furnace, and reappear in some other gentleman's shape. Lately I saw that Melville column rising over Edinburgh; come, good men and true, don't you feel a little awkward and uneasy when you walk under it? Who was this to stand in heroic places? and is yon the man whom Scotchmen most delight to honour? I must own deferentially that there is a tendency in North Britain to over-esteem its heroes. . . .

My brethren, these sermons are professedly short; for I have that opinion of my dear congregation, which leads me to think that were I to preach at great length they would yawn, stamp, make noises, and perhaps go straightway out of church; and yet with this text I protest I could go on for hours. What multitudes of men, what multitudes of women, my dears, pass off their ordinaire for port, their small beer for strong! In literature, in politics, in the army, the navy, the church, at the bar, in the world, what an immense quantity of cheap liquor is made to do service for better sorts!

In an essay, *A Brighton Night Entertainment*, he goes so far as to profess his partiality for 'second-rate beauty in women, second-rate novels' (such as those of George Payne Rainsford James[111] which can be read without the slightest effort), and 'second-rate theatrical entertainments': here the cult of mediocrity becomes a pose.

Thackeray's characters are usually quite ordinary people. In the essay *De Finibus* we read:

My dear good friend, some folks are utterly tired of you, and say, 'What a poverty of friends the man has! He is always asking us to meet those Pendennises, Newcomes, and so forth. Why does he not introduce us to some new characters? Why is he not thrilling like Twostars, learned and profound like Threestars, exquisitely humorous and human like Fourstars? Why, finally, is he not somebody else?' My good people, it is not only impossible to please you all, but it is absurd to try.

So he keeps to his Pendennises and his Newcomes, people who are far from sublime; Pendennis does not aspire to be a hero, but merely a man and a brother, and of Philip Thackeray says: 'Philip did not win crosses and epaulets. He is like us, my dear Sir, not a heroic genius at all.' Colonel Newcome, who, as Thackeray confessed, was supposed to be a mixture of Don Quixote and Sir Roger de Coverley, is a bore, but the convincing, good-natured way in which Thackeray describes him provides the intellectual stimulus which the character, by itself, cannot supply. It is a similar case to that of Goncharov's Oblomov: the pallid character is impressed indelibly upon the memory owing to the manner in which it is presented.[112] Thackeray chose to be the apostle of commonplace, but universal, truths; he preached the gospel of common sense.

A culminating scene in a novel should have, he considered, an air of modesty and unpretentiousness almost like that of a chronicle—such as that which describes the indignation of Mr. Osborne senior at his son's engagement, in *Vanity Fair*. He shuts himself up in his study, goes over all the letters and papers relating to his son, and recalls the most brilliant episodes in the young man's career:

And this, this was the end of all!—to marry a bankrupt and fly in the face of duty and fortune! What humiliation and fury: what pangs of sickening rage, balked ambition and love; what wounds of outraged vanity, tenderness even, had this old worldling now to suffer under!

Having examined these papers, and pondered over this one and the other, in that bitterest of all helpless woe, with which miserable men think of happy past times—George's father took the whole of the documents out of the drawer in which he had kept them so long, and locked them into a writing-box, which he tied, and sealed with his seal. Then he opened the book-case, and took down the great red Bible we have spoken of—a pompous book, seldom looked at, and shining all over with gold. There was a frontispiece to the volume, representing Abraham sacrificing Isaac.[113] Here, according to custom, Osborne had recorded on the fly-leaf, and in his large clerk-like hand, the dates of his marriage and his wife's death, and the births and Christian names of his children. Jane came first, then George Sedley Osborne, then Maria Frances, and the days of the christening of each. Taking a pen, he carefully obliterated George's names from the page; and when the leaf was quite dry, restored the volume to the place from which he had moved it. Then he took a document out of another drawer, where his own private papers were kept; and having read it, crumpled it up and lighted it at one of the candles, and saw it burn entirely away in the grate. It was his will; which being burned, he sate down and wrote off a letter, and rang for his servant, whom he charged to deliver it in the morning. It was morning already: as he went up to bed, the whole house was alight with the sunshine; and the birds were singing among the fresh green leaves in Russell Square.

Thackeray dislikes big scenes. It has been remarked by Percy Lubbock,[114] for example, that the only big scene— that is, dramatic crisis bringing several characters face to face with each other—in *Vanity Fair* is the one between Rawdon who has just been let out of prison, the guilty Becky, and the tempter Lord Steyne. Except on this occasion, Thackeray usually approaches close to the critical point where a big scene appears unavoidable, and then avoids it.[115] In *Esmond*, for example, when the Duke of Hamilton has insulted Esmond, and Lady Castlewood reveals the secret of their benefactor to him. Everything, from the beginning, seems to promise a big scene: there is an interchange of blows and harsh, brilliant repartee, and then, all at once, Thackeray unexpectedly intervenes and confines the flood within one quiet channel: 'And then, in her touching way, and having hold of her daughter's hand and speaking to her rather than my Lord Duke, Lady Castlewood told the story.'[116] Mr. J. W. Dodds[117] observes that 'the lack of scenic tension is basic to Thackeray's method', which 'stems from his own awareness of his limitations as well as from his instinctive recognition that "big scenes" are the more powerful if they are few. . . . He feared dropping melodrama and preferred understatement. . . . With a controlled, precise objectivity he lets a cadenced

sentence carry a heavy weight of implication.' The death
of George Osborne is the best-known example of this:
'No more firing was heard at Brussels—the pursuit rolled
far away. Darkness came down on the field; and Amelia
was praying for George, who was lying on his face, dead,
with a bullet through his heart.' Compare this effective con-
ciseness with the unbridled sentimentality with which the
same theme (in this case a mother waiting for her son to
return from the war, while the son lies dead on the battlefield) is treated by Pierre Loti at the end of the *Roman d'un
Spahi*. At other times Thackeray, instead of fastening upon
the centre of a scene, lingers over its marginal reflections,
from which the centre can be deduced without being
directly seen: thus, instead of describing the death of Sir
Pitt Crawley, the novelist gathers together all the different
signs of disturbance in the house when it is turned upside-
down by the occurrence—'lights go about from window
to window . . . a boy on a pony goes galloping off . . . neighbours and hopeful relatives enter the mansion. . . . Sir
Pitt's housekeeper wildly trying the escritoire with a bunch
of keys. . . .' It is the same technique of indirect presentation
that we have already noted in certain of Breughel's pictures (the *Ascent to Calvary*, the *John the Baptist preaching*,
the *Fall of Icarus*).[118]

In this characteristic too (the indirectly suggested event)
Thackeray remains faithful to himself. We have already
pointed out how he avoids the description of strong
emotions, and so, also, he avoids strong scenes; he prefers
psychological analysis to description of feelings, or rather
he replaces both effect and emotion by a corresponding
logical thread, and prefers a picture to a dramatic scene;
that is, instead of identifying himself with his characters,
he stops to contemplate them, and, as he does so, their
voices die in their throats, as if the sound apparatus of
a film came suddenly to a halt.

Now M. Las Vergnas actually claims that Thackeray
excelled in suggestive silences, almost as though what the
page says in its blank spaces were of more importance than
the printed words: he even finds in Thackeray's work 'un
sens du mystérieux à l'œuvre, et comme une politique du

subconscient'. The novelist, he says, has 'l'art de l'inex-primé'—'silences d'or'. The idea seems paradoxical, and the critic recognizes this: 'Quelque étrange que cela puisse paraître, vu le bavardage presque constant de l'auteur et cette paraphrase personnelle dans laquelle il enveloppe, comme d'un amical manteau, ses personnages, il est, chez Thackeray, un art du non écrit.' There is considerable exaggeration in this judgement on the part of M. Las Vergnas. If one examines the passages which the critic quotes in support of his thesis, one comes to the conclusion that the 'unwritten' page that charms him lives only in his own mind: that the critic, in other words, by dint of wishing to discover admirable qualities in his author, rewrites him in his head in his own fashion, and communicates to us, not the true result, but the impression which that potential result brings about in himself.

Take for instance the scene in chapter lxvi of *Vanity Fair*, in which Amelia asks Becky Sharp for news of her son: 'Écoutez-la, sous les paroles gaies, enjouies de la mauvaise mère, dire, mieux que tous les discours, son égoïsme foncier, son détachement, sa vanité coupable, écoutez cette voix: elle vous apporte un des échos les plus fidèles du grand talent de Thackeray.' Now from the very first words the attitude of the characters does not derive from the circumstances or the dialogue, but is given as an already known, already fixed element: they are like two 'humours' talking to each other in accordance with their own charac-teristics; and the dialogue is merely the corollary of a known theorem. 'Frankness and kindness like Amelia's were likely to touch even such a hardened little reprobate as Becky.' The two women are placed in contrast to each other: one, 'frankness and kindness' personified, the other 'a hardened little reprobate'.

She returned Emmy's caresses and kind speeches with something very like gratitude, and an emotion which, if it was not lasting, for a moment was almost genuine. That was a lucky stroke of hers about the child 'torn from her arms shrieking'. It was by that harrowing misfortune that Becky had won her friend back, and it was one of the very first points, we may be certain, upon which our *poor simple* little Emmy began to talk to her new-found acquaintance.

'And so they took your darling child from you?' our *simpleton*
cried out. 'Oh, Rebecca, my poor dear suffering friend! . . .' 'The
child, my child? Oh yes, my agonies were frightful,' Becky owned,
not perhaps without a twinge of conscience. It jarred upon her, to
be obliged to commence instantly to tell lies in reply to so much
confidence and *simplicity*. But that is the misfortune of beginning
with this kind of forgery.

Then follows a general consideration of the habit of lying.
And a little farther on:

'I know, I know,' Becky cried out, who had in fact quite forgotten all about little Rawdon's age. 'Grief has made me forget so
many things, dearest Amelia. . . .' 'Was he fair or dark?' went on
that *absurd* little Emmy. 'Show me his hair.' Becky almost laughed
at her *simplicity*.

How, in relation to a passage like this, in which the
qualities and intentions of the characters are three or four
times underlined (for no less often than that is Amelia
called a 'simpleton'),[119] how it is possible, in such a passage,
to speak of 'sous-entendus', of 'silences d'or', is one of the
not inconsiderable number of critical mysteries in the work
of M. Las Vergnas. He allows himself to be carried away
by the momentum of his own sentences, and proceeds from
slender pretexts to imposing fabrications which have no
relation whatever to their premises. Had he said this of
Jane Austen, in whom also both scenes and emotions are
restrained or avoided, but in whom the 'art of the un-
expressed' is truly subtle, one could have found no fault.
But that Thackeray, the novelist who has to stick labels on
everything, should be described as a sage magician of suggestive silence, is a matter beyond all credibility. 'Les mots
écrits passent devant nos yeux, mais d'autres bourdonnent
à nos oreilles, que nous savons être les vrais et que la *magie*
de Thackeray nous fait entendre aussi clairement que si les
blancs de la page avaient un langage propre, celui de la
vérité.' It is, rather, the contrary which is true—that is,
that Thackeray takes his reader by the hand and never
stops directing his attention to the point he is anxious to
bring out, with almost the same pedagogic persistence as
Macaulay, whom Taine, as we have seen, imagined as

25. The Prince Regent and Allied Sovereigns at the Review of the Troops in Hyde Park (*engraving of the period*)

26. J. ARCHER. Thomas De Quincey with his daughters and granddaughter
(*drawing*)

saying: 'Be as absent in mind, as stupid, as ignorant as you please; in vain you will be absent in mind, you shall listen to me; in vain you will be stupid, you shall understand; in vain you will be ignorant, you shall learn.'

M. Las Vergnas finds in Thackeray's atmosphere 'une timidité délicieuse, et comme impondérable—tant elle est fine et diluée—une pudeur en suspens'. We have seen that this kind of modesty is nothing more nor less than repression, a repression whose results we do not feel inclined to describe with the epithet of 'delicious', which we might well apply to that of Miss Austen. And when M. Las Vergnas says: 'La prose de Thackeray palpite souvent d'un lyrisme secret! Son art frémit à fleur d'écorce', we feel he is going altogether too far in praising reticences of this type: 'A veil should be thrown over those sacred emotions of love and grief', or again (to quote a passage from chapter li of *Pendennis*):

And as that duty was performed quite noiselessly,—while the supplications, which endowed her with the requisite strength for fulfilling it, also took place in her own chamber, away from all mortal sight,—we, too, must be perforce silent about these virtues of hers, which no more bear public talking about, than a flower will bear to bloom in a ball-room. This only we will say—that a good woman is the loveliest flower that blooms under heaven; and that we look with love and wonder upon its silent grace, its pure fragrance, its delicate bloom of beauty. Sweet and beautiful!—the fairest and the most spotless!—is it not a pity to see them bowed down or devoured by Grief or Death inexorable—wasting in disease—pining with long pain—or cut off by sudden fate in their prime? *We* may deserve grief—but why should these be unhappy? —except that we know that Heaven chastens those whom it loves best; being pleased, by repeated trials, to make these pure spirits more pure.

Do such passages, which find their parallel in the sugary lithographs of the period, deserve the title of 'secret lyricism'?

Let us say, rather: just as the modesty of Thackeray is the modesty of Jane Austen, but without magic, so is his style the style of Addison, but again without magic. Here, in fact, is the eighteenth century turned bourgeois, gone flat. In an article in which he passed severe judgement upon Carlyle's *French Revolution*, Thackeray said: 'Never did ... a man's style so mar his subject and dim his genius. It is stiff, short, and rugged, it abounds with Germanisms and Latinisms, strange epithets, and choking double words, astonishing to the admirers of simple Addisonian English.' And of Swift's style he writes: 'His statement is elaborately simple; he shuns tropes and metaphors, and uses his ideas and words with a wise thrift and economy. ... He never indulges in needless extravagance of rhetoric, lavish epithets, profuse imagery. He lays his opinion before you with a grave simplicity and a perfect neatness.' Here then is the ideal at which Thackeray aimed: simplicity and precision. And evidently he thought he had attained to it, since, in speaking of Dickens's style, he praised the improvement which had come about through Dickens having imitated him, Thackeray: 'greatly simplifying his style and overcoming the use of fine words: by this the public will be the gainer and *David Copperfield* will be improved by taking a lesson from *Vanity Fair*'. Did Thackeray really achieve such perfection? Did the fear of rhetoric, of using 'fine words' like Dickens, or startling ones like Carlyle, really preserve him in an exemplary purity? M. Las Vergnas himself has to admit that Thackeray's simplicity is all too often synonymous with slovenliness and familiarity. Simplicity, to be a virtue, must be 'essential', must be compendious, as it is, in fact, in Swift, in whom style never diverges from its practical purpose of expressing an idea in the most economical way possible: a precise style with a fascination that might be described as geometrical, a style made for communication rather than for magical persuasiveness. Now in Thackeray simplicity is not 'essential': he is familiar, he is verbose; pages of his essays might with advantage be condensed; or rather, as one reads them, one is tempted to skip entire sentences which are mere sequences of *clichés*, paraphrases, and commonplaces. The critic Frederic Harrison said of Thackeray: 'If sometimes below himself in substance, [he is] never below himself in form'— an arbitrary remark, but which has this truth in it: that Thackeray often says things that were not worth saying, and in a form that does not even confer a memorable accent upon commonplaces, as happens, for example, in Pope. But M. Las Vergnas, with his usual arbitrary amplification, hears pure music in Thackeray's style: 'lit chantant, voix du ruisseau'. 'Refermer un livre de Thackeray c'est un peu comme revenir d'un récital.' The sermon becomes, for him, an oratorio: 'Musique non savante, non agencée, qui est plutôt comme une inspiration perpétuelle, comme un tacte inné des voyelles heureuses, des syllabes mélodiques et des chutes fortunées. Grave et tendre, la prose thackerayenne pleure et chante comme une poésie.' This must indeed have been the ideal at which Thackeray aimed; but how rarely he achieves it! M. Las Vergnas even succeeds in discovering a cadence that reminds him of Beethoven, and recalls Keats's *Ode to a Nightingale* and Tennyson's *Lotos-Eaters*. And he quotes, as an example of musical quality, one of the few genuine cases of it, the conclusion—so typically Biedermeier—of the essay *De Juventute*:

It is night now: and here is home. Gathered under the quiet roof, elders and children lie alike at rest. In the midst of a great peace and calm, the stars peep out from the heavens. The silence is peopled with the past; sorrowful remorses for sins and shortcomings— memories of passionate joys and griefs rise out of their graves, both now alike calm and sad. Eyes, as I shut mine, look at me, that have long ceased to shine. The town and the fair landscape sleep under the starlight, wreathed in the autumn mists. Twinkling among the houses a light keeps watch here and there, in what may be a sick chamber or two. The clock tolls sweetly in the silent air. Here is night and rest. An awful sense of thanks makes the heart swell, and my head bow, as I pass to my room through the sleeping house, and feel as though a hushed blessing were upon it.

M. Las Vergnas admits Thackeray's slovenliness, and calls it 'splendide anarchie esthétique'! And he concludes, on the subject of Thackeray's message: 'Si Thackeray n'a point exercé de magnétisme sur les générations littéraires qui lui ont succédé, c'est qu'il lui a manqué l'enthousiasme.' Because of his 'détachement désabusé' he wants to call Thackeray 'le romancier de la critique'; just as Spenser has been called 'a poet's poet', so Thackeray would be 'a critic's novelist'. It is an elegant way of conferring an air of virtue upon his lack of enthusiasm—which means, after all, lack of creative impulse. 'Apostle of mediocrity'—the epithet given to him by Walter Frewen Lord—seems to us more just; and we are reminded again of Horace's: 'mediocribus esse poetis non homines, non di, non concessere columnae.' But that would be going too far. A poet, a great artist, Thackeray is not; but within the compass of an honest, genuine, bourgeois *sermo pedestris* he attains an excellence of his own; he is, as he himself said, *vin ordinaire*, but from a good cask, 'from the right tap'. His charm is the charm of a Dutch picture, as Angellier has said, or of a 'Biedermeier' interior, as we ourselves have tried to show. 'The artist as gentleman'—so Desmond MacCarthy described him; and we would add: 'The artist as *Victorian* gentleman.' Flaubert, who did not worry about being a gentleman, gives a complete portrait of Madame Bovary, pitilessly showing up every corner of her soul. But a modest gentleman like Thackeray could not do the same with Becky Sharp. Charlotte Brontë, taking up one of Thackeray's metaphors, wrote:[120] 'He, I see, keeps the mermaid's tail below water, and only hints at the dead men's bones and noxious slime amidst which it wriggles.' And we seem to see him, this faultlessly dressed gentleman, holding down the mermaid in her pool, with a grappling-hook—for fear the splashes should soil his clothes: and, to tell the truth, we believe in the mermaid's tail only because the placard informs us of it; actually all that we see is a young lady of respectable appearance. So much, and no more, could be done to provide Victorian eyes with a representation of Evil. Imagine the stir that a *Madame Bovary* would have caused in that world, and compare the picturesque, sentimental-romance superficialities of *Pendennis* with the bitter experience of *L'Éducation sentimentale!*

Anthony Trollope

In Dickens the Victorian age seems to be reflected as it were in a curved mirror. With its bold foreshortenings and queer perspectives, a curved mirror gives a bewitched, preternatural image of the scene it reflects. The colours are those of real life, but they are arranged as if in a kaleidoscope, they are assembled and distributed, in that motionless glass whirlpool, in such a way that the reflected scene assumes the quality of a dream or nightmare. So it is with Dickens: in Victorian society as we see it through his artist's eye, certain features are accentuated till they become positively surrealist; from Dickens to the *collages* of Max Ernst, from the benevolence of the Christmas Carols to the cruelty of *Une Semaine de bonté*, the step is shorter than it might appear. Thackeray, at first sight, seems to offer a more truthful image of the Victorian age, an image faithful to the point of disenchantment; and yet there is something in this image that disturbs us, that gives us the embarrassing feeling of being looked at from behind: the photographer has photographed a mirror, and, together with the people and the things in the room, has reproduced himself, behind his black cloth, intent on snapping his subject. This intrusion of the photographer's hooded figure is both awkward and upsetting, and sometimes suffices to take away all magic of illusion from the adventures of the characters.

Now although Trollope, too, sometimes shares—as we shall see—in this trick of Thackeray's, of obtruding himself into the scene with his commentary, he does it in so discreet a measure that he does not compromise his own essential quality, that of acting as the supremely faithful mirror of the Victorian age between the years 1860 and 1880. It is due to this discreetness, and to his unruffled and benevolently realistic estimate of human emotions, so full of shades and subtleties, that Trollope, who had been declared 'stupid' by the wiseacre critics of the end of the last century, has come back into fashion in our own day, whether because the society depicted by him provides, in its relative quietness, a sharp contrast with modern times, or because the reawakened interest in all things Victorian has found more to nourish it in his calm, meticulous little pictures than in the great canvases of Dickens. In Dickens, even when he is speaking of things of everyday reality, there is often a kind of apocalyptic, cataclysmic atmosphere, just as there is in the paintings—the last phase of the heroic landscape—of John Martin. The world of Dickens is indeed a bourgeois world, but from it to Martin's *Joshua commanding the Sun to stand still*; *Last Days of the Antediluvian World*; *Country of the Iguanodon*; *The Great Day of His Wrath*, the transition is not so very abrupt. Those perspectives of precipitous rocks, of monumental citadels, of thousand-pillared halls, beneath threatening skies with livid cloud-processions torn by blinding flashes of lightning, are of the same stamp as the immensely picturesque, squalid, tragic metropolis that forms the background of Dickens's novels. A painter of far greater stature, Constable, speaking of Martin's hostility to the Royal Academy, said that Martin looked at the Academy from the Plains of Nineveh, from the Destruction of Babylon, &c., whereas he, Constable, was content to look at it from a gate, and the highest spot he ever aspired to was a windmill. Something of the kind might be said of Dickens and Trollope. Dickens sought success by way of the melodramatic, the sensational; Trollope did not choose to forsake the commonplace—so much so that someone, alluding to him, has gone so far as to speak of 'novels for young ladies'.[121] And anyone who considers his background of interested motives, of love-affairs opposed by parents, of ambitions that go no farther than a bishopric or a seat in Parliament, anyone who thinks of the usual happy ending to the ups and downs of his plots, with a procession of couples facing the altar, will feel that Trollope's volumes might well form a part of the 'bibliothèque rose'.

But the very absence of too pronounced a character and style were the salvation of this writer. The figure of the man may well disillusion those who seek originality or picturesqueness in an artist. Not that a certain lack of balance was altogether absent in his early youth, when he was oppressed by a sense of inferiority and unworthiness which in other temperaments might have been a source of morbid inspiration. A fixed job in the Post Office, and marriage, marked the beginning of a better life; his restlessness, his continual postponements of the literary work in which, ever since he left school, he had felt that his true career lay (discarding poetry, drama, history, and biography, he decided very early to try the only way that seemed to him profitable, the novel), his indecision, his laziness, were replaced by an activity that has something of the miraculous about it, so that, reviewing the period from 1859 to 1871, he was able to assert: 'I feel confident that in amount no other writer contributed so much during that time to English literature.' The miracle lies not so much in the quantity as in the method—a method which is thoroughly in harmony with the triumphs of industrial civilization and mass production. This is how he speaks of it in his *Autobiography*, which, with its candour and freshness, remains one of his best books:

It was my practice to be at my table every morning at 5.30 a.m.; and it was also my practice to allow myself no mercy. . . . It had at this time become my custom,—and it still is my custom, though of late I have become a little lenient to myself,—to write with my watch before me, and to require from myself 250 words every quarter of an hour. I have found that the 250 words have been forthcoming as regularly as my watch went. . . . This division of time allowed me to produce over ten pages of an ordinary novel volume a day, and if kept up through ten months, would have given as its results three novels of three volumes each in the year.

Nor did the inspections and journeys that he had to undertake in his capacity as a postal official interrupt his activity:

I always had a pen in my hand. Whether crossing the seas, or fighting with American officials, or tramping about the streets of Beverley, I could do a little, and generally more than a little. I had long since convinced myself that in such work as mine the great secret consisted in acknowledging myself to be bound to rules of labour similar to those which an artisan or a mechanic is forced to obey.

Whenever he heard people say that the correct thing for an artist was to wait for inspiration, he was unable to restrain his contempt. The idea appeared to him just as absurd as if a shoemaker had to wait to be inspired before starting to make a shoe, or a tallow-chandler to wait for the divine moment of melting. This was the advice he gave to young writers: 'Let their work be to them as is his common work to the common labourer. . . . I . . . venture to advise young men who look forward to authorship as the business of their lives . . . to avoid enthusiastic rushes with their pens, and to seat themselves at their desks day by day as though they were lawyers' clerks.'

Not merely did he write during sea voyages, but even when he was seasick; not merely did he keep his eye on his watch, but he compiled a register of the pages written each day, and the two pages at the end of the *Autobiography* where he balances up the profits that had accrued to him from his work (profits amounting to a considerable sum, such as were attained by no other novelist of the time simply from novels) make one think of the profit and loss account drawn up by Robinson Crusoe. The recollection of Defoe might invite us to reflect upon the connexion between the puritan spirit and the mercantile spirit; but since such reflections have been made so often by others,[122] a mere mention is all that is needed here. Of more interest to us is another relationship, that between Trollope's tireless bourgeois industry and the golden classic maxims to which it is allied. *Labor omnia vincit improbus, Gutta cavat lapidem, Nulla dies sine linea*: Trollope never tires of repeating these Latin sayings, or of paraphrasing Horace's *utile et dulce*. 'It is the first necessity of [the novelist's] position that he make himself pleasant.' Therefore his style must be correct, clear, intelligible without effort, and harmonious. 'Honesty is the best policy.' The first novel that impressed him was *Pride and Prejudice*, and if, later, he was inclined to consider that its position as the first among English novels was contested by *Ivanhoe*, the whole of Trollope's work is there to prove how Jane Austen, and not Scott, was his model.[123] From Miss Austen he learned the art of what may be called functional dialogue. 'The dialogue', he wrote, 'is generally

the most agreeable part of a novel; but it is only so as long
as it tends in some way to the telling of the main story.'
'The ordinary talk of ordinary people is carried on in short
sharp expressive sentences, which very frequently are never
completed—the language of which even among educated
people is often incorrect. The novel-writer in constructing
his dialogue must so steer between absolute accuracy of
language—which would give to his conversation an air of
pedantry, and the slovenly inaccuracy of ordinary talkers,
which if closely followed would offend by an appearance of
grimace—as to produce upon the ear of his readers a sense
of reality. If he be quite real he will seem to attempt to be
funny.' He must therefore pursue a middle path. The *juste
milieu*, the golden mean in all things. The precepts of
Horace, underlined in England by Pope, find a belated
follower in this bourgeois English novelist. Each man has
his own method of work, and we shall not exclude, *a priori*,
the possibility that the man who follows Trollope's method
may be a great artist, just as we shall not agree that a man
is necessarily a great artist because he has in front of him,
for his inspiration, an enchanting landscape rather than
a timepiece, or derives stimulus from a drug instead of from
the persistent repetition of a maxim such as *Nulla dies sine
linea*. In Trollope the method of work is so completely in
harmony with the work itself, and the work so completely
in harmony with its period, that we are not in the least surprised at his now appearing to us as the most typical representative of the Victorian spirit, or—to adopt a term of
European scope—of the Biedermeier spirit.

All he proposed to himself was to look at the world
honestly and to portray men exactly as they were, so that
his readers should be able to recognize themselves in his
books and not feel that they had been transported amongst
divinities and demons. Through the mouth of one of his
characters, Brooke Burgess (in *He Knew He Was Right*),
he declared: 'It is a great mistake to think that anybody is
either an angel or a devil.' To these books the title of *novel*
is suitable, but not that of *romance*: the elements of suspense, of mystery, are lacking in them, as they are in the
novels of Jane Austen. As Henry James wrote about him

(in *Partial Portraits*): 'There are two kinds of taste in the
appreciation of imaginative literature: the taste for emotions
of surprise and the taste for emotions of recognition. It is
the latter that Trollope gratifies.' If, occasionally, the reader
imagines he has discerned a theme of mystery, as in the
secret nature of George Vavasor's dwelling in *Can You
Forgive Her?*, he is very quickly brought back to the domain
of ordinary reality: the mysterious figure received by
Vavasor in this abode which is unknown to his most
intimate friends proves to be nothing more diabolical than
an election agent. It is like Charles Lamb dreaming of the
triumph of Neptune and Amphitrite; and then gradually
the great breakers sink down, the swell changes to flat calm
and then to the flow of a river, and the river is simply the
gentle Thames which lands him, rolling him up on one or
two placid waves 'alone, safe and inglorious, somewhere
at the foot of Lambeth Palace'. A mysterious room like
that of George Vavasor would have become, in Dickens,
the scene of some dark plot or other, directed, perhaps,
against an orphan whose life was bound up with the fate of
a great inheritance. And again, in *The Eustace Diamonds*,
at a certain point (chap. xliv) the course of the quiet narrative appears to be ruffled, all of a sudden, by a sensational
occurrence, the theft of the famous necklace from Lizzie
Eustace's bedroom. But all possible reasons for mystery
are dissipated in a few pages: Lizzie had taken the necklace
out of the jewel-box, and it was only the latter that the
thieves had stolen. Had Lizzie then planned a faked robbery? Not at all! The robbery had been genuine enough;
it was merely that Lizzie had at first been ashamed to
say that, for fear of being robbed, she had brought the
jewel-case empty and concealed the necklace about her
person, then had at once seen, in a flash, that the circumstance might lead people to believe that the necklace really
had been stolen, and only later had realized that this would
create difficulties for her, but since she had not told the
truth from the beginning, could not now retrace her steps.
There is no suspense, no mystery: how differently matters
would have turned out in Wilkie Collins! But Trollope
says (chap. xlviii): 'He who recounts these details has

scorned to have a secret between himself and his readers.'
And again, in the case of the second, and genuine, theft of
the diamonds (chap. lii), when the affair really seems to be
becoming mysterious, Trollope states clearly in whose possession they are to be found, adding: 'The chronicler states
this at once, as he scorns to keep from his reader any secret
that is known to himself.'

On the question of suspense, Trollope expounds an
important principle of his artistic technique at the end of
the fifteenth chapter of *Barchester Towers*:

And here, perhaps, it may be allowed to the novelist to explain
his views on a very important point in the art of telling tales. He
ventures to reprobate that system which goes so far as to violate all
proper confidence between the author and his readers, by maintain-
ing nearly to the end of the third volume a mystery as to the fate
of their favourite personage. Nay, more, and worse than this, is too
frequently done. Have not often the profoundest efforts of genius
been used to baffle the aspirations of the reader, to raise false hopes
and false fears, and to give rise to expectations which are never to be
realized? Are not promises all but made of delightful horrors, in lieu
of which the writer produces nothing but most commonplace realities
in his final chapter? And is there not a species of deceit in this
to which the honesty of the present age should lend no countenance?

And what can be the worth of that solicitude which a peep into
the third volume can utterly dissipate? What the value of those
literary charms which are absolutely destroyed by their enjoyment?
When we have once learnt what was that picture before which was
hung Mrs. Ratcliffe's[124] solemn curtain, we feel no further interest
about either the frame or the veil. . . .

Nay, take the last chapter if you please—learn from its pages all
the results of our troubled story, and the story shall have lost none
of its interest, if indeed there be any interest in it to lose. Our
doctrine is, that the author and the reader should move along
together in full confidence with each other. Let the personages of
the drama undergo ever so complete a comedy of errors among
themselves, but let the spectator never mistake the Syracusan for
the Ephesian. . . .[125]

Honesty is the best policy. No deception with regard either
to events or characters. No mystery, and no hero. The
abolition of the hero is a salient feature in Trollope, no

less—perhaps even more—than in Thackeray. Neither are his likeable characters perfect, nor do his scoundrels and wrongdoers lack some sympathetic traits; neither are the female protagonists of his love-stories dazzling beauties, nor yet are his eminent statesmen geniuses. At the end of *The Three Clerks* he declares:

> So much must be done in order that our readers may know something of the fate of those who perhaps may be called the hero and heroine of the tale. The author does not so call them; he professes to do his work without any such appendages to his story—heroism there may be, and he hopes there is—more or less of it there should be in a true picture of most characters; but heroes and heroines, as so called, are not commonly met with in our daily walks of life.

Doctor Thorne, in the novel of the same name, is a modest country doctor, and 'most far from perfect'. Like many other of Trollope's characters, he 'had within him an inner, stubborn, self-admiring pride . . . and he had a special pride in keeping his pride silently to himself'. As for Lord Lufton, with whom Lucy Robarts is madly in love (in *Framley Parsonage*), 'I know it will be said of Lord Lufton himself that, putting aside his peerage and broad acres, and handsome, sonsy face, he was not worth a girl's care and love':

> That will be said because people think that heroes in books should be so much better than heroes got up for the world's common wear and tear. I may as well confess that of absolute, true heroism there was only a moderate admixture in Lord Lufton's composition; but what would the world come to if none but absolute true heroes were to be thought worthy of women's love? What would the men do? and what,—oh! what would become of the women? (chap. xxi).

And in fact Lucy Robarts, in a moment of desperation, reproves herself for having fallen in love with a 'young popinjay lord'. Another leading *amoroso*, Major Grantly, in the *Last Chronicle of Barset*, may at one moment appear to be no more than a weak, irresolute youth; and John Eames, a second constant lover in the same novel, is excused for flirting with the usual announcement that he was 'certainly no hero,—was very unheroic in many phases of his life; but then, if all the girls are to wait for heroes, I fear that the difficulties in the way of matrimonial arrangements, great as they are at present, will be very seriously enhanced. Johnny was not ecstatic, nor heroic, nor transcendental, nor very beautiful in his manliness; he was not a man to break his heart for love, or to have his story written in an epic; but he was an affectionate, kindly, honest young man; and I think most girls might have done worse than take him' (chap. lxxvi). Another lover, Harry Gilmore in *The Vicar of Bullhampton*, 'is not handsome, nor clever, nor rich, nor romantic, nor distinguished in any way', observed Henry James; 'he is simply rather a dense, narrow-minded, stiff, obstinate, common-place, conscientious modern Englishman . . . he is interesting because he suffers and because we are curious to see the form that suffering will take in that particular nature'.

Trollope's best ecclesiastics are far from faultless. Robarts, in *Framley Parsonage* (chap. xlii),

had within him many aptitudes for good, but not the strengthened courage of a man to act up to them. The stuff of which his manhood was to be formed had been slow of growth, as it is with most men; and, consequently, when temptation was offered to him, he had fallen. But he deeply grieved over his own stumbling, and from time to time, as his periods of penitence came upon him, he resolved that he would once more put his shoulder to the wheel as became one who fights upon earth that battle for which he had put on the armour.

There is much of the heroic in another clergyman, Crawley, as we shall see; but the character that comes closest to an ideal of goodness, the purest clerical figure in Trollope, is Mr. Harding, the Warden; and he is a Biedermeier hero. The Archdeacon says of him, near the end of the book:

I feel sure that he never had an impure fancy in his mind, or a faulty wish in his heart. His tenderness has surpassed the tenderness of woman; and yet, when an occasion came for showing it, he had all the spirit of a hero. . . . He never was wrong. He couldn't go wrong. He lacked guile, and he feared God,—and a man who does both will never go far astray. I don't think he ever coveted aught in his life,—except a new case for his violoncello and somebody to listen to him when he played it.'

At the end of *Barchester Towers* (chap. liii) Mr. Harding is recommended to readers:

... not as a hero, not as a man to be admired and talked of, not as a man who should be toasted at public dinners and spoken of with conventional absurdity as a perfect divine, but as a good man without guile, believing humbly in the religion which he has striven to teach, and guided by the precepts which he has striven to learn.

On this character Trollope wrote some of his most moving pages: we shall come back to them later.

Plantagenet Palliser, the politician, central figure of the group of novels to which a modern reprint has given the title of 'The Palliser Novels', bears no resemblance whatever to a soaring eagle:

He was a tall thin man, apparently not more than thirty years of age, looking in all respects like a gentleman, but with nothing in his appearance that was remarkable. It was a face that you might see and forget, and see again and forget again; and yet when you looked at it and pulled it to pieces, you found that it was a fairly good face, showing intellect in the forehead, and much character in the mouth. The eyes, too, though not to be called bright, always had something to say for themselves, looking as though they had a real meaning. But the outline of the face was almost insignificant, being too thin . . . Mr. Palliser was one of those politicians in possessing whom England has perhaps more reason to be proud than of any other of her resources, and who, as a body, give to her that exquisite combination of conservatism and progress which is her present strength and best security for the future (*Can You Forgive Her?* chaps. xxii, xxiv).[126]

Although extremely rich, Palliser had dedicated himself to work with the tenacious energy of a penniless young lawyer toiling for a dowerless wife, and this he did for no more selfish purpose than that of being enrolled amongst the government officials of England.

He was not a brilliant man, and understood well that such was the case. He was now listened to in the House, as the phrase goes; but he was listened to as a laborious man, who was in earnest in what he did, who got up his facts with accuracy, and who, dull though he be, was worthy of confidence. And he was very dull. He rather prided himself on being dull, and on conquering in spite of his dulness. He never allowed himself a joke in his speeches, nor attempted even the smallest flourish of rhetoric. . . . He had taught himself to believe that oratory, as oratory, was a sin against that honesty in politics by which he strove to guide himself. He desired to use words for the purpose of teaching things which he knew and which others did not know; and he desired also to be honoured for his knowledge. But he had no desire to be honoured for the language in which his knowledge was conveyed. He was an upright, thin, laborious man. . . . If he was dull as a statesman he was more dull in private life. . . .

Just as the external appearance and pedestrian tone of the great politician may deceive the reader as to his qualities, so may the aspect of Trollope's chief feminine figures be at first sight deceptive; to discover their charms a discerning eye is needed. If we think of the Romantic heroes and heroines, whose presence is immediately striking, whose appearance, once seen, is never forgotten (Byron's characters are a typical example), we realize how much the point of view has changed in the course of the nineteenth century. The eye has come to avoid big canvases, in order to enjoy the realistic details of small Dutch pictures. Charlotte Brontë had been the first to make the protagonist of her novel, Jane Eyre, a plain, colourless woman. Trollope's novels are designed to encourage gentle, modest, not very passionate girls. Lucy Robarts (*Framley Parsonage*) is lacking in beauty except for her teeth, which are like pearls, and her eyes, which are of an indescribable colour, somewhere between green and grey, and animated by a fire which is surprising; apart from this, she is dark and small and retiring, and to most people might appear plain. To Lady Lufton she seems positively insignificant. But if one looks at her closely, one discovers that her brow has an expression which is full of poetry. Grace Crawley (*Last Chronicle of Barset*), who is the most beautiful girl in the neighbourhood, does not, at first sight, strike one as such, either because of the carelessness of her dress or because of her thin, emaciated appearance and her features that lack fullness. Her beauty is 'unobtrusive', is only discovered slowly. When Archdeacon Grantly goes to see her, his first idea is that his son must be a fool if he is going to sacrifice his

inheritance for love of a creature 'so slight and unattractive'
as the girl now standing in front of him:

But this idea stayed with him only for a moment. As he continued
to gaze at her during the interview he came to perceive that there
was very much more than he had perceived at the first glance, and
that his son, after all, had had eyes to see. . . . She was so slight, so
meek, so young; and yet there was about her something so beautifully feminine,—and, withal, so like a lady,—that he felt instinc-
tively that he could not attack her with harsh words. Had her lips
been full, and her colour high, and had her eyes rolled; had she put
forth against him any of that ordinary artillery with which youthful
feminine batteries are charged, he would have been ready to rush
to the combat. But this girl, about whom his son had gone mad, sat
there as passively as though she were conscious of the possession of
no artillery. There was not a single gun fired from beneath her
eyelids. . . . It was a noble face, having in it nothing that was poor,
nothing that was mean, nothing that was shapeless. It was a face
that promised infinite beauty, with a promise that was on the very
verge of fulfilment. . . . No man in England knew better than the
archdeacon the difference between beauty of one kind and beauty
of another kind in a woman's face,—the one beauty, which comes
from health and youth and animal spirits, and which belongs to the
miller's daughter, and the other beauty, which shows itself in fine
lines and a noble spirit,—the beauty which comes from breeding
(chap. lvii).

And when at last, towards the end of the novel, Grace
consents to say 'yes' to Major Grantly, she does so with
a truly Biedermeier humility, thanking her lover ('I do not
know why you should be so good to me. . . . Why should
you love me? I am such a poor thing for a man like you to
love'), instead of exhibiting the usual triumph of the long-
courted, finally conquered girl. Phineas Finn (in the novel
of the same name), who has been in love with beautiful and
brilliant women, ends by succumbing to the fascination of
the modest, docile Mary Flood Jones:

A thousand times he had told himself that she had not the spirit
of Lady Laura, or the bright wit of Violet Effingham, or the beauty
of Madame Goesler. But Mary had charms of her own that were
more valuable than them all. Was there one among the three who
had trusted him as she trusted him,—or loved him with the same
satisfied devotion? (chap. lxxiv).

But, after all, Violet lacked that sweet, clinging, feminine softness which made Mary Flood Jones so pre-eminently the most
charming of her sex (chap. lxviii).

If it could be well to lose the world for a woman, it would be well
to lose it for her. . . . The best charm of a woman is that she should
be soft, and trusting, and generous (chap. lxix).

Mary Flood Jones, in the sphere of amorous emotion,
corresponds to the upright, conscientious Mr. Monk in
the sphere of political conduct: under the influence of the
two of them Phineas Finn sacrifices the brilliant career
upon which he has entered, sacrifices marriage with a rich
and beautiful woman and a political position of the first
rank, and retires to a remote provincial town, to the quiet,
modest happiness of a Biedermeier official. We recall those
well-known lines of Wordsworth:

> Among thy mountains did I feel
> The joy of my desire:
> And she I cherished turned the wheel
> Beside an English fire.

Another modest girl is Lucy Morris in *The Eustace
Diamonds*, 'hardly even pretty, small, in appearance almost
insignificant' (chap. xviii):

She was not beautiful. She had none of the charms of fashion.
He had never seen her well dressed,—according to the ideas of dress
which he found to be prevailing in the world. She was a little thing,
who, as a man's wife, could attract no attention by figure, form, or
outward manner,—one who had quietly submitted herself to the
position of a governess, and who did not seem to think that in doing
so she obtained less than her due. But yet he knew her to be better
than all the rest (chap. xiii).

Frank is torn between the desire to make a career and the
Biedermeier ideal—of the sweet wife comforting her husband when he comes home tired in the evening.

In other cases, the female protagonist is not even an
unobtrusive beauty like Grace; she has characteristics
which are not at all admirable, like Alice Vavasor (*Can
You Forgive Her?*)—'. . . nothing that was girlish in her
manners. . . . In person she was tall and well made, rather
large in her neck and shoulders. . . . Her nose was somewhat broad, and retroussé too, but to my thinking', says

the novelist, 'it was a charming nose, full of character, and giving to her face at times a look of pleasant humour, which it would otherwise have lacked'.

Trollope has no liking for beauties of the classical type, such as the irresistible Madame Neroni in *Barchester Towers* and the statuesque Griselda Grantly in *Framley Parsonage*: beauty, for him, is in inverse ratio to good sense, to spirituality. Griselda Grantly is insipid and cold, and the splendidly handsome Burgo Fitzgerald is almost a half-wit. An exception seems to be Madame Max Goesler, the fascinating, wealthy Austrian, albeit of humble origin, who first appears in *Phineas Finn* as an adventuress, to display later on, during the course of the novel, the virtues of a sensible, generous woman. In reality it is quite possible, since Trollope was in the habit of trusting to the inspiration of the moment ('As to the incidents of the story, the circumstances by which these personages were to be affected, I knew nothing. They were created for the most part as they were described. I never could arrange a set of events before me', he declared, with regard to this novel)—it is possible that Madame Goesler at first seemed to him like a kind of Becky Sharp; but later, when put to the proof, she throws over the aged and eminent Duke of Omnium and is ready to offer herself and all her substance to the charming but unreliable Finn. 'With all her ambition, there was something of genuine humility about her' (chap. lvii). As to her beauty, it is of an irregular, exotic type (chap. xl); her nose, for instance, 'was not classically beautiful, being broader at the nostrils than beauty required, and, moreover, not perfectly straight in its line'.

Another beautiful adventuress, a calculating woman of the Becky Sharp type, as even the author himself proclaimed ('that opulent and aristocratic Becky Sharp'), is Lizzie Eustace in *The Eustace Diamonds*; but here too, beauty is not an external sign of spiritual perfection—far from it! This is how her cousin Frank Greystock and Lucy Morris speak of her (chap. xii): 'Sometimes to me she is almost frightful to look at', says Lucy. 'In what way?' asks Frank. 'Oh, I can't tell you. She looks like a beautiful animal that you are afraid to caress for fear it should bite you;—an animal that would be beautiful if its eyes were not so restless, and its teeth so sharp and so white.' Frank is of the same opinion, and compares her to a cat.

Just as we shall never find, in Trollope, a character who is an absolute paragon of beauty or virtue, so also we shall never find any of those grim scoundrels, those thorough-paced rascals, who, in the world of Dickens, form an inevitable complement to his angels incarnate.

As man is never strong enough to take unmixed delight in good, so may we presume also that he cannot be quite so weak as to find perfect satisfaction in evil.

Thus wrote Trollope (*The Eustace Diamonds*, chap. i) of the intriguer Lizzie Eustace. And in the same novel (chap. xviii) he speaks of mixed characters, upon whom Satan has an 'intermittent grasp', and who, when this grasp is relaxed, rise, on the rebound, to a display of virtuous resolutions and a genuine love of good and noble things. Slope, the intriguing chaplain in *Barchester Towers*, 'was not in all things a bad man. His motives, like those of most men, were mixed; and though his conduct was generally very different from that which we would wish to praise, it was actuated perhaps as often as that of the majority of the world by a desire to do his duty.' Madeline Neroni, the diabolical and improbable *femme fatale* in the same novel, shows a streak of goodness when she decides to leave Arabin to the woman he loves. Colonel Osborne (in *He Knew He Was Right*), of whom Louis Trevelyan is jealous, even though he passes in Lady Milborough's eyes as an 'eminent, notorious, and experienced Lothario', is not a shameless lady-killer, a *bel-ami* out of a French novel. 'He was not a man who boasted of his conquests. He was not a ravening wolf going about seeking whom he might devour, and determined to devour whatever might come in his way; but he liked that which was pleasant; and of all pleasant things the company of a pretty clever woman was to him the pleasantest.' 'He was not especially a vicious man, and had now, as we know, reached a time of life when such vice as that in question might be supposed to have lost its charm for him. . . . [He] could hardly have wished to run away with his neighbour's wife, or to have destroyed the happiness of his old friend's daughter. . . . But he had a certain pleasure in being the confidential friend of a very pretty woman; and when he heard that that pretty woman's husband was jealous, the pleasure was enhanced rather than otherwise.' When the husband has made a jealous scene, Osborne walks home with a 'jauntier step than usual', because he knows himself to have been the cause of the scene: 'This was very wrong; but there is reason to believe that many such men as Colonel Osborne, who are bachelors at fifty, are equally malicious.' Of the scapegrace Sowerby, in *Framley Parsonage*: '. . . reckless as this man always appeared to be, reckless as he absolutely was, there was still within his heart a desire for better things and in his mind an understanding that he had hitherto missed his career as an honest English gentleman.' And when, at the end of the novel, Lord Lufton behaves extremely harshly to Sowerby, the author remarks that, in spite of all the latter's rogueries, 'I have for him some tender feeling knowing that there was still a touch of gentle bearing round his heart, an abiding taste for better things within him. . . . There was yet within him the means of repentance.' Sowerby, the liar, the sponger, is shown to us in a sympathetic, touching light when, for the last time, he revisits the estate which has been lost to him by his own recklessness. Even the adventurer Lopez, in *The Prime Minister*, 'was not naturally an ill-natured man'. Trollope, furthermore, is not given to devising exemplary and melodramatic punishments for his villains—unless the knocking of Lopez's body 'into bloody atoms' by the railway-engine be such an one. Sowerby vanishes, the true perpetrators of the theft of the cheque for which the Reverend Crawley had been held guilty disappear and are never brought to justice; and the reader, after seeing him emigrate to America, loses sight of George Vavasor (in *Can You Forgive Her?*), an egoist and a man of violence, whose revolting character is as it were symbolized by the grisly scar that disfigures his face, a scar which, when he loses his temper, swells and opens. Vavasor is a kind of bourgeois, realistic version of the Byronic outlaw. Unpopular, unable to form intimate relationships with other men, capable of relaxing only in the company of women, he is always pursuing some interested aim: 'Nature, I think, had so fashioned George Vavasor that he might have been a good, and perhaps a great, man. . . . Vavasor had educated himself to badness with his eyes open. He had known what was wrong, and had done it, having taught himself to think that bad things were best.' Murderous ideas often cross his mind, but Trollope hastens to extenuate: it was not that Vavasor really wanted to kill Scruby, but that 'he received some secret satisfaction in allowing his mind to dwell upon the subject, and in making those calculations'. And when the banks in the City refuse to cash Alice's bills for him, 'George Vavasor cursed the City and made his calculation about murdering it. Might not a river of strychnine be turned on round the Exchange about luncheon time?' Vavasor's criminal qualities melt away in caricature.[127] A Biedermeier of the type of Trollope was unable to arrive at the representation of the abysses of the criminal soul: the farthest point he could reach was brutal behaviour to women, a thing that disqualified George Vavasor as a gentleman and in a way placed him outside the pale of society. The scene in which Vavasor throws his sister to the ground, and she, as she falls, breaks her arm, is the worst a Trollope can conceive in the representation of evil in action. Almost equally brutal and ruthless is Vavasor's behaviour towards his ex-mistress when she begs a meal from him—an episode that contrasts sharply with Burgo Fitzgerald's conduct towards the little prostitute whom he meets casually in the street: both men, Vavasor and Fitzgerald, are financially ruined, but whereas the cad brutally drives away the faded woman who has been his mistress, the gentleman helps the unknown strumpet from an innate sense of chivalry towards the weaker sex. Nevertheless, women sacrifice themselves for George Vavasor. Alice is ready to waste her fortune on him, his sister Kate idolizes him, would give up her own inheritance for him, and even performs, for love of him, an evil act of which she never ceases to repent: all this being a sign that even George Vavasor must possess some sort of virtue. When Alice and

Kate are speaking of him after he has vanished, Kate says: 'But he will never come back. He will never ask us to forgive him, or even wish it. He has no heart.' 'He has longed for money, till the Devil has hardened his heart', says Alice. 'And yet how tender he could be in his manner when he chose it;—how soft he could make his words and his looks!'

With Vavasor, Trollope came near to portraying a criminal, tracing, in dark colours, the likeness of a type of ambitious politician and parasite already sketched in Sowerby (and the part played by Miss Dunstable in relation to the latter is brought to perfection in the role assigned to Alice in *Can You Forgive Her?*): but, as we have seen, he stops at the threshold of tragedy. This watering-down of tragedy is already discernible in one of Trollope's earliest novels, *The Three Clerks* (1858), in which there enters upon the scene the type of unrestrained, evil sponger that was to be later reincarnated in various forms in successive novels. Truly diabolical is the work of corruption that Undy Scott carries into effect upon Alaric Tudor, who, starting as an honest official, finally turns into an untrustworthy Stock Exchange speculator and the fraudulent administrator of a young girl's patrimony. But if Undy Scott is a devil, if this first of Trollope's villains is genuinely evil, there is nothing truly terrible about him: this jovial figure, this imperturbable cynic is a vile character, certainly, but is of mediocre stature, and appears positively mean under the fire of accusations from the lawyer Chaffanbrass; his machinations ruin Alaric, but also fall back upon his own head, like those of Ben Jonson's Volpone, in a scene (the trial of Alaric) which is one of the few dramatic scenes in Trollope. Alaric does not perish entirely, but finds support and comfort in his wife, and after serving his light prison sentence, makes a new life for himself in Australia: his adventures, we note, correspond exactly in spirit to the cycles of pictures (in the Hogarth tradition) by Augustus Egg and William Powell Frith—for instance, the series of five paintings by the latter entitled *The Race for Wealth*;[128] and the description of Alaric's last breakfast at home before he is condemned is a picture in the true Egg manner. Trollope (chap. xliv) compares his wicked Undy Scott to Dickens's

Bill Sikes; both 'had taught themselves to believe that that which other men called virtue was, on its own account, to be regarded as mawkish, insipid, and useless for such purposes as the acquisition of money or pleasure; whereas vice was, on its own account, to be preferred, as offering the only road to those things which they were desirous of possessing'. But, although they held in common this faith in the *prospérités du vice*, Sikes and Scott, in Trollope's opinion, differed in this, that Sikes was an ignorant man, whereas Scott, who through education had the power of choosing between good and evil, had deliberately chosen to serve the Devil. And yet, in the eyes of the world, Bill Sikes passes for the more odious scoundrel of the two. 'Lady, you now know them both. Is it not the fact, that, knowing him as you do, you could spend a pleasant hour enough with Mr. Scott, sitting next to him at dinner; whereas your blood would creep within you, your hair would stand on end, your voice would stick in your throat, if you were suddenly told that Bill Sikes was in your presence?' Poor Bill! Trollope professes a sort of liking for him and, if it is inevitable that he should be hanged, allows him the extenuating circumstance of the social setting in which he was born; but with what zest he would hang Undy Scott! 'Fate, however, and the laws are averse.' Scott, expelled from his club and from the House of Commons, betakes himself to the Continent and drags out a more and more sordid and degrading existence in various watering-places and gambling-casinos, until at last 'his wretched life will ooze out from him in some dark corner, like the filthy juice of a decayed fungus'. It is rather like the end of Thackeray's woman-demon, Becky Sharp—an anti-heroic end *par excellence*. In *The Three Clerks* we have a further example of watered-down tragedy. Katie seems to be on the point of dying like a Dickens heroine, like Little Nell; we are present at what appear to be her touching last moments, the moving scene with Charley at the sick girl's bedside; but then she recovers and ends by marrying the young man for love of whom she was languishing. In *Phineas Redux* the convergence of circumstances clearly indicates that Yosef Mealyus, the Bohemian adventurer who has become

a priest in England under the name of Joseph Emilius and
has craftily insinuated himself into the good graces of Lady
Eustace, even to the point of making her his bride (although
he already has a wife in Bohemia), is the murderer of Bon-
teen the M.P. But the decisive test is never reached, and
Mealyus is condemned merely for bigamy. We recall how
Dickens cheerfully sent his Jew to the gallows in *Oliver
Twist*: indeed, the climax of that novel was the episode of
Fagin in the condemned cell. But Trollope avoids melodrama and offers his reader the *anticlimax* of another Jew,
cleverer than Fagin, condemned indeed, but for the least
grave of his crimes.

Another watering-down of a dramatic situation occurs
in the case of Colonel Osborne and Mrs. Trevelyan in
He Knew He Was Right. When Osborne (chap. xx) learns
of the separation of Louis Trevelyan from his wife, and that
the latter has been banished to a remote corner of Devon-
shire near the prison on Dartmoor, while he feels a certain
private satisfaction at knowing himself to be the cause of
this family tragedy, 'he began to think that if Trevelyan
were out of the way, he might,—might perhaps be almost
tempted to make this woman his wife'. What follows is
typically Trollopian:

The reader is not to suppose that Colonel Osborne meditated any
making-away with the husband. Our Colonel was certainly not the
man for a murder. Nor did he even think of running away with his
friend's daughter. Though he told himself that he could dispose of
his wrinkles satisfactorily, still he knew himself and his powers
sufficiently to be aware that he was no longer fit to be the hero of
such a romance as that. He acknowledged to himself that there was
much labour to be gone through in running away with another
man's wife; and that the results, in respect to personal comfort, are
not always happy. But what if Mrs. Trevelyan were to divorce
herself from her husband on the score of her husband's cruelty? . . .
He did not probably declare to himself that a divorce should be
obtained, and that, in such event, he would marry the lady,—but
ideas came across his mind in that direction.

And now the dramatic situation becomes tinged with
Biedermeier humour:

Trevelyan was a cruel Bluebeard; Emily—as he was studious to call Mrs. Trevelyan,—was a dear injured saint. And as for himself, though he acknowledged to himself that the lumbago pinched him now and again, so that he could not rise from his chair with all the alacrity of youth, yet, when he walked along Pall Mall with his coat properly buttoned, he could not but observe that a great many young women looked at him with admiring eyes.

In another case, that of the portrait of Miss Van Siever in *The Last Chronicle of Barset*, there is a detail from which one can easily imagine what a French Romantic, of the 'frénétique' or decadent type, would have made of it. Miss Van Siever 'was handsome as may be a horse or a tiger, but there was about her nothing of feminine softness'. The painter Conway Dalrymple thinks of painting her as Jael in the act of driving the nail into Sisera's head. 'You may observe', says the painter to the girl, 'that artists in all ages have sought for higher types of models in painting women who have been violent or criminal, than have sufficed for them in the portraitures of gentleness and virtue. Look at all the Judiths, and the Lucretias, and the Charlotte Cordays; how much finer the women are than the Madonnas and the Saint Cecilias' (chap. xxvi). This, in Trollope, is no more than a hint; for this woman with a fierce, pitiless appearance turns out to be a girl of great good sense, with a character of the most completely practical kind. When Dalrymple tells her of a nail with which she has pierced his heart, she does not feel in the least flattered; but when (chap. lx) the painter takes off his apron, puts down his palette, and declares flatly, without circumlocutions: 'I am going to ask Clara Van Siever to be my wife'—this abrupt request, with its complete lack of sentimentality, convinces her. Clara is certainly no *diabolique* in the d'Aurevilly manner. There is no excess in Trollope, either in virtue or, even less, in vice. And in the case of the proposed marriage of Lucinda Roanoke to Sir Griffin Tewett (in *The Eustace Diamonds*), a marriage that might have led to the most tragic consequences owing to the girl's loathing for her brutal *fiancé*, Trollope adopts a tragi-comic solution: the wedding is called off at the last moment, and the farce of the wedding-presents, and of the bankruptcy of the girl's aunt, Mrs. Carbuncle, puts to flight the tragic shadows of

Lucinda's desperation, and she is left brandishing a poker instead of a dagger. Lucinda is a cold, hard type like Clara Van Siever, and the two of them have in common the fact that they both sit to painters:

> She had sat for her portrait during the last winter, and her picture had caused much remark in the Exhibition. Some said that she might be a Brinvilliers [the famous poisoner], others a Cleopatra, and others again a Queen of Sheba (chap. xxxvi).

Towards the end of *The Last Chronicle of Barset* (chap. lxxxiv) Trollope takes exception to those who, in literature, 'love a colouring higher than nature justifies. We are, most of us, apt to love Raphael's madonnas better than Rembrandt's matrons. But, though we do so, we know that Rembrandt's matrons existed; but we have a strong belief that no such woman as Raphael painted ever did exist.' Similarly in *The Eustace Diamonds* (chap. xxxv), with regard to the mixed character of Frank Greystock:

> It is very easy to depict a hero,—a man absolutely stainless, perfect as an Arthur,—a man honest in all his dealings, equal to all trials, true in all his speech, indifferent to his own prosperity, struggling for the general good, and, above all, faithful in love. At any rate, it is as easy to do that as to tell of the man who is one hour good and the next bad, who aspires greatly, but fails in practice, who sees the higher, but too often follows the lower course. There arose at one time a school of art, which delighted to paint the human face as perfect in beauty; and from that time to this we are discontented unless every woman is drawn for us as a Venus, or at least a Madonna. I do not know that we have gained much by this untrue portraiture, either in beauty or in art. There may be made for us a pretty thing to look at, no doubt;—but we know that that pretty thing is not really visaged as the mistress whom we serve, and whose lineaments we desire to perpetuate on the canvas. The winds of heaven, or the flesh-pots of Egypt, or the midnight gas,—passions, pains, and, perhaps, rouge and powder, have made her something different. But still there is the fire of her eye, and the eager eloquence of her mouth, and something, too, perhaps, left of the departing innocence of youth, which the painter might give us without the Venus or the Madonna touches. But the painter does not dare to do it. Indeed, he has painted so long after the other fashion that he would hate the canvas before him, were he to give way to the rouge-begotten roughness or to the flesh-pots,—or even to the winds. . . .

And so also has the reading world taught itself to like best the
characters of all but divine men and women. Let the man who
paints with pen and ink give the gaslight, and the flesh-pots, the
passions and pains, the prurient prudence and the rouge-pots and
pounce-boxes of the world as it is, and he will be told that no one
can care a straw for his creations. With whom are we to sympathize?
says the reader, who not unnaturally imagines that a hero should
be heroic. Oh, thou, my reader, whose sympathies are in truth the
great and only aim of my work, when you have called the dearest of
your friends round you to your hospitable table, how many heroes
are there sitting at the board?

And so on, in a style that closely recalls that of Thackeray,
concluding with remarks on the mediocrity of the things
and the people that go to make up our daily experience:

The persons whom you cannot care for in a novel, because they
are so bad, are the very same that you so dearly love in your life,
because they are so good. To make them and ourselves somewhat
better,—not by one spring heavenwards to perfection, because we
cannot so use our legs,—but by slow climbing, is, we may presume,
the object of all teachers, leaders, legislators, spiritual pastors, and
masters. He who writes tales such as this, probably also has, very
humbly, some such object distantly before him. A picture of sur-
passing godlike nobleness,—a picture of a King Arthur among men,
may perhaps do much. But such pictures cannot do all. When such
a picture is painted, as intending to show what a man should be, it
is true. If painted to show what men are, it is false. The true picture
of life as it is, if it could be adequately painted, would show men
what they are, and how they might rise, not, indeed, to perfection,
but one step first, and then another on the ladder.

The novelist writes in the same manner (in chap. lxxvi),
still about Frank Greystock's character, that he was a young
man without 'heroic attributes', but, on the whole, 'nobler
than his friends'.

Apart from the extravagance of Trollope's assertion on
the subject of the women painted by Raphael (he was
evidently unfamiliar with a type of beauty not so very rare
in Italy), the principle of honest, meticulous reproduction
of the world around him holds good in his case. And anyone
who may say to me at this point that Trollope is therefore
photographic, and that his charm for us is that of the old

daguerreotypes, will be taking the words out of my mouth. Photography was born of the period. Just as a genius is usually born at the right moment, the supreme flower, as it were, of a tradition, of a school, so also certain technical inventions seem to crown the aspirations of an entire age. I do not mean to say that the invention of photography had as much importance as that of oil painting, which permitted the attainment of previously impossible effects of colour and light: but think of how, about the middle of the nineteenth century, thanks to the gospel of Ruskin, the meticulous rendering of the most insignificant details of a scene, without either selection or rejection, became the main preoccupation of the Pre-Raphaelites; think of the Ruskinian formula for the 'historic landscape'—that is, a picture whose object was to provide those who could not go there with a faithful image of a place; compare the landscapes of Ruskin with the first photographs of the countryside; think of Ford Madox Brown's answer to someone who asked him why he had chosen 'such a very ugly subject' for his last picture: 'Because it lay out of a back window.' It was not by mere chance that photography was born; it was just at the moment when the tendency of art was towards a minute and faithful reproduction of reality. Dickens rebelled against the realism that does not shun mean human detail, even in matters with which some transcendental significance is connected. His reaction to Millais's *Christ in the Carpenter's Shop* is well known—a picture in which Christ's family is depicted as a real, ordinary family of humble artisans. A Holy Family, for him, demanded the application of all the most ennobling, the most gracious, the most beautiful ideas that the brush of man could devise. Trollope, like the Pre-Raphaelites, was concerned, on the other hand, with verisimilitude; to the idealized Madonnas of Raphael he preferred the real matrons of Rembrandt.

Absolute objectivity, of course, does not exist even in photography, and if it did exist, one would miss in it that 'imponderable something more', as Edith Wharton calls it, which is the very essence, the flower, of reality, which makes life circulate within reality and endows it with a permanent value. Trollope was well aware of this when he remarked, in *Barchester Towers* (chap. xx), that it was to be regretted that no mental method of daguerreotype or photography had yet been discovered, but that in any case photographs were never entirely satisfying, since they missed that touch of the divine which illuminates the human face ('they will never achieve a portrait of the human face divine'): the true likeness could not be obtained by mechanical means. If indeed Trollope had achieved nothing more than what Hawthorne considered to be his chief characteristic—it is 'as if some giant had hewn a great lump out of the earth and put it under a glass case, with all its inhabitants going about their daily business, and not suspecting that they were being made a show of'—then he would really have achieved what is supposed to be achieved by a photographic objective. In *Doctor Thorne* (chap. viii), when Frank is holding Mary's hand, one has the impression that Trollope feels the need of some rapid means such as photography or cinematography to convey the actual *tempo* of their movements.

From my tedious way of telling it, the reader will be led to imagine that the hand-squeezing had been protracted to a duration quite incompatible with any objection to such an arrangement on the part of the lady; but the fault is all mine: in no part hers. Were I possessed of a quick spasmodic style of narrative, I should have been able to include it all—Frank's misbehaviour, Mary's immediate anger, Augusta's arrival, and keen, Argus-eyed inspection, and then Mary's subsequent misery—in five words and half a dozen dashes and inverted commas. The thing should have been so told; for, to do Mary justice, she did not leave her hand in Frank's a moment longer than she could help herself.

The effort to prove himself adequate to the changeableness of life is continual in Trollope:

In writing *Phineas Finn* I had constantly before me the necessity of progression in character,—of marking the changes in men and women which would naturally be produced by the lapse of years. . . . I was continually asking myself how this woman would act when this or that event had passed over her head, or how that man would carry himself when his youth had become manhood, or his manhood declined to old age.

Thus Phineas Finn, who one year earlier would have done anything for one word of love from Lady Laura, when at last the word came, felt that all it did was to create an embarrassment for him (chap. xxxiii).

Not that Trollope does not sometimes give the impression of the photographic objective; but these are the least vivid parts of his work. Certain descriptions of individuals and of landscapes are no more animated than topographical charts. Here is a short example from *Barchester Towers* (chap. xxi):

She was standing at the lattice of a little room upstairs, from which the view certainly was very lovely. It was from the back of the vicarage, and there was nothing to interrupt the eye between the house and the glorious gray pile of the cathedral. The intermediate ground, however, was beautifully studded with timber. In the immediate foreground ran the little river which afterwards skirted the city; and, just to the right of the cathedral, the pointed gables and chimneys of Hiram's Hospital peeped out of the elms which encompass it.

It is a rather dull, generalized stage direction. Trollope gives, on the contrary, a precise description, admirable in its close correspondence with observed reality, of the desolate country house near Siena—Casalunga, where the half-crazed Louis Trevelyan has shut himself up with his little son. Dry, photographic—any other English novelist would have either heightened the colours, or introduced a personal point of view, alien to the landscape—this description of a utilitarian corner of the Tuscan countryside helps to convey the inhuman desolation of the place better than a richer palette would have done (*He Knew He Was Right*, chap. lxxviii):

On this side of the house the tilled ground, either ploughed or dug with the spade, came up to the very windows. There was hardly even a particle of grass to be seen. A short way down the hill there were rows of olive trees, standing in prim order and at regular distances, from which hung the vines. . . . Olives and vines have pretty names, and call up associations of landscape beauty. But here they were in no way beautiful. The ground beneath them was turned up, and brown, and arid, so that there was not a blade of grass to be seen. On some furrows the maze or Indian corn was sprouting, and there were patches of growth of other kinds,—each patch closely marked by its own straight lines; and there were narrow paths, so constructed as to take as little room as possible. But all that had been done had been done for economy, and nothing for beauty. . . .

The sun was blazing fiercely hot, hotter on this side, Sir Marmaduke thought, even than on the other; and there was not a wavelet of a cloud in the sky. A balcony ran the whole length of the house, and under this Sir Marmaduke took shelter at once, leaning with his back against the wall. 'There is not a soul here at all,' said he.

'The men in the barn told us that there was,' said Mr. Glascock; 'and, at any rate, we will try the windows.' So saying, he walked along the front of the house, Sir Marmaduke following him slowly, till they came to a door, the upper half of which was glazed, and through which they looked into one of the rooms. Two or three of the other windows in this frontage of the house came down to the ground, and were made for egress and ingress; but they had all been closed with shutters, as though the house was deserted. But they now looked into a room which contained some signs of habitation. There was a small table with a marble top, on which lay two or three books, and there were two arm-chairs in the room, with gilded arms and legs, and a morsel of carpet, and a clock on a shelf over a stove, and—a rocking-horse. 'The boy is here, you may be sure,' said Mr. Glascock. . . .

The rocking-horse in the desolate house is all we need to make us understand the life of the child that has been snatched away from its mother by Louis Trevelyan; a more emphatic and precise statement—such as Dickens would have given us—would not have succeeded in being so moving. Trollope, by stressing one detail, here achieves an effect which the cinema obtains by isolating an object in the foreground of the picture.

Trollope's art comes most fully into play at moments when he discovers the beauty of people who are not at all striking, or even positively insignificant, in appearance (we have already seen the case of Grace Crawley), when he reveals the noble or even heroic aspects of individuals whose stature does not seem to rise above the average (Mr. Harding, for instance), or the charm, difficult to specify, of landscapes not particularly favoured by nature. In this choice of unheroic human types and 'unpoetic' landscapes we find an expression of the same democratic spirit which, in nineteenth-century France, animated painters like Courbet and Daumier. Such is the description of Vavasor Hall in *Can You Forgive Her?*—situated 'on the intermediate ground between the mountains of the lake country and the plains':

For myself, I can find, I know not what of charm in wandering over open, unadorned moorland. It must be more in the softness of the grass to the feet, and the freshness of the air to the lungs, than in anything that meets the eye. You might walk for miles and miles to the north-east, or east, or south-east of Vavasor without meeting any object to arrest the view. The great road from Lancaster to Carlisle crossed the outskirt of the small parish about a mile from the church, and beyond that the fell seemed to be interminable. Towards the north it rose, and towards the south it fell, and it rose and fell very gradually. Here and there some slight appearance of a valley might be traced which had been formed by the action of the waters; but such breakings of ground were inconsiderable, and did not suffice to interrupt the stern sameness of the everlasting moorland.

This is a type of landscape devoid of the beauty that tourists seek; it forms the background of a winter walk undertaken by Alice and Kate (chap. xxxi):

The air was clear and cold, but not actually frosty. The ground beneath their feet was dry, and the sky, though not bright, had that appearance of enduring weather which gives no foreboding of rain. There is a special winter's light, which is very clear, though devoid of all brilliancy,—through which every object strikes upon the eye with well-marked lines, and under which almost all forms of nature seem graceful to the sight if not actually beautiful. But there is a certain melancholy which ever accompanies it. It is the light of the afternoon, and gives token of the speedy coming of the early twilight. It tells of the shortness of the day, and contains even in its clearness a promise of the gloom of night. It is absolute light, but it seems to contain the darkness which is to follow it. I do not know that it is ever to be seen and felt so plainly as on the wide moorland, where the eye stretches away over miles, and sees at the world's end the faint low lines of distant clouds settling themselves upon the horizon.

It is not a spectacular landscape, it might even be called dull; but its intimate charm, its 'imponderable something

27. W. P. FRITH. The Railway Station (*London, Royal Holloway College. By courtesy of the College*)

28. PETER BREUGHEL. John the Baptist preaching (*Budapest, Fine Arts Museum*)

more', its touch of the divine, has been caught by Trollope. From the same novel comes this lovingly painted hunting-scene, a scene not in the grand manner but full of a gay thoughtfulness of its own (chap. xvii):

Of all sights in the world there is, I think, none more beautiful than that of a pack of foxhounds seated, on a winter morning, round the huntsman, if the place of meeting has been chosen with anything of artistic skill. It should be in a grassy field, and the field should be small. It should not be absolutely away from all buildings, and the hedgerows should not have been clipped and pared, and made straight with reference to modern agricultural economy. There should be trees near, and the ground should be a little uneven, so as to mark some certain small space as the exact spot where the dogs and servants of the hunt should congregate.

There are well-known grand meets in England, in the parks of noblemen, before their houses, or even on what are called their lawns; but these magnificent affairs have but little of the beauty of which I speak. Such assemblies are too grand and too ornate, and, moreover, much too far removed from true sporting proprieties. At them, equipages are shining, and ladies' dresses are gorgeous, and crowds of tradesmen from the neighbouring town have come there to look at the grand folk. To my eye there is nothing beautiful in that. The meet I speak of is arranged with a view to sport, but the accident of the locality may make it the prettiest thing in the world. Such, in a special degree, was the case at Edgehill.

And he proceeds to describe this eminently picturesque and popular place for a meet. But it is not so much the picturesque that attracts Trollope as the dull, neutral landscape, the type of landscape that was the constant study of the Dutch painters. Again in *Can You Forgive Her?* (chap. lxxiv), we hear John Grey declaring that he prefers the flat, 'ugly' landscape of Cambridgeshire to the beauties of the Lake of Lucerne 'partly because all beauty is best enjoyed when it is sought for with some trouble and difficulty, and partly because such beauty, and the romance which is attached to it, should not make up the staple of one's life. Romance, if it is to come at all, should always come by fits and starts.'

George Eliot, too, at the beginning of her career, had similar aims in view to those of Trollope—to discover the 'silver lining' in ordinary people and things; but in her, later, the ethical purpose gained the upper hand, whereas Trollope, who accepted, without discussion, the main corner-stones of the Victorian social structure, was able to preserve the crystalline purity of his lens of observation. Indeed Trollope, with his passion for the traditional English sport of fox-hunting, is the champion of Old England. Speaking in *Barchester Towers* of Squire Thorne of Ullathorne and his sister, figures that might have stepped straight out of *The Spectator*, so closely related do they seem to the immortal Sir Roger de Coverley, Trollope says: 'Such, we believe, are the inhabitants of many an English country home. May it be long before their number diminishes.' In *The Eustace Diamonds* (chap. iv) he says, of conservatives of the old type: 'There is a large body of such men in England, and, personally, they are the very salt of the nation.' And how much sympathy seeps through the humorous description of another *Spectator* Club figure, Miss Jemima Stanbury in *He Knew He Was Right*, who is truly worthy of a place amongst the Canterbury Pilgrims, beside the Prioress, and very closely related, as well, to Aunt Betsy in *David Copperfield*![129] A Tory of the old school, a fierce opponent of reform, a friend of those clergymen in whom she found 'a flavour of the unascetic godliness of ancient days', she revered a bust of Lord Eldon 'before which she was accustomed to stand with hands closed and to weep—or to think that she wept', and detested the *chignon* of the latest feminine fashion to such a degree that she refused even to mention the word.[130] With regard to the clergy, Miss Jemima reflects the taste of Trollope himself who, at the end of *The Last Chronicle of Barset*, after protesting, in the passage already quoted about Raphael's Madonnas and Rembrandt's matrons, against those who found fault with him for having painted portraits of bad clergymen rather than exemplary ones, concludes: 'For myself I can only say that I shall always be happy to sit, when allowed to do so, at the table of Archdeacon Grantly, to walk through the High Street of Barchester arm-in-arm with Mr. Robarts of Framley, and to stand alone and shed a tear beneath the modest black stone in the north transept

of the cathedral on which is inscribed the name of Septimus
Harding.' Apart from the last, who in his way is a very
good Christian, both Archdeacon Grantly—dominated by
his instinct as a landowner and a fanatical devotee of fox-
hunting, and also a secret reader of Rabelais—and Robarts
who, in his ambition to make a career, sets himself to move
in high society and, by renewing bills of exchange, brings
his family to the brink of ruin, are types of Old England
that would not be out of place in a novel by Fielding or
Smollett. In a pleasing little scene in *The Last Chronicle of
Barset*—a real Biedermeier *genre* picture—the two worldly
clergymen, Mark Robarts and Caleb Oriel, driving away
in a smart private gig, are followed by the envious eyes of
two poor clergymen who have to hire a conveyance at their
own expense; and there is no doubt as to where Trollope's
sympathies lie. The awkward Mr. Thumble remarks to
the prolific and ever-needy Mr. Quiverful (chap. liv):

> 'Did you ever see such a fellow as that Robarts,—just look at
> him;—quite indecent, wasn't he? He thinks he can have his own
> way in everything, just because his sister married a lord. I do hate
> to see all that meanness.'
> Mark Robarts and Caleb Oriel left Silverbridge in another gig
> by the same road, and soon passed their brethren, as Mr. Robarts
> was in the habit of driving a large, quick-stepping horse. The last
> remarks were being made as the dust from the vicar of Framley's
> wheels saluted the faces of the two slower clergymen.

Mr. Thumble, later on, was to be the victim of an adventure in the picaresque manner, for, having fallen from his
horse and been unsuccessful in obtaining a place in Mr.
Grantly's carriage, he is forced to lead his old hack on foot
all the way from Hogglestock to Barchester. And there are
ways and types from the picaresque novel to be found also
in the episode of the quintain contest in *Barchester Towers*,
and in the secondary plot of *Can You Forgive Her?*, the
courting of Mrs. Greenow on the part of Captain Bellfield
and the farmer Cheesacre—humorous sketches in the
eighteenth-century tradition. Scenes of action do not
abound in the pages of Trollope, but there is one type of
scene of action of which he is particularly fond, and he puts

all the salty humour of good old England into the describing of it—a rascal getting what he deserves: Mr. Moffat being thrashed by Frank in *Doctor Thorne*, George Vavasor being kicked out of John Grey's house in *Can You Forgive Her?*

Trollope is for the old order; he mistrusts reforms, and the very idea of progress, so popular amongst the Victorians, provokes his ridicule. In *Framley Parsonage* Mr. Harold Smith makes a grotesque declamatory speech which is simply a hymn to civilization from beginning to end; in *The Warden* there is a caricature of Dickens's campaigns against systems and institutions, in the figure of Mr. Popular Sentiment who with his novel *The Almshouse* makes an onslaught against the prevailing system of workhouses. Towards the end of the novel we see how Hiram's Hospital, which is one of these same almshouses, languishes and decays as soon as the spirit of reform seeks to refashion it: the old institution, with all its injustices, was adequate; all that reform accomplishes is the destruction of what is beautiful in the traditional order—'the beauty of the place is gone'.

In his attitude of *laudator temporis acti*, in the disillusioned kind-heartedness with which he looks upon human actions, in the very way in which he insinuates his opinions, Trollope recalls Thackeray, of whom he was a great admirer.[131] In his *Autobiography* he gives Thackeray first place amongst modern novelists: 'His knowledge of human nature was supreme, and his characters stand out as human beings, with a force and a truth which has not, I think, been within the reach of any other English novelist in any period.' He goes so far as to compare Colonel Newcome with Don Quixote for the intimate knowledge of him that the reader finally achieves, and he has an exclamation of wonder for each of the great characters in Thackeray's novels. Thackeray's tone when, with tears in his eyes, he shakes his head over certain touching aspects of human affairs, is to be met with again, sometimes, in Trollope. Thus in *Doctor Thorne*, when speaking of the tears shed by Sir Roger Scatcherd after he has been cruelly disappointed by his son: 'Such tears as those which wet that pillow are the bitterest which human eyes can shed'; in *The Last Chronicle of Barset*, of Crosbie's forced smile in reply to Sir Raffle Buffle's astonishment at meeting him in the City where he has gone, in vain, to try and raise money: 'Who can tell, who has not felt it, the pain that goes to the forcing of such smiles?'; or when he turns directly to one of his characters with an admonition: 'Ah! Mrs. Woodward, my friend, my friend, was it well that thou shouldst leave that sweet unguarded rosebud of thine to such perils as these?' (*The Three Clerks*), 'Oh, Frank, . . . what a fool thou art! Was any word necessary for thee? Had not her heart beat against thine?' &c. (*Doctor Thorne*), 'Ah, thou weak man; most charitable, most Christian, but weakest of men! Why couldst thou not have asked herself? Was she not the daughter of thy loins, the child of thy heart?' &c. (*Barchester Towers*); or in considerations like the following (*Framley Parsonage*, chap. xxxiii), as to how much a husband's troubles are relieved when he makes his wife acquainted with them ('A burden that will crush a single pair of shoulders will, when equally divided,—when shared by two, each of whom is willing to take the heavier part,—become light as a feather. Is not that sharing of the mind's burdens one of the chief purposes for which a man wants a wife?'), or, in the same novel (chap. xlviii), reflections upon the aroma of love, the undefinable delicacy of flavour that is lost immediately after the nuptial ceremony: these and similar observations, suffused with a delicate sadness that comes from experience —pedestrian variations upon *Sunt lacrymae rerum*—show clearly how much Trollope had learnt in the school of his much-admired Thackeray. From Thackeray he learned also the use of symbolical names for his characters, a use which in Trollope is not generally very felicitous: for instance, Clementina Golightly, Lord Mount-Coffeehouse, Victoire Jaquetanapes, the Misses Neverbend, the lawyer Githemthruet; and the telling of humorous fairy-tales (in *The Three Clerks*, chap. xix, 'Sir Anthony Allan-a-dale and the Baron of Ballyporeen', and chap. xxii, 'Crinoline and Macassar').

Sometimes Trollope assumes Thackeray's cynical tone, as in chapter i of *The Eustace Diamonds*, in his account of the engagement of Lizzie Greystock and Sir Florian Eustace; for instance when the latter, who is consumptive, speaks to the girl of his illness:

As he spoke of his danger, there came a gurgling little trill of wailing from her throat, a soft, almost musical, sound of woe, which seemed to add an unaccustomed eloquence to his words. When he spoke of his own hope the sound was somewhat changed, but it was still continued. When he alluded to the disposition of his fortune, she was at his feet. 'Not that,' she said; 'not that!' He lifted her, and with his arm round her waist he tried to tell her what it would be his duty to do for her. She escaped from his arm and would not listen to him. But,—but—! When he began to talk of love again, she stood with her forehead bowed against his bosom. Of course the engagement was then a thing accomplished.

But still the cup might slip from her lips. . . .

And when Lizzie, at the end of the novel, yields, in a moment of weakness, to the rapacious, unctuous Mr. Emilius, she is not so intoxicated by his poetical language as to forget to protect her own interests:

It was a delicious moment to her, that in which she was weeping. She sobbed forth something about her child, something about her sorrows, something as to the wretchedness of her lot in life, something of her widowed heart,—something also of that duty to others which would compel her to keep her income in her own hands; and then she yielded herself to his entreaties.

Lizzie is not an all-of-a-piece character like Becky Sharp; there is a certain softness in her, a want of boldness, a low-grade sentimentality, which make her sometimes worthy of pity, although she remains despicable. Her ideal, nourished on cheap romanticism, is the type of Byron's Corsair; her dream of love is to wander amongst islands in the delicious warmth of a Mediterranean sun; the flowery declarations of the unctuous Emilius, with their Biblical flavour, remind her of Don Juan's words to Haidée; and when she is in despair, she breaks out into the phrases of melodrama: 'At any rate, I can die!' she exclaims like a tragedy heroine in her most passionate scene with Frank (chap. xxxi). Her intelligence has, as it were, patches of dimness in it, which make her behave like a fool; nor is there any other way of explaining her choice, as a *pis aller*, of the repulsive Emilius, a Jewish clergyman (a revised and worsened version of Slope in *Barchester Towers*) for her husband. The courtship and marriage of the snake-like, shop-soiled Lizzie with this mellifluous, false, sinister Jew, are material for satire, not so much in the Thackeray as in the Hogarth manner. There is also a Hogarthian flavour to the tender episode between Lizzie and the discredited Lord George, 'a pinchbeck lord and a pinchbeck lady' (chap. li). The contrast between the perfidious Lizzie and the virtuous Lucy recalls the Becky-Amelia duet in *Vanity Fair*. Again, in his description of a dubious social circle in *The Eustace Diamonds*, Trollope comes very near to the caustic quality of Thackeray. Just as Becky finishes by pretending to a philanthropic vocation, so Lizzie marries an upstart preacher, the incarnation of a Byronic adventurer turned bourgeois and made into a caricature—of the Corsair himself, in fact, with raven-black (and greasy) hair, a beak-like nose, and a sinister look. Even the feigned tenderness of Lizzie for the son she has had by Florian Eustace is modelled on that of Becky Sharp for little Rawdon: the part of the affectionate mother is acted by both women in order to attract sympathy to themselves. And how can we help thinking of the author of *The Book of Snobs* when we read of the way in which Mrs. Carbuncle manages to extort wedding presents for her niece?

But the homage paid by Trollope to Thackeray's characters, and particularly to Colonel Newcome, appears to us, nowadays, to be excessive. Thackeray's characters, or those of George Eliot, are certainly well observed, but in fixing themselves upon the page they often assume an air of being artificially constructed. In Trollope the opposite happens —if it is true, as he maintains in his *Autobiography*, that *The Warden* was *not* the fruit of a minute observation of clerical life:

I have been often asked in what period of my early life I had lived so long in a cathedral city as to have become intimate with the ways of a Close. I never lived in any cathedral city,—except London, never knew anything of any Close, and at that time had enjoyed no peculiar intimacy with any clergyman. My archdeacon, who has been said to be life-like, and for whom I confess that I have all a parent's fond affection, was, I think, the simple result of an effort of my moral consciousness. It was such as that, in my opinion, that an archdeacon should be,—or, at any rate, would be with such advantages as an archdeacon might have; and lo! an archdeacon was produced, who has been declared by competent authorities to be a real archdeacon down to the very ground. And yet, as far as I can remember, I had not then even spoken to an archdeacon.

Even if Archdeacon Grantly issued entirely from Trollope's brain, the incarnation of this platonic idea of an archdeacon is more alive than many of the observed characters of George Eliot or Thackeray. I would dare to say that George Eliot, with all the fineness of her analyses, never created a single human being as memorable as Mr. Harding or Grace Crawley, never painted so penetrating a portrait of a soul torn between pride, humility, sacrifice, envy, and exalted faith, as that of the Reverend Aidan Crawley; I would even dare to say that the famous character of Thackeray's Becky Sharp has in it something of a marionette moved by visible strings, when compared with that other changeable feminine creature, that mixture of passion, of abandonment, of impetuosity and frivolity, of caprice and of sarcasm, that is Lady Glencora in *Can You Forgive Her?*

Even those moralistic limitations that weighed so heavily upon Victorian novels (compare *Vanity Fair* with *Madame Bovary*, *Pendennis* with *L'Éducation sentimentale*) do not succeed in dimming the clearness of Trollope's vision. It is true, indeed, that the *femme fatale* posturings of Madeline Neroni in *Barchester Towers*, and the illicit relationship between Mrs. Dobbs Broughton and the painter Conway Dalrymple in *The Last Chronicle of Barset*, are presented in a light of genial caricature which takes from them all seriousness—and, so far, Trollope does not differ very greatly from Thackeray. The love-game between Mrs. Dobbs Broughton and Conway Dalrymple is like a contest in a game of skill; the heart, the feelings, are not involved: the pair can play without danger.

When I say that as regarded these two lovers there was nothing of love between them, and that the game was therefore so far innocent, I would not be understood as asserting that these people had no hearts within their bosoms. Mrs. Dobbs Broughton prob-

ably loved her husband in a sensible, humdrum way, feeling him to
be a bore, knowing him to be vulgar, aware that he often took a
good deal more wine than was good for him, and that he was almost
as uneducated as a hog. Yet she loved him, and showed her love by
taking care that he should have things for dinner which he liked to
eat. But in this alone there were to be found none of the charms of
a fevered existence, and therefore Mrs. Dobbs Broughton, requiring
those charms for her comfort, played her little game with Conway
Dalrymple. And as regarded the artist himself, let no reader presume him to have been heartless because he flirted with Mrs. Dobbs
Broughton. Doubtless he will marry some day, will have a large
family for which he will work hard, and will make a good husband
to some stout lady who will be careful in looking after his linen.

With characters as little serious as Madame Neroni and
Mrs. Dobbs Broughton passion shows itself under the
melodramatic, declamatory aspect of Byronic romanticism.
Madame Neroni, like all the Stanhopes, 'had no real feelings, could feel no true passion'; Mrs. Dobbs Broughton
was an insensitive woman, and showed it when learning of
the death of her husband and also in the cool way in which
she arranged to get married again—actually to the dead
man's partner whose interests were in conflict with hers.
They are empty, bored souls, inquisitive about the love
they are incapable of feeling; and therefore they imagine
themselves to be in Byronic situations, they act the tragi-
comedy of passion, without the slightest intention of letting
it translate itself into reality. Mrs. Dobbs Broughton,
'though she expected Conway Dalrymple to marry, she
expected also that he should be Byronically wretched after
his marriage on account of his love for herself' (chap. li).
Treated as a caricature, the illicit passion loses its sting,
and Victorian morality cannot consider itself offended. In
the case of Lady Glencora, however, illegitimate love shows
itself without disguise and in the accents of true passion;
but there is an extenuating circumstance: Lady Glencora
had been torn away from her natural inclination for Burgo
Fitzgerald and compelled to marry a man she did not love.
In the end, it is true, the husband wins, but through a series
of chances and psychological situations so natural that the
modern reader never feels the uneasiness produced in him

by an analogous 'moral' solution in Dickens (I recall, for
instance, the episode of the young wife of the old pedant
Dr. Strong in *David Copperfield*). Lady Glencora's passion
for Burgo Fitzgerald in *Can You Forgive Her?* (like, also,
Lucy Robarts's *not* illicit passion for Lord Lufton in *Framley Parsonage*) has accents of a vehemence and a truth that
we meet with in no other Victorian except Emily Brontë.
We must admit though, that the dreams in her romantic
head are scattered by Trollope with a hand far less light
than that of Flaubert when he shows us the wretched,
yet moving, childishness of Madame Bovary's similar
fantasies:

Would it not even be better to be beaten by [Burgo] than to have
politics explained to her at one o'clock at night by such a husband as
Plantagenet Palliser? The British Constitution, indeed! Had she
married Burgo they would have been in sunny Italy and he would
have told her some other tale than that as they sat together under
the pale moonlight. She had a little water-coloured drawing called
Raphael and Fornarina, and she was infantine enough to tell herself that the so-called Raphael was like her Burgo—no, not her
Burgo, but the Burgo that was not hers. At any rate, all the romance
of the picture she might have enjoyed had they allowed her to
dispose as she had wished of her own hand. She might have sat in
marble balconies, while the vines clustered over her head, and he
would have been at her knee, hardly speaking to her, but making
his presence felt by the halo of its divinity. He would have called
upon her for no hard replies. With him near her she would have
enjoyed the soft air, and would have sat happy, without trouble,
lapped in the delight of loving. It was thus that Fornarina sat. And
why should not such a lot have been hers? Her Raphael would have
loved her, let them say what they would about his cruelty.

Poor, wretched, overburthened child, to whom the commonest
lessons of life had not yet been taught, and who had now fallen into
the hands of one who was so ill-fitted to teach them! Who would
not pity her? Who could say that the fault was hers?

Trollope shakes his head over these romantic daydreams
just as Thackeray would have done. But would Thackeray
have given free rein to the passion of one of his own female
characters in accents so unrestrained as these of Lady
Glencora, when, roaming amongst the ruins of an ancient
priory on a moonlight night, she unburdens herself to Alice

Vavasor, who had been unwilling to countenance her flight with Burgo when the opportunity had presented itself?

'Oh, Alice! dear Alice! I don't know why I should love you, for if you had not been hard-hearted that night,—stony cruel in your hard propriety, I should have gone with him then, and all this icy coldness would have been prevented.'

Trembling, not with cold but with passion, Glencora, to Alice's words: 'But Glencora,—you cannot regret it', replies:

'Not regret it! Alice, where can your heart be? Or have you a heart? Not regret it! I would give everything I have in the world to have been true to him. They told me that he would spend my money. Though he should have spent every farthing of it, I regret it; though he should have made me a beggar, I regret it. They told me that he would ill-use me, and desert me,—perhaps beat me. I do not believe it; but even though that should have been so, I regret it. It is better to have a false husband than to be a false wife.'

'Glencora, do not speak like that. Do not try to make me think that anything could tempt you to be false to your vows.'

'Tempt me to be false! Why, child, it has been all false throughout. I never loved him. How can you talk in that way, when you know that I never loved him? They browbeat me and frightened me till I did as I was told;—and now;—what am I now?'

'You are his honest wife. Glencora, listen to me.' And Alice took hold of her arm.

'No,' she said, 'no; I am not honest. By law I am his wife; but the laws are liars! I am not his wife. I will not say the thing that I am. When I went to him at the altar, I knew that I did not love the man that was to be my husband. But him,—Burgo,—I love him with all my heart and soul. I could stoop at his feet and clean his shoes for him, and think it no disgrace! . . . I am always talking to Burgo in my thoughts; and he listens to me. I dream that his arm is round me—'.

Later on, when Glencora has not the courage to run away with Burgo, and yet does not wish to part from him unkindly, and allows herself to be kissed by him on the mouth, she says, to Alice who seeks to comfort her:

I am not such a fool as to mistake what I should be if I left my husband, and went to live with that man as his mistress. You don't suppose that I should think that sort of life very blessed. But why have I been brought to such a pass as this? And as for female purity! Ah! What was their idea of purity when they forced me, like ogres, to marry a man for whom they knew I never cared? Had I gone with him,—had I now eloped with that man who ought to have been my husband,—whom would a just God have punished worst,—me, or those two old women and my uncle, who tortured me into this marriage?'

And, to her friend who says that at least she has not lost her self-respect: 'How?—When he kissed me, and I could hardly restrain myself from giving him back his kiss tenfold, could I respect myself? But it is all sin. I sin towards my husband, feigning that I love him; and I sin in loving that other man, who should have been my husband.' Glencora refuses to be ashamed of having danced passionately with Burgo while everyone was staring at her in astonishment and horror—'mad, like a wild woman'—and when Alice has listened in surprise to this confession, she flings in her face: 'Of all things in the world, I hate a prude the most.'

A parallel case of conjugal relations is that of Lady Laura with Kennedy, in *Phineas Finn*. Kennedy is a more rigid, more jealous Palliser, Lady Laura a less passionate Glencora.

As for the common saying that 'the woman who doubts is lost', Trollope reacts against it with his own realistic, balanced point of view, which admits shades of difference and compromises (chap. l): 'They who have said so . . . have known but little of women. Women doubt every day, who solve their doubts at last on the right side, driven to do so, some by fear, more by conscience, but most of them by that half-prudential, half-unconscious knowledge of what is fitting, useful, and best under the circumstances.' This is the 'photographic' realism of Trollope, as opposed to the false, melodramatic moralizings of Dickens and the reticences of Thackeray. The wild love-accents of Catherine for Heathcliff are not unknown to him; but he is too conscious of pedestrian reality to allow the atmosphere of *Wuthering Heights* to invade his scene: it is enough to know that this atmosphere exists somewhere, like the episode of the storm in Beethoven's *Pastoral*

Symphony. His landscape retains its calm, its restfulness, its Biedermeier quality, even though away in the distance, behind a mountain, looms a dark, lightning-shot cloud.

* * * * *

Like every other novelist, Trollope elaborates certain types, which are presented in forms sometimes more, sometimes less complete and perfect in his various novels. Parallel situations abound. Phineas Finn fails to mention his engagement when Madame Goesler offers herself to him, and Frank Greystock does the same thing when Lizzie tries to bespeak him as a husband. Lily Dale (in *The Last Chronicle of Barset*), torn between Crosbie and Eames, is reincarnated, in *Can You Forgive Her?*, in Alice Vavasor, hesitating between her cousin and John Grey; Alice also reproduces a trait from Miss Dunstable who, in *Framley Parsonage*, is disposed to give financial help in the elections to the man who aspires to her hand—which, however, she does not wish to bestow upon him. Lady Laura and Madame Goesler, too, offer money to Finn for his election expenses, and Lizzie Eustace offers financial support to her cousin. Sowerby, of *Framley Parsonage*, comes back, in stronger colours, as George Vavasor, and another type of unscrupulous character, Crosbie, is allied to them; and when Vavasor, in order to win at the elections, asks for financial assistance from other people, one is reminded of the similar case of Undy Scott in *The Three Clerks*, who compromises the economic situation of Alaric Tudor, just as Sowerby compromises that of Robarts, as Fitzgibbon reduces Phineas Finn to a state of serious embarrassment, and as Ferdinand Lopez (in *The Prime Minister*) ruins Sextus Parker. Burgo Fitzgerald is the perfection of the type of popinjay who is incapable of any kind of useful activity but is yet innocent and likeable, the type foreshadowed in Bertie Stanhope in *Barchester Towers*; John Grey is the perfection of the type of loyal man suggested in Johnny Eames, and he discourses like the latter when he is making his final attempt to obtain the consent of the woman he loves. George Vavasor wants Alice mainly in order to get his own back on John Grey, who has taken her from him; Burgo plans to run away with Glencora in order, also, to avenge himself on Palliser, who has taken her from him. There is a persistent recurrence of the theme of a marriage obstructed by the parents of the man, whose social position is superior to that of the girl; there is a strong resemblance between the behaviour of Frank towards Mary Thorne and that of another Frank, Frank Greystock, towards Lucy Morris (in *The Eustace Diamonds*), also that of Lord Lufton towards Lucy Robarts, and that of Major Grantly towards Grace Crawley; analogous, too, are the reactions of the girls, and analogous the figures of the mothers who long for marriages of profit and prestige for their sons—though Lady Lufton in *Framley Parsonage* is a highly attenuated version of Lady Arabella (*Doctor Thorne*). There is a recurrence, too, of the father who threatens to disinherit, or does in fact disinherit, his rebellious son (Archdeacon Grantly, Squire Vavasor). And the situation of the man who is in love with one of two sisters, and then puts her aside for the other, is to be found in *The Three Clerks* (Alaric Tudor who, after courting Linda, becomes engaged to Gertrude Woodward) and in the comic secondary plot of *He Knew He Was Right* (the clergyman Gibbon, who changes twice between the sisters French—first Arabella, then Camilla, then Arabella again). Louis Trevelyan in *He Knew He Was Right* presents a case similar to that of Kennedy in *Phineas Redux*.

But Trollope's speciality is for perversely obstinate characters, clergymen who jib and fume over a question of conscience, girls who, from pride or a spirit of sacrifice, reject the men they love, married couples who, out of stubbornness, allow their relationship to become poisoned, friends who, having become enemies, are relentless in their bitterness. It is Septimus Harding who, shaken by the newspaper campaign accusing him of leading an easy life on money intended for the welfare of the old people in the almshouse, sees the veil of illusion torn away which had hitherto been the comfort of his life, and insists on resigning from his sinecure although it is not necessary and implies great sacrifices for himself and his family. The day that Harding spends in London, waiting for the interview with the lawyer Sir Abraham Haphazard to whom he intends to communicate his irrevocable decision, forms the most moving, and the most *mouvementé*, chapter in the book. The brilliant lawyer, who 'sparkled, whether in society, in the House of Commons, or the courts of law . . . glittering sparkles, as from hot steel; but no heat'—this cold, friendless man sees in front of him the timid clergyman 'cowed into such an act of extreme weakness by a newspaper article', and considers him 'so contemptible an object that he hardly knew how to talk to him as to a rational being'. Harding's behaviour, he judges, is 'sheer Quixotism'. But this weak, timid Harding, who in moments of agitation accompanies his conversation with passes of an imaginary bow on an imaginary 'cello,[132] rises, as we have already said, to almost heroic stature—as far as a Biedermeier figure can be a hero—and the silent playing of his 'cello becomes, as it were, one of those symbols that are the accompanying attributes of saints, becomes his own intimate motif, the poetry of the whole personage, established unforgettably, as we shall see, in a scene which is the most touching in the whole work of this novelist.

Phineas Finn, too, gives up a brilliant career and a fine salary for a question of conscience and of consistency with his own opinions. 'Phineas, though he had many misgivings as to the prudence of what he had done, was not the less strong in his resolution of constancy and endurance' (chap. lxvii). Having become a member of Parliament through the expedients of a corrupt electoral system, the moment comes when he considers 'that he had no business to be in Parliament, that he was an impostor, that he was going about the world under false pretences, and that he would never set himself aright, even unto himself, till he had gone through some *terrible act of humiliation*'. I emphasize this last phrase which is characteristic of what I may call the masochistic aspect of many of Trollope's characters. Finn's act, too—considering the ways of political life—is, in a way, 'sheer Quixotism'. Common sense says to him (chap. xxxi): 'You must take the world as you find it, with a struggle to be something more honest than those around you.'

Another stubborn creature is Mark Robarts, who, having been unable to refuse his signature to the bills of the unscrupulous Sowerby, is then determined to endure the consequences of his act to the utmost limit. In a violent scene with the man who has been the cause of his ruin, Mark refuses to come to any arrangement with the creditors: 'You shall be asked in a court of law how much of that money I have handled. You know that I have never touched—have never wanted to touch—one shilling. I will make no attempt at any settlement. My person is here, and there is my house. Let them do their worst.' He refuses the suggestion of the banker Forrest, to recognize the debt as his own and pay it off in two years; he wishes also to give up the prebend at Barchester because it had been obtained through the good offices of Sowerby. Finally the bailiffs install themselves in his house, and catastrophe is only avoided thanks to the intervention of Lord Lufton, who interrupts the taking of the inventory and assumes responsibility for the debt.

Stubborn, also, is Lord Chiltern in *Phineas Finn*: his attempts to win the hand of Violet Effingham are rendered clumsy and ungracious by pride; he makes it a point of honour to refuse stiffly when the girl implores him to find some occupation which will ennoble his life, that of an idle aristocrat devoted only to hunting. 'He thinks it a fine thing not to give way' (chap. xxxiii). Violet is stubborn, too, for it is only with a great effort that she allows the enamoured Chiltern to extort a confession of reciprocated love from her. They are similar characters, violent and stubborn, both of them. And Lizzie Eustace is stubborn in not wishing to restore the diamond necklace which is a Eustace heirloom and which she claims to have received as a gift from her dead husband. Perseverance on an initially wrong course brings her to ruin, as also the protagonist of *He Knew He Was Right*.

The most complex case of stubbornness is that of the Reverend Aidan Crawley, with his scholarly mind and his saintly temper, both of these, however, flawed by his envy of other people's success and darkened by diabolical pride; a character full of oddities, in fact actually lacking some little wheel in the mechanism of his brain, seeing that,

29. Thackeray (*from a photograph taken during his second American tour*)

30. DELACROIX. Naufrage de Don Juan (*Paris, Louvre*)

failing to remember the way in which he had come by a cheque for twenty pounds with which he pays a tradesman, he finds himself accused of theft and ends by almost persuading himself of his own guilt. Very subtle is the analysis of his soul and of that of his wife which Trollope makes (*Last Chronicle of Barset*, chap. xli):

She knew that he was good and yet weak, that he was afflicted by false pride and supported by true pride, that his intellect was still very bright, yet so dismally obscured on many sides as almost to justify people in saying that he was mad. She knew that he was almost a saint, and yet almost a castaway through vanity and hatred of those above him. But she did not know that he knew all this of himself also. She did not comprehend that he should be hourly telling himself that people were calling him mad and were so calling him with truth. It did not occur to her that he could see her insight into him. She doubted as to the way in which he had got the cheque, —never imagining, however, that he had wilfully stolen it;— thinking that his mind had been so much astray as to admit of his finding it and using it without wilful guilt,—thinking also, alas, that a man who could so act was hardly fit for such duties as those which were entrusted to him. But she did not dream that this was precisely his own idea of his own state and of his own position;— that he was always inquiring of himself whether he was not mad; whether, if mad, he was not bound to lay down his office; that he was ever taxing himself with improper hostility to the bishop,— never forgetting for a moment his wrath against the bishop and the bishop's wife, still comforting himself with his triumph over the bishop and the bishop's wife,—but, for all that, accusing himself of a heavy sin and proposing to himself to go to the palace and there humbly to relinquish his clerical authority. . . . And then he prayed, —yes, prayed, that in his madness the Devil might not be too strong for him, and that he might be preserved from some terrible sin of murder or violence. What, if the idea should come to him in his madness that it would be well for him to slay his wife and his children? Only that was wanting to make him of all men the most unfortunate.

There is, in Crawley's continual chafing of his own wound, in his 'over-indulgence in his grief' (chap. xii), something of the perverse pleasure of an ascetic tormenting his own flesh: 'He did give way to it till it became a luxury to him. . . . During those long hours, in which he would sit speechless, doing nothing, he was telling himself from minute to minute that of all God's creatures he was the most heavily afflicted, and was revelling in the sense of the injustice done to him.'[133] He glories in appearing before the bishop mud-bespattered and weary from walking; with great difficulty does he let himself be persuaded by his wife to make use of a farmer's cart for part of the way, and he will not accept the bishop's hospitality: in his wilful refusal of all comfort, of all convenience, there is something of the stubborn attitude of Thoreau. This humble, proud parson compares himself to the most famous 'agonists', to the blind giants, Polyphemus, Belisarius, Samson, Milton: thus he rises to the heroic, to the tragic, but not without a vein of comedy in an occasional high-sounding phrase, Biblical or pedantic (as when he says to Mr. Toogood who brings him some good news: 'It seemeth to me that you are a messenger of glad tidings, whose feet are beautiful upon the mountains') and not without, also, a suggestion of Don Quixote, as when, in bestowing his daughter upon Major Grantly, he makes use of expressions as solemn as if he were conferring upon his future son-in-law the privilege of courting a king's daughter. And yet this man, who can be so lofty, is also so humble that when Arabin denies he has given him the cheque (as, without knowing it, he had done, because Mrs. Arabin had herself added the cheque to some other money sent in an envelope by her husband to Crawley), he doubts himself rather than doubt his friend. Anyone who acts like that, thinks Grantly, must be a hero.

I never quite knew what makes a hero, [*says Toogood*] if it isn't having three or four girls dying in love for you at once [*this suggests the Byronic hero*]. But to find a man who was going to let everything in the world go against him, because he believed another fellow better than himself! There's many a chap thinks another man is wool-gathering, but this man has thought he was wool-gathering himself. It's not natural; and the world wouldn't go on if there were many like that.

Stubbornness is actually mixed with madness in Louis Trevelyan, the protagonist of *He Knew He Was Right*, who provides the opposite case to that of Crawley: if the latter ended by convincing himself that he was wrong, Trevelyan

never ceases to believe that he is right. Having become
suspicious because of the familiar terms upon which his
wife appears to be with a middle-aged but still gallant friend
of her father's, Colonel Osborne, he exacts a humiliating
promise from her that she will have nothing more to do
with him, and since she, though she obeys him, obstinately
refuses to acknowledge any guilt in the matter, he becomes
gradually transformed, one suspicion leading to another,
into a kind of Othello (an Othello turned bourgeois who
finds a stimulus to his *idée fixe* in the detective Bozzle, a
Biedermeier Iago). The situation, starting from one slight
incident, comes very near to tragedy, as Henry James
noted, particularly in a chapter towards the end of the
novel, in which there is a powerful picture of the 'insanity
of stiff-neckedness': 'Louis Trevelyan, separated from his
wife, alone, haggard, suspicious, unshaven, undressed,
living in a desolate villa on a hill-top near Siena and returning doggedly to his fancied wrong, which he has nursed
until it becomes an hallucination, is a picture worthy of
Balzac.' The same might be said of Kennedy in *Phineas
Redux*.

But it is Trollope's young women, particularly, who are
stubborn. The central theme of *Can You Forgive Her?* is,
for example, the grievous dilemma of Alice, who, considering herself to be spiritually too inferior to her betrothed,
John Grey, leaves him and becomes engaged a second
time to her cousin, the more human George Vavasor, for
whose political career she is prepared to sacrifice her own
patrimony—until she discovers that George is a repulsive
scoundrel, and that she still loves the other man; and yet
she denies her own right to happiness, and cannot forgive
herself for her apostasy. A parallel case is that of Emily
Wharton (in *The Prime Minister*), who, having married, for
love, a sinister speculator, Ferdinand Lopez, shuts herself
up, after he has committed suicide, in a kind of cocoon of
thick black crape veils, and for a long time, even though
she has fallen in love with him, spurns the love of Arthur
Fletcher, who had aspired to her hand even before her
unhappy marriage, on the grounds that, because of it, she
considers herself to be contaminated, soiled, unworthy

(chap. lxxiv: 'I am disgraced and shamed. I have been among the pots till I am foul and blackened'). Souls like that of Alice or Emily, or the Reverend Aidan Crawley, wear themselves out and tear themselves to pieces by wearing mental hair-shirts. Alice considers she is a 'fallen creature', and relishes her own position of not being able to forgive herself. Towards the end of the novel, when she has allowed herself to be won over by John Grey's constancy, Lady Glencora says to her: 'I know that it is quite a misery to you that you should be made a happy woman of at last. . . . You are so hard and so proud. . . . You are hard to yourself, and, upon my word, you have been hard to him. What a deal you will have to make up to him!' To which Alice replies: 'I feel that I ought to stand before him always as a penitent—in a white sheet.' This girl, obstinate as a mule, is perhaps the least likeable of all the many whom Trollope portrayed. She is the perfection of pig-headedness: we find ourselves faced with an idiosyncrasy in which intelligence plays little part. Nor is it to be wondered at that some people, thinking of this and similar cases, have gone so far as to call this novelist 'stupid'. But, in his novels, it is, more or less, a case of 'così fan tutte'. They are all proud, these young women, and later become mild as doves, as soon as they are vanquished and won. Lucy Robarts is proud, but behind the severity of her calm she might almost have died of love. Grace Crawley, who in the end is the humblest of *fiancées*, persistently denies herself love: Major Grantly has made her confess that she loves him, but she tells him she will never be his wife. Mary Thorne withholds herself, with pretended coldness, from Frank Gresham. In *Framley Parsonage* Lord Lufton refuses to take his leave until Lucy Robarts places her hand on her heart and says she is unable to love him. Lucy does so, Lord Lufton retires in despair, and Lucy goes and throws herself on her bed and weeps because she has told a lie for which she cannot forgive herself. Either from pride, or social propriety, or mistaken generosity, or fear of straitened economic circumstances, all these young women, intent as they are upon self-repression or self-punishment—whether they are called Alice Vavasor, Grace Crawley, Mary Thorne, Lily Dale, Nora

Rowley, or Emily Wharton—all of them reach the point of lacerating their own hearts by professing not to love their lovers. To put it shortly: there is in them a considerable degree of masochism.[134] This trait corresponds exactly with what we should have suspected to exist behind the whalebone, the steel hoops and the yards of material which went to make up the clothes of the Victorian woman: a self-torturing fashion, and postures cramped by draperies, lead one to expect inner conflicts such as those analysed by Trollope. We recognize in both the imprint of the same style, of the same culture. In him alone can we see the soul of the Victorian woman, distorted in Dickens, and in Thackeray eclipsed by the shadow of the moralist-commentator.

Trollope has been reproached for a lack of lofty imagination and poetry. Mr. Raymond Mortimer, for instance, wrote:[135]

His characters are like the persons one meets in a ship or an hotel; their ways become familiar, you feel you have known them always, and a week after leaving you can't remember a thing about them. . . . If knowledge of human nature were the first virtue in a novelist, Trollope would be a Himalaya, and Dickens only a foothill. It is this knowledge that allows him wonderfully to survive, the only writer to do so without style, wit, trenchancy, fire or poetic feeling.

And he concludes by saying that he reads him as a precious fount of information upon the Victorian age.

That poetic feeling is rare in the pages of Trollope is incontestable; but when we do find it, it strikes us all the more intensely just because of its rarity. And also for a sober, a chaste quality that it has, for its scarcely articulate eloquence: like the almost involuntary poetic feeling (and I say 'almost' because in some way the point of view of the photographer is responsible) that is given off by a particularly successful photograph.[136] For example, in *The Last Chronicle of Barset* (chap. xxxv), the scene in which Lily Dale refuses John Eames's proposal because she is still in love with Crosbie, whom, however, she does not wish to marry, is conducted with a delicacy of touch for whose equal one would seek in vain in Dickens; Thackeray is indeed capable of it in his best moments, and this scene has in fact Thackeray's quality of disconsolate tenderness, of emotion barely contained within the bounds of tears. And a few pages later (Trollope must have happened to be in a moment of particular grace) a sober comment on the first love-letter that Grace Crawley receives brings us back again to the same kind of poetic feeling, the kind of feeling that is experienced when life is looked at from an angle outside itself, when everything seems consummated and fixed for ever, and extremely fragile and human: a kind of feeling that Trollope has in common with Thackeray. 'As she held the letter in her hand she felt that it was a possession. It was a thing at which she could look in coming years, when he and she might be far apart,—a thing at which she could look with pride in remembering that he had thought her worthy of it.'

In moments like these the lives of his characters are lit up for an instant, as a flash of lightning reveals a whole countryside; it is the ending of a tale, and this is the faint perfume of poetry that it exhales—like the perfume which rises, in certain conditions of the atmosphere, from even the humblest flowers. And what constitutes the peculiar poetry of such moments is that we are conscious of their extreme fragility and transitoriness. Trollope, more discreet than Thackeray, avoids over-emphasis at these delicate moments, does not intrude with such reflections as: 'So this poor little flower had bloomed for its little day, and pined, and withered, and perished' (*The Newcomes*, chap. lxxx). Even characters who have nothing poetical about them may, in such moments, be transfigured. See, in *Framley Parsonage* (chap. xxxvii), the scene in which Sowerby, ruined and without resources, revisits the woods which in a short time will no longer be his:

It was a melancholy, dreary place now, that big house of Chaldi-cotes; and though the woods were all green with their early leaves, and the garden thick with flowers, they also were melancholy and dreary. The lawns were untrimmed and weeds were growing through the gravel and here and there a cracked Dryad, tumbled from her pedestal and sprawling in the grass, gave a look of disorder to the whole place. The wooden trellis-work was shattered here and bending there, the standard rose-trees were stooping to the ground and the leaves of the winter still encumbered the borders. Late in the evening of the second day Mr. Sowerby strolled out, and went through the gardens into the wood. Of all the inanimate things of the world this wood of Chaldicotes was the dearest to him. He was not a man to whom his companions gave much credit for feelings or thoughts akin to poetry, but here, out in the Chace, his mind would be almost poetical. While wandering among the forest trees, he became susceptible of the tenderness of human nature: he would listen to the birds singing, and pick here and there a wild flower on his path. He would watch the decay of the old trees and the progress of the young, and make pictures in his eyes of every turn in the wood. He would mark the colour of a bit of road as it dipped into a dell, and then, passing through a water-course, rose brown, rough, irregular, and beautiful against the bank on the other side. And then he would sit and think of his own family: how they had roamed there time out of mind in those Chaldicotes woods, father and son and grandson in regular succession, each giving them over, without blemish or decrease, to his successor. So he would sit, and so he did sit even now, and, thinking of those things, wished that he had never been born.

It was in this vein of tender, human sadness that Trollope wrote what is perhaps the most famous page in his whole work, the episode of old Mr. Harding paying a visit to his 'cello (*The Last Chronicle of Barset*, chap. xlix):

It was sometimes sad enough to watch him as he sat alone. He would have a book near him, and for a while would keep it in his hands. . . . And he had a habit, when he was sure that he was not watched, of creeping up to a great black wooden case, which always stood in one corner. . . . Mr. Harding, when he was younger, had been a performer on the violoncello, and in this case there was still the instrument from which he had been wont to extract the sounds which he had so dearly loved. Now in these latter days he never made any attempt to play. Soon after he had come to the deanery there had fallen upon him an illness, and after that he had never again asked for his bow . . . but even before that illness his hand had greatly failed him. . . . It had become known to Mrs. Arabin, through the servants, that he had once dragged the instrument forth from its case when he had thought the house to be nearly deserted; and a wail of sounds had been heard, very low, very short-lived, recurring now and again at fitful intervals. . . .

In these latter days of which I am now speaking he would never draw the instrument out of its case. Indeed he was aware that it was too heavy for him to handle without assistance. But he would open the prison door, and gaze upon the thing that he loved, and he would pass his fingers among the broad strings, and ever and anon he would produce from one of them a low, melancholy, almost unearthly sound. And then he would pause, never daring to produce two such notes in succession,—one close upon the other. . . . He imagined that his visits to the box were unsuspected,—that none knew of the folly of his old fingers which could not keep themselves from touching the wires; but the voice of the violoncello had been recognized by the servants and by his daughter, and when that low wail was heard through the house,—like the last dying note of a dirge,—they would all know that Mr. Harding was visiting his ancient friend.

The figure of old Mr. Harding, with its melancholy, resigned expression, is a presence that one continually meets with in the *Last Chronicle of Barset*, until, in the pages describing his death, Trollope succeeds in excelling the last chapter of Thackeray's *The Newcomes* which he must certainly have had in mind. Old Colonel Newcome, during his illness, loves to have with him one of the little boys from the orphanage, who amuses him by his 'archness and merry ways'; 'and the Colonel would listen to him for hours, and hear all about his lessons and his play, and prattle, almost as childishly, about Dr. Raine and his own early school-days'. Old Mr. Harding is comforted by a little girl, Posy, who plays cat's-cradle with him:

What was there left to him now in the world? Posy and cat's-cradle! Then, in the midst of his regrets, as he sat with his back bent in his old easy-chair, with one arm over the shoulder of the chair, and the other hanging loose by his side, on a sudden there came across his face a smile as sweet as ever brightened the face of man or woman. He had been able to tell himself that he had no ground for complaint,—great ground rather for rejoicing and grati-tude. Had not the world and all in it been good to him; had he not children who loved him, who had done him honour, who had been to him always a crown of glory, never a mark for reproach? . . . Whose latter days had ever been more blessed than his? And for the future——? It was as he thought of this that that smile came across his face,—as though it were already the face of an angel.

And then he muttered to himself a word or two. 'Lord, now lettest Thou Thy servant depart in peace. Lord, now lettest Thou Thy servant depart in peace.'

The picture belongs to the same Biedermeier school as that of the death of Colonel Newcome, and Trollope has the good taste not to insist, as Thackeray does, on the *noble* figure of his subject ('the *noble* old gentleman's touching history', 'the *noble* careworn face'):

> At the usual evening hour the chapel bell began to toll, and Thomas Newcome's hands outside the bed feebly beat time. And just as the last bell struck, a peculiar sweet smile shone over his face, and he lifted up his head a little, and quickly said, 'Adsum!' and fell back. It was the word we used at school, when names were called; and lo, he, whose heart was as that of a little child, had answered to his name, and stood in the presence of The Master.

The child at the bedside of the dying old man is an exquisitely Victorian feature; Trollope, however, makes a more sober use of it than Dickens would have done, and its poetical purpose, if mannered, is not without a certain grace.

Knowledge of human nature is not enough, in Mr. Raymond Mortimer's opinion, to communicate a thrill of poetry to Trollope's pages. And yet there are episodes in which his skill in culling the essential elements of a situation in itself constitutes poetry. Take for instance the reaction of Mrs. Dobbs Broughton when the news of her husband's death is given her by Conway Dalrymple (*The Last Chronicle of Barset*, chap. lxiv):

> Then he took both her hands in his, and looked into her face without speaking a word. And she gazed at him with fixed eyes, and rigid mouth, while the quick coming breath just moved the curl of her nostrils. It occurred to him at the moment that he had never before seen her so wholly unaffected, and had never before observed that she was so totally deficient in all the elements of real beauty. She was the first to speak again. 'Conway,' she said, 'tell it me all. Why do you not speak to me?'
> 'There is nothing further to tell,' said he.
> Then she dropped his hands and walked away from him to the window, and stood there looking out upon the stuccoed turret of

a huge house that stood opposite. As she did so she was employing herself in counting the windows. Her mind was paralysed by the blow, and she knew not how to make any exertion with it for any purpose. Everything was changed with her,—and was changed in such a way that she could make no guess as to her future mode of life. She was suddenly a widow, a pauper, and utterly desolate,— while the only person in the whole world that she really liked was standing close to her. But in the midst of it all she counted the windows of the house opposite. Had it been possible for her she would have put her mind altogether to sleep.

The picture of that house opposite with its stuccoed turret, and of the woman with staring eyes and tight lips, counting its windows, remains imprinted on the memory with the clear truth of a moment of poetry—the melancholy poem of a soul incapable of feeling true sorrow, a soul impotent and numb—and if anyone objects to the use of the word poetry in this case, let him consider how much of the greatness of Flaubert is made up of essential moments of this kind, observed in a spirit of careful precision.[137]

And whether we give the name of poetry or of humour to the sense of a perfectly played game which we derive from so many of Proust's scenes of society life, we shall still have to admit that Trollope preceded him along this road. An example: the meeting of two implacable enemies, Lady Lufton and the Duke of Omnium at Miss Dunstable's reception in *Framley Parsonage* (chap. xxix). As soon as Lady Lufton hears the voice of the Duke, who, in the crowd of guests, suddenly happens to find himself beside her—

... she turned round quickly, but still with much feminine dignity, removing her dress from the contact. In doing this she was brought absolutely face to face with the duke, so that each could not but look full at the other. 'I beg your pardon', said the duke. They were the only words that had ever passed between them, nor have they spoken to each other since; but simple as they were, accompanied by the little by-play of their speakers, they gave rise to a considerable amount of ferment in the fashionable world. Lady Lufton, as she retreated back on to Dr. Easyman, curtsied low; she curtsied low and slowly, and with a haughty arrangement of her drapery that was all her own; but the curtsy, though it was eloquent, did not say half so much,—did not reprobate the habitual iniquities of the duke with a voice nearly as potent, as that which was expressed in the gradual fall of her eye and the gradual pressure of her lips. When she commenced her curtsy she was looking full in her foe's face. By the time that she had completed it her eyes were turned upon the ground, but there was an ineffable amount of scorn expressed in the lines of her mouth. She spoke no word, and retreated, as modest virtue and feminine weakness must ever retreat, before barefaced vice and virile power, but nevertheless she was held by all the world to have had the best of the encounter. The duke, as he begged her pardon, wore in his countenance that expression of modified sorrow which is common to any gentleman who is supposed by himself to have incommoded a lady. But over and above this—or rather under it—there was a slight smile of derision, as though it were impossible for him to look upon the bearing of Lady Lufton without some amount of ridicule. All this was legible to eyes so keen as those of Miss Dunstable and Mrs. Harold Smith, and the duke was known to be a master of this silent inward sarcasm; but even by them—by Miss Dunstable and Mrs. Harold Smith— it was admitted that Lady Lufton had conquered.

'It will be years before she has done boasting of her triumph, and it will be talked of by the young ladies of Framley for the next three generations', remarks Mrs. Harold Smith.[138] In the same novel Mrs. Proudie's comment on Griselda's marriage (chap. xl), and in *Can You Forgive Her?* (chap. xxii) the silly Duchess of St. Bungay's way of talking and the manner in which Lady Glencora is made to imitate her,[139] are passages which Proust, with his fine sense of social comedy, could not have bettered.

Although Trollope in his *Autobiography*, speaking of *The Claverings*, felt himself bound to admit that 'humour has not been my forte', Lord David Cecil sees, in his very humour, 'his greatest glory'.[140] We certainly do not look for this humour in facile sketches of eighteenth-century type such as the figures and adventures of Mrs. Greenow's suitors in *Can You Forgive Her?* or in conventional devices which aim at provoking laughter by means of a repeated phrase put into the mouth of some character or other, such as, for instance, the Widow Greenow's 'with a buried heart' or 'the rocks and the valleys', or Captain Cuttwater's 'craving the ladies' pardon' (in *The Three Clerks*), or Mrs. Proudie's 'the souls of the people'. In such tricks of the trade Trollope is easily surpassed by Dickens, as he is also whenever he tries to follow in his footsteps as a describer of odd corners of London (see for instance the descriptions of the gloomy offices in *Framley Parsonage*, chap. xxvii, and in *The Last Chronicle of Barset*, chap. xxxvii; of the popular eating-house and the Cigar Divan in *The Warden*, chap. xvi; and of the Bremen Coffee House in *He Knew He Was Right*, chap. lxii). Even in his most successful popular sketches (such as that of the publican Grimes in *Can You Forgive Her?*, chap. xiii) Trollope never achieves the irresistible comic quality of Dickens; we always feel, with him, that he is sticking closely to real life, with its mixture of contrasting elements, whereas Dickens justifies his obvious exaggerations, his grotesque metaphysics, by the inimitable oddity of the results. Dickens's comic characters can be recalled by dozens; in Trollope one remembers, particularly, Mrs. Proudie, the typical 'woman who wears the trousers', whose interruptions in the conversations between clergymen and the feeble bishop, her husband, lead to scenes of a grotesque pungency which are more reminiscent of Ben Jonson than of Dickens: indeed in the struggle between Mrs. Proudie and her former *protégé* Dr. Slope in *Barchester Towers* there is something of the acrid spirit of that contemporary of Shakespeare, with his rascals who plot and counterplot against each other. Trollope was perfectly right in hesitating to kill off Mrs. Proudie, for when the reader learns that this difficult woman was suffering from heart trouble and had confided her ailments to no one except her maid, he might be tempted to protest at this touching detail having been kept hidden from him all the time he was amusing himself with the pugnacious lady's outbursts of passion.

Trollope's anti-heroic point of view led him, as it did Thackeray, to see the other side of every situation, to prick every bladder he saw with a sharp pin: the self-sufficiency and the touchiness of doctors, the ordinariness of politicians and journalists, the melodramatic, romantic poses of heartless women—all these provided him with material for delectable scenes, flavoured with the ironical bourgeois common sense which counts, in its tradition, such glorious names as those of Boccaccio, Chaucer, and Molière.

In Hawthorne's judgement upon Trollope of which we have already quoted a part, the American novelist confessed that his own individual taste was 'for quite another class of works than those which I myself am able to write. ... Have you ever read the novels of Anthony Trollope? They precisely suit my taste—solid and substantial, written on the strength of beef and through the inspiration of ale, and just as real as if some giant...' &c.—and he continued with the comparison we have already quoted. I am not sure that the reference to beefsteaks and beer is the most obviously suitable one for emphasizing the 'Old England' solidity that distinguishes Trollope's novels. Just as, with Jane Austen, one is reminded of the functional elegance of certain English instruments and pieces of furniture—the kind of English furniture that has polished surfaces, strong, delicate joints and unemphatic mouldings and that is adorned by the names of Hepplewhite and Sheraton—so, with Trollope, one thinks of the solidity of English mahogany furniture of the nineteenth century—not the kind that displays the oddities of the fashion for Gothic, but the kind that honestly, if indeed weightily, carries on the noble tradition of functional beauty which had started a century earlier. For the relationship that can be traced between Miss Austen and Trollope is exactly the same as that between a simple, slender piece of Hepplewhite furniture and a Victorian piece, bare and massive: they are members of the same family, and they have the common qualities of honesty of workmanship, absence of emphasis, and fitness to their purpose. There is nothing showy about him, but much that is worthy of admiration for a practised eye. His qualities are rather like those of the statesman Plantagenet Palliser, who looked like a gentleman, but had nothing remarkable in his appearance,[141] and a face that you might see and then forget; and yet when you looked at it bit by bit . . .: 'a face like a boot', to adopt an expression used by Siegfried Sassoon in his *Memoirs of a Fox-hunting Man* to describe certain typical faces of English sportsmen. You may read Trollope and find, like Mr. Raymond Mortimer, that his characters are people you seem always to have known; and you may fail to remember them with precision when you have turned your back upon them. For none of these characters will take you outside your ordinary everyday life; the impression of truth that they leave upon you is so profound that you will not be able to distinguish between them and the persons of your acquaintance any better than the birds in the story managed to distinguish between the real grapes and the ones painted by Zeuxis. His novels, said Henry James, are not so much stories as pictures: groups of people in everyday life, making themselves known through dialogue. Just as the seventeenth-century Dutch painters, in their *genre* pictures, did not so much tell stories as present types of men and women who were in no way exceptional, just as they presented pictures of social life, constantly repeating themselves, so also does Trollope obtain his results through a slow accumulation of little pictures of ordinary life, with nothing spectacular about them—often, in fact, varied by only slight alterations. And both the Dutch painters and the English novelist knew how to make monotony lively, and how to bring a universal character into the portraiture of everyday things.

George Eliot

MARY ANN EVANS was almost forty when, encouraged by her friend and, in effect, illegitimate husband, George Henry Lewes, she wrote and began to publish her *Scenes of Clerical Life* in *Blackwood's Magazine* in 1857. The 'scenes' are three: *The Sad Fortunes of the Rev. Amos Barton, Mr. Gilfil's Love Story,* and *Janet's Repentance.* The first of these 'long short stories' presents us with a character who could not be more Biedermeier. The protagonist might well have been taken bodily from one of Spitzweg's pathetic-humorous little pictures. Here he is on his way home (chap. ii):

Look at him as he winds through the little churchyard! The silver light that falls aslant on church and tomb, enables you to see his slim black figure, made all the slimmer by tight pantaloons, as it flits past the pale gravestones.

George Eliot, like Thackeray, does not seek her characters amongst exceptional beings, amongst heroes. In *Amos Barton* it is not the type of the adventuress-Countess Czerlaski which forms the main theme, as might have happened in an eighteenth-century novel, but rather the dull, grotesque, and at the same time pitiable parish priest and the handsome housewife to whom he is married. At a certain point (chap. v) George Eliot expresses herself, with regard to her central character, in words that contain a whole programme:

The Rev. Amos Barton, whose sad fortunes I have undertaken to relate, was, you perceive, in no respect an ideal or exceptional character; and perhaps I am doing a bold thing to bespeak your sympathy on behalf of a man who was so very far from remarkable, —a man whose virtues were not heroic, and who had no undetected crime within his breast; who had not the slightest mystery hanging about him, but was palpably and unmistakably commonplace; who was not even in love, but had had that complaint favourably many years ago. 'An utterly uninteresting character!' I think I hear a lady reader exclaim—Mrs. Farthingale, for example, who prefers the ideal in fiction; to whom tragedy means ermine tippets, adultery, and murder; and comedy, the adventures of some personage who is quite a 'character'.

But, my dear madam, it is so very large a majority of your fellow-countrymen that are of this insignificant stamp. At least eighty out of a hundred of your adult male fellow-Britons returned in the last census are neither extraordinarily silly, nor extraordinarily wicked, nor extraordinarily wise; their eyes are neither deep and liquid with sentiment, nor sparkling with suppressed witticisms; they have probably had no hairbreadth escapes or thrilling adventures; their brains are certainly not pregnant with genius, and their passions have not manifested themselves at all after the fashion of a volcano. They are simply men of complexions more or less muddy, whose conversation is more or less bald and disjointed. Yet these common-place people—many of them—bear a conscience, and have felt the sublime prompting to do the painful right; they have their unspoken sorrows, and their sacred joys; their hearts have perhaps gone out towards their first-born, and they have mourned over the irreclaim-able dead. Nay, is there not a pathos in their very insignificance— in our comparison of their dim and narrow existence with the glorious possibilities of that human nature which they share? [Earlier, George Eliot had confessed that she 'had a sympathy for mongrel ungainly dogs' such as Amos Barton.]

Depend upon it, you would gain unspeakably if you would learn with me to see some of the poetry and the pathos, the tragedy and the comedy, lying in the experience of a human soul that looks out through dull grey eyes, and that speaks in a voice of quite ordinary tones. In that case, I should have no fear of your not caring to know what farther befell the Rev. Amos Barton, or of your thinking the homely details I have to tell at all beneath your attention. As it is, you can, if you please, decline to pursue my story farther; and you will easily find reading more to your taste, since I learn from the newspapers that many remarkable novels, full of striking situations, thrilling incidents, and eloquent writing, have appeared only within the last season.

In which words there can be observed the same reaction to the novels of Bulwer Lytton and his like, with their mysterious, criminal heroes, as we have already noticed in Thackeray. And indeed George Eliot, in a letter to the publisher Blackwood dated June 11th, 1857,[142] admitted that to be reminded of Thackeray was not inadmissible:

There are too many prolific writers who devote themselves to the production of pleasing pictures, to the exclusion of all disagreeable truths, for me to desire to add to their number. In this respect, at least, I may have some resemblance to Thackeray, though I am not conscious of being in any way a disciple of his, unless it constitute discipleship to think him, as I suppose the majority of people of any intellect do, on the whole the most powerful of living novelists.

But George Eliot goes farther than Thackeray: she tones down the colour, she avoids the picturesque that is observable in Thackeray, who, after all, as we have already said, still conforms to the theory of Ben Jonson's 'humours' and delights to exercise his pungent satire upon eccentric characters, upon 'snobs'. Even closer to George Eliot is Charlotte Brontë, who in her first novel, *The Professor*, also published in 1857, wrote (chap. xix):

Novelists should never allow themselves to weary of the study of real life. If they observed this duty conscientiously, they would give us fewer pictures chequered with vivid contrasts of light and shade; they would seldom elevate their heroes and heroines to the heights of rapture—still seldomer sink them to the depths of despair . . . the man of regular life and rational mind never despairs.

Amos Barton is absolutely mediocre; he is a Vicar of Wakefield[143] translated into terms of a more bourgeois, a duller age than was the eighteenth century, when a picaresque air still breathed. He is not an ascetic; he likes brandy-and-water; but even this homage to the power of Bacchus is incapable of becoming a vice (chap. v):

After all, the Rev. Amos never came near the borders of a vice. His very faults were middling—he was not *very* ungrammatical. It was not in his nature to be superlative in anything; unless, indeed, he was superlatively middling, the quintessential extract of mediocrity.

A Dickens, undoubtedly, would have exploited Barton's tendency to commit errors of grammar; he would have made him into a figure of fun, a caricature; we can imagine how he would have put into his mouth sermons and discourses full of irresistible solecisms. But George Eliot passes lightly over this opportunity for caricature, and comments thus upon his other idiosyncrasy, his maize-coloured dressing-gown: 'Maize is a colour that decidedly did *not* suit his complexion, and it is one that soon soils; why, then, did Mr. Barton select it for domestic wear? Perhaps because he had a knack of hitting on the wrong thing in garb as well as in grammar.' But George Eliot, as I have said, avoids the picturesque. Her aim is a different one—not so far removed, fundamentally, from that of Jules Romains when, in times closer to our own, he wrote *Mort de quelqu'un*. It is an aim which she expressed in these words: 'I wish to stir your sympathy with commonplace troubles—to win your tears for real sorrow: sorrow such as may live next door to you—such as walks neither in rags nor in velvet, but in very ordinary decent apparel.'

This passage makes it quite clear to whom George Eliot is related: to the Wordsworth of *Peter Bell*, of *The Idiot Boy*, of all those poems in which the poet sought to bring to light the workings of the 'dread spirits' of conscience in humble souls:

> From men of pensive virtue go,
> Dread Beings! and your empire show
> On hearts like that of Peter Bell.

George Eliot's declarations are, moreover, explicit:

If art does not enlarge men's sympathies, it does nothing morally. ... The only effect I ardently long to produce by my writings is, that those who read them should be better able to *imagine* and to *feel* the pains and the joys of those who differ from themselves in everything but the broad fact of being struggling, erring human creatures.[144]

Wordsworth, in *The Prelude* (xiii), had sought contact with the humble people whom he met by the wayside, 'souls that appear to have no depth at all, to careless eyes'. He had made the feelings of these humble people interesting by instilling the atmosphere of the ideal world into situations and incidents which had been deprived of all lustre by their everyday, ordinary character, thus transfiguring the most familiar kind of reality by appropriate and significant language. And thus George Eliot takes up, in prose, the programme announced in Wordsworth's part of the manifesto of *Lyrical Ballads*.[145] Peter Bell, the idiot boy, the old leech-gatherer, the reaper, the old Scotch pedlar of *The Excursion*, the blind Highland boy—the role of all these was the translation into action of Wordsworth's desire to bring to light, in the humble human story, its nucleus of loftiest spiritual message. And all these find a parallel, in George Eliot's work, in characters such as Silas Marner, the rough weaver whose heart is softened through the compassion of others for him, and at last humanized altogether through his love for the orphan child (chap. xiv: 'As the child's mind was growing into knowledge, his mind was growing into memory: as her life unfolded, his soul, long stupefied in a cold narrow prison, was unfolding too, and trembling gradually into full consciousness');[146] in Adam Bede, who also feels himself awakened to a 'full consciousness' by grief for Hetty's guilt—Hetty, who was to feel her own soul thawing at the warm contact of Dinah's sympathy; in Rosamond Vincy, who, after her conversation with Dorothea, feels her soul to be set free beneath the action of impulses she had never known before; in Gwendolen Harleth regenerated by remorse for a criminal thought which she has seen, almost without her own intervention, translated into action:[147] all these are minutely careful studies in which the 'Spirits of the mind', the 'Dread Beings' of Wordsworth, are awakened in humble or erring souls. Quite understandably, then, did George Eliot write to Blackwood (February 24th, 1861)[148] on the subject of *Silas Marner*: 'I don't wonder at your finding my story, as far as you have read it, rather sombre: indeed, I should not have believed that any one would have been interested in it but myself (since Wordsworth is dead) if Mr. Lewes had not been strongly arrested by it.' In any case Lewes himself had directed George Eliot's imagination into this channel. Before the time of his intimate friendship with the future novelist, he had written (in July 1852) in the *Westminster Review* an essay on *The Lady Novelists*, in which he had outlined the theory that was later to become hers, that the literature of imagination must be based on real experience, and must enable readers to become more profoundly aware of the feelings and sufferings of common humanity.[149] As Lewes declared later in another essay, *Realism in Art*

(*Westminster Review*, October 1858), it was a question of not distorting or falsifying the facts of real life, but of conferring upon them a special intensity, of focusing them: the ordinary appearance of everyday life would furnish the necessary basis. A simple recipe, yet not easy to recognize, even for admirers of Wordsworth. Ruskin, for example, who carried on the Wordsworth tradition of calling attention to the minutest details of nature, went so far as to repeat, when writing of *The Mill on the Floss* (in *Fiction, Fair and Foul*), exactly the same objection that George Eliot had put into the mouth of the imaginary female reader in chapter v of *Amos Barton*: 'There is not a single person in the book', says Ruskin, 'of the smallest importance to anybody in the world, except themselves, and whose qualities deserve so much as a line of printer's type in their description.'[150]

In a passage in *Adam Bede* (chap. xvii)—contrary to the opinion of some, according to whom, if you wish to retain the slightest faith in human heroism, you should never make a pilgrimage to see the hero—George Eliot maintains that the way in which she has reached the conclusion 'that human nature is lovable', the way by which she has 'learnt something of its deep pathos, its sublime mysteries —has been by living a great deal among people more or less commonplace and vulgar, of whom you would perhaps hear nothing very surprising if you were to inquire about them in the neighbourhood where they dwelt'. It is a passage that paraphrases what Wordsworth had said in the thirteenth book of *The Prelude* concerning the contact that should be cultivated with 'souls that appear to have no depth at all, to careless eyes'.

Another passage in *Adam Bede* (chap. xvii) touches upon the same theme of 'realism in art' that had formed the subject of Lewes's essay quoted above, which was written at the precise moment when George Eliot was engaged on the composition of that same novel:

I am content to tell my simple story, without trying to make things seem better than they were; dreading nothing, indeed, but falsity, which, in spite of one's best efforts, there is reason to dread. Falsity is so easy, truth so difficult. The pencil is conscious of a delightful facility in drawing a griffin—the larger the claws, and the larger the wings, the better; but that marvellous facility which we mistook for genius is apt to forsake us when we want to draw a real unexaggerated lion. . . . It is for this rare precious quality of truthfulness that I delight in many Dutch paintings, which lofty-minded people despise. I find a source of delicious sympathy in these faithful pictures of a monotonous homely existence, which has been the fate of so many more among my fellow-mortals than a life of pomp or of absolute indigence, of tragic suffering or of world-stirring actions. I turn, without shrinking, from cloud-borne angels, from prophets, sibyls and heroic warriors, to an old woman bending over her flower-pot, or eating her solitary dinner, while the noonday light, softened perhaps by a screen of leaves, falls on her mob-cap, and just touches the rim of her spinning-wheel, and her stone jug, and all those cheap common things which are the precious neces-saries of life to her;—or I turn to that village wedding, kept between four brown walls, where an awkward bridegroom opens the dance with a high-shouldered, broad-faced bride, while elderly and middle-aged friends look on, with very irregular noses and lips, and probably quart-pots in their hands, but with an expression of unmistakable contentment and goodwill. 'Foh!' says my idealistic friend, 'what vulgar details! What good is there in taking all these pains to give an exact likeness of old women and clowns? What a low phase of life!—what clumsy, ugly people!'

But bless us, things may be lovable that are not altogether hand-some, I hope? I am not at all sure that the majority of the human race have not been ugly. . . . Yes! thank God; human feeling is like the mighty rivers that bless the earth: it does not wait for beauty— it flows with resistless force and brings beauty with it. All honour and reverence to the divine beauty of form! Let us cultivate it to the utmost in men, women, and children—in our gardens and in our houses. But let us love that other beauty too, which lies in no secret of proportion, but in the secret of deep human sympathy.[151] Paint us an angel, if you can . . . paint us yet oftener a Madonna, turning her mild face upward and opening her arms to welcome the divine glory; but do not impose on us any aesthetic rules which shall banish from the region of Art those old women scraping carrots with their work-worn hands, those heavy clowns taking holiday in a dingy pot-house, those rounded backs and stupid weather-beaten faces that have bent over the spade and done the rough work of the world—those homes with their tin pans, their brown pitchers, their rough curs, and their clusters of onions. . . . Therefore let us always have men ready to give the loving pains of a life to the faithful representing of commonplace things—men who see beauty in those commonplace things, and delight in showing how kindly the light of heaven falls on them.

These pages form another manifesto, and this time the reference is not to Wordsworth, but to Dutch painting, the painting which, as has been said in the introductory chapter to this book, first discovered beauty in humble, everyday things, in creatures plebeian and anonymous, the painting which initiated democratic art. It was to a Dutch picture that George Eliot compared her first story, *Amos Barton*, in a letter to Blackwood dated February 4th, 1857;[152] and in a passage of her diary, dated Ilfracombe, May 1856,[153] she describes an ugly landscape transfigured to beauty by the evening light—describes it as a Dutch painter might have painted it:

From our windows we had a view of the higher part of the town, and generally it looked uninteresting enough; but what is it that light cannot transfigure into beauty? One evening after a shower, as the sun was setting over the sea behind us, some peculiar arrangement of clouds threw a delicious evening light on the irregular cluster of houses, and merged the ugliness of their forms in an exquisite flood of colour—*as a stupid person is made glorious by a noble deed.*

These last words are worth italicizing, so clearly do they give us the key to George Eliot's inspiration. We have seen Trollope exalting Rembrandt's matrons above the Madonnas of Raphael, and Thackeray singing the praises of small beer: in George Eliot this recurrent fundamental theme of nineteenth-century bourgeois literature takes on an ethical urgency, in a way that may remind us of Tolstoy. Just as Rembrandt had been the first to invest awkward models, women whose features and figures were far from impeccable, with an atmosphere of love and compassion (Caravaggio too had chosen vulgar models, but there is little sign of love or compassion in his impassive renderings of light and shade!), so did Tolstoy glorify, with gentleness of spirit and dignity of bearing, beings who would have appeared despicable and 'to have no depth at all, to careless eyes' (from Generalissimo Kutusov, mocked by the courtiers, down to the humble soldier Karataiev, in *War and Peace*). And how can we help thinking again of Tolstoy when George Eliot concludes *Middle-march* by saying that the good of the world is dependent on 'unhistoric acts', and that if things are not so ill as they might have been, this 'is half owing to the number who lived faithfully a hidden life, and rest in unvisited tombs'? Or when, in *Felix Holt* (chap. xvi) she writes:

We see human heroism broken into units, and say this unit did little,—might as well not have been. But in this way we might break up a great army into units; in this way we might break the sunlight into fragments, and think that this and the other might be cheaply parted with. Let us rather raise a monument to the soldiers whose brave hearts only kept the ranks unbroken, and met death,— a monument to the faithful who were not famous, and who are precious as the continuity of the sunbeams is precious, though some of them fall unseen and on barrenness—

how can we help thinking of Tolstoy, who, in *War and Peace* (Book IV, Part I, 4), insists upon the importance of the anonymous crowd, of the deeds that do not pass into history; who maintains that only unconscious activity bears fruit, and that the man who plays a part in an historical event never understands its significance?[154] We think of Tolstoy, but, even more, of Wordsworth in the *Ode to Duty* and of Gray in the *Elegy written in a Country Churchyard*: two other poems whose theme was to echo throughout the work of George Eliot.

It was Wordsworth who had insisted upon the importance of the humble round of accomplished duty—duty, a support and a joyfully accepted rule, which brings man into harmony with the universe, with the stars in their changeless courses, with the patient hills that bear without complaint the heat of the sun and the violence of the storm, with the days and the seasons in their comings and goings, with the birds, the flowers, the clouds—all of them things that are joyful because they are subject to the law of their own being, which they obey without murmuring.

> Turn to private life
> And social neighbourhood; look we to ourselves;
> A light of duty shines on every day
> For all.

(*The Excursion*, Book V, 381–4)

In conformity with Wordsworth's teaching George Eliot speaks in *Daniel Deronda* (chap. xv) of the 'want of regulated channels for the soul to move in,—good and sufficient ducts of habit without which our nature easily turns to mere ooze and mud, and at any pressure yields nothing but a spurt or a puddle'. The lines from the *Ode to Duty*: 'Stern lawgiver! . . . Thou dost preserve the stars from wrong; And the most ancient heavens through Thee, are fresh and strong' form the heading to chapter lxxx of *Middlemarch*. In a conversation which she had with F. W. H. Myers[155] in the garden of Trinity College, Cambridge, in 1873, George Eliot,

stirred somewhat beyond her wont, and taking as her text the three words which have been used so often as the inspiring trumpet-calls of men,—the words *God*, *Immortality*, *Duty*,—pronounced with terrible earnestness, how inconceivable was the *first*, how unbelievable the *second*, and yet how peremptory and absolute the *third*. Never, perhaps, have sterner accents affirmed the sovereignty of impersonal and unrecompensing Law. I listened, and night fell; her grave, majestic countenance turned towards me like a Sibyl's in the gloom; it was as though she withdrew from my grasp, one by one, the two scrolls of promise, and left me the third scroll only, awful with inevitable fates. And when we stood at length and parted, amid that columnar circuit of forest-trees, beneath the last twilight of starless skies, I seemed to be gazing, like Titus at Jerusalem, on vacant seats and empty halls,—on a sanctuary with no Presence to hallow it, and heaven left lonely of a God.

A contributing factor to this hegemony of Duty in George Eliot's conception of life was clearly, as V. S. Pritchett remarks,[156] the country surroundings in which she was brought up, which must have impressed upon her the sense—the true peasant's sense—of the laws and repetitions of Nature, of the exact place that each man holds in the system of things, and also of the evocative, poetic value of ancient institutions. Of her own Deronda, who, as we shall see, was an ideal projection of herself, she wrote (*Daniel Deronda*, chap. xxxii):

I have said that under his calm exterior he had a fervour which made him easily feel the presence of poetry in every-day events; and the forms of the Juden-gasse, rousing the sense of union with what is remote, set him musing on two elements of our historic life which that sense raises into the same region of poetry,—the faint beginnings of faiths and institutions, and their obscure lingering decay; the dust and withered remains with which they are apt to be covered, only enhancing for the awakened perception the impressiveness either of a sublimely penetrating life, as in the twin green leaves that will become the sheltering tree, or of a pathetic inheritance in which all the grandeur and the glory have become a sorrowing memory.

This innate feeling for tradition in George Eliot was to receive an articulate confirmation in the message of Wordsworth's *Ode to Duty*, which itself, also, was an emanation of a rural world. After a complete reading of Wordsworth George Eliot wrote to Miss Lewis on November 22nd, 1839:[157] 'I never before met with so many of my own feelings expressed just as I could like them.'

George Eliot's morality assumed, therefore, the aspect of a law of Nature, of a kind of Fate whose decrees were as ineluctable as the changes of the seasons. The result of this was that her situations and characters are often drawn in hard, massive outlines, with clear, sharp corners as though cut with an axe: it is a robust, rural art, in which Retribution holds accurate scales and the tread of Nemesis is unfaltering. Not that she ignores the subtler shades, for, as we shall see, she investigated complexities of character more profoundly than her predecessors: she was to write in *Felix Holt* (chap. xxii): 'Very close and diligent looking at living creatures, even through the best microscope, will leave room for new and contradictory discoveries.' But her investigation often reveals the cast-iron pattern of a casuistry as precise as a set of pigeon-holes, and a sense of limits as clear as a surveyor's records.[158] And if it was to these same rural surroundings that George Eliot owed her respect for the ancient traditions that find their sanctuary in the country village, so that her reforming zeal wore always a conservative air, on the other hand the sense of unchangeable laws which these surroundings had instilled into her must have predisposed her to the acceptance of Comte's positivism, with its conception of human processes being governed by natural laws which man can assist but

not alter, of tendencies that assert themselves independently of individuals, so that the individual becomes merely
the agent of a superior force (a conception that finds a
parallel in the Tolstoy of *War and Peace*).[159] If, under the
influence of such doctrines, George Eliot did not become
more rigid than she did, it was due to the mild, beneficent
manner in which her childish world lingered in her memory
—the world of childhood reminiscence which makes the
first part of *The Mill on the Floss* into one of the masterpieces
of narrative: and here too there is a striking analogy with
what happened in the case of Wordsworth: just as Silas's
feeling of reverence in front of the child who suddenly
appears in his hut is a reflection of Wordsworth's reverence
for infancy.[160] It was the survival of this childish world, like
a secret spring, in George Eliot, that allowed her, even if
rather late, to assert herself as an imaginative writer, after
years of arid labour as a translator and reviewer. Comte,
with his new religion that substituted Humanity for God,
Love and Sympathy for Faith, that eliminated the supernatural and elevated the natural, that, in a word, demo-
cratized Heaven, did no more than place the final seal upon
the tendency towards democratization of the heroic which,
in George Eliot, already had its roots in her surroundings
and her culture.

*   *   *   *   *

Amongst the works of Wordsworth George Eliot expressed a special liking for his sonnet to the minor hero
Toussaint l'Ouverture, unhappy negro proclaimer of freedom, and also for that other sonnet *I grieved for Buonaparte*,
which later[161] she was to regret that Arnold had not included in his selection—a sonnet in which the poet declares
that—

> Wisdom doth live with children round her knees:
> Books, leisure, perfect freedom, and the talk
> Man holds with week-day man in the hourly walk
> Of the mind's business: those are the degrees
> By which true Sway doth mount; this is the stalk
> True Power doth grow on; and her rights are these.

Wordsworth had made his *Excursion* hinge upon this 'talk

Man holds with week-day man in the hourly walk Of the mind's business'. But there had been another poet, before Wordsworth, who had exalted the dignity of humble things, Gray. The following lines from the *Elegy written in a Country Churchyard*, although extremely well known, may be quoted here because of their precise applicability to George Eliot:

> Perhaps in this neglected spot is laid
>   Some heart once pregnant with celestial fire;
> Hands, that the rod of empire might have sway'd,
>   Or waked to ecstasy the living lyre.
>
> But Knowledge to their eyes her ample page
>   Rich with the spoils of time did ne'er unroll;
> Chill Penury repress'd their noble rage,
>   And froze the genial current of the soul.
>
> Full many a gem of purest ray serene
>   The dark unfathom'd caves of ocean bear:
> Full many a flower is born to blush unseen,
>   And waste its sweetness on the desert air.
>
> Some village Hampden that with dauntless breast
>   The little tyrant of his fields withstood,
> Some mute inglorious Milton here may rest,
>   Some Cromwell guiltless of his country's blood. . . .
>
> Far from the madding crowd's ignoble strife
>   Their sober wishes never learn'd to stray;
> Along the cool, sequester'd vale of life
>   They kept the noiseless tenor of their way.

The Prelude to *Middlemarch* is but a natural consequence of the concept contained in these lines of Gray's: in it, after referring to the episode of Saint Theresa who, as a little girl, wished to go with her little brother and seek martyrdom amongst the Moors, and after saying that she 'found her epos in the reform of a religious order', George Eliot continues as follows:

That Spanish woman who lived three hundred years ago, was certainly not the last of her kind. Many Theresas have been born who found for themselves no epic life wherein there was a constant unfolding of far-resonant action; perhaps only a life of mistakes, the offspring of a certain spiritual grandeur ill-matched with the meanness of opportunity; perhaps a tragic failure which found no sacred poet and sank unwept into oblivion. With dim lights and tangled circumstance they tried to shape their thought and deed in noble agreement; but after all, to common eyes their struggles seemed mere inconsistency and formlessness; for these later-born Theresas were helped by no coherent social faith and order which could perform the function of knowledge for the ardently willing soul. Their ardour alternated between a vague ideal and the common yearning of womanhood; so that the one was disapproved as extravagance, and the other condemned as a lapse.

The concept is taken up again in the conclusion to the story of Dorothea, that village Saint Theresa:

Certainly those determining acts of her life [her first marriage with Casaubon and her second with Ladislaw] were not ideally beautiful. They were the mixed results of young and noble impulse struggling amidst the conditions of an imperfect social state, in which great feelings will often take the aspect of error, and great faith the aspect of illusion. For there is no creature whose inward being is so strong that it is not greatly determined by what lies outside it. A new Theresa will hardly have the opportunity of reforming a conventual life, any more than a new Antigone will spend her heroic pity in doing all for the sake of a brother's burial: the medium in which their ardent deeds took shape is forever gone. . . . Her [Dorothea's] finely touched spirit had still its fine issues, though they were not widely visible. Her full nature, like that river of which Cyrus broke the strength, spent itself in channels which had no great name on the earth. But the effect of her being on those around her was incalculably diffusive: for the growing good of the world is partly dependent on unhistoric act; and that things are not so ill with you and me as they might have been, is half owing to the number who lived faithfully a hidden life, and rest in unvisited tombs.[162]

With Gray, with Wordsworth, with George Eliot, the setting of tragedy moves to the abodes of the humble. The democratic tendency was so pronounced in the nineteenth century that its expression does not, after all, seem so very original in the lines of Walt Whitman, whose loftiest poetry springs not from the grandiose, but from the humble and the ordinary:[163] the very title of *Leaves of Grass* suggests something not in the least precious, something, in fact, of the most everyday kind (he had written in the opening pages of his first notebook: 'Bring all the art and science of the world, and baffle and humble it with one spear of grass'), and yet full of freshness, and yet 'no less than the journey-work of the stars' (*Song of Myself*, section 31): the leaf of grass, the humble leaf of grass:

Painters have painted their swarming groups and the centre-figure of all,
From the head of the centre-figure spreading a nimbus of gold-color'd light,
But I paint myriads of heads, but paint no head without its nimbus of gold-color'd light,
From my hand from the brain of every man and woman it streams, effulgently flowing forever.

And in the poem *Crossing Brooklyn Ferry*:

Diverge, fine spokes of light, from the shape of my head, or any one's head, in the sunlit water!

Every individual can be his hero, his own Messiah.

At the beginning of Book IV of *The Mill on the Floss* George Eliot compares the ruins of humble villages devastated by the waters along the banks of the Rhône with the splendid ruins of the castles on the Rhine:

I have a cruel conviction that the lives those ruins are traces of, were part of a gross sum of obscure vitality, that will be swept into the same oblivion with the generations of ants and beavers. Perhaps something akin to this oppressive feeling may have weighed upon you in watching this old-fashioned family life on the banks of the Floss, which even sorrow hardly suffices to lift above the level of the tragi-comic. It is a sordid life, you say, this of the Tullivers and Dodsons—irradiated by no sublime principles, no romantic visions, no active, self-renouncing faith—moved by none of those wild, uncontrollable passions which create the dark shadows of misery and crime—without that primitive rough simplicity of wants, that hard submissive ill-paid toil, that childlike spelling out of what nature has written, which gives its poetry to peasant life. Here, one has conventional worldly notions and habits without instruction and without polish—surely the most prosaic form of human life: proud respectability in a gig of unfashionable build: worldliness without side-dishes. Observing these people narrowly, even when the iron hand of misfortune has shaken them from their unquestioning hold on the world, one sees little trace of religion, still less of a distinctively Christian creed. . . . You could not live among such people, you are stifled for want of an outlet towards something beautiful, great, or noble, you are irritated with these dull men and women, as a kind of population out of keeping with the earth on which they live. . . . I share with you this sense of oppressive narrowness; but it is necessary that we should feel it, if we care to understand how it acted on the lives of Tom and Maggie—how it has acted on young natures in many generations, that in the onward tendency of human things have risen above the mental level of the generation before them, to which they have been nevertheless tied by the strongest fibres of their hearts. The suffering, whether of martyr or victim, which belongs to every historical advance of mankind, is represented in this way in every town, and by hundreds of obscure hearths; and we need not shrink from this comparison of small things with great; for does not science tell us that its highest striving is after the ascertainment of a unity which shall bind the smallest things with the greatest? In natural science, I have understood, there is nothing petty in the mind that has a large vision of relations, and to which every simple object suggests a vast sum of conditions. It is surely the same with the observation of human life.

Thus the tragedy of Tulliver the miller has its own dignity (*Mill on the Floss*, Book III, chap. i):

Tulliver . . . though nothing more than a superior miller and maltster, was as proud and obstinate as if he had been a very lofty personage, in whom such dispositions might be a source of that conspicuous, far-echoing tragedy, which sweeps the stage in regal robes, and makes the dullest chronicler sublime. The pride and obstinacy of millers, and other insignificant people, whom you pass unnoticingly on the road every day, have their tragedy too; but it is of that unwept, hidden sort, that goes on from generation to generation and leaves no record—such tragedy, perhaps, as lies in the conflict of young souls, hungry for joy, under a lot made suddenly hard to them, under the dreariness of a home where the morning brings no promise with it, and the unexpectant discontent of worn and disappointed parents weighs on the children like a damp, thick air, in which all the functions of life are depressed; or such tragedy as lies in the slow or sudden death that follows on a bruised passion, though it may be a death that finds only a parish funeral.

'Let the high Muse chant loves Olympian', run the lines placed as a heading to chapter xxvii of *Middlemarch*; 'We are but mortals, and must sing of man.'

At one point in *The Mill on the Floss* (Book V, chap. ii) George Eliot compares Maggie's internal conflicts, and Tom's struggles against more substantial obstacles, to the toilsome adventures of Homer's heroes. To Deronda (chap. xix) the finding of Mirah 'was as heart-stirring as anything that befell Orestes or Rinaldo'. There is nothing commonplace in the tragedies of mediocre souls; the paltry tragedy of the pedant Casaubon, intent upon a muddled and unrealizable work which has been spurious from its very beginning, is redeemed by the fact that in it 'everything is below the level of tragedy except the passionate egoism of the sufferer'. The love-approaches between Dinah and Adam Bede seem commonplace, but are no more so than the ever-recurring first signs of spring, to which the shy glances, the tremulous touches by which two human souls are brought together so closely correspond. When Esther comes to know Felix better (*Felix Holt*, chap. xxii), 'her conception of what a happy love must be had become like a dissolving view, in which the once-clear images were gradually melting into new forms and new colours. The favourite Byronic heroes were beginning to look something like last night's decorations seen in the sober dawn.' She felt now that if an imperfect being like Felix were to love her, 'her life would be exalted into something quite new,— into a sort of difficult blessedness, such as one may imagine in beings who are conscious of painfully growing into the possession of higher powers'.

Any 'low subject' may be elevated: all that is needed is to consider it a parable in order to ennoble it, writes George Eliot in *Middlemarch* (chap. xxxv). But absolute greatness, hundred per cent. heroism—do they really exist? she asks; and in this question, and in the inferences she derives from her own doubtful answer, she finds herself in agreement with Thackeray and Trollope, with—in short—the Biedermeier conception of human potentialities. 'There are few prophets in the world; few sublimely beautiful women; few heroes', she writes in *Adam Bede* (chap. xvii), continuing the passage already quoted:[164]

I can't afford to give all my love and reverence to such rarities: I want a great deal of those feelings for my everyday fellow-men, especially for the few in the foreground of the great multitude, whose faces I know, whose hands I touch, for whom I have to make way with kindly courtesy. Neither are picturesque lazzaroni or romantic criminals half so frequent as your common labourer, who gets his own bread, and eats it vulgarly but creditably with his own pocket-knife. It is more needful that I should have a fibre of sympathy connecting me with that vulgar citizen who weighs out my sugar in a vilely-assorted cravat and waistcoat, than with the handsomest rascal in red scarf and green feathers,—more needful that my heart should swell with loving admiration of some trait of gentle goodness in the faulty people who sit at the same hearth with me, or in the clergyman of my own parish, who is perhaps rather too corpulent, and in other respects is not an Oberlin or a Tillotson, than at the deeds of heroes whom I shall never know except by hearsay, or at the sublimest abstract of all clerical graces that was ever conceived by an able novelist.

George Eliot wrote those words about the clergyman Irwine, who will appear to the reader to be very far from fulfilling what would seem to be the requisites for the character of a priest. And we are reminded of what Trollope wrote a few years later in the *Last Chronicle of Barset* (1867) to defend himself against those who reproved him for not having painted portraits of exemplary clergymen.[165] Like Thackeray, George Eliot disliked the kind of heroism that is loudly acclaimed and celebrated by monuments in public squares. Maggie does not like Madame de Staël's *Corinne*; nor does she wish to be a tenth Muse (*Mill on the Floss*, Book V, chap. iv). 'Nothing in all literature moved her [George Eliot] more than the pathetic situation and the whole character of Gretchen. It touched her more than anything in Shakespeare.'[166] And she saw Shakespeare himself from the visual point of view of everyday life:[167]

The writers who dare to be thoroughly familiar are Shakespeare, Fielding, Scott (where he is expressing the popular life with which he is familiar), and indeed every other writer of fiction of the first class. Even in his loftiest tragedies—in *Hamlet*, for example— Shakespeare is intensely colloquial. One hears the very accent of living men.

In George Eliot's skill in extracting tragedy from 'moral mediocrity' F. R. Leavis[168] sees a sign of her greatness as

31. W. P. FRITH. The Good Pastor

32. DAVID. Leonidas at Thermopylae (*Paris, Louvre*)

a writer. 'There is nothing sentimental about George Eliot's vision of human mediocrity and "platitude", but she sees in them matters for compassion, and her dealings with them are assertions of human dignity. To be able to assert human dignity in this way is greatness: the contrast with Flaubert is worth pondering.'

Indeed if we imagine how the author of *Bouvard et Pécuchet*, on the one hand, and, on the other, the author of *Uncle Vanya* might have presented the figure of Casaubon, we shall come to understand the characteristic position of George Eliot, who, however original she may look beside a Flaubert or a Tchekov, appears much less so if we think of Thackeray and Trollope, and of characters like the former's Colonel Newcome and the latter's Doctor Harding. The theme of *Middlemarch* seems, in truth, to invite comparison with *Uncle Vanya*: in both of them a hero, in the first Casaubon, in the second Professor Serebriakov, is finally unmasked; but whereas in Tchekov's play the victim, Uncle Vanya, sinks feebly, after a first impulse of revolt, into a situation which is patently grotesque and immoral, George Eliot, who seems to start by considering Dorothea's exalted feeling for Casaubon from a humorous point of view, later, as we have said, concentrates upon the truly tragic element in the figure of this paltry man, so that he escapes without being distorted either by sentimentality or caricature. To Dorothea it seems at first as if marrying Casaubon will be like marrying Pascal; she imagines that she will be able to collaborate with him by reading aloud to him Latin and Greek texts as Milton's daughters did to their father, and she throws herself metaphorically at his feet, 'kissing his unfashionable shoe-ties as if he were a Protestant Pope' (chap. v). 'There would be nothing trivial about our lives. Everyday things with us would mean the greatest things'; and Dorothea plunges into a work annotated by Casaubon and absorbs it 'taking it in as eagerly as she might have taken in the scent of a fresh bouquet after a dry, hot, dreary walk' (chap. iv). Are we being confronted with a bourgeois version of the story of Bottom and Titania? In the meantime the reader, who has also been allowed to see passages from Casaubon's letters that are grotesque in their pomposity, is under no illusion. Later, bit by bit, the scales fall from Dorothea's eyes, until the day when her husband exacts an unconditional promise from her and it becomes clear that he expects her to devote herself completely to the sifting of masses of material collected by him, material which was to be 'the doubtful illustration of principles still more doubtful': then the poor woman, like Psyche in front of the heap of barley and peas and poppy-seeds which she had to sort out by command of Venus, sees before her days, months, and years of toil in the result of which she has lost all faith. Seeing the uselessness of her task, will Dorothea give the fatal promise to the man who now, in her eyes, is nothing more than a selfish, jealous pedant? Tchekov, perhaps, would have made her give it, and would have shown us a picture of a woman withering away in morbid resignation. George Eliot brings it about that, when Dorothea goes to Casaubon to give him the fatal promise, she finds him dead in the garden.

Dorothea's hero falls from his pedestal; but as he gradually sinks in her estimation, his character loses its suggestion of caricature, and he is merely a poor wretch more worthy of pity than anything else, as he wanders round the garden, conscious, now, of the illness that will carry him to the grave (chap. xlii):

> The black figure with hands behind and head bent forward continued to pace the walk where the dark yew-trees gave him a mute companionship in melancholy, and the little shadows of bird or leaf that fleeted across the isles of sunlight, stole along in silence as in the presence of a sorrow.

The figure of Casaubon has here none of the grotesque angularity, *à la* Spitzweg, with which the figure of Amos Barton crossing the churchyard was presented.[169] It is, on the contrary, as though we were present at Nature's own suffering, at her participation in human sorrow, as it is to be found later in certain famous pages of D. H. Lawrence's *The White Peacock*.

Casaubon's life is a failure, in a novel which is a whole story of ill-assorted marriages and thwarted lives: the life of Casaubon, sacrificed to a futile task; that of Lydgate, who fails in his learned career owing to his wife and becomes merely a doctor with a large practice; that of Bulstrode, whose ambition to become an ideal figure of piety and beneficence is frustrated by the impure source of his wealth. There would indeed have been material, in this novel, for a conclusion *à la* Tchekov! But for George Eliot each of these stories suggests a piece of ethical instruction: in each of these cases there is to be seen the corruption of a character that yet has noble aspects: and in the study of processes of corruption such as these, as also in the study of the dawning of higher moral standards in uncouth souls, lies the main theme—we shall return to it shortly— of George Eliot's work.

Meanwhile let us observe the manner in which her anti-heroic tendency is limited. This limit is constituted by the more or less conscious desire of the writer to project herself in figures that are idealizations of herself: with a greater sense of reality in Maggie, with a lesser in Dinah and Dorothea, with little or none in Romola and Daniel Deronda. The idealization of herself is obvious in *The Mill on the Floss* and *Middlemarch*: in both novels the central figure is a type of woman such as she would have liked to be, with beauty of rather an unusual kind, great simplicity of manners, acute moral sensibility. Maggie at the charity bazaar (Book VI, chap. ix) is both beautiful and simple at the same time, and makes all the people round her look artificial. But in Maggie there is little stylization, thanks mainly to the fresh spring of the novelist's childhood memories which steep the figure of the protagonist in poetry. The stylization of Dinah, Dorothea, and Romola, on the other hand, makes them altogether too like the *cliché* of the Victorian angel-woman, as we found her, for instance, in Dickens's Agnes Wickfield. Seen through the eyes of Will Ladislaw in the Vatican Museum (chap. xix), Dorothea is presented to us like a Victorian portrait, in which elements of classicism are attenuated with a kind of Biedermeier conscientiousness:

A breathing, blooming girl, whose form, not shamed by the Ariadne, was clad in Quakerish grey drapery; her long cloak, fastened at the neck, was thrown backward from the arms, and one beautiful ungloved hand pillowed her cheek, pushing somewhat backward the white beaver bonnet which made a sort of halo to her face around the simply braided dark-brown hair.

Later on in the novel Dorothea's cloak takes on the veritable form of a protecting Madonna's outspread mantle, beneath which imploring devotees take shelter. 'This young creature has a heart large enough for the Virgin Mary', reflects Lydgate. And indeed, at the very beginning of her portrayal of the character of Dorothea, George Eliot had written (chap. i):

Miss Brooke had that kind of beauty which seems to be thrown into relief by poor dress. Her hand and wrist were so finely formed that she could wear sleeves no less bare of style than those in which the Blessed Virgin appeared to Italian painters; and her profile as well as her stature and bearing seemed to gain the more dignity from her plain garments, which by the side of provincial fashion gave her the impressiveness of a fine quotation from the Bible,—or from one of our elder poets—in a paragraph of to-day's newspaper.

Place this figure against the background of the Italian Renaissance and you will have Romola, who, when she appears in a village that has been decimated by plague, holding in her arms the child she has saved, is taken by the inhabitants for an actual apparition of the Virgin with the Divine Child (chap. lxviii). The affinity between Romola and Dorothea is revealed also in their acts; just as Romola helps Tessa's family after Tito has been killed, so Dorothea, after her husband's death, makes plans for the hospital and proposes to reinstate Lydgate and later to save Rosamond. George Eliot's imagination, as we shall see later, moves in an extremely limited and repetitive circle of invention. Dinah, in *Adam Bede* (chap. x), looks like an angel, but with traces of human toil, a working-class angel. Adam's mother, who sees her unexpectedly in front of her in the room which she has entered like a spirit, says to her: 'Ye've got a'most the face o' one as is a-sittin' on the grave i' Adam's new Bible', and is astonished that such an apparition should have the hands of a working woman. When Hetty is in prison, Dinah performs her function as a comforting, redeeming angel; Dorothea, when Ladislaw announces to her that he has refused Bulstrode's money, gives her approval with the speech and bearing of an allegorical figure of Virtue in a medieval mystery play in the act of judging Everyman (*Middlemarch*, chap. lxxxiii): ' "You acted as I should have expected you to act", said Dorothea, her face brightening and her head becoming a little more erect on its beautiful stem.' Here Dorothea is an incarnate allegory of Duty. All these feminine figures, besides responding to a particular myth of George Eliot's, conform, as I have said, to the Victorian conception of woman as a creature whose goodness should serve as a guide to men. When Gwendolen asks Deronda why it appears to him improper for a woman to sit down at a gaming-table, Deronda replies (chap. xxix): 'Perhaps because *we* need that you should be better than we are.'

But the most curious projection of her ideal self that George Eliot has given us is the character of Deronda himself, that kind of *shaman* with an eye as blandly and sinisterly fascinating as that of a wizard (Gwendolen does in fact, at a certain moment, accuse him of having given her the evil eye at the gaming-table). Deronda serves another purpose besides that of reflecting the ideal George Eliot, with whom he has in common, amongst other things, an ability to 'find poetry and romance among the events of everyday life' (chaps. xix and xxxii) and in the relics of tradition,[170] and an aptitude for feeling interest in people in proportion to the possibility of exercising a redeeming influence upon them (chap. xxviii);[171] he also serves to bestow a heroic quality not, this time, upon a humble figure (the programme announced in *Amos Barton* was 'to stir your sympathy with *commonplace* troubles'), but upon a man who was rejected by the English society of the period, upon a Jew. It has been observed[172] that Deronda does not at all possess the characteristics of a Jew (the Jew has a pronounced personality, whereas he is 'featureless'); but this matters little. What matters is the avowed intention of George Eliot to make a Jew into a hero, in face of the then current prejudices which she enumerates in her introduction to the novel. A sign of these prejudices can be seen in Dickens's Fagin, who in the first version of *Oliver Twist* is stamped throughout with the qualification of 'Jew', until the novelist, in consequence of the protests of a Jewish lady, Mrs. Davis, not merely cut out the insistence on the racial characteristic from the 1867 and later editions, substituting, in many cases, the word 'Fagin' for 'the Jew', but actually, in *Our Mutual Friend*, created the character of a good Jew.[173]

It was to the authoress of *Uncle Tom's Cabin*, champion of the negro race, that George Eliot dedicated *Daniel Deronda*, and to her she wrote a letter (October 29th, 1876)[174] which was partly quoted later in her introduction to the book:

As to the Jewish element in 'Deronda' I expected from first to last, in writing it, that it would create much stronger resistance, and even repulsion, than it has actually met with. But precisely because I felt that the usual attitude of Christians towards Jews is—I hardly know whether to say more impious or more stupid, when viewed in the light of their professed principles, I therefore felt urged to treat Jews with such sympathy and understanding as my nature and knowledge could attain to. . . . There is nothing I should care more to do, if it were possible, than to rouse the imagination of men and women to a vision of human claims in those races of their fellow-men who most differ from them in customs and beliefs.

The 'inability to find interest in any form of life' that is not familiar to us 'lies very close to the worst kind of irreligion' and is a sign of 'intellectual narrowness—in plain English . . . stupidity'. What the ideas then current in England on the subject of the Jews were, is illustrated by the conversation of Gwendolen's sisters in the house of Mrs. Davilow (chap. lviii): to those narrow British minds the idea of living Jews, existing independently from those in books, 'suggested a difference deep enough to be almost zoological, as of a strange race in Pliny's *Natural History* that might sleep under the shade of its own ears'. George Eliot actually brings it about that a fascinating English-woman, Gwendolen, throws herself at Deronda's feet like Mary Magdalene at the feet of Jesus (chap. lvii: 'I will bear any penance, I will lead any life you tell me. But you must not forsake me. You must be near'). But Deronda, who has something of the knight errant in his nature (chap.

xxviii), is an Ivanhoe who chooses Rebecca rather than Rowena. At the end of the novel the English, converted to an understanding of the Jews, are present at the wedding of Mirah and Deronda: 'Sir Hugo and Lady Mallinger had taken trouble to provide a complete equipment for Eastern travel' for the bridal couple, who were to visit the Israelite communities in those parts, to find out about their living conditions. To complete the casuistry of her theme, George Eliot in *Daniel Deronda* also combats the prejudice against mixed marriages, making a young Englishwoman of very good family defy the wishes of her relations and marry a genial Jewish musician, Klesmer (described by the girl's mother as 'a gipsy, a Jew, a mere bubble of the earth'; chap. xxii).

But, as its authoress noted, *Daniel Deronda* did not create that fierce resistance or repulsion in the English public that she had expected, had in fact hoped for (the more violent the fever, the more beneficial would have been the reaction): and she was forced regretfully to admit that readers usually 'cut the book up into scraps' and were interested in nothing but Gwendolen.[175] From the artistic point of view, we know that they were perfectly right.

* * * * *

More interesting to readers than her idealized, heroic characters, who, as has been remarked,[176] 'suffer from the unqualified approval' of their creator, were the characters who were in conflict with themselves; and it was precisely in the portrayal of imperfect souls that George Eliot excelled:

My artistic bent is directed not at all to the presentation of eminently irreproachable characters, but to the presentation of mixed human beings in such a way as to call forth tolerant judgment, pity, and sympathy.[177]

I wish less of our piety were spent on perfect goodness, and more given to real imperfect goodness.[178]

And, in the passage from *Adam Bede* (chap. xvii), forming part of George Eliot's declared programme with regard to realism in art, which we have quoted above:[179]

There are few prophets in the world; few sublimely beautiful women; few heroes. I can't afford to give all my love and reverence to such rarities: I want a great deal of those feelings for my everyday fellow-men, *etc.*

One side of George Eliot's work shows us the process of refinement and sublimation of character under life's trials: a Wordsworthian theme, as we have seen, which she co-ordinates with her own Comtist faith in the progress, the perfectibility of mankind. Cross[180] wrote of her: 'In her general attitude towards life George Eliot was neither optimist nor pessimist. She held to the middle term, which she invented for herself, of "meliorist".' But if the intention that animates her is to display the possibility of good and of the power of the will, the prevailing colour of her work looked at as a whole—the observation is P. Bourl'honne's[181] —is pessimistic, and the general impression that emerges is of the powerlessness of man against circumstances and of the checkmate of the will. Dyspeptic, inclined to a melancholy point of view,[182] afflicted with depression during the drafting of many of her novels (it was not until November 1876, in the decline of her life, that she wrote to Sara Hennell:[183] 'It is remarkable to me that I have entirely lost my *personal* melancholy.[184] I often, of course, have melancholy thoughts about the destinies of my fellow-creatures, but I am never in that *mood* of sadness which used to be my frequent visitant even in the midst of external happiness'), her attitude of mind sometimes approached the pessimism of Leopardi in *La Ginestra*[185]—an avowal of Nature's indifference, and an exhortation to mankind to make up for it by piety and reciprocal love. In *Adam Bede* (chap. xxvii) she wrote:

If it be true that Nature at certain moments seems charged with a presentiment of one individual lot, must it not also be true that she seems unmindful, unconscious at another? For there is no hour that has not its births of gladness and despair, no morning brightness that does not bring new sickness to desolation as well as new forces to genius and love. There are so many of us, and our lots are so different: what wonder that Nature's mood is often in harsh contrast with the great crisis of our lives? We are children of a large family, and must learn, as such children do, not to expect that our hurts will be made much of—to be content with little nurture and caressing, and help each other the more.

We are reminded of Leopardi's:

> ... Tutti fra se confederati estima
> Gli uomini, e tutti abbraccia
> Con vero amor, porgendo
> Valida e pronta ed aspettando aita
> Negli alterni perigli e nelle angosce
> Della guerra comune.[186]

Being accustomed to scientific analysis, George Eliot gave full weight to the influence of circumstances which put character to the test:[187]

There is a terrible coercion in our deeds which may first turn the honest man into a deceiver, and then reconcile him to the change; for this reason—that the second wrong presents itself to him in the guise of the only practicable right. The action which before commission has been seen with that blended common-sense and fresh untarnished feeling which is the healthy eye of the soul, is looked at afterwards with the lens of apologetic ingenuity, through which all things that men call beautiful and ugly are seen to be made up of textures very much alike. Europe adjusts itself to a *fait accompli*, and so does an individual character,—until the placid adjustment is disturbed by a convulsive retribution. No man can escape this vitiating effect of an offence against his own sentiment of right.

Circumstances exercise an insidious pressure; evil propagates itself like an infection:[188]

There is no sort of wrong deed of which a man can bear the punishment alone: you can't isolate yourself, and say that the evil which is in you shall not spread. Men's lives are as thoroughly blended with each other as the air they breathe: evil spreads as necessarily as disease.

George Eliot's works pay much attention to the study of 'diseases of the character': 'Character is not cut in marble —it is not something solid and unalterable. It is something living and changing, and many become diseased as our bodies do.'[189] And so, side by side with the souls which rise and are uplifted, such as Silas Marner, Adam Bede, Esther Lyon, side by side with those who, like Maggie, struggle between their own inclinations and the duty not to make others unhappy, and are triumphant, we have those which degenerate and become corrupted; and to describe their corruption George Eliot often finds powerful images, as for instance when, speaking of the slow process of defilement that had come about in the mind of Bulstrode, she writes (*Middlemarch*, chap. lxi): 'Mentally surrounded with that past again, Bulstrode had the same pleas,—indeed the years had been perpetually spinning them into intricate thickness, like masses of spider-webs padding the moral sensibility.' Bulstrode, Tito Melema, Donnithorne—they all try to justify themselves to themselves, and so, little by little, the germ of goodness there had been within them comes to be stifled.

For with George Eliot, as with Trollope, there are no absolutely wicked people; her sinners have their human, their amiable sides. The seducer Donnithorne, cause of Hetty's ruin, is no more wicked than was Colonel Osborne in *He Knew He Was Right* (1869), who caused so tragic a misunderstanding between the Trevelyans:[190]

Arthur Donnithorne had an agreeable confidence that his faults were all of a generous kind—impetuous, warm-blooded, leonine; never crawling, crafty, reptilian. It was not possible for Arthur Donnithorne to do anything mean, dastardly, or cruel. 'No, I'm a devil of a fellow for getting myself into a hobble, but I always take care the load shall fall on my own shoulders.' Unhappily there is no inherent poetical justice in hobbles, and they will sometimes obstinately refuse to inflict their worst consequences on the prime offender, in spite of his loudly-expressed wish. It was entirely owing to this deficiency in the scheme of things that Arthur had ever brought any into trouble besides himself. He was nothing, if not good-natured, and all his pictures of the future, when he should come into his estate, were made up of a prosperous, contented tenantry, adoring their landlord, who would be the model of an English gentleman—mansion in first-rate order, all elegance and high taste—jolly housekeeping, finest stud in Loamshire—purse open to all public objects—in short, everything as different as possible from what was now associated with the name of Donnithorne. . . .

You perceive that Arthur Donnithorne was 'a good fellow'—all his college friends thought him such: he couldn't bear to see anyone uncomfortable. . . . Whether he would have self-mastery enough to be always as harmless and purely beneficent as his good-nature led him to desire, was a question that no one had yet decided against him. . . . We use round, general, gentlemanly epithets about a young man of birth and fortune; and ladies, with that fine intuition which is the distinguishing attribute of their sex, see at once that he is 'nice'. The chances are that he will go through life without scandalising any one; a sea-worthy vessel that no one would refuse to insure. Ships, certainly, are liable to casualties, which sometimes make terribly evident some flaw in their construction, that would never have been discoverable in smooth water; and many a 'good fellow', through a disastrous combination of circumstances, has undergone a little betrayal. But we have no fair ground for entertaining unfavourable auguries concerning Arthur Donnithorne, who this morning proves himself capable of a prudent resolution founded on conscience. One thing is clear: Nature has taken care that he shall never go far astray with perfect comfort and satisfaction to himself: he will never get beyond that borderland of sin, where he will be perpetually harassed by assaults from the other side of the boundary. He will never be a courtier of Vice, and wear her orders in his button-hole.[191]

The bitterly ironical tone of this portrait of Donnithorne is lowered in the description of Tito Melema, the 'bad lot' in *Romola*. He, too, is not an entirely evil character, but has amiable sides to his nature which had at first procured him the affection of Baldassare Calvo; he hates the sight of blood and has an instinctive repugnance for spectacles of death and pain (*Romola*, chap. lx), and he acts like a tender father to Tessa's children; but his talent for dissimulation, favoured by circumstances, brings him to ruin; he manages to convince himself that he has a right to make use, for his own purposes, of the jewels confided to him by Baldassare to ransom him from slavery, and this sophism becomes, in his mind, 'as active as a virulent acid, eating its rapid way through all the tissues of sentiment' (chap. xi). And so this fascinating, cultivated, pleasure-loving young Greek becomes a traitor, a traitor to his adoptive father, a traitor to the various parties to which he lends his services, a traitor to his wife Romola and a deceiver of Tessa, the simple country girl who becomes his concubine. His reaction is characteristic when, in circumstances suitable to a romantic novel, Baldassare turns up again right under his nose. He could have recognized him and easily obtained his freedom, now that he was in Florence amongst the prisoners of the French. But Tito Melema 'had no sense that there was strength and safety in truth; the only strength he trusted to lay in his ingenuity and his dissimulation' (chap. xxiii). He 'was experiencing that inexorable law of human souls that we prepare ourselves for sudden deeds by the reiterated choice of good or evil which gradually determines character'. Nor, on the other hand, does he think of 'ridding himself' of Baldassare; 'his dread generated no active malignity, and he would still have been glad not to give pain to any mortal'.

If he had only not been wanting in the presence of mind necessary to recognize Baldassare under that surprise!—it would have been happier for him on all accounts; for he still winced under the sense that he was deliberately inflicting suffering on his father: he would very much have preferred that Baldassare should be prosperous and happy. But he had left himself no second path now: there could be no conflict any longer: the only thing he had to do was to take care of himself.[192]

And, farther on in the book (chap. xxxix), when Tito denies Baldassare, who presents himself at a supper-party in the Rucellai gardens:

He had never yet done an act of murderous cruelty even to the smallest animal that could utter a cry, but at that moment he would have been capable of treading the breath from a smiling child for the sake of his own safety.

The study of the gradual debasement of Tito's soul is reminiscent of similar studies in Hawthorne (*Ethan Brand*, for instance); and indeed the whole atmosphere of *Romola*, and especially the appearance of Baldassare like a ghost of the past, a Nemesis incarnate, recalls the mysterious apparition that pursues Miriam in *Transformation* (*The Marble Faun*)—which was published in 1860, three years before *Romola*. The comparison might be carried farther, though perhaps not without forcing it, if one sees in the metamorphosis of the fascinating Tito, creature of the Renaissance, into a reprobate, a reflection of the metamorphosis of the pagan Donatello, in Hawthorne's novel, into a moral man, under the stimulus of a crime. The two authors have in common a subtlety in the study of the successive degrees of moral transformation, a faith in the uplifting force of suffering, and a puritan love of allegory of which we shall later see examples in George Eliot.

No character is wholly good or wholly bad: circumstances will develop this or that side, but the germ of goodness is extremely delicate. Of the old miser Featherstone we read in *Middlemarch* (chap. xxxiv):

If any one will here contend that there must have been traits of goodness in old Featherstone, I will not presume to deny this; but I must observe that goodness is of a modest nature, easily discouraged, and when much elbowed in early life by unabashed vices, is apt to retire into extreme privacy, so that it is more easily believed in by those who construct a selfish old gentleman theoretically, than by those who form the narrower judgements based on his personal acquaintance.

Gwendolen, in *Deronda*, has criminal tendencies, and her appearance of pale, serpent-like beauty, Lamia-like, and her long, narrow eyes (chap. i) ally her to the type of cold *femme fatale* which was to be met with so often in the Decadents, towards the end of the century. As a child, she had strangled a canary which had exasperated her by interrupting her singing with its shrill warblings. Yet with all this her nature was not ruthless. The consciousness of evil, of having contributed to, if not actually caused, the drowning of the odious Grandcourt, was to act in her as a leaven of redemption, in much the same way as in one of Hawthorne's characters.

Analysis of the conflicts of conscience is tantamount to saying formulation of a moral casuistry; and this pervades the work of George Eliot to such an extent that her main defect as a novelist has often been considered to consist in the heaviness, the pedagogic aridity with which she usually conducts such casuistry. The instructional aspect is often underlined at the end of her novels. We are to learn from *The Mill on the Floss* that modest, quiet virtues are the most beneficial, and that the wise man is the perfectly balanced man,[193] as Wordsworth had already concluded in the *Ode to Duty*; we see in Adam Bede the model of a hard-working, intelligent man who accepts life as it is and has a deep respect for the social organism, and in Felix Holt another man of the people who is a paragon of loyalty to his own social class, an incarnation of the dignity of labour. What do the two marriages of Dorothea in *Middlemarch* illustrate? 'They were the mixed results of young and noble impulse struggling amidst the conditions of an imperfect social state, in which great feelings will often take the aspect of error, and great faith the aspect of illusion.' Even more is this novel a handbook of matrimonial casuistry. The Rosamond-Lydgate couple illustrates an opposite case to that of Dorothea and Casaubon: in the latter, an idealistic woman had sought her own spiritual elevation by uniting herself with a man whom she revered as a genius and who then revealed himself as an arid pedant, in the former a woman who longed for luxury and success had united herself to Lydgate in the expectation of material advantages and had destroyed, in him, the seeds of a higher vocation. Dorothea, Rosamond, Harriet Bulstrode illustrate different types of reactions of wives to husbands. Gwendolen's choice in *Deronda* (Book IV: *Gwendolen gets her Choice*), Esther's choice in *Felix Holt* (chap. xlix) between the mountain air of a pure love and a compromise with circumstances, are other lessons in casuistry. Further instructive examples are provided by Lydgate's uncertainties in face of corrupting temptations (instead of voting for the worthiest candidate as hospital chaplain, he votes for the candidate put up by the powerful, useful Bulstrode, and later accepts a large sum of money to make him close an eye to Bulstrode's part in hastening the death of the man who is blackmailing him, Raffles). Sometimes a dilemma put before the reader at the beginning of a novel allows him to foresee the conclusion and takes away from the interest of the story. Thus, from the moment when Mirah and Gwendolen are both waiting for Deronda's next move, we guess which of the two alternatives he will choose. And when Deronda stands at the parting of the ways between Mordecai and Gwendolen, who does not guess which way the scales will turn? (*Daniel Deronda*, chap. xlv):

There was a foreshadowing of some painful collision: on the one side of Mordecai's dying hand on him, with all the ideals and prospects it aroused; on the other this fair creature in silk and gems, with her hidden wound and her self-dread, making a trustful effort to lean and find herself sustained. It was as if he had a vision of himself besought with outstretched arms and cries, while he was caught by the waves and compelled to mount the vessel bound for a far-off coast.

*   *   *   *   *

This last image, which occurs again in similar terms elsewhere in *Deronda*,[194] invites us to linger for a moment over the types of emblematic image that are recurrent in George Eliot's work. Rarely are these images enlivened by poetic imagination. More often they are images from the books of emblems which for two centuries past had formed no mean part of the pious literature even of Protestants.[195] They are clear images, in which allegory and the thing it suggests fit closely together: the terms are reversible, but what *tertium quid* springs forth from the translation of a situation into an allegorical cipher?

In *The Mill on the Floss* (Book VI, chap. xiii) Stephen urges Maggie to unite herself with him in marriage, and points to the current that is carrying their boat down the river:

We never thought of being alone together again: it has all been done by others. See how the tide is carrying us out—away from all those unnatural bonds that we have been trying to make faster round us—and trying in vain. . . . Maggie listened—passing from her startled wonderment to the yearning after that belief, that the tide was doing it all—that she might glide along with the swift, silent stream, and not struggle any more.

The image of the stream occurs again in *Felix Holt* (chap. xxvii):

So our lives glide on: the river ends we don't know where, and the sea begins, and then there is no more jumping ashore.

In *Adam Bede* (chap. xxxi) another nautical comparison is applied to Hetty:

Yes, the actions of a little trivial soul like Hetty's, struggling amidst the serious, sad destinies of a human being *are* strange. So are the motions of a little vessel without ballast tossed about on a stormy sea. How pretty it looked with its particoloured sail in the sunlight, moored in the quiet bay! 'Let that man bear the loss who loosed it from its moorings'. But that will not save the vessel—the pretty thing that might have been a lasting joy.

We have already seen the comparison of Donnithorne's soul to a ship made only for smooth waters. Elsewhere in *Adam Bede* (chap. xxxv) George Eliot draws an emblem of the troubles of girls like Hetty, which take place behind the scenes in a countryside of joyful aspect, from an image of certain roads on the Continent (in southern Germany, for instance) where, amongst sunny fields, there is to be seen, here and there, at the edge of the road, a Crucifix. 'If there came a traveller to this world who knew nothing of the story of man's life upon it, this image of agony would seem to him strangely out of place in the midst of this joyous nature.' In the same novel again (chap. xlv) it seems to Hetty, as she is running away with the intention of getting rid of her baby, that the moon is looking at her out of the clouds in an unusual way: she is fascinated by the moon, one would say, just as Raskolnikov was while going upstairs in the house where his crime had been committed: the moon becomes, as it were, an image of remorse.

Silas Marner is simply an allegorical fairy-tale: Silas finds the gold of the little girl's hair instead of the material gold he had been longing for. He comes back to his cottage and thinks he sees gold on the floor in front of the fireplace (chap. xii):

Gold!—his own gold—brought back to him as mysteriously as it had been taken away! He felt his heart begin to beat violently, and for a few moments he was unable to stretch out his hand and grasp the restored treasure. The heap of gold seemed to glow and get larger beneath his agitated gaze. He leaned forward at last, and stretched forth his hand; but instead of the hard coin with the familiar resisting outline, his fingers encountered soft warm curls.

The metaphor is worthy of a school-teacher; the spiritual phenomenon has to be indicated by the image: just as gold has a cold, hard outline, so the child's hair feels soft and warm; and this leads us to the moral, which is that cold avarice, inadequate nourishment for a human soul, is to be replaced by love of one's neighbour, which is soft and warm.

33. SIR EDWIN LANDSEER. Fido's bath

REX   LUDOVICUS   LUDOVICUS REX

AN HISTORICAL STUDY

34. Illustration to Thackeray's *Meditations at Versailles*

In *Middlemarch* the avenue of lime-trees that can be seen from Dorothea's window, leading towards the sunset, becomes a symbol of the idea of progress.[196]

In *Daniel Deronda* (chap. xlviii) the passing of Gwendolen from the shade into the sunlight is accompanied by a movement of her soul towards relief from oppressive feeling. Later on (chap. lxiii) the effect of the ardent words of Deronda, hitherto so reserved, upon Mirah, is like that of 'a breaking of day around her which might show her other facts unlike her forebodings in the darkness'. And shortly afterwards (at the end of the chapter) an image which recalls a famous one of William Cowper's, of the fawn saved from the arrows of the huntsmen, serves to illustrate a psychological situation in which Mirah finds herself; and this is reinforced by the comparison of Deronda's words to 'a soft warm rain of blossoms'.

In *Middlemarch* (chap. lxxxiii) a thunderstorm breaks out during a conversation between Dorothea and Ladislaw: 'While he was speaking there came a vivid flash of lightning which lit each of them up for the other—and the light seemed to be the terror of a hopeless love.' Deronda's song on the river, 'Nessun maggior dolore...' becomes symbolic of the tragedy of Mirah; Gwendolen's gambling at *roulette* at the beginning of the novel is an emblem of her attitude towards life (chap. lvi: 'I wanted to make my gain out of another's loss'); the coat of mail that Tito Melema puts on to protect himself becomes a symbol of his hardened soul. Sometimes the comparison is as complicated as a conceit in a seventeenth-century sermon, as in chapter xxvii of *Middlemarch*:

An eminent philosopher among my friends, who can dignify even your ugly furniture by lifting it into the serene light of science, has shown me this pregnant little fact. Your pier-glass or extensive surface of polished steel made to be rubbed by a housemaid, will be minutely and multitudinously scratched in all directions; but place now against it a lighted candle as a centre of illumination, and lo! the scratches will seem to arrange themselves in a fine series of concentric circles round that little sun. It is demonstrable that the scratches are going everywhere impartially, and it is only your candle which produces the flattering illusion of a concentric arrangement, its light falling with an exclusive optical selection. These things are a parable. The scratches are events, and the candle is the egoism of any person now absent. . . .

Sometimes the images have an exquisitely Victorian and slightly grotesque flavour, like the then popular emblems of Mrs. Gatty or of G. S. Cautley, vicar of Nettleden, for whom—

> A fish, a ship, the night and day
> Some Christian truth declare,
> And e'en the winging crows display
> Black crosses in the air.[197]

Dorothea (*Middlemarch*, chap. lv) is 'still in that time of youth when the eyes with their long full lashes look out after their rain of tears unsoiled and unwearied as a freshly-opened passion-flower'. The souls of Hetty and Donnithorne (*Adam Bede*, chap. xii) come close together:

> Such young unfurrowed souls roll to meet each other like two velvet peaches that touch softly and are at rest; they mingle as easily as two brooklets that ask for nothing but to entwine themselves and ripple with ever-interlacing curves in the leafiest hiding-places.

Images and allegories of this kind reveal a pedestrian, a Biedermeier imagination; no light of poetry ever emanates from them; the very sense of fate, as V. S. Pritchett has written,[198] was, in George Eliot, 'prosaic, not majestic; prosaic in the sense of unpoetical'. And whatever Mr. Leavis may say of the inferiority of Hardy[199] in comparison with George Eliot, in one thing he is far superior to her— in having been able to bestow a sinister and poetical majesty upon that figure of Fate which dominates his work, clumsily introduced though it may sometimes be, from the logical point of view.

The images of George Eliot, then, are neither one thing nor another; they are semi-poetical or downright prosaic, just as her characters are neither wholly good nor wholly bad; and the latter are so, not because she is incapable of rising to heights, but because observation of human nature becomes, with her, ever closer and more precise, though still directed along fixed lines of casuistry.[200] We shall never find in her those rapt, inspired images which throw a beam of light upon an entire situation. Her rhythm is pedestrian, it is the measured step of a solid, grey phalanx. Not that she feels no inspiration: how, otherwise, could she have been a novelist, and a novelist of her stature? Cross wrote:[201] 'She told me that, in all that she considered her best writing, there was a "not herself" which took possession of her, and that she felt her own personality to be merely the instrument through which this spirit, as it were, was acting.' And he adds: 'With this sense of "possession", it is easy to imagine what the cost to the author must have been of writing books, each of which has its tragedy.' But this spirit which 'possessed' her was exacting, severe, and left no margin for joy. She herself confessed:[202]

> We have no sorrow just now, except my constant inward 'worrit' of unbelief in any future of good work on my part. Everything I do seems poor and trivial in the doing; and when it is quite gone from me, and seems no longer my own, then I rejoice in it and think it fine. That is the history of my life.

And one often feels, indeed, from her pages, that George Eliot did not compose with joy.[203] This does not affect the solidity of her work, but it takes away from it the glow, the happy tension, the temperature, in fact, from which alone are born images that strike the mark with the speed of lightning. Her sky is never, by nature, the sky of St. Lawrence's Eve, furrowed by shooting stars; I should say that her sky is also wanting in transparency. Hers is the serene sky of a fine English night, which is never bright and pellucid: it is an effective serenity, but it is prosaic, not poetic. Or, to make use of an image from Milton's *Comus*, her 'sable cloud' is very rarely wont to 'turn forth her silver lining on the night', and 'cast a gleam'.

*　　*　　*　　*　　*

Just as George Eliot is akin to Trollope in what may be termed her 'meliorist' conception of character, so is she also in her attitude to feminine beauty. Much has been said of the severity with which George Eliot treats beautiful women, and people have seen in it the reflection of a highly personal irritation (beautiful, she herself could truly not be called), or a transference of punishment for the sense of guilt felt by the authoress herself[204]—apart from the more general, puritan suspicion of beauty as the Devil's bait. The description of Hetty who, in *Adam Bede* (chap. vii), personifies the foolish, frivolous beauty that leads to disaster, is written with a caustic pen:

> There are various orders of beauty, causing men to make fools of themselves in various styles, from the desperate to the sheepish; but there is one order of beauty which seems made to turn the heads not only of men, but of all intelligent mammals, even of women. It is a beauty like that of kittens, or very small downy ducks making gentle rippling noises with their soft bills, or babies just beginning to toddle and to engage in conscious mischief—a beauty with which you can never be angry, but that you feel ready to crush for inability to comprehend the state of mind into which it throws you. Hetty Sorrel's was that sort of beauty.

Obvious prettiness conceals danger: 'Hetty's was a spring-tide beauty; it was the beauty of young frisking things, round-limbed, gambolling, circumventing you by a false air of innocence.' George Eliot describes her charming attitudes and movements while she is making butter, with an accompanying play of pouting lips and dark eyes. And she insists upon presenting the girl to us as devoid of any warmth of feeling, and upon underlining her horror in face of the fact that this pretty shape is indeed that of a woman, that is, of a moral being. Here is Hetty examining her ear-rings (chap. xxii):

> Perhaps water-nixies, and such lovely things without souls, have these little round holes in their ears by nature, ready to hang jewels in. And Hetty must be one of them: it is too painful to think that she is a woman, with a woman's destiny before her—a woman spinning in young ignorance a light web of folly and vain hopes which may one day close round her and press upon her, a rancorous poisoned garment, changing all at once her fluttering, trivial butter-fly sensations into a life of deep human anguish.

George Eliot insists several times upon the comparison with a kitten, with a round, soft pet animal (chap. xxxvii: 'Hetty had the luxurious nature of a round, soft-coated pet animal'). Akin to Hetty is Tessa in *Romola*; and, in *Middle-march*, the lovely Rosamond, luxury-loving, superficial, in-different to her husband's nobler aspirations, is also com-pared to a 'water-nixie' (chap. lxiv) and to a cat (chap. xvi: she touches her plaits of hair with a gesture 'as pretty as any movements of a kitten's paw'), as well as to a snake (symbol of the tempting, destructive power that she exercises over Lydgate); and certain lively movements of the serpent-like Gwendolen (*Deronda*, chap. xxxi) recall those of a kitten that 'will not sit quiet to be petted'. Gwendolen is caught kissing her own reflection in the mirror (chap. ii), Hetty recovers for a moment from her distress (*Adam Bede*, chap. xxxvii) and kisses her own arms 'with the passionate love of life'. Beautiful women, with George Eliot, are generally silly, superficial, insensitive; the tragedy of human life lies precisely in the capacity of beautiful forms to have a signi-ficance that by far transcends the being they enclose, in the same way that the words of a genius have a wider meaning than the thought that prompted them (*Adam Bede*, chap. xxxiii). 'To be permissibly beautiful,' Graham Hough has wittily written,[205] 'a woman must be a Methodist saint or a drowning Jewess.'

But if one recalls Trollope's estimation of physical beauty (the irresistible Madame Neroni, the statuesque Griselda Grantly, the splendidly handsome Burgo Fitzgerald),[206] the intimate personal reasons to which George Eliot's aversion to beauty has been ascribed lose something of their validity. All the more so, since the discredit under which good-looking people labour is contrasted, both in George Eliot and in Trollope, with the exaltation of the humble character, whose endowments shrink from any shameless exhibitionism. Mary Garth, in *Middlemarch* (chap. xl), a good, virtuous girl, has few attractions:

If you want to know more particularly how Mary looked, ten to one you will see a face like hers in the crowded street to-morrow, if you are there on the watch: she will not be among those daughters of Zion who are haughty, and walk with stretched-out necks and wanton eyes, mincing as they go: let all those pass, and fix your eyes on some small plump brownish person of firm but quiet carriage, who looks about her, but does not suppose that anybody is looking at her. If she has a broad face and square brow, well-marked eye-brows and curly dark hair, a certain expression of amusement in her glance which her mouth keeps the secret of, and for the rest features entirely insignificant—take that ordinary but not disagreeable person for a portrait of Mary Garth. If you made her smile, she would show you perfect little teeth; if you made her angry, she would not raise her voice, but would probably say one of the bitterest things you have ever tasted the flavour of; if you did her a kindness, she would never forget it.

Mrs. Vincy's surprise (chap. lxiii) when confronted with her son's fiancée is similar to Archdeacon Grantly's at the sight of Grace Crawley in Trollope's *The Last Chronicle of Barset*: 'Mrs. Vincy . . . looked at Mary's little figure, rough wavy hair, and visage quite without lilies and roses, and wondered.' In *Deronda* (chap. vii) Mrs. Gascoigne says: 'There are things in Gwendolen I cannot reconcile myself to. My Anna is worth two of her, with all her beauty and talent.'

We have already seen how, for George Eliot, even an uninteresting or ugly landscape can, in a certain light, be transfigured, and we have noted her liking for the Dutch painters, who had been able to perceive the beauty of ordinary things. This does not imply that she did not also feel admiration for a kind of absolute beauty. Her tastes, in this direction, were for the monumental, the severe, the weighty. We have seen how simple clothes gave to Dorothea the dignity of a quotation from the Bible. 'The Bible and our elder English poets', says Cross,[207] 'best suited the organ-like tones of [George Eliot's] voice, which required, for their full effect, a certain solemnity and majesty of rhythm. Her reading of Milton was especially fine.' The Temple of Neptune at Paestum seemed to her 'the finest thing . . . we had yet seen in Italy'.[208] Dorothea makes her think of a Christian Antigone or Ariadne, of a Saint Barbara (*Middlemarch*, chap. x)—obviously the one painted by Palma Vecchio, in Santa Maria Formosa at Venice, of which she wrote in her diary:[209] 'It is an almost unique presentation of a hero-woman, standing in calm preparation for martyrdom, without the slightest air of pietism, yet with the expression of a mind filled with serious conviction.' Her taste for the monumental led her to admire even the

colossal statue of Bavaria by Schwanthaler at Munich:[210]
'I have never seen anything, even in ancient sculpture, of
a more awful beauty than this dark colossal head, looking
out from a background of pure, pale-blue sky.' An impression of solemnity, also, emanates from Deronda's mother,
although in this case there is no reference to any particular
artist (Reynolds's Michelangelesque portrait of Mrs.
Siddons as the Tragic Muse comes to mind): 'In her dusky
flame-coloured garment, she looked like a dreamed visitant
from some region of departed mortals' (*Deronda*, chap. liii).
The noble pose taken up by Grandcourt beside the hearth
reminds her of one of Moroni's aristocratic portraits
(*Deronda*, chap. xxviii); and the contrast between the
figures of Deronda and Mordecai recalls Titian's *Tribute
Money* (chap. xl). On the other hand she found that
Raphael's early Madonnas had a 'somewhat stupid expression' (*Mill on the Floss*, chap. ii).

George Eliot's artistic tastes are reflected in the prints
that adorn Mrs. Meyrick's drawing-room (*Deronda*, chap.
xx)—Dürer's *Melancholy*, Michelangelo's prophets and
sibyls, Raphael's *School of Athens*, Holbein, Rembrandt.
Of foreign poets, she was impressed particularly by Dante;
she constantly quotes him in *Daniel Deronda*, and Deronda
himself is compared (chap. xxxvi), for his gravity, to the
spiriti magni . . . con occhi tardi e gravi of Canto IV of the
Inferno. In the same novel Leopardi's song 'O patria mia'
is sung, to the music of Leo; and Rossetti's translation of
Guinizelli's song 'Al cor gentil . . .' is quoted (chap. lxi).
Her great favourite was Molière; she considered *Le Misanthrope* 'the finest, most complete production *of its kind* in
the world'.[211]

George Eliot shares the predilection for Dutch painting
with Thackeray and Trollope, and like them tends towards
genre painting in her novels. Mr. Pritchett has written:[212]

When she wrote of the peasants, the craftsmen, the yeomen, the
clergy and squires of Warwickshire, George Eliot was writing out
of childhood, from that part of her life which never betrayed her
or any of the Victorians. The untutored sermons of Dinah have the
same pastoral quality as the poutings of Hetty at the butter churn,
the harangues of Mrs. Poyser at her cooking, or the remonstrances

of Adam Bede at his carpenter's bench. In the mid-Victorian England of the railway and the drift to the towns, George Eliot was harking back to the last of the yeomen, among whom she was born and who brought out the warmth, the humour, the strength of her nature. We seem to be looking at one of Morland's pictures, at any of those domestic or rustic paintings of the Dutch school, where every leaf of the elm trees or the limes is painted, every gnarl on the bark inscribed, every rut followed with fidelity.

Besides the Dutch painters, naturally, and—less naturally —Morland (a pastoral painter, certainly, but with a pallid idyllic flavour), one is reminded of the nineteenth-century *genre* painters, and not only the English ones, who infused sentiment and pathos into pictures of this type. The tavern conversations in *Silas Marner* and *Felix Holt*, the successful groupings of local characters, the old women's chatter and the parish gossip may make one think of Brouwer, of Teniers, of Jan Steen; but only a nineteenth-century *genre* painter could have produced the equivalent of the scene (in *Silas Marner*, chap. xii) in which Godfrey Cass's wife goes off into a fatal sleep in the snow while her little girl opens her eyes wide to the cold starlight; or that other scene in which Silas comes into his hovel and thinks that he sees gold, the gold being the child's hair; or the scene (in *The Mill on the Floss*, Book V, chap. vi) when Tom tells his father of the money he has earned, and the father bursts into sobs, and thinks of getting his own back on Wakem, and wants to celebrate the event with a glass of brandy; or the scene in *Amos Barton* with Amos at the bedside of his dying wife, or that other one, of the funeral (chap. ix), with the afflicted father and, beside him, the boy 'with great rosy cheeks, and wide open blue eyes, looking first up at Mr. Cleves and then down at the coffin, and thinking he and Chubby would play at that when they got home'; and finally the melancholy group of Amos and his daughter Patty, now grown up, revisiting the mother's grave twenty years afterwards. In England an Augustus Egg, a Peter Fendi in Austria, might have provided the pictorial equivalents of such scenes. Think, too, of Lisbeth, in *Adam Bede*, making the preparations for her husband's funeral, or of Mr. Irwine in his breakfast-room (*Adam Bede*, chap. xvi):

It was a small low room, belonging to the old part of the house—dark with the sombre covers of the books that lined the walls; yet it looked very cheery this morning as Arthur reached the open window. For the morning sun fell aslant on the great glass globe with gold fish in it, which stood on a scagliola pillar in front of the ready-spread bachelor breakfast-table, and by the side of this breakfast-table was a group which would have made any room enticing. In the crimson damask easy-chair sat Mr. Irwine, with that radiant freshness which he always had when he came from his morning toilet; his finely-formed plump white hand was playing along Juno's brown curly back; and close to Juno's tail, which was wagging with calm matronly pleasure, the two brown pups were rolling over each other in an ecstatic duet of worrying noises. On a cushion a little removed sat Pug, with the air of a maiden lady, who looked on these familiarities as animal weaknesses, which she made as little show as possible of observing. On the table, at Mr. Irwine's elbow, lay the first volume of the Foulis Aeschylus, which Arthur knew well by sight; and the silver coffee-pot, which Carroll was bringing in, sent forth a fragrant steam which completed the delights of a bachelor breakfast.

The Bachelor's Breakfast might well be the title of this little *genre* picture.

The effect which Donnithorne's letter produces upon Hetty is not observed directly, but in the reflection of a mirror, as in a Dutch painting (*Adam Bede*, chap. xxxi):

Slowly Hetty had read this letter; and when she looked up from it there was the reflection of a blanched face in the old dim glass—a white marble face with rounded childish forms, but with something sadder than a child's pain in it. Hetty did not see the face —she saw nothing—she only felt that she was cold and sick and trembling. . . .

How many nineteenth-century painters tried to portray the effect of bad news upon the tragic face of a woman bending over a letter! More sophisticated, and worthy of a minutely exact Pre-Raphaelite (e.g. Holman Hunt in *The Awakening Conscience*) is the picture in *Deronda* (chap. xxxi) of Gwendolen who, when the casket of diamonds which her rival has sent her with a terrible letter has fallen to the floor and the diamonds have been scattered, falls back in her chair in a fit of hysterics:

She could not see the reflections of herself then: they were like so many women petrified white; but coming near herself you might have seen the tremor in her lips and hands. . . . Truly here were poisoned gems, and the poison had entered into this poor young creature.

Title of the picture: *The Poisoned Diamonds*. In each diamond is the bewitched image of the woman cursed by her rival: the figure is a symbol.

Of a humorous kind, on the other hand, is the scene in which Bartle Massey (*Adam Bede*, chap. xxi) is teaching grown-up labourers to write: the gentle expression of the schoolmaster, the studies of the various grimaces of his pupils; or the series of astonished, worried faces of those attending the funeral of the old miser Featherstone at the appearance of an 'unknown mourner', in *Middlemarch* (chap. xxxv) (title: *The Unknown Relation*), and, immediately after the funeral, the reading of the will and the sentiments expressed upon the countenances of the listeners (will-reading, as a subject, is reminiscent of Wilkie or Danhauser); or Mr. Brooke's and Mr. Dagley's dogs (*Middlemarch*, chap. xxxix), Monk and Fag, who transfer the hostility between their masters on to the animal plane, and while Mr. Brooke warns and Mr. Dagley protests, Fag starts growling at his master's heels when the latter raises his voice, and Monk also draws close 'in silent dignified watch'. Mary Garth scolding the dog (*Middlemarch*, chap. lii) forms the subject of another tasty little *genre* picture: the dog persists in walking on a sheet upon which Mary is scattering rose-petals, and the girl takes the dog's forepaws in one hand and holds up the forefinger of the other, while the dog frowns and looks embarrassed. Another dog, in *Daniel Deronda* (chap. lii), sits beside the tea-table round which is 'a complete bouquet of young faces', and 'with large eyes on the alert' regards 'the whole scene as an apparatus for supplying his allowance of milk'.

*　　*　　*　　*　　*

In such *genre* pictures George Eliot comes close to Dickens, to Thackeray, and to Trollope. We have already pointed out how much she admired Thackeray as the most powerful of contemporary novelists, and how close she came to him in the theme that Thackeray developed in the *Small-Beer Chronicle*: 'There are few prophets in the world; few sublimely beautiful women; few heroes', or: 'A great deal of life goes on without strong passion' (*Deronda*, chap. xv)—in the acceptance, in fact, of the 'down to earth', of the banality of everyday life. Her affinities with Trollope are even more noteworthy, as we have had occasion to observe. Just as readers of Trollope's *The Warden* imagined him to be very familiar with such circles, whereas he confessed that he had never, at that time, been on terms of intimate friendship with any clergyman and had built up his archdeacon simply by an effort of his own moral consciousness,[213] so there were some who, on reading *Scenes of Clerical Life*, thought that their author must actually be a clergyman.[214] Clever, like Trollope, at giving an impression of minutely observed reality; capable, like him, of seeing the passing beauty of a commonplace person or landscape, she is also closely related to him in her study of difficult or desperate matrimonial situations.

The Grandcourt-Gwendolen part of *Deronda* has been very highly praised, so much so, indeed, that Mr. Leavis[215] could even say that 'there is, lost under that damning title, an actual great novel to be extricated. And to extricate it for separate publication as *Gwendolen Harleth* seems to me the most likely way of getting recognition for it.'[216] But Trollope, in the story of Glencora and in *He Knew He Was Right*, had portrayed matrimonial situations of equal force. Indeed Grandcourt in *Deronda* behaves to his wife in a cold, tyrannical manner reminiscent of Louis Trevelyan in *He Knew He Was Right*, and the words that Gwendolen says to him (chap. liv): 'You had better leave me at liberty to speak with any one I like. It would be better for you', might have issued from the mouth of Mrs. Trevelyan. And if we feel that George Eliot surpasses Trollope in tragic intensity (though the situation in Trollope's novel comes very near to tragedy), we must not, on the other hand, forget that *He Knew He Was Right* belongs to 1869 and *Daniel Deronda* to 1876, and that before Trollope no one in England had studied the special hell of an unhappy marriage with so much truth. If we wish to push the comparison farther, it has to be pointed out that Trollope, with surer taste, did not burden his novel with a plot (the Jewish complication) which is a mere dead weight.

And George Eliot's novels contain far more dead portions than Trollope's; in this she is second only, amongst great novelists, to Dickens, and by reason of the same vice (to which Trollope is much less subject) of indulging the Victorian vogue for the sensational and the melodramatic.[217] This vice becomes accentuated in George Eliot from *Romola* onwards, but even *Mr. Gilfil's Love-Story*, *The Lifted Veil*, and parts of the novels previous to *Romola* show this tendency; and when George Eliot goes too far in this direction there is not much difference between her and the authoresses of those 'novelettes' of which England is full (*The Lifted Veil* and chapter xxi of *Felix Holt* might easily be translated into strip cartoons).

It cannot be said that George Eliot was prolific in the invention of plots: she moves, in fact, in a rather restricted circle of subjects, not all of them her own. The situation of Dorothea at the feet of old Casaubon, while Casaubon's cousin, Will Ladislaw, falls in love with her, is similar to the episode, in *David Copperfield*, of young Mrs. Strong and her old pedant husband;[218] and the brilliant cousin Jack Maldon, in love with her, anticipates Ladislaw. *David Copperfield* is also brought to our minds by the plot of *Adam Bede*. Adam, the working man, is in desperation, wishing to come to Hetty's support, while Arthur Donnithorne, the gentleman, fails to appear at the trial and seems to be abandoning her (later, it is true, having learned of Hetty's tragedy, he obtains the commutation of her sentence and himself departs on a journey of expiation). One is reminded of the unscrupulous Steerforth who seduces Little Em'ly, while the honest working man, her betrothed, goes so far as to sacrifice his own life in order to save the wretched seducer from the shipwreck. The very theme of honest working-man and wicked gentleman bears the stamp of Dickens. Hetty's infanticide is probably a reflection of the story of Gretchen which, as we have seen, made a deep impression upon George Eliot. In *Felix Holt* we have another man of the people compared favourably with a gentleman, Harold Transome, who, though he redeems himself at the end with a noble gesture, is nevertheless throughout the novel a living accusation against the superficiality and unscrupulousness of the upper classes. Mrs. Holt is a Dickensian figure; Dickensian, too, is the Meyrick family in *Deronda*; so is the blackmailer Raffles in *Middlemarch*, as Mr. Leavis has recognized,[219] and so is the whole plot with Bulstrode as its centre. Dark family secrets, recognition-scenes, marks of identification, all these are old trappings in the repertory of narrative, which the sensational novelists, and Dickens in particular, had brought back into fashion. And George Eliot, as we shall soon see, makes all too much use of them.

To return, however, to the limited nature of her inventive imagination, let us look at a few more cases. In *Romola* Baldassare Calvo has adopted little Tito Melema, hoping to be loved by him. 'I was a loving fool. . . . I took a helpless child and fostered him; and I watched him as he grew, to see if he would care for me only a little—care for *me* over and above the good he got from me' (chap. xxx). With exactly the same intention Silas Marner had adopted the little girl, and, differently from Baldassare, had received affection in return. And Rufus Lyon and his putative daughter Esther, and the circumstances in which he finds her, again recall *Silas Marner*, while the marriage of Rufus with the woman who yields to him out of pure gratitude, as her saviour, is analogous to that of Mr. Gilfil (in *Mr. Gilfil's Love-Story*) with Tina, to whose broken soul this good parson restores peace; in both cases the woman, worn out by trouble, languishes and dies at an early age. We hear, in the disillusionment of Baldassare, the same voice of thwarted nature calling for justice that we hear in the jealousy of Casaubon.[220] The exhortations of Savonarola's followers to women to divest themselves of vain ornaments, and their taking away of Tessa's baubles, re-echoes, against a different historical background, Dinah's preaching against vanities in *Adam Bede*; and Bessy who, ashamed of her own frivolity, casts away her ear-rings, is reincarnated in Tessa (is the similar sound of their names due to pure chance?). Gwendolen marries Grandcourt, who already has a mistress,

Lydia Glasher, with children; Romola marries Tito, who is secretly bound to Tessa, by whom he too has children. And in *Silas Marner* Godfrey Cass has a secret tie (like Grandcourt) all the time he is paying court to Miss Lammeter. Later she, having become Godfrey Cass's wife, wants to adopt the daughter of the other woman, just as Romola, at the end of the novel, acts as mother to Lillo, the son of Tito and Tessa. Gwendolen feels remorse at the death of her husband, whom she had longed to kill, just as Tina, in *Mr. Gilfil's Love-Story*, is deeply troubled when she finds the unfaithful lover whom she had intended to stab lying dead in the wood. Deronda is told by Mordecai of his race and his mission, just as *The Spanish Gypsy* (in the dramatic poem of this title), on the point of marrying a nobleman, is confronted by duty in the garb of her gipsy father who orders her to abandon her country, her religion and her lover so as to follow him in his undertaking as the Moses or Mahomet of his gipsy tribe. And again: Lydia Glasher, anxious to appear to Gwendolen as a Nemesis, a petrifying Medusa, echoes Baldassare's determination to present himself to the unrecognizing Tito as the very personification of remorse. Dorothea, we have seen, is a Madonna with a cloak, like Romola and Dinah.

Themes sometimes multiply themselves by a system of figures and counter-figures, like Boulle furniture, such as we have already observed in Dickens,[221] with positive inlay and negative inlay, *premier effet* and *deuxième effet*. There are two recognition-scenes in *Felix Holt*, on the part of Esther and on the part of Harold Transome. Harold, who hates his mother's legal adviser, the old lawyer Jermyn, discovers that the latter is his father; Esther, who adores the old dissenting minister Rufus Lyon, discovers that he is *not* her father. Both Rufus Lyon and Lady Transome have concealed the names of their real fathers from their respective children. But behind the poor minister's secret lies a whole story of love and sacrifice and virtue; behind the secret of the proud titled lady is a story of guilt, of tyranny, of vice. Rufus's secret, when revealed, gives the virtuous man the prize of virtue; Lady Transome's, when discovered, leads to catastrophe for all that she holds most dear. In

Deronda we have also two parallel discoveries of parents.
Premier effet: Deronda at last finds the mother for whom
he has been searching; *deuxième effet*: Mirah—unfortunately—rediscovers the father whom she never wished
to meet again; Mirah's father had wanted to bring her up
to despise the Jews, but the girl had remained devoted to
her own people; Deronda's mother had rebelled against
his father, a fanatical Jew, and had wanted her son to be
brought up like a gentleman, but in him too the spirit of
his race had remained irrepressible. In *Deronda* we have
also a further 'pendant': two Jewish artists who assert the
exclusive rights of their vocation, Klesmer and Deronda's
mother, Leonora Alcharisi. There is, again, a parallel case
between *Adam Bede* and *Deronda*: in both there are two
women, one pure and religious (Dinah, Mirah), the other
a woman of the world, a sinner, a criminal (Hetty who
commits infanticide; Gwendolen who meditates the murder
of her husband). The hero (Bede, Deronda) is late in
realizing that he loves the first one. In *Middlemarch*, as
we have seen, Dorothea overrates Casaubon's scientific
abilities (*premier effet*), while Rosamond extinguishes Lydgate's devotion to science (*deuxième effet*)—pale on a dark
ground, dark on a pale ground, brass on tortoiseshell, tortoiseshell on brass. Mrs. Bulstrode becomes aware that the
husband she has revered for twenty years has deceived
her by concealing his dishonest past; Dorothea not merely
discovers that her pedantic husband is a pathetic nonentity,
but also finds, from his will, that he had been harbouring
odious suspicions about her; Rosamond discovers that her
husband is hiding his financial ruin from her. Bulstrode is
unmasked, and his wife envelops him with affectionate,
silent understanding; Lydgate is ruined, and his wife cannot find a single gesture of affection for him.

George Eliot's mind appears to be positively fascinated
by one particular theme; and that is, death by water.[222]
Brother and sister are drowned in *The Mill on the Floss*; and
their mother had had an obscure presentiment of this death
(Book I, chap. x): 'They're such children for the water,
mine are,' she said, 'they'll be brought in dead and
drownded some day. I wish that river was far enough'), as

also had Philip, who dreams that Maggie is drowned in a canal (Book VI, chap. viii), and Maggie herself, in a prophetic dream (Book VI, chap. xiv). Hetty thinks of drowning herself in some dark pool in the woods (*Adam Bede*, chap. xxxv); Romola takes a boat at Viareggio with the intention of setting herself adrift and being drowned; in *Mr. Gilfil's Love-Story* (chap. xvii), when Caterina disappears the people at Cheverel Manor think she is drowned in the big pool; Mirah is on the point of throwing herself into the river; Grandcourt is drowned in the sea. George Eliot's mind—like, indeed, the minds of all novelists—falls back continually upon certain original models, upon situations to be repeated with variations. Only, in her case, the situations are not many in number, and soon begin to show a family resemblance.

In order to enliven her pictures of everyday, monotonous life (and as we shall see, it was here that her greatest contribution as a novelist really lay), George Eliot adopted certain melodramatic expedients such as were beloved of her contemporaries, but which in her—in her more than anyone—are out of tune. That this tendency existed in her from the very beginning is proved by the short story *The Lifted Veil*, of the year 1859, the attribution of which to George Eliot would appear difficult if her signature were not appended to it. A servant-girl is dying of peritonitis: there is a secret between her and her mistress, which it is important to the mistress not to have disclosed. The servant dies, but Dr. Meunier gives her a blood-transfusion which produces a momentary return of life, during which the dying woman reveals that her mistress is intending to poison her husband. 'You mean to poison your husband ... the poison is in the black cabinet. . . . I got it for you.' The curtain falls: this, surely, is a one-act Grand Guignol play; a recent scientific discovery is being exploited to make a sensational case. This is the school which, starting from Poe and Villiers de l'Isle Adam, was to develop into the surrealism of Raymond Roussel.

In *Mr. Gilfil's Love-Story* the girl who is preparing to kill the lover who has betrayed her, finds him dead, and almost goes out of her mind with remorse.[223] In *Silas*

Marner, Silas thinks to touch a heap of gold and finds it is the hair of a little girl who has appeared mysteriously in his room. The finding of the corpse of Dunstan Cass and the simultaneous discovery that it was he who had stolen Silas's hoard, are stage effects in the best (or rather, the worst) style of the sensational novelette. Shocked by the discovery, Dunstan's brother, Godfrey Cass, says to his wife: 'Everything comes to light, Nancy, sooner or later. When God Almighty wills it, our secrets are found out. I've lived with a secret on my mind, but I'll keep it from you no longer' (chap. xviii); and he discloses to Nancy that the woman whom Marner had found dead was his first wife, and that Eppie is his daughter. The discovery of a corpse leads to a confession about the mystery of another corpse, and to a recognition-scene.

The recognition-scene was the *deus ex machina* of the Victorian novel, just as it was of the *feuilleton*-romances of the whole of the nineteenth century. George Eliot abused it, especially in *Felix Holt* and *Daniel Deronda*. In the first, the chance finding of a pocket-book puts the Rev. Rufus Lyon on the track of the father of his adopted daughter Esther (who had been picked up in circumstances, as we have seen, that recall *Silas Marner*) by means of a medal which was the twin of one possessed by Annette, Esther's mother; in consequence of this, Lyon discloses to Esther who her real father is; the story is complicated by an exchange of names and by a dispute over a property. Even more sensational[224] is the discovery of the real father of Harold Transome. Harold (chap. xlvii) strikes Jermyn across the face with his whip when the latter asks to speak to him in private; 'you will repent else—for your mother's sake'. Jermyn, a powerful man, seizes Harold by his coat just below the throat, making him stagger; the attention of everyone in the inn room is drawn to what is happening, but the two enemies 'were beyond being arrested by any consciousness of spectators':

'Let me go, you scoundrel! said Harold, fiercely, 'or I'll be the death of you.'

'Do', said Jermyn, in a grating voice; '*I am your father.*'

In the thrust by which Harold had been made to stagger backward a little, the two men had got very near the long mirror. They were both white; both had anger and hatred in their faces; the hands of both were upraised. As Harold heard the last terrible words he started at a leaping throb that went through him, and in the start turned his eyes away from Jermyn's face. He turned them on the same face in the glass with his own beside it, and saw the hated fatherhood reasserted.

The reflection in the mirror has a symbolic and a 'terror' value like the reflection of Gwendolen in the accursed diamonds:[225] the sensational revelation is reinforced by the sensational circumstance.

Melodramatic, too, is the way in which Deronda learns from his mother (chap. li: 'Her worn beauty had a strangeness in it as if she were not quite a human mother, but a Melusina, who had ties with some world which is independent of ours') the secret of his birth; and this happens actually in the same town—Genoa—in which Grandcourt's tragic death takes place. By chance the protagonists of the novel find themselves in one and the same unlikely point in space at the critical moment of their respective lives. By a sensational chance, in *Middlemarch*, Raffles, in order to reinforce his flask inside its leather case, makes use of a piece of paper which he finds beside the firescreen in Rigg's room—a piece of paper with Bulstrode's signature upon it; by chance the pocket-book containing Bycliffe's medallion falls into the hands of Rufus Lyon, in *Felix Holt*; by chance Tito Melema finds himself face to face with his adoptive father, when the latter escapes from the group of prisoners captured by the French, and by chance Tito Melema, a fugitive in his turn, lands, exhausted, on the embankment of the Arno just at the point to which Baldassare, full of his plans for revenge, has come down. Tito opens his eyes and sees the terrible face of the old man who, the moment Tito gives signs of life, strangles him: the old man dies also, and the two bodies remain locked together; the painter Piero di Cosimo recognizes the old man whom he had used as a model for the figure of Terror, in a picture in which the other figure is a portrait of Tito. Mirrors and diamonds reflecting distorted human faces, prophetic pictures—all this nineteenth-century sen-

sationalism was in the end to form the mainstay of popular
novels such as, in Italy, those of Carolina Invernizio ('The
Accursed Diamonds' or 'The Jewels of Dishonour' might
well have been the title of one of that lady's romances),
before it was submitted to surrealist transplantation in the
collages of Max Ernst.

It is fair to say that George Eliot has in common with
Dickens not only her sensationalism, but also a vein of
humour which, if not devoid of crudity in her early works,
had become refined and subtle by the time she wrote *The
Mill on the Floss*. Of all the other Victorians, only a Dickens
could have created a Mrs. Linnet (in *Janet's Repentance*,
chap. iii) who, in her reading of religious books and the
lives of celebrated preachers, took an interest chiefly in the
details of their diseases, and paused over passages that contained such words as smallpox, pony, or boots and shoes,
skipping pages in which the words Zion, or the River of
Life, and notes of exclamation predominated. Only a
Dickens could have created a character like Adam Bede's
mother, or given so strong a vernacular flavour to the conversation of the drinkers in the country inns; and a sentence
like that of Mrs. Barton (chap. ii) about her children's shoes:
'Really, boots and shoes are the greatest trouble of my life.
Everything else one can turn and turn about, and make old
look like new; but there's no coaxing boots and shoes to
look better than they are', seems to come from the same pen
that had made the boarding-house keeper, Mrs. Todgers,
exclaim:[226] 'The gravy alone is enough to add twenty years
to one's age, I do assure you.... The anxiety of that one item
... keeps the mind continually upon the stretch. There is
no such passion in human nature, as the passion for gravy
among commercial gentlemen. It's nothing to say a joint
won't yield—a whole animal wouldn't yield—the amount
of gravy they expect each day at dinner...'; and a character
like Mr. Fitchett, again in *Amos Barton* (chap. ii), the ex-
footman whose decline had been due to his contempt for
boiled beef, who 'when he was on field-work, carted and
uncarted the manure with a sort of flunkey grace, the ghost
of that jaunty demeanour with which he used to usher in
my lady's morning visitors'—this ex-flunkey is a brother

of Littimer, Steerforth's manservant,[227] who arranged a guest's shoes, after cleaning them, in the first position of the dance and put down his jacket as though it were a baby in swaddling-clothes. Reminiscent of Dickens, too, is Mrs. Glegg (*The Mill on the Floss*, Book I, chap. vii), with her collection of false curls for every occasion; and reminiscent of Dickens are some of Casaubon's grotesquely pompous expressions, such as those in his proposal of marriage (chap. v): 'It was, I confess, beyond my hope to meet with this rare combination of elements both solid and attractive, adapted to supply aid in graver labours and to cast a charm over vacant hours . . .'), or the phrase in which he denies that Ladislaw has any thirst for travelling (chap. ix: 'No, he has no bent towards exploration, or the enlargement of our geognosis').[228]

George Eliot's eye is almost as sharp as Dickens's in picking out people's little habits and whimsies; she fixes them in our minds with a quick, sure touch: in *The Mill on the Floss*, for instance (Book I, chap. ix), Mr. Pullet began 'to nurse his knee and shelter it with his pocket-handkerchief, as was his way when the conversation took an interesting turn'. More rarely her humour has the quiet good-nature of Scott, as in the speeches that Bartle Massey addresses to his bitch Vixen, just as if she were a woman.

*   *   *   *   *

But, although George Eliot presents us with humorously observed figures of rural society, we are not left with the feeling that humour is her predominant quality, as happens in the case of Dickens; and as for her sensational and melo-dramatic episodes, we feel them to be alien to her true nature, which was that of an observer of humble, mono-tonous, everyday existence, of one who watches a grey sky to catch the moment when the sable cloud 'turns forth her silver lining on the night' (to make use of Milton's phrase once more), of one who contemplates a flat and perhaps ignoble landscape, which the light of sunset may trans-figure into beauty. She declared she had found a source of agreeable sympathy in the faithful Dutch pictures of 'monotonous homely existence', and in *The Mill on the Floss* (Book I, chap. v) she wrote:

Life did change for Tom and Maggie; and yet they were not wrong in believing that the thoughts and loves of these first years would always make part of their lives. We could never have loved the earth so well if we had had no childhood in it,—if it were not the earth where the same flowers come up again every spring that we used to gather with our tiny fingers as we sat lisping to ourselves on the grass—the same hips and haws on the autumn hedgerows—the same redbreasts that we used to call 'God's birds', because they did no harm to the precious crops. What novelty is worth that sweet monotony where everything is known, and *loved* because it is known?

The wood I walk in on this mild May day, with the young yellow-brown foliage of the oaks between me and the blue sky, the white star-flowers and the blue-eyed speedwell and the ground ivy at my feet—what grove of tropic palms, what strange ferns or splendid broad-petalled blossoms, could ever thrill such deep and delicate fibres within me as this home-scene? These familiar flowers, these well-remembered bird-notes, this sky, with its fitful brightness, these furrowed and grassy fields, each with a sort of personality given to it by the capricious hedgerows—such things as these are the mother-tongue of our imagination, the language that is laden with all the subtle inextricable associations the fleeting hours of our childhood left behind them. Our delight in the sunshine on the deep-bladed grass to-day, might be no more than the faint perception of wearied souls, if it were not for the sunshine and the grass in the far-off years which still live in us, and transform our perception into love.

And further on in the same novel (Book II, chap. ii) she speaks of the affection one has for 'old inferior things' because they have roots in the memory and awaken associations.

With this Wordsworthian cult of the memories of a childhood spent in the country—which the poet exalted in his *Lines Composed a few miles above Tintern Abbey* as a source of serenity and faith for the whole of life—is linked George Eliot's conservative aspect. She wrote in *Deronda* (chap. iii):

A human life, I think, should be well rooted in some spot of a native land, where it may get the love of tender kinship for the face of earth, for the labours men go forth to, for the sounds and accents that haunt it, for whatever will give that early home a familiar unmistakable difference amidst the future widening of knowledge.

Daniel Deronda belongs to 1876; in 1878 Walter Pater wrote *The Child in the House*, and the way in which he dwells upon this attachment to the place of childhood's first impressions has by this time acquired an 'inward' or spiritual quality, a quality of 'intimism':

How insignificant, at the moment, seem the influences of the sensible things which are tossed and fall and lie about us, so, or so, in the environment of early childhood. How indelibly, as we afterwards discover, they affect us; with what capricious attractions and associations they figure themselves on the white paper, the smooth wax, of our ingenuous souls, as 'with lead in the rock for ever',[229] giving form and feature, and as it were assigned house-room in our memory, to early experiences of feeling and thought, which abide with us ever afterwards, thus, and not otherwise. The realities and passions, the rumours of the greater world without, steal in upon us, each by its own special little passage-way, through the wall of custom about us; and never afterwards quite detach themselves from this or that accident, or trick, in the mode of their first entrance to us. Our susceptibilities, the discovery of our powers, manifold experiences—our various experiences of the coming and going of bodily pain, for instance—belong to this or the other well-remembered place in the material habitation—that little white room with the window across which the heavy blossoms could beat so peevishly in the wind, with just that particular catch or throb, such a sense of teasing in it, on gusty mornings; and the early habitation thus gradually becomes a sort of material shrine or sanctuary of sentiment; a system of visible symbolism interweaves itself through all our thoughts and passions; and irresistibly, little shapes, voices, accidents—the angle at which the sun in the morning fell on the pillow—become parts of the great chain wherewith we are bound.

'Sweet monotony where everything is known, and loved because it is known', influences that seem insignificant yet are indelibly impressed upon the soul, old, everyday things that have their own beauty: George Eliot's minute, realistic observation is transformed into intimism, so repeating the transition which had already taken place in Holland, from the realism of Caravaggio, impassive to the point of appearing devoid of human feeling, to that other realism, warm, shot through with muted poetry, the realism of a Vermeer. The Dutch, indeed, as we noted at the beginning of this

book, had been the first to bring out the poetry of the dull
landscape, the poetry of the humble interior, of the not-
beautiful face. In the best parts of her novels, George
Eliot's chief study was to represent the gradual action of
ordinary causes, the cumulative weight of imponderables,
the slow course of life, the insensible alteration of character
with the years that stiffen it or blunt it, the tergiversations
of conscience, the progressive slippings into acts not truly
desired, the imperceptible touch that crystallizes the scattered elements of a situation, the tragedies that are like the
slow dripping of water day by day, the melancholy waste
of energy in those of feeble will. 'If we had a keen vision
and feeling of all ordinary human life', she wrote in *Middlemarch* (chap. xx), 'it would be like hearing the grass grow
and the squirrel's heart beat, and we should die of that roar
which lies on the other side of silence. As it is, the quickest
of us walk about well wadded with stupidity.'[230]

Here then is a development which becomes gradually
accentuated in this democratic art: lacking heroes and
heroines, attention becomes concentrated on the details of
common life, and these aspects of life are closely studied;
the most ordinary things, by dint of being looked at with
intensity, acquire an important significance, an intimate
beauty of their own, more profound for the very reason
that it is muted.

Let us come back for a moment to the description of the
Rev. Irwine in *Adam Bede* (chap. xvii). The writer tells us
that she could have portrayed a different clergyman 'if I
held it the highest vocation of the novelist to represent
things as they never have been and never will be':

But it happens, on the contrary, that my strongest effort is to
avoid any such arbitrary picture, and to give a faithful account of
men and things as they have mirrored themselves in my mind. The
mirror is doubtless defective; the outlines will sometimes be
disturbed, the reflection faint or confused; but I feel as much bound
to tell you as precisely as I can what that reflection is, as if I were
in the witness-box narrating my experience on oath.

Out of this profession of rigid realism George Eliot
develops her penetrating vision of human life, of life laden

with a spiritual significance of its own even in its humble and ordinary aspects. From Caravaggio to Vermeer, from George Eliot to Proust, realism has become intimism.

André Maurois,[231] referring to a phrase of Proust's, 'Deux pages du *Moulin sur la Floss* me font pleurer . . .', remarked:

On est surpris qu'aucun commentateur n'ait signalé, bien que la ressemblance soit criante, l'analogie entre le début de *Swann* et celui du *Moulin sur la Floss*: 'Je m'éveille, pressant de mes coudes les bras de mon fauteuil: je m'étais endormi et je croyais être sur le pont, devant le moulin de Dorlecote, le voyant tel que je l'avais vu dans une après-midi de février, il y a longtemps de cela. . . .' Sur quoi le lecteur est transporté dans le passé. Remplacez la Floss par la Vivonne: les deux paysages mentaux sont superposables.[232]

It may be that the two pages which made Proust weep are not precisely those at the beginning of *The Mill on the Floss*, but rather those I have previously quoted, where she speaks of the 'sweet monotony where everything is known, and loved because it is known'. Who indeed, more than Proust, has stressed monotony as a source of deep-seated sensations? The gentle flow of the first part of *The Mill on the Floss* must have left a deep imprint upon the mind of the author of the *Recherche*.

Even closer affinities between him and George Eliot might be traced. Combray is a paradise of monotony. The church at Combray is not beautiful, but is beloved because of its childhood associations which give it the position of a source of experience and feeling such as Pater recognized in the house where the child had first grown up. In *Scenes of Clerical Life*, too, Shepperton church is ugly, but the impressions of childhood invest it with charm. George Eliot was in fact able to serve as a model to Proust for the minute study of small provincial environments, for the portrayal of a whole section of society displayed organically in its every aspect (in *Middlemarch*), even though the world of the *Recherche* is entirely different from the one described by her.

And a certain type of unusual, out-of-the-way, ironical comparison, for the unexpected bringing together of two different things—did Proust derive this, too, from George Eliot? Albert Feuillerat[233] employed the name Góngora for a certain metaphysical habit of Proust's, as an example of which we may take the case of the cook Françoise who, when about to make *bœuf à la gelée*,[234] attached extreme importance to the materials which were to enter into the composition of her production, and would betake herself to the market—

se faire donner les plus beaux carrés de romsteck, de jarret de bœuf, de pied de veau, comme Michel-Ange passant huit mois dans les montagnes de Carrare à choisir les blocs de marbre les plus parfaits pour le monument de Jules II. Françoise dépensait dans ces allées et venues une telle ardeur que maman voyant sa figure enflammée craignait que notre vieille servante ne tombât malade de surmenage comme l'auteur du Tombeau des Médicis dans les carrières de Pietrasanta.[235]

Or this, of the tables in the Rivebelle restaurant:[236]

... pareil à ces industries chimiques grâce auxquelles sont débités en grandes quantités des corps qui ne se rencontrent dans la nature que d'une façon accidentelle et fort rarement, ce restaurant de Rivebelle réunissait en un même moment plus de femmes au fond desquelles me sollicitaient des perspectives de bonheur que le hasard des promenades ne m'en eût fait rencontrer en une année.

Or, in *Du côté de chez Swann*:[237]

C'étaient de ces chambres de province qui, — de même qu'en certains pays des parties entières de l'air ou de la mer sont illuminées ou parfumées par des myriades de protozoaires que nous ne voyons pas, — nous enchantent des mille odeurs qu'y dégagent les vertus, la sagesse, les habitudes, toute une vie secrète, invisible, surabondante et morale que l'atmosphère y tient en suspens. ...

Or in *Sodome et Gomorrhe*:[238]

'Si nous allions faire quelques pas dans le jardin, monsieur', dis-je à Swann, tandis que le comte Arnulphe, avec une voix zézayante qui semblait indiquer que son développement, au moins mental, n'était pas complet, répondait à M. de Charlus avec une précision complaisante et naïve: 'Oh! moi, c'est plutôt le golf, le tennis, le ballon, la course à pied, surtout le polo.' Telle Minerve, s'étant subdivisée, avait cessé, dans certaine cité, d'être la déesse de la Sagesse et avait incarné une part d'elle-même en une divinité purement sportive, hippique, 'Athéné Hippia' . . .

Such unusual and witty comparisons may remind us of the poets of the seventeenth century, or of the mock-heroic poets (*The Rape of the Lock*, for instance); but we can find examples nearer to Proust in the novelist whom he admired, George Eliot:[239]

Mrs. Tulliver had lived thirteen years with her husband, yet she retained in all the freshness of her early married life a facility of saying things which drove him in the opposite direction to the one she desired. Some minds are wonderful for keeping their bloom in this way, as a patriarchal gold-fish apparently retains to the last its youthful illusion that it can swim in a straight line beyond the encircling glass. Mrs. Tulliver was an amiable fish of this kind, and, after running her head against the same resisting medium for thirteen years, would go at it again to-day with undulled alacrity.[240]

Here is another zoological comparison in *The Mill on the Floss* (Book II, chap. i) regarding the uniformity of Mr. Stelling's methods of teaching:

Perhaps it was because teaching came naturally to Mr. Stelling, that he set about it with that uniformity of method and independence of circumstances, which distinguish the actions of animals understood to be under the immediate teaching of nature. Mr. Broderip's amiable beaver, as that charming naturalist tells us, busied himself as earnestly in constructing a dam, in a room up three pair of stairs in London, as if he had been laying his foundation in a stream or lake in Upper Canada. It was 'Binny's' function to build: the absence of water or of possible progeny was an accident for which he was not accountable. With the same unerring instinct Mr. Stelling set to work at his natural method of instilling the Eton grammar and Euclid into the mind of Tom Tulliver.

And here is a botanical simile, in the same novel (Book IV, chap. i):

Certain seeds which are required to find a nidus for themselves under unfavourable circumstances, have been supplied by nature with an apparatus of hooks, so that they will get a hold on very unreceptive surfaces. The spiritual seed which had been scattered over Mr. Tulliver had apparently been destitute of any corresponding provision, and had slipped off to the winds again, from a total absence of hooks.

In *Adam Bede* (chap. xxxi) we find Mrs. Poyser 'knitting with fierce rapidity, as if that movement were a necessary function, like the twittering of a crab's antennae'.

In *Felix Holt* (chap. xxxviii):

Mrs. Transome hardly noticed Mr. Lyon, not from studied haughtiness, but from sheer mental inability to consider him—as a person ignorant of natural history is unable to consider a fresh-water polype otherwise than as a sort of animated weed, certainly not fit for table.

In *Middlemarch* (chap. vii) we find a completely Proustian comparison to designate the tepidity of Casaubon's amorous experience:

As in droughty regions baptism by immersion could only be performed symbolically, so Mr. Casaubon found that sprinkling was the utmost approach to a plunge which his stream would afford him; and he concluded that the poets had much exaggerated the force of masculine passion.

A little farther on, in the same chapter, Mr. Brooke thinks that after all it would be a good thing if Casaubon becomes a bishop, without taking into consideration that he himself, later on, would be led to make a Radical speech against the incomes of the bishops. Thus Henry of Navarre, 'when a Protestant baby, little thought of being a Catholic monarch', and Alfred the Great, 'when he measured his laborious nights with burning candles, had no idea of future gentlemen measuring their idle days with watches'.

More elaborate, again, is this passage, full of ironical parallels (*Middlemarch*, chap. vi):

Now, why on earth should Mrs. Cadwallader have been at all busy about Miss Brooke's marriage; and why, when one match that she liked to think she had a hand in was frustrated, should she have straightway contrived the preliminaries of another? Was there any ingenious plot, any hide-and-seek course of action, which might be detected by a careful telescopic watch? Not at all: a telescope might have swept the parishes of Tipton and Freshitt, the whole area visited by Mrs. Cadwallader in her phaeton, without witnessing any interview that could excite suspicion, or any scene from which she did not return with the same unperturbed keenness of eye and the same high natural colour. In fact, if that convenient vehicle had existed in the days of the Seven Sages, one of them would doubtless have remarked, that you can know little of women by following them about in their pony phaetons. Even with a microscope directed on a water-drop we find ourselves making interpretations which turn out to be rather coarse; for whereas under a weak lens you may seem to see a creature exhibiting an active voracity into which other smaller creatures actively play as if they were so many animated tax-pennies, a stronger lens reveals to you certain tiniest hairlets which make vortices for these victims while the swallower waits passively at his receipt of custom. In this way, metaphorically speaking, a strong lens applied to Mrs. Cadwallader's match-making will show a play of minute causes producing what may be called thought and speech vortices to bring her the sort of food she needed.

In *Deronda* (chap. xlviii) Grandcourt has insinuated the suspicion into Gwendolen's mind that Deronda is Mirah's lover; Gwendolen tries to find out the truth from Mirah, and the young Jewess is disgusted and indignant at the idea that Deronda's virtue can possibly be suspected; on her return from her visit to Mirah, Gwendolen is assailed by her husband's sneers:

Gwendolen did not, for all this, part with her recovered faith;—rather, she kept it with a more anxious tenacity, as a Protestant of old kept his Bible hidden or a Catholic his crucifix, according to the side favoured by the civil arm. . . . The one result established for her was, that Deronda had acted simply as a generous benefactor, and the phrase 'reading Hebrew' had fleeted unimpressively across her sense of hearing, as a stray stork might have made its peculiar flight across her landscape without rousing any surprised reflection on its natural history.

In the same novel (chap. lviii) the state of mind of Rex, who has little reason to hope that Gwendolen returns his love, is illustrated by an historical comparison: 'His inward peace was hardly more stable than that of republican Florence,[241] and his heart no better than the alarm-bell that made work slack and tumult busy.'[242]

In its manner of observing peculiarities in individual characters Proust's eye looks at its object from an angle very close to that of George Eliot. Caleb Garth in *Middle-*

march (chap. xl) might well be a Proust character; it was one of his 'quaintnesses' that—

> In his difficulty of finding speech for his thought, he caught, as it were, snatches of diction which he associated with various points of view or states of mind; and whenever he had a feeling of awe, he was haunted by a sense of Biblical phraseology, though he could hardly have given a strict quotation.

The stubbornness of a servant in not wishing to recognize the possibility of learning anything from other people, which is one of the traits of Françoise (in *À l'ombre des jeunes filles en fleurs*) and of the lift-attendant in the hotel at Balbec (*Sodome et Gomorrhe*, i), can also be found in the manservant Pummel, in the chapter *The Watch-Dog of Knowledge* in *The Impressions of Theophrastus Such*.[243] Pummel was never surprised at anything, and received the strangest pieces of information with a 'So I suppose, Sir,' and 'with an air of resignation to hearing [his master's] poor version of well-known things.' The Balbec lift-attendant would answer with a 'Vous penzez! — ou — Pensez! — qui semblait signifier que ma remarque était d'une telle évidence que tout le monde l'eût trouvée, ou bien reporter sur lui le mérite comme si c'était lui qui attirait mon attention là-dessus.' And Françoise 'ne voulait pas avoir l'air étonné. On aurait dit devant elle que l'Archiduc Rodolphe dont elle n'avait jamais soupçonné l'existence était non pas mort, comme cela passait pour assuré, mais vivant, qu'elle eût répondu: "Oui" comme si elle le savait depuis longtemps.' Characteristics such as those just referred to, and curious conversations, like the grotesque variations on the subject of Mrs. Renfrew's health in *Middlemarch* (chap. x), or the chatter in *The Mill on the Floss* (Book I, chap. ix), evidently left an impression upon Proust's mind.

It is, above all, in the degree of subtlety of observation that George Eliot shows how nineteenth-century realism prepared the way to intimism. In *Adam Bede* (chap. iv) she wrote:

> Family likeness has often a deep sadness in it. Nature, that great tragic dramatist, knits us together by bone and muscle, and divides us by the subtler web of our brains; blends yearning and repulsion;

and ties us by our heart-strings to the beings that jar us at every movement. We hear a voice with the very cadence of our own uttering the thoughts we despise; we see eyes—ah! so like our mother's—averted from us in cold alienation; and our last darling child startles us with the air and gestures of the sister we parted from in bitterness long years ago. The father to whom we owe our best heritage—the mechanical instinct, the keen sensibility to harmony, the unconscious skill of the modelling hand—galls us, and puts us to shame by his daily errors; the long-lost mother, whose face we begin to see in the glass as our own wrinkles come, once fretted our young souls with her anxious humours and irrational persistence.[244]

And in the same novel (chap. xxvi):

There are faces which nature charges with a meaning and pathos not belonging to the single human soul that flutters beneath them, but speaking the joys and sorrows of foregone generations—eyes that tell of deep love which doubtless has been and is somewhere, but not paired with these eyes—perhaps paired with pale eyes that can say nothing; just as a national language may be instinct with poetry unfelt by the lips that use it.

Here are other observations which also point the way to an art that pays close attention to the imperceptible, the imponderable. In *Middlemarch* (chap. xxxiv):

Scenes which make vital changes in our neighbours' lot are but the background of our own, yet, like a particular aspect of the fields and trees, they become associated for us with the epochs of our own history, and make a part of that unity which lies in the selection of our keenest consciousness.

When, in *Daniel Deronda* (chap. xxi), Gwendolen arrives at the station where she has to wait for a carriage to go to Offendene, she catches sight of the vehicle, which at once gives her a sense of the changed fortunes of her family— 'a dirty old barouche . . . being slowly prepared by an elderly labourer'. George Eliot observes:

Contemptible details these, to make part of a history; yet the turn of most lives is hardly to be accounted for without them. They are continually entering with cumulative force into a mood until it gets the mass and momentum of a theory or a motive. Even philosophy is not quite free from such determining influences. . . .

The mind of George Eliot, brought up in the positivist school, knew that in natural science 'there is nothing petty to the mind that has a large vision of relations, and to which every single object suggests a vast sum of conditions. It is surely the same with the observation of human life' (*Mill on the Floss*, Book IV, chap. i). Minute positivist observation thus brought her to the exploration of that 'unmapped country within us which would have to be taken into account in an explanation of our gusts and storms' (*Deronda*, chap. xxiv). The way was open from the realist to the intimist novel. Disillusioned observation of life as it really was, led to the eclipse of the hero and the disclosure of man's swarming interior world, made up of disparate and contradictory things. And from the observation of this world, thus almost scientifically initiated by George Eliot (but let us remember, if one of her divinities was Comte, the other was Wordsworth) there was to arise later a new magic, with Henry James[245] and Marcel Proust.

NOTES TO PART II

1 'This scene, which is one of the worst in Dickens,' writes Edmund Wilson (*The Wound and the Bow*, p. 67), 'must be one of the passages in fiction most completely conceived in terms of the stage.' Equally theatrical and false is Jasper's outburst of passion for Rose in *The Mystery of Edwin Drood* (chap. xix). In such scenes, passion is represented as odious and bestial by Dickens, who here completely shares the point of view of Victorian respectability as expressed in the allegory of the hawk and the dove. In Dickens's private life, however, as we shall see later, things went differently.

2 Trollope also, in *The Prime Minister* (1875–6: therefore contemporary with *Anna Karenina*) makes the adventurer Ferdinand Lopez commit suicide under an express train, and his body is 'knocked into bloody atoms' (the description of Tenway Junction is given with a vivid minuteness worthy of Frith: the railway-scape was then a novelty).

3 Examples might be multiplied. Thus, in the first chapter of *The Old Curiosity Shop*, Dickens describes Covent Garden in spring and summer, when the scent of the flowers succeeds in 'overpowering even the unwholesome streams of last night's debauchery'.

4 An episode as early as the end of the eighteenth century (1794) provides an illustration of the contrast which was to become so acute in the

Victorian era. Coleridge was on a walking tour with his friend Joseph Hucks, and while, at the end of a day's walk, they were dining at an inn on lamb, green peas, and salad, 'a little girl with a half-famished sickly baby in her arms' looked in at the open window and begged a bit of bread and meat. Coleridge was affected with pity, and with anger at the system which permitted such poverty, but he was diverted from these reflections by Hucks's reaction. Hucks was annoyed at an impertinent intrusion; no doubt it was bad that such things could be, but he had paid for his dinner, and a gentleman ought to be free to eat in peace. Hucks, said Coleridge, was 'a man of cultivated, though not vigorous understanding,' with feelings 'all on the side of humanity', but he was occasionally capable of such want of feeling owing to 'the lingering remains of aristocracy'. (See Malcolm Elwin, *The First Romantics*, p. 113). Note also, in this passage, the improper use of the term 'aristocracy' by Coleridge who was at that time infatuated with revolutionary ideas from France.

⁵ Una Pope-Hennessy, *Charles Dickens*, London, 1945. See also Ada Nisbet, *Dickens and Ellen Ternan*, with a Foreword by Edmund Wilson (University of California Press, 1952) for full details of the relations between Dickens and Ellen Ternan.

⁶ Mr. Edmund Wilson has given a plausible justification of this appeal to the public by calling attention to the close relationship between novelist and public at that period.

⁷ An idealized portrait of her can be seen in the heroines of Dickens's later novels, in Lucie Manette, Estella, Bella Wilfer, and, especially, Rosa Bud. The actual name of Ellen Lawless Ternan can be seen thinly disguised in the names Estella Provis, Bella Wilfer, Helena Landless.

⁸ See George Orwell, *Critical Essays*, London, 1946, for the attitude of Dickens in cases of love-affairs between persons of different classes, and his Victorian feeling for the moral elevation of woman. What disgusts Dickens in the love of Uriah Heep for Agnes is not so much that Uriah is a rascal as the fact, unpardonable to a Victorian, that his accent is that of a man of low extraction: 'It is the thought of the "pure" Agnes in bed with a man who drops his aitches that really revolts Dickens.'

⁹ When Oliver realized that the adventure into which his companions were dragging him was housebreaking for the purpose of robbery,

he clasped his hands together, and involuntarily uttered a subdeud exclamation of horror. A mist came before his eyes; the cold sweat stood upon his ashy face; his limbs failed him; and he sunk upon his knees. 'Get up!' murmured Sikes, trembling with rage, and drawing the pistol from his pocket. 'Get up, or I'll strew your brains upon the grass.' 'Oh! for God's sake let me go!' cried Oliver; 'let me run away and die in the fields. I will never come near London; never, never! Oh! pray have mercy on me, and do not make me steal. For the love of all the bright Angels that rest in Heaven, have mercy upon me!'

Here then is a scene of violence between diabolical murderer and angelic victim, making use again of the persecution motif so dear to the writers of the 'tales of terror' at the end of the eighteenth century. Elsewhere we see Oliver engaged in tasks much more suitable to his Biedermeier-angel nature, in the quiet atmosphere of a country visit (chap. xxxii):

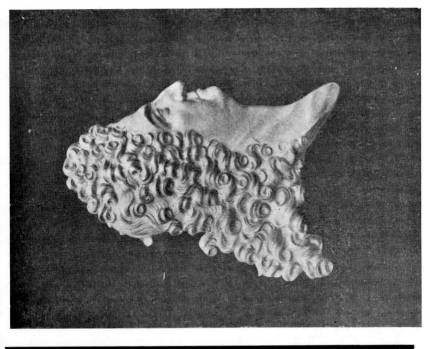

35. BENOIST. Louis XIV (wax) (*Versailles*)

36. BENOIST. Louis XIV (bronze)

37. N. MAES. Grace before Meat (*Paris, Louvre*)

In the morning, Oliver would be a-foot by six o'clock, roaming the fields, and plundering the hedges, far and wide, for nosegays of wild flowers, with which he would return laden, home; and which it took great care and consideration to arrange, to the best advantage, for the embellishment of the breakfast-table. There was fresh groundsel, too, for Miss Maylie's birds, with which Oliver, who had been studying the subject under the able tuition of the village clerk, would decorate the cages, in the most approved taste.

As for Cruikshank, he does not illustrate the most terrifying of the scenes, such as that in which Sikes accidentally hangs himself, still brandishing the knife intended for cutting the rope; he illustrates only comic, grotesque, or sentimental scenes; Sikes meditating killing the dog is the highest point of terror reached by this perfect Biedermeier illustrator.

¹⁰ See Humphry House, *The Dickens World* (Oxford University Press, 1942), where he quotes what Frederic Harrison wrote in 1895: 'Here is a writer who is realistic, if ever any writer was, in the sense of having closely observed the lowest strata of city life, who has drawn the most miserable outcasts, the most abandoned men and women in the dregs of society, who has invented many dreadful scenes of passion, lust, seduction and debauchery; and yet in forty works and more you will not find a page which a mother need withhold from her grown daughter.'

¹¹ In 'Marsyas', iv. 162 (June 1934), pp. 760–2. Alexander Blok declared, in his famous essay on the decay of Humanism (1919): 'These cosy (*uiutnye*: cosy, snug, *gemütlich*) novels of Dickens are made of very terrible, explosive stuff; I have sometimes, in reading Dickens, felt a horror such as not even Edgar Poe himself inspires.' With regard to the sadistic elements in Dickens, one has only to think of Miss Dartle's savage attack on Emily, of little Estella who enjoys seeing Pip suffer and Pocket beating him, of Miss Havisham who takes pleasure in Estella's cruelty, of characters like the Murdstones and Creakle, of Uriah Heep tormenting old Mr. Wickfield in *David Copperfield*, of Quilp and Miss Sally Brass in *The Old Curiosity Shop*: and the end of his monsters is contemplated by Dickens with sadistic pleasure. See also how the novelist's pen lingers over the excesses of the Gordon Riots in *Barnaby Rudge* and over those of the Terror in *A Tale of Two Cities*, and how, in his pages on Rome (*Pictures from Italy*), Santo Stefano Rotondo and the Mamertine Prison form as it were the first movements of the funeral symphony which Dickens gradually develops, giving glimpses of the horrors of the Colosseum and the catacombs, and culminating, like the *Symphonie fantastique* of Berlioz, in a 'marche au supplice' and an execution, which he went to see at San Giovanni Decollato. And he gives details of the long wait, of the blood-stained epilogue, with a mixture of attraction and repulsion that naturally recalls the accounts of English sadism, the more or less legendary 'milords' who, for large sums, rented windows with a good view over the place where the gallows stood. And, amongst all the antiquities in the Vatican galleries or the collections of princes, what does he stop to describe but, of course, the so-called portrait of Beatrice Cenci? 'Through the transcendent sweetness and beauty of the face, there is a something shining out, that haunts me.' See the chapter *Rome and the Victorians*, Appendix II of this volume, in which further

information is to be found on the morbid attraction exercised on these
writers by the figure of Beatrice Cenci.

¹² See for example the macabre description, in *The Old Curiosity Shop*,
of the corpse of the drowned Quilp, carried away by the current and flung
on a swamp,

a dismal place where pirates had swung in chains, through many a wintry night
[and had then been] left there to bleach. . . . And there it lay, alone. The sky was
red with flame, and the water that bore it there had been tinged with the sullen
light as it flowed along. The place the deserted carcase had left so recently, a
living man, was now a blazing ruin. There was something of the glare upon its
face. The hair, stirred by the damp breeze, played in a kind of mockery of death
—such a mockery as the dead man himself would have revelled in when alive—
about its head, and its dress fluttered idly in the night wind.

There is a kind of humorous-macabre quality, such as was dear to the
Romantics, in the sententious 'tailor and funeral furnisher' in *David Copperfield*, beside whose shop can be heard the sound of hammering on a coffin,
and, even more, in the kiss which Joram, who has just finished nailing up
a coffin, steals from one of the tailor's daughters—an episode that recalls a
celebrated one in *L'Âne mort* by Jules Janin (chap. xxiv, *Le Baiser*: the
carpenter who, having finished hammering at the guillotine he is making,
ties his mistress to it for a joke and gives her a kiss). Although Dickens finds
his true province in the description of friendless individuals, reprobates,
murderers, *heautontimoroumeni*, monsters, and grotesques, it must, however, be pointed out that his involvement in the macabre is never complete:
he is conscious of his own brilliance as a descriptive writer and overdoes it,
displaying, often, a forcible-feeble quality (except when his intensity becomes lyric, as in a passage in *Great Expectations*: 'Dry rot and wet rot and
all the silent rots that rot in neglected roof and cellar'); or again he cannot
resist the temptation of the humorous touch, as in the description of Miss
Havisham's frightful room, where the spiders were running up and down
'as if some circumstance of the greatest public importance had just trans-
pired in the spider community.' Besides, Pip's continual visits to Miss
Havisham end by making the surroundings familiar, by depriving them of
their mystery, so that Miss Havisham beside her wedding cake is no more
formidable than a wicked fairy with her customary attributes. See also the
grotesque-macabre quality of Durdles the maker of gravestones, with his
diabolical urchin Deputy (*Edwin Drood*, chap. v).

¹³ See also House, op. cit., p. 202. Dickens's arrangement with Wills
to make nocturnal rounds of visits to gaslit police-stations, the meeting of
the detectives in the Household Words office, the excursion along the
Thames in the launch of the river police, his interest in prisons and execu-
tions, all show very clearly his morbid curiosity about all forms of crime
and death. In one of the essays in *The Uncommercial Traveller*, written in
his last years, Dickens tells how he had been obsessed by the swollen corpse
of a drowned man that he had seen in the Morgue in Paris. Edmund
Wilson in his study 'Dickens: the two Scrooges' (in *The Wound and the
Bow*) records other examples of this obsession in Dickens, the fascination
that photographs of criminals had for him, the performance of the French

actor Lemaître in the part of a murderer. The obsession is explained by
Mr. Wilson as an effect of the psychic trauma received by Dickens as a
boy, as a result of his father's ruin and of his own despair at having to work
in the boot-blacking factory—a trauma which gave him an urge towards
vengeance and crime which was then transposed into his work ('For the
man of spirit whose childhood has been crushed by the cruelty of organized
society, one of two attitudes is natural: that of the criminal, or that of the
rebel. Charles Dickens, in imagination, was to play the roles of both, and
to continue up to his death to put into them all that was most passionate in
his feeling.') Mr. Wilson also calls attention to the horrific tales interpolated
into the *Pickwick Papers*, which present cases such as might have provided
subjects for writers of the French 'frénétique' school, such as Pétrus Borel,
who was writing during those same years (*Champavert, contes immoraux*,
1833). Although allowing for the convention of the 'tales of terror,' which
still had a following among the public, Mr. Wilson emphasizes the personal
element in these horrific tales.

14 Orwell also observes, however (p. 19): 'One thing which Dickens
seems to have recognised, and which most of his contemporaries did not, is
the sadistic sexual element in flogging. I think this can be inferred from
David Copperfield and *Nicholas Nickleby*.'

15 Since the revelation of Howard Duffield, 'John Jasper—Strangler', in
The American Bookman, Feb. 1930. See Wilson, pp. 85 et seq.

16 The aesthetic value of the *collages* by the Surrealist Max Ernst is open
to discussion, but there can be no doubt that they possess an interpretative
value—and of what power! These gloomy compositions, put together with
pieces taken from illustrations to the popular novels of the last century, and
juxtaposing with sinister wit pictures that are unrelated and that yet have
some secret congruity, reveal fully, as though by the action of a reagent,
a taste which, in that century, remained more or less hidden underground.
The façade of the century was good, practical, bourgeois, but, as in Ernst's
Semaine de bonté, the contents of the house behind the façade were often
far from good. It was the century, it must be remembered, during which
piano-legs and mantelpieces were hidden beneath draperies; the suffocating
hangings, the heavy curtains were merely a symbol of the ethical attitude
of the time.

17 A persistent thread of macabre, funereal fantasy runs through *Edwin
Drood* even to a small detail (chap. vi) like that of the six brothers Crisparkle
who preceded Septimus ('Septimus, because six little brother Crisparkles
before him went out, one by one, as they were born, like six weak little
rushlights, as they were lighted'). The most notable comic passage in the
novel is the epitaph composed by Mr. Sapsea; and when the driver of the
coach replies to intimations of brotherhood on the part of the wrathful
philanthropist Honeythunder: 'The worm will, when . . .', one gets an
unexpected glimpse of the funereal eloquence of the sermons of Donne,
who was haunted by visions of the corpse-devouring worm.

18 *Charles Dickens, The Progress of a Radical*, London, Lawrence &
Wishart, 1937.

19 Lenin, when he went, towards the end of his life, to see a dramatized

version of *The Cricket on the Hearth*, found the bourgeois sentimentality of Dickens so intolerable that he went out half way through a scene. This is reported by N. Krupskaia and quoted by G. Orwell, op. cit., p. 7.

[20] See the similar conclusions in Wilson, op. cit., pp. 29 et seq.

[21] For Mr. Wilson, too (p. 30).

Dickens had at first imagined that he was pillorying abstract faults in the manner of the comedy of humors: Selfishness in *Chuzzlewit*, Pride in *Dombey*. But the truth is that he had already begun an indictment against a specific society: the self-important and moralizing middle class who had been making such rapid progress in England and coming down like a damper on the bright fires of English life—that is, on the spontaneity and gaiety, the frankness and independence, the instinctive human virtues, which Dickens admired and trusted. The new age had brought a new kind of virtues to cover up the flourishing vices of cold avarice and harsh exploitation; and Dickens detested these virtues.

See also the penetrating analysis of *Our Mutual Friend* on pp. 76 et seq. of Edmund Wilson's book.

[22] It was from Dickens the reformer that the Russian novelists derived their inspiration. Marcel Schwob at one time planned a critical study of *Charles Dickens et le roman russe*. What is the fundamental idea in the Russian novel? Schwob asked himself: that the humble have a lesson to teach the ruling classes. That is the novelty, and it is common to Dickens, and Dostoevski, and Tolstoy; and it was Dickens who first proclaimed it, who first proclaimed that 'the heart has its reasons'. Together with the central idea, a quantity of characters and characteristics passed from Dickens into the Russian novel; e.g. in *The Idiot*, Ivolgin, the father of Gania, recalls Micawber with one or two of the characteristics of William Dorrit, the Father of the Marshalsea in *Little Dorrit*; Lebedeff, in the same novel, is drawn from Uriah Heep. Certain of the latter's words might well issue from the mouth of Uriah, for instance:

'Be assured, most honourable, most worthy of princes—be assured that the whole matter shall be buried within my heart!' cried Lebedeff, in a paroxysm of exaltation. 'I'd give every drop of my blood. . . . Illustrious prince, I am a poor wretch in soul and spirit, but ask the veriest scoundrel whether he would prefer to deal with one like himself, or with a noble-hearted man like you, and there is no doubt as to his choice! He'll answer that he prefers the noble-hearted man— and there you have the triumph of virtue! *Au revoir*, honoured prince! You and I together—softly! softly!' (*The Idiot*, newly revised version by Eva M. Martin, Dent, Everyman's Library, p. 441.)

Uriah, who wishes to humiliate himself before David and make him accept his pardon for the blow he has received, is a character who would find himself quite at home in a Russian novel, and the same can be said of the character of Dick, also in *David Copperfield*; while Estella, in *Great Expectations*, with her capricious cruelty, seems to have a family likeness to Dostoevski's Nastasias and Lisavetas. For the deepening of the evil qualities of Steerforth's character in Stavrogin, see G. Katkov, 'Steerforth and Stavrogin; On the Sources of "The Possessed"', in *The Slavonic Review*, 1949, pp. 469–88.

[23] Orwell, op. cit., p. 31.

²⁴ Orwell, op. cit., pp. 42–43.

²⁵ The affinity between Dickens and Spitzweg can, for example, be illustrated by a scene such as the following, at the end of chapter iv of *The Old Curiosity Shop*:

> His wife returned no other reply than the customary 'Yes, Quilp,' and the small lord of the creation took his first cigar and mixed his first glass of grog. The sun went down and the stars peeped out, the Tower turned from its own proper colours to grey and from grey to black, the room became perfectly dark and the end of the cigar a deep fiery red, but still Mr. Quilp went on smoking and drinking in the same position, and staring listlessly out of window with the dog-like smile always on his face, save when Mrs. Quilp made some involuntary movement of restlessness or fatigue; and then it expanded into a grin of delight.

Compare this with the pictures of Spitzweg in which, in the evening air, some grotesque type of misanthrope or little old man appears at a small window and stays staring silently in front of him (but does he really see?) while the twilight sky curves down over the gables and parapets and distant towers of a landscape of roofs (see, for instance, *The Hypochondriac*, Munich, Schack Gallery). Again from *The Old Curiosity Shop*, the old convalescent (chap. xi):

> In a small dull yard below his window, there was a tree—green and flourishing enough, for such a place—and as the air stirred among its leaves, it threw a rippling shadow on the white wall. The old man sat watching the shadows as they trembled in this patch of light until the sun went down, and when it was night and the moon was slowly rising he still sat in the same spot. To one who had been tossing on a restless bed so long, even these few green leaves and this tranquil light, although it languished among chimneys and housetops, were pleasant things. They suggested quiet places afar off, and rest, and peace.

²⁶ Mountains of food become, in Dickens, the symbol, the hieroglyphic, of benevolence; see e.g. *Great Expectations*, chap. xxxvii: 'a haystack of buttered toast'.

²⁷ Satire of the Malthusian point of view is to be found, for instance, in the Christmas story of *The Chimes*, in the advice given by Filer and Sir Joseph Bowley. The former says to a young engaged couple:

> 'Married! Married! The ignorance of the first principles of political economy on the part of these people; their improvidence; their wickedness; is, by Heavens! enough to—. . . A man may live to be as old as Methusaleh . . . and may labour all his life for the benefit of such people as those; and may heap up facts on figures, facts on figures, facts on figures, mountains high and dry; and he can no more hope to persuade 'em that they have no right or business to be married, than he can hope to persuade 'em that they have no earthly right or business to be born. And *that* we know they haven't. We reduced it to a mathematical certainty long ago. . . .' &c.

And Sir Joseph, who sets up to be a patron of the poor:

> 'I will think for you; I know what is good for you; I am your perpetual parent. Such is the dispensation of an all-wise Providence! Now, the design of your creation is: not that you should swill, and guzzle, and associate your enjoyments, brutally, with food . . . but that you should feel the Dignity of Labour; go forth erect into the cheerful morning air, and—and stop there. Live hard and temperately, be respectful, exercise your self-denial, bring up your family on next to

nothing, pay your rent as regularly as the clock strikes, be punctual in your dealings . . . and you may trust me to be your Friend and Father', &c.

28 *Sunday under three heads.*

29 *Histoire de la littérature anglaise,* vol. iv, p. 63.

30 Orwell, op. cit., p. 10, says for instance, of the general tendency of *Hard Times,* which Macaulay refused to review because he disapproved of its 'sullen socialism': 'There is not a line in the book that can properly be called Socialistic; indeed, its tendency if anything is pro-capitalist, because its whole moral is that capitalists ought to be kind, not that workers ought to be rebellious. . . . His whole "message" is one that at first glance looks like an enormous platitude: If men would behave decently the world would be decent.'

31 Orwell, op. cit., p. 17, notes that apologists of revolution usually try to minimize its horrors; Dickens's impulse is to exaggerate them.

32 See above, note 13, pp. 386–7.

33 With regard to characters, take for instance Quilp, who rubs his hands together continuously, and so hard that he looks as if he were busy making little pieces of ammunition for a blowpipe, with the dirt that incrusts them.

34 See above, pp. 129–30.

35 A suitable scene for an opera, for example, would be the mysterious, desolate place beside a swamp, with, in the background, miserable hovels inhabited by criminals, and a ruined house in the foreground, in which, one sultry summer evening, the Bumbles have an appointment with Monks (an offshoot of Mrs. Radcliffe's Schedoni) (*Oliver Twist,* chap. xxxviii). In the theatrical convention, also, is the storm which breaks with thunder and lightning during this meeting of malefactors; in the same convention are the epileptic attacks of Monks at the sound of the thunder; and finally, what more conventionally theatrical could be imagined than the things which are to be bartered in this nefarious thieves' market—the medallion with the hair, and the ring, left by Oliver's mother, which are to serve to identify him? A theatrical effect of lantern-light illumines the scene: 'The sickly rays of the suspended lantern falling directly upon them, aggravated the paleness and anxiety of their countenances: which, encircled by the deepest gloom and darkness, looked ghastly in the extreme.'

36 Cf. E. M. Forster, *Aspects of the Novel,* London, Arnold, 1927, p. 98.

37 *Old Lamps for New Ones.*

38 The majority of these painters are typical of English early-Victorianism: which is as much as to say, of Biedermeier.

39 In this part I am much indebted to the study by W. C. Phillips, *Dickens, Reade, Collins, Sensation Novelists,* New York, 1919.

40 p. 62.

41 See O. Elton, *A Survey of English Literature, 1830–80,* London, 1920, p. 201.

42 Mr. Edmund Wilson has not observed that the theme of the double personality already begins to be visible in *The Old Curiosity Shop,* in the figure of the good old grandfather with a mania for gambling who one night

robs his granddaughter Nell so that he can gamble with her money (chaps. xxx–xxxi): 'She had no fear of the dear old grandfather, in whose love for her this disease of the brain had been engendered; but the man she had seen that night, wrapt in the game of chance, lurking in her room, and counting the money by the glimmering light, seemed like another creature in his shape, a monstrous distortion of his image, a something to recoil from, and be the more afraid of, because it bore a likeness to him, and kept close about her, as he did.'

⁴³ Dickens's plan of interlarding a sensational plot with recognition scenes, humorous patches, and the Christmas spirit, persisted until quite recently in the cinema, in a film such as Charlie Chaplin's *The Kid* (in which the dream of paradise is an interlude in the manner of a Christmas tale). Even in his last, unfinished novel, *The Mystery of Edwin Drood*, at a time when he was reaching out towards a greater psychological subtlety, Dickens, as seems certain, made use, for a case of double personality, of information about the savage practices of the Thug sect, which Sue also had exploited in *The Wandering Jew*, in which he, too, imported a Thug strangler into Europe. Wilkie Collins too, in *The Moonstone* (1868), had introduced a band of Hindu fanatics who committed a secret murder in England.

⁴⁴ In *Bleak House* Dickens develops a new type of novel, the novel of the social group, held together also by an all-pervading symbolism (Wilson, pp. 36 et seq.): the London fog is the symbol of the Court of Chancery, and, in general, of the network of antiquated institutions that stifled English life; and the epidemic that spreads from the slums, owing to bourgeois selfishness, until it infects the leisured classes, is a symbol of the evil that undermines the social edifice. For this symbolism see also p. 187.

⁴⁵ M. L. Cazamian, *Le Roman et les idées en Angleterre, l'influence de la science*, Strasbourg, 1923, p. 268.

⁴⁶ David Cecil, *Early Victorian Novelists*, London, Constable, 1934, p. 29.

⁴⁷ Compare this false pathetic with the genuine pathetic of the funeral in D. H. Lawrence's *The White Peacock*, to get the full measure of Victorian bad taste. The Dickens-type pathetic was in any case widespread during the nineteenth century over the whole of Europe. See e.g. *The Tale of the Toad and the Rose* by the Russian Garzhin.

⁴⁸ Another picture by Breughel, *The Fall of Icarus* (Brussels) seems almost like a puzzle-picture: 'Puzzle; find Icarus.' Looking at it, one sees a tract of sea bathed in an enchanted light, and on land, in the foreground, exquisite details as it might be from a Book of Hours, a ploughman wrapped in sunlight, and, on the promontory amongst his snow-white sheep, a shepherd raising his face towards the sky; lower down is a fisherman intent on his line, in the blue sea a caravel sails by, and in the shadow of the caravel there is a flicker of white legs amongst the curling waves: and that is Icarus. The little marginal figures from Ovid (*Metamorphoses*, viii. 217 et seq.):

> Hos aliquis tremula dum captat harundine pisces,
> Aut pastor baculo stivaque innixus arator
> Vidit et obstupuit . . .

are the ones that emerge most prominently, and Breughel has even managed to slip in an old man's corpse in the wood on the left, to illustrate the German proverb: 'Es bleibt kein Pflug stehen um eines Menschen willen, der stirbt.' The bourgeois anecdotal and moral qualities reduce the heroic theme to a mere pretext. In the *Climb to Cavalry* (Vienna), also, although the group of sorrowing Maries is figured in the foreground, Christ is barely visible amongst the picturesque crowd which, with its profane, holiday-making air, dominates the scene. This has been remarked by Charles de Tolnay in *Pierre Bruegel l'ancien* (Brussels, Nouvelle Société d'Éditions, 1935, pp. 27 et seq.):

> Comme perdue dans ce vaste paysage, la chute du héros [Icarus] reste in-aperçue de tout le monde, petit épisode sans importance dans cette nature immuable, dominée par la magie seule du soleil . . . le tableau met en lumière la subordination de la vie humaine aux lois éternelles de la nature. Sans se préoccuper ni de l'accident d'Icare ni de la mort naturelle d'un vieillard dont le cadavre apparaît à gauche sous un buisson, le paysan continue machinalement son travail quotidien à la charrue, confirmant l'ancien proverbe: 'Aucune charrue ne s'arrête pour un homme qui meurt'. L'événement exceptionnel du mythe se transforme, éclairé par le proverbe populaire, en un événement quotidien et prosaïque, il perd son caractère heroïque.

And on p. 43: 'La conversion de Saint Paul est représentée au second plan comme un épisode sans importance.' In *The Fall of Icarus*, W. H. Auden (in his poem *Musée des Beaux Arts*) sees an illustration of the in-difference of everyday life to such an amazing event as a boy falling out of the sky. The reaction against the convention of the heroic is on the other hand a salient feature in artists of various periods and cultural climates, and should not always be interpreted as a bourgeois feature. There is nothing bourgeois about the everyday, deliberately plebeian treatment of sacred subjects in Caravaggio, who, reacting against conventional rhetorical recipes, comes out with an opposite kind of rhetoric, as in *The Conversion of Saint Paul* (Santa Maria del Popolo, Rome), in which the horse strikes the eye far more than the saint, or in *The Burial of Saint Lucy* (Santa Lucia alla Marina, Syracuse), where the massive figures of the two gravediggers enclose the subject of the picture as if in a vice (See B. Berenson, *Caravaggio: his Incongruity and his Fame*, London, Chapman & Hall, 1954). The anti-rhetorical rhetoric of these pictures, as also Caravaggio's deliberate vulgarity in certain symbolizations of Love (Pitti Gallery, Florence; Kaiser Friedrich Museum, Berlin), may be compared with the pedestrian, every-day treatment which was given, almost contemporaneously, by John Donne to certain themes in lyric love-poetry, and with the latter's combinations of incongruous elements (see M. Praz, *Secentismo e marinismo in Inghilterra*, 1925, pp. 110 et seq.). The history of this anti-heroic current through the centuries, with the various movements that flow into it, leads us to mention certain descriptions of battles from the one-sided point of view of a single individual, by no means conspicuous, who has taken part in them, e.g. in Stendhal's *Chartreuse de Parme* and Tolstoy's *War and Peace*. On the other hand, in the famous picture by Gros, *Napoleon on the Battlefield of Eylau* (in the Salon of 1808), the prominence given to the wounded in the foreground is intended to accentuate the note of horror at the slaughter and the pity expressed by the Emperor himself ('Si tous les rois de la terre pouvaient contempler un tel spectacle, ils seraient moins avides de guerres et de conquêtes'. These bodies, larger than life-size, are certainly not intended in any way to express 'la grandeur de la victoire que les Français ont remportée de leurs ennemis', as J. Tripier le Franc naïvely wrote (*Histoire de la vie et de la mort du Baron Gros*, Paris, Jules Martin, 1880, pp. 254–5).

[49] At one point in *David Copperfield* Dickens himself indicates that his ideal is a Dutch painting. It is in the scene between the decks of the ship carrying the emigrants to Australia—a picturesque crowd that causes the protagonist to exclaim: 'I seemed to stand in a picture by Ostade.' (chap. lvii). A little farther on Dickens paints a picture that recalls Ford Madox Brown's *The Last of England* (the idea for this picture came to the painter at Gravesend in 1857, when he accompanied Woolner, who was going to Australia in search of fortune, on board ship—*David Copperfield* was published in 1849–50: the figures of the two emigrants are portraits of the painter and his wife): Emily, at her uncle's side, her eyes fixed on the slowly receding shore; 'surrounded by the rosy light, and standing high upon the deck, apart together, she clinging to him, and he holding her, they solemnly passed away'. In *Great Expectations*, Mr. Wopsle's school offers another little picture of the type beloved by the Dutch and their nineteenth-century followers, e.g. Wilkie.

[50] In *The London Mercury*, vol. x, p. 35.

[51] Orwell, op. cit., p. 37, after remarking that one remembers pages of Dickens, but never the central story, says:

Dickens sees human beings with the most intense vividness, but he sees them always in private life, as 'characters', not as functional members of society; that is to say, he sees them statically. Consequently his greatest success is *The Pickwick Papers*, which is not a story at all, merely a series of sketches; there is little attempt at development—the characters simply go on and on, behaving like idiots, in a kind of eternity. As soon as he tries to bring his characters into action, the melodrama begins. He cannot make the action revolve round their ordinary occupations; hence the crossword puzzle of coincidences, intrigues, murders, disguises, buried wills, long-lost brothers, etc. etc. . . . . Wonderfully as he can describe an *appearance*, Dickens does not often describe a *process*. The vivid pictures that he succeeds in leaving in one's memory are nearly always the pictures of things seen in leisure moments, in the coffee-rooms of country inns or through the windows of a stage-coach.

[52] What C. Brandi (essay on Picasso, in *Carmine*, Florence, Vallecchi, 1947, p. 257) says of Daumier, might also be said of Dickens, that 'he confessed that he was unable to draw from life, but with one infallible stroke took possession of the object at the first instant'.

[53] See Earle R. Davis, 'Dickens and the Evolution of Caricature', in *P.M.L.A.* lv (1940), for the influence of the performances of the comedian Charles Mathews the Elder. Mr. Davis concludes:

The influence which seems plain in the case of Mr. Jingle was undoubtedly extended in a major or minor way to the mannerisms and tags of other characters and led to Dickens's own distinctive type of caricature. It seems fair to say that all the comic characters of Dickens retain some of this early influence, an influence which lasted into the days when Dickens read publicly and acted out his many characters which provoked laughter by their mannerisms.

54 *The Old Curiosity Shop*, chap. xix.

55 *David Copperfield*, chap. iii.

56 *Great Expectations.*

57 *The Old Curiosity Shop*, chap. xvi. Another piquant contrast in this same novel—children playing amongst the tombs: 'Some young children sported among the tombs, and hid from each other, with laughing faces. They had an infant with them, and had laid it down asleep upon a child's grave, in a little bed of leaves.' And in *David Copperfield* there is the contrast between the surroundings of the undertaker Mr. Omer and his lively grandchildren, a contrast which leaps to the eye like an epigram of Victor Hugo when Mr. Omer says: ' "And Joram's at work, at this minute, on a grey one with silver nails, not this measurement"—the measurement of the dancing child upon the counter—"by a good two inches".'

58 His pleasure in the sinister-picturesque contrasts in a curious manner with his unfavourable reaction to the new, just-built, appearance of American towns and houses; as a reformer, Dickens should, on the contrary, have approved of the newness which implied improved social conditions. This is observed by Dorothy Carrington, *The Traveller's Eye*, London, The Pilot Press Ltd., 1947, p. 315.

Robert Liddell, in *A Treatise on the Novel*, London, Cape, 1947, p. 115, in estimating the great quantity of descriptive matter in the novels of Dickens—matter which he considers to be alien to the medium of the novel, the definition of which should be 'representation of character in action'— maintains that 'it is for the sake of the human drama that the background is provided' by Dickens, that it is symbolic and related to the passions of the characters. He cites as an example the description of the rain in Lincolnshire, in relation to the state of mind of Lady Dedlock in *Bleak House*. But he then observes: 'Unfortunately the actual drama in this case, as so often in Dickens, is strained and impossible.' Powerful as he is when describing atmosphere and surroundings, his art fails, as we have seen, when he goes on to display the passions of his characters in action. This confirms the point of view maintained in the present chapter.

59 This passage is quoted as being typical of the reaction of an artist to the progress of industrial civilization in F. D. Klingender, *Art and the Industrial Revolution*, London, Royle, 1947.

60 See my essay 'Gl'interni di Proust', in *La Casa della Fama*, Milan–Naples, Ricciardi, 1952.

61 See S. Sitwell, *Narrative Pictures*, London, Batsford, 1937, Plate 97.

62 See above, pp. 127–8.

63 With regard to Dickens's dialogue, account must however be taken of the reservation made by V. S. Pritchett (essay on *Edwin Drood* in *The Living Novel*, London, Chatto & Windus, 1946): 'When he attempts this [to make his people talk to each other] he merely succeeds in making them talk *at* each other, like actors. His natural genius is for human soliloquy, not for conversation.'

⁶⁴ Reproduced in *Letters and Private Papers of W. M. Thackeray*, collected and edited by Gordon N. Ray, London, Oxford University Press, 1946, vol. iii, p. 532.

⁶⁵ On the other hand there had been at least nineteen clergymen in the family: this should be borne in mind when we come to speak of Thackeray's tendency to preach.

⁶⁶ The episode is related in the essay on George III in *The Four Georges*.

⁶⁷ See L. Stevenson, *The Showman of Vanity Fair*, London, Chapman & Hall, 1947, p. 116.

⁶⁸ The story of Anne Thackeray's marriages has been told by J. Y. T. Greig, *Thackeray, a Reconsideration*, Oxford University Press, 1950, a book which throws considerable light on the relations between Thackeray and his mother.

⁶⁹ See preceding note.

⁷⁰ Thackeray was aware of the true nature (sexual jealousy) of the possessive instinct of a mother; see Greig, op. cit., p. 23.

⁷¹ Greig, op. cit., p. 77; and p. 29: 'How far Mrs. Carmichael-Smyth made Thackeray the novelist, it is hard to say. That she did much to mar him is beyond question.' In *Esmond*, Thackeray (writes Mr. Greig, p. 164) 'set himself the delicate task of working out the transformation of what was predominantly maternal or filial to begin with, into what was predominantly sexual to end with.' No wonder George Eliot found *Esmond* 'the most uncomfortable book you can imagine'. *Esmond* represented what in Freudian psychology is called a wish-fulfilment.

⁷² This term was used at Cambridge to indicate the population of the town as opposed to that of the University.

⁷³ Cf. the opinions of De Quincey quoted above, p. 79.

⁷⁴ An account of how Thackeray squandered his inheritance by gambling can be found in Appendix IV of vol. i of *Letters and Private Papers*, cited. This circumstance of his own life is reflected in the gambling losses of Lord Castlewood in *Esmond*, and in those of Pendennis. Certain sensations experienced by Thackeray the gambler are related in impersonal form in *The Kickleburys on the Rhine*, 1850.

⁷⁵ Op. cit., p. 153. (See note 67 above.)

⁷⁶ It was Thackeray who gave the word 'snob' the meaning of one who has a mean, vulgar admiration for, and seeks to imitate and frequent, those richer and of higher rank than himself, and who desires to be considered socially important.

⁷⁷ See John W. Dodds, *Thackeray: a Critical Portrait*, Oxford University Press, 1941, pp. 19–20.

⁷⁸ Chapter lx; see above, in the chapter on Dickens, p. 135.

⁷⁹ Thackeray, himself an aspiring painter, looked at this portrait from the pictorial point of view, and in the spirit that animated the canvases of a past period; see, besides the famous passage in chapter vii of Book II on Beatrix's appearance, chapter iii of Book III where Beatrix speaks of her own tastes: 'I love sugar-plums, Malines lace . . . the opera, and everything that is useless and costly. I have got a monkey and a little black boy . . ., a parrot and a spaniel', &c. In portraits of the period we can, in fact, see,

painted upon and around the central figure, similar accessories of 'conspicuous waste'.

⁸⁰ For English precedents of the stock pattern of the varying fortunes and contrasted characters of two closely associated young women, see Kathleen Tillotson, *Novels of the Eighteen-Forties*, Oxford, Clarendon Press, 1954, p. 234 and footnote 2.

⁸¹ R. Las Vergnas, *William Makepeace Thackeray: l'homme, le penseur, le romancier*, Paris, Champion, 1932.

⁸² As Professor Stevenson justly observes (op. cit., p. 240), Thackeray was 'not enough of a Victorian to reprobate the Augustans as Charlotte Brontë would have liked; and yet he was too much of a Victorian to vindicate their frankness'. It is worth while quoting what Carlyle wrote to Emerson on the subject of Thackeray: 'He is a big fellow, soul and body; of many gifts and qualities (particularly in the Hogarth line, with a dash of Sterne superadded), of enormous *appetite* withal, and very uncertain and chaotic in all points except his *outer breeding*, which is fixed enough, and *perfect* according to the modern English style.'

⁸³ This opinion is quoted by H. Sutherland Edwards, *Personal Recollections*, London, 1900, p. 36.

⁸⁴ In Thackeray's defence it may be pointed out that even Sainte-Beuve did not see clearly with regard to his contemporaries. Sainte-Beuve (*Lundis*, ii. 424) calls Charles de Bernard 'le plus spirituel et le plus regrettable' of Balzac's disciples: 'il doutait de tout avec ironie et avec goût, et son œuvre si distinguée s'en est ressentie'. Cf. Henri Peyre, 'The Criticism of Contemporary Writing', in *Lectures in Criticism*, The Johns Hopkins University, Bollingen Series XVI, Pantheon Books, 1949, p. 146: 'He praised Béranger and Ponsard and wasted his attention on even more mediocre poets. He was likewise blind to the originality of Balzac, Stendhal, Mérimée, Flaubert, while he lauded cheaper novelists like Charles de Bernard and Feydeau.' An insignificant novel by Charles de Bernard, whose 'admirable witty tales' Thackeray praised, seemed so good to the English writer that he made an adaptation of it in *The Bedford Row Conspiracy*. On Thackeray's short-sightedness in his judgements on the French literature of the day, see M. Moraud, *Le Romantisme français en Angleterre*, Paris, Champion, 1933, pp. 294 et seq. Thackeray appeared chiefly to appreciate second-rate talent. A friend of Jules Janin (see, however, his article 'Dickens in France', in *Fraser's Magazine*, Mar. 1842, where he attacks Janin for having spoken ill of Dickens's novels—'Ces romans sont le rebut d'une imagination en délire'), the latter's rhetorical style can hardly have been without influence on certain apostrophizings on the part of Thackeray, such as those in his essay on Swift: 'Ah, man! you, educated in Epicurean Temple's library, you whose friends were Pope and St. John —what made you to swear to fatal vows, and bind yourself to a life-long hypocrisy before the Heaven which you adored with such real wonder, humility, and reverence? For Swift's was a reverent, was a pious spirit— for Swift could love and could pray.' And, farther on: 'What had this man done? What secret remorse was rankling at his heart? What fever was boiling in him, that he should see all the world bloodshot? . . . Only a

woman's hair; only love, only fidelity, only purity, innocence, beauty; only the tenderest heart in the world stricken and wounded, and passed away now out of reach of pangs of hope deferred, love insulted, and pitiless desertion:—only that lock of hair left; and memory and remorse, for the guilty lonely wretch, shuddering over the grave of his victim.' See also the essay on Sterne: 'But this man—who can make you laugh, who can make you cry too', &c. And see, too, 'A Gambler's Death' in the *Paris Sketch Book*, written absolutely in the style of Janin, or the attack on the immorality of Georges Sand's novels (*Madame Sand and the New Apocalypse*). At other times his tirades are reminiscent of Soulié—such as the one against lawyers in *Miscellaneous Contributions to 'Punch'*. Another French author admired by Thackeray was Béranger: 'The songs of Béranger are hymns of love and tenderness. I have seen great whiskered Frenchmen warbling the *Bonne Vieille*, the *Soldats, au pas, au pas*, with tears rolling down their mustachios' (*Charity and Humour*). His judgements on English literature were in any case often on the same plane: he praised Hood's *The Song of the Shirt* and called *The Bridge of Sighs* an 'astonishing poem', 'amazing verses'.

85 With regard to an attack in *The Times* reproving *The Newcomes* as a book damaging to morals and religion, Thackeray remarked to Whitwell Elwin: 'With regard to religion, I think, please God, my books are written by a God-loving man; and the morality—the vanity of success, etc., of all but love and goodness—is not that the teaching *Domini nostri?*'

86 Job, vii. 10.

87 J. Brown and H. H. Lancaster, *Thackeray, North British Review*, xl, Feb. 1864.

88 Thomas Sternhold and John Hopkins, sixteenth-century translators of the *Psalms* into English, included in the Prayer Book in 1562.

89 Thomas Walker, 1784–1836, author of the weekly *The Original*, of which twenty-nine numbers appeared in 1835.

90 *Paris Sketch Book*.

91 See the essay on Pope in the *English Humourists*: 'I think of the works of young Pope as I do of the actions of young Bonaparte or young Nelson. In their common life you will find frailties and meannesses, as great as the vices and follies of the meanest men. But in the presence of the great occasion, the great soul flashes out, and conquers transcendent.'

92 In *The Nineteenth Century*, Mar. 1902.

93 See also *Esmond*, Book I, preliminaries: 'I have seen, in his very old age and decrepitude, the old French King, Lewis the Fourteenth, the type and model of kinghood, who . . . persist[ed] in enacting through life the part of Hero; and, divested of poetry, this was but a little, wrinkled old man, pockmarked', &c. The contrast drawn by Thackeray between the real and the heroicized aspects finds a curious confirmation in the wax profile of the King taken from nature, with all its defects, by Benoist, and the idealized bronze profile taken from it by the same artist. The protagonist of Thackeray's novel, comparing Queen Anne's real aspect with that of her statue, goes on: 'Why shall History go on kneeling to the end of time? I am for having her rise up off her knees, and take a natural posture. . . . I would

have History familiar rather than heroic; and I think that Mr. Hogarth and Mr. Fielding will give our children a much better idea of the manners of the present age in England, than the *Court Gazette* and the newspapers which we get thence.' He considers also that a drunken reveller like Charles II should have had an Ostade or a Mieris to paint him, rather than a Kneller or a Le Brun. And in chapter vii he speaks of heroes who grow weary of the artificial atmosphere of etiquette that surrounds them and long to descend from their pedestals, 'as they say the Grand Lama of Thibet is very much fatigued by his character of divinity, and yawns on his altar. . .'. See also the portrait of George IV in *The Four Georges*: 'Nothing but a coat and a wig and a mask smiling below it—nothing but a great simulacrum. . . . I try and take him to pieces, and find silk stockings, padding, stays, a coat with frogs and a fur collar, a star and a blue ribbon, a pocket-handkerchief prodigiously scented, one of Truefitt's best nutty-brown wigs reeking with oil, a set of teeth and a huge black stock, under-waistcoats, more underwaistcoats, and then nothing. . . .' And in Thackeray's review of the *Private Correspondence* of the Duchess of Marlborough (*The Times*, Jan. 6th, 1838): 'The dignity of history sadly diminishes as we grow better acquainted with the materials which compose it. In our ortho-dox history-books the characters move on as a gaudy play-house procession, a glittering pageant of kings and warriors, and stately ladies, majestically appearing and passing away. Only he who sits very near to the stage can discover of what stuff the spectacle is made. The kings are poor creatures, taken from the dregs of the company; the noble knights are dirty dwarfs in tin foil; the fair ladies are painted hags with cracked feathers and soiled trains. One wonders how gas and distance could ever have rendered them so bewitching. The perusal of letters like these produces a very similar disenchantment; and the great historical figures dwindle down into the common proportions as we come to view them so closely.' Remember also Thackeray's description of the view of Constantinople from the Bosphorus in *Rebecca and Rowena* and in *Notes of a Journey from Cornhill to Grand Cairo*, and, in the latter work, his observations on the 'shabbiness' of Athens and the greasy skins of the Oriental beauties, his attack on Byronism, his disappointment at the site of Achilles' tomb, 'a dismal looking mound that lies on a low dreary barren shore—less lively and not more picturesque than the Scheldt or the mouth of the Thames'. Finally he recognizes that such subjects are for great geniuses, for great painters and poets: 'This quill was never made to take such flights; it comes of the wing of an humble domestic bird who walks a common; who talks a great deal (and hisses sometimes); who can't fly far or high, and drops always very quickly; and whose unromantic end is, to be laid on a Michaelmas or Christmas table, and there to be discussed for half an hour—let us hope, with some relish.' Cf. the Rabelaisian motto affixed by Peacock to *Nightmare Abbey*: 'Ay esleu gasouiller et siffler oye,' &c., above, p. 93.

94 See also the essay 'On Men and Pictures' in *Fraser's Magazine*, July 1841: 'Why the deuce will men make light of that golden gift of mediocrity which for the most part they possess, and strive so absurdly at the sublime? But this kind of disbelief in heroes is very offensive to the world, it must

be confessed.' And he quotes the case of *The Times*, which has found fault with him for his account of the 'second funeral' of Napoleon, 'one of the greatest humbugs of modern days'. Farther on he curses uniforms and arms and the vainglory of his own nation in military triumphs, and the hatred between nations that results. In the essay 'On Some French Fashionable Novels' (in the *Paris Sketch Book*) he denounces the absurdity of phrases such as:

Julius Caesar beat Pompey, at Pharsalia; the Duke of Marlborough beat Marshal Tallard, at Blenheim; the Constable of Bourbon beat Francis the First, at Pavia. And what have we here?—so many names, simply. Suppose Pharsalia had been, at that mysterious period when names were given, called Pavia; and that Julius Caesar's family name had been John Churchill;—the fact would have stood, in history, thus: 'Pompey ran away from the Duke of Marlborough at Pavia'. And why not!—we would have been just as wise. Or it might be stated, that: 'The tenth legion charged the French infantry at Blenheim; and Caesar, writing home to his mamma, said: 'Madame, tout est perdu fors l'honneur'. What a contemptible science this is, then, about which quartos are written, and sixty-volumed *Biographies Universelles*, and Lardner's *Cabinet Cyclopaedias*, and the like! the facts are nothing in it, the names everything.

See also the amusing parody of Scott's historical novels in *A Legend of the Rhine* and in *Rebecca and Rowena*; Thackeray diverts himself by plunging historical figures into an atmosphere which is something between the comic-heroic and the bourgeois, and seeks suggestions of the ridiculous in names and anachronisms.

   95 Cf. the famous saying, which goes back to Montaigne: 'Il n'y a pas de héros pour son valet de chambre.'

   96 *The English Humourists*; *Steele.*

   97 See also in *A Legend of the Rhine*: 'On the cold and rainy evening of Thursday, the 26th of October, in the year previously indicated, such travellers as might have chanced to be abroad in that bitter night, might have remarked a fellow-wayfarer journeying on the road from Oberwinter to Godesberg.' It is a typical technique in the historical novel, a technique which, later, Lytton Strachey did not disdain to employ.

   98 *Journey from Cornhill to Grand Cairo.* In any case the anti-heroic tendency was common to the age: in America, for instance, Theodore Parker held Prescott's dramatic pageants to amount to no more than rhetorical *tours de force*; Whitman, later, believed the worship of heroes to be poisonous, and Emerson wrote: 'What is best written or done by genius in the world, was no man's work, but came by wide social labour, when a thousand wrought like one, sharing the same impulse.' See F. O. Matthiessen, *American Renaissance*, Oxford University Press, 1946, pp. 632 et seq.

   99 See Stevenson, *The Showman of Vanity Fair*, cited, p. 267; and p. 268 where he quotes a remark by Clough about this habit of Thackeray.

   100 Op. cit., p. 88.

   101 The lines along which the theme of this ballad developed are already to be found in *A Legend of the Rhine*:

They are passed away:—those old knights and ladies: their golden hair first changed to silver, and then the silver dropped off and disappeared for ever; their elegant legs, so slim and active in the dance, became swollen and gouty, and then, from being swollen and gouty, dwindled down to bare bone-shanks; the roses left their cheeks, and then their cheeks disappeared, and left their skulls, and then their skulls powdered into dust, and all sign of them was gone. And as it was with them, so shall it be with us. Ho, seneschal! fill me a cup of liquor! put sugar in it, good fellow—yea, and a little hot water: a very little for my soul is sad, as I think of those days and knights of old.

[102] Cf. Wordsworth, *Lines composed a few miles above Tintern Abbey,* lines 33 et seq.: 'The best portion of a good man's life, His little, nameless, unremembered acts Of kindness and of love.'

[103] *The Virginians,* lxvi. Thackeray's emblems are often of the most naïvely commonplace type; see, for example, in *Pendennis,* his reflections upon the voyage through life, with sea-going metaphors: 'It has been prosperous [the voyage], and you are riding into port, the people huzzaing and the guns saluting,' &c.

[104] It is Thackeray's usual formula for reticence; cf. *Pendennis*: 'A veil should be thrown over those sacred emotions of love and grief.'

[105] See also, in *Mr. Brown's Letters to a Young Man about Town, Some more Words about the Ladies,* where Thackeray's attitude towards women is the typical Victorian attitude of protectiveness and ceremonious homage: 'It has been my fortune to meet with excellent English ladies—wives graceful and affectionate, matrons tender and good, daughters happy and pureminded; and I urge the society of such on you, because I defy you to think evil in their company.' Previously, however, writing on *Our Batch of Novels for Christmas 1837,* he had said, in connexion with Mrs. Trollope's *Vicar of Wrexhill*: 'Oh! . . . that ladies would make puddings and mend stockings! that they would not meddle with religion (what is styled religion, we mean), except to pray to God, to live quietly among their families, and move lovingly among their neighbours!'

[106] J. B. Cabell, *Beyond Life,* 1925, vol. ii, p. 33.

[107] Isambard Kingdom Brunel (1806–59), famous engineer, son of Sir Marc Isambard Brunel (1769–1849, born in Normandy, emigrated to America in 1793, came to England in 1799, where he had a distinguished career as an engineer and inventor). Isambard Brunel was the designer of the Clifton Suspension Bridge (1831), he built the Great Western Railway (1833 and following years), and, in particular, built big ships, e.g. the *Great Western,* a transatlantic liner of 1,320 tons, 450 steam horse-power, which crossed the ocean in 14 days (hence 'Brunel's vast deck').

[108] 'Montaigne and "Howell's Letters" are my bedside books. If I wake at night, I have one or the other of them to prattle me to sleep again. They talk about themselves for ever, and don't weary me. . . . I read them in the dozy hours, and only half remember them. . . . I hope I shall always like to hear men, in reason, talk about themselves. What subject does a man know better?'

[109] Richard Bentley (1662–1742), famous Latin and Greek scholar, Master of Trinity College, Cambridge (and not, therefore, an 'Oxford don', as Thackeray calls him), observed: 'Claret would be port if it could.'

38. TENIERS. Village Fête (*Paris, Louvre*)

39. HOLMAN HUNT. The Awakening of Conscience (*Coll. Sir Colin Anderson. By courtesy of the owner*)

¹¹⁰ A character in *The Adventures of Philip*, which was appearing in the *Cornhill Magazine*.

¹¹¹ He lived from 1799 to 1860. His novels are unread today.

¹¹² Consider also the well-known beginning of chapter vii of Part I of Gogol's *Dead Souls*, where he contrasts the happy lot of those writers who depict heroic characters with that of the writer (such as himself) who dares to stress all the meannesses of our daily life, meannesses which are under the eyes of all and observed by none, and to describe the ordinary characters which grow thickly along our sometimes bitter and tedious way through the world. Also the beginning of chapter i of Part II of the same novel, where the author, asked why he describes misery upon misery and all the imperfections of life, and why he goes and digs up obscure characters from the remote corners of the countryside, answers that this is inevitable because it is his nature to do so: a reply similar to that of Thackeray now quoted.

¹¹³ Here the Bible illustration has a symbolic value closely connected with the present episode: in this detail of his picture Thackeray is following Hogarth's method. Thus in the big scene which we shall be quoting shortly, Becky's arms and hands are 'all covered with serpents and rings and baubles', which appear as a symbol of the frivolous, fraudulent woman.

¹¹⁴ *The Craft of Fiction*, pp. 101–2.

¹¹⁵ See above, p. 224.

¹¹⁶ *Esmond*, Book III, chap. iv.

¹¹⁷ Op. cit., p. 110.

¹¹⁸ See above, pp. 169, 391.

¹¹⁹ See also, in the big scene in chapter liii of *Vanity Fair*, when Rawdon catches his wife with Lord Steyne: 'The wretched woman was in a brilliant full toilette, her arms and all her fingers sparkling with bracelets and rings. . . .' The ethical verdict is impressed upon the reader by the epithet 'wretched'.

¹²⁰ See above, p. 204.

¹²¹ Marco Lombardi (Aldo Camerino) in the *Corriere Padano* of Jan. 16th, 1940.

¹²² See the well-known studies by Max Weber, *Die protestantische Ethik und der Geist des Kapitalismus*, which appeared first in the *Archiv für Sozialwissenschaft und Sozialpolitik*, vols. xx and xxi, 1904 and 1905, and were then collected in the first volume of the *Religionssoziologie*, Tübingen, 1921; also R. H. Tawney, *Religion and the Rise of Capitalism*, London, John Murray, 1926.

¹²³ There are many pages in Trollope that make one think of Jane Austen. Chapter xviii of *Doctor Thorne*, for example, with the exchange of letters between George de Courcy and Miss Dunstable. The latter often speaks like one of Miss Austen's sensible, 'rational' girls (see, e.g. chapter xx of *Doctor Thorne*). Chapter xxxii of the same novel, with the figure of the clergyman Oriel and the conversations between Patience and Beatrice, seems also to be an echo of Miss Austen's world. And the remarks of Priscilla Stanbury on the subject of marriage (*He Knew He Was Right*, chap. xvi)

to Mrs. Trevelyan, or the way in which Priscilla and Nora discuss the latter's refusal of Mr. Glascock's proposal (ib., chap. xviii), seem as it were like plaster casts of some of Jane Austen's pages. The limited horizon of parochial quarrels, of parochial love-affairs (see, for example, chapter iii of *Framley Parsonage*), the regular cycle of daily occupations, with breakfast marking the important moment of opening the letters (see *Can You Forgive Her?* chap. x), the misunderstandings which are so difficult to dispel (cf. *Barchester Towers*, chap. xxix), the dialogues between women (*Framley Parsonage*, chap. xxiv), the awkward wooings of clergymen (Dr. Slope in *Barchester Towers* is no more fortunate than the famous Mr. Elton in *Emma*), the absence of picturesque descriptions, the dry, unadorned page —these are some of the points of contact between the polished female novelist of the end of the eighteenth century and Trollope. Miss Austen too, be it noted, wrote in circumstances which to most people would seem highly unpropitious to artistic activity. For fuller details, see my introductory essay to the translation of *Emma*, reprinted in *La Casa della Fama*, Milan–Naples, Ricciardi, 1952.

[124] This refers to a well-known incident in *The Mysteries of Udolpho*.

[125] The allusion is to the plot in Shakespeare's *Comedy of Errors*.

[126] In *Phineas Finn*, too, there is an eminent politician, Turnbull, whose face held no indicating sign of any special talent (chap. xviii).

[127] So also, in *He Knew He Was Right*, Camilla French, who, when deserted by her *fiancé* Mr. Gibson, at first threatens tragedy and arms herself with a kitchen knife, then with a clasp knife, and Gibson reaches the point of considering suicide; but Camilla lets the weapon fall from her hands as soon as she is touched by her uncle, and Gibson ends by submitting to marriage with Bella: and everything comes right.

[128] This series of pictures, painted in 1880, is reproduced and described in the catalogue of the fourth sale of the Ch. Sedelmeyer Collection, Paris, June 12th–14th, 1907. Egg's *Past and Present* series (painted in 1858) is in the Tate Gallery. See Graham Reynolds, *Painters of the Victorian Scene*, London, Batsford, 1953, p. 78 and figs. 48–50.

[129] See *He Knew He Was Right*, chap. vii: 'She did not like a girl who could not drink a glass of beer with her bread and cheese in the middle of the day, and she thought that a glass of port after dinner was good for everybody,' &c.

[130] Reminiscent of *The Spectator* is the postscript to the letter (chap. viii) in which Miss Stanbury asks her sister-in-law to send one of her daughters to live with her: 'I hope the young lady does not have any false hair about her.' She shared this aversion for the *chignon* with another old lady of her own type, Lady Linlithgow in *The Eustace Diamonds*.

[131] Henry James, *Partial Portraits*: 'It is probably not unfair to say that if Trollope derived half his inspiration from life, he derived the other half from Thackeray; his earlier novels, in especial, suggest an honourable emulation of the author of *The Newcomes*.'

[132] This imaginary playing may remind one of Diderot's *Neveu de Rameau*, a character in other ways very different.

The warden still looked mutely in his face, making the slightest possible passes with an imaginary fiddle bow, and stopping, as he did so, sundry imaginary strings with the fingers of his other hand. 'Twas his constant consolation in conversational troubles. While these vexed him sorely, the passes would be short and slow, and the upper hand would not be seen to work; nay the strings on which it operated would sometimes lie concealed in the musician's pocket, and the instrument on which he played would be beneath his chair. But as his spirit warmed to the subject—as his trusting heart, looking to the bottom of that which vexed him, would see its clear way out—he would rise to a higher melody, sweep the unseen strings with a bolder hand, and swiftly fingering the cords from his neck, down along his waistcoat, and up again to his very ear, create an ecstatic strain of perfect music, audible to himself and to St. Cecilia. . . . (*The Warden*, chap. v).

133 Similarly, in *He Knew He Was Right* (chap. lxxxiv), Louis Trevelyan finally decides to sacrifice himself, as though glorying in his own physical decay, imagining that the blame will fall upon his wife and that she will afterwards be consumed with remorse.

134 Henry James, in *Partial Portraits*, also noted a family resemblance between Trollope's young women, adding (to our surprise) that they had nothing morbid about them: 'She has not a touch of the morbid, and is delightfully tender, modest and fresh.'

135 In *The New Statesman and Nation*, Apr. 19th, 1947.

136 See my essay 'Ritratti e illusioni' in *Lettrice notturna*, Rome, Casini, 1952.

137 Trollope may have learned from Thackeray to observe the curious significance that surrounding objects, of no importance in themselves, assume in the recollection of a moment of intense emotional life. In *The Adventures of Philip*, chap. xiv, when Philip hears, on Brighton Pier, that his cousin has become engaged to Captain Woolcomb: 'The pier tosses up to the skies, as though it had left its moorings—the houses on the cliff dance and reel, as though an earthquake was driving them. . . .' But a moment later Philip recovers himself: 'The houses, after reeling for a second or two, reassume the perpendicular, and bulge their bow-windows towards the main. He can see the people looking from the windows, the carriages passing, Professor Spurrier riding on the cliff with eighteen young ladies, his pupils. In long-after days he remembers those absurd little incidents with a curious tenacity.' In *Esmond*, also, recollection goes back again to a scene, apparently quite ordinary, which had remained fixed in the mind more intensely than sights more worthy of note (chap. xiv).

138 Another example may be seen in chapter xlviii of *Phineas Finn*, in a scene into which the Duke of Omnium again enters, to be vanquished, this time, by Madame Goesler.

139 The passage runs as follows:

The Duchess spoke with an enormous emphasis on some special syllable, as almost to bring her voice to a whistle. This she had done with the word 'pipes' to a great degree—so that Alice never afterwards forgot the hot-water pipes of Longroyston. . . . 'We've got no pipes, Duchess, at any rate', said Lady Glencora; and Alice, as she sat listening, thought she discerned in Lady Glencora's pronunciation of the word pipes an almost hidden imitation of the Duchess's whistle.

[140] *Early Victorian Novelists*, p. 278: 'When all is said and done, his humour is his greatest glory.'

[141] See above, pp. 270–1.

[142] J. W. Cross, *George Eliot's Life as related in her Letters and Journals*, William Blackwood, 3-vol. edition, 1885, vol. i, p. 460. The William Blackwood Complete Edition has been used for quotations from George Eliot's novels.

[143] Cf. G. H. Lewes's accompanying letter to John Blackwood with *Scenes of Clerical Life*, Nov. 6th, 1856, Cross, vol. i, pp. 417–18, apropos of *Amos Barton*: 'I don't know what you will think of the story, but according to my judgment, such humour, pathos, vivid presentation, and nice observation, have not been exhibited (in this style) since the "Vicar of Wakefield".' The Rev. Mr. Swayne also wrote to Blackwood saying that *Amos*, with its 'charming tenderness', made him think of the *Vicar of Wakefield* (Cross, vol. i, p. 433).

[144] Cross, vol. ii, p. 118, July 5th, 1859.

[145] Cf. O. Elton, *A Survey of English Literature, 1830–1880*, London, 1920, p. 263; he calls *The Mill on the Floss* and *Silas Marner* 'lyrical ballads in prose'. It has been remarked that in her perception of the dignity of character in humble life George Eliot had been anticipated also by Walter Scott, who has been described as 'probably the greatest single influence on her fiction' by Walter Allen, *The English Novel*, London, Phoenix House, Ltd., 1954, p. 211.

[146] Expressions drawn from poems by Wordsworth, *Three Years She Grew* and *Tintern Abbey*, are to be found in the description (chap. xix) of the state of mind of Silas during the moment of quietness and absorption which follows his finding of the child:

Anyone who has watched such moments in other men remembers the brightness of the eyes and the strange definiteness that comes over coarse features from that transient influence. It is as if a new fineness of ear for all spiritual voices had sent wonder-working vibrations through the heavy mortal frame—as if 'beauty born of murmuring sound' had passed into the face of the listener.

Cf. *Three Years She Grew*:

The stars of midnight shall be dear To her; and she shall lean her ear In many a secret place Where rivulets dance their wayward round, And beauty born of murmuring sound Shall pass into her face.

Moreover Silas, in becoming aware of the child's presence, wonders whether she could be

. . . his little sister come back to him in a dream—his little sister whom he had carried about in his arms for a year before she died, when he was a small boy without shoes or stockings. . . . *Was* it a dream ? . . . It was very much like his little sister. Silas sank into his chair powerless, under the double presence of an inexplicable surprise and a hurrying influx of memories. How and when had the child come in without his knowledge ? He had never been beyond the door. But along with that question, and almost thrusting it away, there was a vision of the old home and the old streets leading to Lantern Yard—and within that vision another, of the thoughts which had been present with him in those far-off scenes.

The method is Wordsworthian; a compact landscape breaks into the consciousness as in *The Reverie of Poor Susan*. And Silas's soul is warmed by the memory of a little girl (his sister), as was Peter Bell's by the memory of his young wife.

147 Cf. Henry James: *Daniel Deronda: a Conversation*. 'Constantius—The universe forcing itself with a slow, inexorable pressure into a narrow, complacent, and yet after all extremely sensitive mind, and making it ache with the pain of the process—that is Gwendolen's story.'

148 Cross, vol. ii, p. 290.

149 Cf. Basil Willey, *Nineteenth Century Studies*, London, Chatto & Windus, 1949, p. 246; P. Bourl'honne, *G. Eliot, Essai de biographie intellectuelle et morale, 1819–1854*, Paris, Champion, 1933, pp. 156 et seq.

150 Ruskin's objection is similar to that which Henry Fuseli (see *The Mind of Henry Fuseli*, op. cit., p. 285), in theory a partisan of ideal and historical painting, made against portrait-painting, against 'the insignificant individual that usurps the centre, one we never saw, care not if we never see, and, if we do, remember not'.

151 Cf. Thackeray's opinions on painting, pp. 217, 219 above.

152 Cross, vol. i, p. 429.

153 Cross, vol. i, p. 397.

154 It is the same theme as the famous epitaph of A. E. Housman on a mercenary army.

155 *Essays—Modern*, 1883, pp. 268–9.

156 V. S. Pritchett, *The Living Novel*, London, Chatto & Windus, 1946, p. 98.

157 Cross, vol. i, p. 61.

158 As Lord David Cecil wrote in *Early Victorian Novelists*, George Eliot 'did not think of a man and then invent what sort of thing was likely to happen to him, she thought of what happened to him and from that evolved what sort of man he was likely to have been'.

159 For the influence of Comte on George Eliot, see Basil Willey, op. cit., pp. 188 et seq.

160 Some lines by Wordsworth are quoted as a heading to *Silas Marner*: 'A child, more than all other gifts That earth can offer to declining man Brings hope with it, and forward-looking thoughts.' See chapter xiii of *Silas Marner*: We 'older human beings, with our inward turmoil, feel a certain awe in the presence of a little child, such as we feel before some quiet majesty or beauty in the earth or sky—before a steady glowing planet, or a full-flowered eglantine, or the bending trees over a silent pathway.' The child performs the miracle which in old days, it was said, was performed by 'angels who came and took men by the hand and led them away from the city of destruction' (chap. xiv).

161 Cross, vol. iii, p. 389.

162 And in *Adam Bede*, chap. liii: 'I am not ashamed of commemorating old Kester: you and I are indebted to the hard hands of such men—hands that have long ago mingled with the soil they tilled so faithfully, thriftily making the best they could of the earth's fruits, and receiving the smallest share as their own wages.'

[163] See F. O. Matthiessen, *American Renaissance*, Oxford University Press, 1946, p. 544.

[164] p. 303.

[165] See above, p. 290.

[166] Cross, vol. iii, p. 421.

[167] Cross, Letter to M. d'Albert, Jan. 22nd, 1861 (vol. ii later editions only).

[168] *The Great Tradition*, London, Chatto & Windus, 1948, p. 60. Gaetano Negri, in his fine essay 'G. Eliot, la sua vita e i suoi romanzi', Milan 1903, vol. i, p. 143, had stressed: 'The contrast between man's mediocrity and the grandeur of sorrow is, to her mind, more tragic than any heroic catastrophe.'

[169] See above, p. 319.

[170] See above, pp. 328–9.

[171] In face of the sad case of Mirah wishing to drown herself, he too—like George Eliot herself who was more deeply moved by the tragedy of Gretchen than by any other—reflects (chap. xvii) upon 'the girl-tragedies that are going on in the world, hidden, unheeded, as if they were but tragedies of the copse or hedgerow, where the helpless drag wounded wings forsakenly, and streak the shadowed moss with the red moment-hand of their own death'.

[172] Elton, op. cit., p. 266.

[173] See Lauriat Lane Jr. ' "Oliver Twist": a Revision', in *The Times Literary Supplement*, July 20th, 1951. Mr. Lane observes that Riah in *Our Mutual Friend* is 'so painfully good that he is almost more of an insult than Fagin'.

[174] Cross, vol. iii, p. 294.

[175] Cross, vol. iii, p. 291: letter of Oct. 2nd, 1876 to Mme. Bodichon.

[176] Gerald Bullett, *George Eliot*, London, Collins, 1947.

[177] Cross, vol. i, p. 431: letter of Feb. 18th, 1857.

[178] Cross, vol. i, p. 392: letter to Miss Sara Hennell, Feb. 25th, 1856.

[179] pp. 313, 314.

[180] Cross, vol. iii, p. 429.

[181] P. Bourl'honne, op. cit., pp. 92–93 and 128.

[182] Cross, vol. iii, p. 262.

[183] Cross, vol. iii, p. 296.

[184] In the period 1842–8, before the time of her real literary activity, she often expressed, on the other hand, her joy in living; see Bourl'honne, p. 66.

[185] She wrote, however, in *Scenes of Clerical Life*: 'We reap what we sow, but Nature has love over and above that justice, and gives us shadow and blossom and fruit that spring from no planting of ours.' But, as M. Bourl'honne remarks (footnote, p. 136), George Eliot did not integrate this idea into the general system of her thought, which continued to be dominated by the idea of necessity, so that she cannot well linger over such a notion.

186 Leopardi, *La Ginestra*. Literal translation: '[That man has a noble nature who] considers all men to be allied together, and embraces all with true love, offering and expecting valid and prompt help in the dangers which befall now one, now another, and in the torments of the war which Nature, their common enemy, wages against them.'

187 *Adam Bede*, chap. xxix.

188 *Adam Bede*, chap. xli.

189 *Middlemarch*, chap. lxxii.

190 See above, p. 280.

191 *Adam Bede*, chap. xii.

192 *Romola*, chap. xxvi.

193 Cf. *Early Essays*, The Westminster Press, 1919, pp. 33–34:

It is only the highest human state at which he [the true philosopher] aims— not anything superhuman. He seeks exercise for all the minor feelings—nay, he holds that these are the only nest in which the ever-aspiring eagle, Nature, can be properly fledged and winged; but he baptizes and hallows them all with the chrism of the diviner soul within him, and regulates their indulgence by his consciousness of the degree in which they encourage or repress the impulses of his moral sentiments.

See Bourl'honne, op. cit., pp. 64 and 132–3.

194 Chapter xlviii: 'The feeling Deronda endured in these moments he afterwards called horrible. Words seemed to have no more rescue in them than if he had been beholding a vessel in peril of wreck—the poor ship with its many-lived anguish beaten by the inescapable storm'. Chapter lxv: 'Deronda felt the look as if she had been stretching her arms towards him from a forsaken shore.'

195 An example from *Amos Barton*: 'A tallow dip . . . is an excellent thing in the kitchen candlestick, and Betty's nose and eye are not sensitive to the difference between it and the finest wax; it is only when you stick it in the silver candlestick, and introduce it into the drawing-room, that it seems plebeian, dim, and ineffectual. Alas for the worthy man, who, like that candle, gets himself into the wrong place!' A vignette and its moral application: an emblem.

196 The metaphors in *Middlemarch* have been studied by Mark Schorer in the essay 'Fiction and the "Matrix of Analogy" ' in the *Kenyon Review* of autumn 1949.

197 *A Century of Emblems*, London, 1878.

198 Op. cit., p. 93.

199 F. R. Leavis, op. cit., p. 124, considers that Hardy, in comparison with George Eliot, is 'a provincial manufacturer of gauche and heavy fictions that sometimes have corresponding virtues'.

200 Pritchett, op. cit., p. 91: 'If we read a novel in order to clarify our minds about human character, in order to pass judgment on the effect of character on the world outside itself, and to estimate the ideas people have lived by, then George Eliot is one of the first to give such an intellectual direction to the English novel. She is the first of the simplifiers, one of the first to cut moral paths through the picturesque maze of human motive. It is the intimidating role of the schoolmistress.'

[201] Vol. iii, pp. 424–5.

[202] Cross, vol. ii, p. 284.

[203] See above, note 184.

[204] See Pritchett, op. cit., pp. 91–92, and his review of Gerald Bullett's Life of George Eliot in the *New Statesman and Nation*, Aug. 9th, 1947; R. H. Hutton, 'George Eliot's Life' in the *Contemporary Review*, Mar. 1885, according to whom the work of George Eliot is an expiation of the guilt of Miss Evans (her extra-conjugal union with Lewes); Bourl'honne, op. cit., pp. 189–90, note, and 191: 'Nous croyons que son œuvre est inspirée d'un sentiment de réparation par rapport à sa vie.'

[205] 'Novelist-Philosophers, XII, George Eliot', in *Horizon*, Jan. 1948, pp. 50–62.

[206] See above, p. 274.

[207] Cross, vol. iii, p. 420.

[208] Cross, vol. ii, p. 209.

[209] Cross, vol. ii, p. 244.

[210] Cross, vol. ii, p. 26.

[211] Cross, vol. ii, p. 148.

[212] Op. cit., p. 93.

[213] See above, p. 295.

[214] Cross, vol. i, pp. 429 et seq.

[215] Op. cit., p. 122.

[216] I fear Mr. Leavis is under an illusion as to the entity which this book would make if purged of its mouldy parts; and even more so with regard to *Felix Holt*, which, if the parts that are unsuccessful (in Mr. Leavis's opinion) of Holt himself, of Rufus Lyon ('a bore' whose discourses occupy 'a large proportion of the book') were removed, and it were reduced merely to the Mrs. Transome–Jermyn–Harold Transome plot, would take little more space than a long-short-story by Maupassant: and yet Mr. Leavis deplores the fact that this book, which according to him is 'one of the finest things in fiction', should be almost unknown to the public of today. In his reaction against current opinion, Mr. Leavis makes assertions which can only be called 'extravagant'. Thus, to him, Dickens's *Hard Times* (p. 47) is a 'great book' 'which combines a perfection of "art" in the Flaubertian sense with an un-Flaubertian moral strength and human richness'. To which one can only remark that Mr. Leavis's throwing of anti-Flaubertian brickbats sometimes leads to very strange excesses. *Hard Times* is a paradigmatic novel like Huxley's *Brave New World*, its aim being to show the inhumanity of industrial civilization. The scenes which Mr. Leavis quotes to convince us that 'Flaubert never wrote anything approaching this in subtlety of achieved art' are brilliant satirical scenes, extremely good in a field in which any comparison with Flaubert would be out of place.

[217] I do not therefore understand how Lord David Cecil (op. cit.) can affirm that 'since the action of George Eliot's stories arises logically from the characters [*but he had previously said something quite different; see above, note 158*] those strokes of fortune, coincidences, sudden inheritances, long-lost wills, which are the stock-in-trade of the ordinary Victorian plot, are inevitably omitted'.

²¹⁸ See above, pp. 127 et seq.

²¹⁹ Op. cit., pp. 52 and 72.

²²⁰ Pritchett, op. cit., p. 99.

²²¹ See above, p. 154.

²²² Cf. Henry James, *Daniel Deronda: a Conversation*. '*Pulcheria*— She is very fond of deaths by drowning. Maggie Tulliver and her brother are drowned. Tito Melema is drowned. Mr. Grandcourt is drowned. It is extremely unlikely that Grandcourt should not have known how to swim. *Constantius*—He did, of course, but he had a cramp. It served him right.'

²²³ Very melodramatic is the way in which Caterina prepares herself for vengeance (chap. xiii)

See how she rushes noiselessly, like a pale meteor, along the passages and up the gallery stairs! Those gleaming eyes, those bloodless lips, that swift silent tread, make her look like the incarnation of a fierce purpose, rather than a woman. The midday sun is shining on the armour in the gallery, making mimic suns on bossed sword-hilts and the angles of polished breastplates. Yes, there are sharp weapons in the gallery. There is a dagger in that cabinet; she knows it well. And as a dragon-fly wheels in its flight to alight for an instant on a leaf, she darts to the cabinet, takes out the dagger, and thrusts it into her pocket. . . .

She has reached the Rookery, and is under the gloom of the interlacing boughs. Her heart throbs as if it would burst her bosom—as if every next leap must be its last. Wait, wait, O heart!—till she has done this one deed. He will be there— he will be before her in a moment. He will come towards her with that false smile, thinking she does not know his baseness—she will plunge that dagger into his heart.

Poor child! poor child! she who used to cry to have the fish put back into the water—who never willingly killed the smallest living thing—dreams now, in the madness of her passion, that she can kill the man whose very voice unnerves her. But what is that lying among the dank leaves on the path three yards before her? Good God! it is he—lying motionless—his hat fallen off. He is ill, then—he has fainted. Her hand lets go the dagger, and she rushes towards him. His eyes are fixed; he does not see her. She sinks down on her knees, takes the dear head in her arms, and kisses the cold forehead. 'Anthony, Anthony! speak to me—it is Tina—speak to me! O God, he is dead!'

²²⁴ Nevertheless Mr. Leavis says about this scene (p. 60): 'This may sound melodramatic as recapitulated here; that it should come with so final a rightness in the actual text shows with what triumphant success George Eliot has justified her high tragic conception of her theme.'

²²⁵ See above, p. 361.

²²⁶ In *Martin Chuzzlewit*.

²²⁷ In *David Copperfield*, see above, p. 172.

²²⁸ At the end of her career George Eliot still retained traces of this Dickensian felicity of humorous phrase. Gwendolen, in a tête-à-tête with her hated husband (chap. xlviii), rather than look at his false 'lizard's eyes' prefers to look at the 'boiled ingenuousness' of the eyes of the prawn she is eating.

²²⁹ Job xix. 24.

²³⁰ See also *The Mill on the Floss*, Book I, chap. vii, on the troubles of children which we grown-ups, forgetful of our childhood, treat 'with a smiling disbelief in the reality of their pain', whereas, 'if we could recall that early bitterness, and the dim guesses, the strangely perspectiveless conception of life that gave the bitterness its intensity, we should not pooh-pooh the griefs of our children'.

²³¹ *À la recherche de Marcel Proust*, Paris, Hachette, 1949, p. 29.

²³² A pupil of mine, Clara Bruner, in a thesis (not published) on the 'Influence of the Victorian novelists on Marcel Proust', observed that Maurois does not quote the phrase preceding the passage from George Eliot cited by him, which shows the identity of the two writers' starting-points: 'It is time, too, for me, to leave off resting my arms on the cold stone of the bridge. . . . Ah, my arms are really benumbed. I have been pressing my elbows on the arms of my chair, and dreaming that I was standing on the bridge in front of Dorlecote Mill, as it looked one February afternoon, many years ago . . . .' 'Thus,' says Miss Bruner, 'the past was partly re-created by George Eliot from the position of the body during sleep: the arms of the chair were replaced by the parapet of the bridge over the Floss and a whole landscape was re-created round this sensation. Various sensations from the past were re-created for Proust from the position of his body during sleep.' For George Eliot's influence on Proust see also L. A. Bisson, 'Proust, Bergson et George Eliot', in the *Modern Language Review*, 1945, and J. M. Cocking, 'English Influences on Proust', in *The Listener*, Aug. 27th, 1953.

²³³ Albert Feuillerat, *Comment Marcel Proust a composé son roman*, New Haven 1934 (Yale Romantic Studies, vii).

²³⁴ *À l'ombre des jeunes filles en fleurs*, vol. i, p. 26, in the edition *Œuvres complètes, Nouvelle Revue française*, 1929 et seq.

²³⁵ The text here is incorrect (Pietraganta), as often, unfortunately, occurs in this typographically fine edition.

²³⁶ *À l'Ombre des jeunes filles en fleurs*, vol. iii, p. 64.

²³⁷ Vol. i, p. 75.

²³⁸ Vol. i, p. 144.

²³⁹ George Eliot was in any case a diligent reader of Donne; she quotes lines from Donne as a heading to chapter xxxix of *Middlemarch*.

²⁴⁰ *The Mill on the Floss*, Book I, chap. viii. George Eliot's partiality for zoological similes may have been due to Lewes's zoological interests.

²⁴¹ Cf. Dante, *Purg.* vi. 148 et seq.

²⁴² Proust speaks in *Sodome et Gomorrhe* (vol. i, p. 292) of the new interest one feels in writers of the past when one finds that they have, 'dans un simple morceau, réalisé quelque chose qui ressemble à ce que le maître peu à peu s'est rendu compte que lui-même avait voulu faire. Alors il voit en cet ancien comme un précurseur; il aime chez lui, sous une autre forme, un effort momentanément, partiellement fraternel. Il y a des morceaux de Turner dans l'œuvre de Poussin, une phrase de Flaubert dans Montesquieu.' If the metaphors of George Eliot that we have quoted seem to be those of a Proust *avant la lettre*, others have a family resemblance to Meredith.

Adam Bede and *The Ordeal of Richard Feverel* were published in the same year, 1859. Describing the idyll of Arthur and Hetty (*Adam Bede*, vol i, chap. xiii) George Eliot writes: 'He is bending his face nearer and nearer to the round cheek, his lips are meeting those pouting child-lips, and for a long moment time has vanished. He may be a shepherd in Arcadia for aught he knows, he may be the first youth kissing the first maiden, he may be Eros himself, sipping the lips of Psyche—it is all one.' In the idyll between Richard and Lucy on the river, in Meredith's novel, the scene changes by enchantment into that of Shakespeare's *Tempest*: 'He had landed on an island of the still-vexed Bermoothes. The world lay wrecked behind him. . . . Hark how Ariel sang overhead ! . . . Fair Flame, by whose light the glories of being are now first seen. . . . Radiant Miranda ! Prince Ferdinand is at your feet.' In *Middlemarch* (chap. viii) we read of 'solid imperturbable ease and good-humour which is infectious, and like great grassy hills in the sunshine, quiets even an irritated egoism'. The portrait of Clara Middleton in *The Egoist* contains similar transpositions into terms of landscape: 'Aspens imaged in water, waiting for the breeze, would offer a susceptible lover some suggestion of her face.' Of similar Meredithian characteristics, several are to be found in George Eliot's work. In *Middlemarch* (chap. xxii) a remark by Ladislaw shows 'such originality as we all share with the morning and the spring-time and other endless renewals'. In chapter xxxix of the same novel:

For effective magic is transcendent nature; and who shall measure the subtlety of those touches which convey the quality of soul as well as body, and make a man's passion for one woman differ from his passion for another as joy in the morning light over valley and river and white mountain-top differs from joy among Chinese lanterns and glass pannels ? Will, too, was made of very impressible stuff. The bow of a violin drawn near him cleverly, would at one stroke change the aspect of the world for him, and his point of view shifted as easily as his mood. Dorothea's entrance was the freshness of morning.

It is curious to note these momentary contacts between the prosaic and somewhat ponderous woman novelist and the most poetical, the most volatile, of English story-tellers. And also with another, very different, sister of the future. The moment in which the flirtation between Lydgate and Rosamond (*Middlemarch*, chap. xxxi) turns into love, when Lydgate stoops to pick up the girl's chain from the floor, and rising again finds himself very close to her face and discovers in it an expression which gives him a new feeling, 'at this moment she was as natural as she had ever been when she was five years old: she felt that her tears had risen, and it was no use to try to do anything else than let them stay like water on a blue flower or let them fall over her cheeks, even as they would. That moment of naturalness was the crystallising feather-touch: it shook flirtation into love.' It is interesting to compare this passage with one from Virginia Woolf (*The Common Reader*, London, 1925, p. 178) in which she is commenting upon an episode in Jane Austen's *Mansfield Park*: 'From triviality, from commonplace, their words become suddenly full of meaning, and the moment for both one of the most memorable in their lives. It fills itself; it shines: it glows; it hangs before us, deep, trembling, serene for a second. . . .' But

George Eliot did no more than catch a glimpse of what was to be Virginia Woolf 's central problem, the expression of the moment in which all life seems to be contained at its greatest intensity (G. Melchiori, in an essay not yet published, 'The Moment as a Time Unit in Fiction', has examined this preoccupation of modern narrative). Meredithian, too, is the image with which George Eliot's passage concludes: 'Remember that the ambitious man who was looking at those Forget-me-nots under the water was very warm-hearted and rash.' George Eliot, without extracting the consequences from it in the way Virginia Woolf was to do, had already noticed the sense of time as a purely personal and psychological condition: 'Extension, we know, is a very imperfect measure of things. . .' (*Deronda*, chap. lviii).

243 The comparison is Miss Bruner's, in the thesis quoted in note 232.

244 The sense of the affinity of certain aspects of character in different members of the same family is illustrated, for example, in *The Mill on the Floss*, Book II, chap. ii.

245 For the influence of George Eliot on Henry James, see Leavis, op. cit.

APPENDIX I

The Epic of the Everyday

'The Angel in the House'

by COVENTRY PATMORE

He thinks of writing a poem to be *the* poem of the age.

Letter from ALFRED FRYER,
referring to COVENTRY PATMORE

THE poetry of Coventry Patmore again occupies a place of honour in our present century, thanks to its 'discovery' by Paul Claudel and to the translation he made of a group of odes from *The Unknown Eros* in 1911.[1] In this work (published in 1877) Patmore showed how closely related he was to the English religious poets of the seventeenth century, to the 'metaphysical' tradition on one side (Donne, Herbert, Crashaw, Vaughan), and on the other to the whole of the mystical tradition. He therefore found favourable terrain in the rebirth of interest—soon to be transformed into a fashion—for Donne and his school, which had its beginning with Professor Grierson's edition (1912) of the works of the great metaphysical poet of the seventeenth century. But the figure of a mystical, metaphysical Patmore, the only one known to modern readers, is very different from that of the poet who in the eighteen-fifties enjoyed a few years of great popularity with his *Angel in the House*, which seemed like an incarnation of Victorian Biedermeier ideals and identified itself to such a degree with the bourgeois conception of life that Swinburne's description of it as 'idylls of the dining-room and the deanery' was an epigram that fitted it like a glove. In reality, as we shall see, the metaphysical influence is just as strong in this poem as the intention to convey the atmosphere of everyday life in its every detail. This latter element was due—is it necessary to say?—to Wordsworth, one of Patmore's youthful enthusiasms, whom he imitated even more closely in his first volume of verse (*Poems*, 1844), particularly in *The Woodman's Daughter*, which he wrote at the age of sixteen.

Patmore's contemporaries failed to notice, in *The Angel in the House*, the first expression of what was to be the dominant motif of his whole work, of what was, for him, 'the burning heart of the universe'[2]—the conception of earthly love as a first stage, a prefiguration of divine love. The love between God and the Soul is the love between the Spouse and the Espoused, elevated to its highest perfection; the only means of comprehending and achieving supernatural relations is by meditation and by the contemplation of their types in Nature; the invisible is known through the visible; and we are able, even through the gross medium of the senses, when clarified by the spirit, to perceive ultimate perfection:

> Bright with the spirit shone the sense,
> As with the sun a fleecy cloud.

What for Wordsworth had been intimations of immortality through childhood memories, became, for Patmore, intimations of the soul's union with God, communicated through the physical materiality of carnal love.[3] Thus corporal pleasure, to which the poet was exceptionally partial, came to be sublimated through its symbolic interpretation: 'Glorify God in your body.' There was only one Church which seemed to countenance the poet's theory of human love—the Catholic Church, with its symbolic interpretation of the sensual theme of the *Song of Songs*, and its exaltation of Woman as the image of Paradise. The conversion of Patmore to Catholicism was therefore a foregone conclusion.[4]

Patmore's face, no less than that of Thackeray, tells its own story—with its brow wide as Caesar's, the grey eyes of the fanatic beneath curiously circumflex lids, the *nez fureteur* like that of a pointer, and the sensual lips, fleshy, pendulous, again like those of a sporting dog.[5] Some dictatorial and at the same time Don Quixote-like quality is

apparent in the whole emaciated figure, which is like that
of a military man as El Greco might have painted it. And
if we look at him in a scene from everyday life, in a photograph taken on the lawn in front of his house at Hastings,
surrounded by his family at the tea-table, the impression
we get of his domestic life—perhaps owing to the stiffness
of Victorian formality which has shrivelled up the two unmarried daughters standing at the back, and the maid in
cap and apron ready to hand round the cake—is not quite
what one would expect from a reading of *The Angel in the
House*. The old poet lying back in his easy chair, twisting
his face round above the high, stiff collar—a face that tries
to look good-natured—towards the group formed by his
third wife and his beloved son Piffie, has the possessive
air of an ancient patriarch set apart on his own special
throne.[6] And his sensual tastes were indeed those of
the patriarch or the pasha, not limited to women but
extending, as with an Oriental, to precious stones: and not
merely did he enjoy the handling of emeralds, pearls, and
diamonds, but he knew how to estimate the water of jewels,
and for a certain period of his life actually bought and sold
them. His third wife, the one in the picture, who followed
the example of Becky Sharp and rose from governess to
mistress of the house, survived the poet; but the first wife
died of consumption, the second soon became a semi-invalid
and died suddenly in 1880, while Patmore's favourite
daughter, Emily Honoria, who had become a nun and was
obsessed, in her last moments, by the guilty feeling that
she had loved her father too much,[7] also died of consumption, as did the most beloved of the poet's sons, Henry,
himself a poet. So that one comes to wonder whether the
poet was not one of those fatal germ-carriers who, although
they themselves remain immune, sow death all around
them. Anyhow, Patmore's life was not the mirror of felicity
that one might think; it was, in fact, troubled by bereave-
ments, by incomprehension (after he lost his first wife, he
was lacking in tact in his relations with his sons), and, in
his last period, disturbed by a senile passion—not at all
conjugal, this time!—a real, genuine physical passion,
which was not reciprocated, for Alice Meynell.[8] And he

himself remarks 'that the happiest life was a tragedy or a series of tragedies'.[9]

But it is not Patmore's life nor even the very personal type of his mysticism that interests us here, but rather his highly successful poem, and the reasons for which it was bound to have an appeal to contemporaries who saw certain of their own aspirations mirrored in it.

Looked at from the distance from which we now see it, *The Angel in the House*, the epic and paean of conjugal love, no longer seems the bold invention that in truth it was. The reign of Queen Victoria had at its centre a conjugal idyll, the idyll of Victoria and Albert: have not Tennyson's *Idylls of the King* been called in view of this, 'idylls of the Prince Consort'? *The Angel in the House* may therefore seem to us the natural product of a whole society, that of the age of Albert the Good, and to be the poetic mouthpiece of an already acclimatized conception of life. Wordsworth's popularity had lasted almost until 1850. And had not Wordsworth, repudiating his youthful ideals, proclaimed:

> I travelled among unknown men,
>   In lands beyond the sea;
> Nor, England! did I know till then
>   What love I bore to thee.

> 'Tis past, that melancholy dream!
>   Nor will I quit thy shore
> A second time; for still I seem
>   To love thee more and more.

> Among thy mountains did I feel
>   The joy of my desire;
> And she I cherished turned her wheel
>   Beside an English fire.

Had not Wordsworth proclaimed this?[10] And Patmore[11] sang of the interdependence of love and conjugal faithfulness:

> Such perfect friends are truth and love
>   That neither lives where both are not.

40. Victorian Cupid and Psyche (from Thomas Miller's
Poetical Language of Flowers, London 1847)

> Praise then my Song where'er it comes,
>   Ladies, whose innocence makes bright
> England, the land of courtly homes,
>   The world's exemplar and delight.

And the twelfth letter in Book II of the poem that was a sequel to *The Angel in the House*, *The Victories of Love*, an imaginary letter from the protagonist of the *Angel* to his wife, concludes with:

> . . . yet, ere wrath or rot destroy
> Of England's state the ruin fair,
> Oh, might I so its charm declare,
> That, in new Lands, in far-off years,
> Delighted he should cry that hears:
> 'Great is the Land that somewhat best
> Works, to the wonder of the rest!
> We, in our day, have better done
> This thing or that than any one;
> And who but, still admiring, sees
> How excellent for images
> Was Greece, for laws how wise was Rome;
> But read this Poet, and say if home
> And private love did e'er so smile
> As in that ancient English isle!'

Thackeray, as we have seen,[12] wrote in *Pendennis*:

I think it is not national prejudice which makes me believe that a high-bred English lady is the most complete of all Heaven's subjects in this world. In whom else do you see so much grace, and so much virtue; so much faith, and so much tenderness; with such a perfect refinement and chastity? And by high-bred ladies I don't mean duchesses and countesses. Be they ever so high in station, they can be but ladies, and no more. But almost every man who lives in the world has the happiness, let us hope, of counting a few such persons amongst his circle of acquaintance—women in whose angelical natures there is something awful, as well as beautiful, to contemplate; at whose feet the wildest and fiercest of us must fall down and humble ourselves, in admiration of that adorable purity which never seems to do or to think wrong.

And here, in fact, we have the Angel in the house:

> Her disposition is devout,
>   Her countenance angelical . . .
>   .   .   .   .   .

In mind and manners how discreet!
How artless in her very art;
How candid in discourse; how sweet
In concord of her lips and heart;
How simple and how circumspect;

.   .   .   .   .

How humbly careful to attract,
Though crown'd with all the soul desires,
Connubial aptitude exact,
Diversity that never tires.[13]

But, whereas novelists had lingered over the delights of
married life, to poets the subject had always seemed far
from heroic. If English romanticism had not, like the
French variety, reached the point of identifying love with
adultery, even to it the terms passion and matrimony
seemed, if not contradictory, to be certainly an ill-assorted
pair. It has been remarked[14] that, after all, at the time when
The Angel in the House appeared, Shelley's *Epipsychidion*
was still fresh in men's minds, and hardly less fresh was
Byron's *Don Juan*. So that Patmore, in considering love
sanctioned by the Church and State as a theme worthy of
poetry, nay, as the worthiest of all themes, brought about
a parallel revolution to that of the Victorian prose-writers
who proclaimed the dignity and beauty of humble everyday things as against the conventional romantic idea of the
heroic. The Prologue of the First Book of *The Angel in the
House* stresses the humdrum character of its inspiration in
a stanza which reminds us of the programme of George
Eliot's *Scenes of Clerical Life* and of Thackeray's *Small-
Beer Chronicle*. Reminiscent of George Eliot, too, are the
first two lines of Patmore's ode to *Winter*:

I, singularly moved
To love the lovely that are not beloved. . . .

Winter is like a Dutch picture, an unattractive landscape
in which the artist discovers a beauty that is not obvious.
The Prologue of the First Book, then, declares:

Mine is no horse with wings, to gain
The region of the sphered chime;
He does but drag a rumbling wain,
Cheer'd by the silver bells of rhyme;

> And if at Fame's bewitching note
> My homely Pegasus pricks an ear,
> The world's cart-collar hugs his throat,
> And he's too wise to kick or rear.

Patmore imagines a poet of the name of Vaughan (the same name, be it noted, as that of the mystical seventeenth-century poet) who, on the eighth anniversary of his marriage, confides to his wife that he has undertaken a poem on an entirely new subject:

> I, meditating much and long
> What I should sing, how win a name,
> Considering well what theme unsung,
> What reason worth the cost of rhyme
> Remains to loose the poet's tongue
> In these last days, the dregs of time,
> Learn that to me, though born so late,
> There does, beyond desert, befall
> (May my great fortune make me great!)
> The first of themes sung last of all.
> In green and undiscover'd ground,
> Yet near where many others sing,
> I have the very well-head found
> Whence gushes the Pierian Spring.

It is curious to note that in those same years (*The Angel in the House* appeared in two parts, *The Betrothal* in 1854, *The Espousals* in 1856) another poet, in France, feeling, also, that he had arrived as it were too late, when the main subjects of inspiration had all been exploited, went in search of it 'à l'extrémité du Kamtchatka littéraire', into an unexplored province where he found—oh, a very different subject from Patmore's—the beauty of evil, *Les Fleurs du mal*!

Vaughan's wife, in the Prologue to *The Angel in the House*, asks the poet what theme he has chosen:

> 'What is it, Dear? The Life
> Of Arthur, or Jerusalem's Fall?'
> 'Neither: your gentle self, my wife,
> And love, that grows from one to all.'

Conjugal love: this is 'the most heart-touching theme'

that voice of poet ever intoned; he will live as long as those
poets who sang the praises of Laura and Beatrice, and com-
mentators will dispute over his lines, attributing a 'mytho-
logical intent' to his praises of Woman, in whom some will
see a symbol of Faith, others of Charity, others of Hope,
and others again, wiser, of all three.[15] The pedestrian
tone of the octosyllabics with alternate rhymes confers no
solemnity at all upon these declarations, so that the reader
skims over them, as it were, as if they were the voluble
chit-chat of some humble, provincial Muse. And the poem,
as it proceeds, seems to confirm him in this provincialism:

> 'Your arm's on mine! these are the meads
>   In which we pass our living days;
> There Avon runs, now hid with reeds,
>   Now brightly brimming pebbly bays;
> Those are our children's songs that come
>   With bells and bleatings of the sheep;
> And there, in yonder English home,
>   We thrive on mortal food and sleep!'

It is a rustic, Wordsworthian world, it is a provincial
poet trying to fit the laurels of Dante or Petrarch on to his
own brow, rather like the 'newly made knight' in Fedotov's
picture who, proud of his title, strikes an attitude like
an ancient Roman. Each canto consists of short preludes
which contain considerations of metaphysical character
intended to form the intellectual background of the poem,
and of narrative sections characterized by a realism which
is minute, caressing, and often unintentionally grotesque
in its attempt to relate itself closely to everyday existence.
Patmore chose an elastic form, as T. S. Eliot was to do in
our own day for *The Cocktail Party*, the metre of which had
to be capable of throbbing with transcendental solemnity
and also of flattening itself out in such a way that the listener
could not tell it was different from prose. Patmore's
quatrains seem indeed to be modelled on the tune of the
'Old Hundredth' psalm, as Professor Grierson and J. C.
Smith[16] point out; but one notices with surprise that the
metre is the same as that of Donne's *Extasie*.

Nevertheless the kinship with Donne and the other

metaphysical poets is not at first apparent. The familiar,
Biedermeier, Wordsworthian tone is what first strikes us:

> If rightly you peruse the Lay,
> You shall be sweetly help'd and warn'd.

The purpose the poet seems to be establishing for himself is to be instructive, practical, and pedestrian.

> Thou Primal Love, who grantest wings
> And voices to the woodland birds,
> Grant me the power of saying things
> Too simple and too sweet for words![17]

How can we fail to hear an echo, in these lines, of Wordsworth's: 'Thoughts that do often lie too deep for tears'
(*Intimations of Immortality*)? The same undertaking that the
poet formulates farther on (Book I, Canto VI, Preludes, 2,
Love Justified):

> This little germ of nuptial love,
> Which springs so simply from the sod,
> The root is, as my Song shall prove,
> Of all our love of man and God—[18]

—this undertaking to soar from conjugal to divine love,
from 'home sweet home' to the Empyrean, is announced
candidly, like the naïve discovery of a country schoolmaster. The provincial, Victorian atmosphere is clearly
conveyed and unalterably fixed in the oft-quoted lines from
the first narrative section, *The Cathedral Close*:

> Once more I came to Sarum Close,
> With joy half memory, half desire,
> And breathed the sunny wind that rose
> And blew the shadows o'er the Spire,
> And toss'd the lilac's scented plumes,
> And sway'd the chestnut's thousand cones,
> And fill'd my nostrils with perfumes,
> And shaped the clouds in waifs and zones,
> And wafted down the serious strain
> Of Sarum bells, when, true to time,
> I reach'd the Dean's, with heart and brain
> That trembled to the trembling chime.

'Twas half my home six years ago.
  The six years had not alter'd it:
Red-brick and ashlar, long and low,
  With dormers and with oriels lit.
Geranium, lychnis, rose array'd
  The windows, all wide open thrown;
And some one in the Study play'd
  The Wedding-March of Mendelssohn.

These last lines, particularly, are as it were the quint-essence of Victorianism, and as such have been often quoted; but there are flowers scattered here and there all over the poem, flowers as vivid as those in a piece of Victorian cross-stitch or a Victorian keepsake. Now it is the geranium, the carnation, and the rose which are used as terms of comparison (Book I, Canto II, Preludes, 1, *The Paragon*; and Canto IV, *The Morning Call*, 2: 'geranium-plots, a rival glow of green and red': Patmore is the first poet who ever sang of the geranium, that exquisitely Victorian plant), now it is the buds of the foxglove, opening by couples, which provide an image of 'confidences' between a young man and a young woman that 'heavenwards blew' (Book I, Canto II, *Mary and Mildred*); and elsewhere it is the yellow water-flags (Book I, Canto I, Preludes, 6), clematis (Book I, Canto IV, *The Morning Call*, 1), hyacinths and primroses (Book II, Canto VII, *The Revulsion*, 1), violets blue and white (Book I, Canto V, *The Violets*, 2), guelder-roses (Book I, Canto VII, *Aetna and the Moon*, 2) harebells (Book I, Canto VIII, *Sarum Plain*, 5). This taste for flowers, evocative, to us, of the Victorian atmosphere, must have given pleasure to Patmore's contemporaries—not so much to the learned ones, as to readers of only moderate culture, amongst whom the poem was especially popular (250,000 copies of it were printed during the poet's lifetime);[19] and readers of this type saw mirrored in *The Angel in the House* even the quiet Victorian domesticity, even the conversations with their commonplace phrases that were their own daily experience, without minding whether such passages in the body of the poem were regarded by critics as examples of extreme bathos, as illustrations of the category of the grotesque. Like Wordsworth in the first place, and

George Eliot later, Patmore had no fear of being over-pedestrian: in fact he deliberately insisted upon the pedestrian, thus falling in with the general tendency of Victorian poetry, which cultivated the subdued note in opposition to the heroic, the everyday in place of the eccentric, such as had formed the stock-in-trade of the Romantic Muse. In *The Angel in the House* the subject itself has nothing apparently heroic or dramatic about it. A young man of good family, Felix Vaughan, with six hundred a year, falls in love with Honoria, one of the daughters of the Dean of Sarum, Dr. Churchill, she herself having a dowry of three thousand pounds; he woos her, and after some mild rivalry on the part of the girl's cousin, Frederick Graham, a naval officer, finds his love recipro-cated, asks the Dean for his daughter's hand in marriage, obtains it and leads her to the altar. The minute events of this wooing, the visits, the dinners, the departures by train, all are registered with a realism which, as happens with writers of the second rank, with the minor masters, has preserved the whole flavour of the period and to us seems amusing or charming (although the charm here lies more in the manners than in the poetry): it was pleasing to Pat-more's contemporaries, as I have said, because they saw reflected in it their own habits and their taste for moral orderliness and neatness.

> For something that abode endued
>   With temple-like repose, an air
> Of life's kind purposes pursued
>   With order'd freedom sweet and fair.
> A tent pitch'd in a world not right
>   It seem'd, whose inmates, every one,
> On tranquil faces bore the light
>   Of duties beautifully done,
> And humbly, though they had few peers,
>   Kept their own laws, which seem'd to be
> The fair sum of six thousand years'
>   Traditions of civility.[20]

And again, speaking of men of exemplary character (Book I, Canto x, Preludes, I):

They live by law, not like the fool,
　　But like the bard, who freely sings
In strictest bonds of rhyme and rule,
　　And finds in them, not bonds, but wings.
Postponing still their private ease
　　To courtly custom, appetite,
Subjected to observances,
　　To banquet goes with full delight;
Nay, continence and gratitude
　　So cleanse their lives from earth's alloy,
They taste, in nature's common food,
　　Nothing but spiritual joy.
They shine like Moses in the face,
　　And teach our hearts, without the rod,
That God's grace is the only grace,
　　And all grace is the grace of God.

The principle is the same as that of Wordsworth's *Ode to Duty*, that happiness is to be sought not in 'unchartered freedom' but in strict adherence to a rule, to a law. Read again the last but one stanza of the *Ode to Duty*:

Stern Lawgiver! yet thou dost wear
The Godhead's most benignant grace;
Nor know we anything so fair
As is the smile upon thy face—

and compare it with the image which concludes this prelude by Patmore: the very rhyme *grace–face* reveals the source to which Patmore's accents can be traced.

As regards its ethical basis, then, *The Angel in the House* was grafted upon the Wordsworthian tradition, which was at the height of its renown during the first half of the nineteenth century and was diffused amongst all grades of society, not limited to literary circles. There was to be found, in this poem, Wordsworth's loftiest note, and there was also his pedestrian side, his bathos, carried to the point of the most deliberate carelessness. Scattered throughout the poem are specifications and conversations of the most banal type, such as to challenge the conventional concept of the poetic. We find put into verse the 'luncheon-bell' (Book I, Canto II, *Mary and Mildred*, 3), 'tea on the lawn'

(Book I, Canto vi, *The Dean*, 4), plans for the day announced at breakfast (Book I, Canto viii, *Sarum Plain*, 1 :
'Breakfast enjoy'd . . .'), rent-collecting (Book I, Canto iv,
The Morning Call, 2 : 'Three hundred pounds for half the
year'), an invitation to dinner (Book I, Canto v, *The Violets*,
2 : 'Papa had bid her send his love, And would I dine with
him next day ?'); and we find a passage like this (Book I,
Canto iii, *Honoria*, 1):

> I rode to see
> The church-restorings; lounged awhile
> And met the Dean; was ask'd to tea,
> And found their cousin, Frederick Graham,
> At Honor's side—

which, if it does not represent the whole of Trollope in a
nutshell, if it does not condense the whole of the Barchester
Novels into one epigram, as has been said, nevertheless
gives the quintessence of England round about 1850. The
following lines, in other respects, are no less typical (Book I,
Canto iv, *The Morning Call*, 2):

> Her sisters in the garden Walk'd,
> And would I come? Across the Hall
> She took me; and we laugh'd and talk'd
> About the Flower-show and the Ball.
> Their pinks had won a spade for prize;
> But this was gallantly withdrawn
> For 'Jones on Wiltshire Butterflies':
> Allusive! So we paced the lawn,
> Close-cut, and, with geranium-plots,
> A rival glow of green and red;
> Then counted sixty apricots
> On one small tree; the gold-fish fed;
> And watch'd where, black with scarlet rings,
> Proud Psyche stood and flash'd like flame,
> Showing and shutting splendid wings;
> And in the prize we found its name.[21]

And in Book I, Canto vi, *The Dean*, 2, 3:

> Towards my mark the Dean's talk set:
> He praised my 'Notes on Abury',
> Read when the Association met
> At Sarum; he was glad to see

I had not stopp'd, as some men had,
    At Wrangler and Prize Poet; last,
He hoped the business was not bad
    I came about: then the wine pass'd.

A full glass prefaced my reply:
    I loved his daughter, Honor; he knew
My estate and prospects; might I try
    To win her? To mine eyes tears flew.
He thought 'twas that. I might. He gave
    His true consent, if I could get
Her love. A dear, good Girl! she'd have
    Only three thousand pounds as yet;
More bye and bye. . . .

The subdued tone, the 'undrest, familiar style' (Book II,
Canto III, Preludes, I), the *enjambements* give the passage
a laboured, lurching rhythm, like prose put on the Pro-
crustes' bed of verse rather than a natural *sermo pedestris,*
and with a forced effect that reminds one of Goethe's *Her-
mann und Dorothea,* the poem that sought to adapt bourgeois material and everyday conversation to the heroic
metres of Homer.[22] *The Angel in the House* abounds in
banal conversations. Thus in Book II, Canto I, *Accepted,* 2:

I paced the streets; a pistol chose,
    To guard my now important life
When riding late from Sarum Close;
    At noon return'd. Good Mrs. Fife,
To my, 'The Dean, is he at home?'
    Smiled, 'No, Sir; but Miss Honor is';
And straight, not asking if I'd come,
    Announced me, 'Mr. Felix, Miss',
To Mildred, in the Study. There
    We talk'd, she working. We agreed
The day was fine; the Fancy-Fair
    Successful; 'Did I ever read
De Genlis?' 'Never.' 'Do! She heard
    I was engaged.' 'To whom?' 'Miss Fry.
Was it the fact?' 'No!' 'On my word?'
    'What scandal people talk'd!' 'Would I
Hold out this skein of silk?' So pass'd
    I knew not how much time away.

It might almost be a page from Jane Austen, with its typical indirect remarks, put into verse. Of the same kind are these warnings from the aunt, who is against her niece marrying Vaughan (Book II, Canto II, *The Course of True Love*, 3):

'You, with your looks and handsome air,
　　To think of Vaughan! You fool! You know,
You might, with ordinary care,
　　Ev'n yet, be Lady Harrico.[23]
You're sure he'll do great things some day!
　　Nonsense, he won't; he's dress'd too well.
Dines with the Sterling Club, they say;
　　Not commonly respectable!
Half Puritan, half Cavalier!
　　His curly hair I think's a wig;
And, for his fortune, why, my Dear,
　　It's not enough to keep a gig.
Rich Aunts and Uncles never die;
　　And what you bring won't do for dress;
And so you'll live on "Bye-and-bye",
　　With oaten-cake and water-cress!'

But later the aunt calms down a little on hearing that Honoria's *fiancé* has bought her 'a carriage and a pair of bays'. The speech of the housekeeper (Book II, Canto v, *The Queen's Room*, 2) illustrates the same pedestrian tendency, and a tiresome complacency, like that of one of the mimiambi of Herodas, in following the mental processes of a person of humble position. On the other hand a gossipy dialogue with a friend, Charles Barton (Book II, Canto III, *The County Ball*, 4) was cut out almost entirely in the final version; and the same thing happened to a banal conversation with another friend, Frank (Book II, Canto IX, *The Friends*, 3), and to the following words exchanged between the young woman and her father (Book II, Canto XI, *The Wedding*, 3):

'Adieu, dear, dear Papa, adieu!
　　To-morrow I'll write.' 'No, Pet, —'. 'I will!
You know I'm very happy; and you
　　Have Mary and Mildred with you still!

> Mary, you'll make Papa his tea
>   At eight exactly. Au revoir!
> Only six weeks! How soon 'twill be!'
> Then on us two they shut the door.

Later on Patmore was to be put on his guard against the prosaic quality of many passages and expressions by Hopkins, who considered them *infra dignitatem*.[24] But the poet did not change his point of view, and in the final edition, as in the first, we find this perfect example of realism *à outrance* (Book II, Canto VI, *The Love-Letters*, 2):

> I ended. 'From your Sweet-Heart, Sir,'
>   Said Nurse, 'The Dean's man brings it down.'
> I could have kiss'd both him and her!
>   'Nurse, give him that, with half-a-crown.'

It would be difficult to find in the poetry of the period— for poetry usually keeps to a vaguer, more universal tone than narrative—pictures which so fully portray the customs of the age: but only the poetry of the period that marked the triumph of the *genre* picture could have produced them. The train (Book I, Canto IX, *Sahara*, 1–3):

> I stood by Honor and the Dean,
>   They seated in the London train . . .
>
>   .   .   .   .   .
>
> The bell rang, and, with shrieks like death,
>   Link catching link, the long array,
>
> With ponderous pulse and fiery breath,
>   Proud of its burthen, swept away;
> And through the lingering crowd I broke,
>   Sought the hill-side, and thence, heart-sick,
> Beheld, far off, the little smoke
>   Along the landscape kindling quick.[26]

The hedgehog and the children (Book II, Prologue, 4): the poet has scarcely begun to read the second book of the poem about his wooing, when the children burst into the corner of the garden where he is:

But, with a roar,
In rush'd the Loves; the tallest roll'd
A hedgehog from his pinafore,
Which saved his fingers; Baby, bold,
Touch'd it, and stared, and screamed for life,
And stretch'd her hand for Vaughan to kiss,
Who hugg'd his Pet, and ask'd his wife,
'Is this for love, or love for this?'
But she turn'd pale, for, lo, the beast
Found stock-still in the rabbit-trap,
And feigning so to be deceased,
And laid by Frank upon her lap,
Unglobed himself, and show'd his snout,
And fell, scatt'ring the Loves amain,
With shriek, with laughter, and with shout;
And peace at last restored again,
The Bard, who this untimely hitch
Bore with a calm magnanimous,
(The hedgehog kick'd into a ditch,
And Venus sooth'd), proceeded thus. . . .

The poet's betrothed, dancing (Book II, Canto iii, *The
County Ball*, 2):

Her ball-dress seem'd a breathing mist,
From the fair form exhaled and shed,
Raised in the dance with arm and wrist
All warmth and light, unbraceleted.
Her motion, feeling 'twas beloved,
The pensive soul of tune express'd,
And, oh, what perfume, as she moved,
Came from the flowers in her breast! . . .

The following little scene of the buying of the sand-shoes
(Book II, Canto xii, *Husband and Wife*) is truly a *poesia
scritta col lapis*, a poem written in pencil, as this product of
a minor Muse has been described by an Italian poet of the
present day, Marino Moretti:

I while the shop-girl fitted on
The sand-shoes, look'd where, down the bay,
The sea glow'd with a shrouded sun.
'I'm ready, Felix; will you pay?'

> That was my first expense for this
>   Sweet stranger whom I call'd my wife: [27]
> How light the touches are that kiss
>   The music from the chords of life!
> Her feet, by half-a-mile of sea,
>   In spotless sand left shapely prints;
> With agates, then, she loaded me,
>   (The lapidary call'd them flints);
> Then, at command, I hail'd a boat,
>   To take her to the ships-of-war,
> At anchor, each a lazy mote
>   Black in the brilliance, miles from shore.

In *The Kites* (Book II, Preludes, 2) a naïve symbolism which is at the same time Hellenistic and Biedermeier permeates the *genre* picture. Three cupids launch three kites, on one of which is written 'Plato', on another 'Anacreon', on the third 'Vaughan': the first falls 'for want of tail', the second fails to rise because it has a lump of earth tied to it, the third, 'freighted . . . with a long streamer made of flowers, the children of the sod' (but not the sod itself) rises in the sunlight. An emblem of earthly passion spiritualized.

The following passage, which has become famous and has been included in many anthologies, is a compendium of nineteenth-century fashion-books (Book I, Canto IV, Preludes, 2, *The Tribute*):

> Boon Nature to the woman bows.
>   She walks in all its glory clad,
> And, chief herself of earthly shows,
>   Each other helps her, and is glad.
> No splendour 'neath the sky's proud dome
>   But serves for her familiar wear;
> The far-fetch'd diamond finds its home
>   Flashing and smouldering in her hair;
> For her the seas their pearls reveal;
>   Art and strange lands her pomp supply
> With purple, chrome, and cochineal,
>   Ochre, and lapis lazuli;
> The worm its golden woof presents;
>   Whatever runs, flies, dives, or delves,
> All doff for her their ornaments,
>   Which suit her better than themselves;

And all, by this their power to give,
  Proving her right to take, proclaim
Her beauty's clear prerogative
  To profit so by Eden's blame.[28]

English literature is not rich in poems upon feminine clothes, and, if one looks for further examples, one is naturally reminded of the seventeenth-century Herrick's *Delight in Disorder*, from which Patmore, as he himself confessed (final note to the 1858 edition) borrowed the last two lines of *The Pearl* (Book II, Canto VII, Preludes, 1). In other respects *Delight in Disorder* has nothing in common with *The Tribute* except for the generic theme:

A sweet disorder in the dress
Kindles in clothes a wantonness:
A lawn about the shoulders thrown
Into a fair distraction:
An erring lace, which here and there
Enthrals the crimson stomacher:
A cuff neglectful, and thereby
Ribbands to flow confusedly:
A winning wave, deserving note,
In the tempestuous petticoat:
A careless shoe-string, in whose tie
I see a wild civility:
Do more bewitch me than when art
Is too precise in every part.

But that Herrick's poem was present in Patmore's mind is revealed by a more exact imitation of it, to be found in the poem that forms a sequel to *The Angel in the House*, *The Victories of Love*, where we read (Book, I, Canto XIII, letter from Lady Clitheroe to Mary Churchill):

The indolent droop of a blue shawl,
Or gray silk's fluctuating fall,
Covers the multitude of sins
In me.

*   *   *   *   *

Actually Patmore drew far more inspiration from the English poets of the seventeenth century than has been recognized even by our own contemporaries who have restored these poets to a position of honour—not to mention Patmore's own contemporaries, who were entirely unaware of any such vein of inspiration.[29]

We need only read the fourth section of *The Koh-i-Noor* in Canto VIII of *The Angel in the House* to become aware of a double inspiration:

> 'You have my heart so sweetly seized,
>   And I confess, nay, 'tis my pride
> That I'm with you so solely pleased,
>   That, if I'm pleased with aught beside,
> As music, or the month of June,
>   My friend's devotion, or his wit,
> A rose, a rainbow, or the moon,
>   It is that you illustrate it.
> All these are parts where you're the whole!
>   You fit the taste for Paradise,
> To which your charms draw up the soul
>   As turning spirals draw the eyes.
> Nature to you was more than kind;
>   'Twas fond perversity to dress
> So much simplicity of mind
>   In such a pomp of loveliness!
> But, praising you, the fancy deft
>   Flies wide and lets the quarry stray,
> And when all's said, there's something left,
>   And that's the thing I meant to say.'
> 'Dear Felix!' 'Sweet, sweet love!' But there
>   Was Aunt Maude's noisy ring and knock!
> 'Stay, Felix; you have caught my hair.
>   Stoop! Thank you!' 'May I have that lock?'
> 'Not now. Good morning, Aunt!' 'Why, Puss,
>   You look magnificent to-day.'
> 'Here's Felix, Aunt.' 'Fox and green goose!
>   Who handsome gets should handsome pay.'
> 'Aunt, you are friends!' 'O, to be sure!
>   Good morning! Go on flattering, Sir;
> A woman's like the Koh-i-Noor,
>   Worth just the price that's put on her.'

While the second part (from 'Dear Felix' to the end) is simply the verse rendering of a conversation such as we have seen earlier, the first part, with its argumentative character, its out-of-the-way images ('As turning spirals draw the eyes') recalls Donne's love lyrics.[30] And as for the central conceit, we find it is a conceit taken straight from Donne's *Good-morrow*, and diluted:

> . . . But this, all pleasures fancies bee.
> If ever any beauty I did see,
> Which I desir'd, and got, t'was but a dreame of thee.

The line 'All these are parts where you're the whole!' is particularly reminiscent of Donne. We find the same argumentative, metaphysical turn in a passage in Book I, Canto v, *The Violets*:

> I thought how love, whose vast estate
>   Is earth and air and sun and sea,
> Encounters oft the beggar's fate
>   Despised on score of poverty;
> How Heaven, inscrutable in this,
>   Lets the gross general make or mar
> The destiny of love, which is
>   So tender and particular;
> How nature, as unnatural
>   And contradicting nature's source,
> Which is but love, seems most of all
>   Well-pleased to harry true love's course;
> How, many times, it comes to pass
>   That trifling shades of temperament,
> Affecting only one, alas,
>   Not love, but love's success prevent.

A line like 'Not love, but love's success prevent', if isolated, might well be ascribed to Donne. In the same way, the lines from the Second Prelude (*Love Justified*) of Book I, Canto vi: 'Is that elect relationship Which forms and sanctions all the rest' seem to breathe the atmosphere of *The Extasie*; while the following comparison from Book I, Canto ii, Preludes, i:

> And as geranium, pink, or rose
>   Is thrice itself through power of art,
> So may my happy skill disclose
>   New fairness even in her fair heart—

manifestly derives from:

> A single violet transplant,
>   The strength, the colour, and the size,
> (All which before was poore, and scant),
>   Redoubles still, and multiplies.
> When love, with one another so
>   Interinanimates two soules,
> That abler soule, which thence doth flow,
>   Defects of loneliness controules.

Even more obvious is the derivation of this passage (Book I, Canto VII, *Aetna and the Moon*, 3):

> But, now and then, in cheek and eyes,
>   I saw, or fancied, such a glow
> As when, in summer-evening skies,
>   Some say 'It lightens', some say 'No'—

from *A Valediction: forbidding mourning:*

> As virtuous men passe mildly away,
>   And whisper to their soules, to goe,
> Whilst some of their sad friends doe say,
>   The breath goes now, and some say, no . . .[31]

In *Going to Church*, 4 (Book I, Canto x) we read:

> If oft, in love, effect lack'd cause
>   And cause effect, 'twere vain to soar
> Reasons to seek for that which was
>   Reason itself, or something more—

which is in the metaphysical tradition of the love lyric based on syllogisms. The same could be said of the Second Prelude in Book II, Canto II:

> That ugly good is scorn'd proves not
>   'Tis beauty lies, but lack of it, &c.

The following are word-plays in the manner of Donne: 'And did for fear my fear defy' (Book I, Canto XI, *The Dance*, 3),[32] and 'He thought I thought he thought I slept' (Book II, Canto VIII, *Preludes*, 3):[33] and we constantly encounter metaphors derived from astronomy or from everyday circumstances, such as the metaphysical poets employed. In *The Dance*, 1:

> He who would seek to make her his
>   Will comprehend that souls of grace
> Own sweet repulsion, and that 'tis
>   The quality of their embrace
> To be like the majestic reach
>   Of coupled suns, that, from afar,
> Mingle their mutual spheres, while each
>   Circles the twin obsequious star.

And in the first of the Preludes in Book II, Canto III:

> And let the sweet, respective sphere
>   Of personal worship there obtain
> Circumference for moving clear,
>   None treading on another's train.

In the First Prelude of Book II, Canto II:

> And, like that fatal 'I am thine',
>   Comes with alternate gush and check
> And joltings of the heart, as wine
>   Pour'd from a flask of narrow neck.[34]

Farther on in the same prelude, a military comparison recalls another famous one in one of Donne's Holy Sonnets ('Batter my heart, three person'd God . . .'):

> With her, as with a desperate town
>   Too weak to stand, too proud to treat,
> The conqueror, though the walls are down,
>   Has still to capture street by street. . . .[35]

The allusion to an exotic geographical circumstance which occurs in *The Course of True Love*, 7 (Book II, Canto II):

> She pass'd, and night was a surprise,
>   As when the sun at Quito dips—

is also in the taste of Donne, whereas the legal terminology which we find farther on in the same poem may point to Donne as well as to Shakespeare's sonnets:

> 'At best, can longest life afford
>   That tyranny should thus deduct
> From this fair hand, which calls me lord,
>   A year of the sweet usufruct!'

But no one else except Donne could have written (Book II, Canto IV, *Love in Idleness*, 4):

> . . . love, which is the source of law,
> And, like a king, can do no wrong.

Donne's rugged syntax, together with unusual metaphors, is to be found in a passage in *The County Ball* (Book II, Canto III), which in the final version has disappeared. It indicates the self-contained isolation of the two lovers as they dance together:

> If either for all else but one
>   Was blinder than the mole that delves,
> Dark-lanterns for all else, we shone
>   But to each other and ourselves.

And the following stanza (Book II, Canto IV, *Love in Idleness*, 4):

> 'A road's a road, though worn to ruts;
>   They speed who travel straight therein;
> But he who tacks and tries short cuts
>   Gets fools' praise and a broken shin'—

seems to repeat the scheme of this one of Donne's (*A Valediction; forbidding mourning*):

> Moving of th' earth brings harmes and feares,
>   Men reckon what it did and meant,
> But trepidation of the spheares,
>   Though greater farre, is innocent.

Once we are aware of this metaphysical influence, it is an easy game to detect its traces in *The Angel in the House*. Thus at the end of Canto IV of Book II:

> For as the worm whose powers make pause
>   And swoon, through alteration sick,
> The soul, its wingless state dissolved,
>   Awaits its nuptial life complete.

In Canto vi of Book II, *The Love-Letters*, Preludes, i :

> Yet 'tis a postulate in love
> That part is greater than the whole.[36]

And in the first of the love-letters:

> 'I'll nobly mirror you too fair,
> And, when you're false to me your glass,
> What's wanting you'll by that repair,
> So bring yourself through me to pass.'[37]

In *The Revulsion*, i (Book II, Canto vii):

> I sigh'd, 'Immeasurable bliss
> Gains nothing by becoming more!
> Millions have meaning; after this
> Cyphers forget the integer.'[38]

The Fourth Prelude of Book II, Canto x contains this *Demonstration* (the very title has a Donneish air about it):

> Nature, with endless being rife,
> Parts each thing into 'him' and 'her',
> And, in the arithmetic of life,
> The smallest unit is a pair;
> And thus, oh, strange, sweet half of me,
> If I confess a loftier flame,
> If more I love high Heaven than thee,
> I more than love thee, thee I am;
> And, if the world's not built of lies,
> Nor all a cheat the Gospel tells,
> If that which from the dead shall rise
> Be I indeed, not something else,
> There's no position more secure
> In reason or in faith than this,
> That those conditions must endure,
> Which, wanting, I myself should miss.

In *The Wedding*, 2 (Book II, Canto xi):

> '. . . recollect
> The eye which magnifies her charms
> Is microscopic to defect.
> Fear comes at first; but soon, rejoiced,
> You'll find your strong and tender loves,
> Like holy rocks by Druids poised,
> The least force shakes, but none removes.'[39]

And finally, the First Prelude to the last Canto, *Husband and Wife*, contains a long comparison derived from the custom of subjects' kissing the queen's hand on Court reception-days; this, too, is reminiscent of Donne.

In *The Victories of Love* Marvell's influence is revealed not only by the metre, but also by the recurring echo of the famous lines *To his Coy Mistress*:

> But at my back I always hear
> Time's wingèd chariot hurrying near—

in:

> . . . I hear
> Under her life's gay progress hurl'd,
> The wheels of the preponderant world—[40]

and in:

> . . . hear
> At dawn the carriage rolling near—[41]

and in the word *ambergris* in proximity to the word *shore*:

> With here and there cast up, a piece
> Of coral or of ambergris,
> Which, boasted of abroad, we ignore
> The burden of the barren shore—[42]

reminding one of the well-known passage in Marvell's *Bermudas*:

> Proclaim the ambergris on shore.

Why did Patmore, unlike the other Victorians,[43] seek his inspiration in the metaphysical tradition which had died out after the close of the seventeenth century? Was he attracted to Donne by the theory expounded in *The Extasie* which maintained the necessity and dignity of the sensual part of love ('To our bodies turne wee then, that so Weake men on love reveal'd may looke')? This is likely; but he must also have been attracted by the fact that Donne had been the first to do away with the courtly tradition which banished from Parnassus all common things and common expressions, the first to introduce everyday life into verse, and to find a form of verse which lent itself equally well to the expression of that life and to the rendering of abstract, metaphysical thought in terms which the senses could apprehend.

But who thought of the seventeenth-century metaphysical poets when *The Angel in the House* first appeared? People spoke of derivations from Tennyson, Browning, Keats. Of the real model no one was aware. And it is precisely because of its attempt to find a poetical language of the greatest possible elasticity and modernity that Patmore's experiment, representing, as it does, one aspect of the Victorian anti-heroic reaction, has seemed to us worthy of illustration, whereas usually critics linger over its message, over its spiritualization of sexual love—a fixation which is common to this poet and to a very different writer of our own century, D. H. Lawrence: to both of them divinity is revealed in carnal union.[44]

Considered from this point of view, Patmore's work may seem strangely alien to the atmosphere of Victorianism, and the poet's figure, thus isolated, thus magnified, has been exalted (thanks mainly to Claudel and the fashion which followed him) to a height which is in truth superior to his merits.

The Angel in the House, and to a lesser degree *The Victories of Love*, have the merits of minor poetry that we have sought and found in them: a few groups of lines, a mild impression of the 'household round of duties' (*The Victories of Love*, Book II, Canto xi) and of a comfortable, ordered existence pervaded by affectionate, thoughtful sensuality ('On settl'd poles turn solid joys, And sunlike pleasures shine at home') are all that survives from a poem which diffuses a Victorian 'keepsake' atmosphere over the cult of Priapus.[45]

NOTES TO APPENDIX I

[1] In the *Nouvelle Revue française*, Sept. and Oct. 1911, with a biographical essay on Patmore by V. Larbaud.

[2] See *Further Letters of Gerard Manley Hopkins* including his Correspondence with Coventry Patmore, ed. Claude Colleer Abbott, Oxford University Press, 1938, p. xxxii.

³ On the subject of love in general he wrote to his friend Henry Sutton: 'A minute of the sense of love is better than a play of Shakespeare's' (quoted in Derek Patmore, *The Life and Times of Coventry Patmore*, London, Constable, 1949, p. 64). To Théophile Gautier, Shakespeare's plays had served as a comparison for a different kind of spectacle—the bullfight: for Gautier the situation of the *matador* face to face with the bull 'vaut tous les drames de Shakespeare'.

⁴ He found flashes of Catholic intuition even in the licentious novelists of the French eighteenth century, and—perhaps in one of those outbursts of paradox in which he took pleasure—declared that Crébillon *fils* was a good Catholic. Hidden behind the shelves of his library at Heron's Ghyll was a complete set of the privately printed books of the Eroticon Biblion Society. See D. Patmore, op. cit., p. 148.

⁵ As an adolescent, still uncertain of his vocation, Patmore consulted the phrenologist Deville, in Paris, who exhorted him to think of himself as a poet, 'and this perhaps gives us the date, Oct. 1839, for Patmore's sudden burst into verse', observes Frederick Page (quoted by D. Patmore, op. cit., p. 39).

⁶ This patriarch could at times assume the aspect of the Old Man of the Mountains in the *Arabian Nights*. In 1894, unable to go out alone on account of weakness and vertigo, he used to grasp his son Francis by the neck and lean on him for support. Francis Patmore relates:

> I was thus a human walking-stick, and though I often reached home almost broken by fatigue, for he was heavy to support, it pleases me to know that I never let him suspect the often acute suffering he quite unwittingly caused. During these walks he would often exclaim aloud: 'My God, how cold, how cold!' One hot July night, as I was sweating under his weight, I ventured to protest that he could not possibly be cold, especially as he always wore at night a heavy ulster. He said, 'Oh, it is a spiritual cold I feel.' And in this internal, spiritual life, his last years were far from happy, and his soul longed, I think, for death and to see his God face to face. (D. Patmore, op. cit., p. 237.)

Of this he had no doubt. He wrote to Alice Meynell shortly before he died: 'Our meeting again in Heaven depends on your fidelity to the highest things you have known.' (D. Patmore, op. cit., p. 238.)

⁷ D. Patmore, op. cit., pp. 173–4: 'Especially she was haunted by a conviction that she had loved her father too much, and had been too proud of him.'

⁸ D. Patmore, op. cit., p. 233. In Nov. 1895 he wrote to Francis Thompson, another of Alice Meynell's unsuccessful lovers: 'My heart goes forth to you as it goes to no other man; for are we not singularly visited by a great common delight, and a great common sorrow? Is not this to be one in Christ?' Patmore sees religious sentiment even in the brotherhood of two rejected lovers.

⁹ D. Patmore, op. cit., p. 4.

¹⁰ See above, p. 43.

¹¹ *The Angel in the House*, 1858 edition, Book I, Canto x, Preludes, 2, *Truth and Love*.

¹² See above, p. 239.

¹³ Book I, Canto ɪv, Preludes, ɪ, *The Rose of the World.* But the whole of this Prologue deserves to be quoted. And in Canto x of the same Book, *Going to Church,* 6: 'And when she knelt, she seem'd to be An angel teaching me to pray'. Compare her with Dickens's Agnes Wickfield (see above, pp. 135–6).

¹⁴ By Osbert Burdett, *The Idea of Coventry Patmore,* Oxford University Press, 1921, p. 12.

¹⁵ Thus in the original version, which we follow. In the final form of the poem there are a great number of transpositions and alterations, some of them due to suggestions by G. M. Hopkins.

¹⁶ Herbert J. C. Grierson and J. C. Smith, *A Critical History of English Poetry,* London, Chatto & Windus, 1944, p. 453: 'the tune of the Old Hundredth'; the hundredth psalm is the famous old Puritan hymn.

¹⁷ Book I, Canto ɪ, Preludes, 5, *The Impossibility.*

¹⁸ See also Book II, Canto vɪɪ, Preludes, 3: 'But fools shall feel like fools to find (Too late inform'd), that angels' mirth Is one in cause, and mode, and kind With that which they despised on earth.'

¹⁹ G. M. Hopkins wrote, on May 14th, 1885, to Patmore that 'to dip into it [*The Angel in the House*] was like opening a basket of violets' (an appropriate comparison, in view of what I have just observed regarding the flowers with which the poem is besprinkled), and that the fact of the poem being in its sixth edition showed a 'steady popularity or a steadily reading public': 'But it is a popularity and a public rather below the surface' (see *Further Letters,* cited, pp. 214–15).

²⁰ *The Cathedral Close,* 5.

²¹ In the final version in the *Collected Poems* this passage has been altered here and there. Instead of 'But this was gallantly withdrawn', &c. we read: 'And stepping like the light-foot fawn, She brought me "Wiltshire Butterflies", The Prize-book', &c.

²² See, for example, chapter v, 'Mir ist lästig, noch länger dies wunderliche Beginnen Anzuschauen. Vollendet es selbst! Ich gehe zu Bette.' And in chapter iii the conversation of the chemist: 'Manches hätt'ich getan, allein wer scheut nicht die Kosten Solcher Veränderung, besonders in diesen gefährlichen Zeiten! Lange lachte mir schon mein Haus im modischen Kleidchen, Lange glänzten durchaus mit grossen Scheiben die Fenster...'

²³ 'Clitheroe' in the final text.

²⁴ See *Further Letters of Gerard Manley Hopkins,* cited. Hopkins's chief observations, however, are concerned with points of religion.

²⁵ Cf. *The Victories of Love,* Book I, Letter xvɪɪɪ: 'My wife . . . gave him his hire, and sixpence more.'

²⁶ Hopkins (op. cit., p. 255) observed, with regard to 'link catching link': 'Only goods trains do this; passenger trains are locked rigidly.'

²⁷ In the final edition: 'Sweet Stranger, now my three days' Wife.'

²⁸ The final version offers a few variants. 'To profit so by Eden's blame' —i.e. the covering of the body after the Fall. Similar in subject, but with a different moral, is the sonnet by Alberto Ròndani quoted by B. Croce, *La Letteratura della nuova Italia,* vol. ii, p. 242.

²⁹ Some of Patmore's declarations might in any case put one on the

wrong track: for instance in 1864 he described, from Paris, his enthusiasm for Gérard's *Cupid and Psyche*: 'Certainly love has never been expressed with more force, delicacy, and spiritual science than in the *Cupid and Psyche* of Gérard. As I mean to have a vignette of this picture for the title-page of the next edition of *The Angel in the House*, I will say no more about it' (D. Patmore, op. cit., p. 122). The vignette might have been more suitable for the ode *Eros and Psyche*.

30 I have illustrated the character of Donne's lyric poetry in *Secentismo e marinismo in Inghilterra*, Florence, 1925, reprinted later in *La poesia metafisica inglese del Seicento, John Donne*, Rome, Edizioni italiane, 1945.

31 It is odd to find, close beside an imitation of Donne, another passage in the familiar style: ' "Honoria", I began—No more. The Dean, by ill or happy hap, Came home; and Wolf burst in before, And put his nose upon her lap.'

32 Cf. Donne, *The Good-morrow*: 'For love, all love of other sights controules.'

33 One is reminded also of Dante (*Inferno*, xiii. 25): 'Cred'io ch'ei credette ch'io credesse'; in Donne's *The Dreame*: 'But when I saw thou sawest my heart'; in *Love's Exchange*: 'Let me not know that others know That she knowes my paines. . . .'

34 It has been observed that the image is already to be found in Ariosto, *Orlando Furioso*, xxiii. 113: 'His violent sorrow remained within him because it all wished to come out with too great haste. So sometimes we see water stay in the bottle that has a large belly and a narrow neck, because when it is turned upside down, the water that wishes to get out hastens so much and is so confined in the narrow passage that it comes out with difficulty, drop by drop.' (Trans. Professor Allan H. Gilbert; New York, Vanni, 1954, vol. i, p. 399.)

35 Cf., in Donne's sonnet: 'I, like an usurpt towne, to'another due, Labour to'admit you. . . .'

36 Cf. Donne, *Lovers Infinitenesse*: 'Loves riddles are, that though thy heart depart, It stayes at home. . . .' The last part of this prelude of Patmore's consists of a series of paradoxes of love: 'He worships her, the more to exalt The profanation of a kiss. . . .'

37 Cf. Donne, *A Valediction: of my name, in the window*: ' 'Tis much that Glasse should bee As all confessing, and through-shine as I, 'Tis more, that it shewes thee to thee, And cleare reflects thee to thine eye. But all such rules, loves magique can undoe, Here you see mee, and I am you.' See also, in *The Victories of Love*, Book II, Canto viii: 'She bade me then, in the crystal floor, Look at myself no more; And bright within the mirror shone Honoria's smile, and yet my own!' A similar theme was treated by D. G. Rossetti in *Willowwood*.

38 Cf. the argument in Donne's *Lovers Infinitenesse*. The last line of this passage of Patmore and the last line of the Second Prelude of Book II, Canto iii: 'Or beauty's apparition so Puts on invisibility', sound like anticipations of Emily Dickinson.

39 These are the words of the Dean to the husband.

40 Book I, Canto iii.

⁴¹ Book I, Canto xiv.

⁴² Book I, Canto ix.

⁴³ With the exception of Browning, upon whom the influence of Donne worked in a very different and much less ascertainable way.

⁴⁴ Husband and wife were, to Patmore, 'priest and priestess to one another of the divine womanhood and divine manhood which are inherent in original Deity'. In the exaltation of their finite union the veil is lifted for an instant, and they understand infinity. We are not concerned here with Patmore's odes, in which he 'dared to describe feelings and emotions that tore the veil away from subjects which Victorian Society considered both "unpleasant" and "unmentionable" ' (D. Patmore, op. cit., p. 195) but, though I once thought so, I now doubt whether Patmore should be considered 'no longer the slightly ridiculous poet of matrimony, but *a mystic and a religious poet of the highest order*', as Derek Patmore maintains he appears to the moderns, or actually, as Desmond MacCarthy claimed, 'the greatest religious poet in the English language since the seventeenth century' (D. Patmore, op. cit., p. 5).

⁴⁵ Newman disapproved of Patmore's poetry for 'mixing up amorousness with religion'—elements which to him appeared irreconcilable; and Housman went so far as to speak of a 'nasty mixture of piety and concupiscence'.

APPENDIX II

Rome and the Victorians

THE Roman impressions of the Victorians provide a characteristic example of their anti-heroic point of view, of their fondness for the picturesque and the humorous, of their social preoccupations. If there was one place that had at all times caused the epic trumpet to be blown, that had inspired feelings of veneration or sad, solemn thoughts on the passing of human greatness, that place was Rome. The last word had been said by Byron: 'Oh, Rome! my country! city of the soul!' The Niobe of nations, he had called her, lone mother of dead empires, evoking an image desolate indeed, but still venerable. But this traditional point of view could not continue in a period which nowhere expressed its own spirit so well as in Thackeray's *Small-Beer Chronicle*, which launches out against all those who try to deceive others or themselves into thinking that their own humble *vin ordinaire* is a rich port wine.

The great luminary and charming essayist of *The Spectator*, Joseph Addison, has been called by a witty critic, Bonamy Dobrée, 'the first of the Victorians', since he bestowed a harmoniously classical patina upon the dictates of bourgeois common sense, and—a lay preacher full of good-nature and shrewdness—disseminated philosophy, religion, and morality in a gentlemanly manner, for the use of the tea-table. But his impressions of Italy, and especially of Rome, his *Remarks on Several Parts of Italy* (1705), are at the opposite pole from anything a Victorian could have written: so completely at the opposite pole, indeed, that a brief glance at them will help us to a definition, by contrast, of the Victorian point of view. I have allowed myself to make use of the word 'impressions'; but in reality the word could not be more inappropriate. There is no freshness of impression whatever in the remarks of Addison, who carries about with him his library of classical authors and verifies his quotations on the spot: 'I must confess it was not one of the least entertainments that I met with in travelling, to examine those several descriptions [of the classics] as it were upon the spot, and to compare the natural face of the Country with the Landskips that the Poets have given us of it.' For antiquarian interest the *Remarks* are much nearer to the *Hypnerotomachia* of Polyphilus than to any modern travel book. And just as Polyphilus found, in his dream country, continual evidences of his own classics, so also did Addison, who, rather than tell us of his arrival in Rome, starts straight off with an observation of an archaeological nature: modern Rome is higher than ancient Rome, because the former rises upon the ruins of the latter. He goes on to classify the antiquities of Rome into Christian and pagan; which latter give great pleasure to anyone who has come across them before in the ancient writers. In Rome his attention is attracted by the statues; and upon the clothes they wear, the musical instruments they carry in their hands, the passages of Juvenal that allude to them, he gives an agreeable disquisition which leaves us completely cold. He speaks of statues and obelisks, he mentions the splendid scenes presented by the churches: but in all this there is not a single breath of the air of Rome; it is flavoured with sterility and it smells of the museum. It is as though the gentlemanly Addison had never trodden the streets of Rome in his wish to avoid their dust and mud: it is as though he had flown through the air with winged, golden sandals, enveloped in a protective cloud like those that encircled the gods of Homer. Enclosed in a crystal casket, he observes, from his diving-bell, things that are protected by glass cases and labelled with quotations.

The Victorians, on the other hand, plunge, kicking and protesting, into the atmosphere of Rome; for them there is no preliminary stage of reverence. Rome, however much her praises have been sung, is, for them, a city to be judged by the standard of all other cities. It was impossible that modern Rome should not have come between even Addison and his beloved statues and venerable obelisks; but he ignored it. But the Victorians had no such *parti pris*;

and modern Rome seized upon them even in its more repellent aspects, with its filth and its beggars and its disgusting smells. They are not silent on this subject; in fact they talk about it altogether too much. But not without an artistic purpose. For from the contrast between present squalor and the noble past springs the picturesque.

Take Dickens, who was in Rome in 1845. He will tell you that not a day passed without his going to see the Colosseum; but he tells you this at the end of his chapter on Rome, and in an incidental way, in connexion with an effect of night amongst the ruins. He speaks of the Colosseum at the beginning, too, and from its summit takes a general look at the ruins, as if to discharge all obligations for the rest of his stay in Rome: 'Look down on ruin, ruin, ruin, all about it.' 'It is the most impressive, the most stately, the most solemn, grand, majestic, mournful sight, conceivable. . . . Here was Rome indeed at last; and such a Rome as no one can imagine in its full and awful grandeur!' After this opening bow to the Rome of tradition, and a brave show of a vignette of the Colosseum on the title-page, and after remembering to mention the Colosseum again as a last word, Dickens fills his Roman album, not with the notes of an archaeologist, but with a series of sketches in the manner of a Romantic artist—in fact of a Biedermeier artist. The apse of St. Peter's decorated for a *festa*, with its 'intolerable reds and crimsons' and gold-bordered hangings, makes him think of a 'stupendous bonbon'; the procession with candles reminds him irresistibly of the Fifth of November in England—Guy Fawkes' Day, when boys carry round the grotesque puppet of the preposterous conspirator (the figure of the puppet is here provided by the Pope), and light bonfires and let off fireworks and crackers. From this spectacle, which to Dickens's eyes had something of the carnival about it, we pass on to the real Carnival, the Roman Carnival celebrated by Goethe and Hoffmann: and here, naturally, the author of *Christmas Books* finds himself perfectly at home, and enthusiastically describes the lively scenes, even to the *moccoletti*, the lighted tapers, which must have presented a picture so like the vignettes of Christmas-trees which adorn many editions

of Dickens that we are not surprised at his going into
ecstasies over them. His pen, which had followed the religious ceremonies in St. Peter's with reluctance, and not
without some admixture of acid in the ink, here runs away
with him in one of those *bravura* passages, swarming with
action and with figures, that are the speciality of Dickens:
the cry '*Senza moccolo! senza moccolo!*', in Italian, punctuates
the swelling flow of the Dickensian prose, until 'in the
wildest enthusiasm of the cry, and fullest ecstasy of the
sport, the Ave Maria rings from the church steeples, and
the Carnival is over in an instant—put out like a taper, with
a breath!' Between the end of Carnival and the beginning
of Holy Week, Dickens starts conscientiously seeing the
sights of Rome, and tells us that he has explored every
corner of it, and has had his fill of looking at churches: but
of these explorations he gives us no details, stopping instead
to describe a typical company of English tourists, the
Davises and their friends, with the comic Mr. Davis, who
had the habit of 'taking the covers off urns in tombs, and
looking in at the ashes as if they were pickles', and of
always tracing out inscriptions with the ferrule of his 'great
green umbrella'. This curious vignette is followed by
another—the parade of artists' models on the steps of the
Piazza di Spagna; immediately afterwards, the picturesque
is succeeded by the macabre, with an episode illustrating
the lack of care with which they used to bury the dead in
Rome; and the macabre is again followed by the grotesque,
with the miraculous Bambino of Aracoeli providing the
material. The ceremonies at St. Peter's had made Dickens
think of a pantomime; the Aracoeli chapel reminded him
of certain aspects of an English fair. The face of the Bambino, he says, very much resembled that of 'General Tom
Thumb, the American Dwarf'. Another comic vignette
follows shortly afterwards: the seminarists kneeling down
in a group. 'These boys always kneel down in single file,
one behind the other, with a tall grim master in a black
gown, bringing up the rear: like a pack of cards arranged
to be tumbled down at a touch, with a disproportionately
large Knave of clubs at the end . . . so that if anybody *did*
stumble against the master, a general and sudden over-

throw of the whole line must inevitably ensue.' Here
Dickens is anticipating the agreeable *genre* pictures of the
contemporary Italian painter, Nino Caffè. In the churches
Dickens, like Goldoni, discovers endless suggestions of
comedy: the 'preposterous crowns of silver stuck upon the
painted heads' of saints or Virgins, the unbelievable pious
persons who interrupt their devotions to 'beg a little, or to
pursue some other worldly matter'. 'In one church, a kneeling lady got up from her prayers, for a moment, to offer us
her card, as a teacher of Music; and in another, a sedate
gentleman with a very thick walking-staff, arose from his
devotions to belabour his dog, who was growling at another
dog: and whose yelps and howls resounded through the
church, as his master quietly relapsed into his former train
of meditation—keeping his eye upon the dog, at the same
time, nevertheless.' The shaking of the collecting-box 'for
the souls in Purgatory' seems to him not unlike the rattling
of the cracked bell by Punch in the English Punch and
Judy show. Of all the churches in Rome, the author of
Oliver Twist assures us that he was most deeply impressed
by Santo Stefano Rotondo. 'St. Stefano Rotondo, a damp,
mildewed vault of an old church in the outskirts of Rome,
will always struggle uppermost in my mind, by reason of
the hideous paintings with which its walls are covered.'
The Victorians, in the matter of horrors, did not go in very
much for subtlety; and a picture on the outside of a booth
at a fair (for, as regards artistic merit, the frescoes in Santo
Stefano Rotondo are little more than that) had the power
to impress them as much as a genuine work of art. Let us
remember that this was the period of Madame Tussaud's
waxworks and the 'Chamber of Horrors'; and we shall no
longer be surprised that Nathaniel Hawthorne and William Wetmore Story made a great fuss about the collection
of human bones at the Cappuccini. The chapel of the
Mamertine prison also filled Dickens with horror. 'It is
very small and low-roofed; and the dread and gloom of the
ponderous, obdurate old prison are on it, as if they had
come up in a dark mist through the floor.' He sees hanging
on the walls, amongst votive offerings, 'rusty daggers,
knives, pistols, clubs, divers instruments of violence and

murder, brought here, fresh from use, and hung up to pro-
pitiate offended Heaven: as if the blood upon them would
drain off in consecrated air, and have no voice to cry with.
It is all so silent and so close, and tomb-like; and the
dungeons below are so black and stealthy, and stagnant,
and naked; that this little dark spot becomes a dream within
a dream: and in the vision of great churches which come
rolling past me like a sea, it is a small wave by itself, that
melts into no other wave, and does not flow on with the
rest.' Santo Stefano Rotondo and the Mamertine Prison
are but the first movements of the funeral symphony which
Dickens unfolds in the following pages, giving glimpses of
the horrors of the Colosseum and the catacombs, and culminating, like the *Symphonie fantastique* of Berlioz, in a
marche au supplice and an execution, which he goes to see
in the neighbourhood of San Giovanni Decollato. In his
description of the gloomy, tumbledown houses overlooking
the macabre scene, he brings to bear all his well-known skill
as a painter of London slums. And he gives us details of the
long wait, of the blood-stained epilogue, with a mixture of
attraction and repulsion that naturally recalls the accounts
of English sadism, the more or less legendary 'milords'
who, for large sums, rented windows with a good view of
the place where the gallows stood. And, amongst all the
antiquities in the Vatican galleries or the collections of
princes, what does he stop to describe but, of course, the
so-called portrait of Beatrice Cenci? 'Through the transcendent sweetness and beauty of the face, there is a something shining out, that haunts me.' Shelley, before him,
had been captivated by that face, as, not long after Dickens,
was Herman Melville. Melville, in fact, was to be truly
haunted by it, as can be seen in the last two books of his
novel *Pierre*, and in certain lines of *Clarel*, where he discovers upon the lips of the so-called Beatrice a trembling
as of lustful pleasure in pain, a quiver of algolagnia. To
such an extent were the Romantics able to clothe with their
dark imaginings even the most innocent and positively
stupid facial expressions: they tried with the so-called
Beatrice Cenci of Guido Reni, and they succeeded fully
with Leonardo's Gioconda. 'The guilty palace of the Cenci:

blighting a whole quarter of the town, as it stands withering away by grains: had that face, to my fancy, in its dismal porch, and at its black blind windows, and flitting up and down its dreary stairs, and growing out of the darkness of its ghostly galleries.' It is like a page out of one of the 'tales of terror'; but, in order to re-establish the balance between gloomy and grotesque, Dickens gives us, a few pages later, a comic little picture of the foreigners crowding into the Sistine Chapel to hear the *Miserere* on Thursday in Holy Week.

Hanging in the doorway of the chapel, was a heavy curtain, and this curtain, some twenty people nearest to it, in their anxiety to hear the chaunting of the Miserere, were continually plucking at, in opposition to each other, that it might not fall down and stifle the sound of the voices. The consequence was, that it occasioned the most extraordinary confusion, and seemed to wind itself about the unwary, like a Serpent. Now, a lady was wrapped up in it, and couldn't be unwound. Now, the voice of a stifling gentleman was heard inside it, beseeching to be let out. Now, two muffled arms, no man could say of which sex, struggled in it as in a sack. Now, it was carried by a rush, bodily overhead into the chapel, like an awning. Now, it came out the other way, and blinded one of the Pope's Swiss Guard who had arrived, that moment, to set things to rights.

This comic spectacle, and the anguished voices of the struggling sightseers, are of course far more diverting to him than the *Miserere*. And Dickens catches glimpses of other comic little scenes during other Holy Week ceremonies: the Englishman who 'seemed to have embarked the whole energy of his nature in the determination to discover whether there was ... a mustard-pot' on the table set out for the Apostles, the cardinals who 'smiled to each other, from time to time, as if the thing were a great farce', the ridiculous spectacle of the ascending of the Holy Staircase on Good Friday, with one man helping himself up with an umbrella. ... This Rome of Dickens's is obviously not the Rome of Piranesi, but rather that of Cruikshank.

Not that there was any lack, in the Victorian age, of those for whom Rome was still Ancient Rome, full of classical reminiscences and of monuments which, even in ruin, retained all their traditional fascination. A few years before Dickens's *Pictures from Italy* there had appeared, in 1842, Macaulay's *Lays of Ancient Rome*, whose inspiration came from the same classical Roman source that had suggested, to the painter David, the famous canvases of the Horatii and the Sabine women; and Felicia Hemans had re-evoked the last banquet of Antony and Cleopatra, and Marius among the ruins of Carthage, and Arthur Hugh Clough had sung (*Amours de voyage*, Canto III):

Yet to the wondrous S. Peter's and yet to the solemn Rotunda
  Mingling with heroes and gods, yet to the Vatican walls,
Yet we may go, and recline, while a whole mighty world seems above us
  Gathered and fixed to all time into one roofing supreme;
Yet may we, thinking on these things, exclude what is meaner around us.

But, even without going to the extremes of Mark Twain's deliberately humorous presentation in *The Innocents Abroad* (1869)—Mark Twain found that 'St. Peter's did not look nearly so large as the Capitol [at Washington], and certainly not a twentieth part as beautiful, from the outside', and that the bronze *baldacchino* was like the framework which upholds a mosquito-bar, or 'a considerably magnified bedstead—nothing more', but he enjoyed 'the picturesque horrors of the Capuchin convent'—the Victorians in general looked at Rome with a critical eye; and then St. Peter's no longer looked quite so 'wondrous' nor the Pantheon so 'solemn'. Although he was an American and therefore does not, strictly speaking, form part of the theme of this chapter, Herman Melville deserves to be quoted on the subject. He was in Rome in February 1857. 'Rome fell flat on me. Oppressively flat.' His first glance at Rome left him completely cold. He went on foot to St. Peter's. 'Front view disappointing . . . dome not so wonderful as St. Sophia's.' Coventry Patmore went to Rome in 1864, and found that there was only one good-sized street, the Corso, and that 'scarcely as good as the Rue St. Honoré. . . . Of the great towns, Rome is certainly the meanest I have yet seen.' Even the ruins left him cold: '. . . the ruins of

Imperial Rome are scarcely better worth seeing than the modern city.' Here are his impressions on his first walk:

> After breakfast on Friday I went out, not knowing where I was going, and almost the first building I passed [Patmore had taken rooms at the Hotel Minerva] was a circular edifice of brick, with a mean façade, which I went by without giving it more than a glance. It struck me, however, when I had passed it, that it might be the Pantheon. . . . I went some way further, and was for several minutes approaching a good-sized church, without anything in its appearance to attract attention; but at last came to a colonnade, with two fountains and an obelisk, and I asked Mr. Monsell, who went with me—as he told Mr. de Vere, to witness my enthusiasm —if that was St. Peter's? Have you ever stepped down a step without being prepared for it? Probably you have. But have you ever stepped down four or five steps at once in such a way? If not you cannot understand quite the unexpectedness of the 'drop' from my very moderate expectation to the reality.

Rome disappointed Thackeray too, who was there in the winter of 1853–4; the works of art aroused no enthusiasm in him, the façade of St. Peter's seemed to him ugly, and the only things that pleased him were sunsets from the Pincio and picturesque streets: 'I think the street is always the best sight in Rome: it is always bright new and nobly picturesque—much more to my taste than churches smelling of stale perfumes and statued all over with lies.'

Depressing, also, was the first impression that Hawthorne had of Rome. He arrived there a year after Melville, in January 1858; and his impression was of cold, of squalor, of the lack of all comfort. 'I vainly try to get down upon paper the dreariness, the ugliness, shabbiness, un-home-likeness of a Roman street.' A few passages will suffice to give an idea of the prevailing tone of his Roman diary:

> The first observation which a stranger is led to make, in the neighbourhood of the Roman ruins, is that the inhabitants seem to be strangely addicted to the washing of clothes; for all the precincts of Trajan's Forum, and of the Roman Forum, and wherever else an iron railing affords opportunity to hang them, were whitened

with sheets, and other linen and cotton, drying in the sun. It must be that washerwomen burrow among the old temples. The second observation is not quite so favourable to the cleanly character of the modern Romans; indeed, it is so very unfavourable, that I hardly know how to express it. But the fact is, that, throughout the Forum . . . and anywhere out of the commonest foot-trade and road-way, you must look well to your steps. . . . If you tread beneath the triumphal arch of Titus or Constantine, you had better look downward than upward, whatever be the merit of the sculptures aloft. . . . After a while the visitant finds himself getting accustomed to this horrible state of things; and the associations of moral sublimity and beauty seem to throw a veil over the physical meanness to which I allude. Perhaps there is something in the mind of the people of these countries that enables them quite to dissever small ugliness from great sublimity and beauty. They spit upon the glorious pavement of St. Peter's, and wherever else they like; they place paltry-looking wooden confessionals beneath its sublime arches, and ornament them with cheap little colored prints of the crucifixion; they hang tin hearts and other tinsel and trumpery at the gorgeous shrines of the saints, in chapels that are incrusted with gems, or marble almost as precious; they put pasteboard statues of saints beneath the dome of the Pantheon; in short, they let the sublime and the ridiculous come together, and are not in the least troubled by the proximity. It must be their sense of the beautiful is stronger than in the Anglo-Saxon mind, and that it observes only what is fit to gratify it.

Clough, in a famous poem, *O land of Empire, art and love!* had been struck by the same contrast; and, knowing how Hawthorne was his friend, we may imagine that he was recalling this same poem:[1]

> O land of Empire, art and love!
>   What is it that you show me?
> A sky for Gods to tread above,
>   A soil for pigs below me!
> O in all place and shape and kind
>   Beyond all thought and thinking,
> The graceful with the gross combined,
>   The stately with the stinking!
> Whilst words of mighty love to trace,
>   Which thy great walls I see on,
> Thy porch I pace or take my place
>   Within thee, great Pantheon,

What sights untold of contrast bold
  My ranging eyes must be on!
What though uprolled by young and old
  In slumbrous convolution
Neath pillared shade must lie displayed
  Bare limbs that scorn ablution,
Should husks that swine would never pick
  Bestrew that patterned paving,
And sores to make a surgeon sick
  For charity come craving?
Though oft the meditative cur
  Account it small intrusion
Through that great gate to quit the stir
  Of market-place confusion,
True brother of the bipeds there,
  If Nature's need requireth,
Lifts up his leg with tranquil air
  And tranquilly retireth:
Though priest think fit to stop and spit
  Beside the altar solemn,
Yet, boy, that nuisance why commit
  On this Corinthian column?—
O richly soiled and richly sunned,
Exuberant, fervid and fecund!
  Are these the fixed condition
On which may Northern pilgrim come
To imbibe thine ether-air, and sum
  Thy store of old tradition?
Must we be chill, if clean, and stand
Foot-deep in dirt in classic land?

Clough finally concluded that perhaps this mixture of squalor and grandeur was intended by Mother Nature for a metaphysical reason not so very different from the *grande synthèse* which, in those same years, was sending Gustave Flaubert into ecstasies.

As for the Roman ruins, Hawthorne found that, apart from the immense difference in size, they were no more picturesque than an old American cellar with a brick chimney that had collapsed inside it.

It is to the negative aspects of Rome that especial attention is devoted by the brilliant journalist George Augustus Sala, descendant of a certain Claudio Sebastiano Sala who had emigrated to London in the eighteenth century in order to organize ballets in the theatres. Sala's articles on Italy, which appeared in the *Daily Telegraph* in the years 1866 and 1867, were later collected in book form in *Rome and Venice*, in 1869. Shortly before that, in 1864, there had appeared the first edition of the extremely successful book by the American sculptor William Wetmore Story, with its Italian title, *Roba di Roma*; and in a way the two volumes are complementary, since they present the same spectacles from two different, and often opposing, points of view, Story being optimistic, good natured, enamoured of his subject, while Sala is caustic, outrivalling Dickens in his emphasis on the grotesque, and not mincing matters—to say the least—in speaking of the Roman clergy. Sala arrived in Rome in the dark, and the commissionaire from the Hotel d'Angleterre asked him whether he wanted to proceed by omnibus or by cab. 'An omnibus! Couldn't they keep a *decemjugis* or a *harmamaxa* at the terminus, for the sake of appearances? Mrs. Hemans was right. Rome is no more as she has been.' And he alludes to the vision of the decay of Rome that Marius had among the ruins of Carthage in Mrs. Hemans's lines. Sala mocks at those who expect to find ancient Rome in the modern city.

I have met [he says,] a great many travellers professing an ex-pectation to find the streets of Rome with precisely the same con-figuration, containing the same houses, and presenting the same characteristics, as they may have done under the Twelve Caesars. They require their inn or their greengrocer's-shop to be in exact accordance with the canons of Vitruvius. They look for the *atrium*, the *impluvium*, and the *alae*. They want statues of the Lares and Penates in the peristyle, fresco arabesques in the *cubicula*, 'Cave canem' on the door-jamb, and '*Salve*' on a slab of mosaic to serve as a door-mat; and if they don't find these things, they cry out that Rome is very much fallen indeed.

This, he says, is the fault of Bulwer Lytton's *Last Days of Pompeii*, which had so vividly re-evoked the pagan world to the eyes of the Victorians. But to expect all this would be like expecting modern Romans to wear the *toga*, or the *peplum* or the *tunicopallium*. And yet even a tourist who was far from obtuse, Herman Melville, had declared, at the

sight of the elegant parade on the Pincio: 'Fashion everywhere ridiculous, but most so in Rome.' Story had said:
'It was dirty, but it was Rome; and to anyone who has long
lived in Rome even its very dirt has a charm which the
neatness of no other place ever had. . . . But the soil and
stain which many call dirt I call colour, and the cleanliness
of Amsterdam would ruin Rome for the artist. Thrift and
exceeding cleanness are sadly at war with the picturesque.
. . . The Romantic will not consort with the Monotonous,
—Nature is not neat,—Poetry is not formal,—and Rome
is not clean.' But Sala does not look at it like that; he detests
the wretched, dirty, picturesque hovels, he does not in the
least regret the disappearance of much decrepit minor
architecture, and he never ceases to call down upon Rome
a Saint George who will destroy the old Roman dragon of
dirt and bad smells and malaria. He would like to see
modern lodging-houses in place of filthy huts, and the cult
of 'St. Saponax and St. Aquarius' initiated. To him, it is
the Papacy that has brought Rome's catastrophe to its
crowning height. It had reduced Rome to one of the most
neglected cities on the face of the earth; but the neglect
and filth of Rome are things that can be remedied, he adds,
when a more enlightened and a better government comes
into power. It is very much to be feared that, in times closer
to our own, Sala would have been one of the many foreigners
who sang the praises of Fascism merely because it watered
the streets, cleared out decrepit quarters of the town, and
managed to make the trains run punctually. He proclaims
that he had never seen anything 'so forlorn and so revolting,
so miserable and so degraded, as the "humbler classes" of
Rome'. Do not the priests, who speak so unctuously of the
Madonna, realize that the hovel only two steps away from
their magnificent churches is a denial of God? 'The filthiest
streets of Rome are in the Borgo, and the Borgo is composed of the streets immediately surrounding St. Peter's.
Tu es Petrus . . . but underneath the rock of the Church
priestcraft has built up a dunghill.' Enormous wealth has
been expended upon the decoration of San Paolo fuori le
Mura, but not one penny on the repair of the sordid street
that leads to that sumptuous building, or upon the washing

and clothing of the wretches who trail themselves about the splendid basilica begging alms. None of the principal streets of Rome, the Via Condotti, or the Via Babuino, or the Via Fontanella Borghese or the Via di Ripetta, or the Via della Scrofa, is really a street in the proper sense of the word, and as for the Corso, it is a long, narrow, dirty lane. 'There are streets in Rome whose names are more poignant in their suggestiveness than the fiercest satire of Juvenal. The Vicolo Gesù-Maria is close to the Via degl'Incurabili. The Street of the Guardian Angel is the most abandoned place you ever saw', the Via del Paradiso recalls one of the most squalid streets in London, 'the Street of Death skirts the wall of a grand palace'. In the names of some streets 'now and then plain truth peeps out to the discomfiture of fiction, as in the "Street of the Old Shoes"² and the "Street of the Dark Shops".' Sala even goes so far as to suggest the selling of all the treasures of the churches in order to build a few model lodging-houses, a few baths and wash-houses. In this crusade in the name of cleanliness and progress Sala is representative of the Victorian trends towards social reform, and is nearer to George Eliot than to Dickens. The satirical vein is predominant through all his pages, and his caricatures are not kindly like those of Dickens, with whom otherwise he has many tastes and reactions in common. He ridicules the Bambino of Aracoeli, a hideous wooden idol like the Mumbo Jumbo which he supposes to be wor-shipped by the negroes. The picture presented by eccle-siastical Rome at certain periods of the year is no different from that of a fair, and if those English people who are so crazy about ritualism could see the ceremonies on the spot, they would realize what a pitiful, gaudy image of rags and bones and glaring colours is the object of their admiration. He ridicules the sacred music with its sudden transitions from *Adeste fideles* to a waltz, from an operatic motif to the Dead March in Saul, and sees little difference between the sacristan who lights the candles in the Cappella Paolina and the workman who lights the gas-jets of the Drury Lane footlights; or between a procession of the Madonna and the pagan procession of the Bona Dea, or Venus Salammbô. Regarding this procession, he says: 'It is ludicrous to know that while these monks are wandering with their idol about a city of a hundred-and-fifty-thousand inhabitants, the most interested sightseers are a few groups of foreign heretics, who, in their heart of hearts, know well enough that the whole thing is a Humbug, yet who suck it up greedily, as they would the sight of Blondin on the tight-rope, or the Widow Stodare with her Sphinx.' Nor does he spare the English tourists his barbs:

They appear to regard the Pope as a kind of show provided by the Roman hotel-keepers, and to be enjoyed by the superior classes in common with cameos, mosaics, Castellani's antique jewelry, Piale's reading-room, and the statues in the Museo Chiaramonti by moonlight. They would walk in and out of the Vatican, if they could, as they do in and out of the painters' and sculptors' studios— half as patrons, half as sneering critics. They would take stock of the benighted old gentleman's furniture, and inquire if he wears a crinoline under his white-flannel petticoat, and gaze curiously on the enormous red-silk pocket-handkerchief with which he mops up the quantity of snuff which he bestows on his venerable countenance.

Sala laughs at 'that wonderful dragoon . . . who rides before the Pope, waving a drawn sword, after the manner of the late Mr. Gomersal in the Astleian spectacle of the *Battle of Waterloo*'. When the streets are muddy, the passersby, in order to avoid kneeling down as the Pope passes, run out of sight of this dragoon-outrider, just as the Spanish bishops used to order their coachmen to fly at full speed as the Most Holy Sacrament passed through the streets, to avoid having to give up their carriages to the priest who was bearing it. The worst thing about the Papal government, says Sala, is not so much its tyranny as its age: it is a government that belongs not to the nineteenth, but to the fourteenth, century. In any case Rome is dominated by an air of dotage and decrepitude—from the costumes of the Pope's and cardinals' servants, designed by Raphael and Michelangelo, down to the swaddling-clothes in which babies are tightly bound up, after the fashion of two thousand years ago. 'Were you ever on familiar terms with a human bas-relief, a Cupid with his wings cut off, who has tumbled into the mud, but has gotten some rags to cover his little bare back withal? That is a Roman boy. Did you ever know an animated cameo, chipped and foul and smirched, but a classical cameo for all that? That cameo is a Roman contadina.' Invasions and historical changes have not changed the Romans much. 'As for their character, I do not imagine they have changed much during the last twenty centuries, and that they would not at all object to a sovereign who gave them plenty of bread and plenty of games. I have little doubt, in fact, that they are the same Roman people, or rather Roman populace, whose ways and manners were intuitively divined by a theatrical manager by the riverside, in London, who did some very capital business in Queen Elizabeth's time—a manager, it is said, who made but a poor actor, but was a dramatist of some note, and wrote the plays of *Julius Caesar* and *Coriolanus*.' Moreover he has no illusions on the subject of ancient Rome: 'The civilisation of old Rome was, it cannot be doubted, grand and sumptuous; but the old Romans were, for all that, I suspect, a nasty, dirty set of people, who had need to go to the bath so often, seeing what pigsties they wallowed in elsewhere, and who wore their togas until— like the Russian peasants, who send their hats to the village oven to be baked, and thus freed from insect life—they were compelled to send them to the fuller's to be made decent again. Depend upon it, bad as modern Rome is, badly built, badly paved, and but half-lit with gas, ancient Rome was even more intolerable.' Even the picturesque side of Rome, as presented by Sala, has a flavour of caricature, conceived in an unfriendly and aggressive spirit. One morning—on Christmas morning, in fact—he peeped into a little 'osteria di vino padronale con cucina' in the Vicolo della Rupe Tarpea (which he calls the 'Vicola della Rocca Tarpeia'). Seated at a rough table were 'seven wagoners in Spanish mantles, brigand-hats, and overalls of goatskins': in the middle an enormous flask of red Velletri wine. 'To them entered a kitchen wench, unwashed, but comely, and with a fine Roman nose and eyes like sloes. She had thrown her white petticoat over her head, where it formed a most artistic coiffure; but her *jupons* not being in duplicate, and her skirt but scanty, her lower limbs rather suffered in consequence. . . . She, from a large pipkin, with a semi-circular handle, emptied *right upon the bare deal boards of the table* a prodigious mountain of maccaroni.' So far, it might be an engraving by Pinelli. But here the caustic spirit of the observer intervenes. This mountain of mac-caroni 'must have been hot, for it smoked. I think it was dressed with cheese, for it smelt so strongly that one of the buffaloes in the wains outside coughed. I conjecture that it was also accommodated with oil, or some other fatty matter, and that some hot splashes thereof reached the floor, for I noticed one of the wagoners' dogs, sitting by, lick his lips and wag his tail approvingly. It was a strange sight, this Campagna of grease, with the oil-flask of wine towering in the midst like St. Peter's.' Sala amuses himself by watching the contortions of the wagoners as they thrust the maccaroni into their mouths with their fingers. 'I never saw a boa-constrictor swallow a rabbit, but here were seven men gorg-ing boa-constrictors.' And he imagines Roman wagoners feasting in just the same way two thousand years before, 'long before the Sibyl of Tivoli revealed to Imperial Caesar the vision of the Christmas-day which was to come'. Story took seriously the *pifferari* or bagpipers who used to come down from the Abruzzi to play their *novena* in front of every shrine in Rome. 'They form a picture which every artist desires to paint.' And at the end of his book he gives the musical score of this highly poetic song of the pipers. But the pipers, according to Sala, are one of the plagues of Rome. 'They begin to blow at five o'clock in the morning, preferably choosing for their performances the neighbour-hood of hotels frequented by heretics.' Sala sees no sort of religious fervour in the *pifferari*, merely greed for money. And as for the costume of these 'villainous-looking fellows', it is 'picturesque in photography, but revolting in an age which prefers untattered coats and clean shirts to parti-coloured rags and mangy goatskin breeches'. Neither pipers nor strolling musicians, who are treated by Story with so much good-nature, find favour in his eyes, or rather, in his ears. 'I fancy the Romans pay them because the discord is grateful to their ears. I think they like cacophony, as that Sultan of Turkey did who only derived pleasure from the performances of his brass-band when his musicians were tuning up their instruments. "Mashallah! let the dogs play that tune again," cried the Sultan to his Italian band-master.'

Not even when the Romans try to ape English customs and be modern does Sala give them any credit. His book ends with impressions of a fox-hunt in the Campagna: he ridicules the Roman princesses' riding-habits, copied from the latest Paris fashion-plates, he ridicules the unsporting way in which the hunt is conducted—a hunt in which there was everything except the fox, which, however, at the end, was found, very appropriately, in one of the tombs on the Via Appia, the latter being thronged, if not with foxes, at least with the eternal, inevitable beggars. Beggars, dirt, bad smells, the theatricality of a decayed religion, obscurant-ism—these are the dominant notes in Sala's caustic pages, which, as I have said, represent the other side of a medal that Story had engraved with gentleness and love. Sala's is a gloomy picture, a pitiless portrait, which errs not so much through exaggeration of the negative elements (which un-doubtedly existed, seeing that every other traveller speaks of them) as through the absence of any allusion to the fascination of Rome, which had its effect upon the majority of travellers in spite of dirt and beggars and reactionary priests and malaria. Indeed, as I have said, a Romantic of the Flaubert type would have felt this fascination all the more because of these maladies: for they were indispensable ingredients to him for the creation of the *grande synthèse* of poetic beauty, as were squalor and death to Baudelaire.

Victorian England did not possess a Romantic poet of this kind; yet Robert Browning, whose imagination was especially stimulated by the picturesque and the bizarre, came very near to something that resembled this point of view. He has many of the gifts of Dickens, with a greater refinement; he, too, loves to mix the beautiful and the grotesque, and never feels himself so much at ease as in crowded, high-coloured, turgid descriptive passages. Italy gave inexhaustible satisfaction to this poet's visual intelli-gence, and he plunged into its *miro gurge*, its 'enchanted eddy', with the same blessed pleasure that he attributes, in one of his poems, to the insect groping amongst the pollen inside the calyx of a flower. In a poem such as *The Englishman in Italy*, which has, as sub-title, *Piano di Sorrento*, he vies with the craftsmen who make little figures for the Nativity cribs of Naples in presenting a world of minute objects, until at last his eye comes to rest in the blue solitudes of the sky, and wanders freely over the ever-changing outline of the mountains and capes of the Sorrento Peninsula as he himself moves. Something extremely ancient combined with something extremely new: a two-faced image of youth and decrepitude: this is the secret of the fascination that Italy holds for Browning. How could he fail to be fascinated by what Ampère called *la ville des contrastes*? In *Two in the Campagna* Browning's eye at first lingers curiously upon the ground close about him, observing the yellowing fennel amongst the brickwork of a ruined tomb, noticing the orange cup of a flower; then it moves to the grassy slopes of the meadows and wanders freely over the whole countryside:

> The champaign with its endless fleece
>   Of feathery grasses everywhere!
> Silence and passion, joy and peace,
>   An everlasting wash of air—
> Rome's ghost since her decease.
>
> Such life there, through such lengths of hours,
>   Such miracles performed in play,
> Such primal naked forms of flowers,
>   Such letting Nature have her way
> While Heaven looks from its towers!

At every step, in Italy, Browning was struck by strange and surprising contrasts. In England the past continues in the present through an uninterrupted ritual tradition: Oxford is ancient, but like a precious garment which is jealously guarded from moth and rust and put on for solemn occasions. And thus continued habit lessens the flow of time, and nothing is very remote, and the past is not so much a museum as a family wardrobe or archive-chest, to which one feels bound by a chain that prevails over time and custom. But, in Italy, what is the past? 'O patria mia,' wrote Leopardi, 'vedo le mura e gli archi. . . .' *I see the walls and the arches*. Italians, indeed, may sometimes think like this, but Browning's feelings about our world were different. He saw the basilica grafted upon the pagan temple and the flocks grazing in the Forum; he saw the great medieval tower rising upon the tomb in the Appian Way and the vegetable-market occupying the Assembly's place: he saw a new life, half-barbarous, perhaps, and wild, flourishing among the ruins, and he saw *Love among the Ruins*:

> Oh, heart! oh, blood that freezes, blood that burns!
> Earth's returns
> For whole centuries of folly, noise and sin!
> Shut them in,
> With their triumphs and their glories and the rest.
> Love is best!

The extremely young beside the extremely old, and the unconscious life that adapts the ancient to modern uses: in this lies the picturesqueness of Italy. These piquant contrasts, which stimulated the humour of Dickens and aroused the sarcasm and disdain of George Augustus Sala, are transposed by Browning on to the lyric plane; and out of the disharmony, out of the harsh clash between the majestic antique and the paltry modern, he draws new poetry, using his own favourite method of complicated, unforeseen, almost punning, rhyme. It is Romantic poetry, belonging to that kind of Victorian Romanticism which prefers the bizarre, the picturesque note to the heroic: of this type of Romanticism Browning was the most conspicuous exponent. Ruin, for him, does not usually exist as a mere spectre of the past, a tragic ghost blighting the present: Byron saw in the past a monument and an admonition, Browning sees in it an evidence of life, of a strange, mysterious life whose secret tempts him. The appearance of the inside of a Roman church such as Saint Praxed's does not arouse gloomy, severe reflections in him; but the rare marbles he admires on the tombs become dramatized, as it were, and invested with a soul; and thus the picturesqueness of the church expresses itself in an actual scene—that of the Bishop of St. Praxed's giving directions to his 'nephews'—in reality his sons—for his own tomb, determined that it shall be more sumptuous than that of Gandolfo, his rival in love and in his career. Browning brings to life this figure of a sixteenth-century prelate, greedy for precious marbles as a woman for jewels: he shows him, in his poem, delighting in the slab of basalt beneath which he will rest, and the nine columns of his tabernacle all of 'peach-blossom marble . . . the rare, the ripe As fresh-poured red wine of a mighty pulse', and jeering at the 'paltry onion-stone' on the tomb of his rival Gandolfo, and conjuring his sons to place between his knees, when he is in his tomb, a precious piece of *lapis lazuli* 'Big as a Jew's head cut off at the nape, Blue as a vein o'er the Madonna's breast.'

> Did I say basalt for my slab, sons? Black—
> 'Twas ever antique-black I meant! How else
> Shall ye contrast my frieze to come beneath?
> The bas-relief in bronze ye promised me,
> Those Pans and Nymphs ye wot of, and perchance
> Some tripod, thyrsus, with a vase or so,
> The Saviour at his sermon on the mount,
> Saint Praxed in a glory, and one Pan
> Ready to twitch the Nymph's last garment off,
> And Moses with the tables . . . but I know
> Ye mark me not! What do they whisper thee,
> Child of my bowels, Anselm? Ah, ye hope
> To revel down my villas while I gasp
> Bricked o'er with beggar's mouldy travertine
> Which Gandolf from his tomb-top chuckles at!
> Nay, boys, ye love me—all of jasper, then!
> 'Tis jasper ye stand pledged to, lest I grieve.
> My bath must needs be left behind, alas!
> One block, pure green as a pistachio-nut,
> There's plenty jasper somewhere in the world—
> And have I not Saint Praxed's ear to pray
> Horses for ye, and brown Greek manuscripts,
> And mistresses with great smooth marbly limbs?
> —That's if ye carve my epitaph aright,
> Choice Latin, picked phrase, Tully's every word,
> No gaudy ware like Gandolf's second line—
> Tully, my masters? Ulpian serves his need!
> And then how I shall lie through centuries,

And hear the blessed mutter of the mass,
And see God made and eaten all day long,
And feel the steady candle-flame, and taste
Good strong thick stupefying incense-smoke!

And the bishop's delirium continues:

All *lapis*, all, sons! Else I give the Pope
My villas . . .

and he concludes in anguish:

There, leave me, there!
For ye have stabbed me with ingratitude
To death—ye wish it—God, ye wish it! Stone—
Gritstone, a-crumble! Clammy squares which sweat
As if the corpse they keep were oozing through—
And no more *lapis* to delight the world!

Here the worldliness of the Roman cleric is fixed, once
for all, in a queer, poetic picture which is undoubtedly far
more effective than a caustic affirmation like this of Sala's:
'The Roman-Catholic clergy are, no doubt, as a body,
learned, virtuous, and pious; yet it needs no Lavater, no
Gall or Spurzheim, to discern that their looks belie them,
and that out of Ireland—where the priest is generally a
hale, comely, cheerful-looking gentleman—your Romish
ecclesiastic, facially at least, has the air not only of having
gone into the Church, but of having just broken into one
with a view to the communion-plate.' And far more effective than the many pages devoted by Story to the persecution of the Jews in Rome, are the lines of *Holy-Cross Day*,
in which Browning imagines conversations between Jews
who are forced to be present, once a year, at a sermon, with
a view to their conversion—a poem which, in its clumsy
cacophonies, sets out to convey the spirit of a people as
oppressed and as wary as an army of cellar rats. And finally
the picturesque and sinister life of Papal Rome was to form
the background of Browning's great dramatic poem inspired by a crime almost as heinous as that of the Cenci:
the massacre by Count Guido Franceschini of his wife and
her relations. And certainly the execution at the end of
The Ring and the Book is very different in tone from the

one described by Dickens in his impressions of Rome. Yet Browning too, like the other Victorians, was struck by the picturesque, sinister, and even the squalid modern Rome rather than by the heroic ancient Rome. To sum up all that the Anglo-Saxons felt about Rome during the last century, it may perhaps be fitting to conclude by quoting a page from the author of *The Marble Faun* (published in England as *Transformation*), Nathaniel Hawthorne:

When we have once known Rome, and left her where she lies, like a long decaying corpse, retaining a trace of the noble shape it was, but with accumulated dust and a fungous growth overspreading all its more admirable features—left her in utter weariness, no doubt, of her narrow, crooked, intricate streets, so uncomfortably paved with little squares of lava that to tread over them is a penitential pilgrimage, so indescribably ugly, moreover, so cold, so alley-like, into which the sun never falls, and where a chill wind forces its deadly breath into our lungs—left her, tired of the sight of those immense seven-storied, yellow-washed hovels, or call them palaces, where all that is dreary in domestic life seems magnified and multiplied, and weary of climbing those staircases, which ascend from a ground floor of cook-shops, cobblers' stalls, stables, and regiments of cavalry, to a middle region of princes, cardinals, and ambassadors, and an upper tier of artists, just beneath the unattainable sky—left her worn out with shivering at the cheerless and smoky fireside by day, and feasting with our own substance the ravenous little populace of a Roman bed at night—left her, sick at heart of Italian trickery, which has uprooted whatever faith in man's integrity had endured till now, and sick at stomach of sour bread, sour wine, rancid butter, and bad cookery, needlessly bestowed on evil meats—left her, disgusted with the pretence of holiness and the reality of nastiness, each equally omnipresent—left her, half lifeless from the languid atmosphere, the vital principle of which has been used up long ago, or corrupted by myriads of slaughters—left her, crushed down in spirit with the desolation of her ruin, and the hopelessness of her future—left her, in short, hating her with all our might, and adding our individual curse to the infinite anathema which her old crimes have unmistakably brought down—when we have left Rome in such a mood as this, we are astonished by the discovery, by and by, that our heart-strings have mysteriously attached themselves to the Eternal City, and are drawing us thitherward again, as if it were more familiar, more intimately our home, than even the spot where we were born.

NOTES TO APPENDIX II

¹ *Amours de voyage* was published for the first time at Boston in the *Atlantic Monthly* from Feb. to May 1858. An incomplete manuscript of the volume, with the title *Roman Hexameters and Roman Elegiacs*, had been sent in Sept. 1854 to C. E. Norton at Boston; Norton wanted Ticknor and Fields to publish Clough's poem, and probably circulated these hexameters amongst his friends, who included Hawthorne, who had known Clough when the latter was in America from November 1852 till June 1853. I owe this information to Rolando Anzilotti, who is preparing a work on Clough.

² Sala was probably thinking of the Via della Scarpaccia, which existed in Trastevere, and still exists under the beautified name of Vicolo della Scarpetta, between Via Lungarina and Via dei Salumi. Bernardini, *Descrizione del nuovo ripartimento de' Rioni di Roma*, 1744, p. 205, registers a Via della Scarpaccia at S. Benedetto in Piscinula, Trastevere (communication from Antonio Muñoz).

INDEX